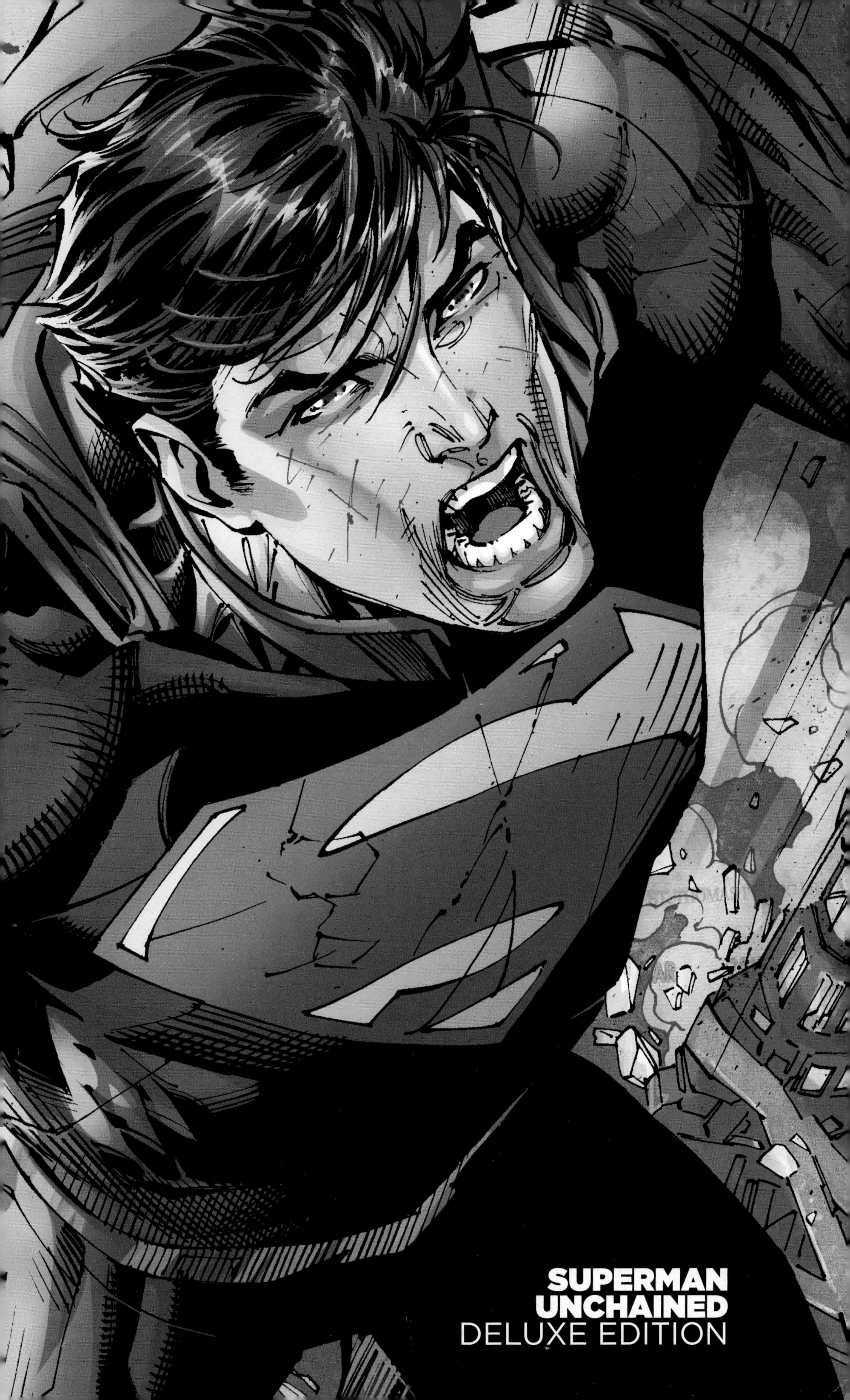
SUPERMAN
UNCHAINED
DELUXE EDITION

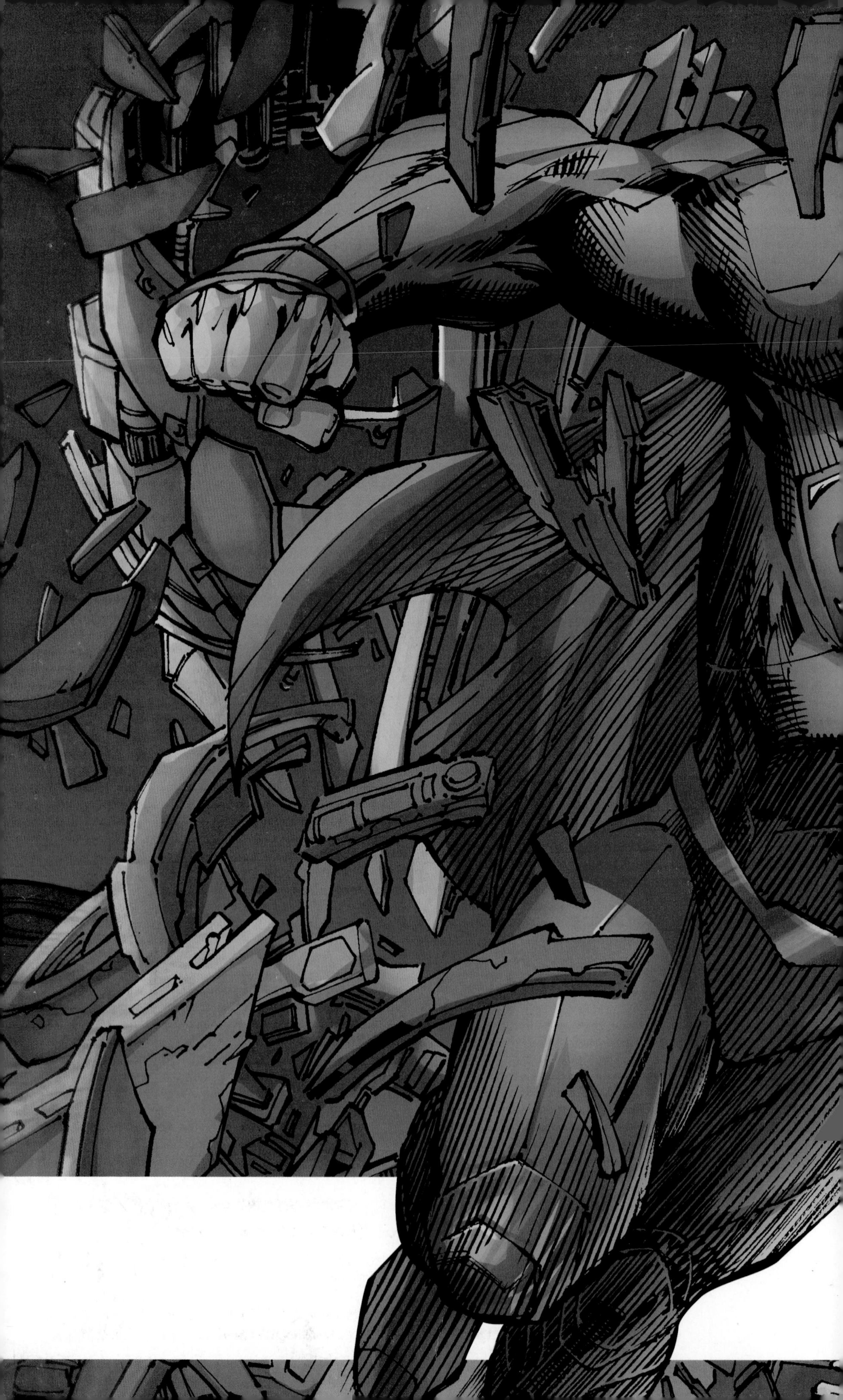

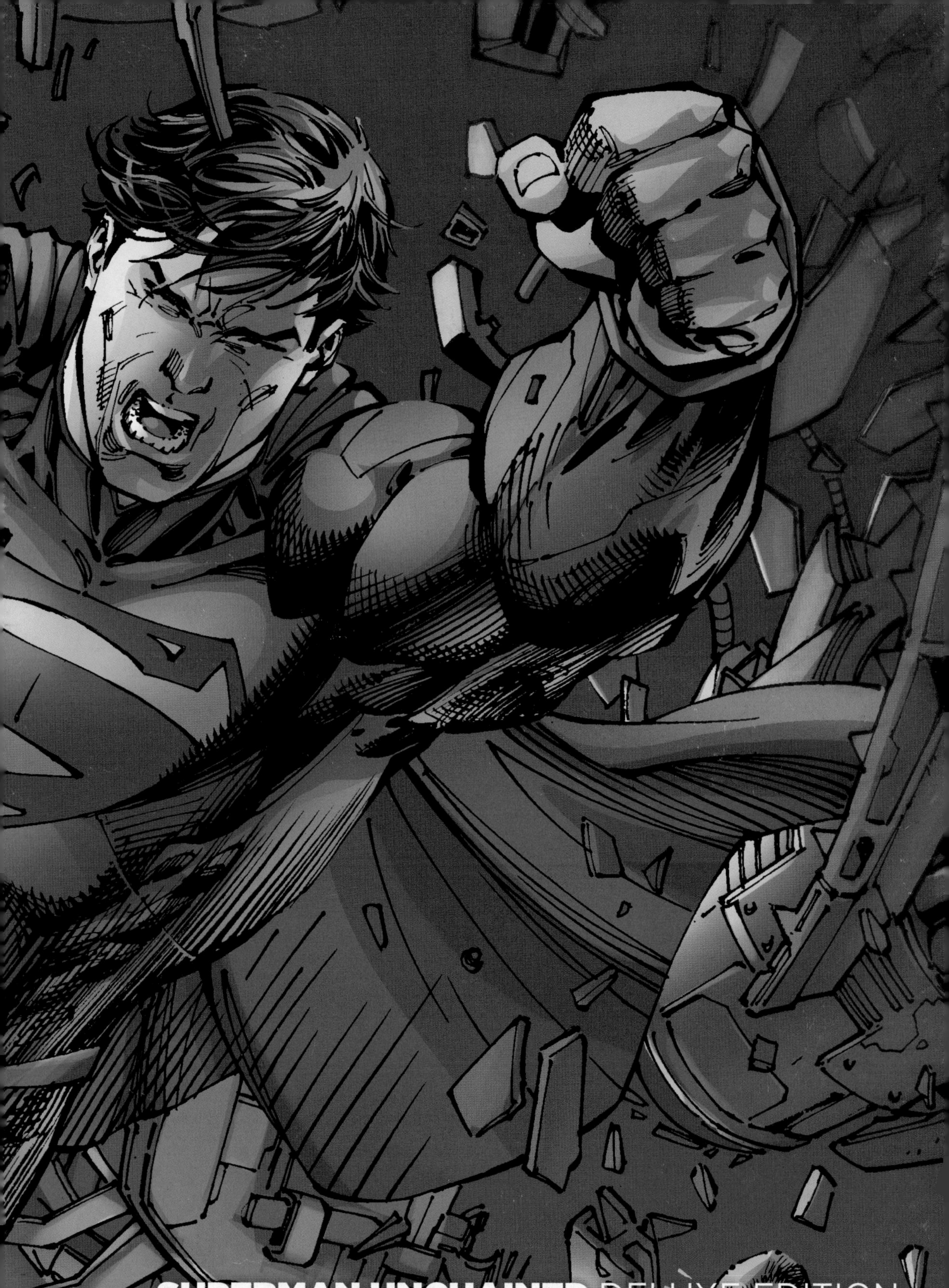

SUPERMAN UNCHAINED DELUXE EDITION

Scott Snyder Writer

Jim Lee Dustin Nguyen Scott Williams Artists

Alex Sinclair **John Kalisz** Colorists **Sal Cipriano** Letterer

Jim Lee, **Scott Williams** and **Alex Sinclair** Cover artists

Superman created by Jerry Siegel and Joe Shuster.
By special arrangement with the Jerry Siegel family.

Matt Idelson Editor – Original Series
Chris Conroy Associate Editor – Original Series
Peter Hamboussi Editor
Robbin Brosterman Design Director – Books
Louis Prandi Publication Design

Bob Harras Senior VP – Editor-in-Chief, DC Comics

Diane Nelson President
Dan DiDio and Jim Lee Co-Publishers
Geoff Johns Chief Creative Officer
Amit Desai Senior VP – Marketing & Franchise Management
Amy Genkins Senior VP – Business & Legal Affairs
Nairi Gardiner Senior VP – Finance
Jeff Boison VP – Publishing Planning
Mark Chiarello VP – Art Direction & Design
John Cunningham VP – Marketing
Terri Cunningham VP – Editorial Administration
Larry Ganem VP – Talent Relations & Services
Alison Gill Senior VP – Manufacturing & Operations
Hank Kanalz Senior VP – Vertigo & Integrated Publishing
Jay Kogan VP – Business & Legal Affairs, Publishing
Jack Mahan VP – Business Affairs, Talent
Nick Napolitano VP – Manufacturing Administration
Sue Pohja VP – Book Sales
Fred Ruiz VP – Manufacturing Operations
Courtney Simmons Senior VP – Publicity
Bob Wayne Senior VP – Sales

SUPERMAN UNCHAINED DELUXE EDITION
Published by DC Comics. Compilation Copyright
© 2014 DC Comics. All Rights Reserved.
Originally published in single magazine form as
SUPERMAN UNCHAINED 1-9 and SUPERMAN
UNCHAINED DIRECTOR'S CUT 1. Copyright
© 2013, 2014 DC Comics. All Rights Reserved.
All characters, their distinctive likenesses and
related elements featured in this publication
are trademarks of DC Comics. The stories, char-
acters and incidents featured in this publication
are entirely fictional. DC Comics does not read
or accept unsolicited ideas, stories or artwork.
DC Comics, 1700 Broadway, New York, NY 10019
A Warner Bros. Entertainment Company.
Printed by RR Donnelley, Salem, VA, USA.
11/7/14. First Printing.
ISBN: 978-1-4012-4522-1

Library of Congress Cataloging-in-Publication
Data is Available.

SUSTAINABLE
FORESTRY
INITIATIVE

Certified Chain of Custody
20% Certified Forest Content,
80% Certified Sourcing
www.sfiprogram.org
SFI-01042
APPLIES TO TEXT STOCK ONLY

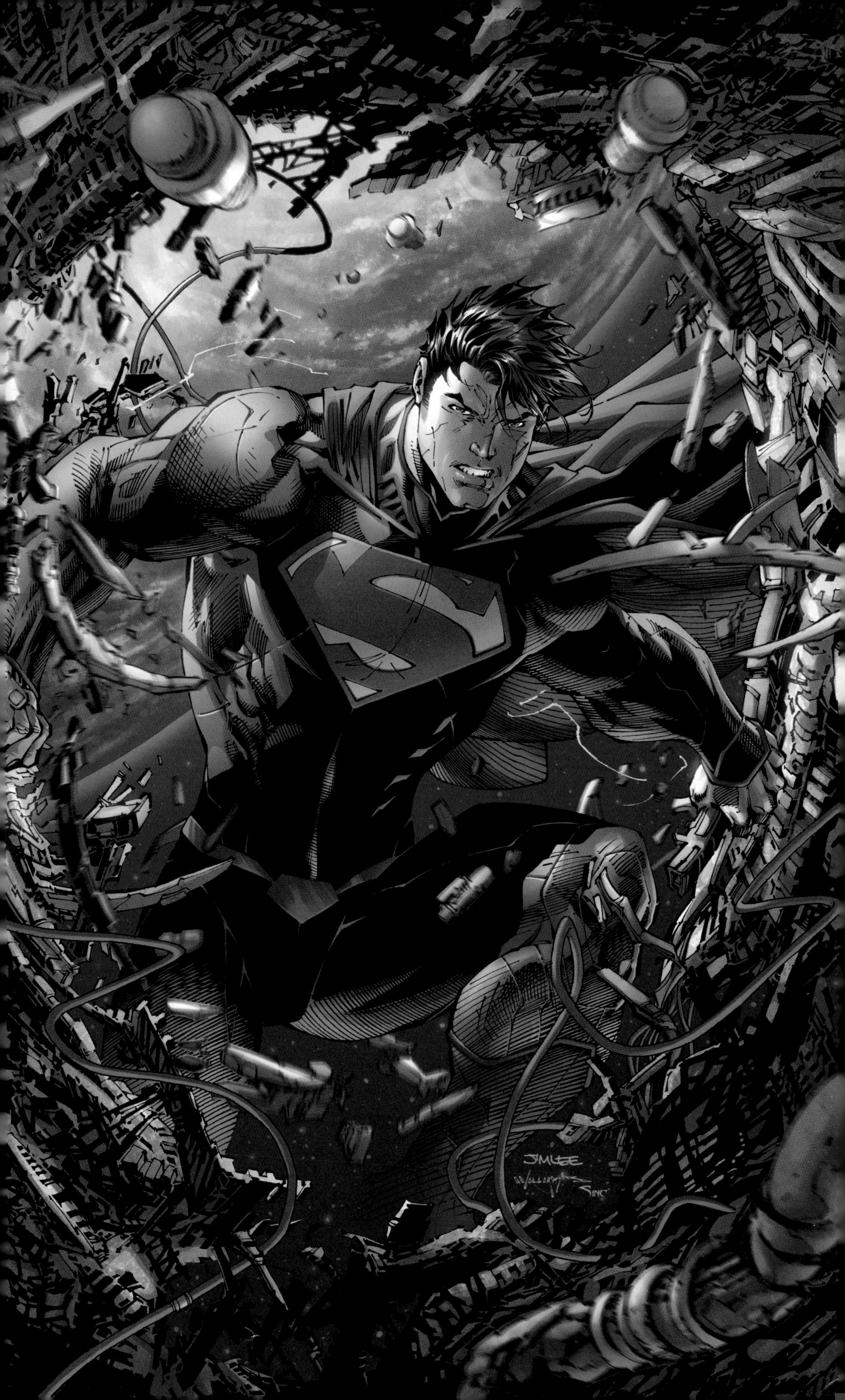

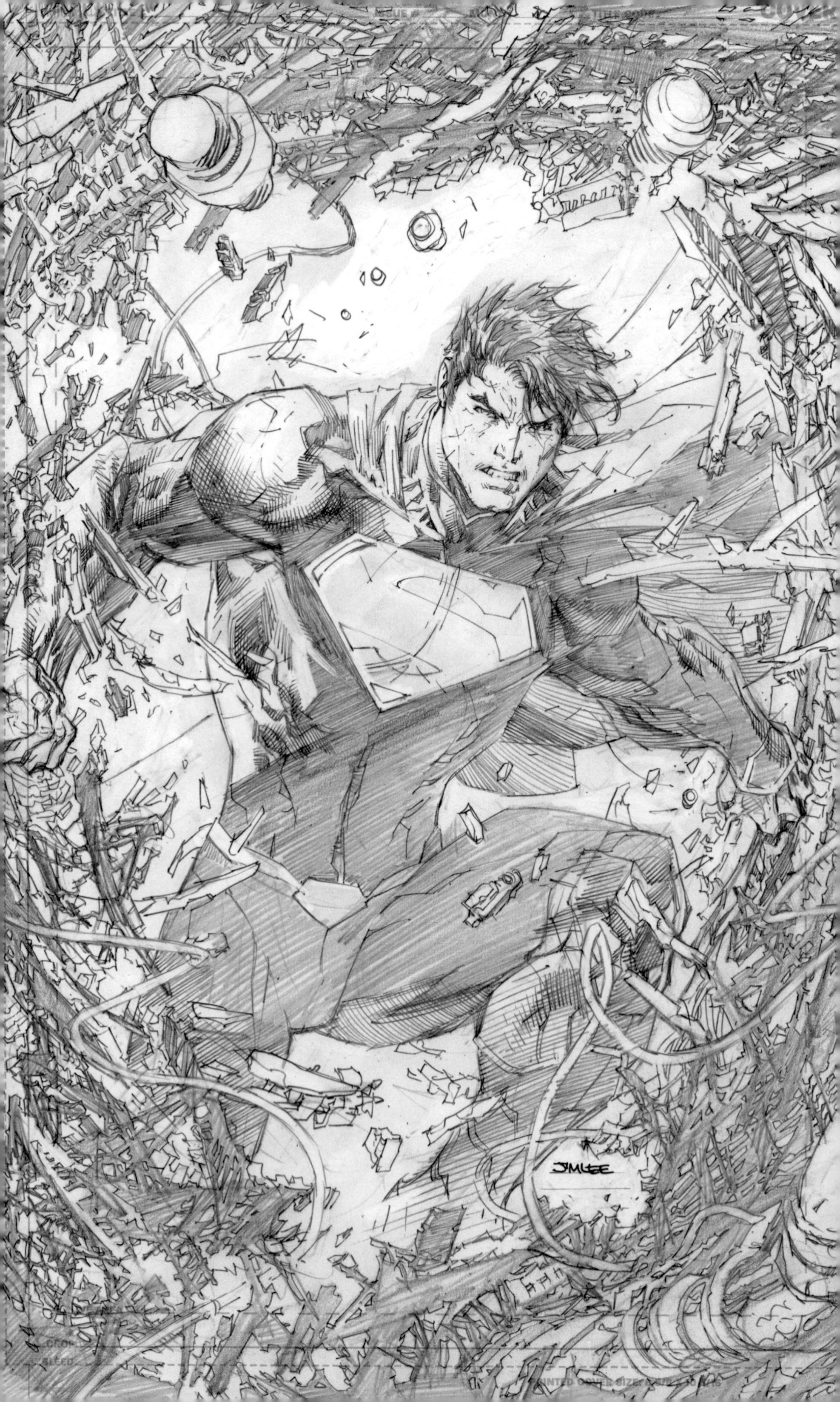
JIM LEE

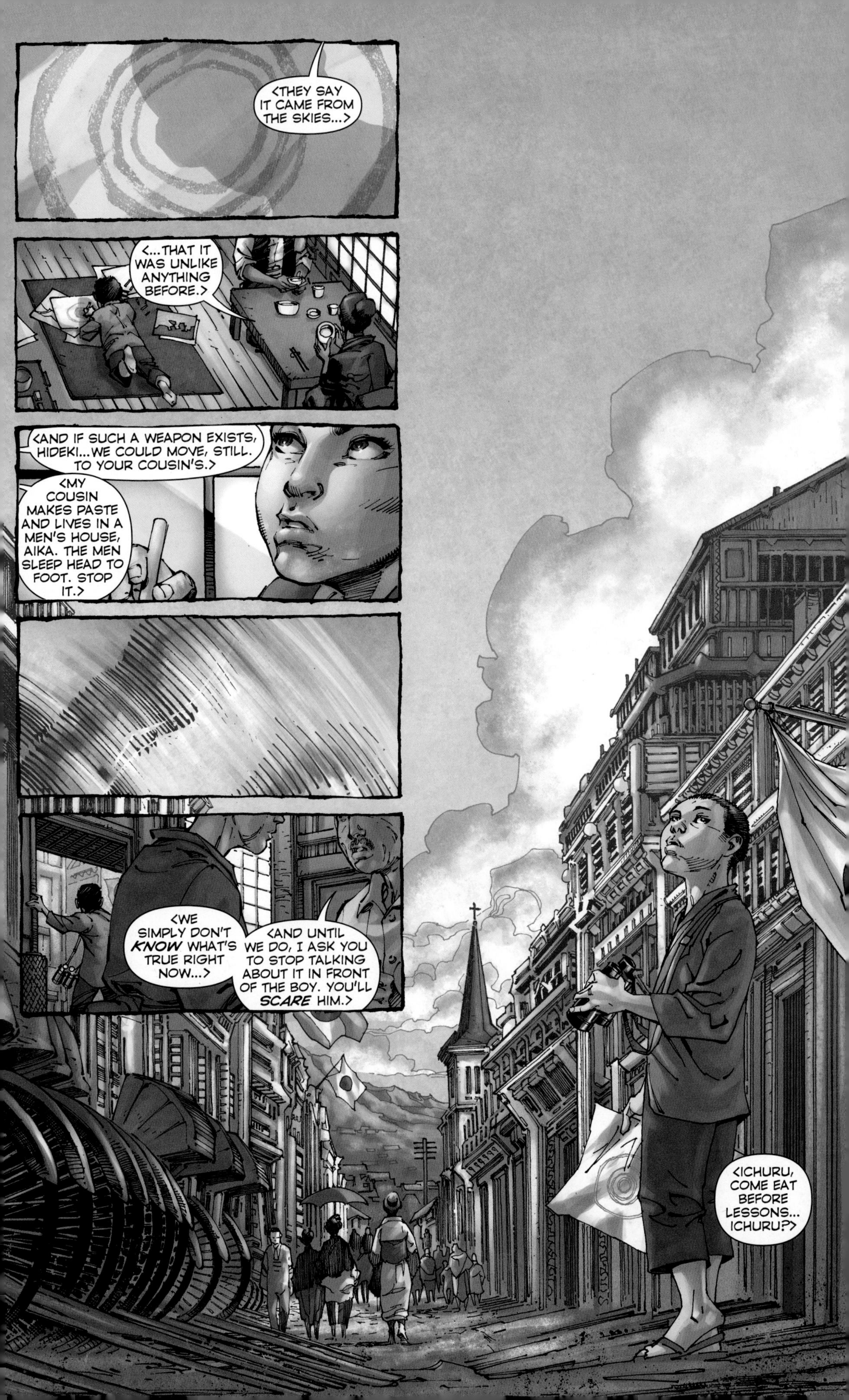
<THEY SAY IT CAME FROM THE SKIES...>
<...THAT IT WAS UNLIKE ANYTHING BEFORE.>
<AND IF SUCH A WEAPON EXISTS, HIDEKI...WE COULD MOVE, STILL. TO YOUR COUSIN'S.>
<MY COUSIN MAKES PASTE AND LIVES IN A MEN'S HOUSE, AIKA. THE MEN SLEEP HEAD TO FOOT. STOP IT.>
<WE SIMPLY DON'T KNOW WHAT'S TRUE RIGHT NOW...>
<AND UNTIL WE DO, I ASK YOU TO STOP TALKING ABOUT IT IN FRONT OF THE BOY. YOU'LL SCARE HIM.>
<ICHURU, COME EAT BEFORE LESSONS... ICHURU?>

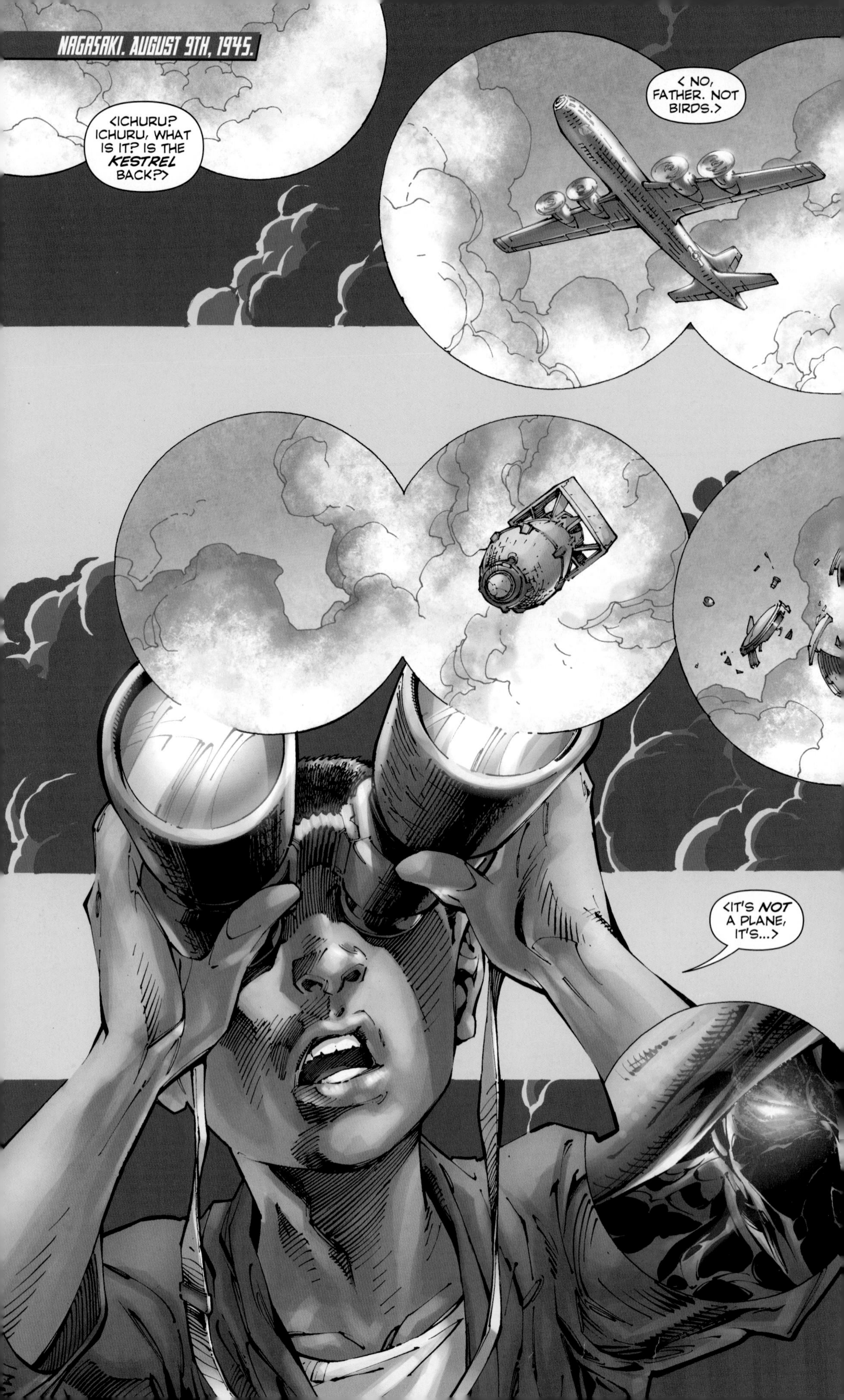
NAGASAKI. AUGUST 9TH, 1945.
<ICHURU? ICHURU, WHAT IS IT? IS THE *KESTREL* BACK?>
< NO, FATHER. NOT BIRDS.>
<IT'S *NOT* A PLANE, IT'S...>

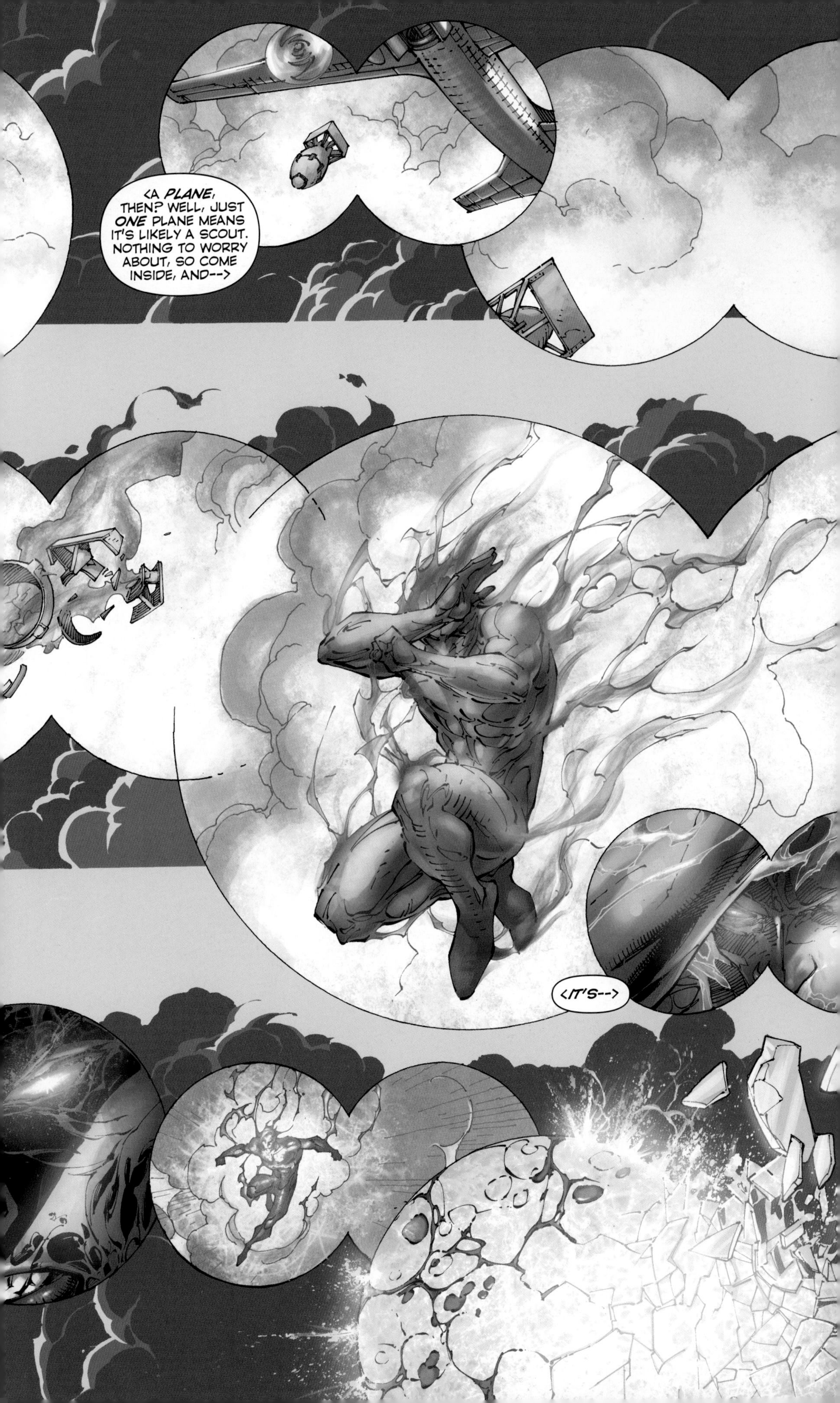
<A *PLANE*, THEN? WELL, JUST *ONE* PLANE MEANS IT'S LIKELY A SCOUT. NOTHING TO WORRY ABOUT, SO COME INSIDE, AND-->
<*IT'S*-->

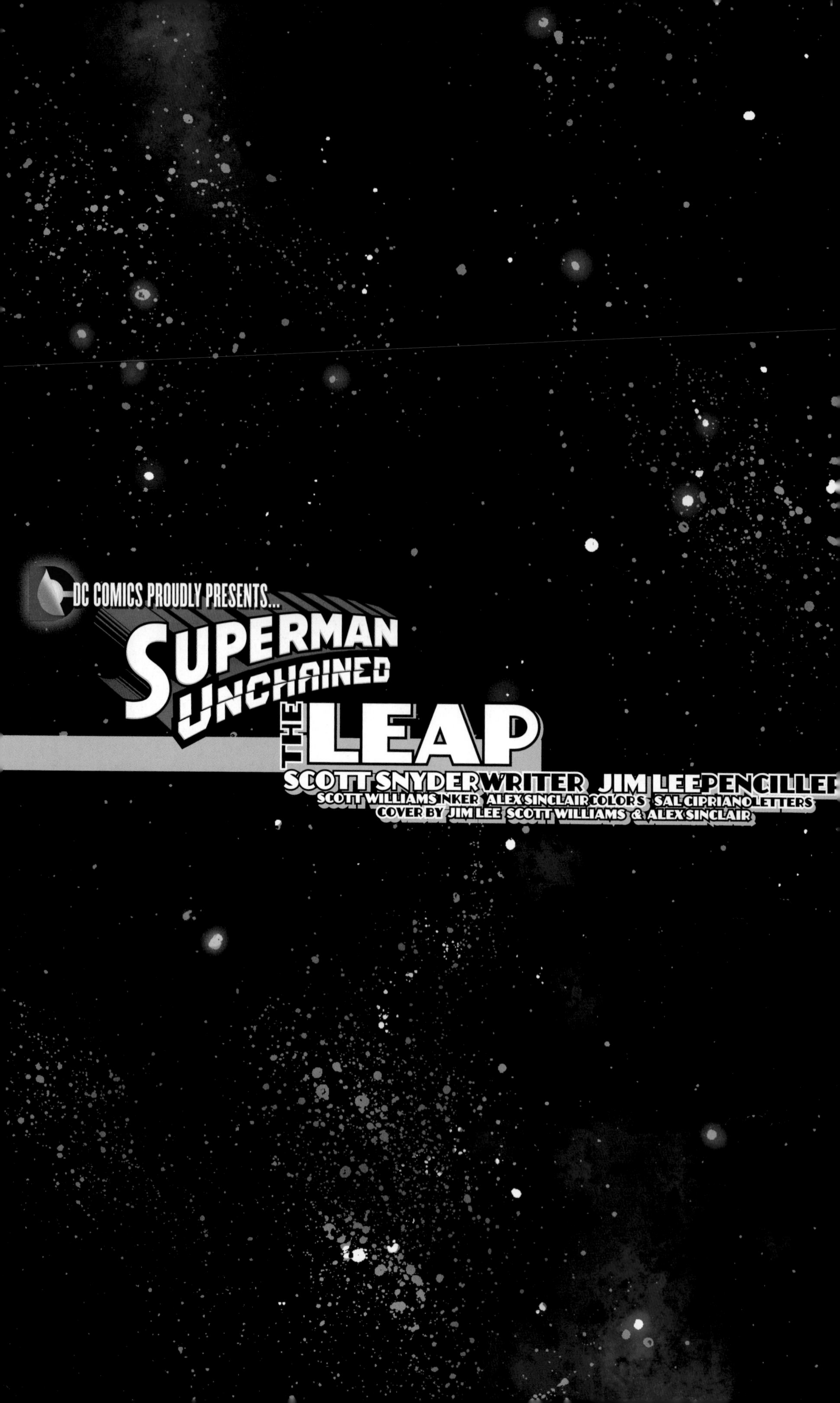
DC COMICS PROUDLY PRESENTS...
SUPERMAN
UNCHAINED
THE LEAP
SCOTT SNYDER WRITER JIM LEE PENCILLER
SCOTT WILLIAMS INKER ALEX SINCLAIR COLORS SAL CIPRIANO LETTERS
COVER BY JIM LEE SCOTT WILLIAMS & ALEX SINCLAIR

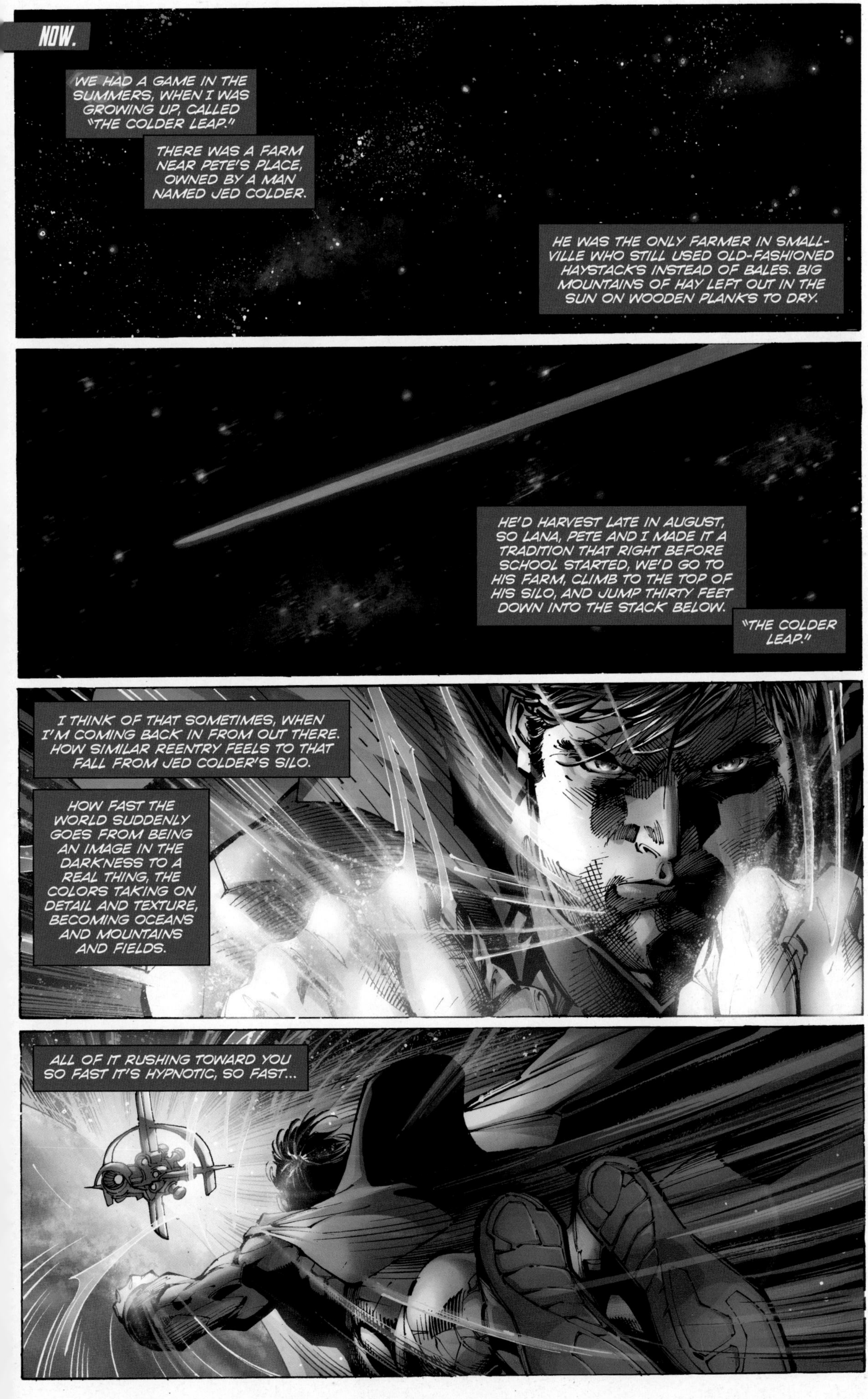
NOW.
WE HAD A GAME IN THE SUMMERS, WHEN I WAS GROWING UP, CALLED "THE COLDER LEAP."
THERE WAS A FARM NEAR PETE'S PLACE, OWNED BY A MAN NAMED JED COLDER.
HE WAS THE ONLY FARMER IN SMALL-VILLE WHO STILL USED OLD-FASHIONED HAYSTACKS INSTEAD OF BALES. BIG MOUNTAINS OF HAY LEFT OUT IN THE SUN ON WOODEN PLANKS TO DRY.
HE'D HARVEST LATE IN AUGUST, SO LANA, PETE AND I MADE IT A TRADITION THAT RIGHT BEFORE SCHOOL STARTED, WE'D GO TO HIS FARM, CLIMB TO THE TOP OF HIS SILO, AND JUMP THIRTY FEET DOWN INTO THE STACK BELOW.
"THE COLDER LEAP."
I THINK OF THAT SOMETIMES, WHEN I'M COMING BACK IN FROM OUT THERE. HOW SIMILAR REENTRY FEELS TO THAT FALL FROM JED COLDER'S SILO.
HOW FAST THE WORLD SUDDENLY GOES FROM BEING AN IMAGE IN THE DARKNESS TO A REAL THING, THE COLORS TAKING ON DETAIL AND TEXTURE, BECOMING OCEANS AND MOUNTAINS AND FIELDS.
ALL OF IT RUSHING TOWARD YOU SO FAST IT'S HYPNOTIC, SO FAST...

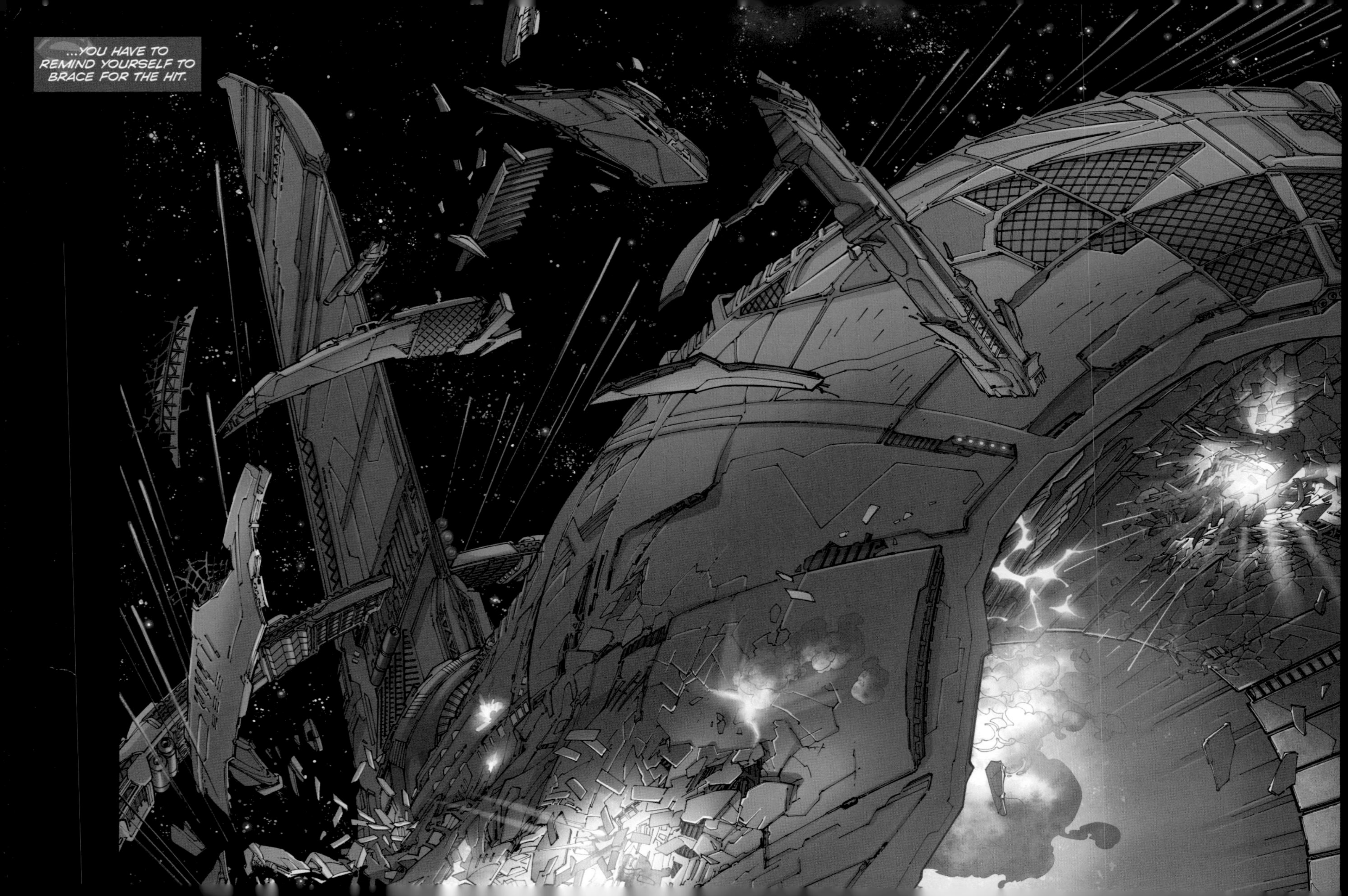
...YOU HAVE TO REMIND YOURSELF TO BRACE FOR THE HIT.

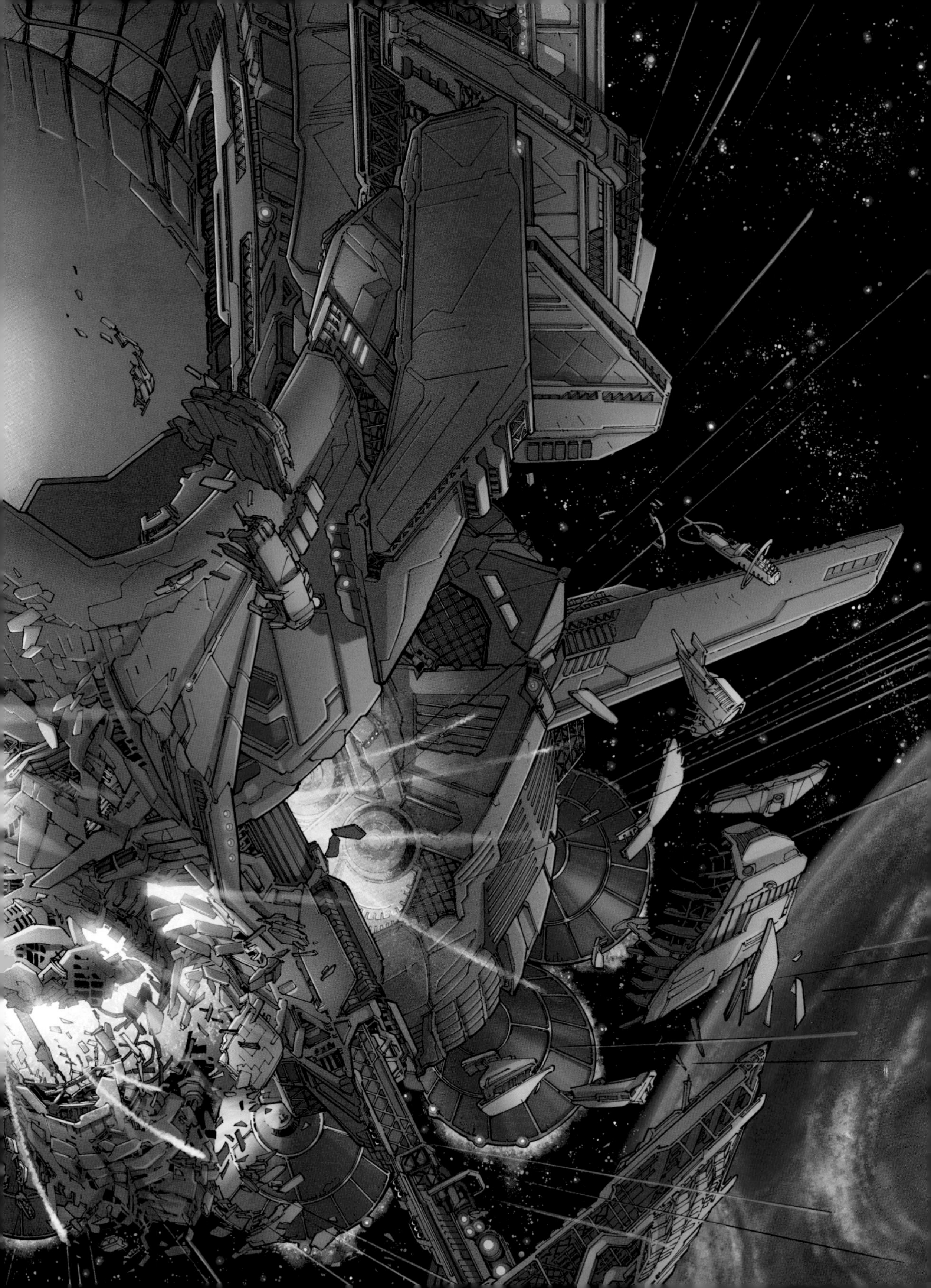

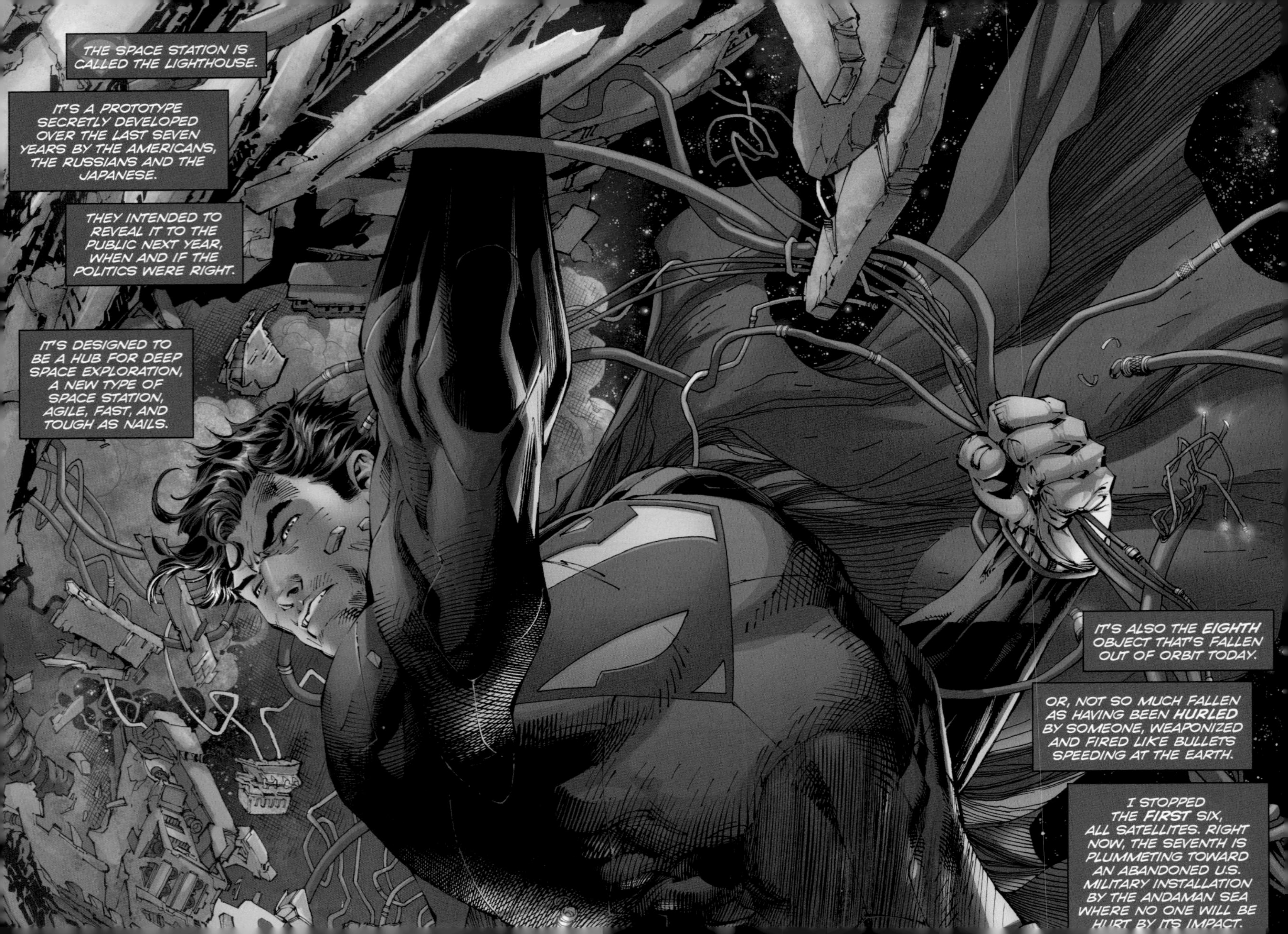

THE SPACE STATION IS CALLED THE LIGHTHOUSE.
IT'S A PROTOTYPE SECRETLY DEVELOPED OVER THE LAST SEVEN YEARS BY THE AMERICANS, THE RUSSIANS AND THE JAPANESE.
THEY INTENDED TO REVEAL IT TO THE PUBLIC NEXT YEAR, WHEN AND IF THE POLITICS WERE RIGHT.
IT'S DESIGNED TO BE A HUB FOR DEEP SPACE EXPLORATION, A NEW TYPE OF SPACE STATION, AGILE, FAST, AND TOUGH AS NAILS.
IT'S ALSO THE EIGHTH OBJECT THAT'S FALLEN OUT OF ORBIT TODAY.
OR, NOT SO MUCH FALLEN AS HAVING BEEN HURLED BY SOMEONE, WEAPONIZED AND FIRED LIKE BULLETS SPEEDING AT THE EARTH.
I STOPPED THE FIRST SIX, ALL SATELLITES. RIGHT NOW, THE SEVENTH IS PLUMMETING TOWARD AN ABANDONED U.S. MILITARY INSTALLATION BY THE ANDAMAN SEA WHERE NO ONE WILL BE HURT BY ITS IMPACT.

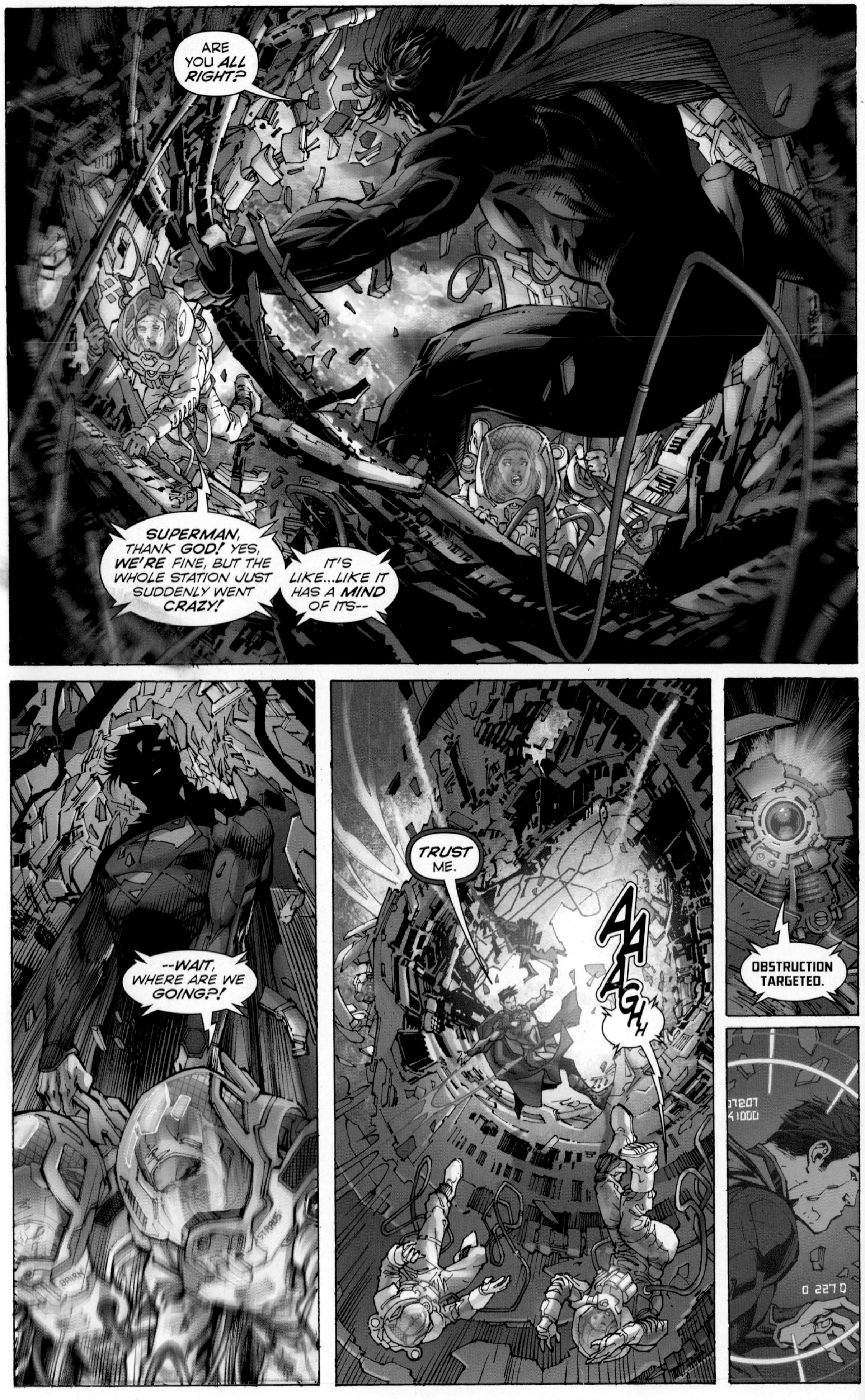
ARE YOU ALL RIGHT?
SUPERMAN, THANK GOD! YES, WE'RE FINE, BUT THE WHOLE STATION JUST SUDDENLY WENT CRAZY!
IT'S LIKE...LIKE IT HAS A MIND OF ITS--
--WAIT, WHERE ARE WE GOING?!
TRUST ME.
AAAGHH
OBSTRUCTION TARGETED.

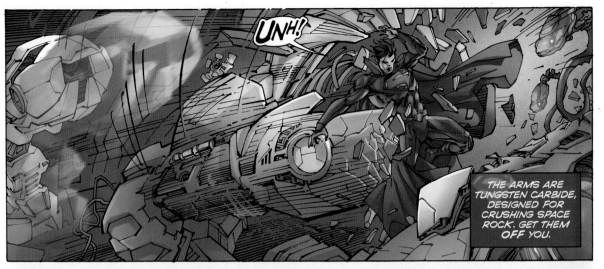

UNH!

THE ARMS ARE TUNGSTEN CARBIDE, DESIGNED FOR CRUSHING SPACE ROCK. GET THEM OFF YOU.

THE ASTRONAUTS ARE TERRIFIED. TALK TO THEM, BEFORE THE STATION'S ATMOSPHERE DISSIPATES. LET THEM HEAR YOUR VOICE.

WE'LL GET THROUGH THIS, DON'T WORRY.

BELIEVE ME, YOU'RE SAFER OUT THERE.

BUT WE'RE GOING TO BURN UP!

NO. YOU'RE NOT.

LISTEN TO ME. MY HEAT VISION ACTIVATED THE REENTRY SHIELD EARLY. YOU'LL BE SAFE BEHIND IT. BUT I NEED YOUR HELP.

THE REPAIR DRONES, SUPERMAN! LOOK OUT, THEY'RE--

NEVER-- *UNH!*

NEVER MIND THEM! I NEED TO SHUT DOWN THE *CORE!* IT'S PROTECTED BY LEADED COPPER CASING. I CAN'T SEE THROUGH IT!

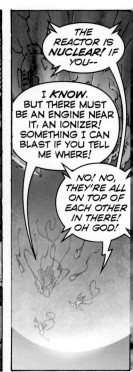

THE REACTOR IS *NUCLEAR!* IF YOU--

I *KNOW.* BUT THERE MUST BE AN ENGINE NEAR IT, AN IONIZER! SOMETHING I CAN *BLAST* IF YOU TELL ME WHERE!

NO! NO, THEY'RE ALL ON TOP OF EACH OTHER IN THERE! OH GOD!

THINK, CLARK! COME ON! THE BATTERY IS NUCLEAR, BUT THE ENGINE...

...IT'S *ELECTRICAL!* MAYBE YOU CAN FRY THE CIRCUITY IF YOU USE YOUR X-RAY VISION...

DAMMIT! NOT WORKING...

THEN GO *STRONGER,* CLARK! INTENSIFY IT!

TURN IT... GAMMA!

ZZZTT

VRRRRRRR

YOU DID IT! THE LIGHTHOUSE IS DEAD WEIGHT, BUT WE'RE TOO FAR INSIDE THE ATMOSPHERE, SUPERMAN! WE'RE GOING TO--

HERE! TAKE MY HAND! I'LL SHIELD YOU FROM THE IMPACT!

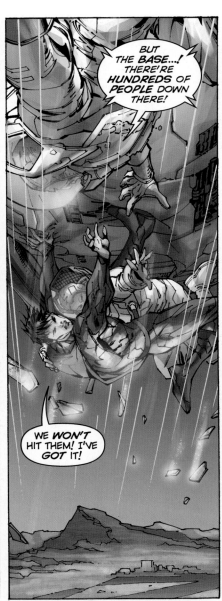

BUT THE BASE...! THERE'RE HUNDREDS OF PEOPLE DOWN THERE!

WE WON'T HIT THEM! I'VE GOT IT!

WE'RE--

LISTEN TO ME!

NO ONE IS GOING TO DIE TOD--

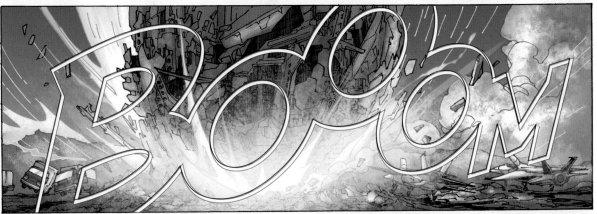

BOOOM

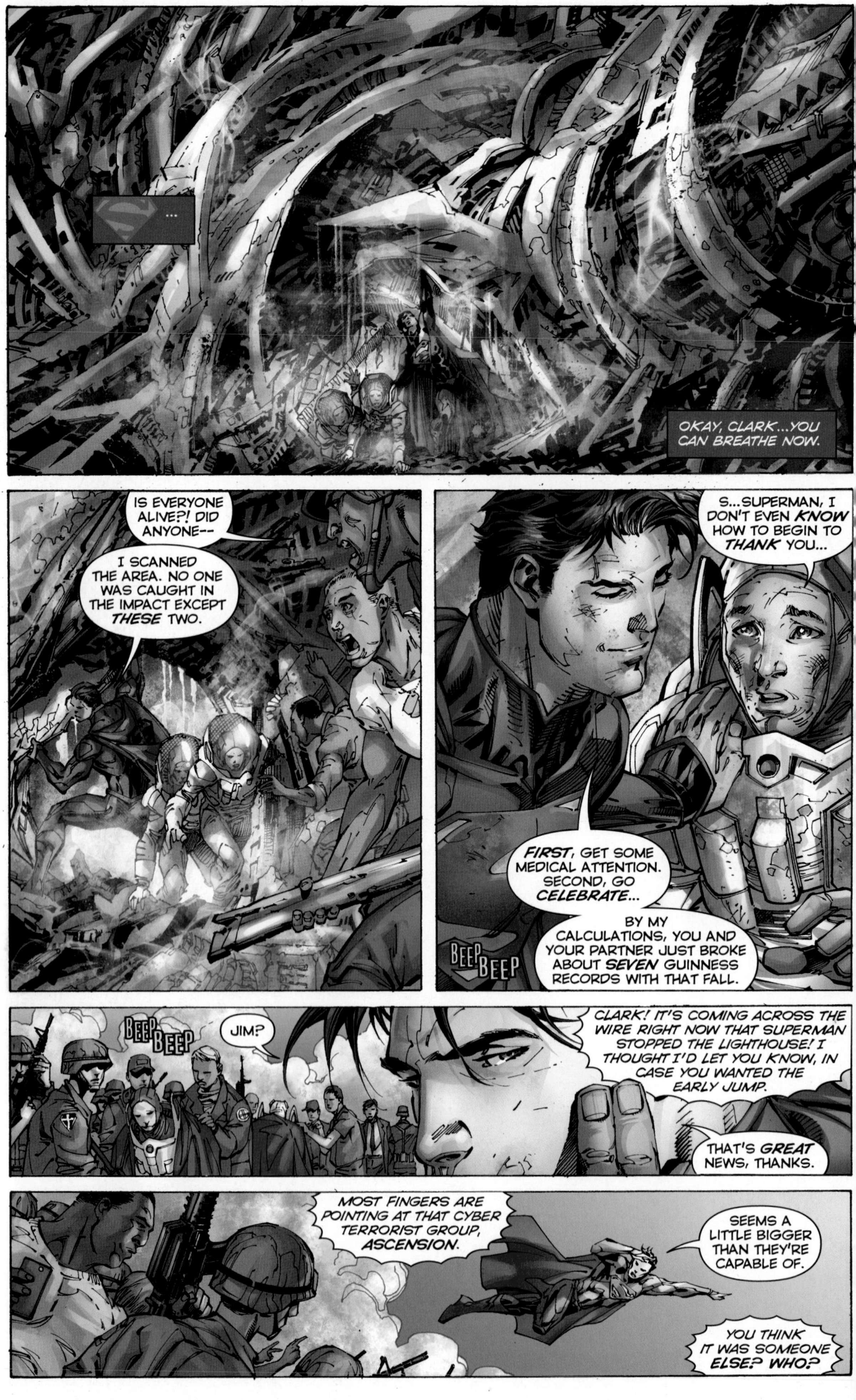

...
OKAY, CLARK...YOU CAN BREATHE NOW.
IS EVERYONE ALIVE?! DID ANYONE--
I SCANNED THE AREA. NO ONE WAS CAUGHT IN THE IMPACT EXCEPT THESE TWO.
S...SUPERMAN, I DON'T EVEN KNOW HOW TO BEGIN TO THANK YOU...
FIRST, GET SOME MEDICAL ATTENTION. SECOND, GO CELEBRATE...
BY MY CALCULATIONS, YOU AND YOUR PARTNER JUST BROKE ABOUT SEVEN GUINNESS RECORDS WITH THAT FALL.
BEEP BEEP
BEEP BEEP
JIM?
CLARK! IT'S COMING ACROSS THE WIRE RIGHT NOW THAT SUPERMAN STOPPED THE LIGHTHOUSE! I THOUGHT I'D LET YOU KNOW, IN CASE YOU WANTED THE EARLY JUMP.
THAT'S GREAT NEWS, THANKS.
MOST FINGERS ARE POINTING AT THAT CYBER TERRORIST GROUP, ASCENSION.
SEEMS A LITTLE BIGGER THAN THEY'RE CAPABLE OF.
YOU THINK IT WAS SOMEONE ELSE? WHO?

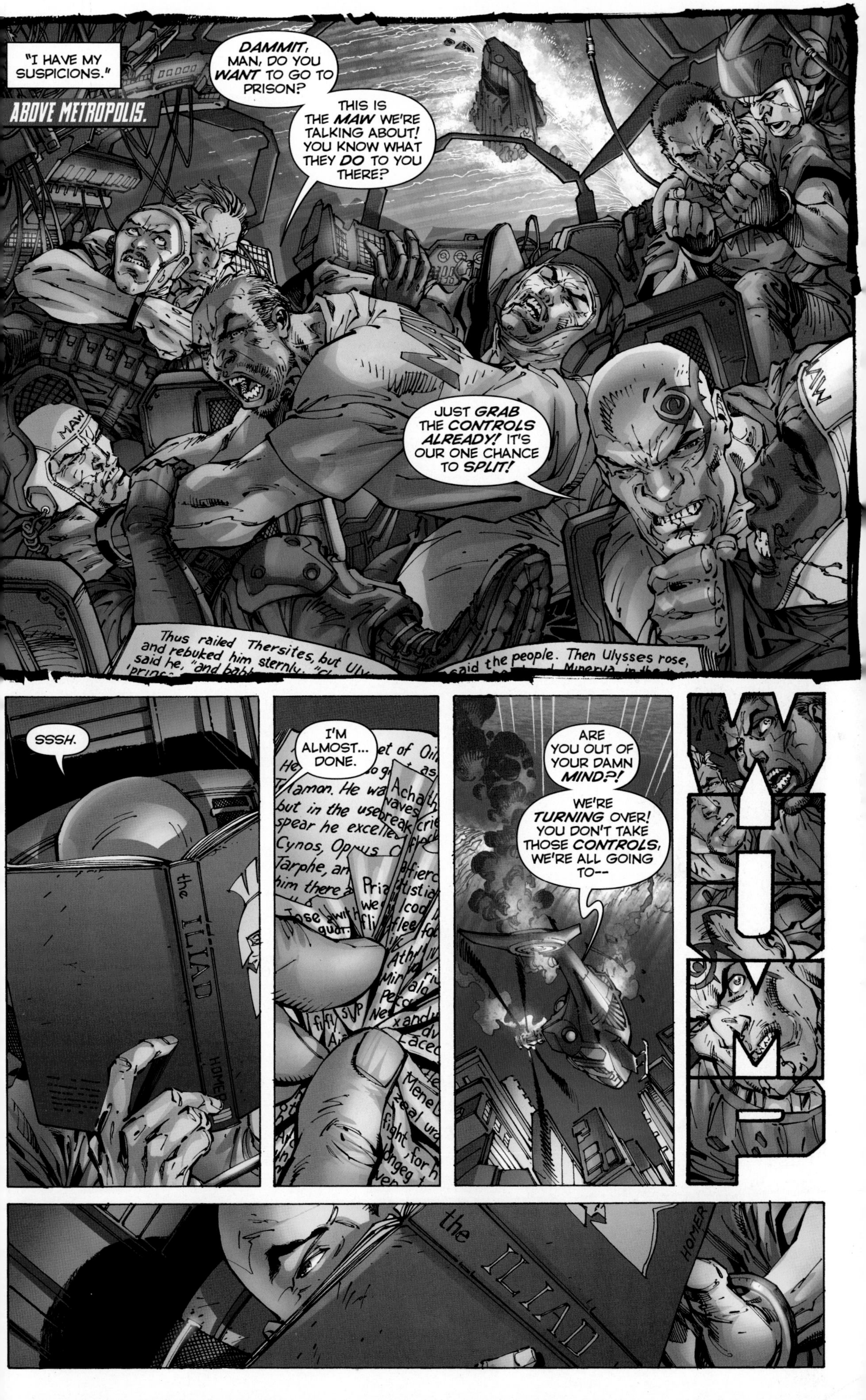

"I HAVE MY SUSPICIONS."
ABOVE METROPOLIS.
DAMMIT, MAN, DO YOU WANT TO GO TO PRISON?
THIS IS THE MAW WE'RE TALKING ABOUT! YOU KNOW WHAT THEY DO TO YOU THERE?
JUST GRAB THE CONTROLS ALREADY! IT'S OUR ONE CHANCE TO SPLIT!
Thus railed Thersites, but Ulysses ... and rebuked him sternly, ... said he, ... said the people. Then Ulysses rose,
SSSH.
I'M ALMOST... DONE.
ARE YOU OUT OF YOUR DAMN MIND?!
WE'RE TURNING OVER! YOU DON'T TAKE THOSE CONTROLS, WE'RE ALL GOING TO--
WUMP
the ILIAD HOMER

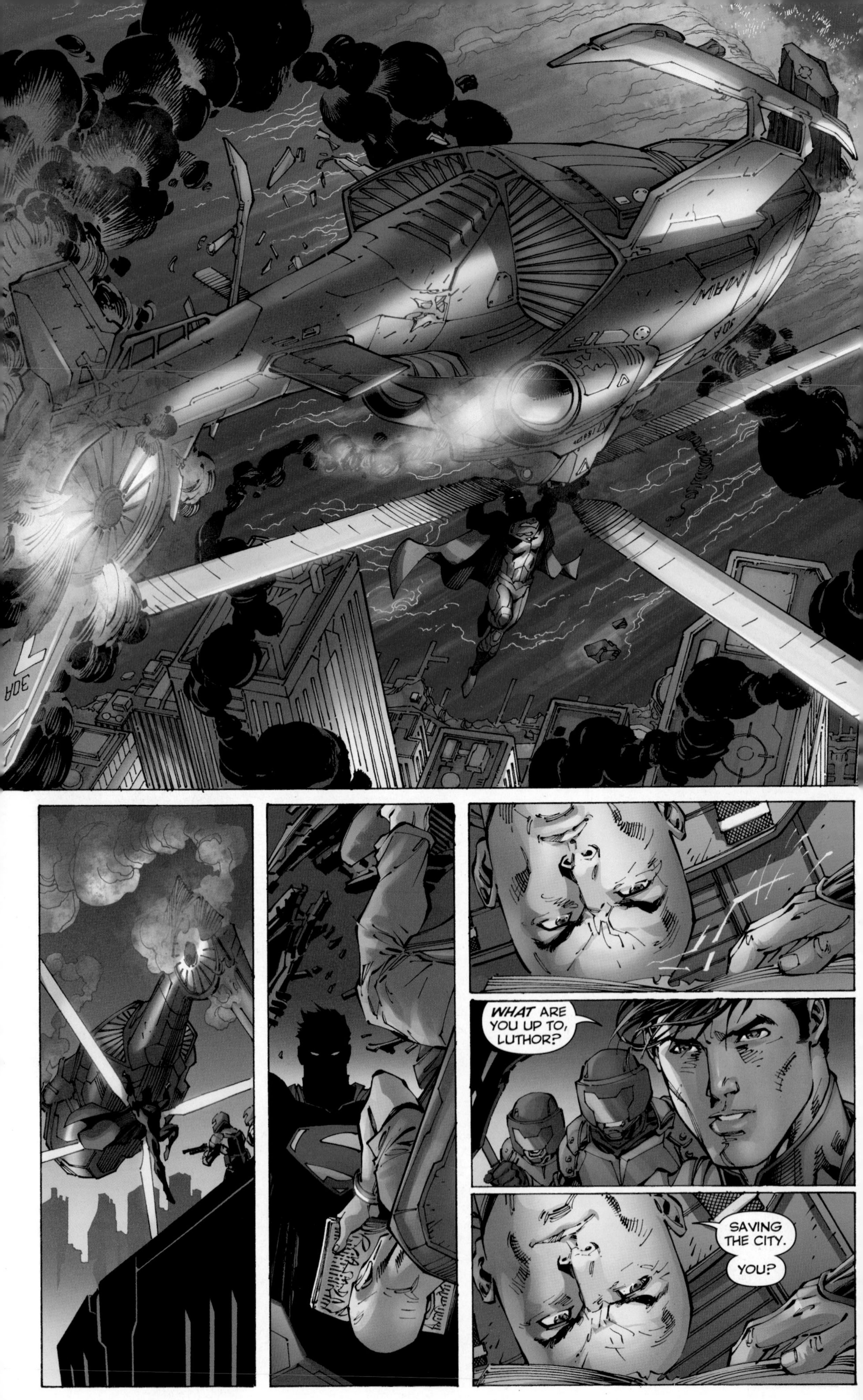

WHAT ARE YOU UP TO, LUTHOR?
SAVING THE CITY.
YOU?

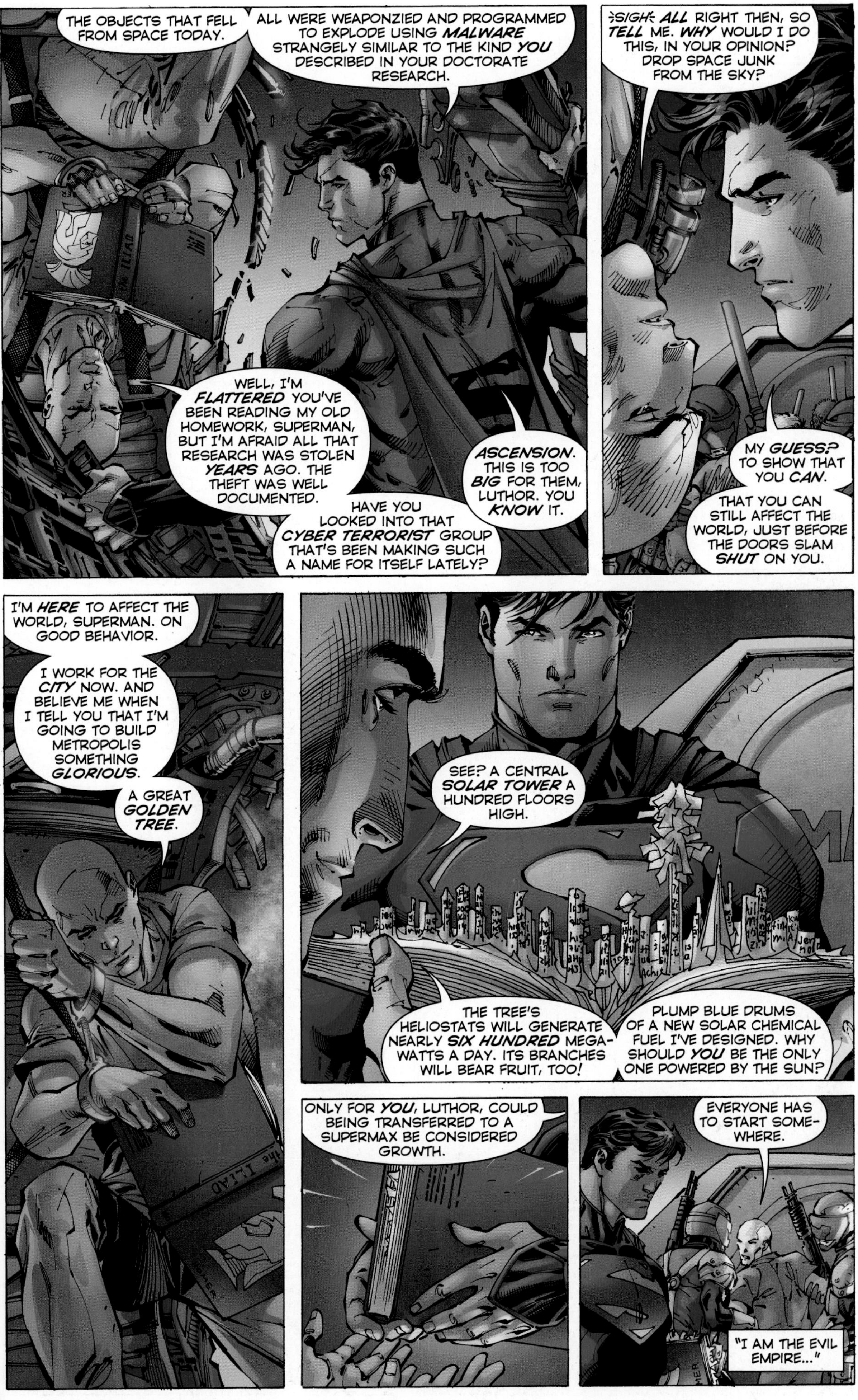

THE OBJECTS THAT FELL FROM SPACE TODAY.
ALL WERE WEAPONZIED AND PROGRAMMED TO EXPLODE USING MALWARE STRANGELY SIMILAR TO THE KIND YOU DESCRIBED IN YOUR DOCTORATE RESEARCH.
WELL, I'M FLATTERED YOU'VE BEEN READING MY OLD HOMEWORK, SUPERMAN, BUT I'M AFRAID ALL THAT RESEARCH WAS STOLEN YEARS AGO. THE THEFT WAS WELL DOCUMENTED.
HAVE YOU LOOKED INTO THAT CYBER TERRORIST GROUP THAT'S BEEN MAKING SUCH A NAME FOR ITSELF LATELY?
ASCENSION. THIS IS TOO BIG FOR THEM, LUTHOR. YOU KNOW IT.
SIGH ALL RIGHT THEN, SO TELL ME. WHY WOULD I DO THIS, IN YOUR OPINION? DROP SPACE JUNK FROM THE SKY?
MY GUESS? TO SHOW THAT YOU CAN.
THAT YOU CAN STILL AFFECT THE WORLD, JUST BEFORE THE DOORS SLAM SHUT ON YOU.
I'M HERE TO AFFECT THE WORLD, SUPERMAN. ON GOOD BEHAVIOR.
I WORK FOR THE CITY NOW. AND BELIEVE ME WHEN I TELL YOU THAT I'M GOING TO BUILD METROPOLIS SOMETHING GLORIOUS.
A GREAT GOLDEN TREE.
SEE? A CENTRAL SOLAR TOWER A HUNDRED FLOORS HIGH.
THE TREE'S HELIOSTATS WILL GENERATE NEARLY SIX HUNDRED MEGA-WATTS A DAY. ITS BRANCHES WILL BEAR FRUIT, TOO!
PLUMP BLUE DRUMS OF A NEW SOLAR CHEMICAL FUEL I'VE DESIGNED. WHY SHOULD YOU BE THE ONLY ONE POWERED BY THE SUN?
ONLY FOR YOU, LUTHOR, COULD BEING TRANSFERRED TO A SUPERMAX BE CONSIDERED GROWTH.
EVERYONE HAS TO START SOME-WHERE.
"I AM THE EVIL EMPIRE..."

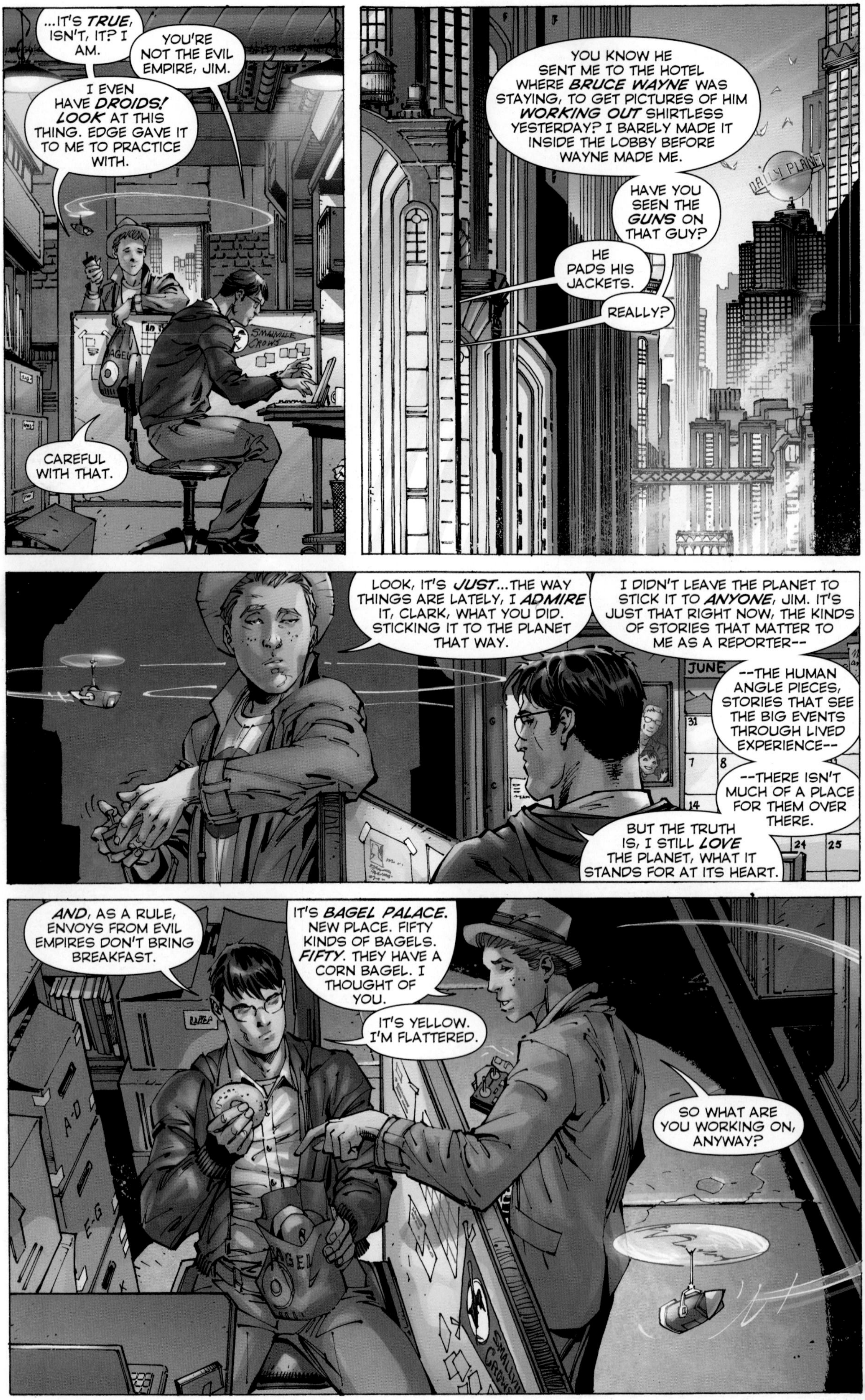

...IT'S TRUE, ISN'T, IT? I AM.
YOU'RE NOT THE EVIL EMPIRE, JIM.
I EVEN HAVE DROIDS! LOOK AT THIS THING. EDGE GAVE IT TO ME TO PRACTICE WITH.
CAREFUL WITH THAT.
YOU KNOW HE SENT ME TO THE HOTEL WHERE BRUCE WAYNE WAS STAYING, TO GET PICTURES OF HIM WORKING OUT SHIRTLESS YESTERDAY? I BARELY MADE IT INSIDE THE LOBBY BEFORE WAYNE MADE ME.
HAVE YOU SEEN THE GUNS ON THAT GUY?
HE PADS HIS JACKETS.
REALLY?
DAILY PLANET
LOOK, IT'S JUST...THE WAY THINGS ARE LATELY, I ADMIRE IT, CLARK, WHAT YOU DID. STICKING IT TO THE PLANET THAT WAY.
I DIDN'T LEAVE THE PLANET TO STICK IT TO ANYONE, JIM. IT'S JUST THAT RIGHT NOW, THE KINDS OF STORIES THAT MATTER TO ME AS A REPORTER--
--THE HUMAN ANGLE PIECES, STORIES THAT SEE THE BIG EVENTS THROUGH LIVED EXPERIENCE--
--THERE ISN'T MUCH OF A PLACE FOR THEM OVER THERE.
BUT THE TRUTH IS, I STILL LOVE THE PLANET, WHAT IT STANDS FOR AT ITS HEART.
AND, AS A RULE, ENVOYS FROM EVIL EMPIRES DON'T BRING BREAKFAST.
IT'S BAGEL PALACE. NEW PLACE. FIFTY KINDS OF BAGELS. FIFTY. THEY HAVE A CORN BAGEL. I THOUGHT OF YOU.
IT'S YELLOW. I'M FLATTERED.
SO WHAT ARE YOU WORKING ON, ANYWAY?

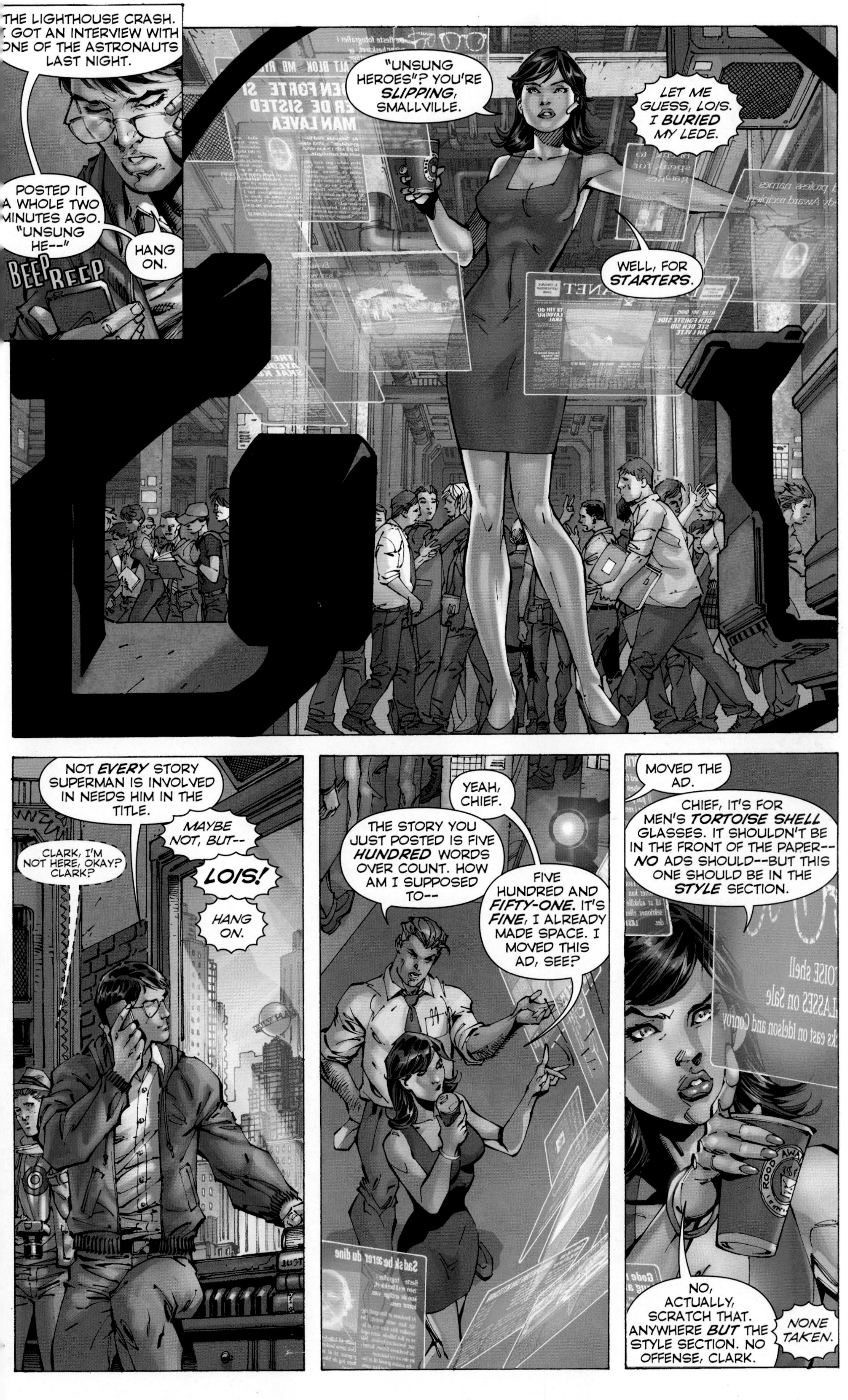
THE LIGHTHOUSE CRASH. I GOT AN INTERVIEW WITH ONE OF THE ASTRONAUTS LAST NIGHT.
POSTED IT A WHOLE TWO MINUTES AGO. "UNSUNG HE--"
BEEP BEEP
HANG ON.
"UNSUNG HEROES"? YOU'RE SLIPPING, SMALLVILLE.
LET ME GUESS, LOIS. I BURIED MY LEDE.
WELL, FOR STARTERS.
NOT EVERY STORY SUPERMAN IS INVOLVED IN NEEDS HIM IN THE TITLE.
MAYBE NOT, BUT--
CLARK, I'M NOT HERE, OKAY? CLARK?
LOIS!
HANG ON.
YEAH, CHIEF.
THE STORY YOU JUST POSTED IS FIVE HUNDRED WORDS OVER COUNT. HOW AM I SUPPOSED TO--
FIVE HUNDRED AND FIFTY-ONE. IT'S FINE, I ALREADY MADE SPACE. I MOVED THIS AD, SEE?
MOVED THE AD.
CHIEF, IT'S FOR MEN'S TORTOISE SHELL GLASSES. IT SHOULDN'T BE IN THE FRONT OF THE PAPER--NO ADS SHOULD--BUT THIS ONE SHOULD BE IN THE STYLE SECTION.
NO, ACTUALLY, SCRATCH THAT. ANYWHERE BUT THE STYLE SECTION. NO OFFENSE, CLARK.
NONE TAKEN.

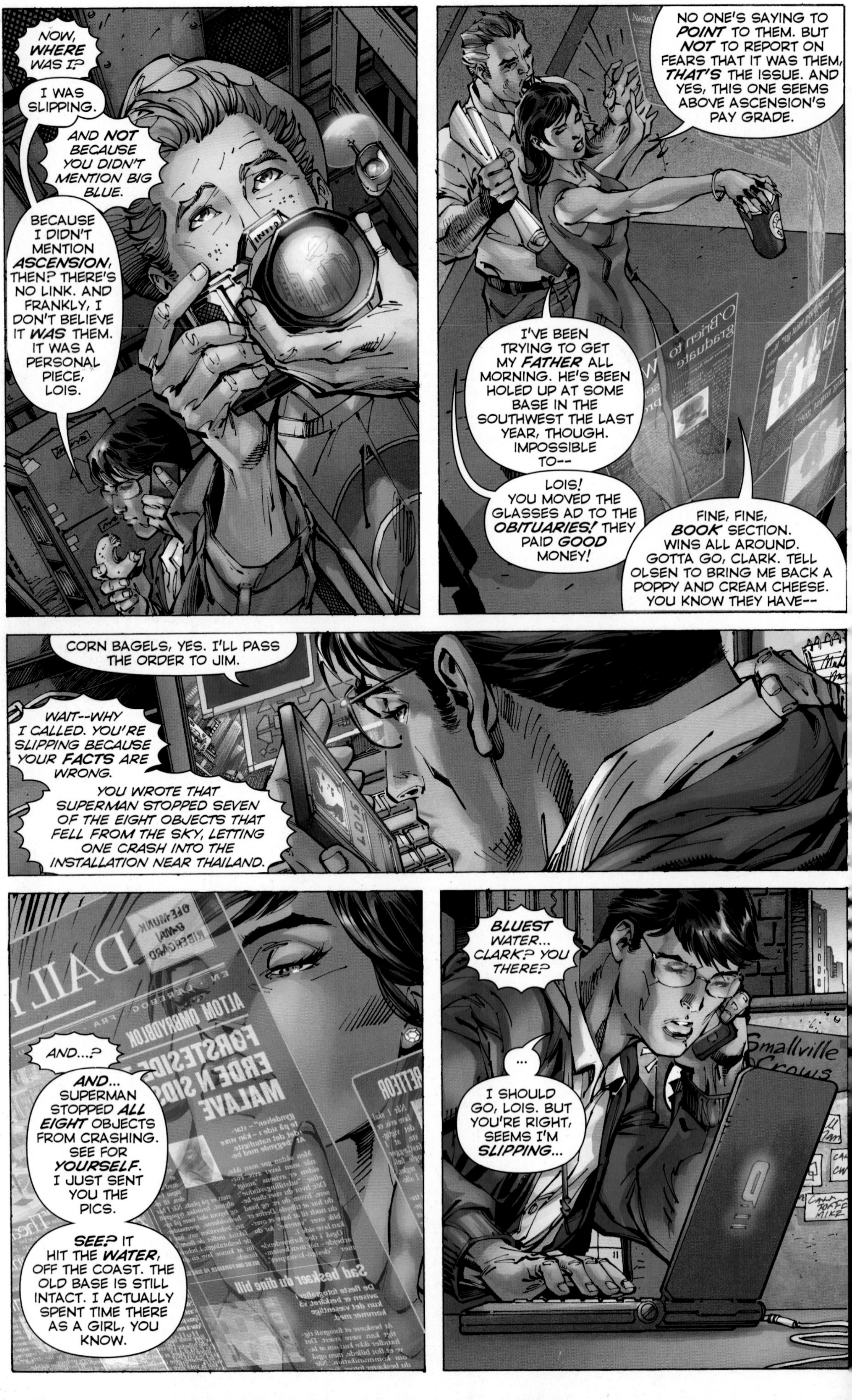
NOW, WHERE WAS I?
I WAS SLIPPING.
AND NOT BECAUSE YOU DIDN'T MENTION BIG BLUE.
BECAUSE I DIDN'T MENTION ASCENSION, THEN? THERE'S NO LINK. AND FRANKLY, I DON'T BELIEVE IT WAS THEM. IT WAS A PERSONAL PIECE, LOIS.
NO ONE'S SAYING TO POINT TO THEM. BUT NOT TO REPORT ON FEARS THAT IT WAS THEM, THAT'S THE ISSUE. AND YES, THIS ONE SEEMS ABOVE ASCENSION'S PAY GRADE.
I'VE BEEN TRYING TO GET MY FATHER ALL MORNING. HE'S BEEN HOLED UP AT SOME BASE IN THE SOUTHWEST THE LAST YEAR, THOUGH. IMPOSSIBLE TO--
LOIS! YOU MOVED THE GLASSES AD TO THE OBITUARIES! THEY PAID GOOD MONEY!
FINE, FINE, BOOK SECTION. WINS ALL AROUND. GOTTA GO, CLARK. TELL OLSEN TO BRING ME BACK A POPPY AND CREAM CHEESE. YOU KNOW THEY HAVE--
CORN BAGELS, YES. I'LL PASS THE ORDER TO JIM.
WAIT--WHY I CALLED. YOU'RE SLIPPING BECAUSE YOUR FACTS ARE WRONG.
YOU WROTE THAT SUPERMAN STOPPED SEVEN OF THE EIGHT OBJECTS THAT FELL FROM THE SKY, LETTING ONE CRASH INTO THE INSTALLATION NEAR THAILAND.
AND...?
AND... SUPERMAN STOPPED ALL EIGHT OBJECTS FROM CRASHING. SEE FOR YOURSELF. I JUST SENT YOU THE PICS.
SEE? IT HIT THE WATER, OFF THE COAST. THE OLD BASE IS STILL INTACT. I ACTUALLY SPENT TIME THERE AS A GIRL, YOU KNOW.
BLUEST WATER... CLARK? YOU THERE?
...
I SHOULD GO, LOIS. BUT YOU'RE RIGHT, SEEMS I'M SLIPPING...
Smallville Crows

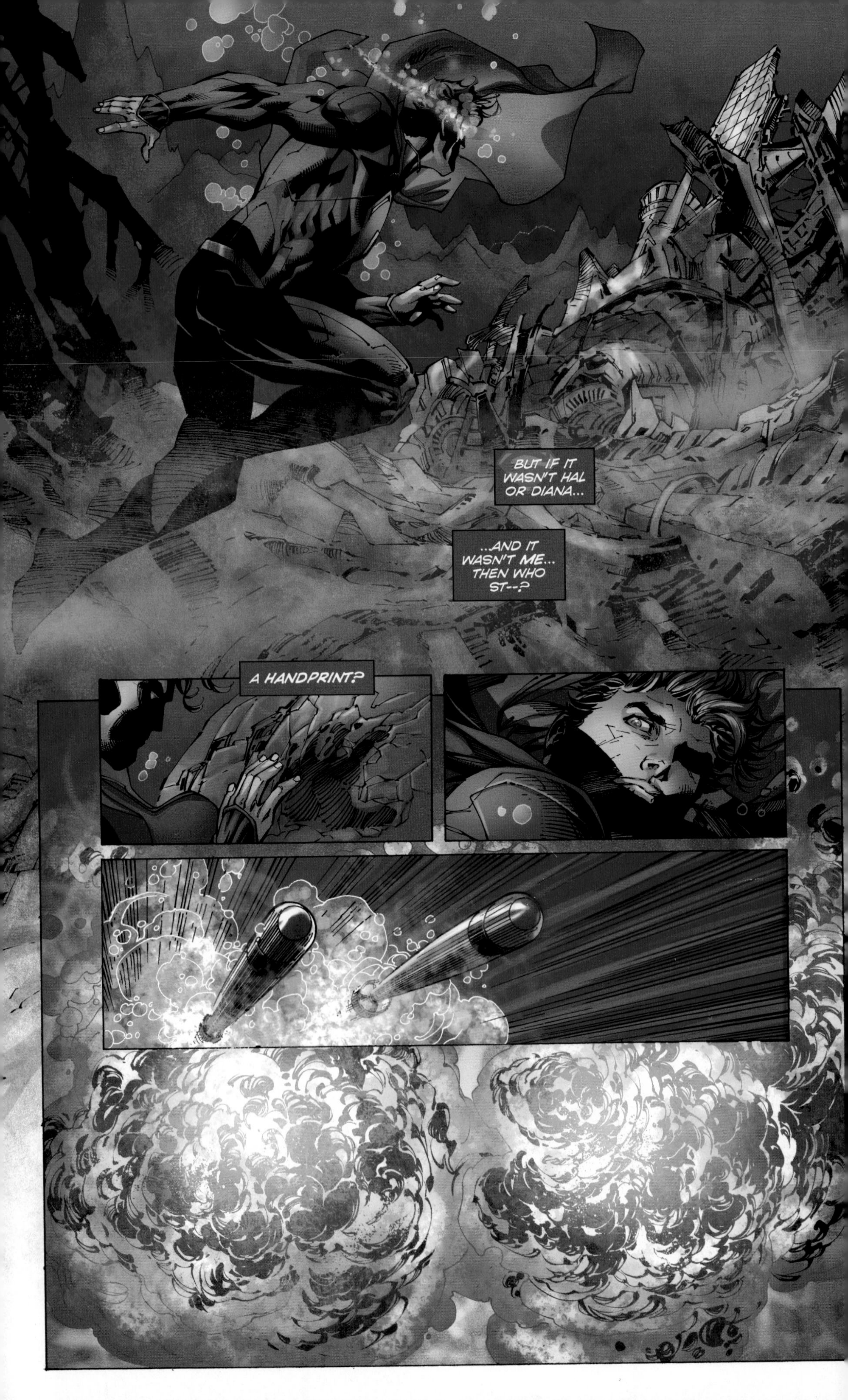

BUT IF IT WASN'T HAL OR DIANA...
...AND IT WASN'T ME... THEN WHO ST--?
A HANDPRINT?

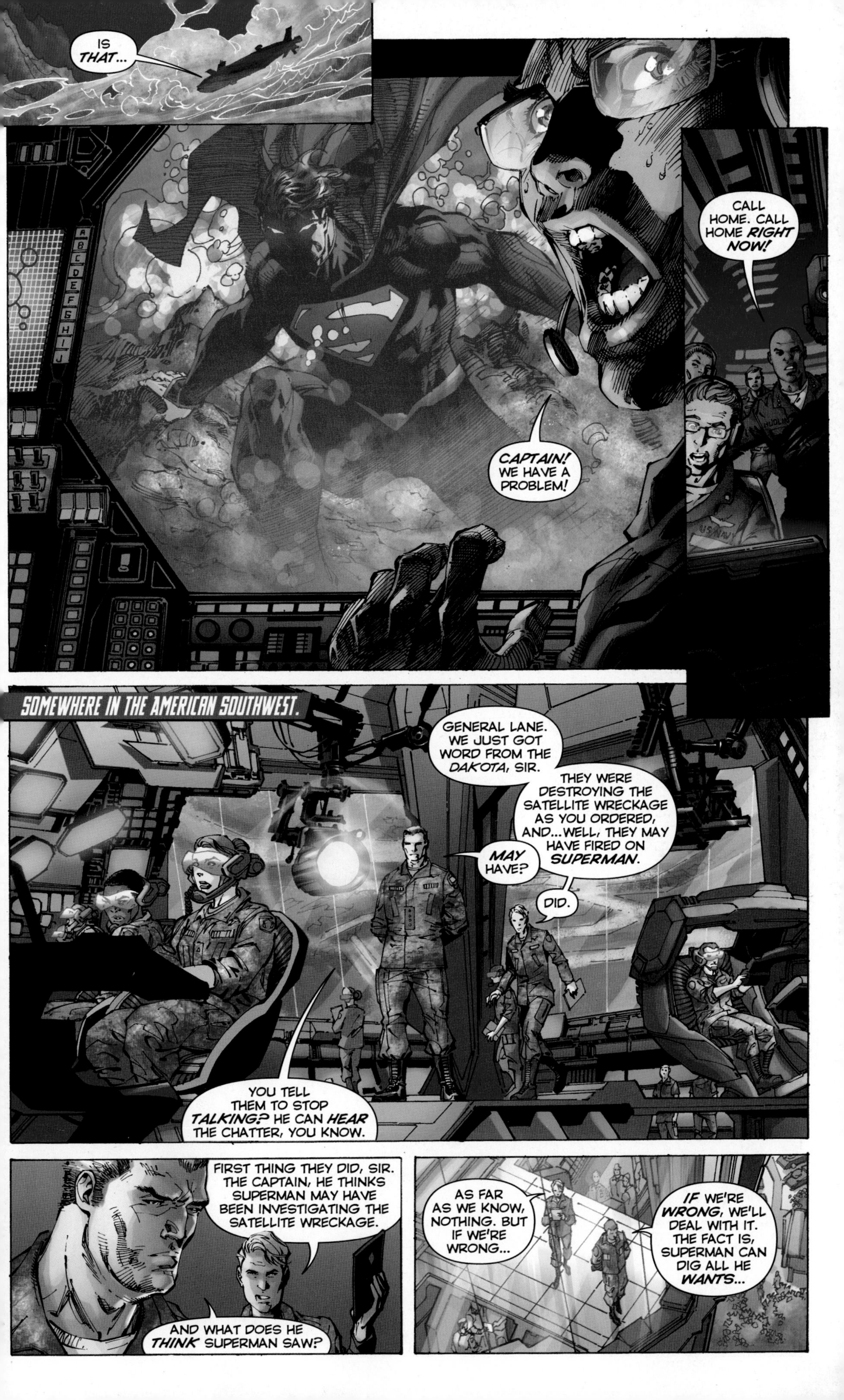
IS THAT...
CALL HOME. CALL HOME RIGHT NOW!
CAPTAIN! WE HAVE A PROBLEM!
SOMEWHERE IN THE AMERICAN SOUTHWEST.
GENERAL LANE. WE JUST GOT WORD FROM THE DAKOTA, SIR.
THEY WERE DESTROYING THE SATELLITE WRECKAGE AS YOU ORDERED, AND...WELL, THEY MAY HAVE FIRED ON SUPERMAN.
MAY HAVE?
DID.
YOU TELL THEM TO STOP TALKING? HE CAN HEAR THE CHATTER, YOU KNOW.
FIRST THING THEY DID, SIR. THE CAPTAIN, HE THINKS SUPERMAN MAY HAVE BEEN INVESTIGATING THE SATELLITE WRECKAGE.
AND WHAT DOES HE THINK SUPERMAN SAW?
AS FAR AS WE KNOW, NOTHING. BUT IF WE'RE WRONG...
IF WE'RE WRONG, WE'LL DEAL WITH IT. THE FACT IS, SUPERMAN CAN DIG ALL HE WANTS...

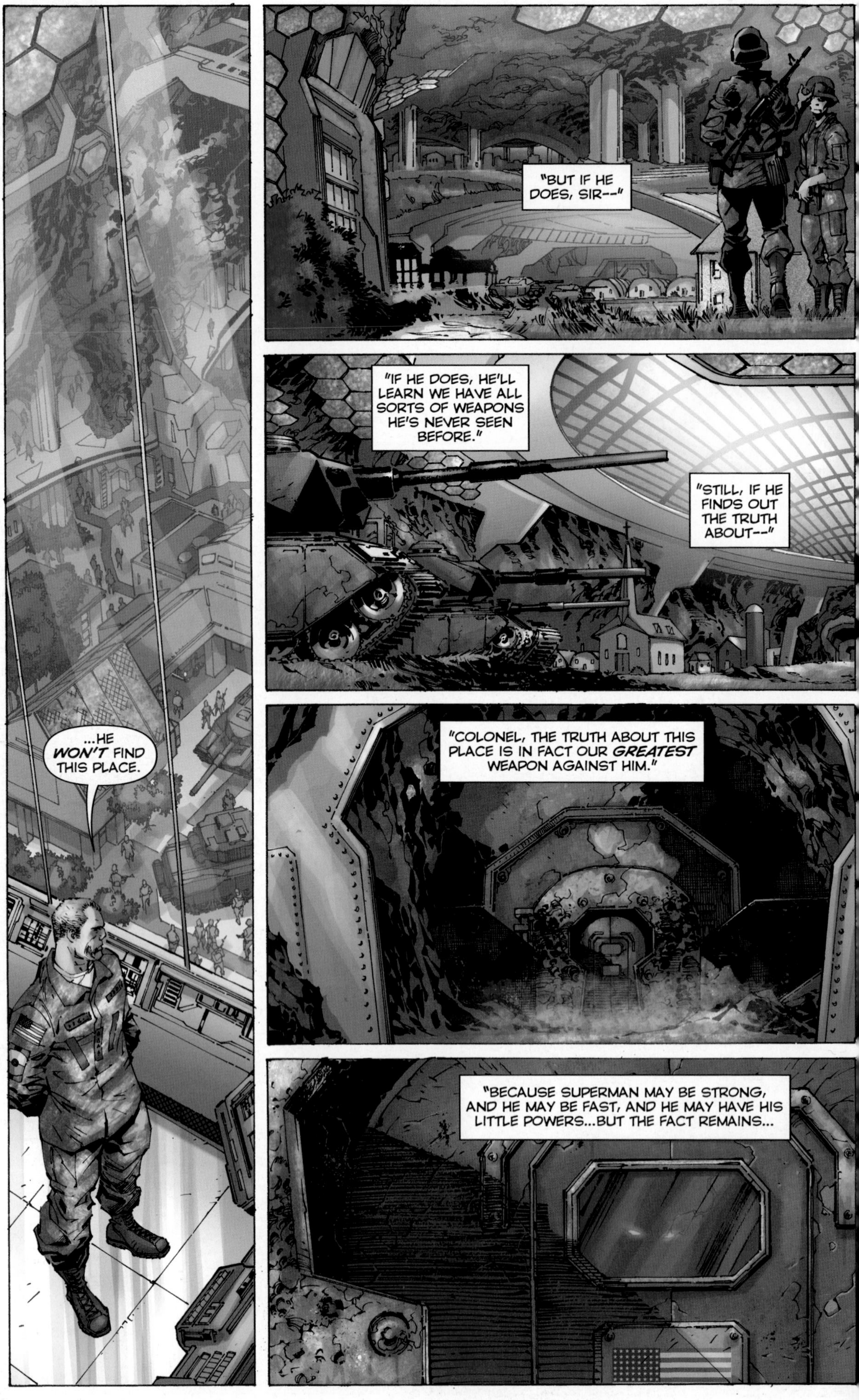

...HE *WON'T* FIND THIS PLACE.
"BUT IF HE DOES, SIR--"
"IF HE DOES, HE'LL LEARN WE HAVE ALL SORTS OF WEAPONS HE'S NEVER SEEN BEFORE."
"STILL, IF HE FINDS OUT THE TRUTH ABOUT--"
"COLONEL, THE TRUTH ABOUT THIS PLACE IS IN FACT OUR *GREATEST* WEAPON AGAINST HIM."
"BECAUSE SUPERMAN MAY BE STRONG, AND HE MAY BE FAST, AND HE MAY HAVE HIS LITTLE POWERS...BUT THE FACT REMAINS...

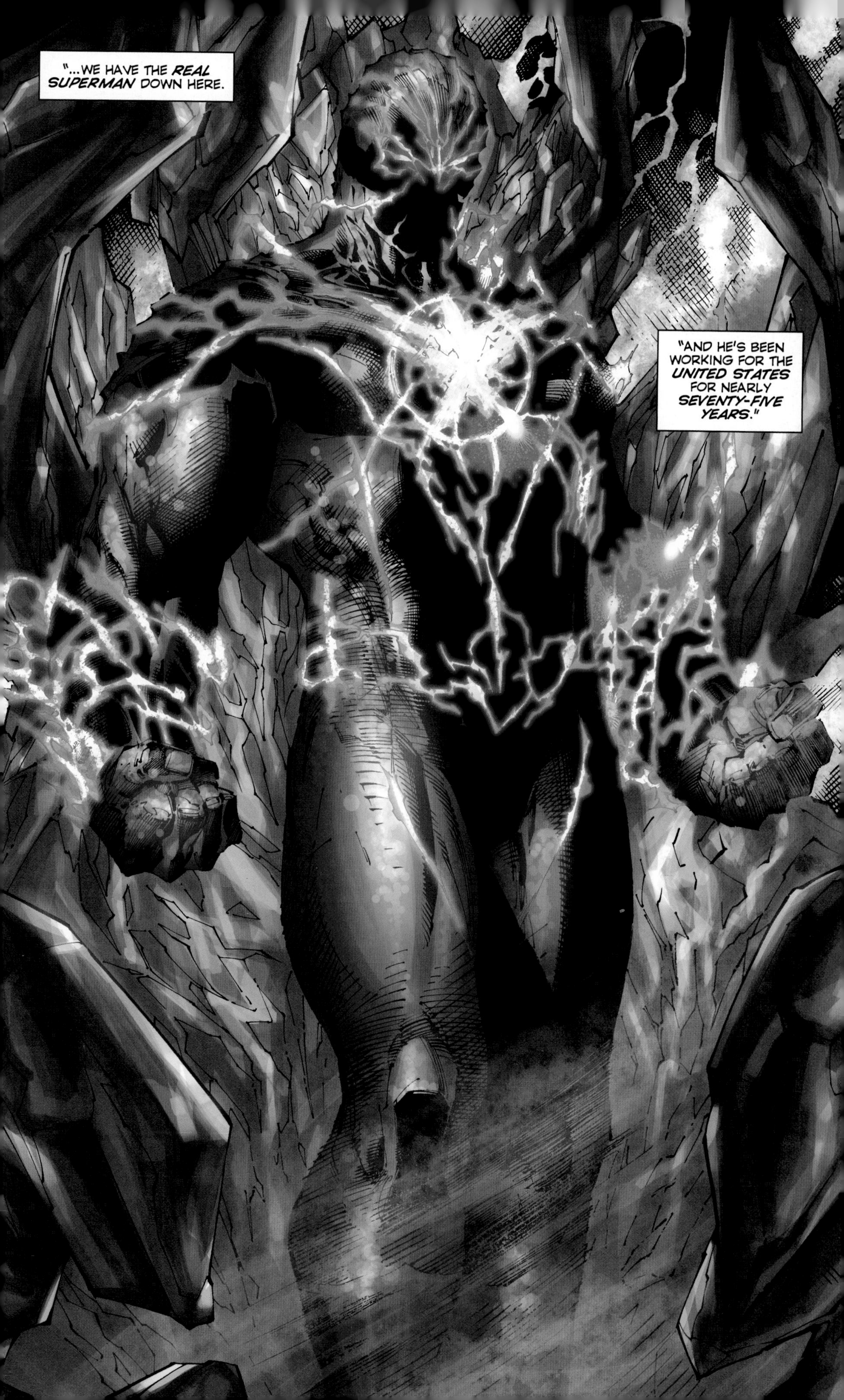
"...WE HAVE THE REAL SUPERMAN DOWN HERE.
"AND HE'S BEEN WORKING FOR THE UNITED STATES FOR NEARLY SEVENTY-FIVE YEARS."

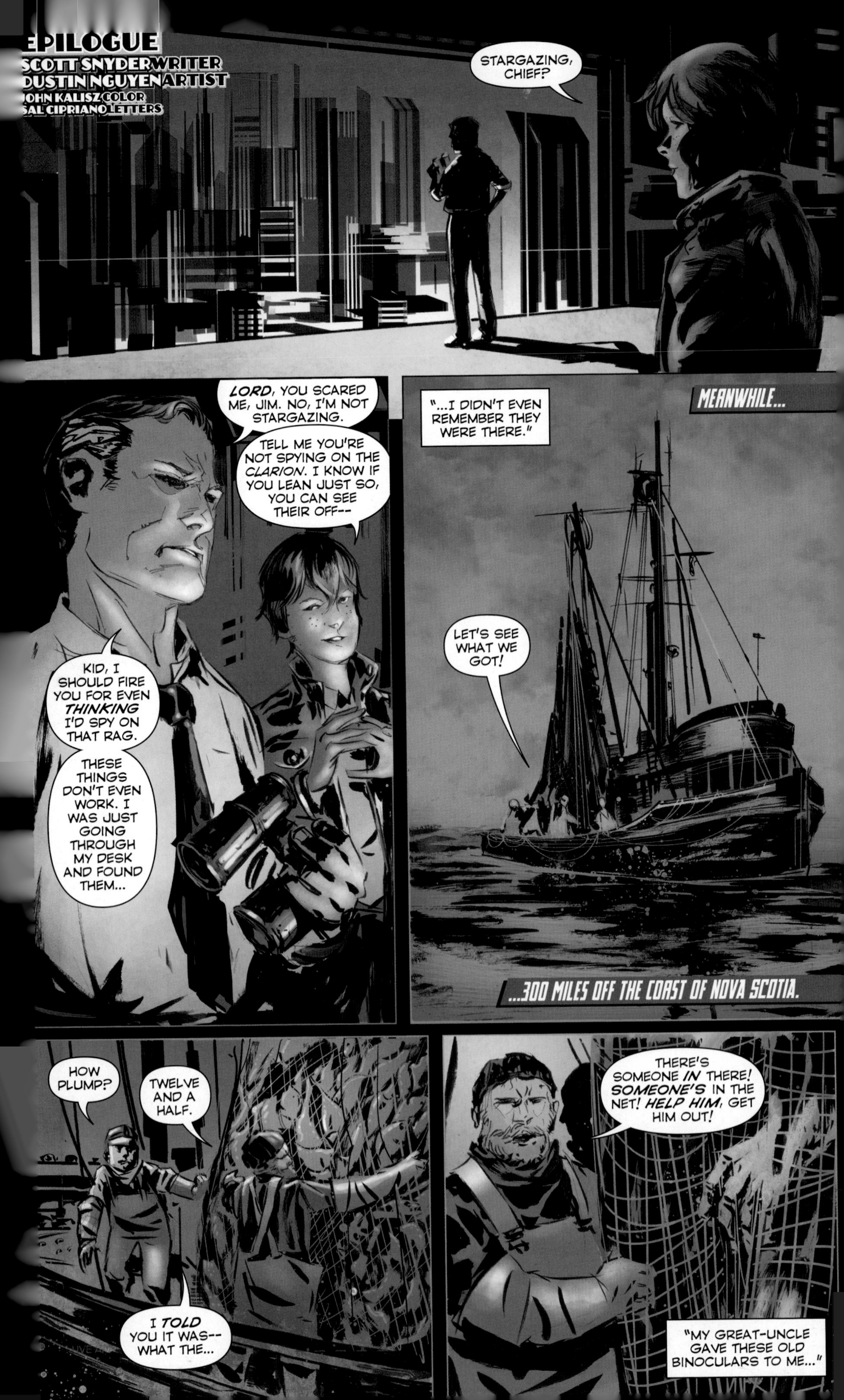
EPILOGUE
SCOTT SNYDER WRITER
DUSTIN NGUYEN ARTIST
JOHN KALISZ COLOR
SAL CIPRIANO LETTERS
STARGAZING, CHIEF?
LORD, YOU SCARED ME, JIM. NO, I'M NOT STARGAZING.
TELL ME YOU'RE NOT SPYING ON THE CLARION. I KNOW IF YOU LEAN JUST SO, YOU CAN SEE THEIR OFF--
KID, I SHOULD FIRE YOU FOR EVEN THINKING I'D SPY ON THAT RAG.
THESE THINGS DON'T EVEN WORK. I WAS JUST GOING THROUGH MY DESK AND FOUND THEM...
"...I DIDN'T EVEN REMEMBER THEY WERE THERE."
MEANWHILE...
LET'S SEE WHAT WE GOT!
...300 MILES OFF THE COAST OF NOVA SCOTIA.
HOW PLUMP?
TWELVE AND A HALF.
I TOLD YOU IT WAS-- WHAT THE...
THERE'S SOMEONE IN THERE! SOMEONE'S IN THE NET! HELP HIM, GET HIM OUT!
"MY GREAT-UNCLE GAVE THESE OLD BINOCULARS TO ME..."

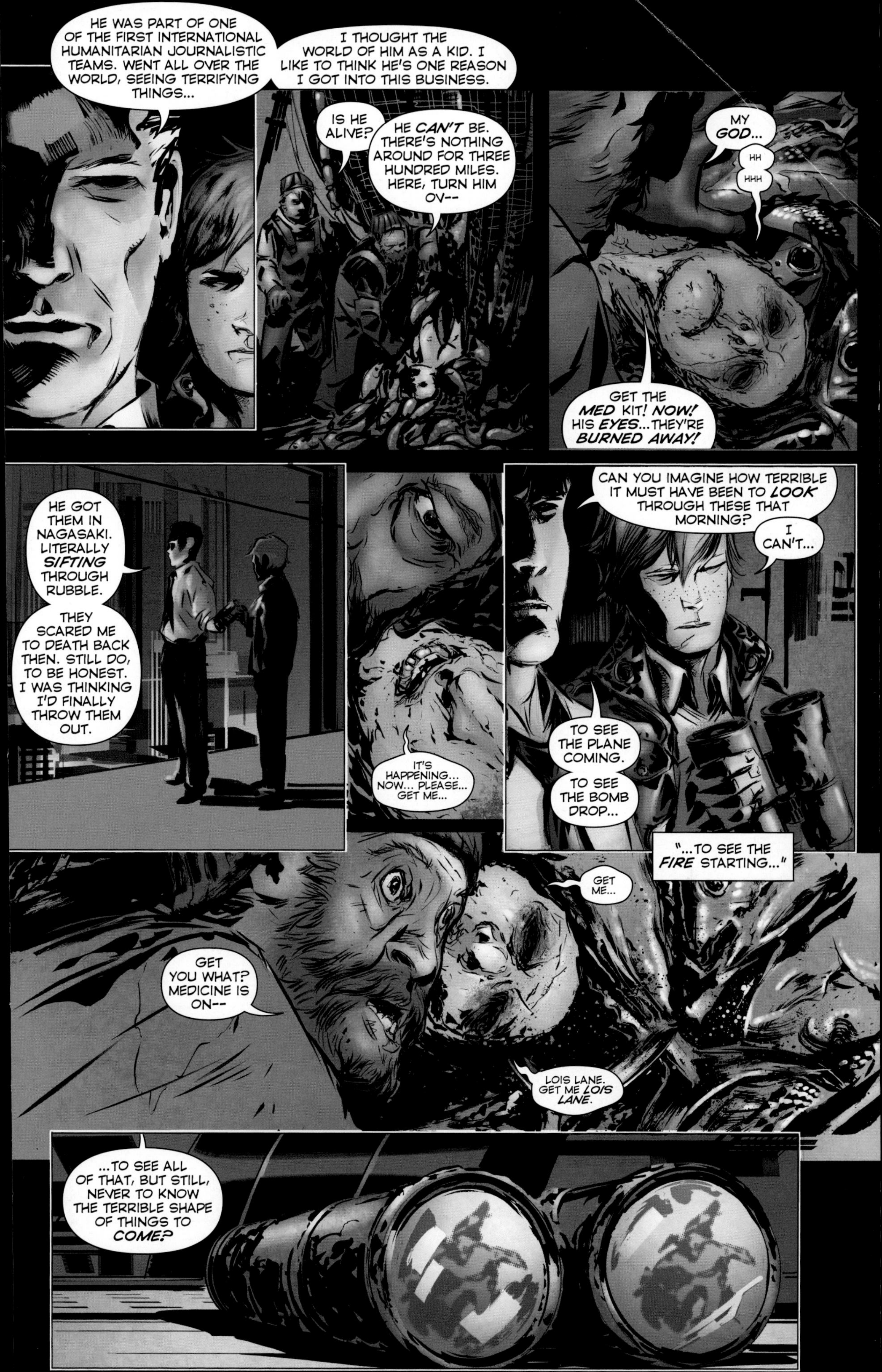
HE WAS PART OF ONE OF THE FIRST INTERNATIONAL HUMANITARIAN JOURNALISTIC TEAMS. WENT ALL OVER THE WORLD, SEEING TERRIFYING THINGS...
I THOUGHT THE WORLD OF HIM AS A KID. I LIKE TO THINK HE'S ONE REASON I GOT INTO THIS BUSINESS.
IS HE ALIVE?
HE *CAN'T* BE. THERE'S NOTHING AROUND FOR THREE HUNDRED MILES. HERE, TURN HIM OV--
MY *GOD*...
HH
HHH
GET THE *MED* KIT! *NOW!* HIS *EYES*... THEY'RE *BURNED AWAY!*
HE GOT THEM IN NAGASAKI. LITERALLY *SIFTING* THROUGH RUBBLE.
THEY SCARED ME TO DEATH BACK THEN. STILL DO, TO BE HONEST. I WAS THINKING I'D FINALLY THROW THEM OUT.
IT'S HAPPENING... NOW... PLEASE... GET ME...
CAN YOU IMAGINE HOW TERRIBLE IT MUST HAVE BEEN TO *LOOK* THROUGH THESE THAT MORNING?
I CAN'T...
TO SEE THE PLANE COMING.
TO SEE THE BOMB DROP...
"...TO SEE THE *FIRE* STARTING..."
GET ME...
GET YOU WHAT? MEDICINE IS ON--
LOIS LANE. GET ME *LOIS LANE*.
...TO SEE ALL OF THAT, BUT STILL, NEVER TO KNOW THE TERRIBLE SHAPE OF THINGS TO *COME?*

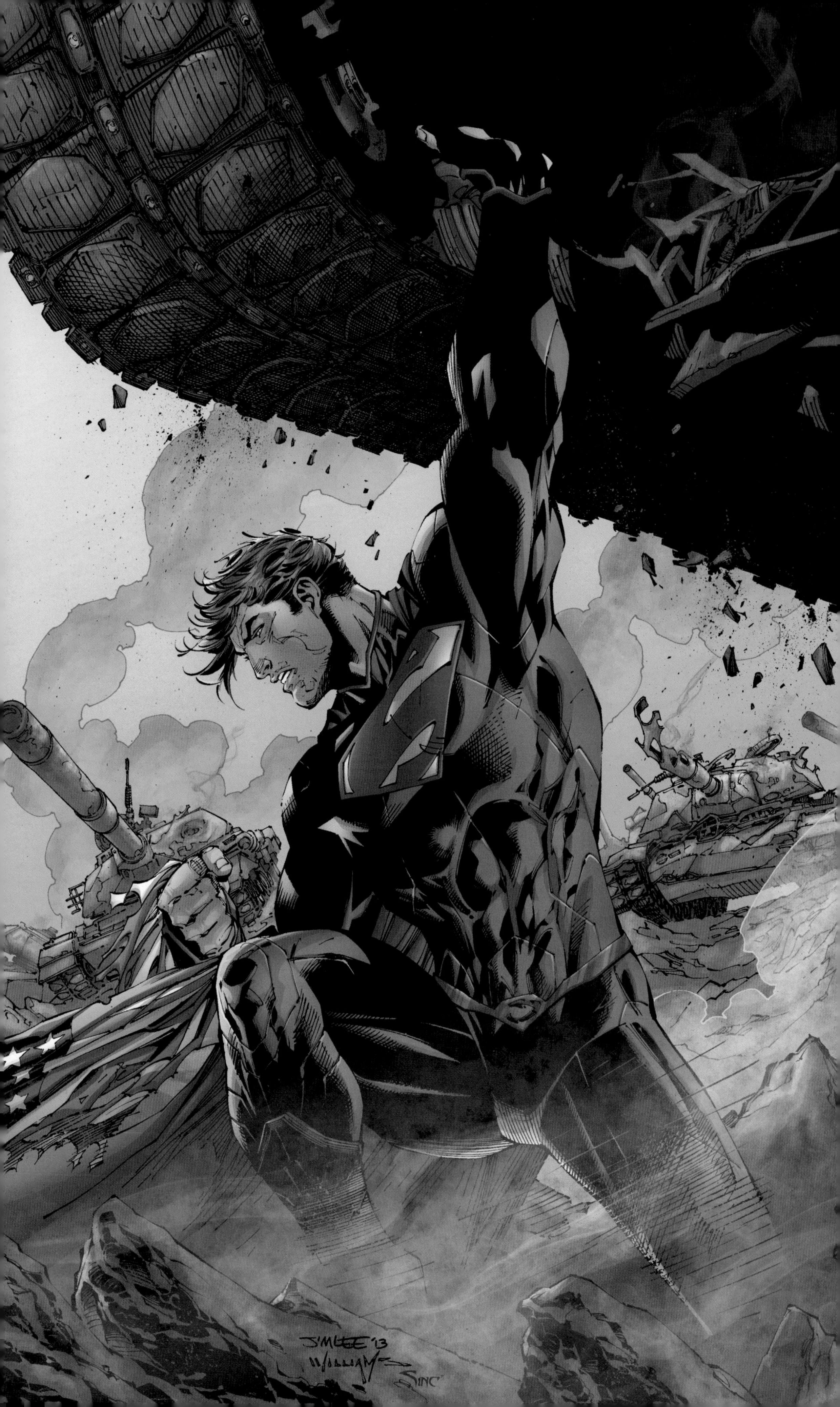
JIM LEE '13
WILLIAMS
SINC

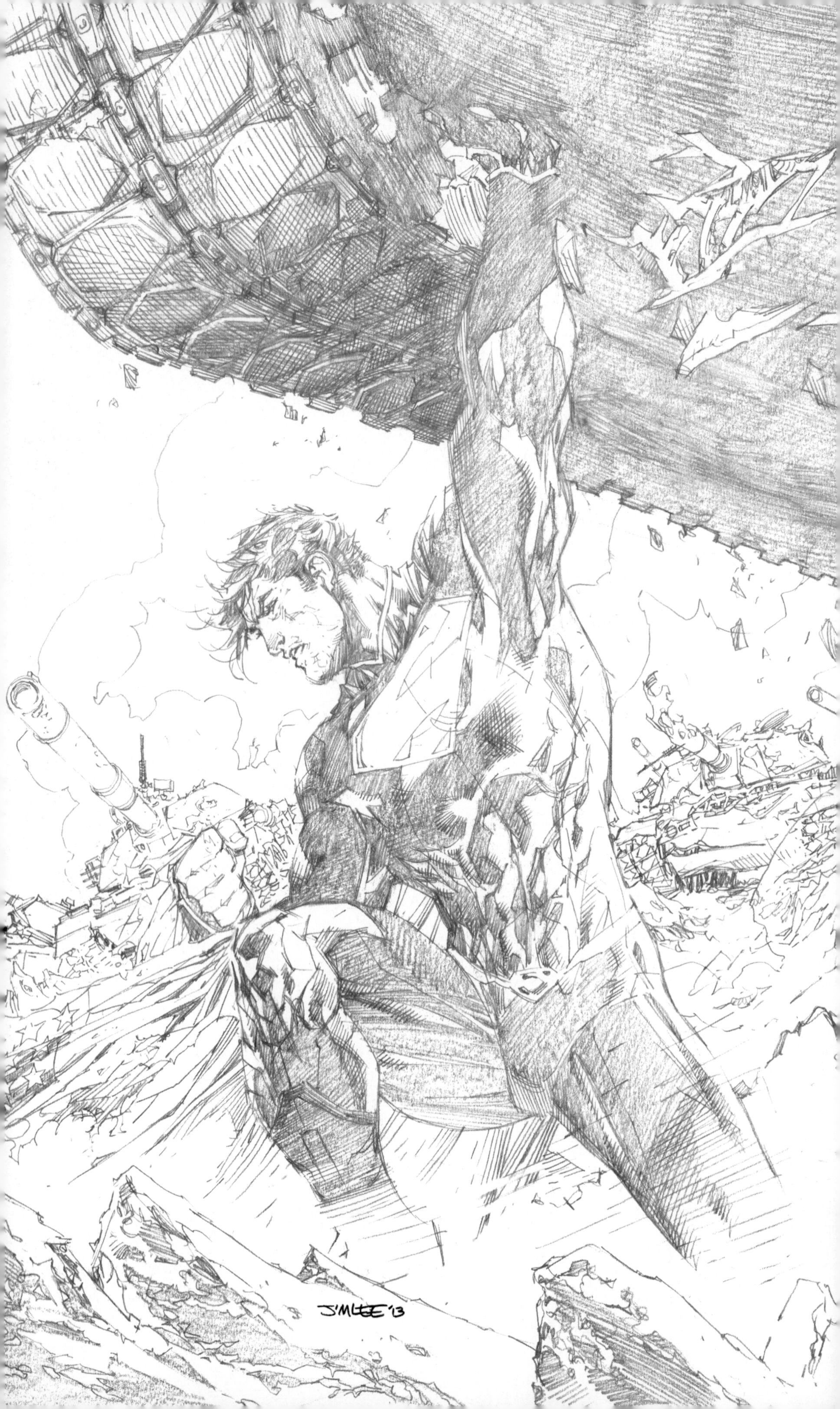

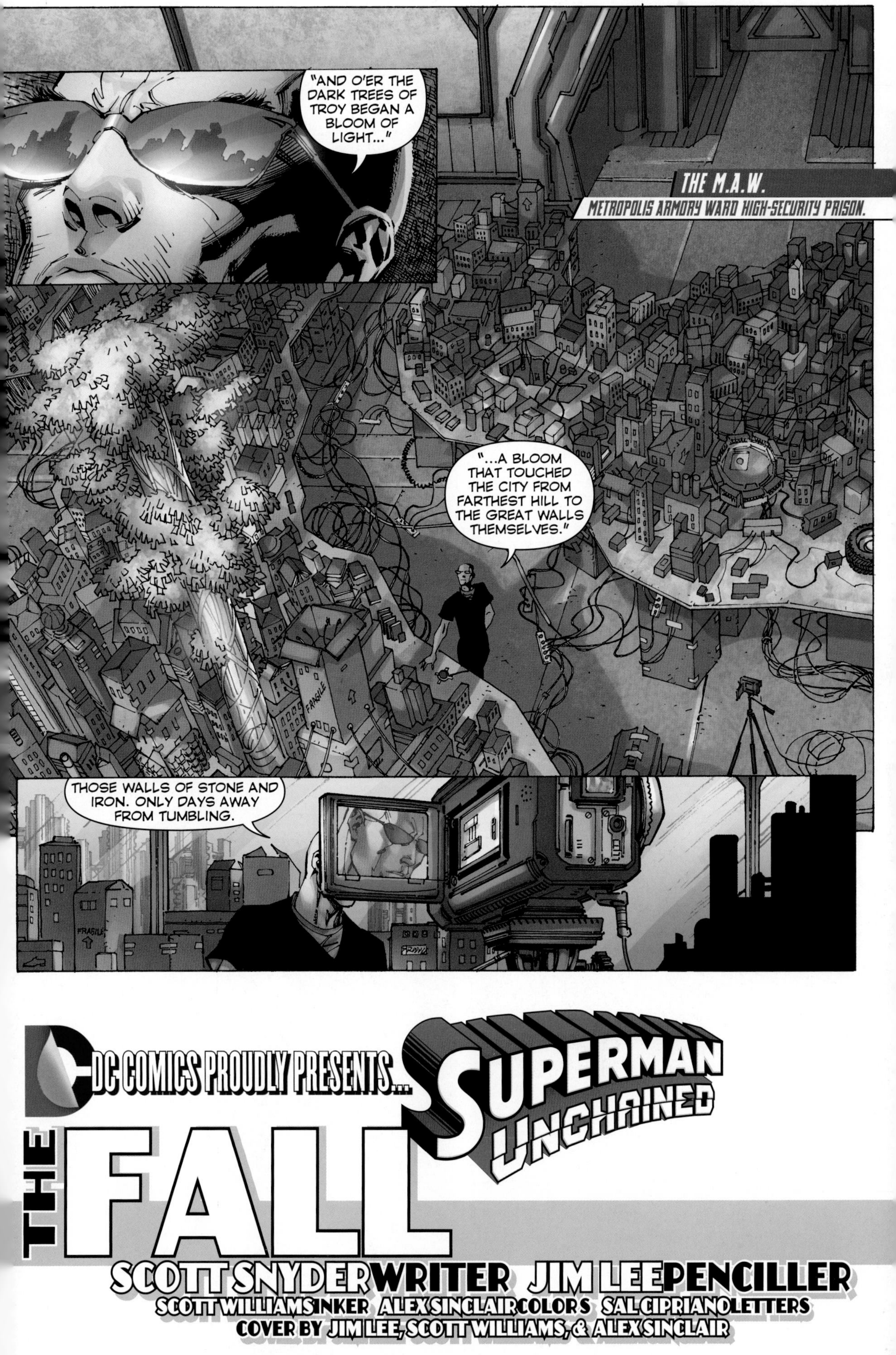

"AND O'ER THE DARK TREES OF TROY BEGAN A BLOOM OF LIGHT..."
THE M.A.W.
METROPOLIS ARMORY WARD HIGH-SECURITY PRISON.
"...A BLOOM THAT TOUCHED THE CITY FROM FARTHEST HILL TO THE GREAT WALLS THEMSELVES."
THOSE WALLS OF STONE AND IRON. ONLY DAYS AWAY FROM TUMBLING.

DC COMICS PROUDLY PRESENTS... SUPERMAN UNCHAINED

THE FALL

SCOTT SNYDER WRITER JIM LEE PENCILLER

SCOTT WILLIAMS INKER ALEX SINCLAIR COLORS SAL CIPRIANO LETTERS

COVER BY JIM LEE, SCOTT WILLIAMS, & ALEX SINCLAIR

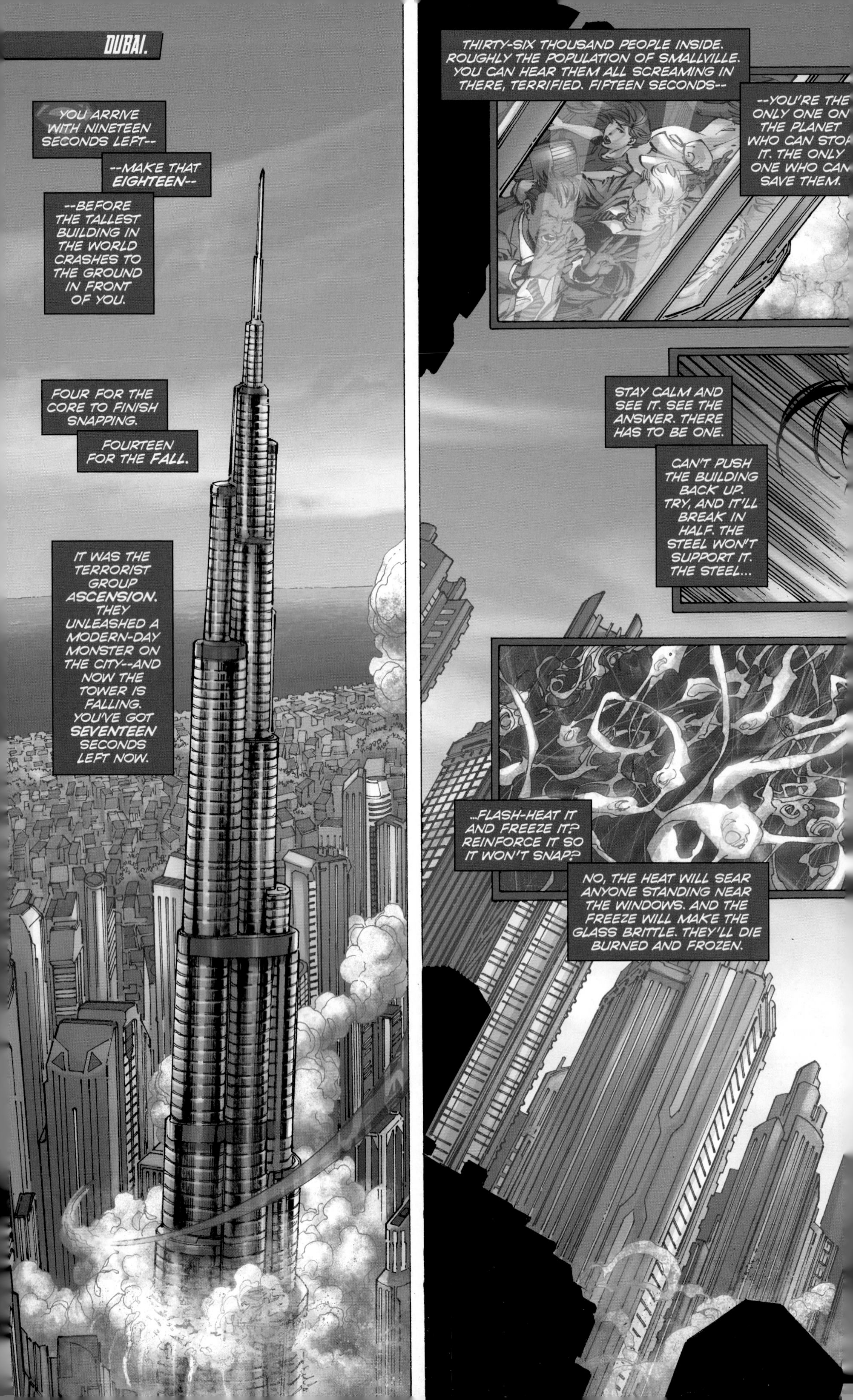
DUBAI.
YOU ARRIVE WITH NINETEEN SECONDS LEFT--
--MAKE THAT EIGHTEEN--
--BEFORE THE TALLEST BUILDING IN THE WORLD CRASHES TO THE GROUND IN FRONT OF YOU.
FOUR FOR THE CORE TO FINISH SNAPPING.
FOURTEEN FOR THE FALL.
IT WAS THE TERRORIST GROUP ASCENSION. THEY UNLEASHED A MODERN-DAY MONSTER ON THE CITY--AND NOW THE TOWER IS FALLING. YOU'VE GOT SEVENTEEN SECONDS LEFT NOW.
THIRTY-SIX THOUSAND PEOPLE INSIDE. ROUGHLY THE POPULATION OF SMALLVILLE. YOU CAN HEAR THEM ALL SCREAMING IN THERE, TERRIFIED. FIFTEEN SECONDS--
--YOU'RE THE ONLY ONE ON THE PLANET WHO CAN STO IT. THE ONLY ONE WHO CAN SAVE THEM.
STAY CALM AND SEE IT. SEE THE ANSWER. THERE HAS TO BE ONE.
CAN'T PUSH THE BUILDING BACK UP. TRY, AND IT'LL BREAK IN HALF. THE STEEL WON'T SUPPORT IT. THE STEEL...
...FLASH-HEAT IT AND FREEZE IT? REINFORCE IT SO IT WON'T SNAP?
NO, THE HEAT WILL SEAR ANYONE STANDING NEAR THE WINDOWS. AND THE FREEZE WILL MAKE THE GLASS BRITTLE. THEY'LL DIE BURNED AND FROZEN.

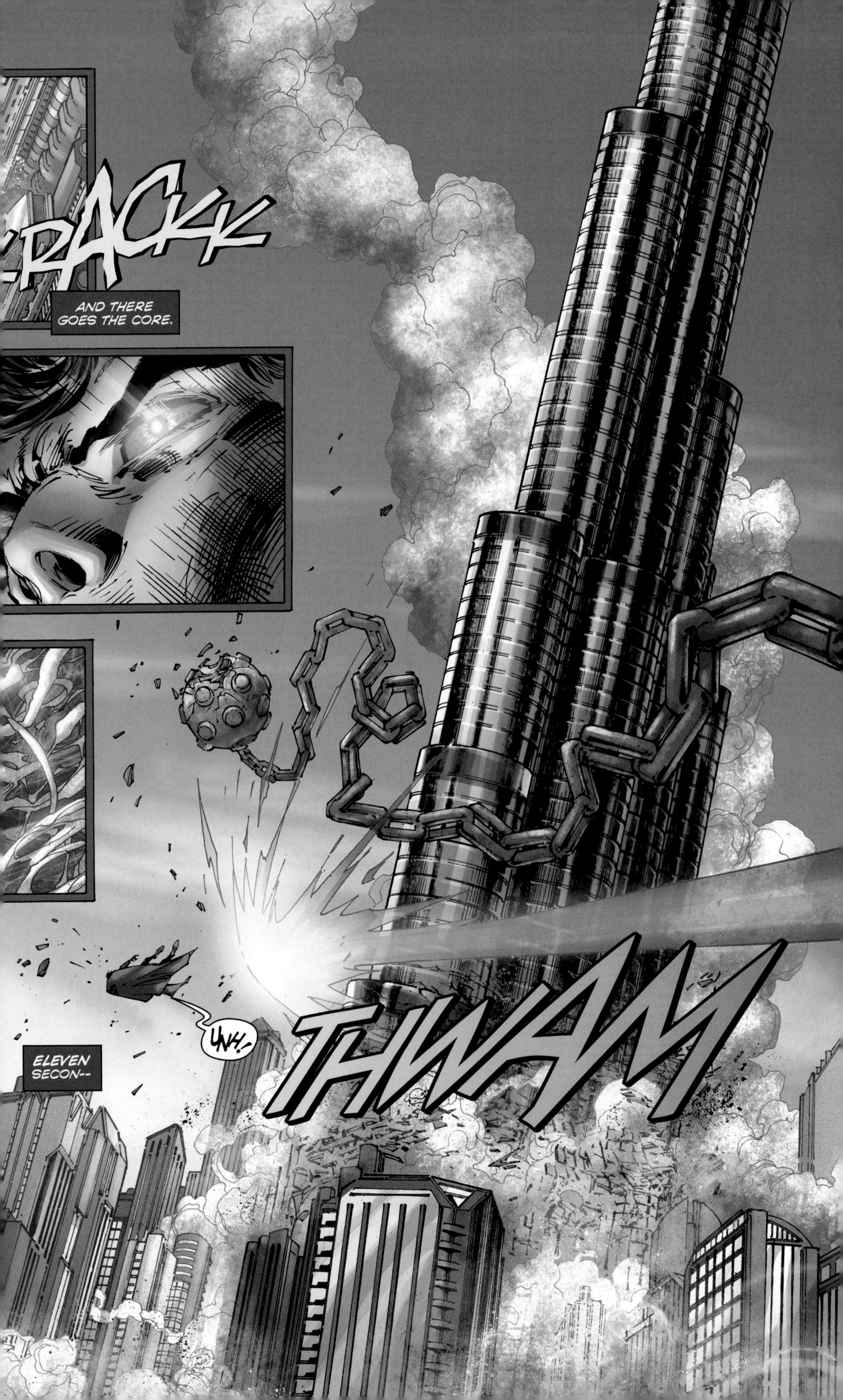

-RACKK
AND THERE GOES THE CORE.
UNH!
THWAM
ELEVEN SECON--

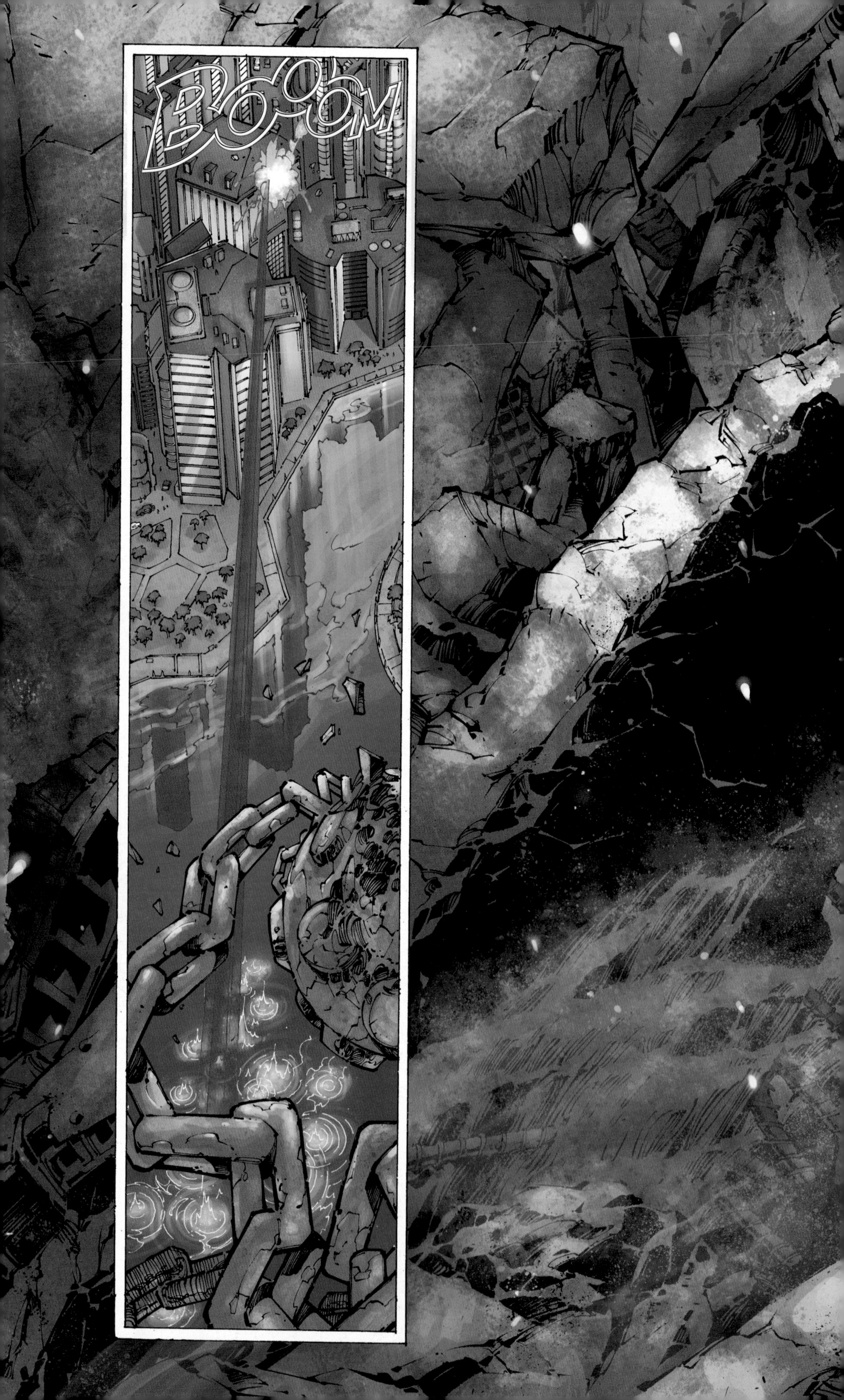
BOOOOM

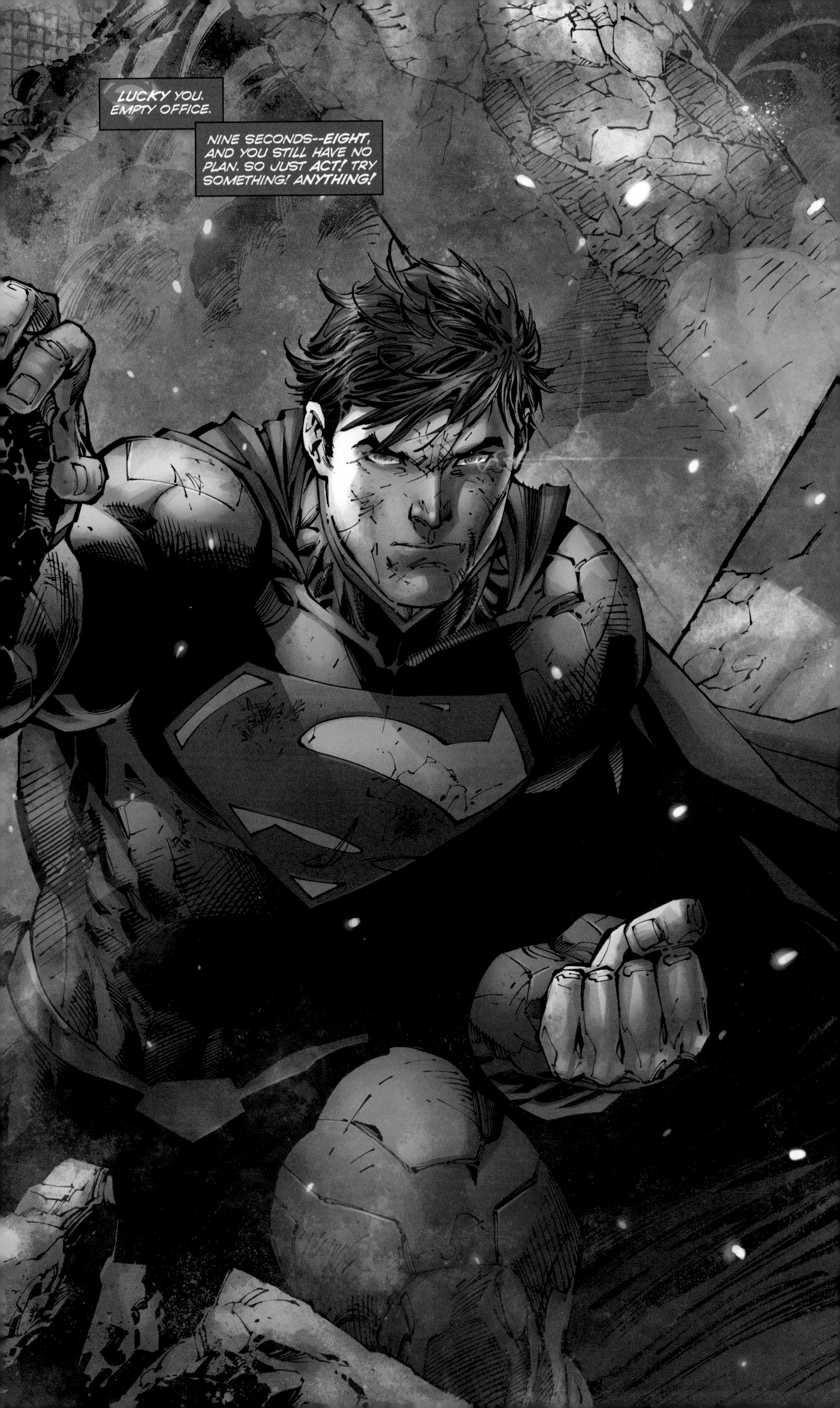
LUCKY YOU. EMPTY OFFICE.
NINE SECONDS--EIGHT, AND YOU STILL HAVE NO PLAN. SO JUST ACT! TRY SOMETHING! ANYTHING!

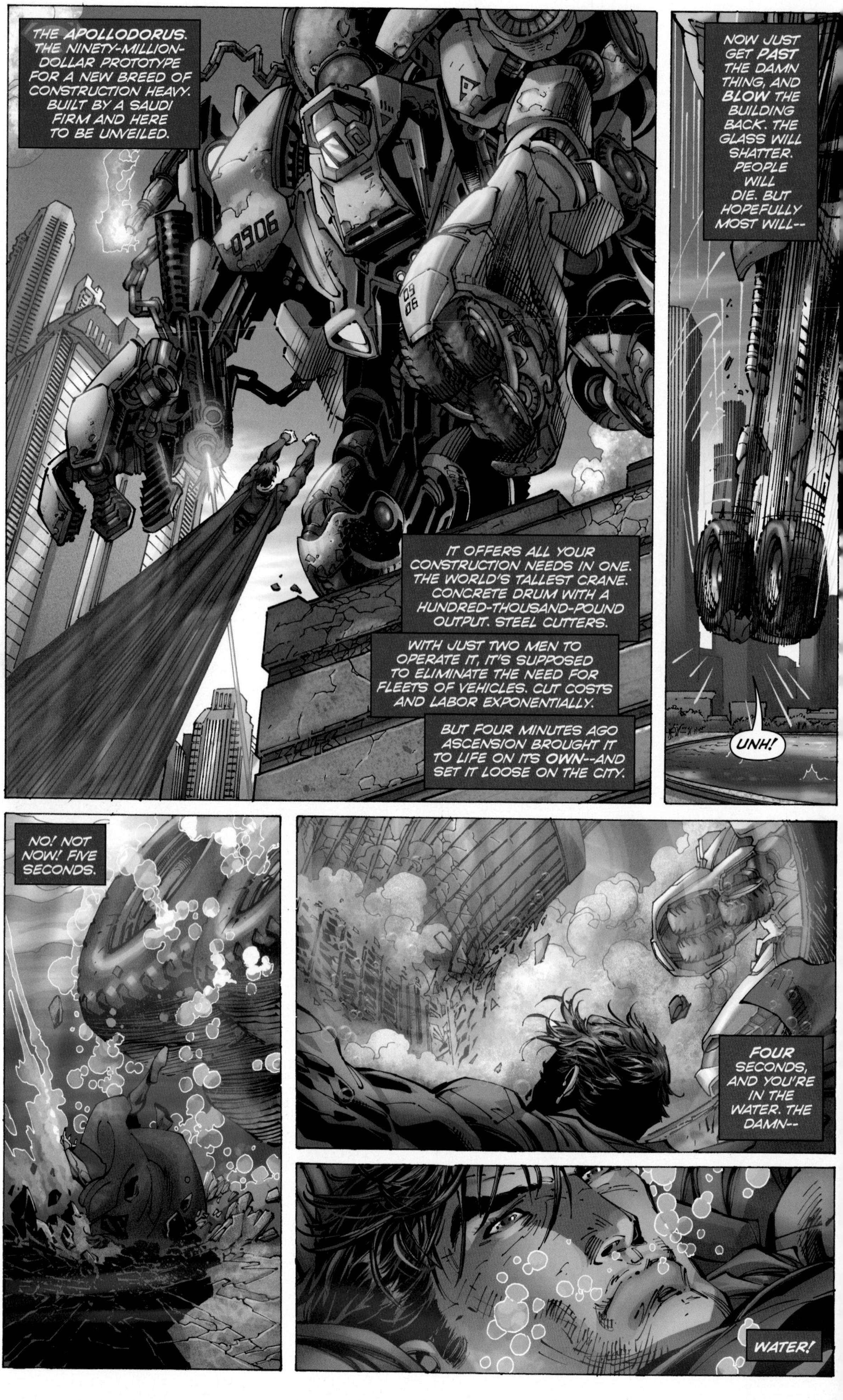
THE APOLLODORUS. THE NINETY-MILLION-DOLLAR PROTOTYPE FOR A NEW BREED OF CONSTRUCTION HEAVY. BUILT BY A SAUDI FIRM AND HERE TO BE UNVEILED.
IT OFFERS ALL YOUR CONSTRUCTION NEEDS IN ONE. THE WORLD'S TALLEST CRANE. CONCRETE DRUM WITH A HUNDRED-THOUSAND-POUND OUTPUT. STEEL CUTTERS.
WITH JUST TWO MEN TO OPERATE IT, IT'S SUPPOSED TO ELIMINATE THE NEED FOR FLEETS OF VEHICLES. CUT COSTS AND LABOR EXPONENTIALLY.
BUT FOUR MINUTES AGO ASCENSION BROUGHT IT TO LIFE ON ITS OWN--AND SET IT LOOSE ON THE CITY.
NOW JUST GET PAST THE DAMN THING, AND BLOW THE BUILDING BACK. THE GLASS WILL SHATTER. PEOPLE WILL DIE. BUT HOPEFULLY MOST WILL--
UNH!
NO! NOT NOW! FIVE SECONDS.
FOUR SECONDS, AND YOU'RE IN THE WATER. THE DAMN--
WATER!

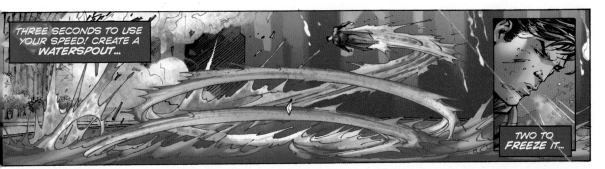

THREE SECONDS TO USE YOUR SPEED! CREATE A WATERSPOUT...

TWO TO FREEZE IT...

...AND ONE TO PRAY IT HOLDS.

THANK YOU UP THERE. THANK Y--

SCREEEEEEEE

RIGHT.

BACK TO WORK.

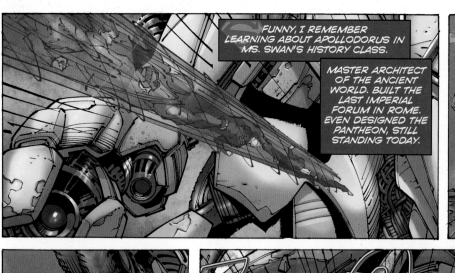

FUNNY, I REMEMBER LEARNING ABOUT APOLLODORUS IN MS. SWAN'S HISTORY CLASS.

MASTER ARCHITECT OF THE ANCIENT WORLD. BUILT THE LAST IMPERIAL FORUM IN ROME. EVEN DESIGNED THE PANTHEON, STILL STANDING TODAY.

BUT UNFORTUNATELY FOR HIM, HE MADE THE WRONG ENEMIES, AND LET'S JUST SAY...

ZZZT

CLICK

ZZZZT

THOOOOM

...IT DIDN'T END WELL FOR HIM.

"YOU'RE BEING WATCHED, CLARK.

"WATCHED FROM THE DARKNESS...

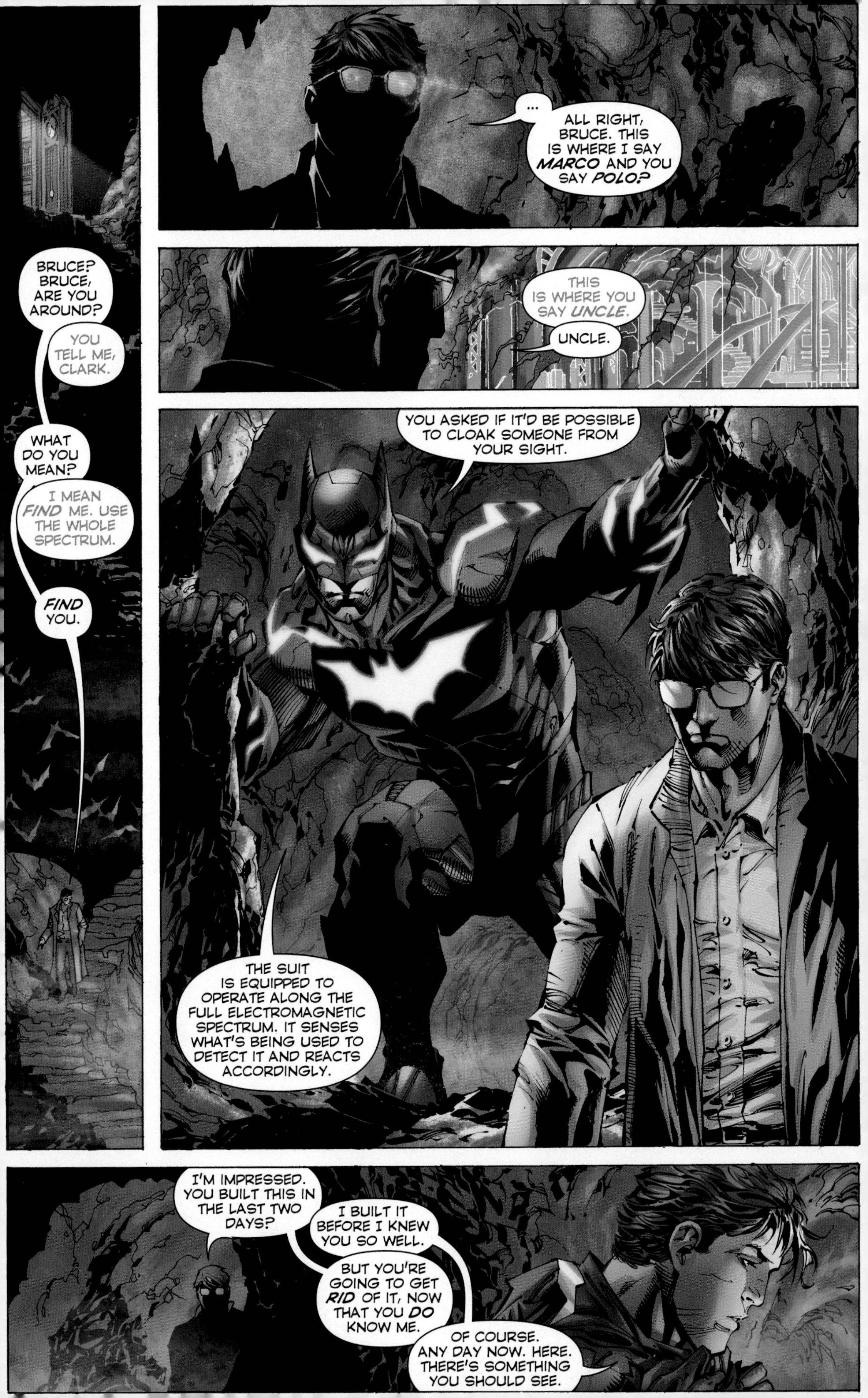
...
ALL RIGHT, BRUCE. THIS IS WHERE I SAY MARCO AND YOU SAY POLO?
BRUCE? BRUCE, ARE YOU AROUND?
YOU TELL ME, CLARK.
WHAT DO YOU MEAN?
I MEAN FIND ME. USE THE WHOLE SPECTRUM.
FIND YOU.
THIS IS WHERE YOU SAY UNCLE.
UNCLE.
YOU ASKED IF IT'D BE POSSIBLE TO CLOAK SOMEONE FROM YOUR SIGHT.
THE SUIT IS EQUIPPED TO OPERATE ALONG THE FULL ELECTROMAGNETIC SPECTRUM. IT SENSES WHAT'S BEING USED TO DETECT IT AND REACTS ACCORDINGLY.
I'M IMPRESSED. YOU BUILT THIS IN THE LAST TWO DAYS?
I BUILT IT BEFORE I KNEW YOU SO WELL.
BUT YOU'RE GOING TO GET RID OF IT, NOW THAT YOU DO KNOW ME.
OF COURSE. ANY DAY NOW. HERE. THERE'S SOMETHING YOU SHOULD SEE.

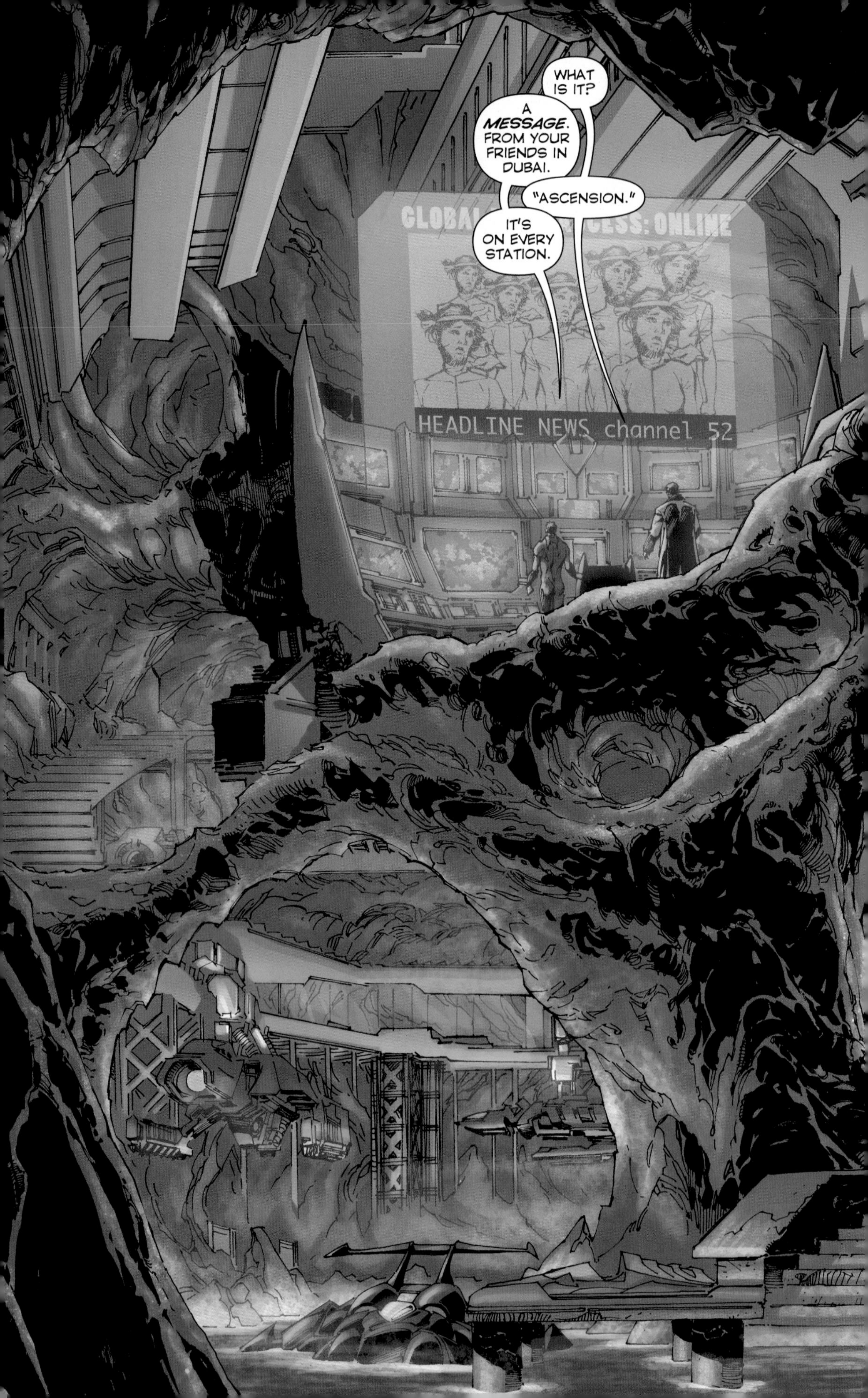
WHAT IS IT?
A *MESSAGE*. FROM YOUR FRIENDS IN DUBAI.
"ASCENSION."
IT'S ON EVERY STATION.
HEADLINE NEWS channel 52

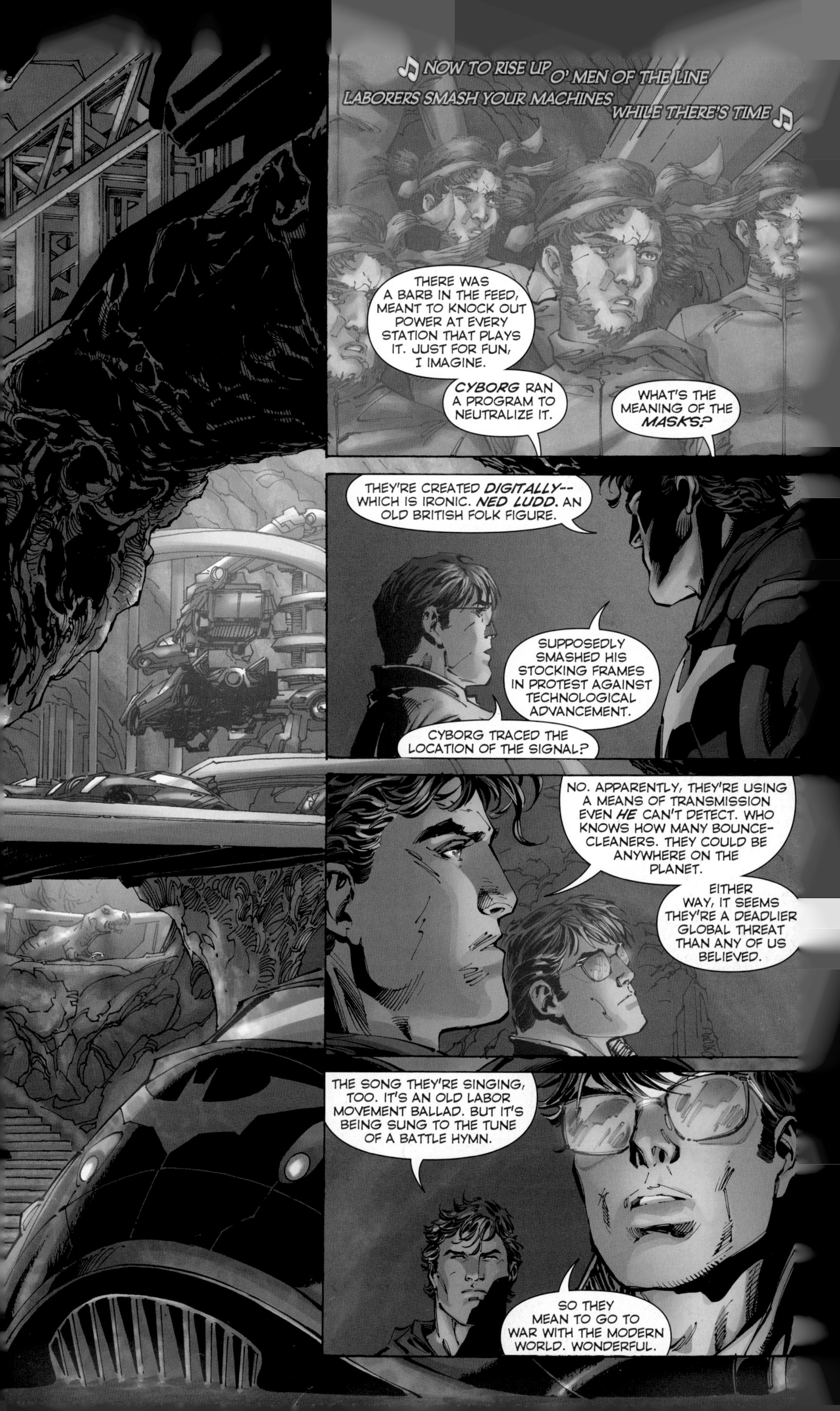
♫ NOW TO RISE UP O' MEN OF THE LINE
LABORERS SMASH YOUR MACHINES WHILE THERE'S TIME ♫
THERE WAS A BARB IN THE FEED, MEANT TO KNOCK OUT POWER AT EVERY STATION THAT PLAYS IT. JUST FOR FUN, I IMAGINE.
CYBORG RAN A PROGRAM TO NEUTRALIZE IT.
WHAT'S THE MEANING OF THE MASKS?
THEY'RE CREATED DIGITALLY--WHICH IS IRONIC. NED LUDD. AN OLD BRITISH FOLK FIGURE.
SUPPOSEDLY SMASHED HIS STOCKING FRAMES IN PROTEST AGAINST TECHNOLOGICAL ADVANCEMENT.
CYBORG TRACED THE LOCATION OF THE SIGNAL?
NO. APPARENTLY, THEY'RE USING A MEANS OF TRANSMISSION EVEN HE CAN'T DETECT. WHO KNOWS HOW MANY BOUNCE-CLEANERS. THEY COULD BE ANYWHERE ON THE PLANET.
EITHER WAY, IT SEEMS THEY'RE A DEADLIER GLOBAL THREAT THAN ANY OF US BELIEVED.
THE SONG THEY'RE SINGING, TOO. IT'S AN OLD LABOR MOVEMENT BALLAD. BUT IT'S BEING SUNG TO THE TUNE OF A BATTLE HYMN.
SO THEY MEAN TO GO TO WAR WITH THE MODERN WORLD. WONDERFUL.

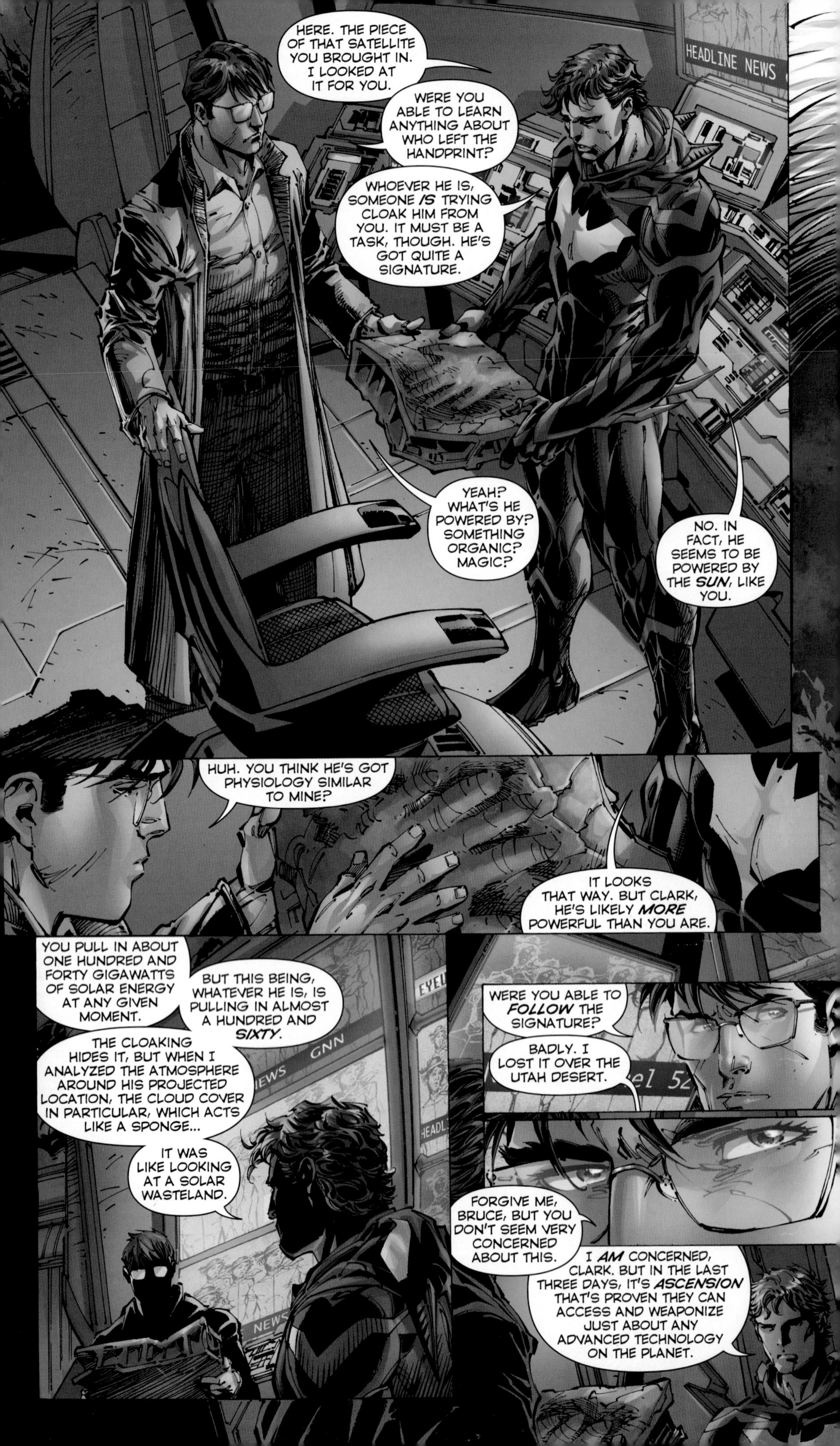
HERE. THE PIECE OF THAT SATELLITE YOU BROUGHT IN. I LOOKED AT IT FOR YOU.
WERE YOU ABLE TO LEARN ANYTHING ABOUT WHO LEFT THE HANDPRINT?
WHOEVER HE IS, SOMEONE IS TRYING CLOAK HIM FROM YOU. IT MUST BE A TASK, THOUGH. HE'S GOT QUITE A SIGNATURE.
HEADLINE NEWS
YEAH? WHAT'S HE POWERED BY? SOMETHING ORGANIC? MAGIC?
NO. IN FACT, HE SEEMS TO BE POWERED BY THE SUN, LIKE YOU.
HUH. YOU THINK HE'S GOT PHYSIOLOGY SIMILAR TO MINE?
IT LOOKS THAT WAY. BUT CLARK, HE'S LIKELY MORE POWERFUL THAN YOU ARE.
YOU PULL IN ABOUT ONE HUNDRED AND FORTY GIGAWATTS OF SOLAR ENERGY AT ANY GIVEN MOMENT.
BUT THIS BEING, WHATEVER HE IS, IS PULLING IN ALMOST A HUNDRED AND SIXTY.
THE CLOAKING HIDES IT, BUT WHEN I ANALYZED THE ATMOSPHERE AROUND HIS PROJECTED LOCATION, THE CLOUD COVER IN PARTICULAR, WHICH ACTS LIKE A SPONGE...
IT WAS LIKE LOOKING AT A SOLAR WASTELAND.
GNN
WERE YOU ABLE TO FOLLOW THE SIGNATURE?
BADLY. I LOST IT OVER THE UTAH DESERT.
FORGIVE ME, BRUCE, BUT YOU DON'T SEEM VERY CONCERNED ABOUT THIS.
I AM CONCERNED, CLARK. BUT IN THE LAST THREE DAYS, IT'S ASCENSION THAT'S PROVEN THEY CAN ACCESS AND WEAPONIZE JUST ABOUT ANY ADVANCED TECHNOLOGY ON THE PLANET.

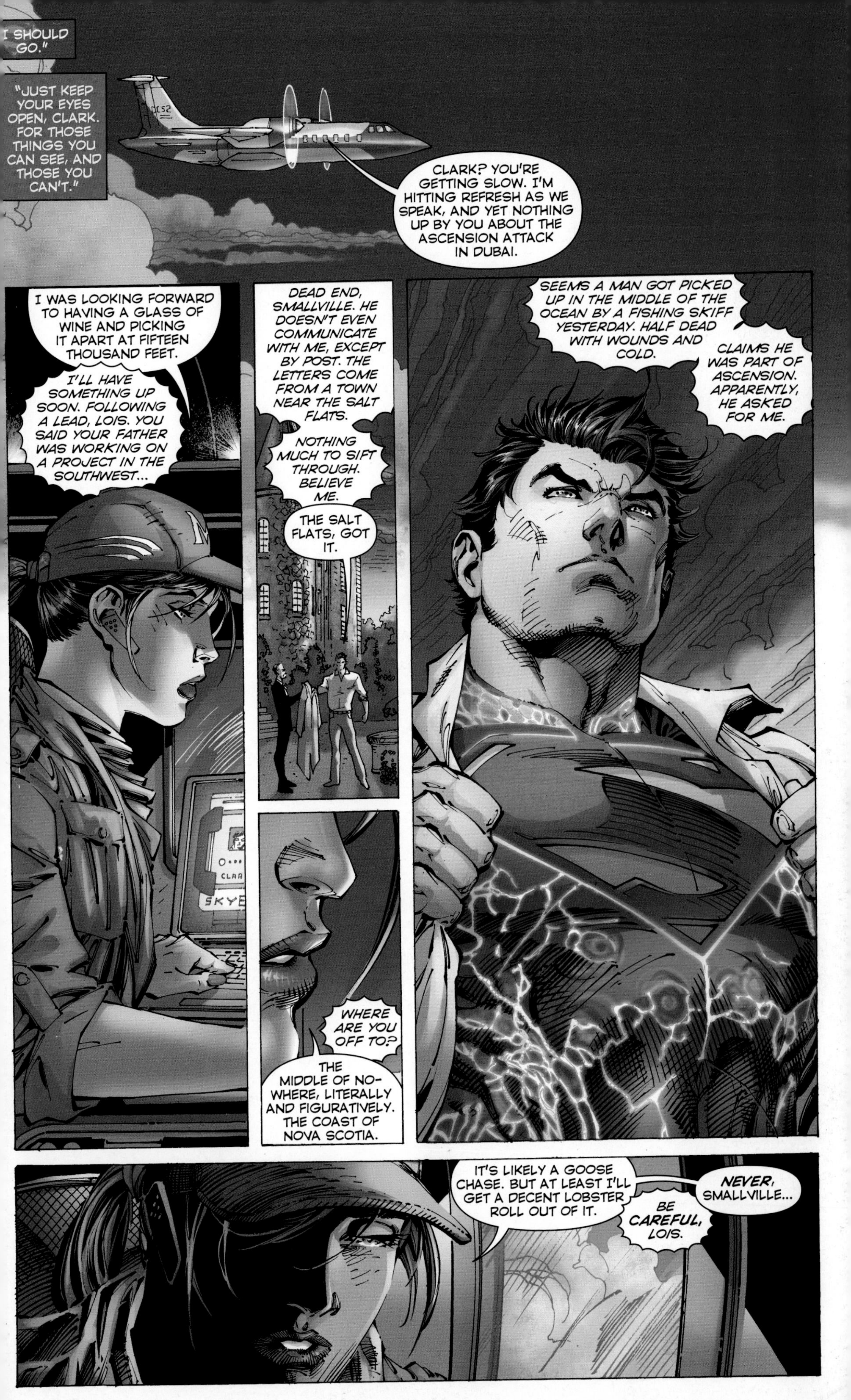

I SHOULD GO."
"JUST KEEP YOUR EYES OPEN, CLARK. FOR THOSE THINGS YOU CAN SEE, AND THOSE YOU CAN'T."
DCS2
CLARK? YOU'RE GETTING SLOW. I'M HITTING REFRESH AS WE SPEAK, AND YET NOTHING UP BY YOU ABOUT THE ASCENSION ATTACK IN DUBAI.
I WAS LOOKING FORWARD TO HAVING A GLASS OF WINE AND PICKING IT APART AT FIFTEEN THOUSAND FEET.
I'LL HAVE SOMETHING UP SOON. FOLLOWING A LEAD, LOIS. YOU SAID YOUR FATHER WAS WORKING ON A PROJECT IN THE SOUTHWEST...
DEAD END, SMALLVILLE. HE DOESN'T EVEN COMMUNICATE WITH ME, EXCEPT BY POST. THE LETTERS COME FROM A TOWN NEAR THE SALT FLATS.
NOTHING MUCH TO SIFT THROUGH. BELIEVE ME.
THE SALT FLATS, GOT IT.
SEEMS A MAN GOT PICKED UP IN THE MIDDLE OF THE OCEAN BY A FISHING SKIFF YESTERDAY. HALF DEAD WITH WOUNDS AND COLD.
CLAIMS HE WAS PART OF ASCENSION. APPARENTLY, HE ASKED FOR ME.
WHERE ARE YOU OFF TO?
THE MIDDLE OF NO-WHERE, LITERALLY AND FIGURATIVELY. THE COAST OF NOVA SCOTIA.
IT'S LIKELY A GOOSE CHASE. BUT AT LEAST I'LL GET A DECENT LOBSTER ROLL OUT OF IT.
NEVER, SMALLVILLE...
BE CAREFUL, LOIS.

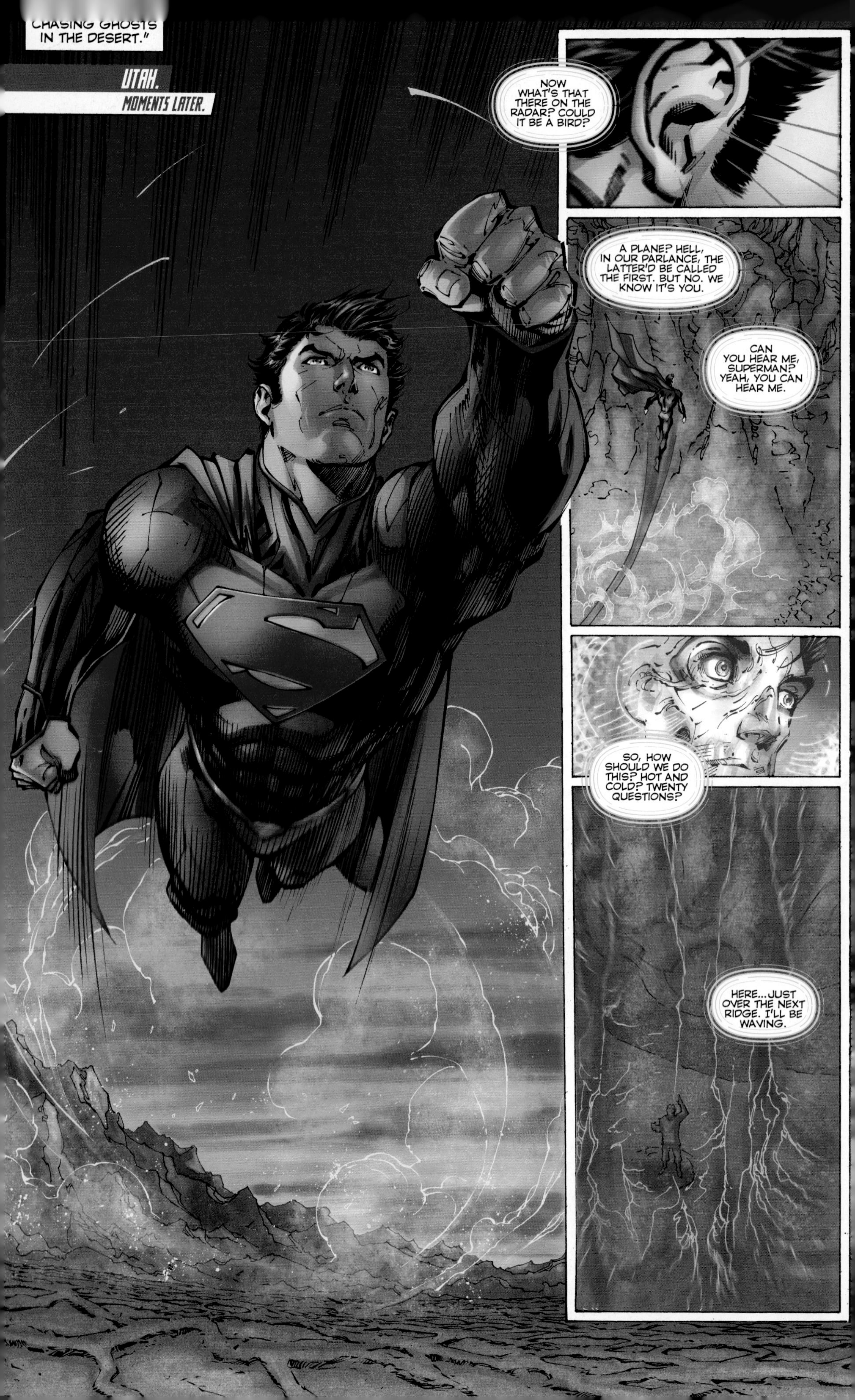
CHASING GHOSTS IN THE DESERT."
UTAH.
MOMENTS LATER.
NOW WHAT'S THAT THERE ON THE RADAR? COULD IT BE A BIRD?
A PLANE? HELL, IN OUR PARLANCE, THE LATTER'D BE CALLED THE FIRST. BUT NO. WE KNOW IT'S YOU.
CAN YOU HEAR ME, SUPERMAN? YEAH, YOU CAN HEAR ME.
SO, HOW SHOULD WE DO THIS? HOT AND COLD? TWENTY QUESTIONS?
HERE...JUST OVER THE NEXT RIDGE. I'LL BE WAVING.

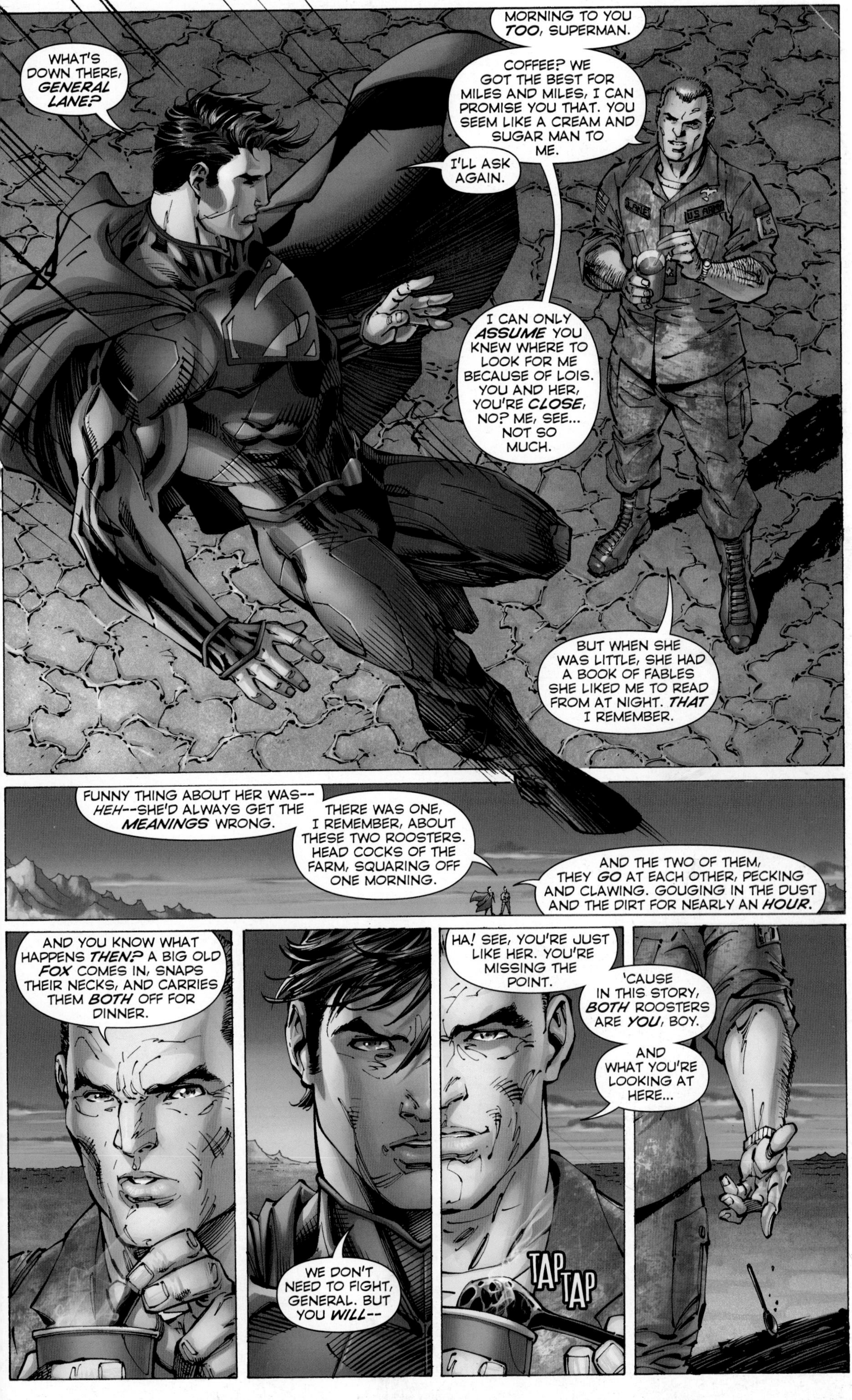
WHAT'S DOWN THERE, GENERAL LANE?
MORNING TO YOU TOO, SUPERMAN.
COFFEE? WE GOT THE BEST FOR MILES AND MILES, I CAN PROMISE YOU THAT. YOU SEEM LIKE A CREAM AND SUGAR MAN TO ME.
I'LL ASK AGAIN.
I CAN ONLY ASSUME YOU KNEW WHERE TO LOOK FOR ME BECAUSE OF LOIS. YOU AND HER, YOU'RE CLOSE, NO? ME, SEE... NOT SO MUCH.
BUT WHEN SHE WAS LITTLE, SHE HAD A BOOK OF FABLES SHE LIKED ME TO READ FROM AT NIGHT. THAT I REMEMBER.
FUNNY THING ABOUT HER WAS-- HEH--SHE'D ALWAYS GET THE MEANINGS WRONG.
THERE WAS ONE, I REMEMBER, ABOUT THESE TWO ROOSTERS. HEAD COCKS OF THE FARM, SQUARING OFF ONE MORNING.
AND THE TWO OF THEM, THEY GO AT EACH OTHER, PECKING AND CLAWING. GOUGING IN THE DUST AND THE DIRT FOR NEARLY AN HOUR.
AND YOU KNOW WHAT HAPPENS THEN? A BIG OLD FOX COMES IN, SNAPS THEIR NECKS, AND CARRIES THEM BOTH OFF FOR DINNER.
WE DON'T NEED TO FIGHT, GENERAL. BUT YOU WILL--
HA! SEE, YOU'RE JUST LIKE HER. YOU'RE MISSING THE POINT.
TAP TAP
'CAUSE IN THIS STORY, BOTH ROOSTERS ARE YOU, BOY.
AND WHAT YOU'RE LOOKING AT HERE...
US ARMY
LANE

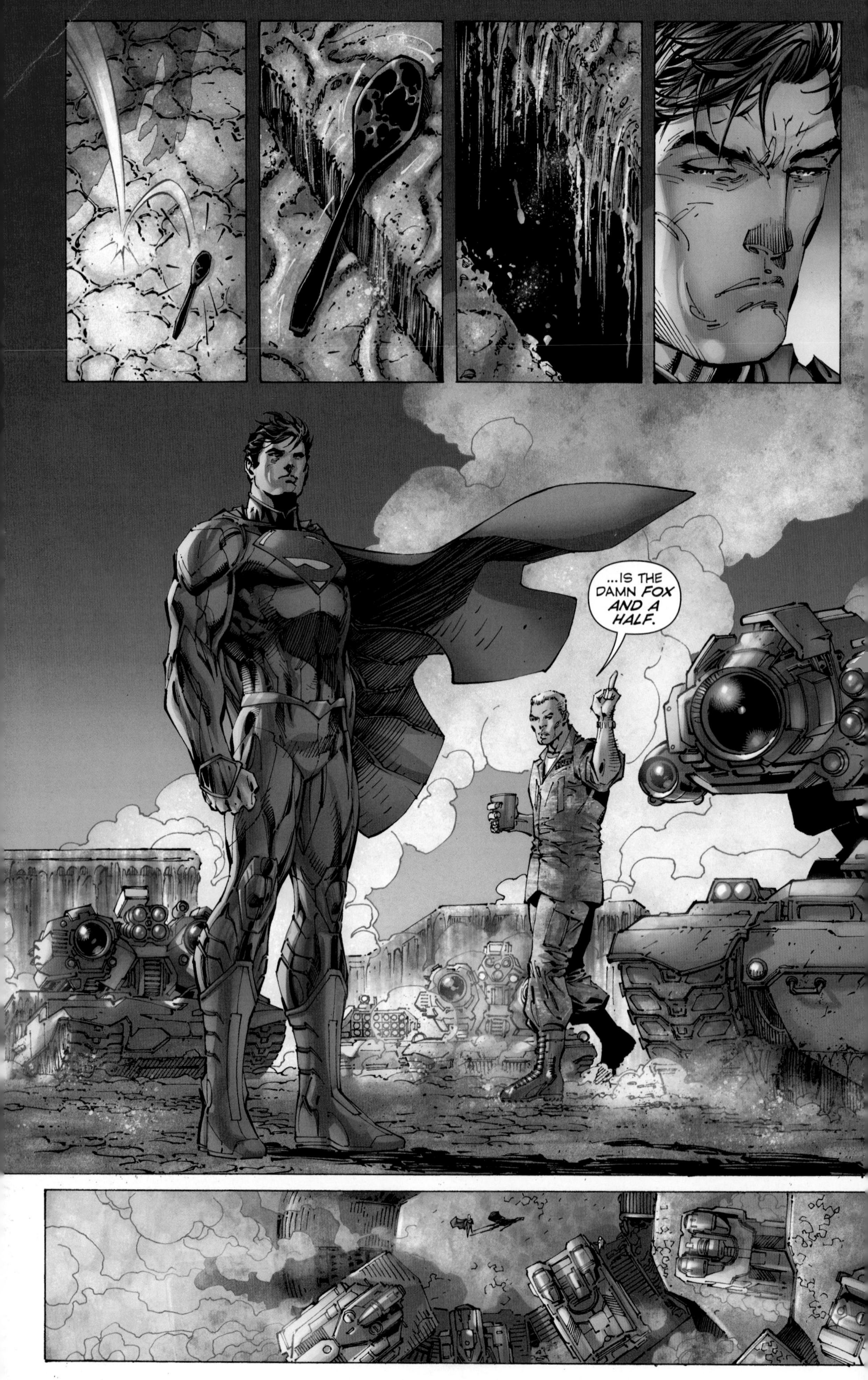
...IS THE DAMN FOX AND A HALF.

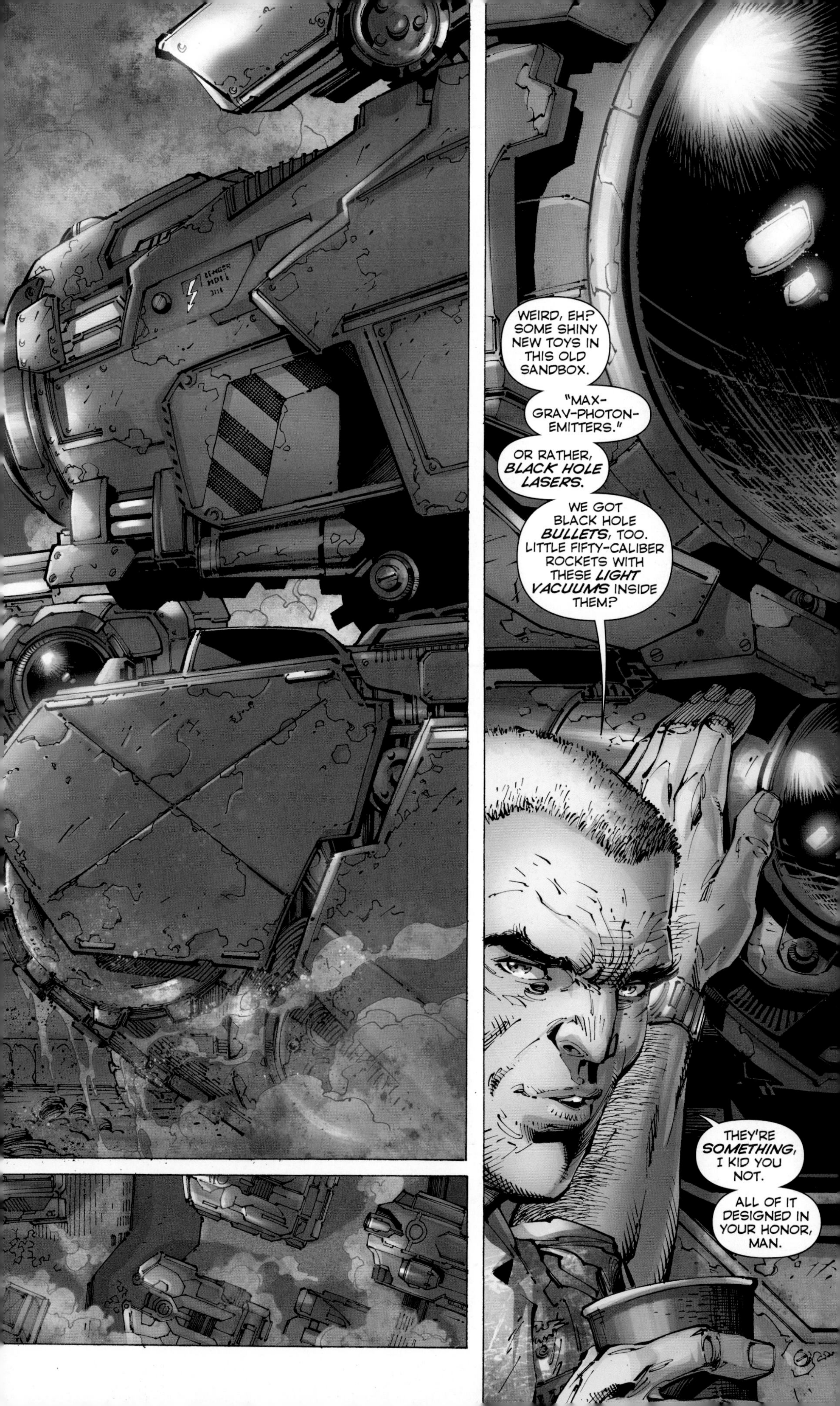
WEIRD, EH? SOME SHINY NEW TOYS IN THIS OLD SANDBOX.
"MAX-GRAV-PHOTON-EMITTERS."
OR RATHER, *BLACK HOLE LASERS.*
WE GOT BLACK HOLE *BULLETS*, TOO. LITTLE FIFTY-CALIBER ROCKETS WITH THESE *LIGHT VACUUMS* INSIDE THEM?
THEY'RE *SOMETHING*, I KID YOU NOT.
ALL OF IT DESIGNED IN YOUR HONOR, MAN.

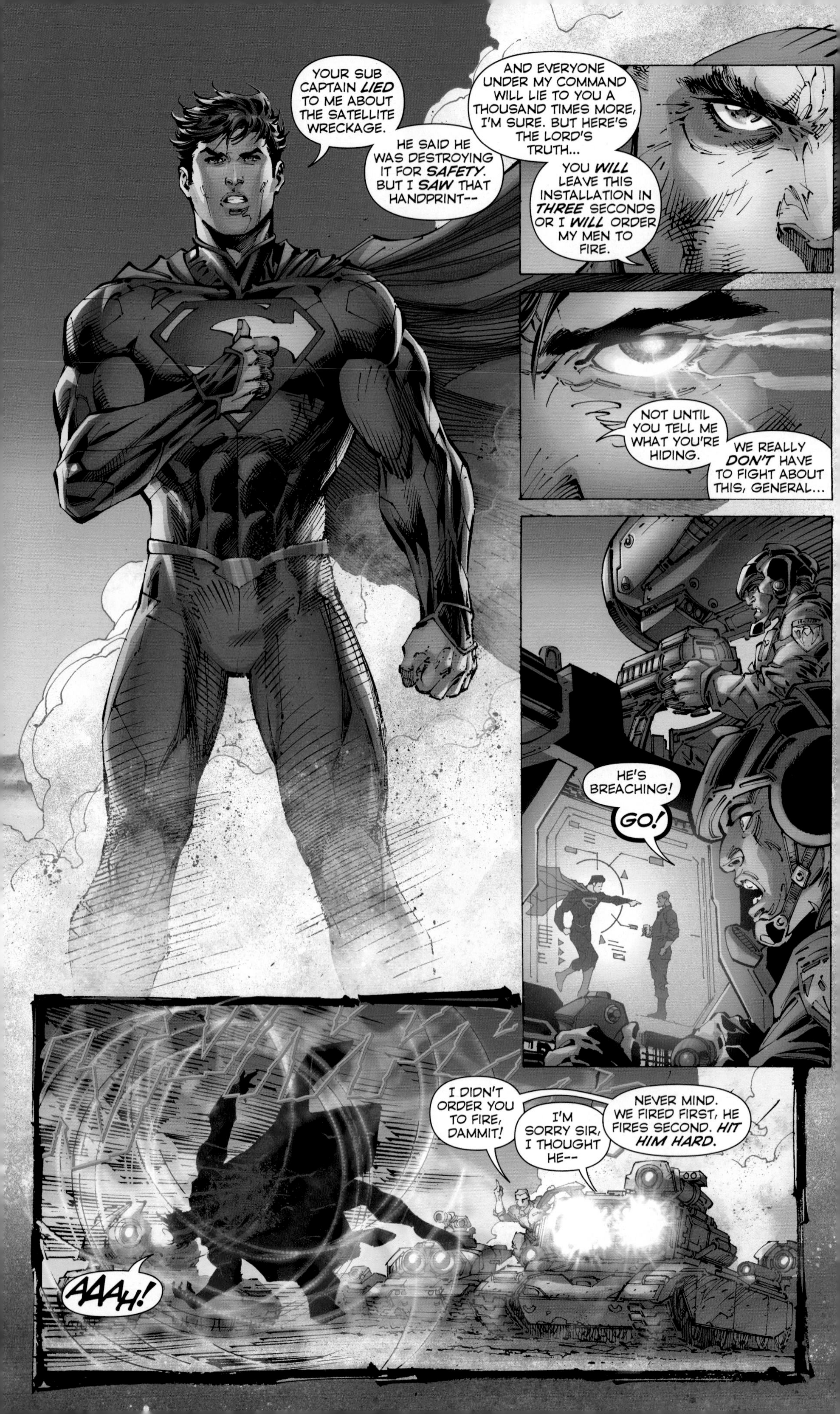

YOUR SUB CAPTAIN *LIED* TO ME ABOUT THE SATELLITE WRECKAGE.
HE SAID HE WAS DESTROYING IT FOR *SAFETY*. BUT I *SAW* THAT HANDPRINT--
AND EVERYONE UNDER MY COMMAND WILL LIE TO YOU A THOUSAND TIMES MORE, I'M SURE. BUT HERE'S THE LORD'S TRUTH...
YOU *WILL* LEAVE THIS INSTALLATION IN *THREE* SECONDS OR I *WILL* ORDER MY MEN TO FIRE.
NOT UNTIL YOU TELL ME WHAT YOU'RE HIDING.
WE REALLY *DON'T* HAVE TO FIGHT ABOUT THIS, GENERAL...
HE'S BREACHING!
GO!
AAAH!
I DIDN'T ORDER YOU TO FIRE, DAMMIT!
I'M SORRY SIR, I THOUGHT HE--
NEVER MIND. WE FIRED FIRST, HE FIRES SECOND. *HIT HIM HARD*.

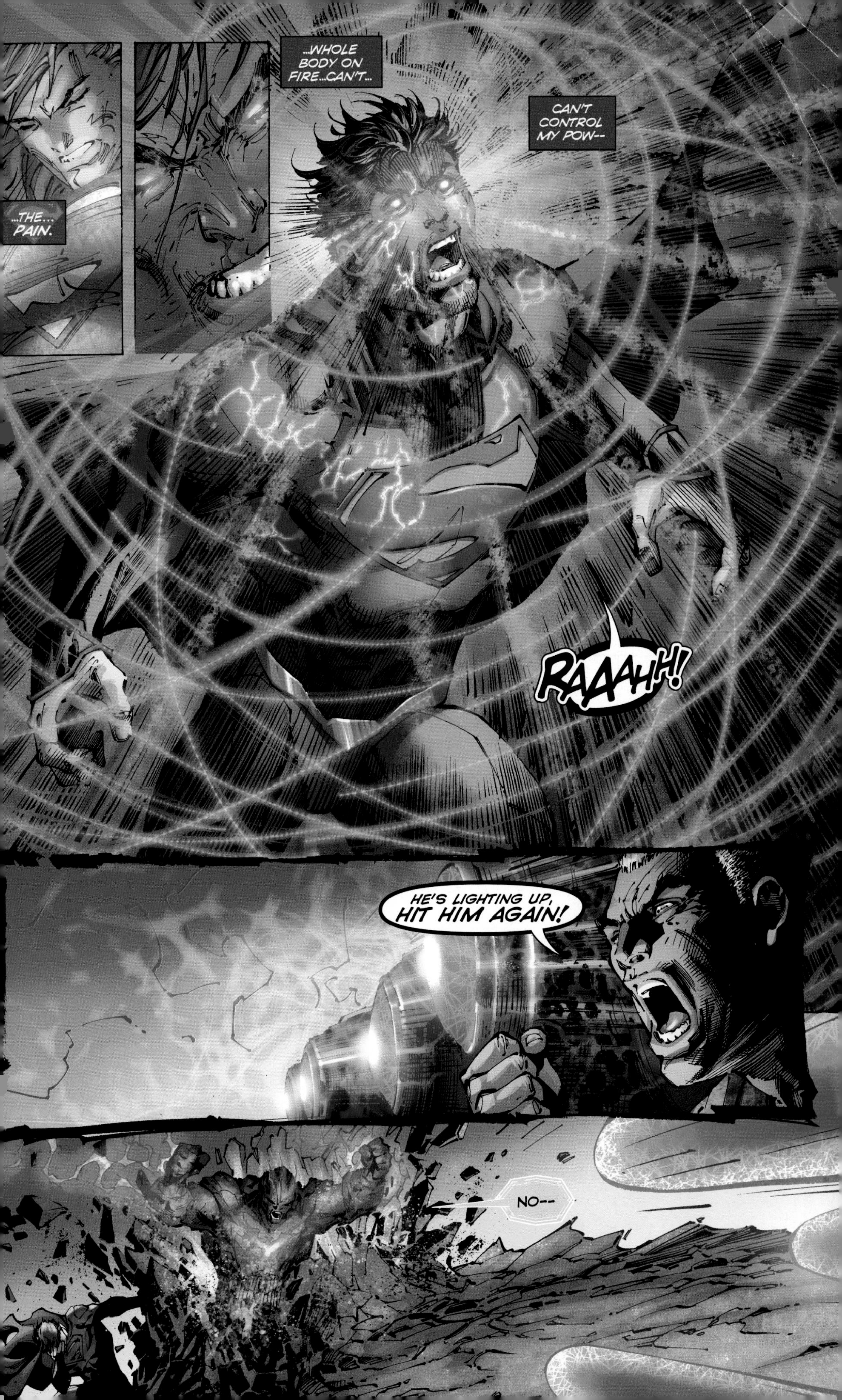
...THE... PAIN.
...WHOLE BODY ON FIRE...CAN'T...
CAN'T CONTROL MY POW--
RAAAHH!
HE'S LIGHTING UP, HIT HIM AGAIN!
NO--

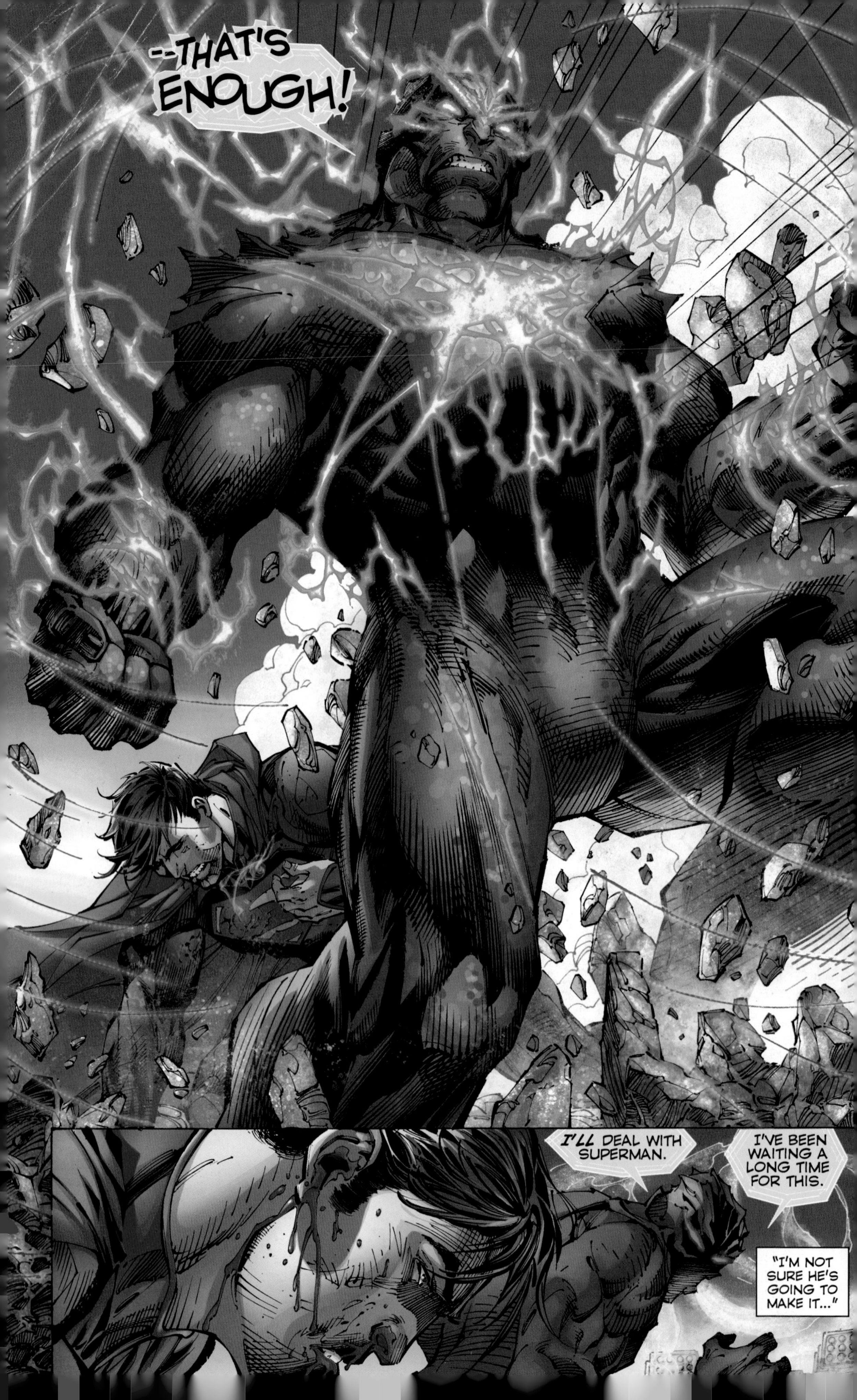
--THAT'S ENOUGH!
I'LL DEAL WITH SUPERMAN.
I'VE BEEN WAITING A LONG TIME FOR THIS.
"I'M NOT SURE HE'S GOING TO MAKE IT..."

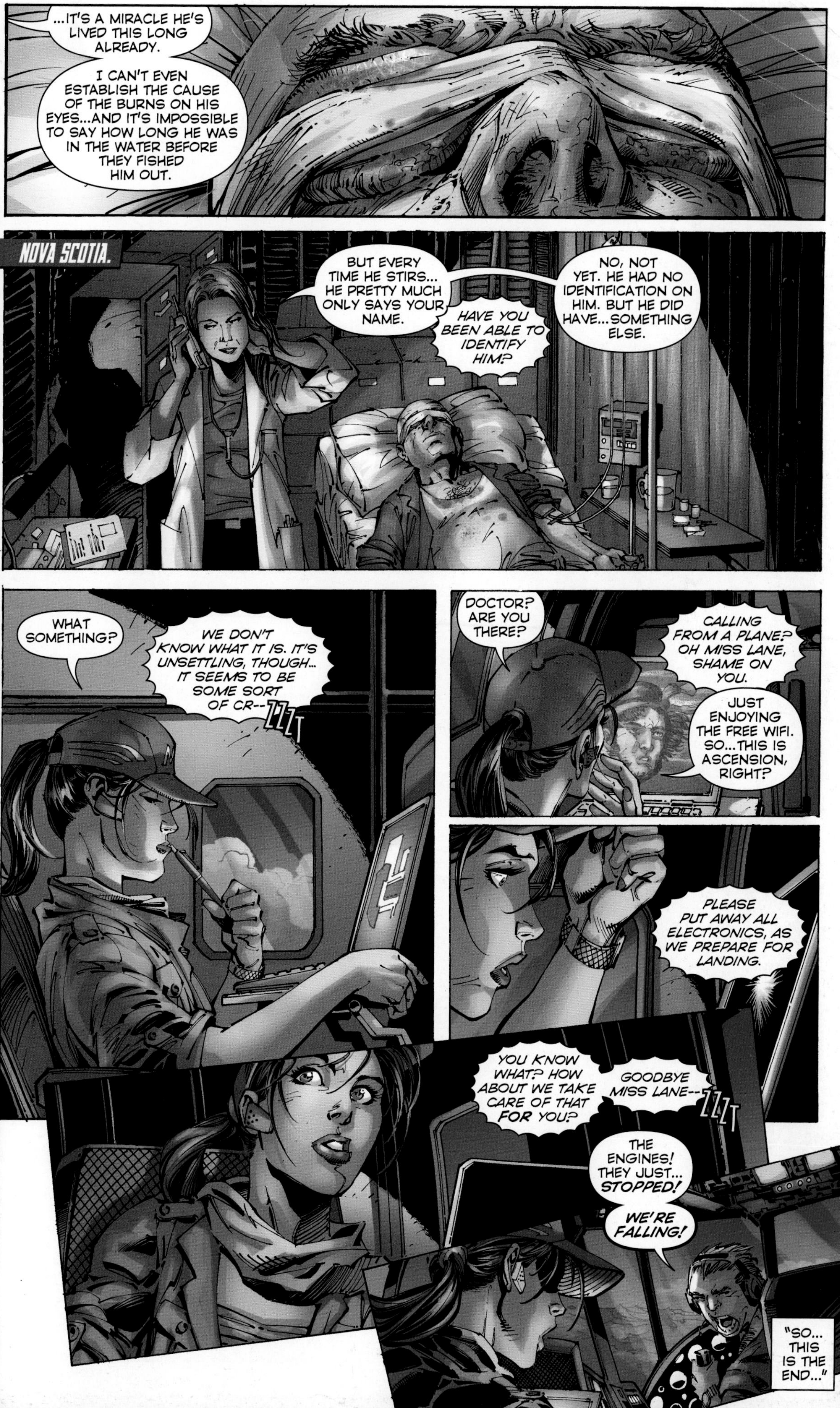
...IT'S A MIRACLE HE'S LIVED THIS LONG ALREADY.
I CAN'T EVEN ESTABLISH THE CAUSE OF THE BURNS ON HIS EYES...AND IT'S IMPOSSIBLE TO SAY HOW LONG HE WAS IN THE WATER BEFORE THEY FISHED HIM OUT.
NOVA SCOTIA.
BUT EVERY TIME HE STIRS... HE PRETTY MUCH ONLY SAYS YOUR NAME.
HAVE YOU BEEN ABLE TO IDENTIFY HIM?
NO, NOT YET. HE HAD NO IDENTIFICATION ON HIM. BUT HE DID HAVE...SOMETHING ELSE.
WHAT SOMETHING?
WE DON'T KNOW WHAT IT IS. IT'S UNSETTLING, THOUGH... IT SEEMS TO BE SOME SORT OF CR--
ZZZT
DOCTOR? ARE YOU THERE?
CALLING FROM A PLANE? OH MISS LANE, SHAME ON YOU.
JUST ENJOYING THE FREE WIFI. SO...THIS IS ASCENSION, RIGHT?
PLEASE PUT AWAY ALL ELECTRONICS, AS WE PREPARE FOR LANDING.
YOU KNOW WHAT? HOW ABOUT WE TAKE CARE OF THAT FOR YOU?
GOODBYE MISS LANE--
ZZZT
THE ENGINES! THEY JUST... STOPPED!
WE'RE FALLING!
"SO... THIS IS THE END..."

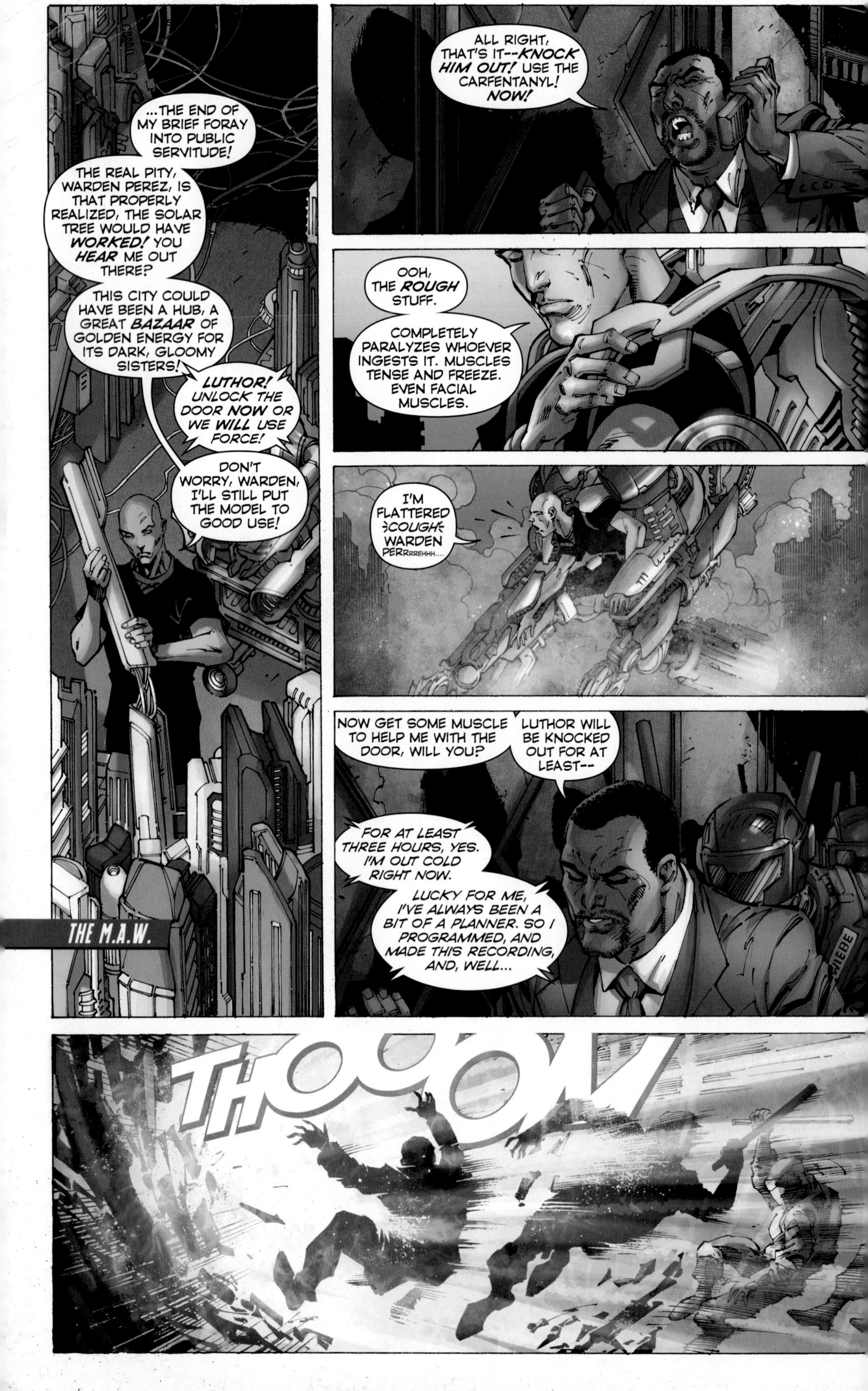

...THE END OF MY BRIEF FORAY INTO PUBLIC SERVITUDE!
THE REAL PITY, WARDEN PEREZ, IS THAT PROPERLY REALIZED, THE SOLAR TREE WOULD HAVE WORKED! YOU HEAR ME OUT THERE?
THIS CITY COULD HAVE BEEN A HUB, A GREAT BAZAAR OF GOLDEN ENERGY FOR ITS DARK, GLOOMY SISTERS!
LUTHOR! UNLOCK THE DOOR NOW OR WE WILL USE FORCE!
DON'T WORRY, WARDEN, I'LL STILL PUT THE MODEL TO GOOD USE!
THE M.A.W.
ALL RIGHT, THAT'S IT--KNOCK HIM OUT! USE THE CARFENTANYL! NOW!
OOH, THE ROUGH STUFF.
COMPLETELY PARALYZES WHOEVER INGESTS IT. MUSCLES TENSE AND FREEZE. EVEN FACIAL MUSCLES.
I'M FLATTERED *COUGH* WARDEN PERRrrrehhh....
NOW GET SOME MUSCLE TO HELP ME WITH THE DOOR, WILL YOU?
LUTHOR WILL BE KNOCKED OUT FOR AT LEAST--
FOR AT LEAST THREE HOURS, YES. I'M OUT COLD RIGHT NOW.
LUCKY FOR ME, I'VE ALWAYS BEEN A BIT OF A PLANNER. SO I PROGRAMMED, AND MADE THIS RECORDING, AND, WELL...
THOOOM

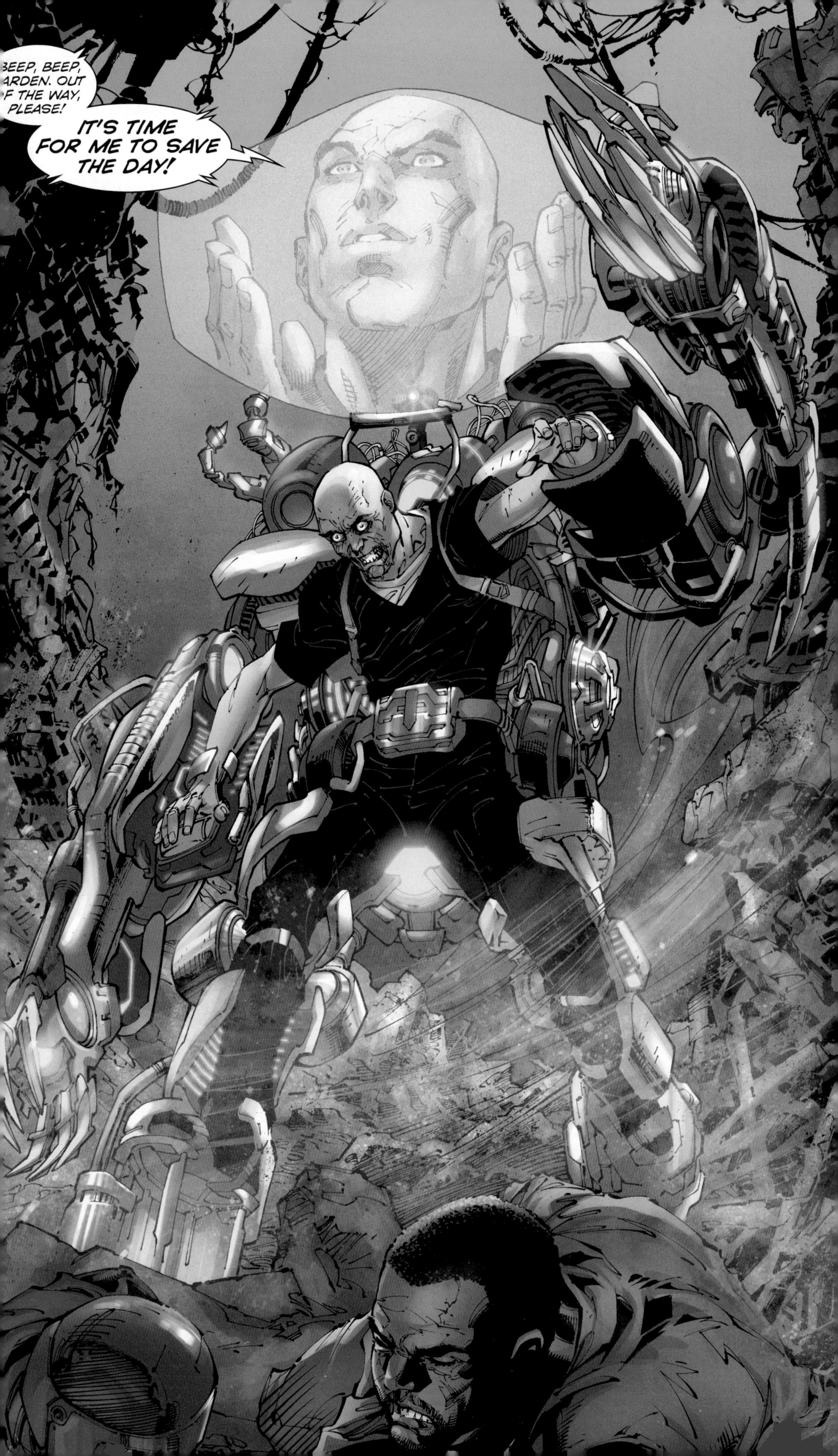
BEEP, BEEP, ARDEN. OUT F THE WAY, PLEASE!
IT'S TIME FOR ME TO SAVE THE DAY!

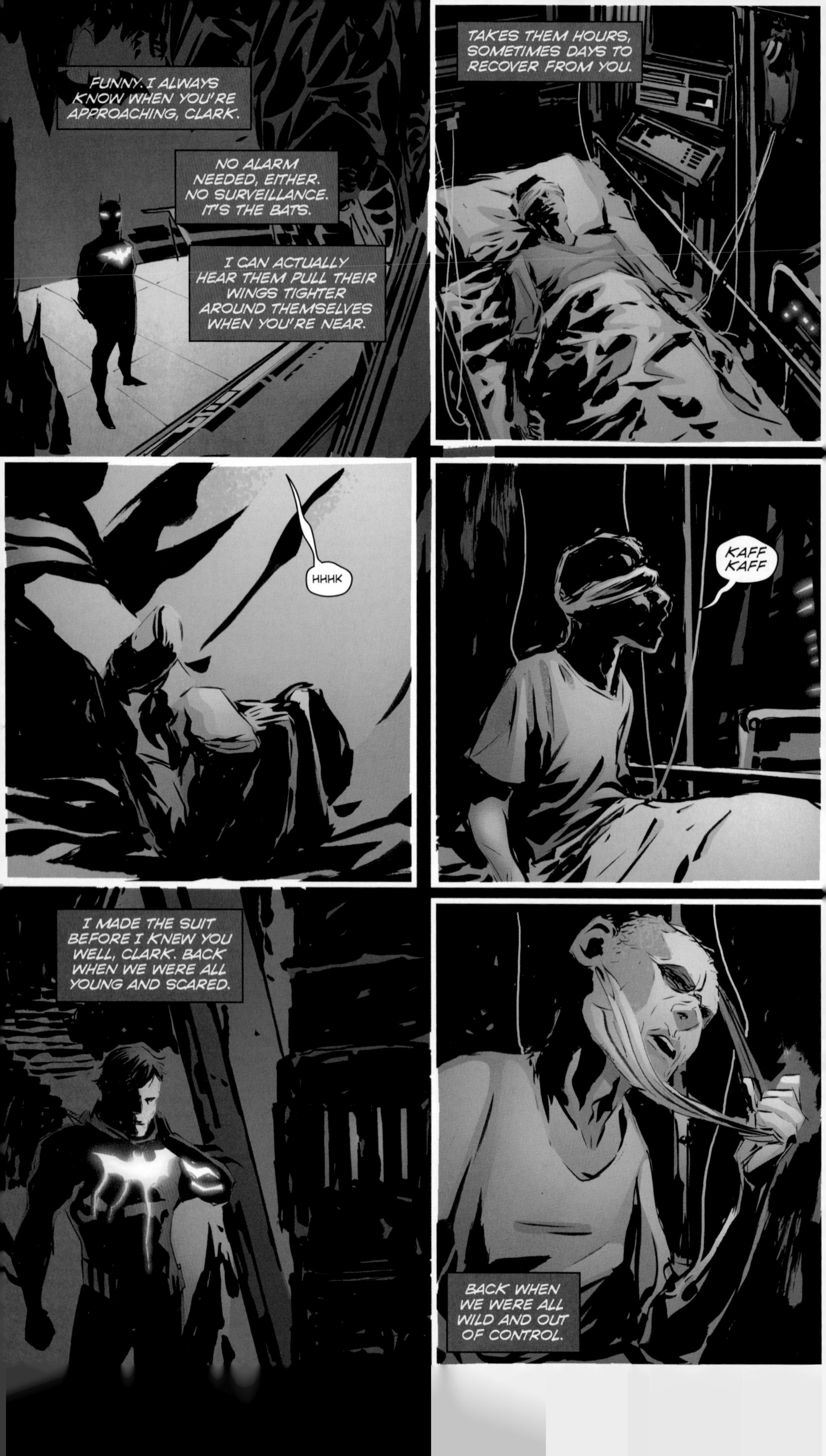
FUNNY. I ALWAYS KNOW WHEN YOU'RE APPROACHING, CLARK.
NO ALARM NEEDED, EITHER. NO SURVEILLANCE. IT'S THE BATS.
I CAN ACTUALLY HEAR THEM PULL THEIR WINGS TIGHTER AROUND THEMSELVES WHEN YOU'RE NEAR.
TAKES THEM HOURS, SOMETIMES DAYS TO RECOVER FROM YOU.
HHHK
KAFF KAFF
I MADE THE SUIT BEFORE I KNEW YOU WELL, CLARK. BACK WHEN WE WERE ALL YOUNG AND SCARED.
BACK WHEN WE WERE ALL WILD AND OUT OF CONTROL.

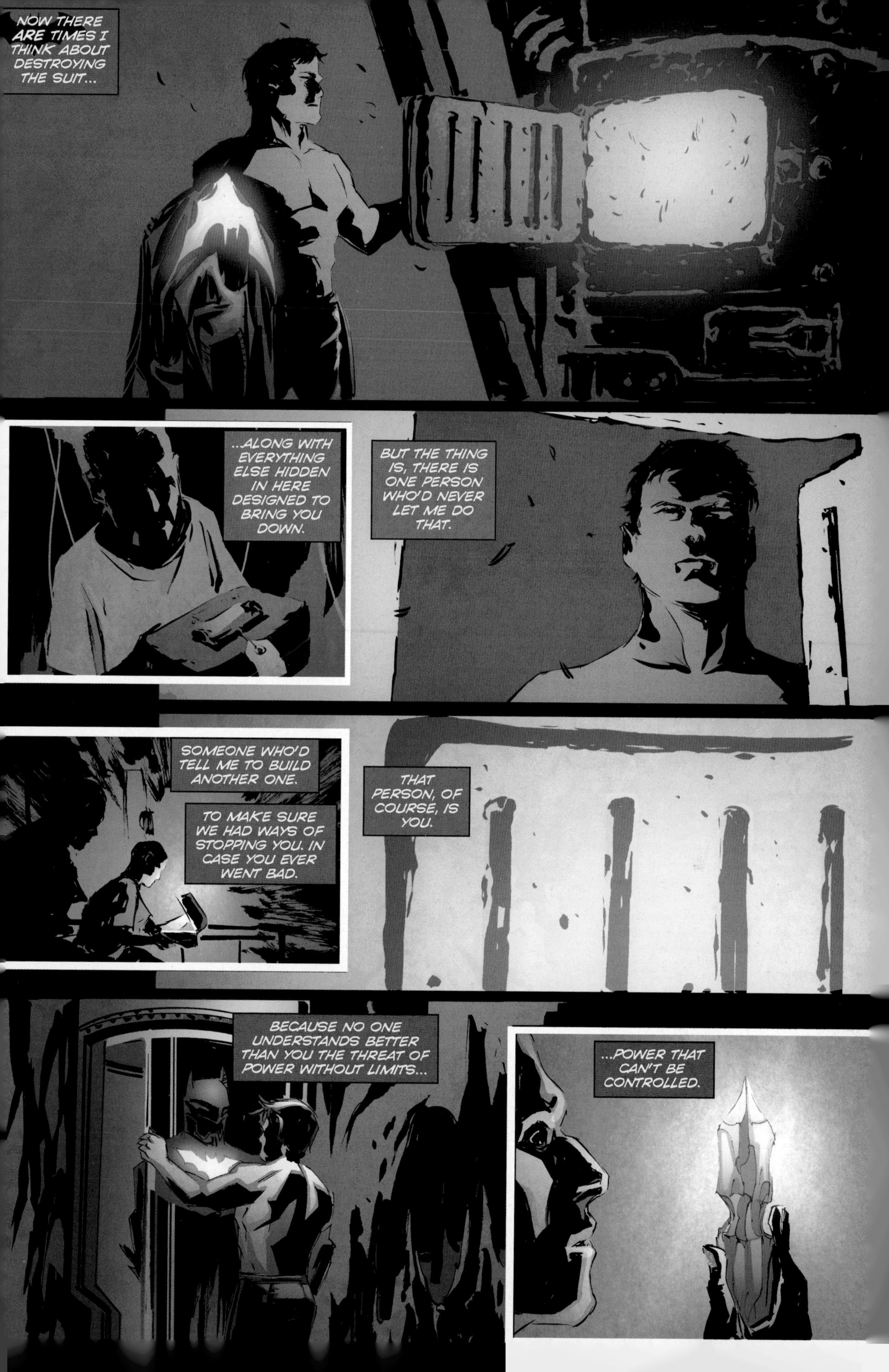
NOW THERE ARE TIMES I THINK ABOUT DESTROYING THE SUIT...
...ALONG WITH EVERYTHING ELSE HIDDEN IN HERE DESIGNED TO BRING YOU DOWN.
BUT THE THING IS, THERE IS ONE PERSON WHO'D NEVER LET ME DO THAT.
SOMEONE WHO'D TELL ME TO BUILD ANOTHER ONE.
TO MAKE SURE WE HAD WAYS OF STOPPING YOU. IN CASE YOU EVER WENT BAD.
THAT PERSON, OF COURSE, IS YOU.
BECAUSE NO ONE UNDERSTANDS BETTER THAN YOU THE THREAT OF POWER WITHOUT LIMITS...
...POWER THAT CAN'T BE CONTROLLED.

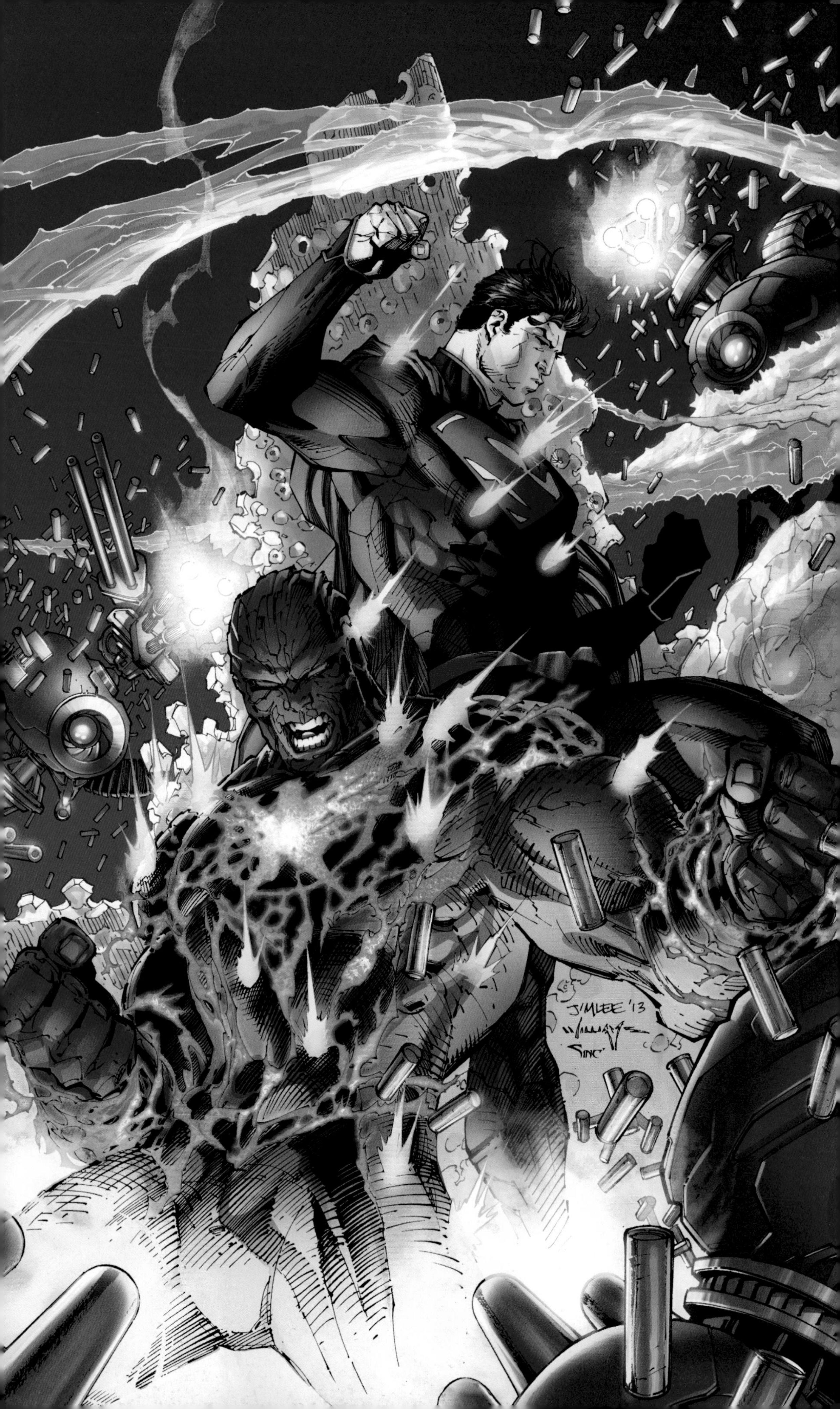
JIMLEE '13

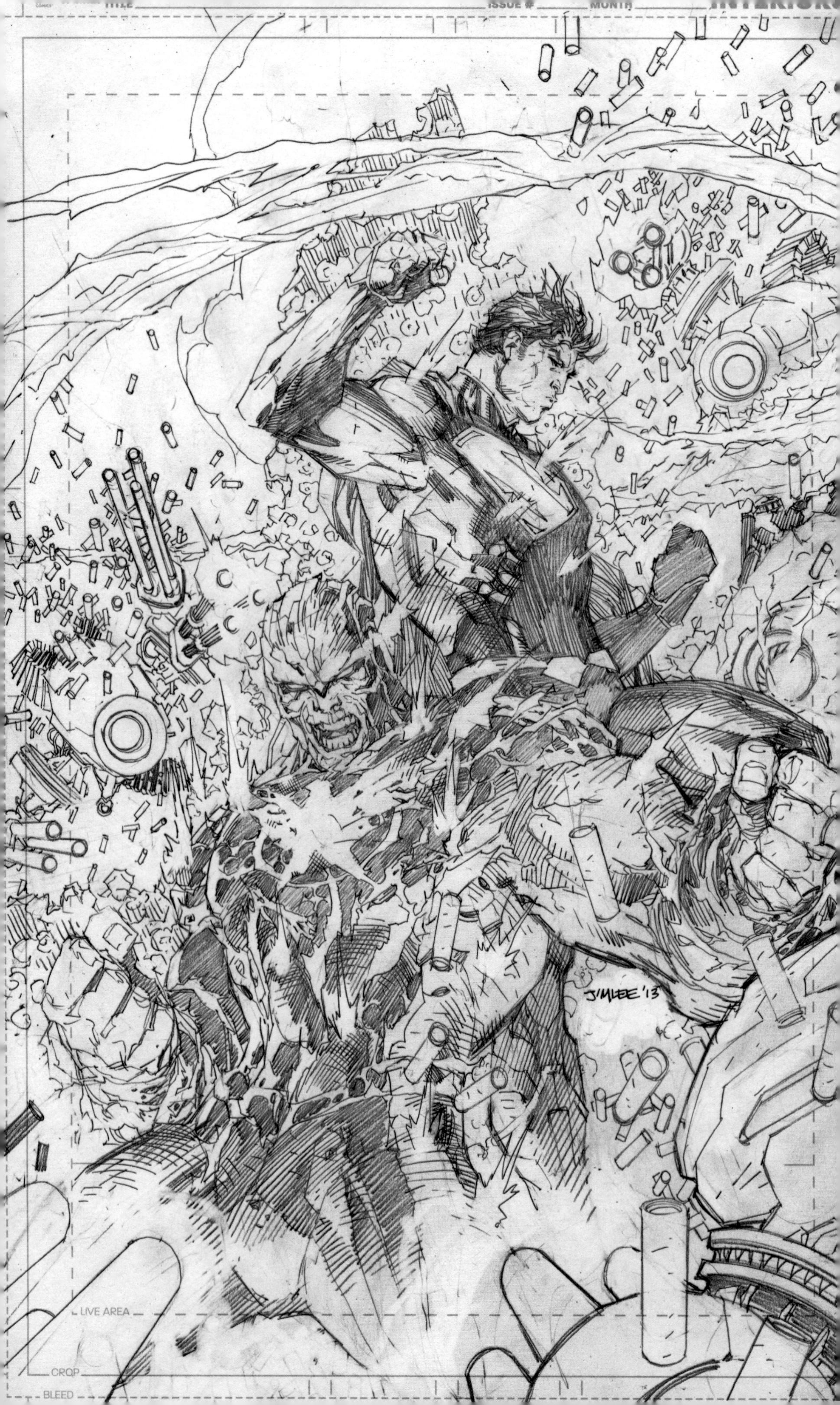
TITLE
ISSUE #
MONTH
J'M LEE '13
LIVE AREA
CROP
BLEED

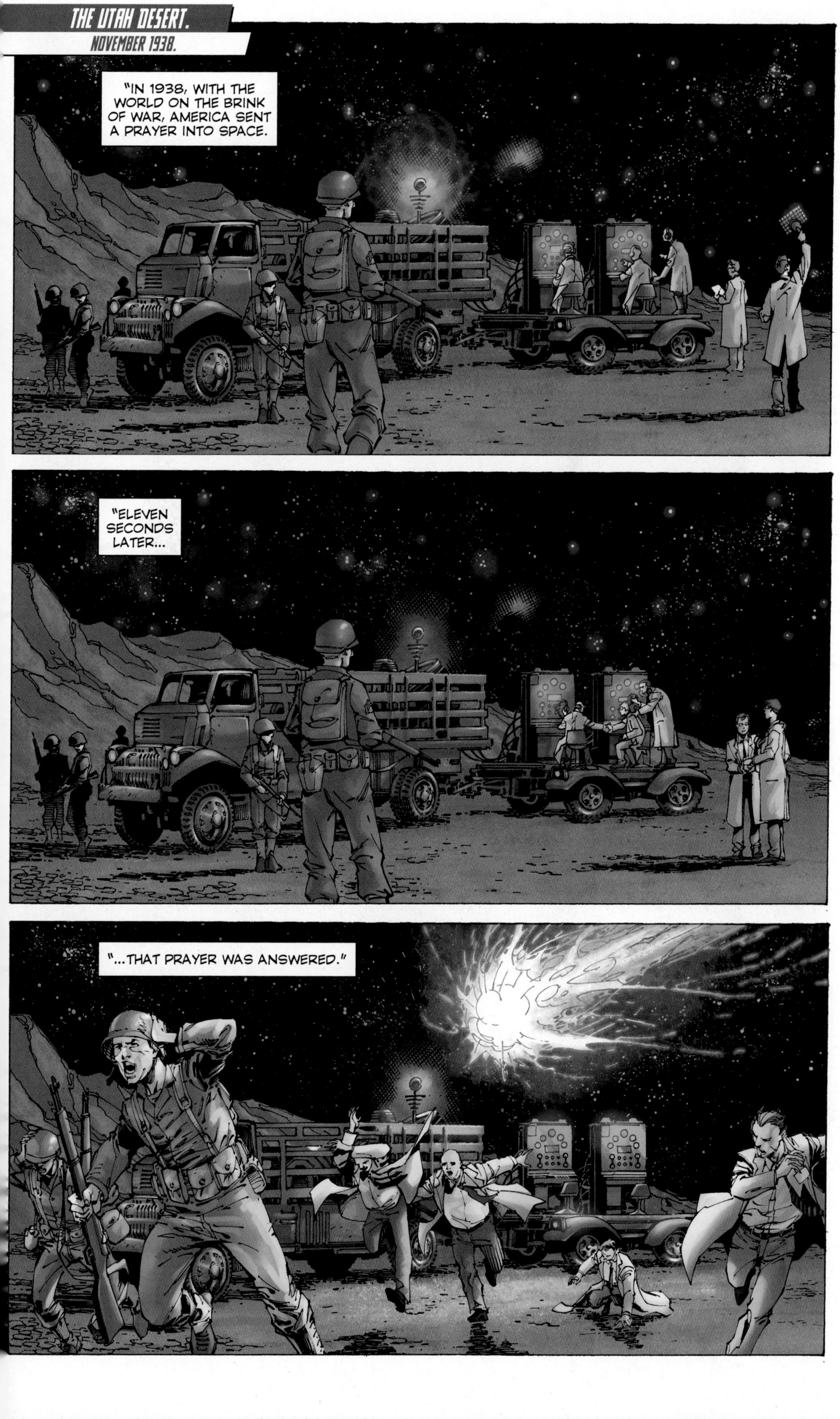
THE UTAH DESERT.
NOVEMBER 1938.
"IN 1938, WITH THE WORLD ON THE BRINK OF WAR, AMERICA SENT A PRAYER INTO SPACE.
"ELEVEN SECONDS LATER...
"...THAT PRAYER WAS ANSWERED."

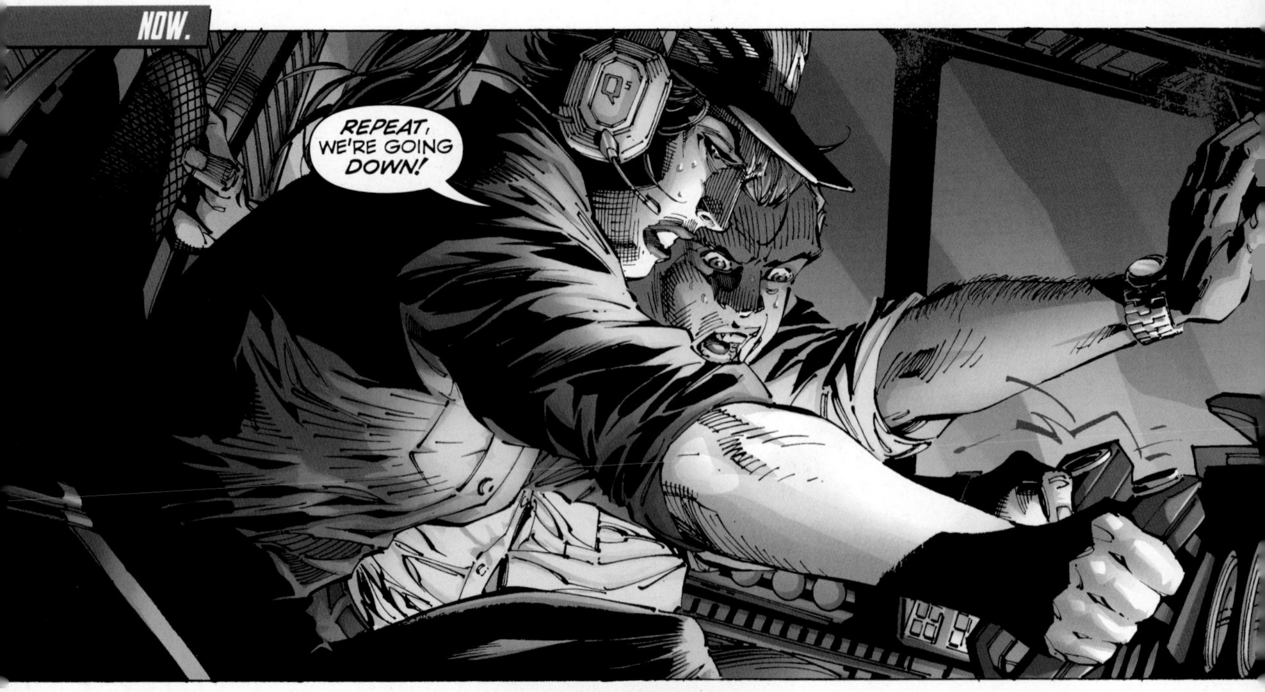
NOW.
REPEAT, WE'RE GOING DOWN!

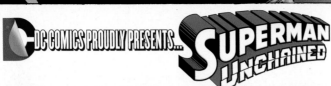

DC COMICS PROUDLY PRESENTS... SUPERMAN UNCHAINED

ANSWERED PRAYERS

SCOTT SNYDER WRITER JIM LEE PENCILLER
SCOTT WILLIAMS INKER
ALEX SINCLAIR & JEROMY COX COLORS SAL CIPRIANO LETTERS
COVER BY JIM LEE, SCOTT WILLIAMS & ALEX SINCLAIR

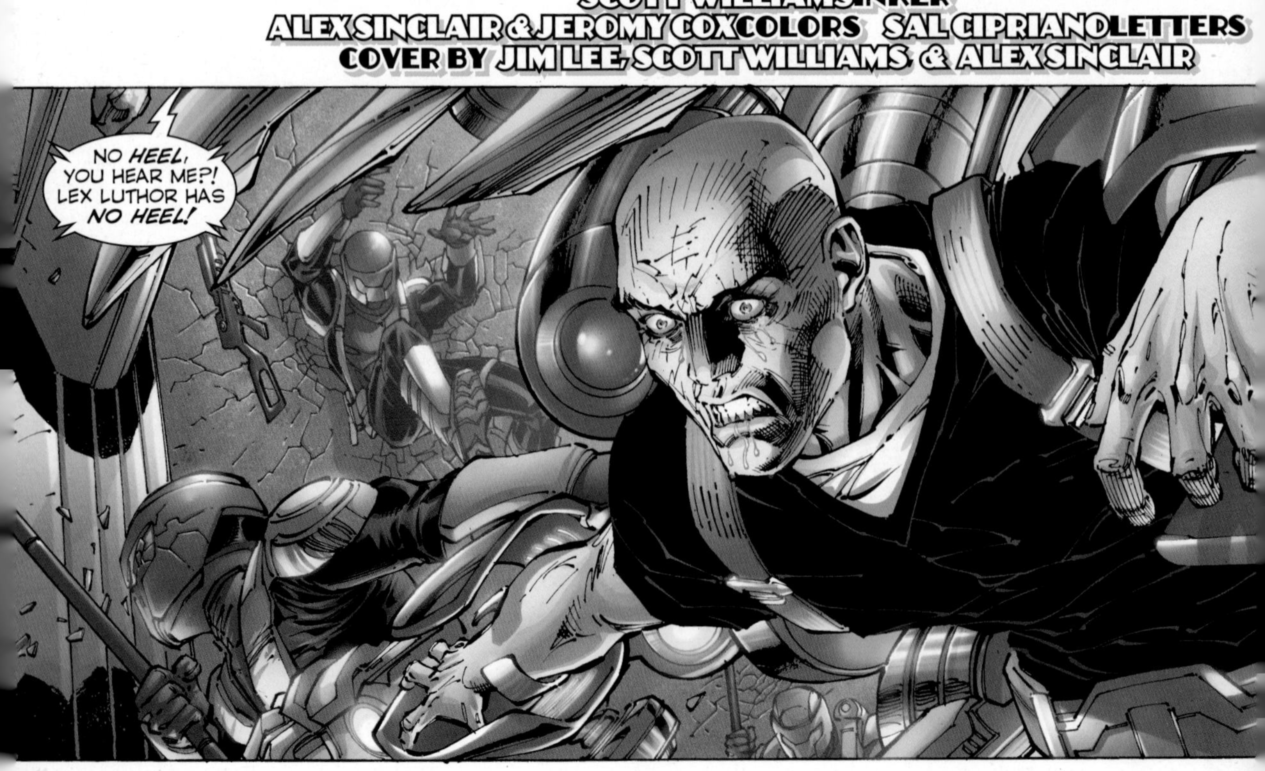
NO HEEL, YOU HEAR ME?! LEX LUTHOR HAS NO HEEL!

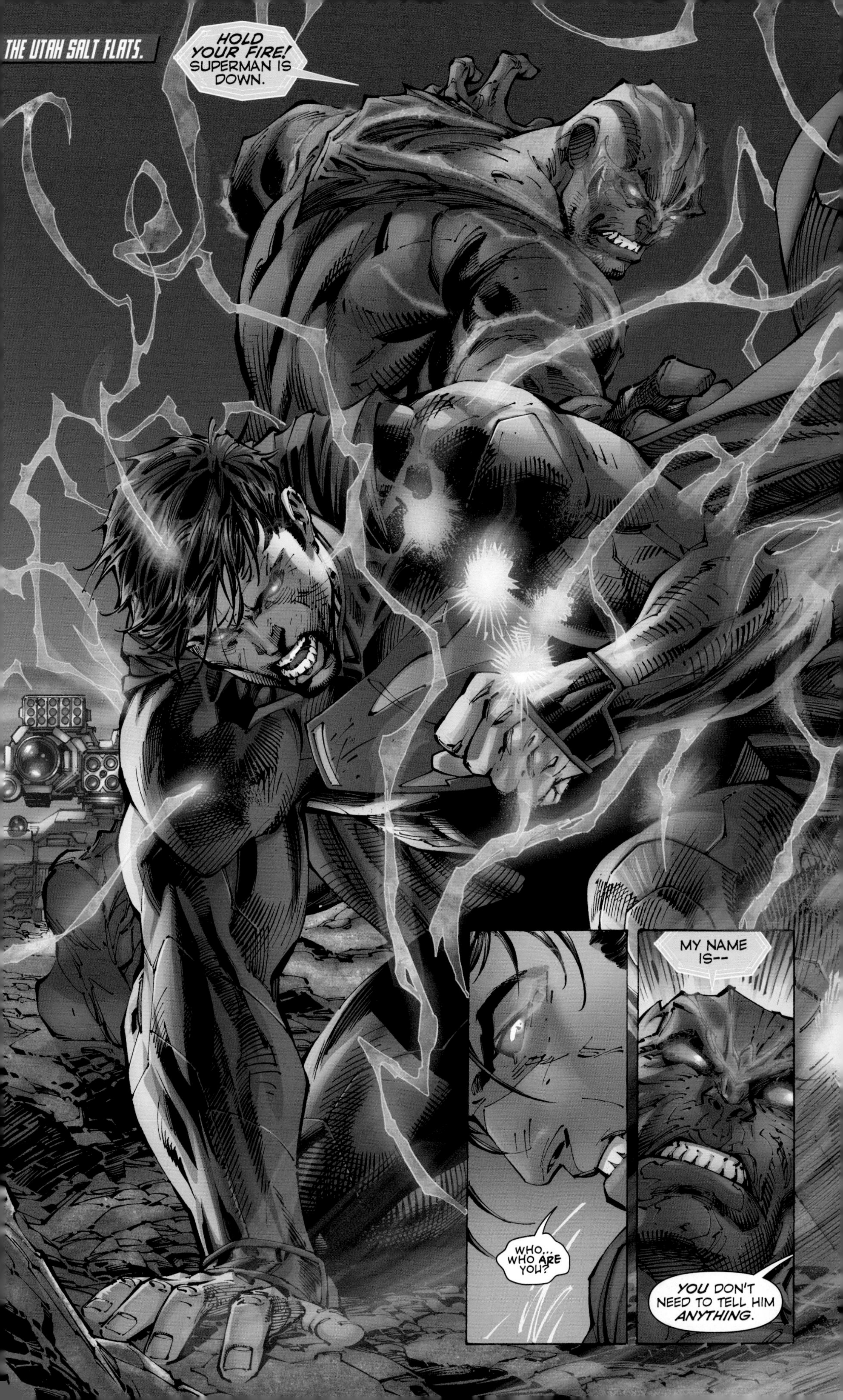
THE UTAH SALT FLATS.
HOLD YOUR FIRE! SUPERMAN IS DOWN.
WHO... WHO ARE YOU?
MY NAME IS--
YOU DON'T NEED TO TELL HIM ANYTHING.

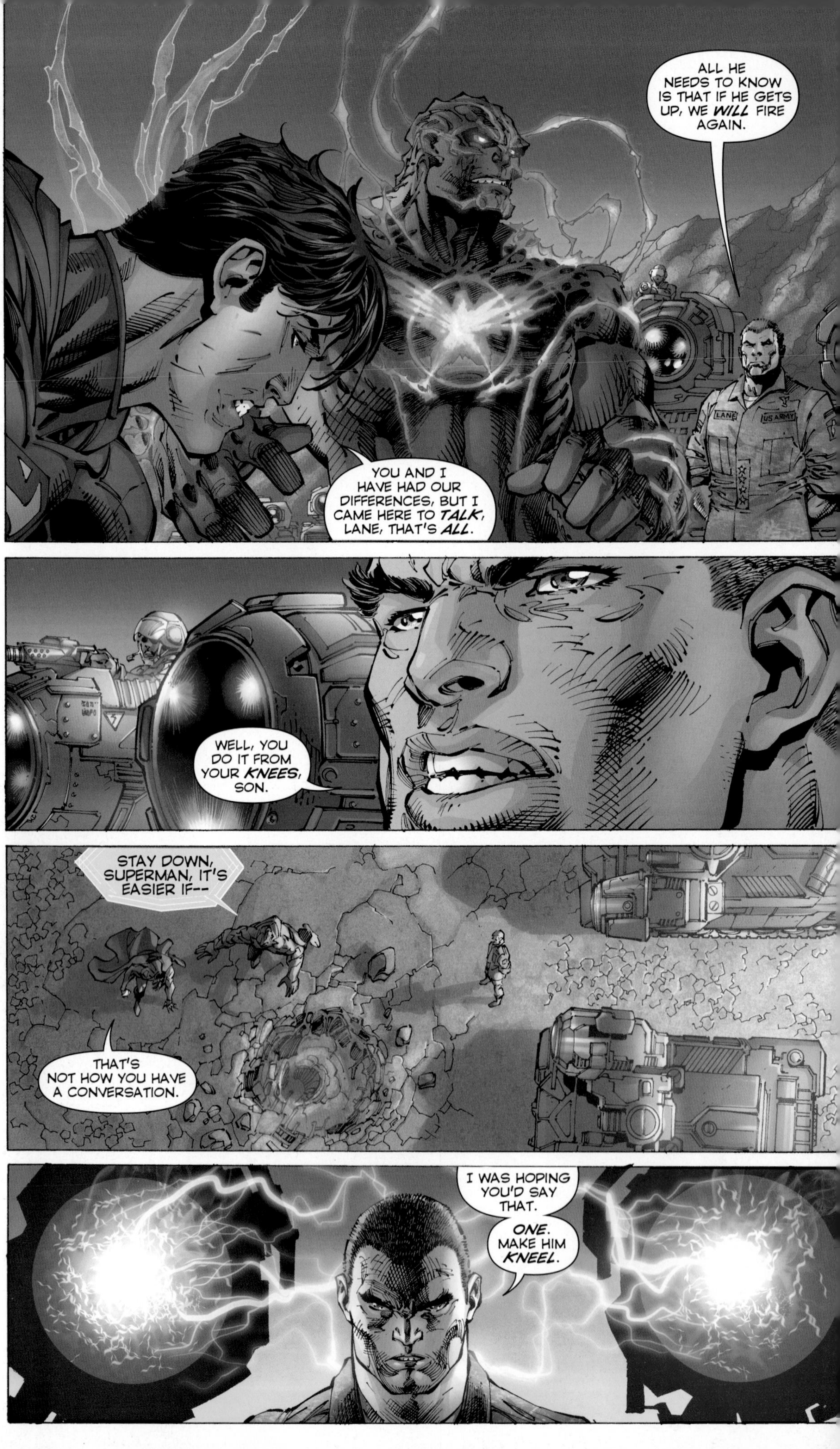
ALL HE NEEDS TO KNOW IS THAT IF HE GETS UP, WE WILL FIRE AGAIN.
YOU AND I HAVE HAD OUR DIFFERENCES, BUT I CAME HERE TO TALK, LANE, THAT'S ALL.
WELL, YOU DO IT FROM YOUR KNEES, SON.
STAY DOWN, SUPERMAN, IT'S EASIER IF--
THAT'S NOT HOW YOU HAVE A CONVERSATION.
I WAS HOPING YOU'D SAY THAT.
ONE. MAKE HIM KNEEL.

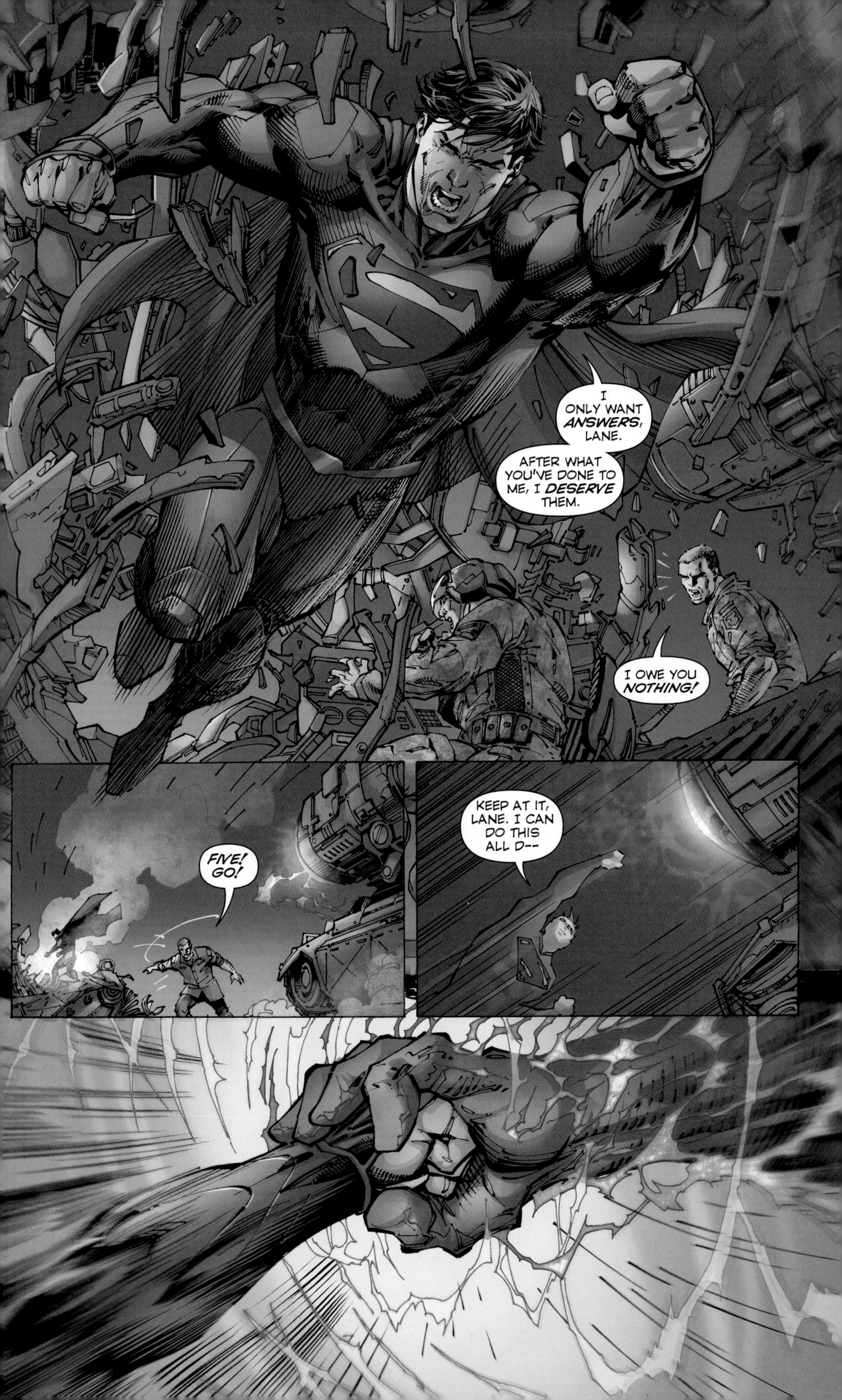

I ONLY WANT ANSWERS, LANE.
AFTER WHAT YOU'VE DONE TO ME, I DESERVE THEM.
I OWE YOU NOTHING!
FIVE! GO!
KEEP AT IT, LANE. I CAN DO THIS ALL D--

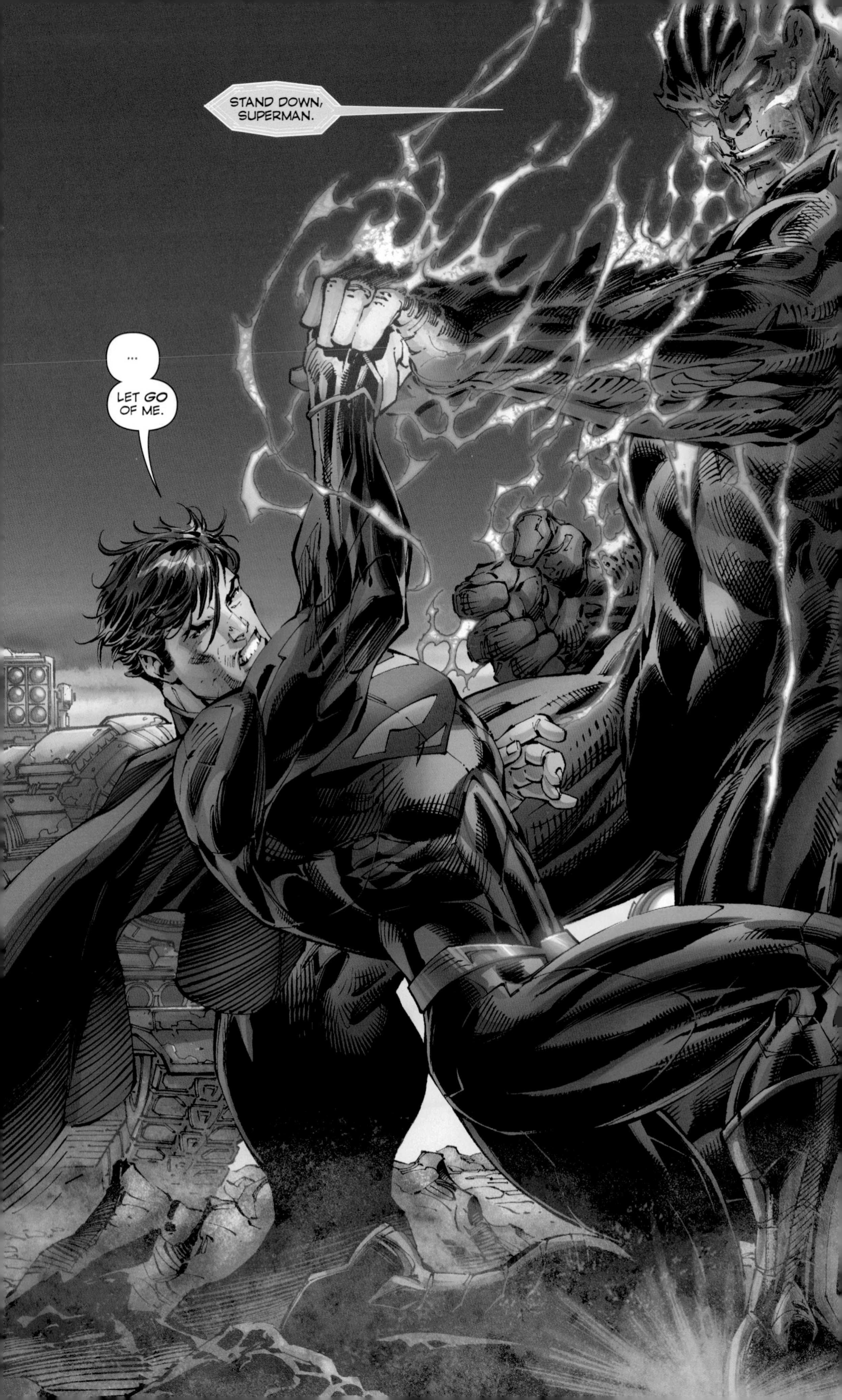
STAND DOWN, SUPERMAN.
...
LET GO OF ME.

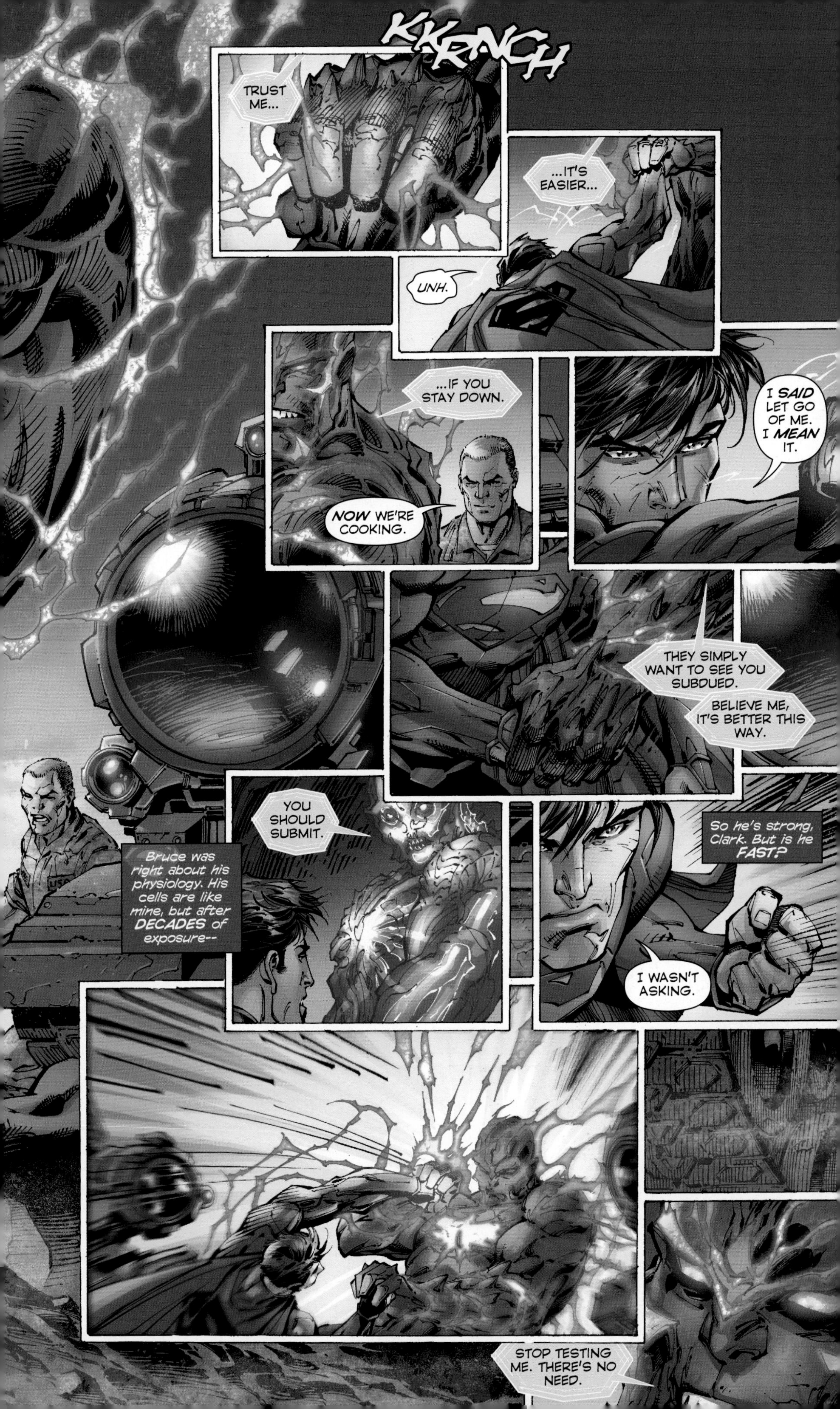
KKRNCH
TRUST ME...
...IT'S EASIER...
UNH.
...IF YOU STAY DOWN.
NOW WE'RE COOKING.
I SAID LET GO OF ME. I MEAN IT.
THEY SIMPLY WANT TO SEE YOU SUBDUED.
BELIEVE ME, IT'S BETTER THIS WAY.
Bruce was right about his physiology. His cells are like mine, but after DECADES of exposure--
YOU SHOULD SUBMIT.
So he's strong, Clark. But is he FAST?
I WASN'T ASKING.
STOP TESTING ME. THERE'S NO NEED.

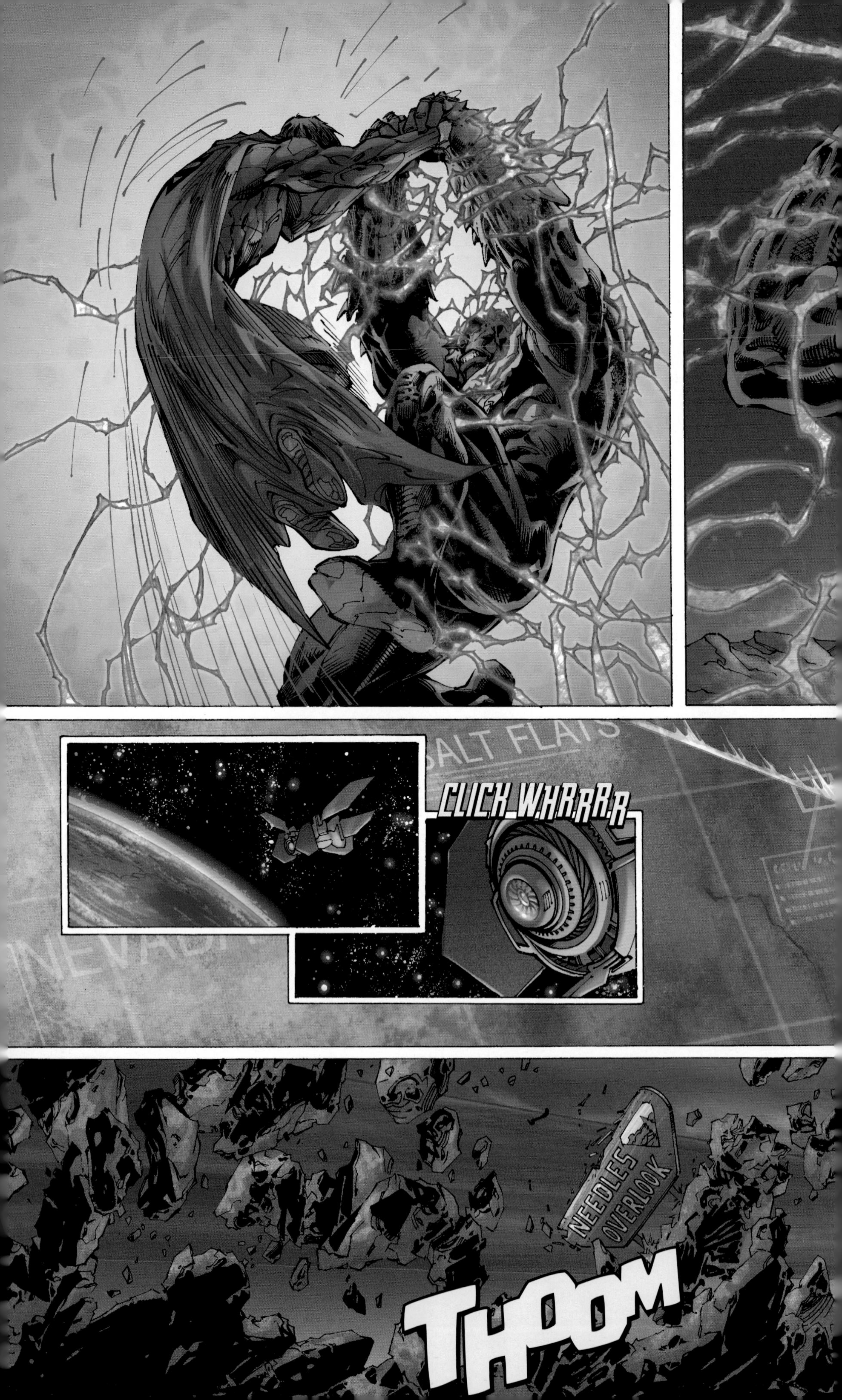
SALT FLATS
CLICK WHRRRR
NEVADA
NEEDLES OVERLOOK
THOOM

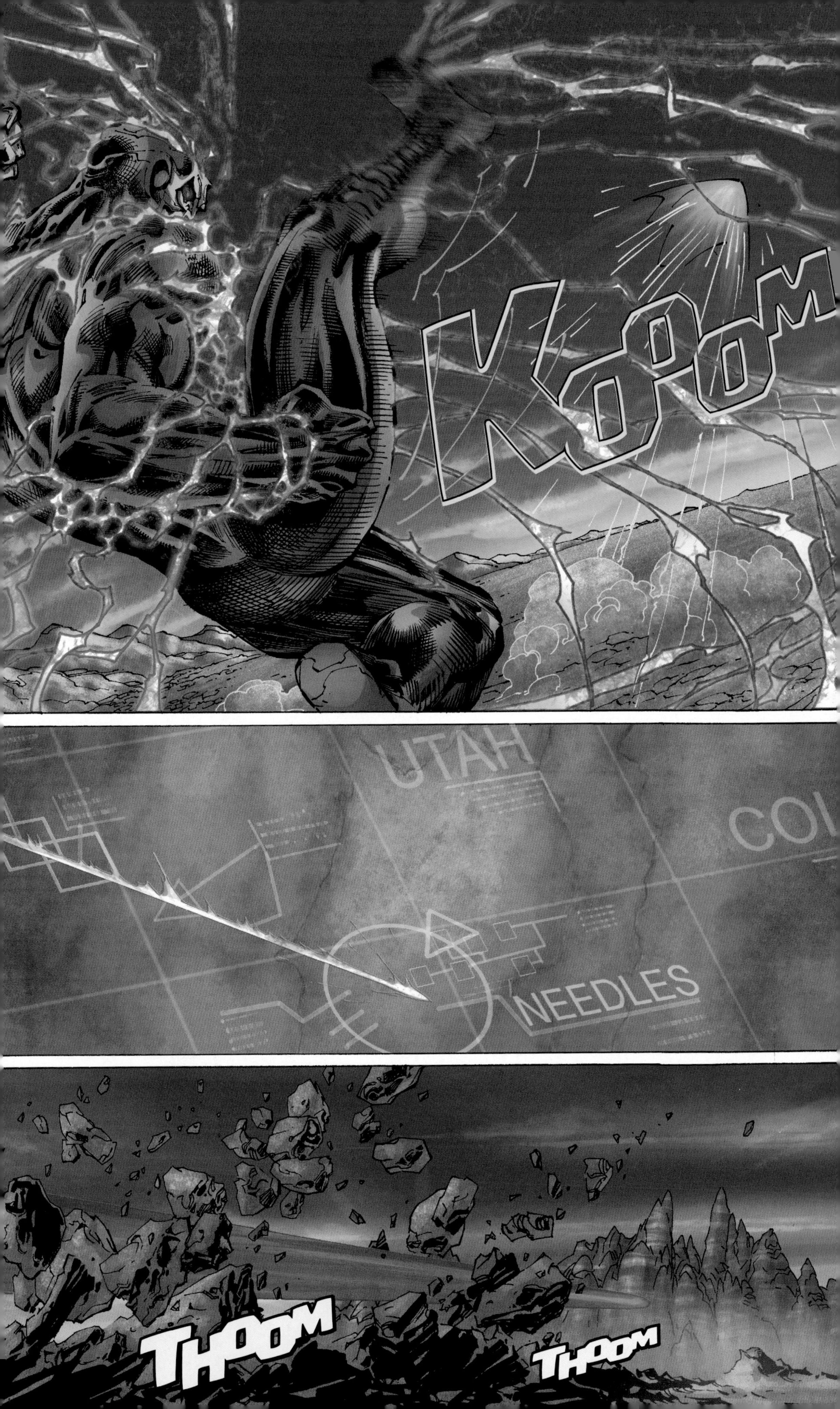
KOOOM
UTAH
CO
NEEDLES
THOOM
THOOM

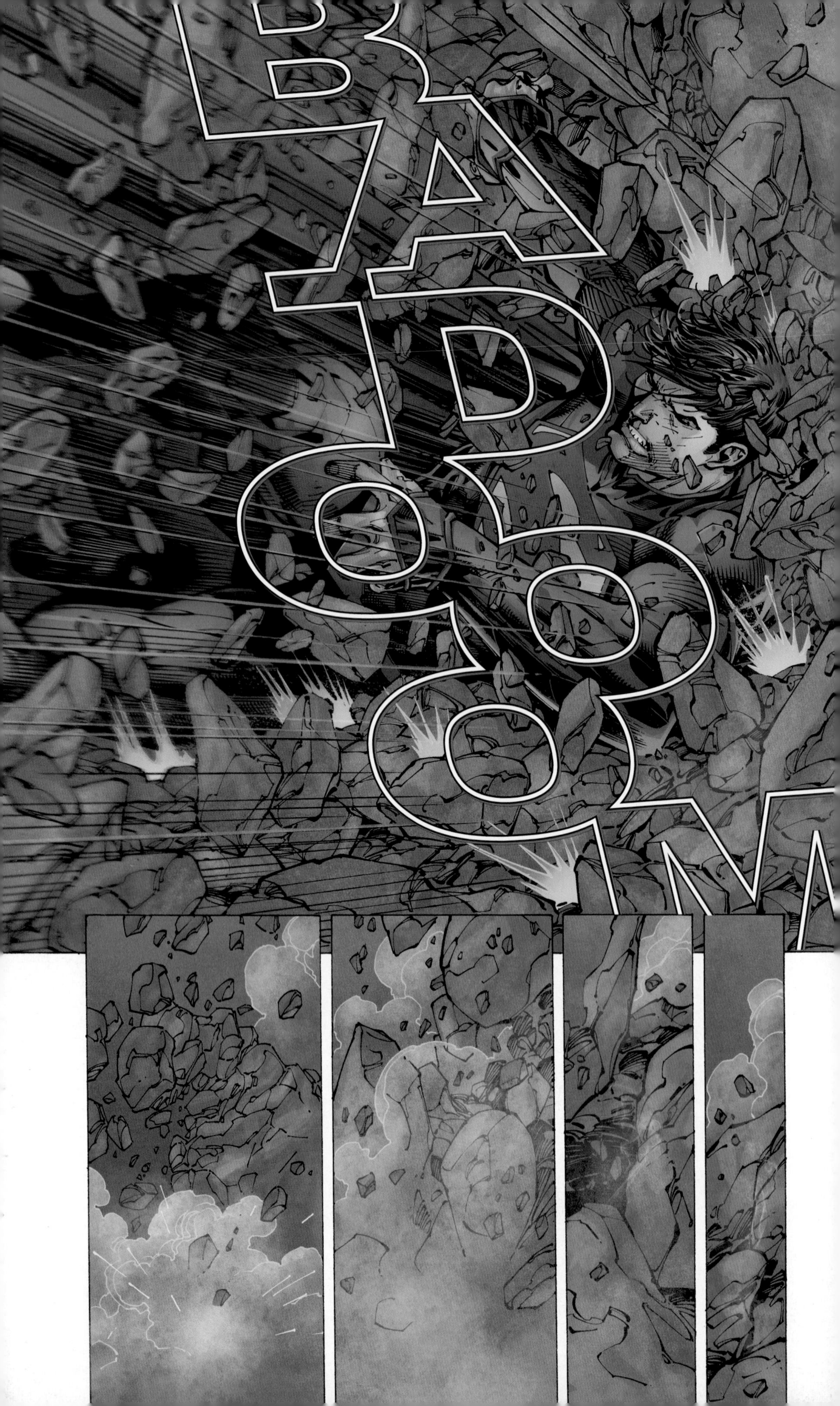
BADOOOM

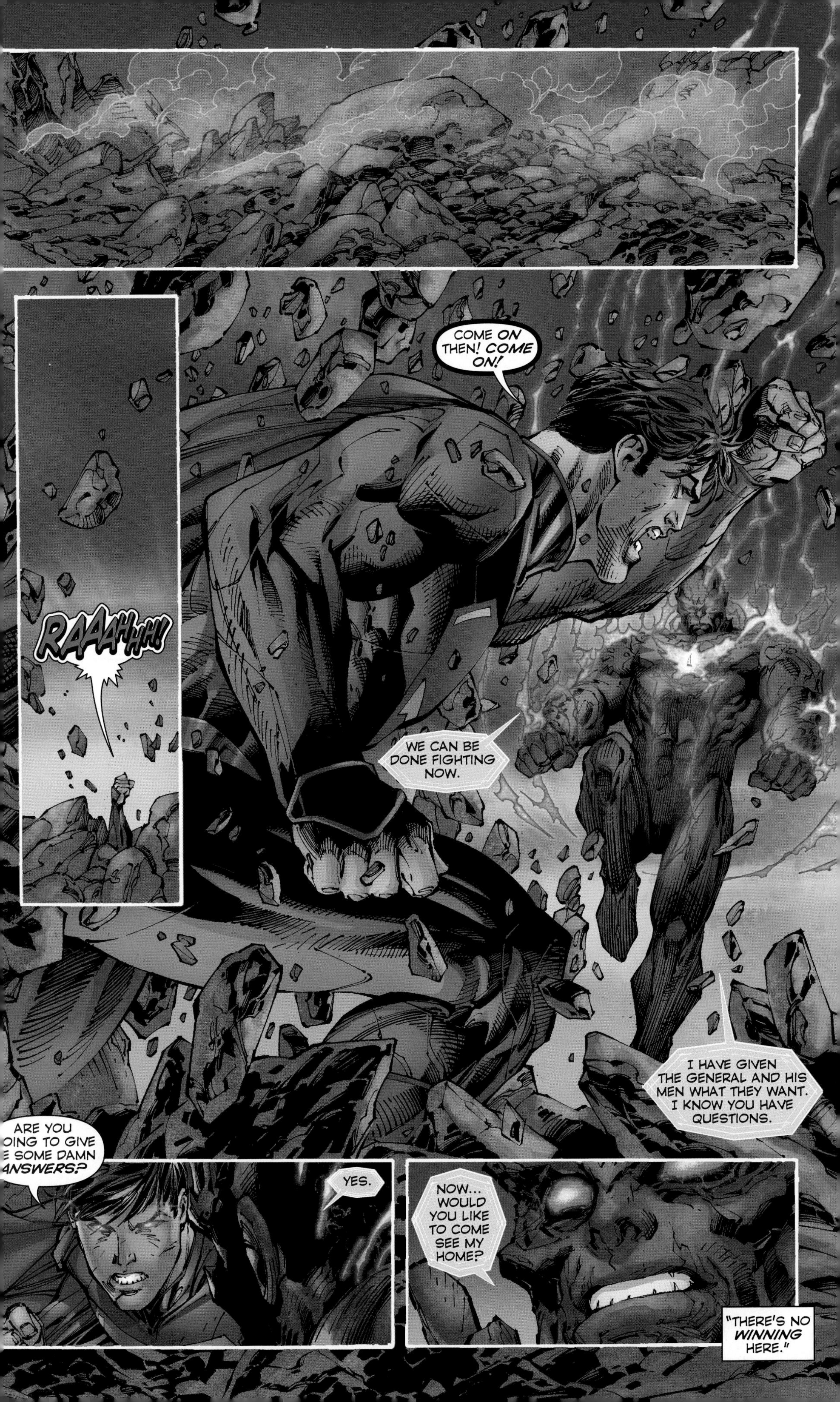
RAAAHHHH!
COME ON THEN! COME ON!
WE CAN BE DONE FIGHTING NOW.
I HAVE GIVEN THE GENERAL AND HIS MEN WHAT THEY WANT. I KNOW YOU HAVE QUESTIONS.
ARE YOU OING TO GIVE E SOME DAMN ANSWERS?
YES.
NOW... WOULD YOU LIKE TO COME SEE MY HOME?
"THERE'S NO WINNING HERE."

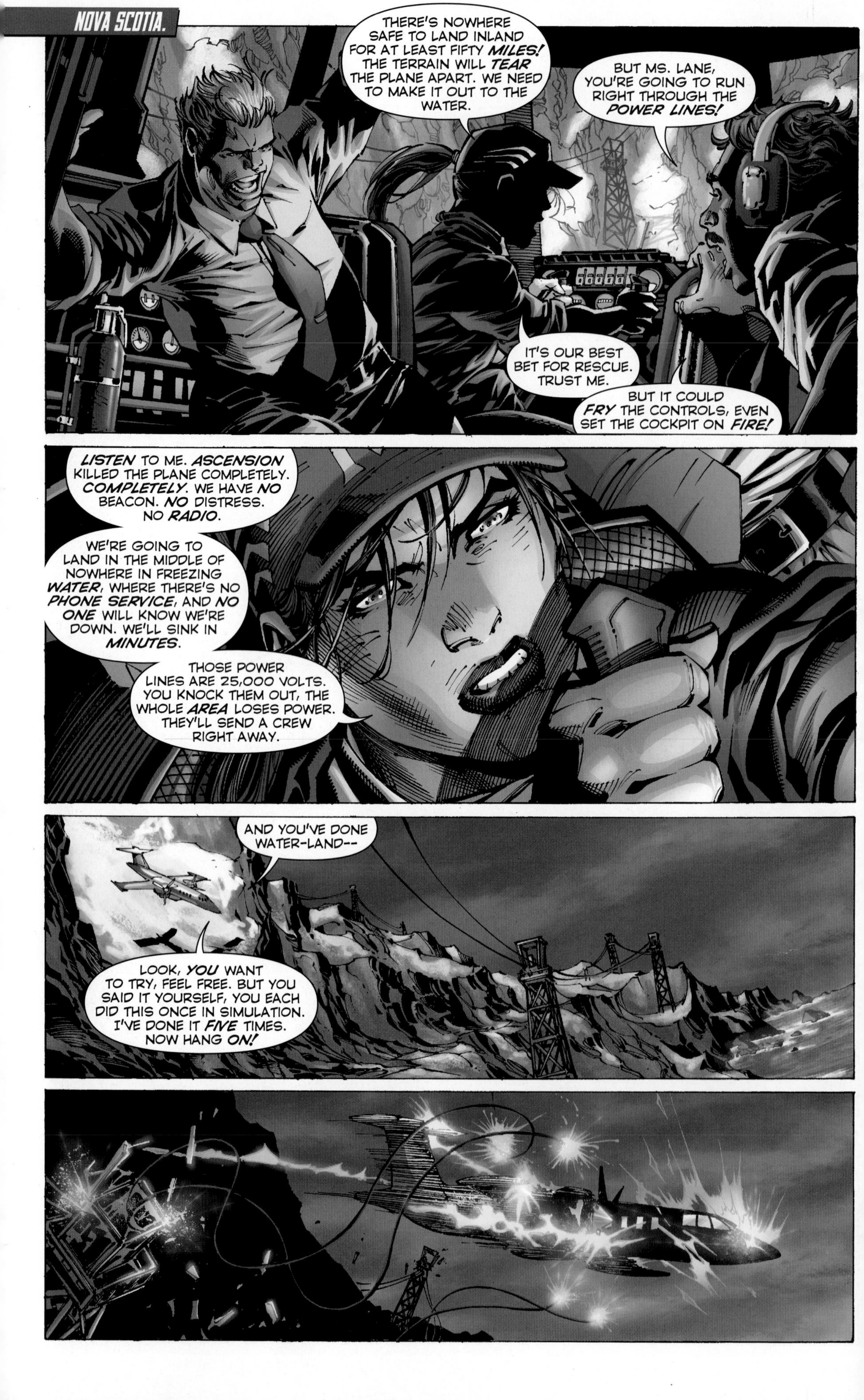
NOVA SCOTIA.
THERE'S NOWHERE SAFE TO LAND INLAND FOR AT LEAST FIFTY MILES! THE TERRAIN WILL TEAR THE PLANE APART. WE NEED TO MAKE IT OUT TO THE WATER.
BUT MS. LANE, YOU'RE GOING TO RUN RIGHT THROUGH THE POWER LINES!
IT'S OUR BEST BET FOR RESCUE. TRUST ME.
BUT IT COULD FRY THE CONTROLS, EVEN SET THE COCKPIT ON FIRE!
LISTEN TO ME. ASCENSION KILLED THE PLANE COMPLETELY. COMPLETELY. WE HAVE NO BEACON. NO DISTRESS. NO RADIO.
WE'RE GOING TO LAND IN THE MIDDLE OF NOWHERE IN FREEZING WATER, WHERE THERE'S NO PHONE SERVICE, AND NO ONE WILL KNOW WE'RE DOWN. WE'LL SINK IN MINUTES.
THOSE POWER LINES ARE 25,000 VOLTS. YOU KNOCK THEM OUT, THE WHOLE AREA LOSES POWER. THEY'LL SEND A CREW RIGHT AWAY.
AND YOU'VE DONE WATER-LAND--
LOOK, YOU WANT TO TRY, FEEL FREE. BUT YOU SAID IT YOURSELF, YOU EACH DID THIS ONCE IN SIMULATION. I'VE DONE IT FIVE TIMES. NOW HANG ON!

OH GOD!

GET THE EXTINGUISHER, QUICK! I CAN *HOLD* US!

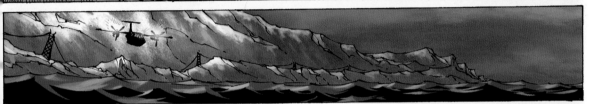

PLEASE. *PLEASE* LET ME PULL THIS ONE OFF.

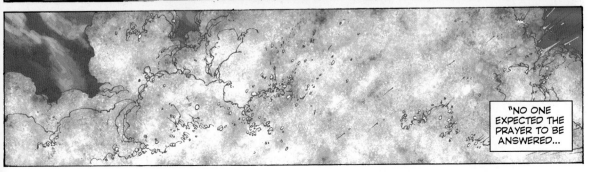

"NO ONE EXPECTED THE PRAYER TO BE ANSWERED...

"...LET ALONE LIKE *THAT*.

"THE ORIGINAL PRAYER THE SCIENTISTS SENT UP WAS A SIMPLE MATHEMATICAL EQUATION.

"BUT AN EQUATION ADDED UP *INCORRECTLY*--TO EQUAL *MORE* THAN THE SUM OF ITS PARTS.

"THE HOPE WAS THAT THE MEANING WOULD BE CLEAR: LET US ADD UP TO MORE, TOGETHER.

"ENGRAVED ON THE INSIDE OF THE SHIP WAS A SIMILAR EQUATION, BUT ONE MUCH MORE *COMPLEX*--

"WITH CODES AND FORMULAS EMBEDDED IN IT, LIKE EDDIES IN A STREAM.

"*GIFTS*.

"IT WAS ONLY WHEN THE SMOKE CLEARED THAT THE SCIENTISTS SAW THE *PASSENGER*.

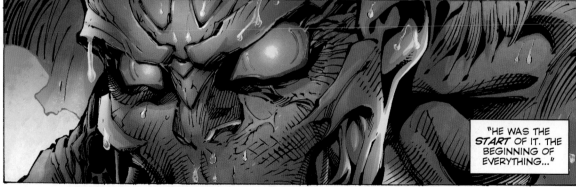

"HE WAS THE *START* OF IT. THE BEGINNING OF EVERYTHING..."

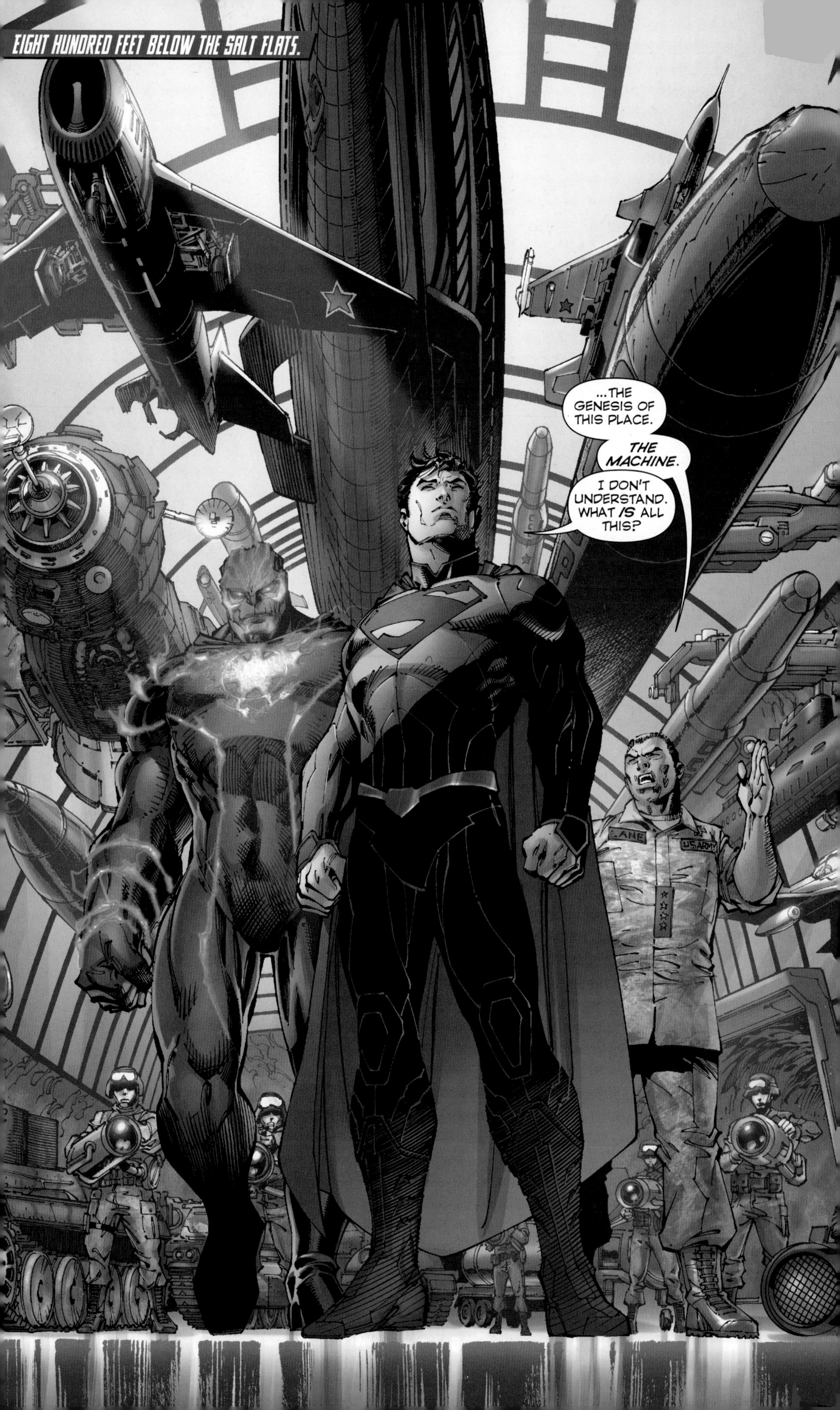
EIGHT HUNDRED FEET BELOW THE SALT FLATS.
...THE GENESIS OF THIS PLACE.
THE MACHINE.
I DON'T UNDERSTAND. WHAT IS ALL THIS?
LANE
U.S. ARMY

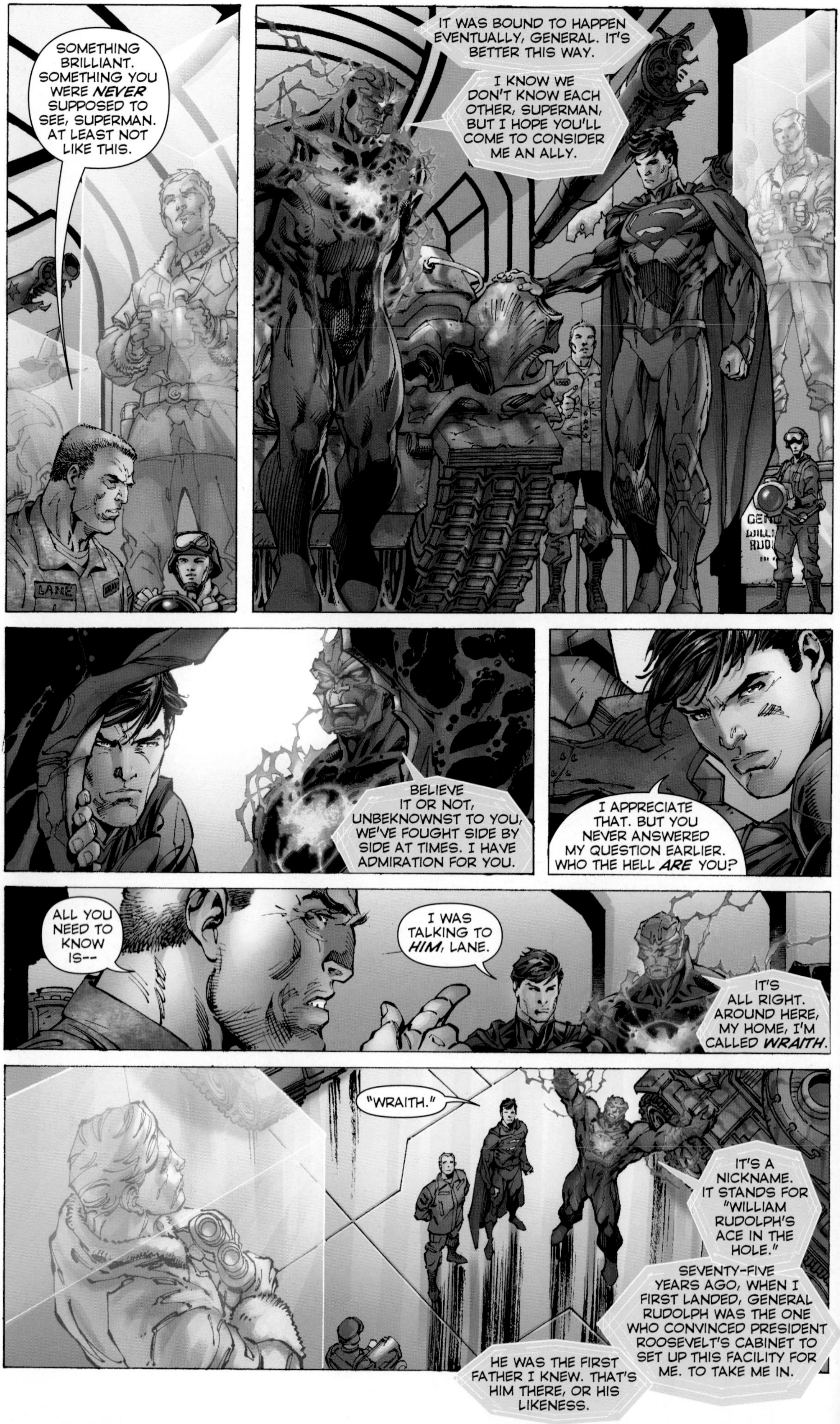
SOMETHING BRILLIANT. SOMETHING YOU WERE NEVER SUPPOSED TO SEE, SUPERMAN. AT LEAST NOT LIKE THIS.
LANE
IT WAS BOUND TO HAPPEN EVENTUALLY, GENERAL. IT'S BETTER THIS WAY.
I KNOW WE DON'T KNOW EACH OTHER, SUPERMAN, BUT I HOPE YOU'LL COME TO CONSIDER ME AN ALLY.
BELIEVE IT OR NOT, UNBEKNOWNST TO YOU, WE'VE FOUGHT SIDE BY SIDE AT TIMES. I HAVE ADMIRATION FOR YOU.
I APPRECIATE THAT. BUT YOU NEVER ANSWERED MY QUESTION EARLIER. WHO THE HELL ARE YOU?
ALL YOU NEED TO KNOW IS--
I WAS TALKING TO HIM, LANE.
IT'S ALL RIGHT. AROUND HERE, MY HOME, I'M CALLED WRAITH.
"WRAITH."
IT'S A NICKNAME. IT STANDS FOR "WILLIAM RUDOLPH'S ACE IN THE HOLE."
SEVENTY-FIVE YEARS AGO, WHEN I FIRST LANDED, GENERAL RUDOLPH WAS THE ONE WHO CONVINCED PRESIDENT ROOSEVELT'S CABINET TO SET UP THIS FACILITY FOR ME. TO TAKE ME IN.
HE WAS THE FIRST FATHER I KNEW. THAT'S HIM THERE, OR HIS LIKENESS.

GENERAL RUDOLPH ESTABLISHED THE MACHINE AS A *RESEARCH* FACILITY, DEDICATED TO UNDERSTANDING AND IMPLEMENTING THE EQUATION AND TECHNOLOGY WRAITH BROUGHT TO US.

BUT IN TIME, THE MACHINE BECAME A MORE AGGRESSIVE OPERATION, AND WRAITH WAS DEPLOYED TO ASSIST AMERICAN INITIATIVES AS NECESSARY.

TROPHIES, SUPERMAN. REMINDERS OF THE WORK WRAITH HAS DONE FOR US OVER THE LAST EIGHT DECADES. THE SUB IS FROM CUBA, 1962. THE MIG 15 FROM VLADIVOSTOK, 1952...

YOU'RE SAYING HE WAS A *SECRET WEAPON*. AND ALL OF THESE OLD THINGS--

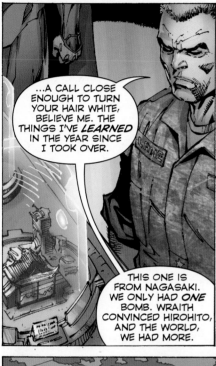

...A CALL CLOSE ENOUGH TO TURN YOUR HAIR WHITE, BELIEVE ME. THE THINGS I'VE *LEARNED* IN THE YEAR SINCE I TOOK OVER.

THIS ONE IS FROM NAGASAKI. WE ONLY HAD *ONE* BOMB. WRAITH CONVINCED HIROHITO, AND THE WORLD, WE HAD MORE.

NAGASAKI.

AND THIS PLACE, ALL OF THIS...WHO KNOWS ABOUT IT?

CHILD'S TOY DIORAMA OF TOKYO WORLD'S FAIR 1922 NAGASAKI

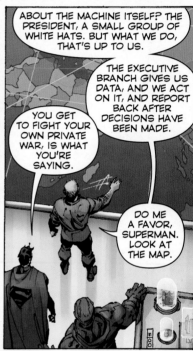

ABOUT THE MACHINE ITSELF? THE PRESIDENT, A SMALL GROUP OF WHITE HATS. BUT WHAT WE DO, THAT'S UP TO US.

THE EXECUTIVE BRANCH GIVES US DATA, AND WE ACT ON IT, AND REPORT BACK AFTER DECISIONS HAVE BEEN MADE.

YOU GET TO FIGHT YOUR OWN PRIVATE WAR, IS WHAT YOU'RE SAYING.

DO ME A FAVOR, SUPERMAN. LOOK AT THE MAP.

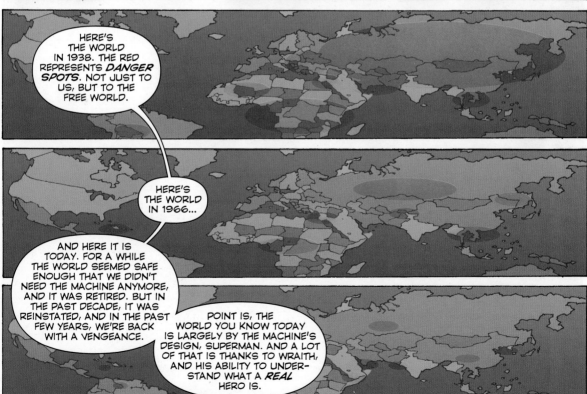

HERE'S THE WORLD IN 1938. THE RED REPRESENTS *DANGER SPOTS*. NOT JUST TO US, BUT TO THE FREE WORLD.

HERE'S THE WORLD IN 1966...

AND HERE IT IS TODAY. FOR A WHILE THE WORLD SEEMED SAFE ENOUGH THAT WE DIDN'T NEED THE MACHINE ANYMORE, AND IT WAS RETIRED. BUT IN THE PAST DECADE, IT WAS REINSTATED, AND IN THE PAST FEW YEARS, WE'RE BACK WITH A VENGEANCE.

POINT IS, THE WORLD YOU KNOW TODAY IS LARGELY BY THE MACHINE'S DESIGN, SUPERMAN. AND A LOT OF THAT IS THANKS TO WRAITH, AND HIS ABILITY TO UNDERSTAND WHAT A *REAL* HERO IS.

THAT MAY BE, BUT THE PUBLIC--

AH, THE "PUBLIC!" SEE, I KNEW IT. I KNEW IT.

YOU KNOW WHAT, I'M GOING TO MAKE MY CASE AGAINST YOU, SUPERMAN. RIGHT HERE, RIGHT NOW.

MAYBE YOU THINK I HATE YOU BECAUSE YOU'RE AN ALIEN. BUT AS YOU CAN SEE, THAT ISN'T MY GRIPE.

OR MAYBE YOU THINK IT'S BECAUSE YOU'RE SOME ALL-POWERFUL THREAT. BUT TURNS OUT, WE'VE ALWAYS HAD THE BIGGER BOY RIGHT HERE.

NO. WHAT I DON'T LIKE ABOUT YOU, SUPERMAN, WHAT GETS ME RIGHT HERE IN MY DAMN THROAT, IS THAT YOU'RE A COWARD.

A COWARD. GENERAL--

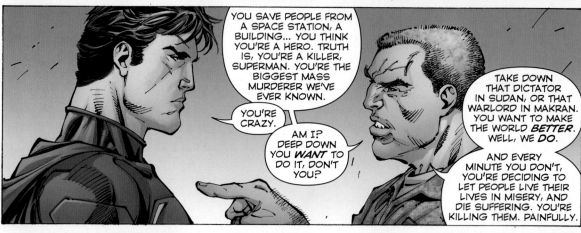

YOU SAVE PEOPLE FROM A SPACE STATION, A BUILDING... YOU THINK YOU'RE A HERO. TRUTH IS, YOU'RE A KILLER, SUPERMAN. YOU'RE THE BIGGEST MASS MURDERER WE'VE EVER KNOWN.

YOU'RE CRAZY.

AM I? DEEP DOWN YOU WANT TO DO IT, DON'T YOU?

TAKE DOWN THAT DICTATOR IN SUDAN, OR THAT WARLORD IN MAKRAN. YOU WANT TO MAKE THE WORLD BETTER. WELL, WE DO.

AND EVERY MINUTE YOU DON'T, YOU'RE DECIDING TO LET PEOPLE LIVE THEIR LIVES IN MISERY, AND DIE SUFFERING. YOU'RE KILLING THEM. PAINFULLY.

AND ALL BECAUSE YOU NEED TO HEAR THIS.

CLAP..CLAP..CLAP...

BECAUSE YOU'RE AFRAID TO DO THE TOUGH THINGS, THE THINGS YOU KNOW YOU SHOULD DO. EASIER TO FLOAT ABOVE IT ALL AND SAVE KITTENS.

I'LL TELL YOU A SECRET, SUPERMAN. SOMETHING I NEVER TOLD ANYONE...

...WHEN YOUR ROCKET LANDED, WHEN MY PREDECESSOR LEARNED ABOUT IT... HE TOLD ME, HE THOUGHT TO HIMSELF, "ANOTHER SOLDIER. ANOTHER HERO."

AND WHAT A DISAPPOINTMENT YOU TURNED OUT TO BE.

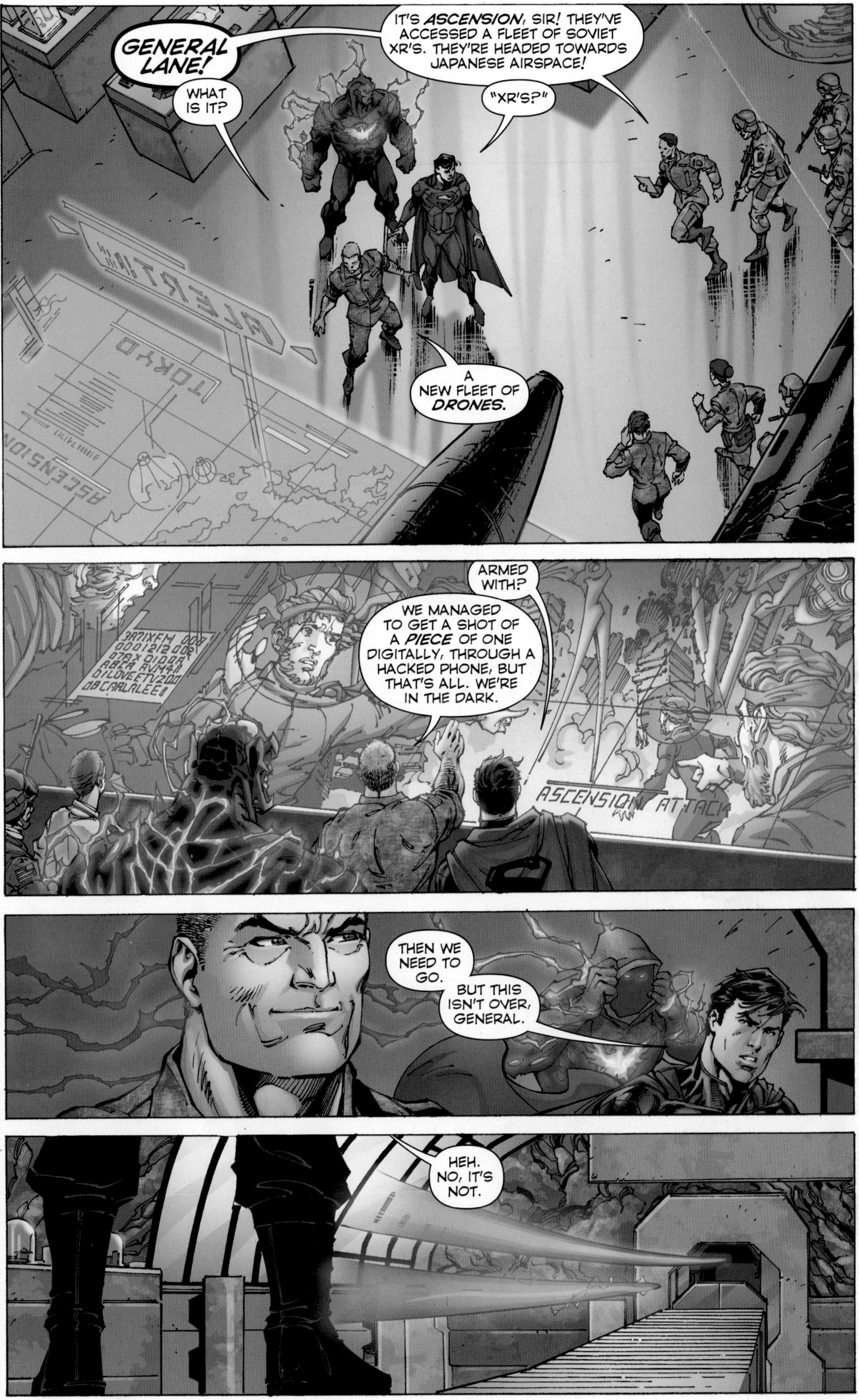
GENERAL LANE!
WHAT IS IT?
IT'S ASCENSION, SIR! THEY'VE ACCESSED A FLEET OF SOVIET XR'S. THEY'RE HEADED TOWARDS JAPANESE AIRSPACE!
"XR'S?"
A NEW FLEET OF DRONES.
ALERT!
TOKYO
ASCENSION
ARMED WITH?
WE MANAGED TO GET A SHOT OF A PIECE OF ONE DIGITALLY, THROUGH A HACKED PHONE, BUT THAT'S ALL. WE'RE IN THE DARK.
ASCENSION ATTACK
THEN WE NEED TO GO.
BUT THIS ISN'T OVER, GENERAL.
HEH. NO, IT'S NOT.

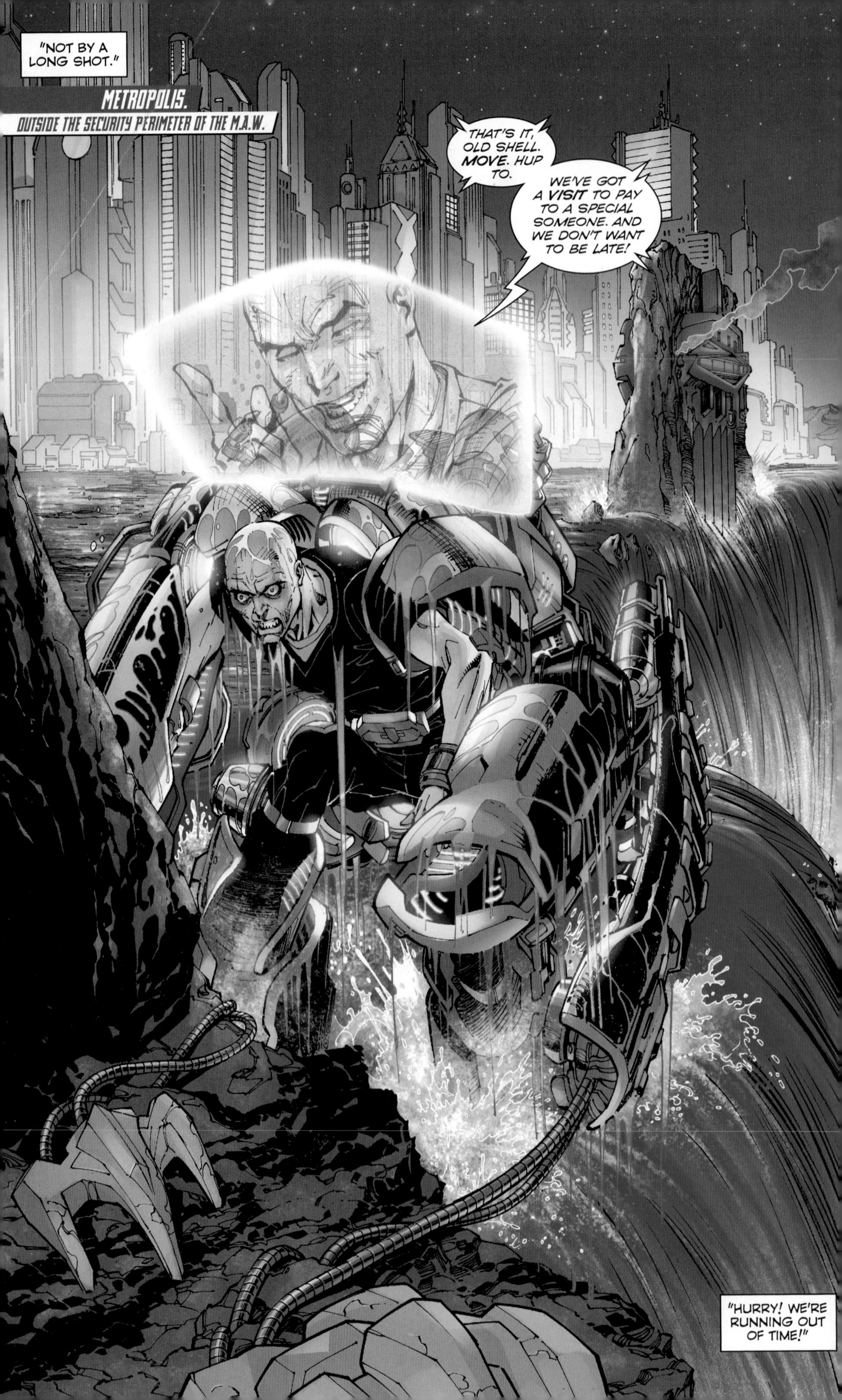
"NOT BY A LONG SHOT."
METROPOLIS.
OUTSIDE THE SECURITY PERIMETER OF THE M.A.W.
THAT'S IT, OLD SHELL. MOVE. HUP TO.
WE'VE GOT A VISIT TO PAY TO A SPECIAL SOMEONE. AND WE DON'T WANT TO BE LATE!
"HURRY! WE'RE RUNNING OUT OF TIME!"

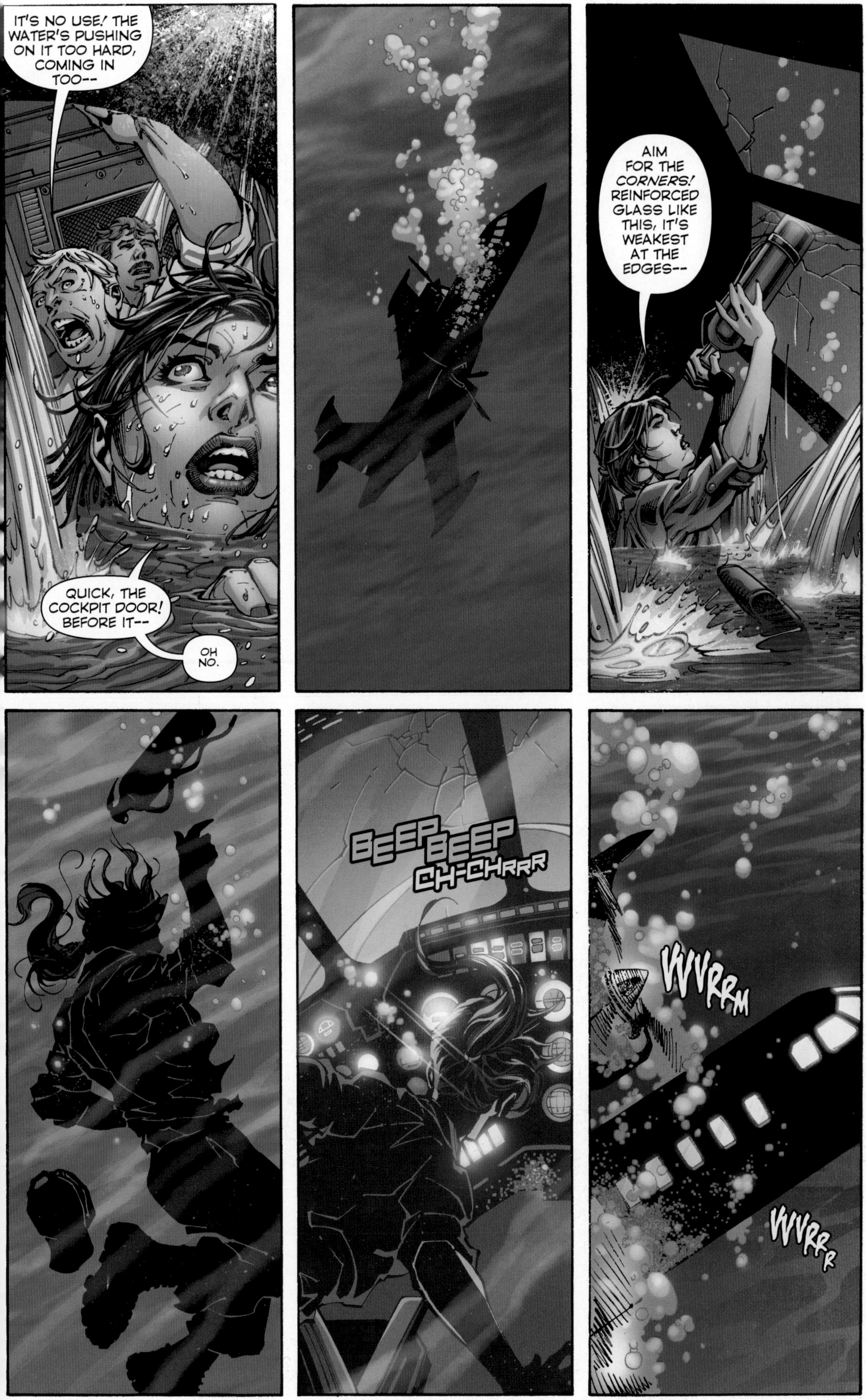
IT'S NO USE! THE WATER'S PUSHING ON IT TOO HARD, COMING IN TOO--
QUICK, THE COCKPIT DOOR! BEFORE IT--
OH NO.
AIM FOR THE CORNERS! REINFORCED GLASS LIKE THIS, IT'S WEAKEST AT THE EDGES--
BEEP BEEP
CH-CHRRR
VVVRRM
VVVRRR

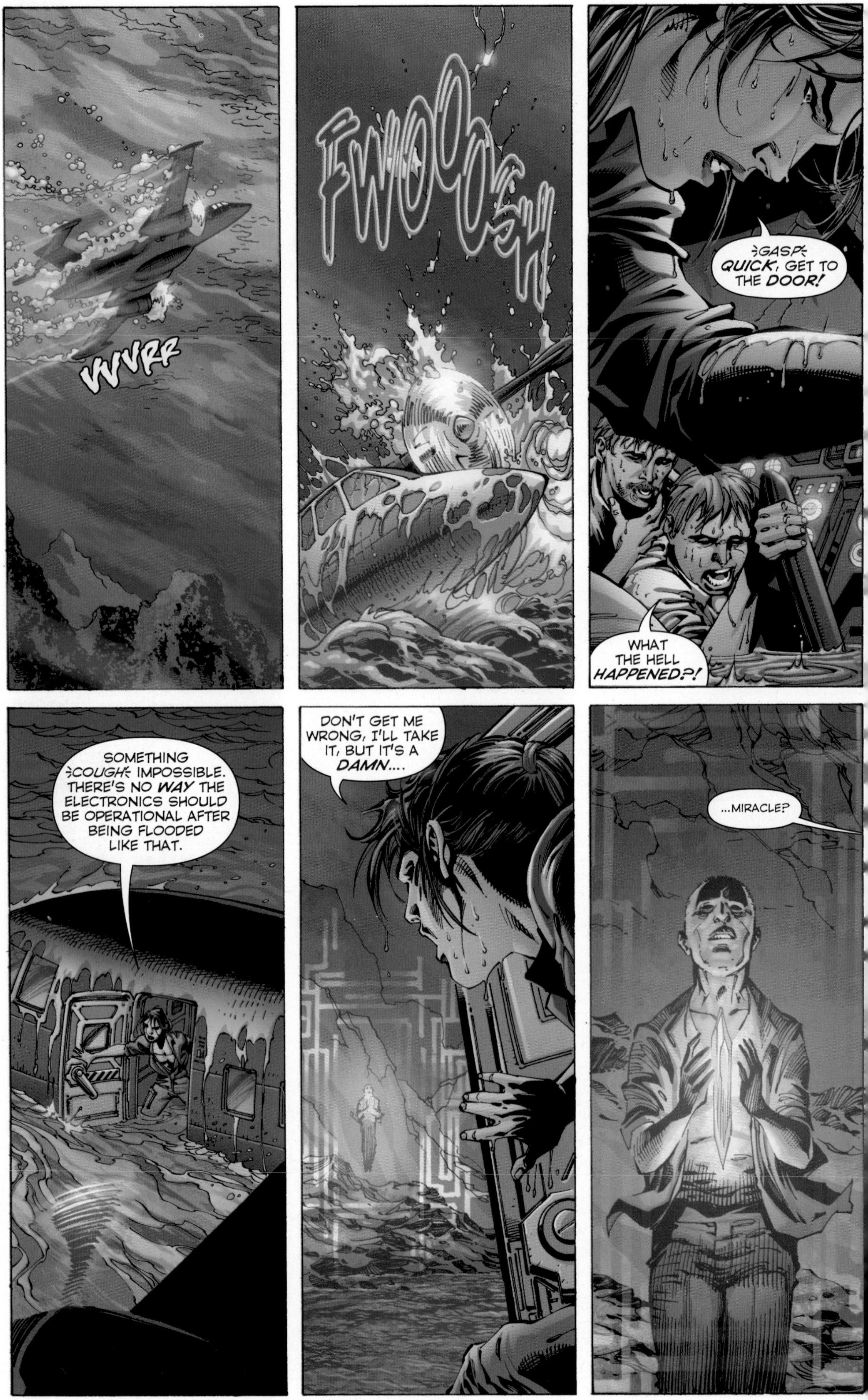
VVVRR
FWOOOOSH
GASP QUICK, GET TO THE DOOR!
WHAT THE HELL HAPPENED?!
SOMETHING *COUGH* IMPOSSIBLE. THERE'S NO WAY THE ELECTRONICS SHOULD BE OPERATIONAL AFTER BEING FLOODED LIKE THAT.
DON'T GET ME WRONG, I'LL TAKE IT, BUT IT'S A DAMN....
...MIRACLE?

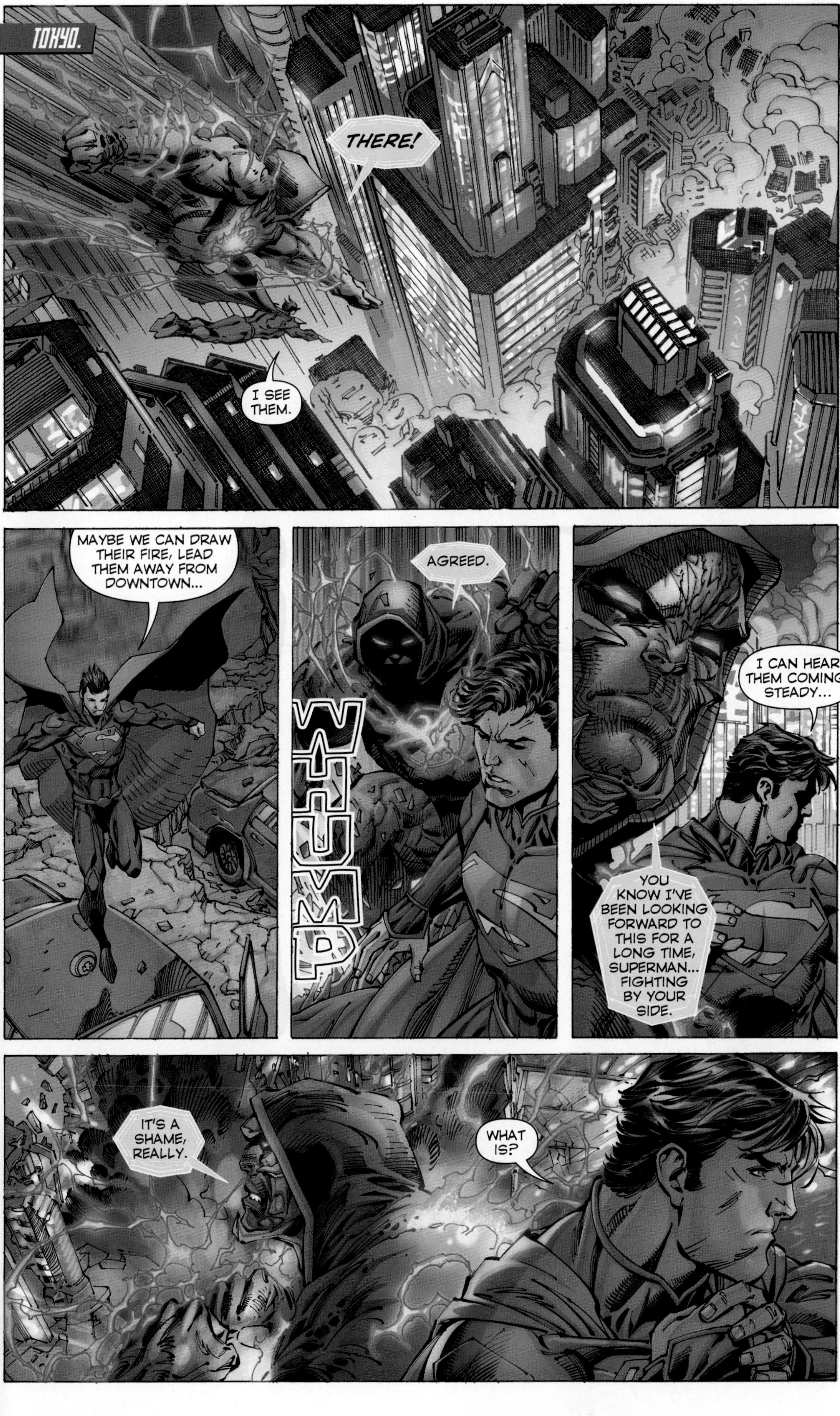
TOKYO.
THERE!
I SEE THEM.
MAYBE WE CAN DRAW THEIR FIRE, LEAD THEM AWAY FROM DOWNTOWN...
AGREED.
FWEESH
I CAN HEAR THEM COMING. STEADY...
YOU KNOW I'VE BEEN LOOKING FORWARD TO THIS FOR A LONG TIME, SUPERMAN... FIGHTING BY YOUR SIDE.
IT'S A SHAME, REALLY.
WHAT IS?

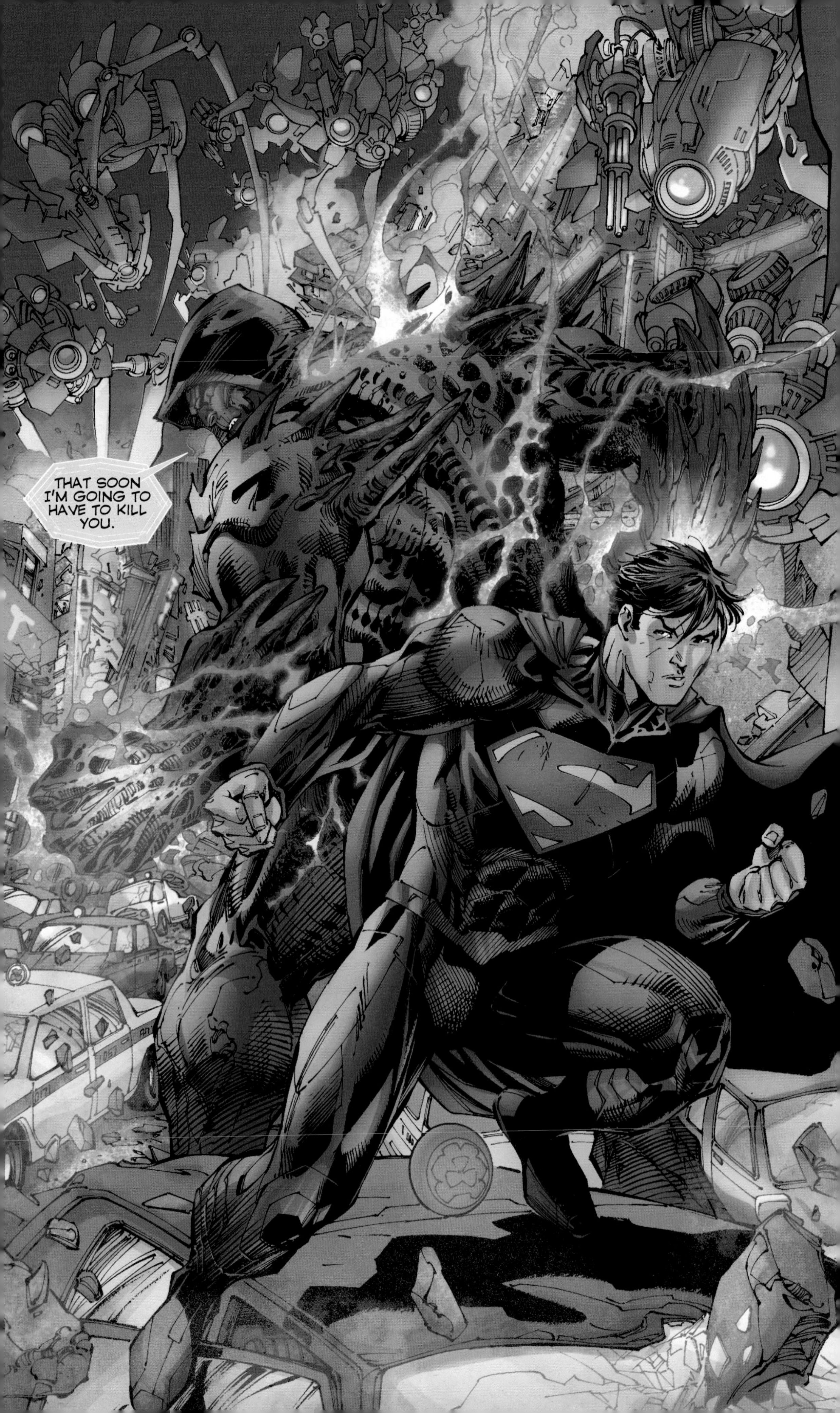
THAT SOON I'M GOING TO HAVE TO KILL YOU.

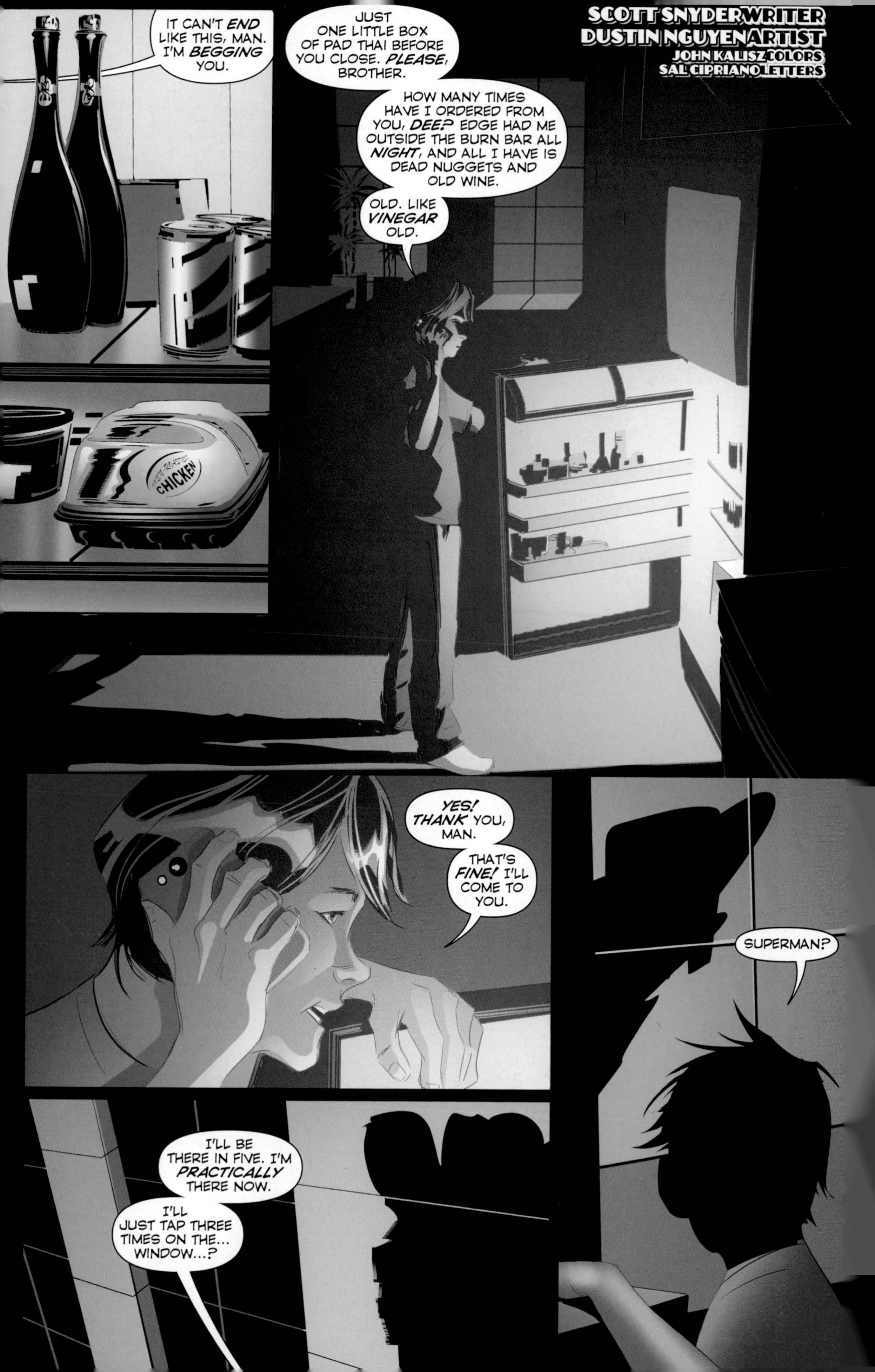
SCOTT SNYDER WRITER
DUSTIN NGUYEN ARTIST
JOHN KALISZ COLORS
SAL CIPRIANO LETTERS
IT CAN'T *END* LIKE THIS, MAN. I'M *BEGGING* YOU.
JUST ONE LITTLE BOX OF PAD THAI BEFORE YOU CLOSE. *PLEASE,* BROTHER.
HOW MANY TIMES HAVE I ORDERED FROM YOU, *DEE?* EDGE HAD ME OUTSIDE THE BURN BAR ALL *NIGHT,* AND ALL I HAVE IS DEAD NUGGETS AND OLD WINE.
OLD. LIKE *VINEGAR* OLD.
CHICKEN
YES! THANK YOU, MAN.
THAT'S *FINE!* I'LL COME TO YOU.
SUPERMAN?
I'LL BE THERE IN FIVE. I'M *PRACTICALLY* THERE NOW.
I'LL JUST TAP THREE TIMES ON THE... WINDOW...?

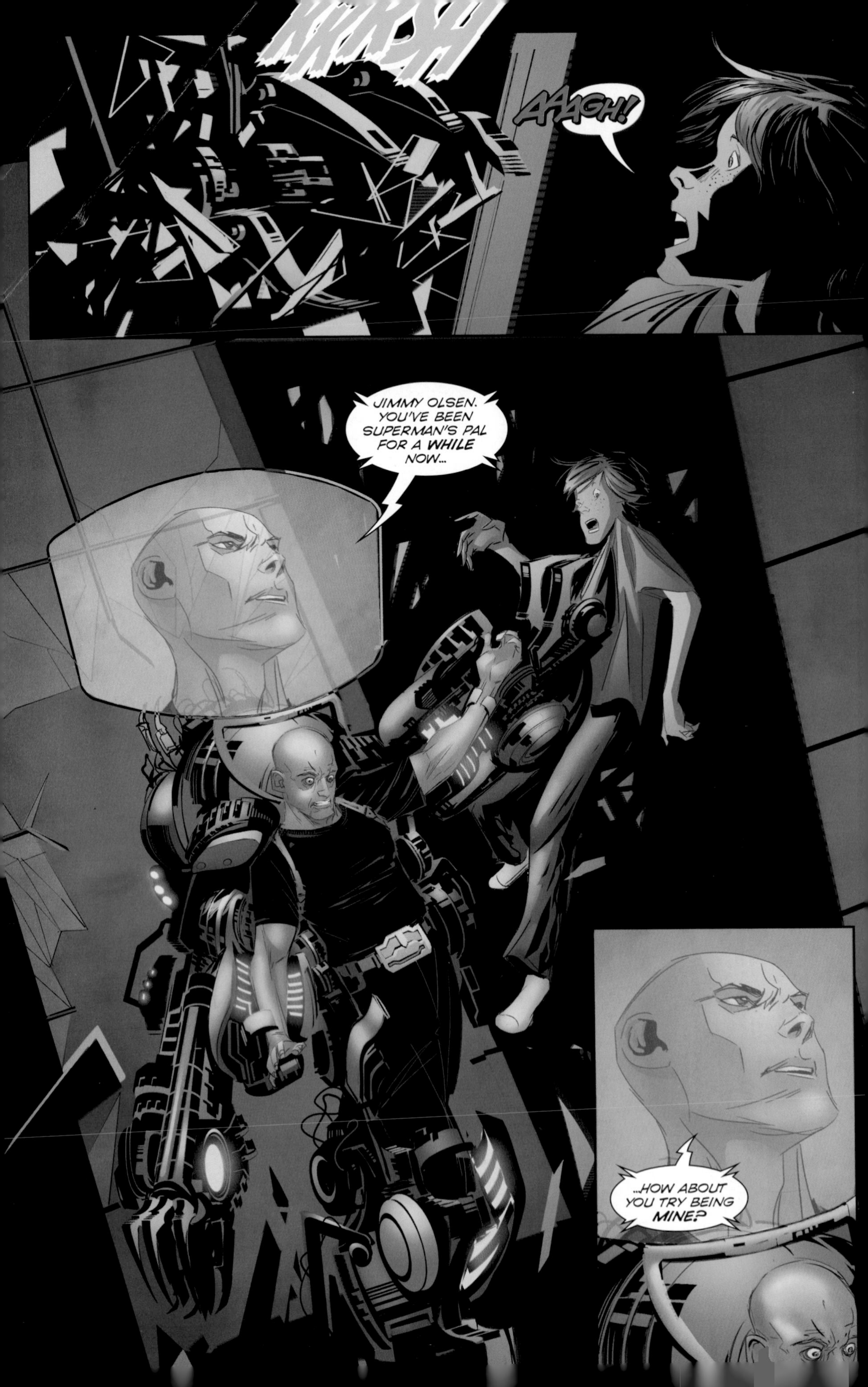
KKRRSH
AAAGH!
JIMMY OLSEN. YOU'VE BEEN SUPERMAN'S PAL FOR A WHILE NOW...
...HOW ABOUT YOU TRY BEING MINE?

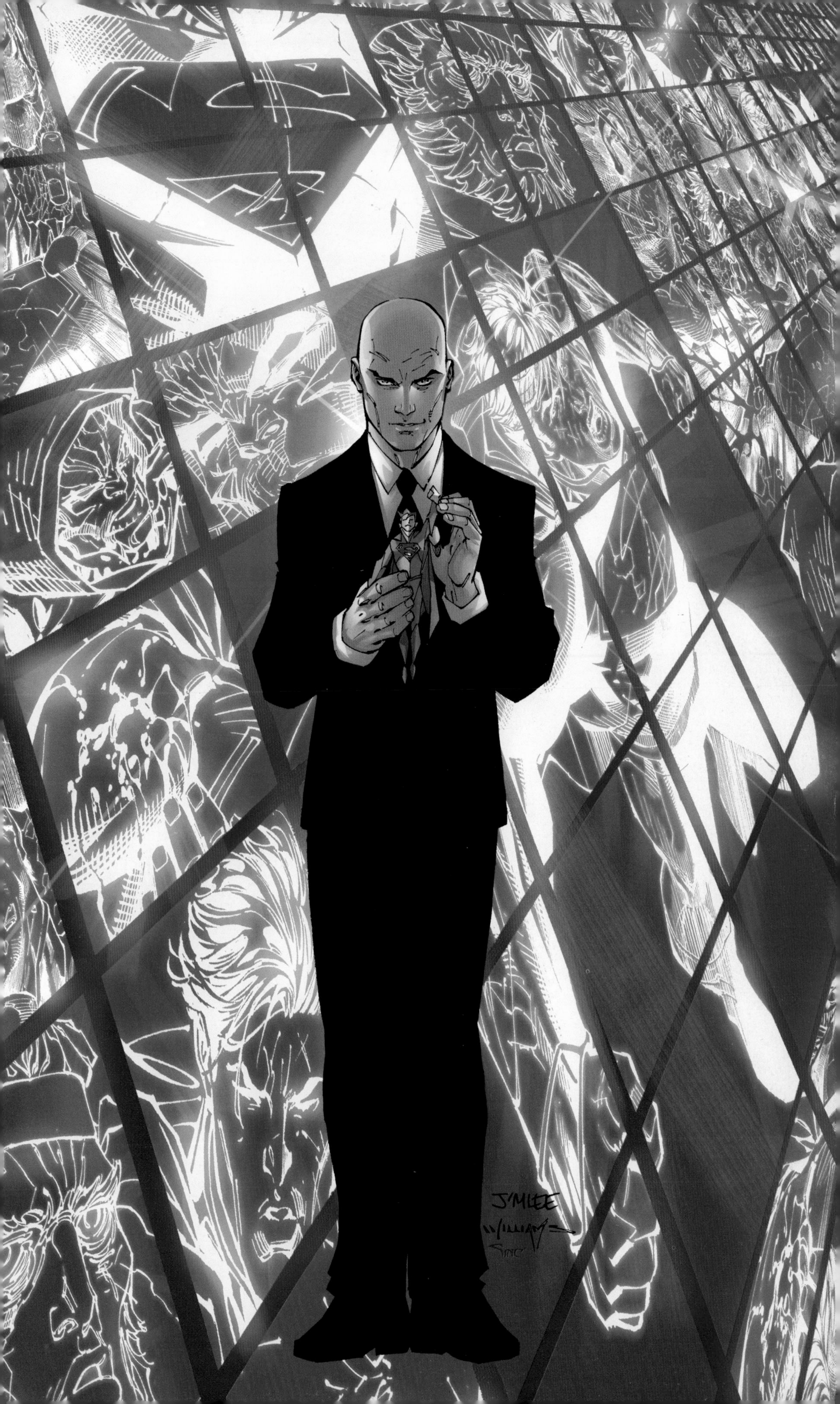
J'MLEE

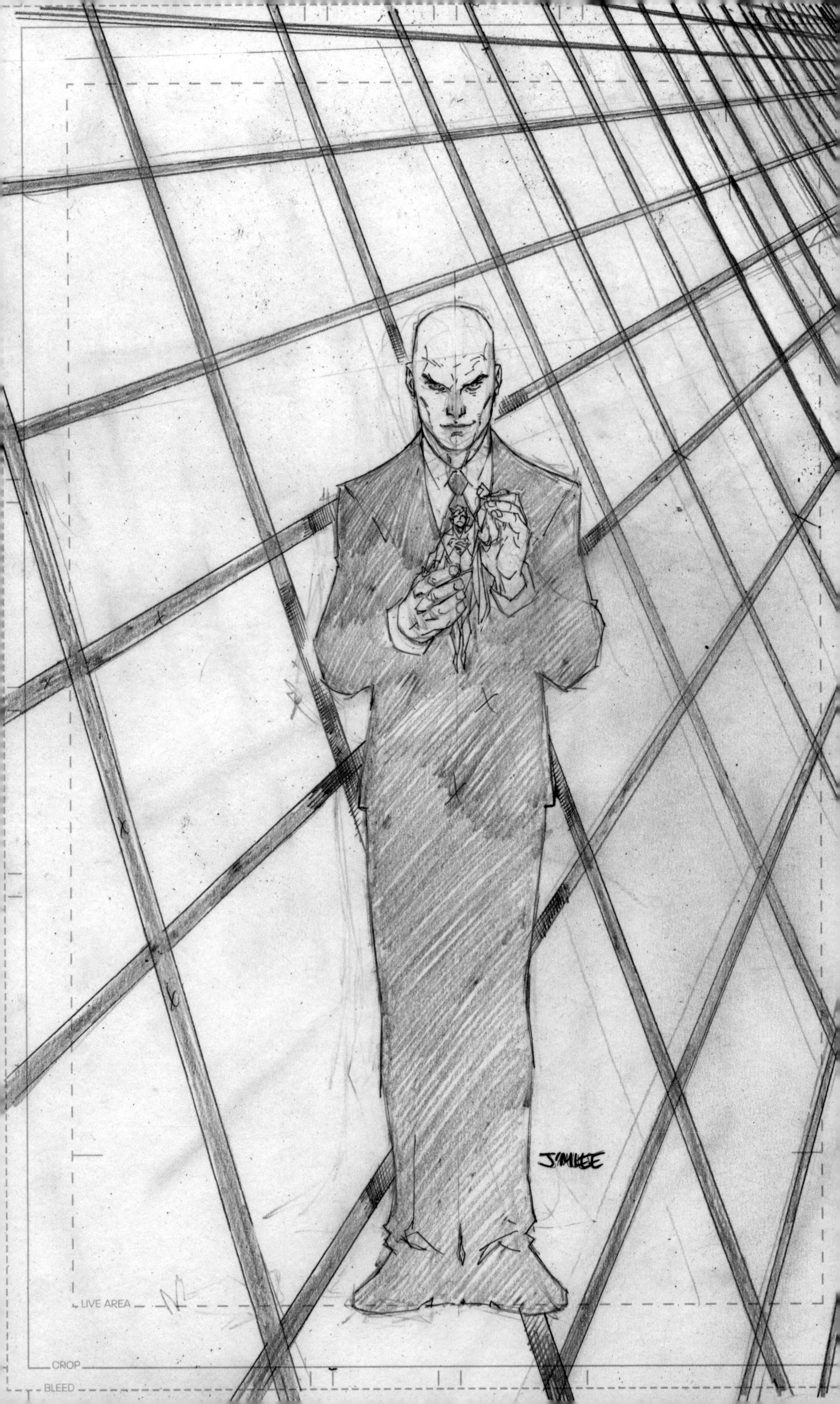
LIVE AREA
CROP
BLEED

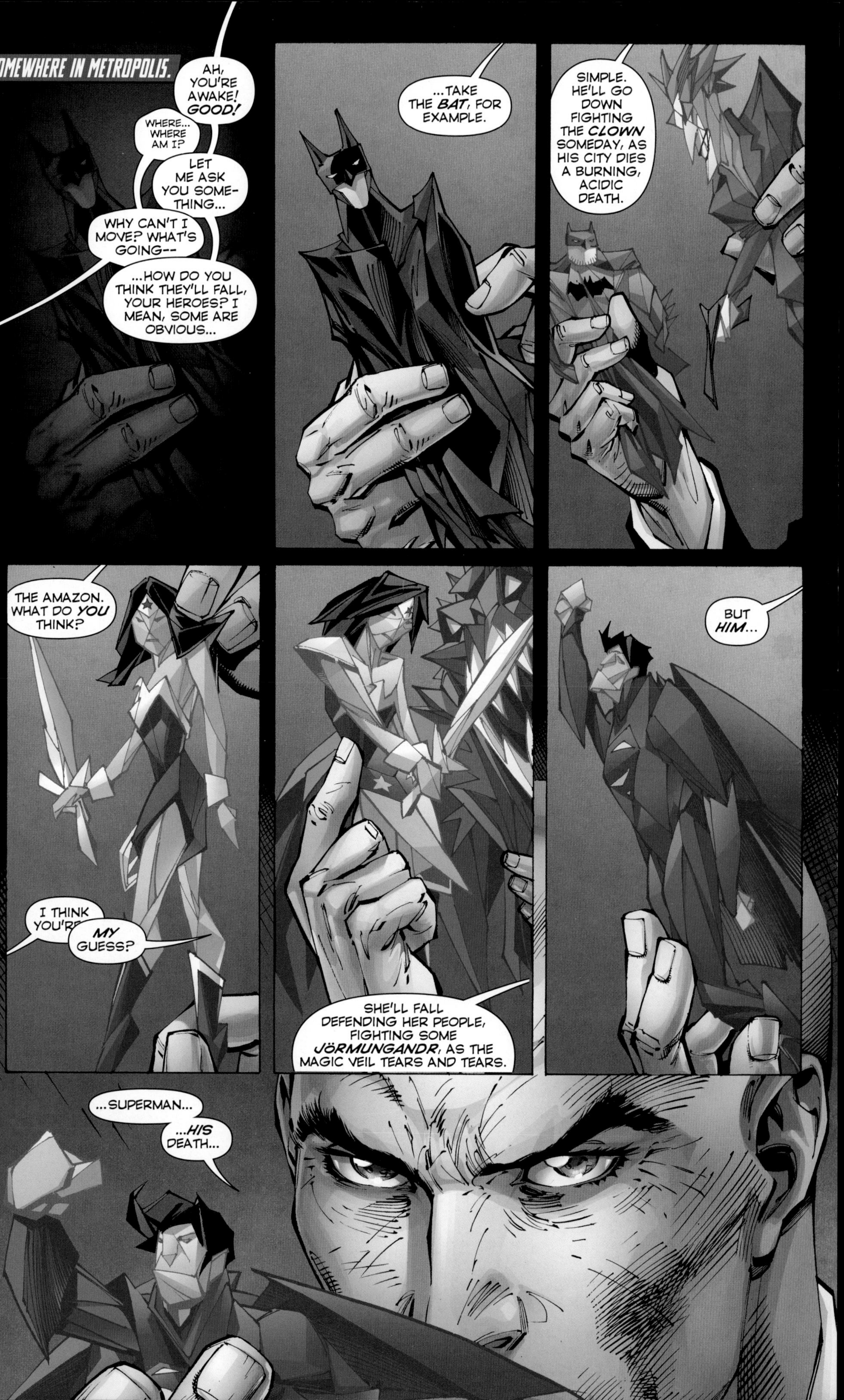

SOMEWHERE IN METROPOLIS.
AH, YOU'RE AWAKE! GOOD!
WHERE... WHERE AM I?
LET ME ASK YOU SOME-THING...
WHY CAN'T I MOVE? WHAT'S GOING--
...HOW DO YOU THINK THEY'LL FALL, YOUR HEROES? I MEAN, SOME ARE OBVIOUS...
...TAKE THE BAT, FOR EXAMPLE.
SIMPLE. HE'LL GO DOWN FIGHTING THE CLOWN SOMEDAY, AS HIS CITY DIES A BURNING, ACIDIC DEATH.
THE AMAZON. WHAT DO YOU THINK?
MY GUESS?
SHE'LL FALL DEFENDING HER PEOPLE, FIGHTING SOME JÖRMUNGANDR, AS THE MAGIC VEIL TEARS AND TEARS.
BUT HIM...
...SUPERMAN...
...HIS DEATH...

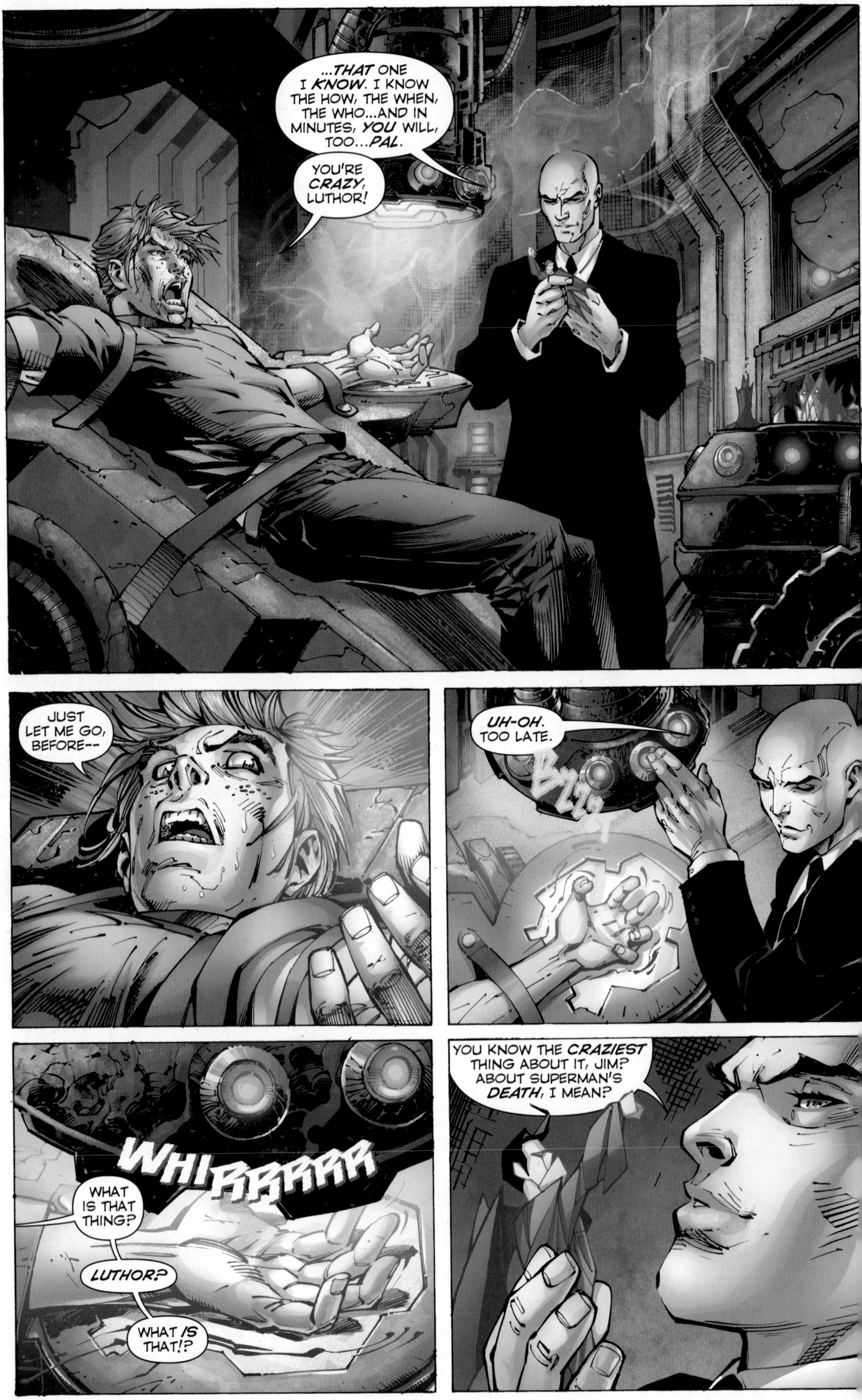
...THAT ONE I KNOW. I KNOW THE HOW, THE WHEN, THE WHO...AND IN MINUTES, YOU WILL, TOO...PAL.
YOU'RE CRAZY, LUTHOR!
JUST LET ME GO, BEFORE--
UH-OH. TOO LATE.
BZZZ
WHIRRRRRR
WHAT IS THAT THING?
LUTHOR?
WHAT IS THAT!?
YOU KNOW THE CRAZIEST THING ABOUT IT, JIM? ABOUT SUPERMAN'S DEATH, I MEAN?

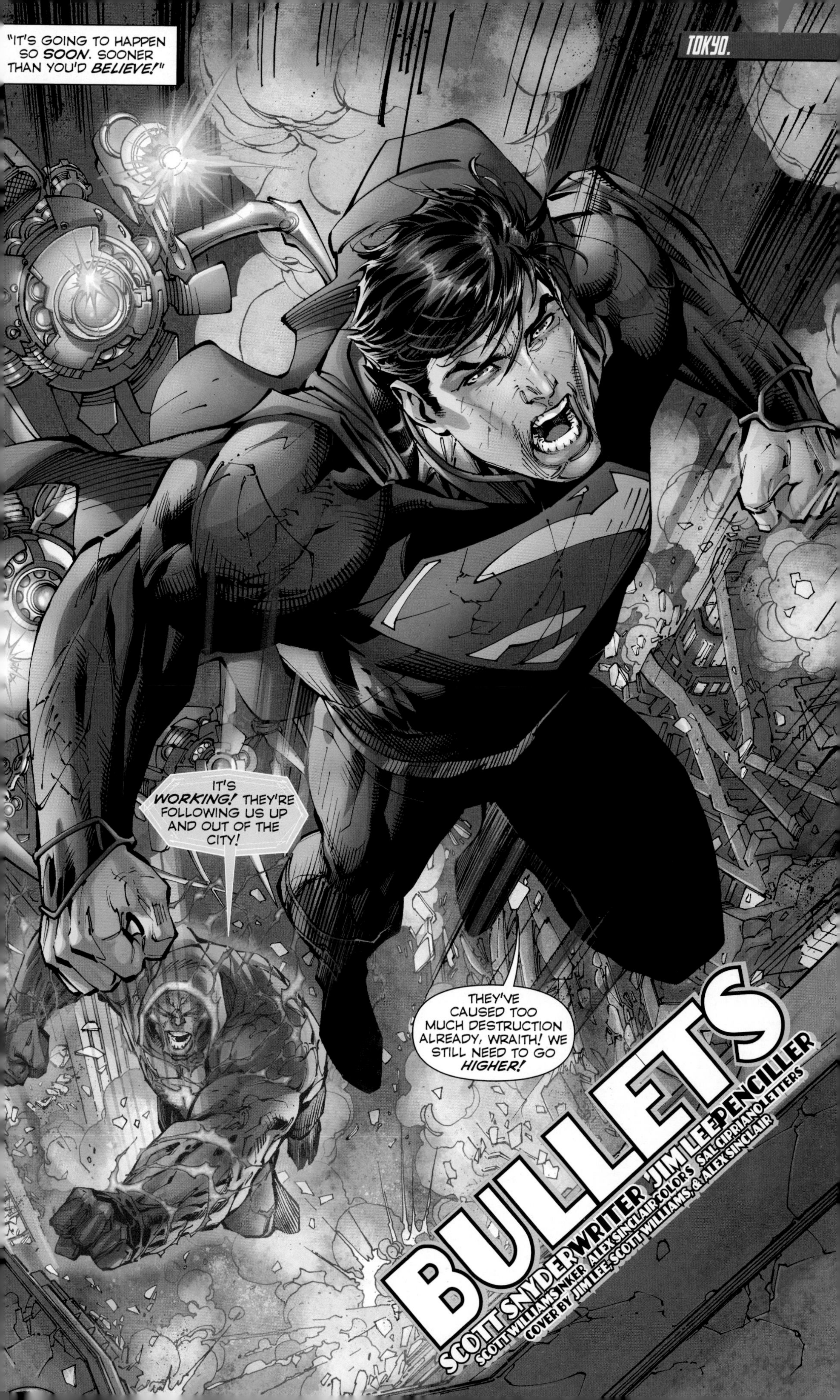
"IT'S GOING TO HAPPEN SO **SOON**. SOONER THAN YOU'D **BELIEVE!**"
TOKYO.
IT'S **WORKING!** THEY'RE FOLLOWING US UP AND OUT OF THE CITY!
THEY'VE CAUSED TOO MUCH DESTRUCTION ALREADY, WRAITH! WE STILL NEED TO GO **HIGHER!**
BULLETS
SCOTT SNYDER WRITER JIM LEE PENCILLER
SCOTT WILLIAMS INKER ALEX SINCLAIR COLORS SAL CIPRIANO LETTERS
COVER BY JIM LEE, SCOTT WILLIAMS, & ALEX SINCLAIR

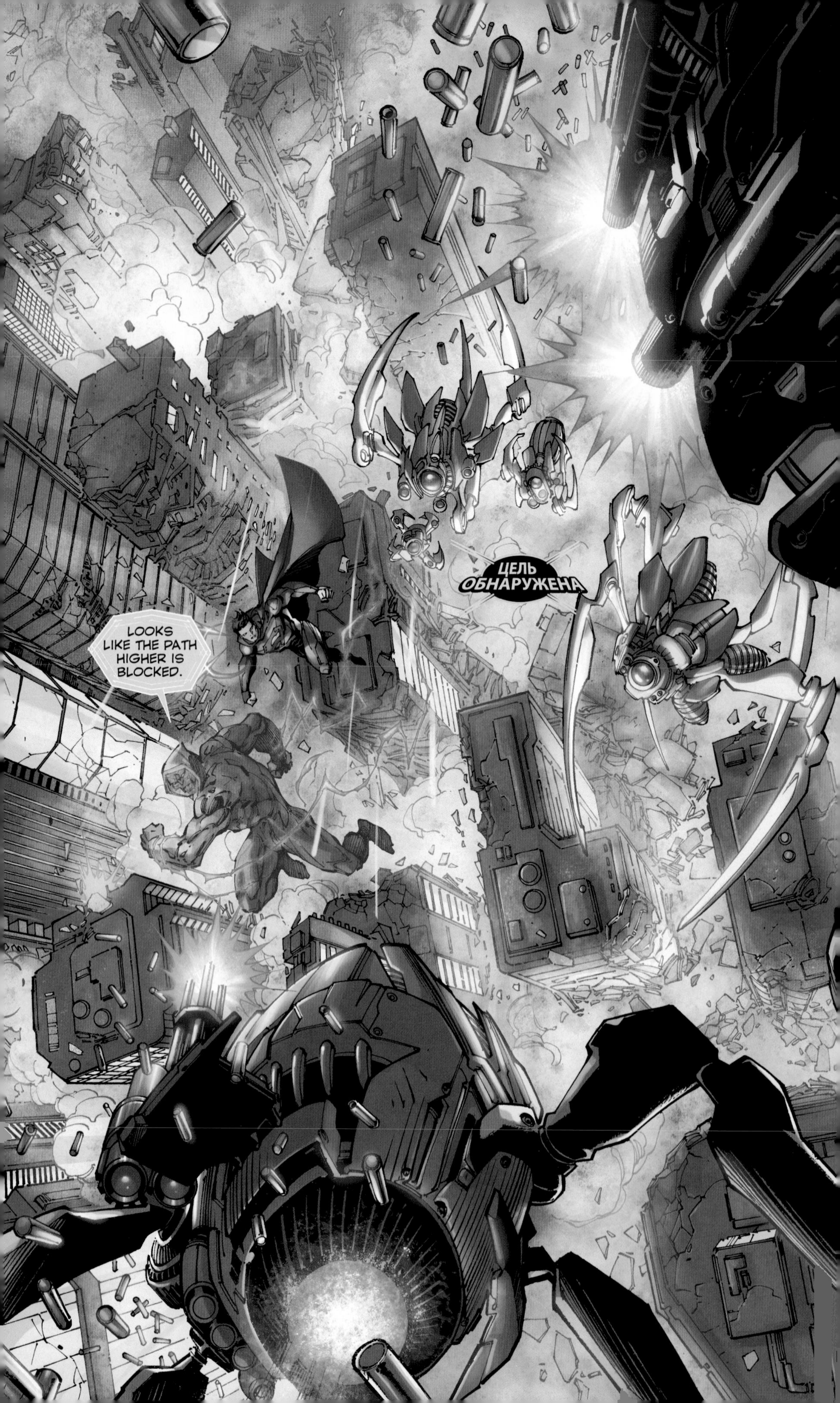
ЦЕЛЬ ОБНАРУЖЕНА
LOOKS LIKE THE PATH HIGHER IS BLOCKED.

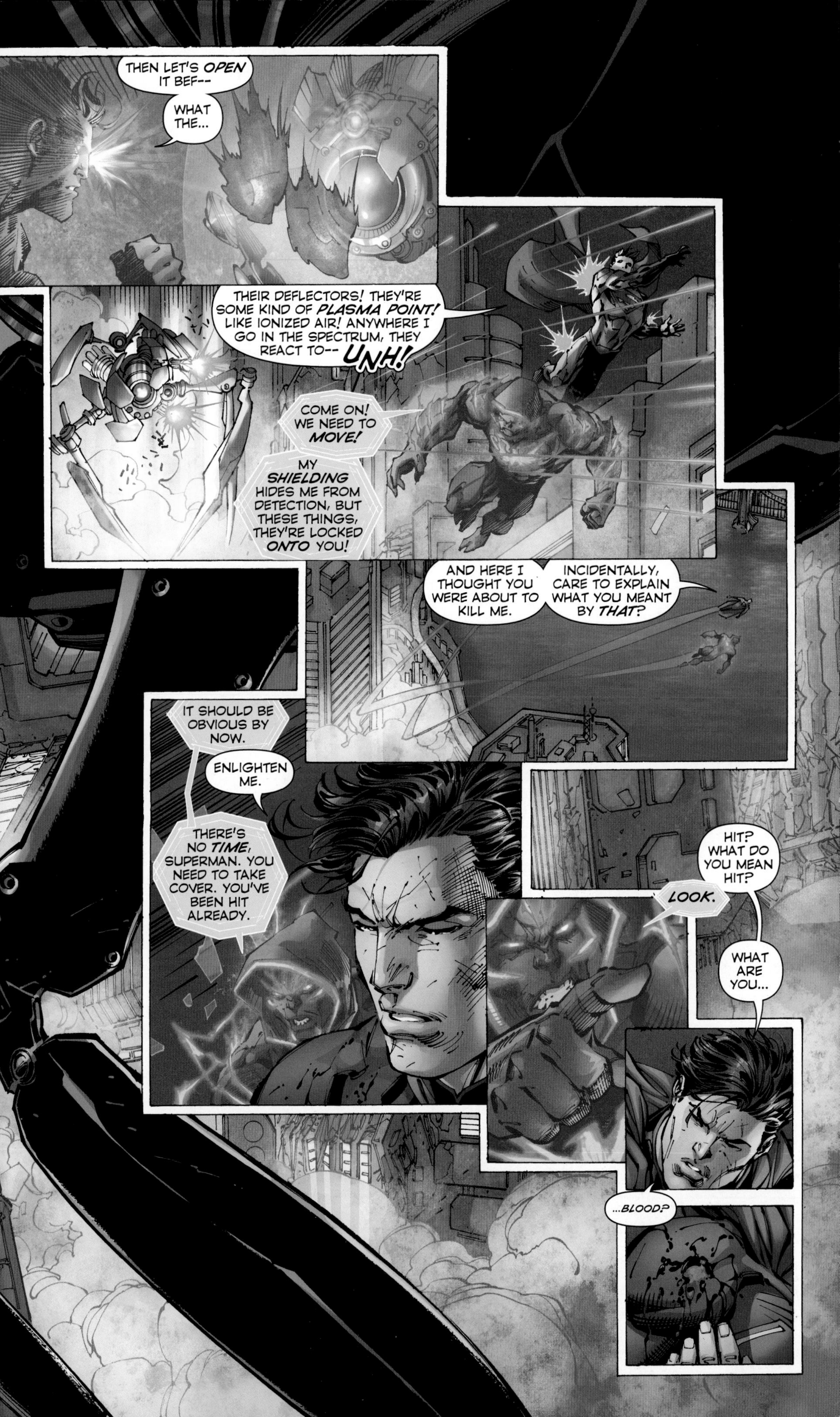
THEN LET'S OPEN IT BEF--
WHAT THE...
THEIR DEFLECTORS! THEY'RE SOME KIND OF PLASMA POINT! LIKE IONIZED AIR! ANYWHERE I GO IN THE SPECTRUM, THEY REACT TO-- UNH!
COME ON! WE NEED TO MOVE!
MY SHIELDING HIDES ME FROM DETECTION, BUT THESE THINGS, THEY'RE LOCKED ONTO YOU!
AND HERE I THOUGHT YOU WERE ABOUT TO KILL ME.
INCIDENTALLY, CARE TO EXPLAIN WHAT YOU MEANT BY THAT?
IT SHOULD BE OBVIOUS BY NOW.
ENLIGHTEN ME.
THERE'S NO TIME, SUPERMAN. YOU NEED TO TAKE COVER. YOU'VE BEEN HIT ALREADY.
LOOK.
HIT? WHAT DO YOU MEAN HIT?
WHAT ARE YOU...
...BLOOD?

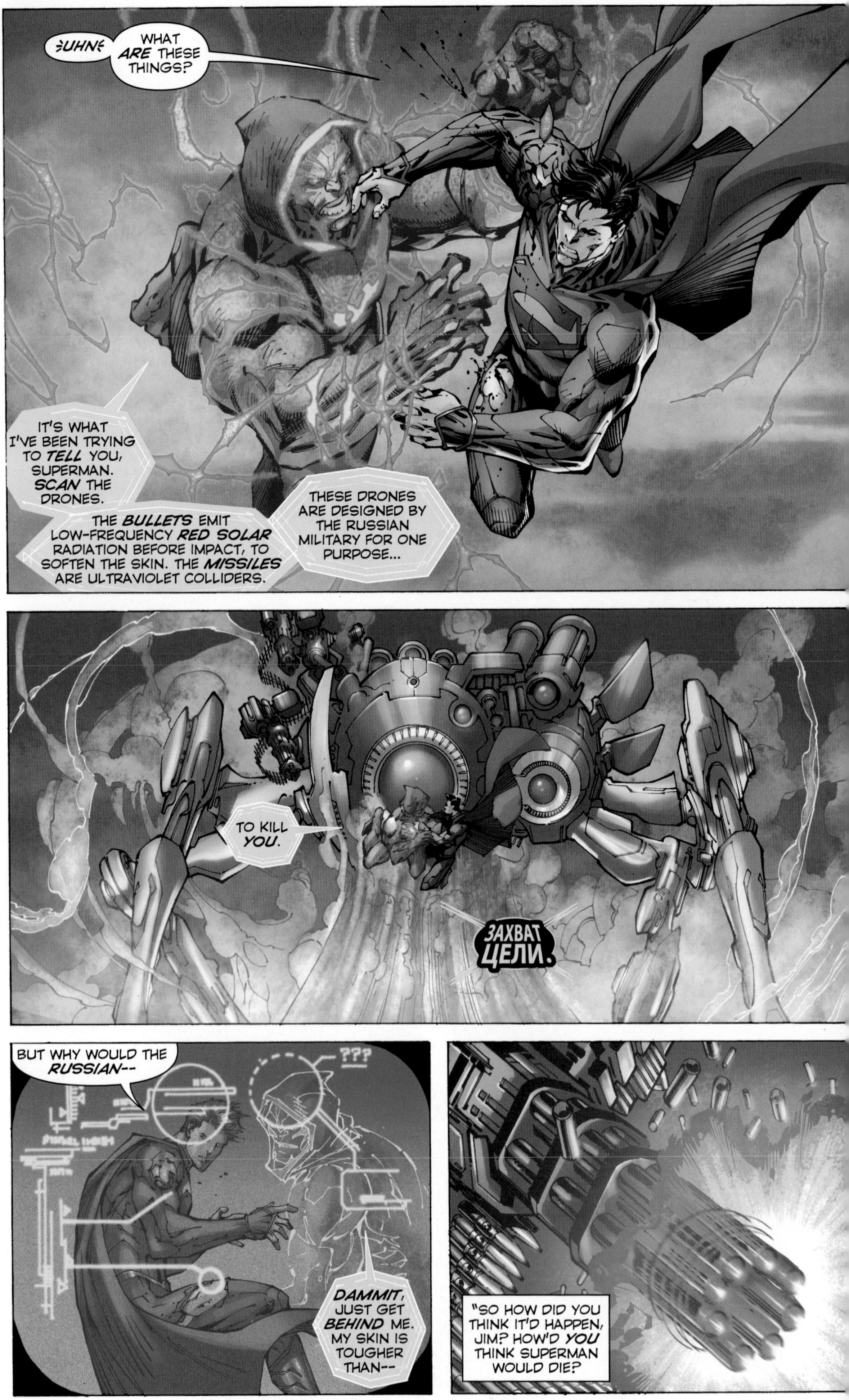

UHN
WHAT ARE THESE THINGS?
IT'S WHAT I'VE BEEN TRYING TO TELL YOU, SUPERMAN. SCAN THE DRONES.
THE BULLETS EMIT LOW-FREQUENCY RED SOLAR RADIATION BEFORE IMPACT, TO SOFTEN THE SKIN. THE MISSILES ARE ULTRAVIOLET COLLIDERS.
THESE DRONES ARE DESIGNED BY THE RUSSIAN MILITARY FOR ONE PURPOSE...
TO KILL YOU.
ЗАХВАТ ЦЕЛИ.
BUT WHY WOULD THE RUSSIAN--
???
DAMMIT, JUST GET BEHIND ME. MY SKIN IS TOUGHER THAN--
"SO HOW DID YOU THINK IT'D HAPPEN, JIM? HOW'D YOU THINK SUPERMAN WOULD DIE?

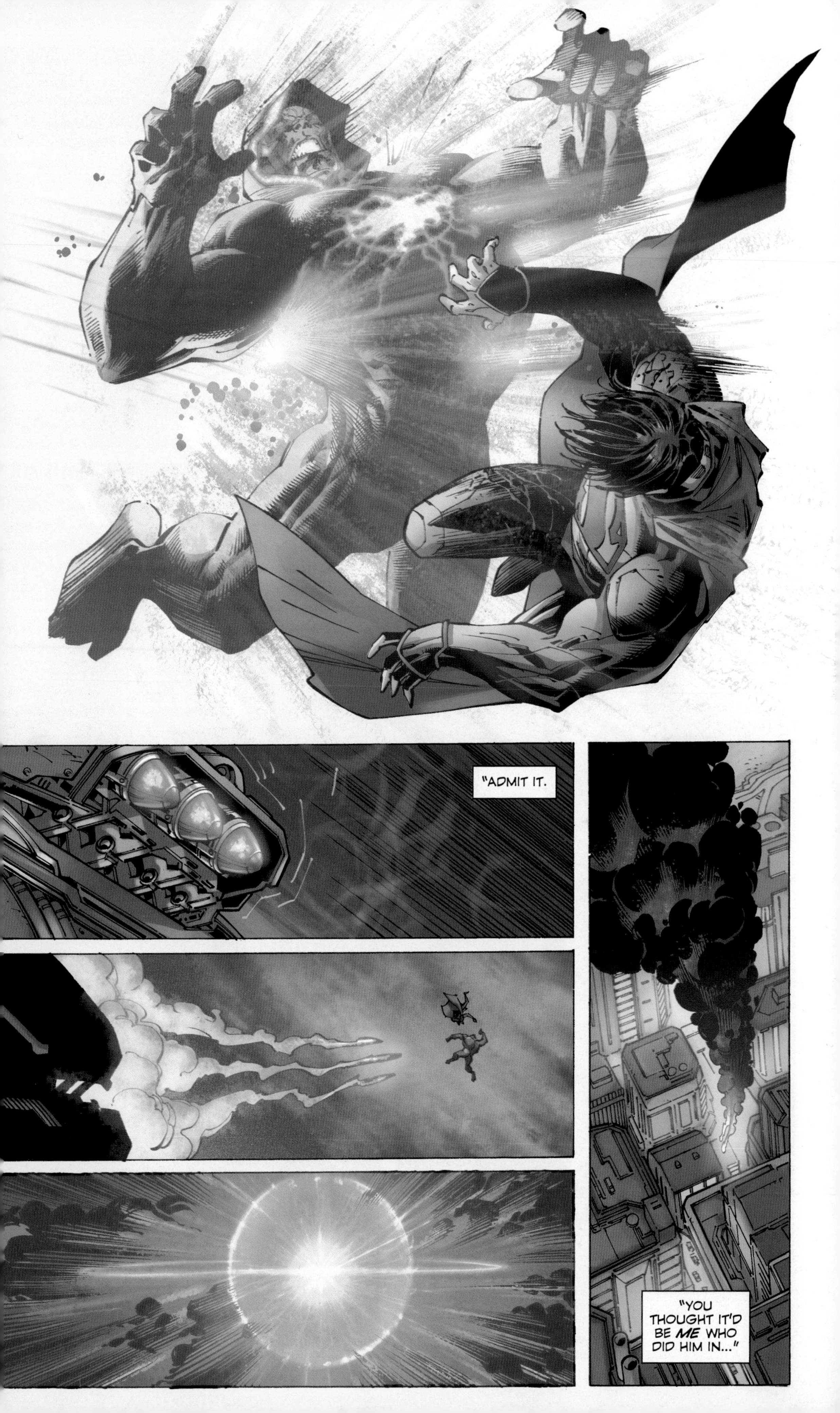
"ADMIT IT.
"YOU THOUGHT IT'D BE ME WHO DID HIM IN..."

...DIDN'T YOU?

THE *PLANET,* THEY'LL REALIZE I'M *MISSING,* LUTHOR. YOU *DON'T* NEED TO--

DAMMIT, LUTHOR! STOP WITH THE PAPER DOLLS AND *LISTEN* TO ME! TURN OFF THE *MACHINE* BEFORE IT COMES *DOWN* ON--

PAPER FOLDING IS A RICH AND *ANCIENT* TRADITION, JIMMY. THERE'S A RECORD OF IT FROM THE FIRST CENTURY A.D., BACK WHEN IT WAS A SPIRITUAL PRACTICE.

THE *REAL* BEAUTY OF THE ART, THOUGH--AND IT TOOK ME A MOMENT TO REALIZE THIS WHILE IN PRISON--

--IS ITS *TRANSIENCE.* THINGS ARE MADE AND THEN *DISAPPEAR.*

I'M NOT GOING TO LIE, THERE WERE MOMENTS I THOUGHT IT MIGHT BE. BUT NO, IN THE END--

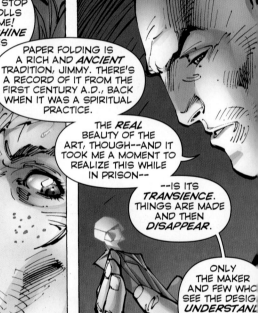

ONLY THE MAKER AND FEW WHO SEE THE DESIG[N] *UNDERSTAN[D]* THE BEAUTY O[F] WHAT WAS MADE.

EVEN THE *TOOLS* USED IN PAPER FOLDING UNDERSCORE THE NOTION--FOLDING *BONES.* CARVE[D] FROM THE BONES OF ELK OR DEER[.]

PAPER CREATIONS ARE OFTEN *EXCHANGED* AT MOMENTS OF TRANSITION, TOO. WARRIORS TRADED THEM BEFORE BATTLE. *NOSHI,* WITH PIECES OF MEAT INSIDE.

SOMETIMES THEY WERE GIVEN BETWEEN *PALS,* TO *CARRY* OVER.

SOMETIMES THEY WERE GIVEN TO A LOVE *LOST.*

"I DON'T UNDERSTAND..."

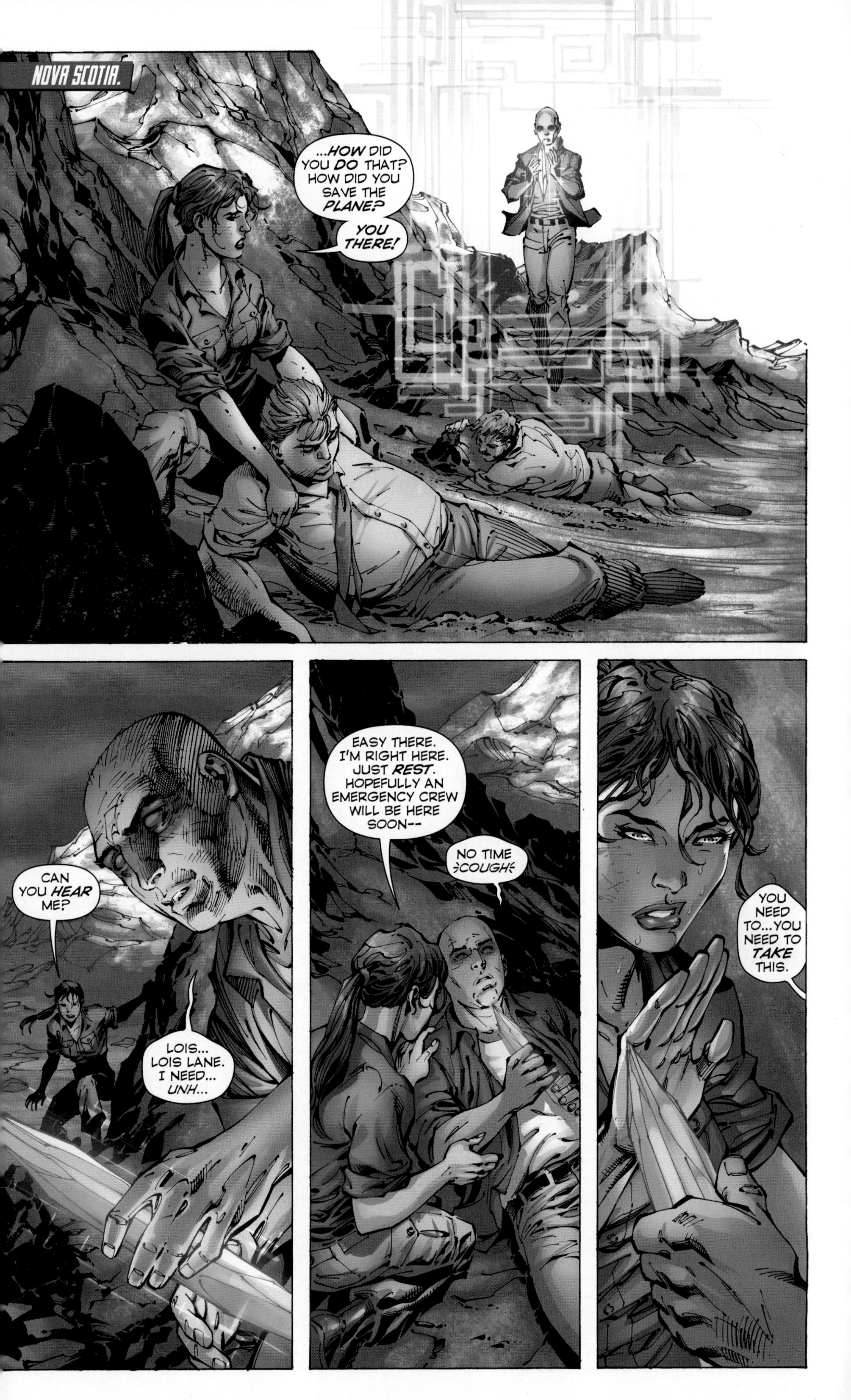
NOVA SCOTIA.
...HOW DID YOU DO THAT? HOW DID YOU SAVE THE PLANE?
YOU THERE!
CAN YOU HEAR ME?
LOIS... LOIS LANE. I NEED... UNH...
EASY THERE. I'M RIGHT HERE. JUST REST. HOPEFULLY AN EMERGENCY CREW WILL BE HERE SOON--
NO TIME *COUGH*
YOU NEED TO...YOU NEED TO TAKE THIS.

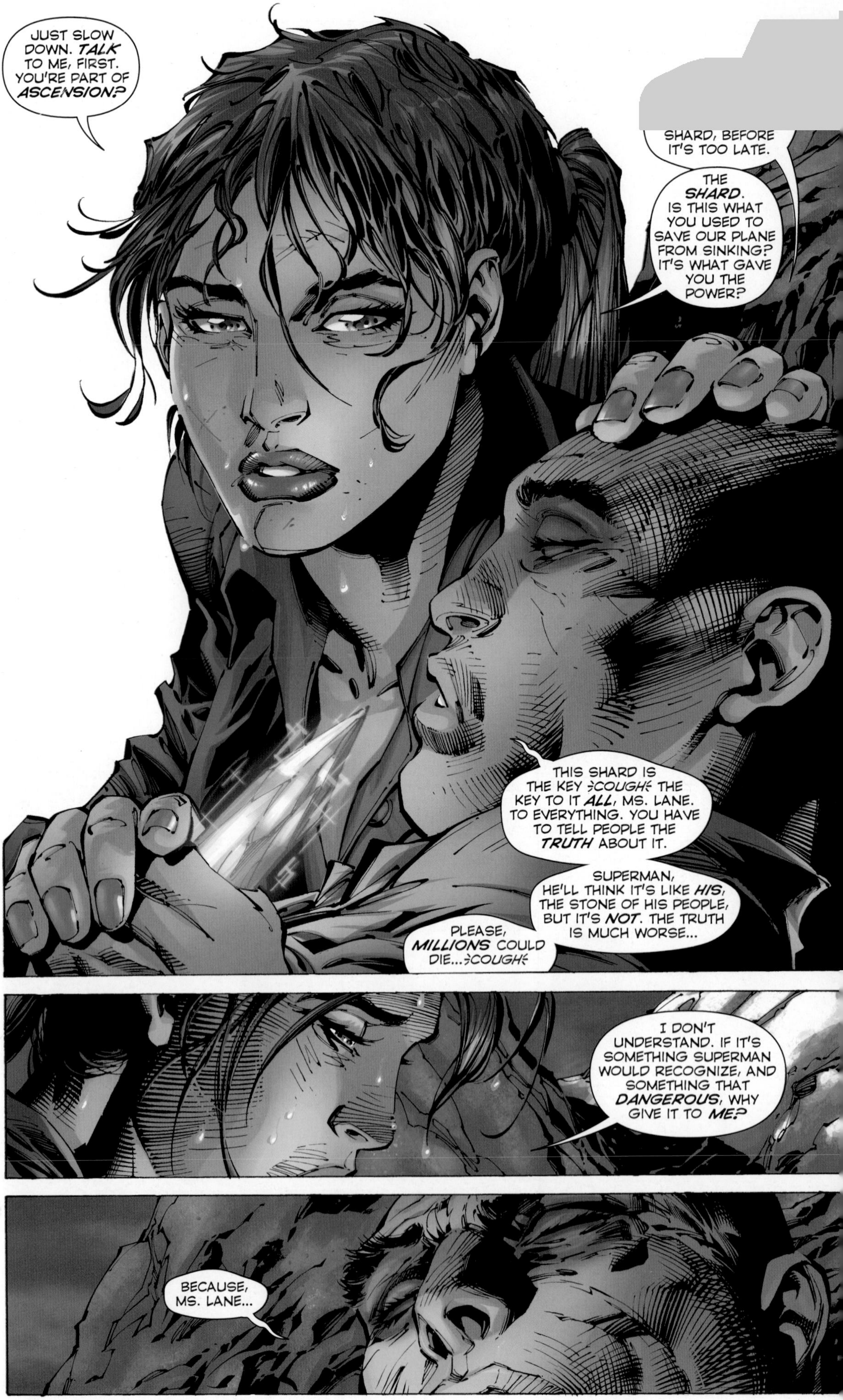
JUST SLOW DOWN. *TALK* TO ME, FIRST. YOU'RE PART OF *ASCENSION?*
SHARD, BEFORE IT'S TOO LATE.
THE *SHARD*. IS THIS WHAT YOU USED TO SAVE OUR PLANE FROM SINKING? IT'S WHAT GAVE YOU THE POWER?
THIS SHARD IS THE KEY *COUGH* THE KEY TO IT *ALL*, MS. LANE. TO EVERYTHING. YOU HAVE TO TELL PEOPLE THE *TRUTH* ABOUT IT.
SUPERMAN, HE'LL THINK IT'S LIKE *HIS*, THE STONE OF HIS PEOPLE, BUT IT'S *NOT*. THE TRUTH IS MUCH WORSE...
PLEASE, *MILLIONS* COULD DIE... *COUGH*
I DON'T UNDERSTAND. IF IT'S SOMETHING SUPERMAN WOULD RECOGNIZE, AND SOMETHING THAT *DANGEROUS*, WHY GIVE IT TO *ME?*
BECAUSE, MS. LANE...

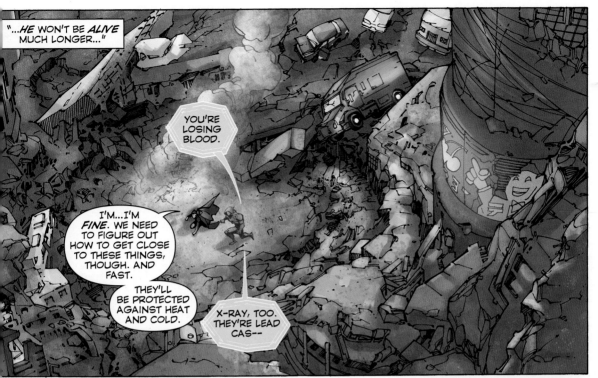

"...HE WON'T BE *ALIVE* MUCH LONGER..."

YOU'RE LOSING BLOOD.

I'M...I'M *FINE*. WE NEED TO FIGURE OUT HOW TO GET CLOSE TO THESE THINGS, THOUGH. AND FAST.

THEY'LL BE PROTECTED AGAINST HEAT AND COLD.

X-RAY, TOO. THEY'RE LEAD CAS--

LEAD CASED, YES. THEY'RE TOUGH, AREN'T THEY?

ASCENSION... WHY DON'T YOU COME OUT AND *FIGHT*, INSTEAD OF TERRORIZING INNOCENT PEOPLE.

INNOCENCE IS IMPOSSIBLE TO *JUDGE*, SUPERMAN, WHEN NO ONE IN QUESTION KNOWS THE *TRUTH*.

ISN'T IT *APPROPRIATE* THEN, THAT YOUR END HAPPENS *HERE?* IN THE COUNTRY WHERE THE *GREAT LIE* BEGAN? WHERE IT *FIRST* STRUCK THE WORLD, NEARLY SEVENTY YEARS AGO.

NOW *DIE* WITH OUR *SONG* IN YOUR EARS:

♪ NOW TO RISE UP O' MEN OF THE LINE

I'LL PASS.

♪ LABORERS SMASH YOUR MACHINES WHILE THERE'S

THEY'LL BE BACK FOR ANOTHER PASS, SUPERMAN. THE DRONES. WE NEED TO MAKE A STAND. HERE AND NOW.

MOST OF THE BUILDINGS WERE EVACUATED. IF WE USE THEM FOR--

NO.

WE CAN'T GET NEAR THOSE THINGS WITHOUT--

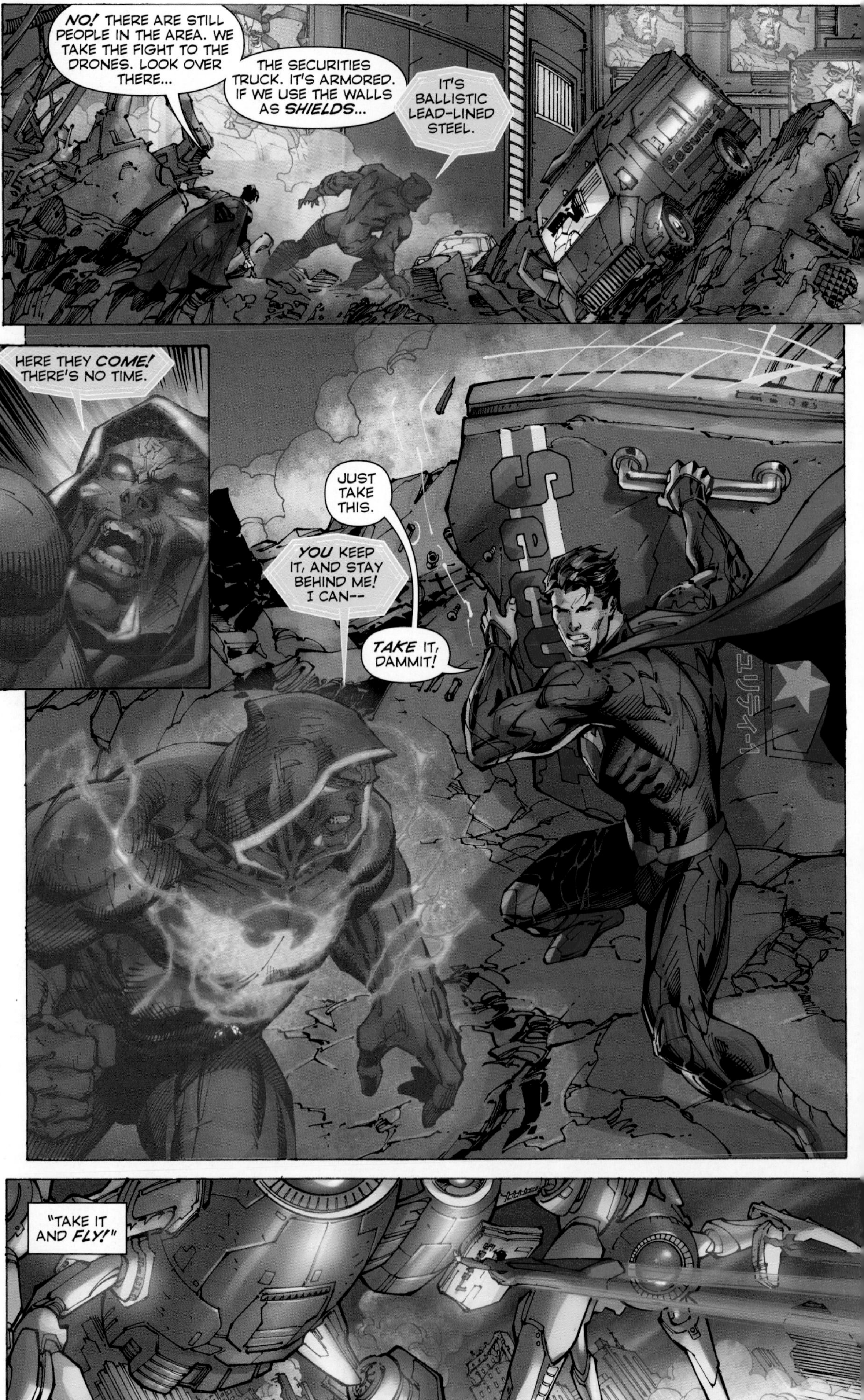
NO! THERE ARE STILL PEOPLE IN THE AREA. WE TAKE THE FIGHT TO THE DRONES. LOOK OVER THERE...
THE SECURITIES TRUCK. IT'S ARMORED. IF WE USE THE WALLS AS SHIELDS...
IT'S BALLISTIC LEAD-LINED STEEL.
HERE THEY COME! THERE'S NO TIME.
JUST TAKE THIS.
YOU KEEP IT, AND STAY BEHIND ME! I CAN--
TAKE IT, DAMMIT!
"TAKE IT AND FLY!"

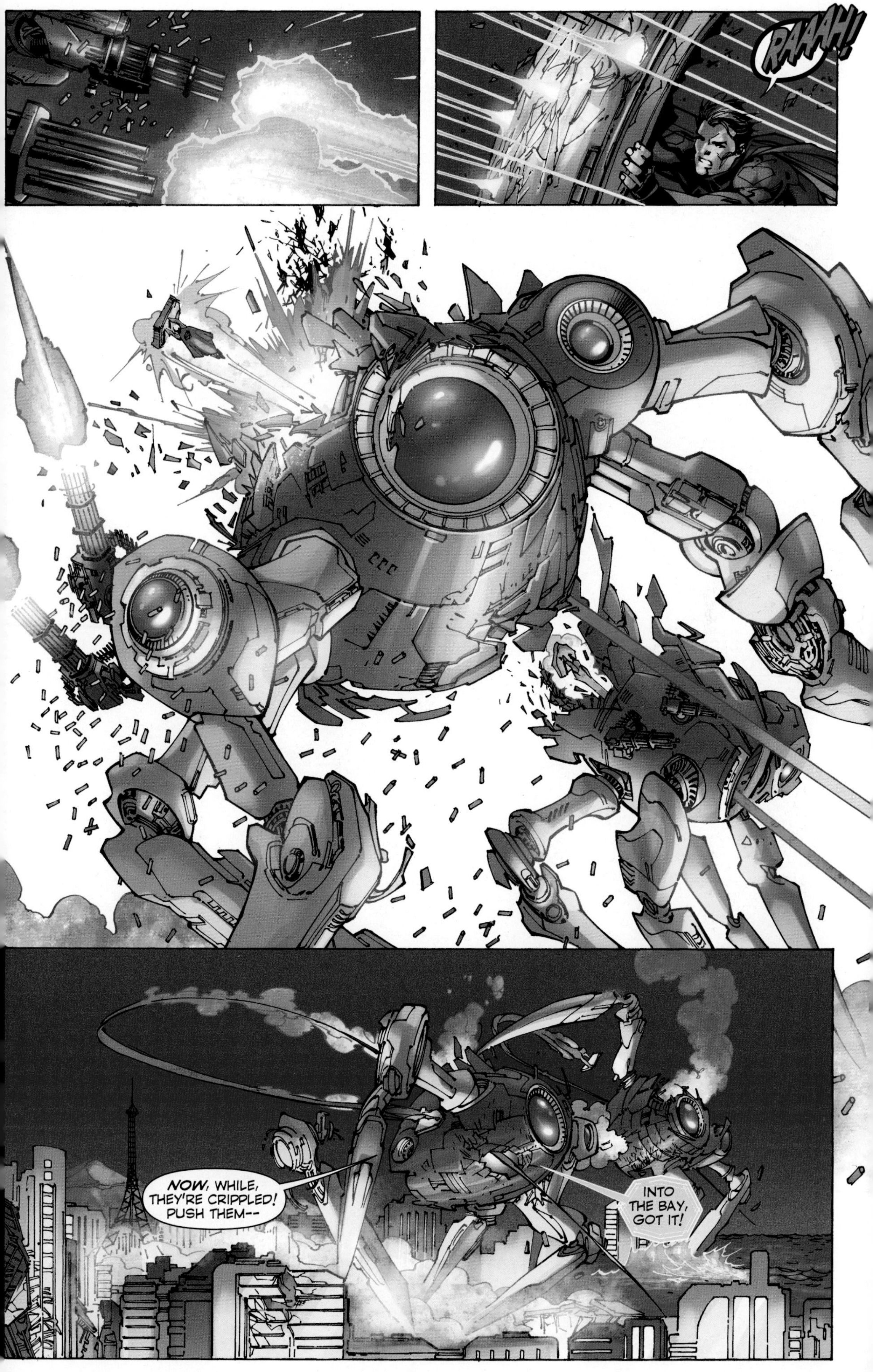
RAAAH!
NOW, WHILE, THEY'RE CRIPPLED! PUSH THEM--
INTO THE BAY, GOT IT!

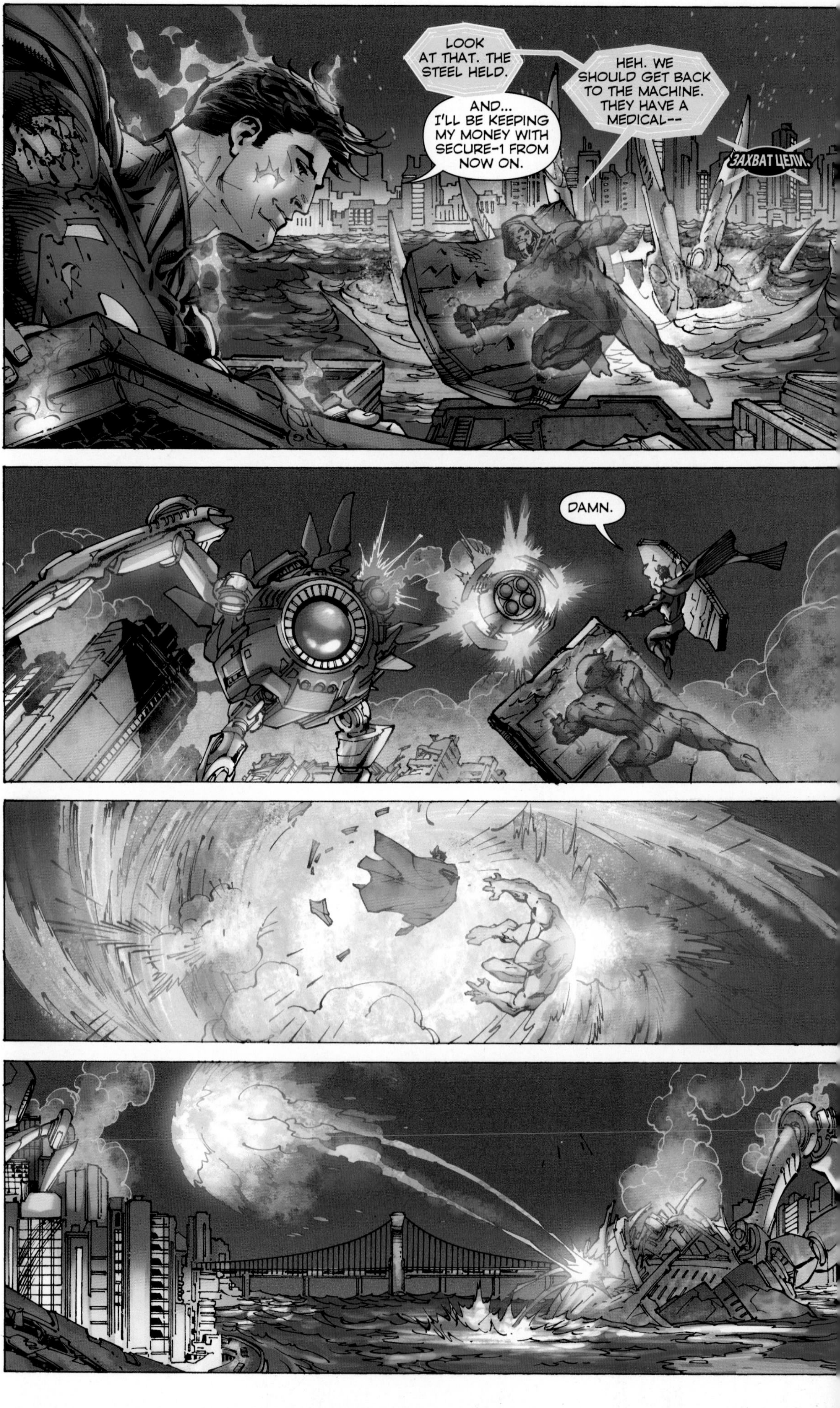
LOOK AT THAT. THE STEEL HELD.
HEH. WE SHOULD GET BACK TO THE MACHINE. THEY HAVE A MEDICAL--
AND... I'LL BE KEEPING MY MONEY WITH SECURE-1 FROM NOW ON.
ЗАХВАТ ЦЕЛИ.
DAMN.

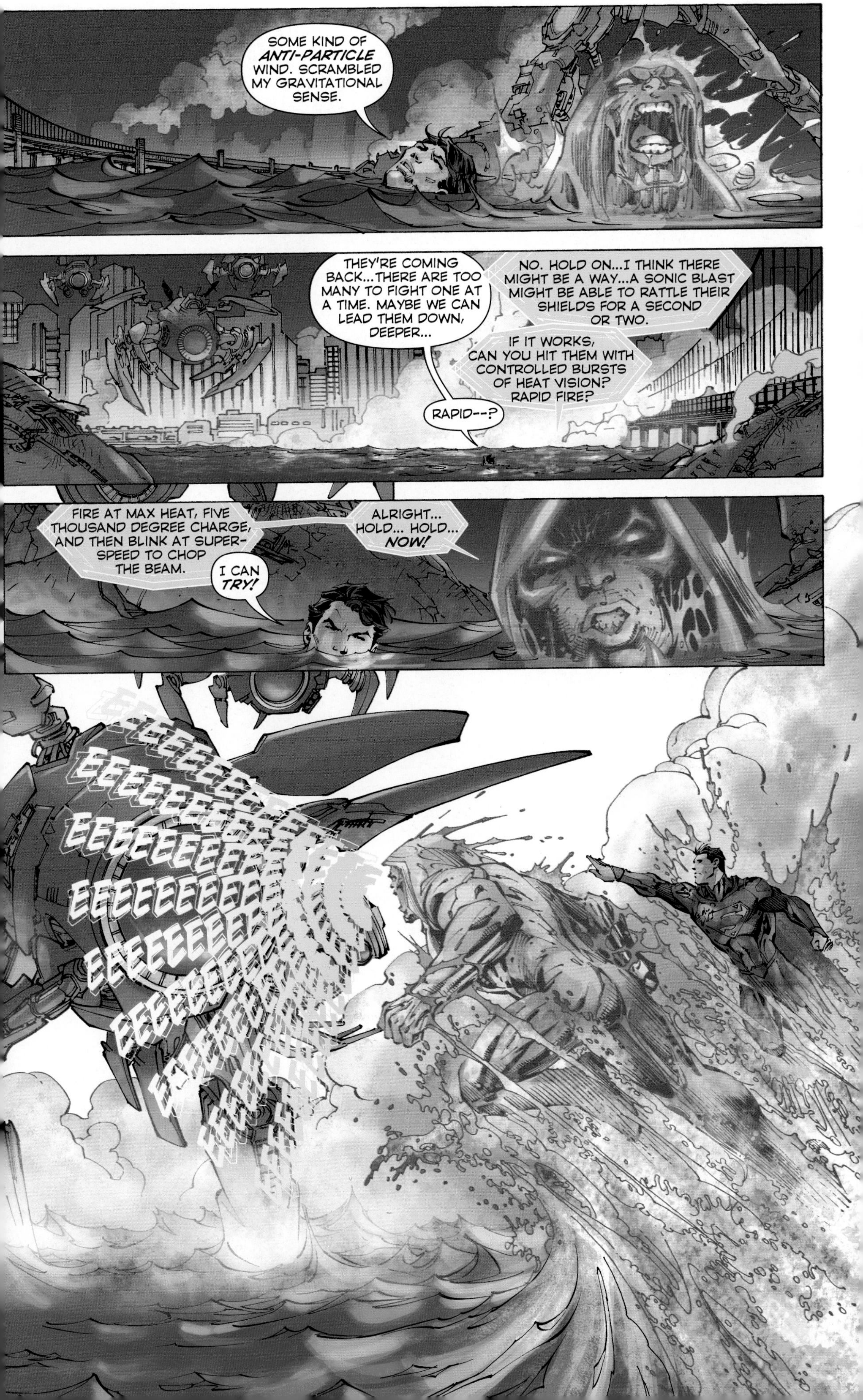

SOME KIND OF ANTI-PARTICLE WIND. SCRAMBLED MY GRAVITATIONAL SENSE.
THEY'RE COMING BACK...THERE ARE TOO MANY TO FIGHT ONE AT A TIME. MAYBE WE CAN LEAD THEM DOWN, DEEPER...
NO. HOLD ON...I THINK THERE MIGHT BE A WAY...A SONIC BLAST MIGHT BE ABLE TO RATTLE THEIR SHIELDS FOR A SECOND OR TWO.
IF IT WORKS, CAN YOU HIT THEM WITH CONTROLLED BURSTS OF HEAT VISION? RAPID FIRE?
RAPID--?
FIRE AT MAX HEAT, FIVE THOUSAND DEGREE CHARGE, AND THEN BLINK AT SUPER-SPEED TO CHOP THE BEAM.
I CAN TRY!
ALRIGHT... HOLD... HOLD... NOW!
EEEEEEEEEEEEEEE

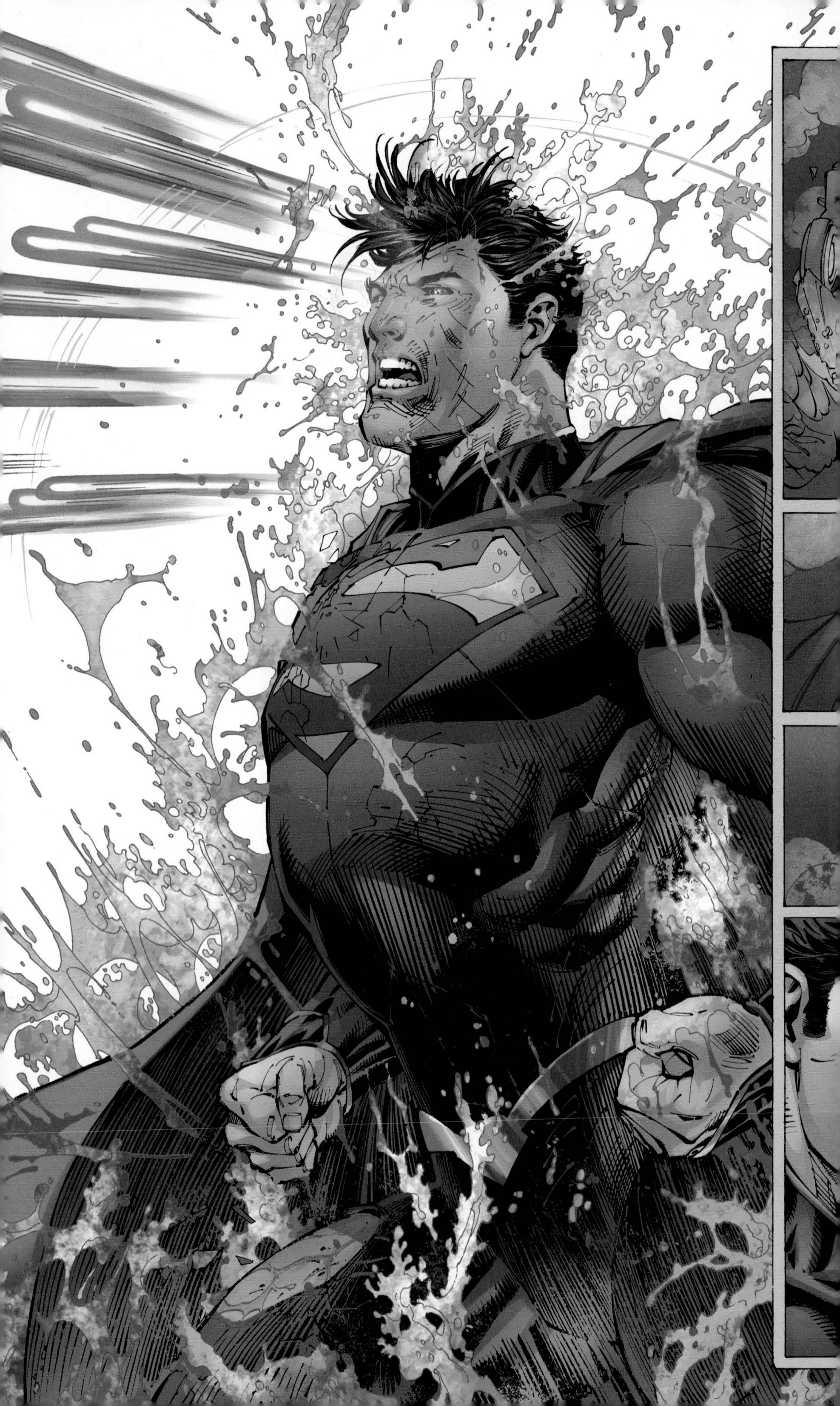

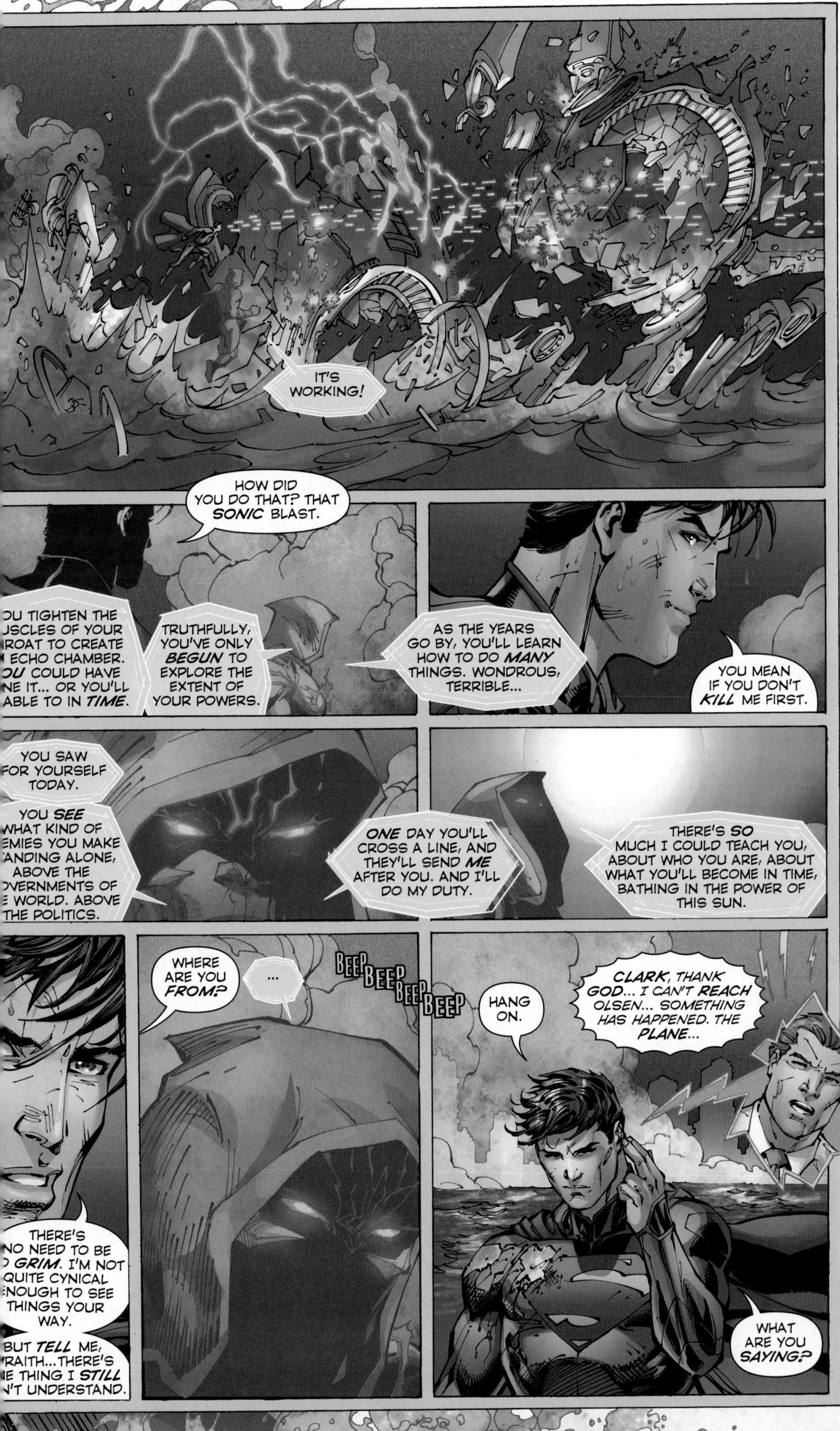
IT'S WORKING!
HOW DID YOU DO THAT? THAT SONIC BLAST.
OU TIGHTEN THE USCLES OF YOUR ROAT TO CREATE ECHO CHAMBER. OU COULD HAVE NE IT... OR YOU'LL ABLE TO IN TIME.
TRUTHFULLY, YOU'VE ONLY BEGUN TO EXPLORE THE EXTENT OF YOUR POWERS.
AS THE YEARS GO BY, YOU'LL LEARN HOW TO DO MANY THINGS. WONDROUS, TERRIBLE...
YOU MEAN IF YOU DON'T KILL ME FIRST.
YOU SAW FOR YOURSELF TODAY.
YOU SEE WHAT KIND OF EMIES YOU MAKE TANDING ALONE, ABOVE THE OVERNMENTS OF E WORLD. ABOVE THE POLITICS.
ONE DAY YOU'LL CROSS A LINE, AND THEY'LL SEND ME AFTER YOU. AND I'LL DO MY DUTY.
THERE'S SO MUCH I COULD TEACH YOU, ABOUT WHO YOU ARE, ABOUT WHAT YOU'LL BECOME IN TIME, BATHING IN THE POWER OF THIS SUN.
THERE'S NO NEED TO BE GRIM. I'M NOT QUITE CYNICAL ENOUGH TO SEE THINGS YOUR WAY.
BUT TELL ME, RAITH...THERE'S E THING I STILL N'T UNDERSTAND.
WHERE ARE YOU FROM?
...
BEEP BEEP BEEP BEEP
HANG ON.
CLARK, THANK GOD... I CAN'T REACH OLSEN... SOMETHING HAS HAPPENED. THE PLANE...
WHAT ARE YOU SAYING?

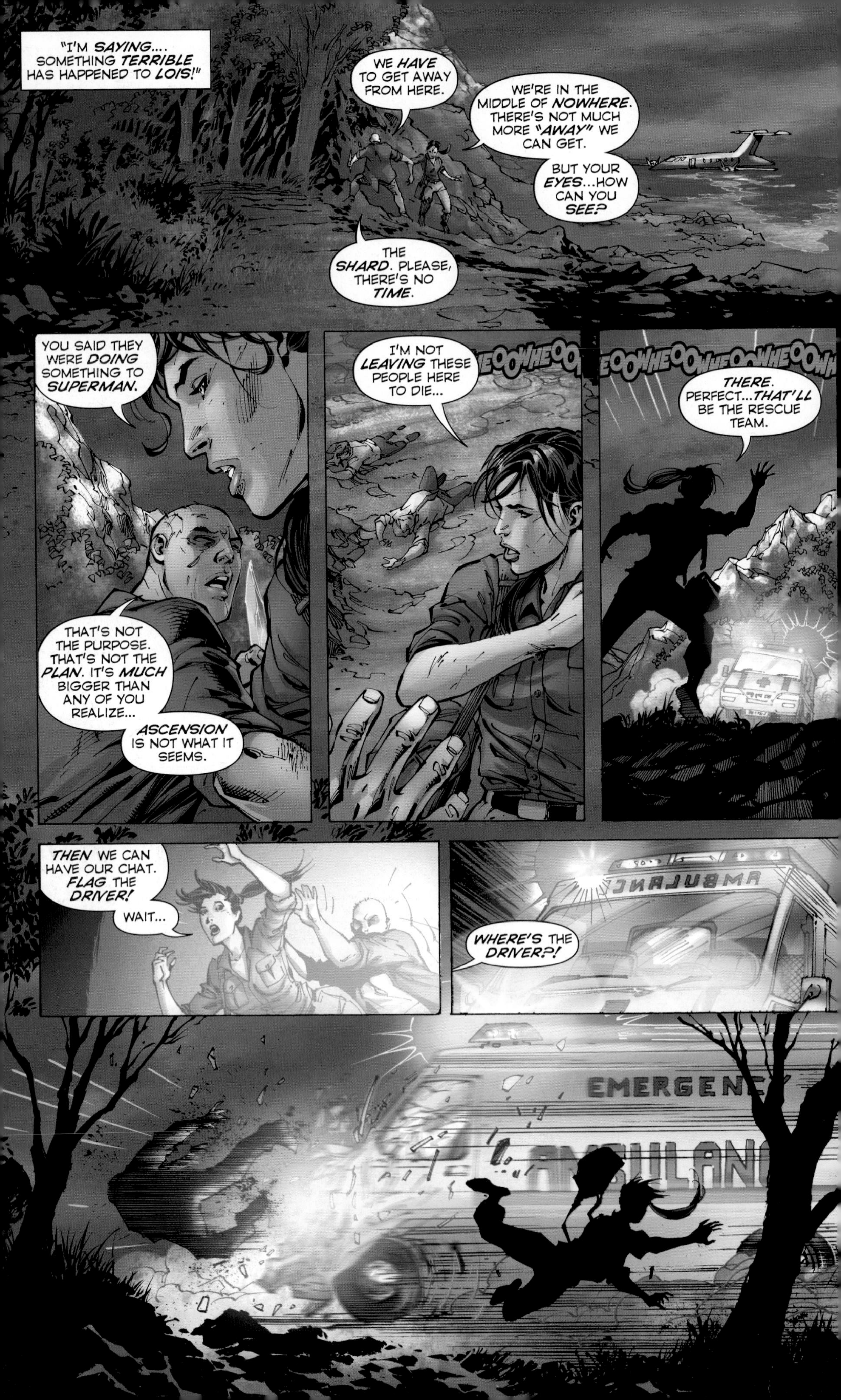

"I'M SAYING.... SOMETHING TERRIBLE HAS HAPPENED TO LOIS!"
WE HAVE TO GET AWAY FROM HERE.
WE'RE IN THE MIDDLE OF NOWHERE. THERE'S NOT MUCH MORE "AWAY" WE CAN GET.
BUT YOUR EYES...HOW CAN YOU SEE?
THE SHARD. PLEASE, THERE'S NO TIME.
YOU SAID THEY WERE DOING SOMETHING TO SUPERMAN.
THAT'S NOT THE PURPOSE. THAT'S NOT THE PLAN. IT'S MUCH BIGGER THAN ANY OF YOU REALIZE...
ASCENSION IS NOT WHAT IT SEEMS.
I'M NOT LEAVING THESE PEOPLE HERE TO DIE...
WHEOOWHEOOWHEOOWHEOOWHEOOWHEOOWH
THERE. PERFECT...THAT'LL BE THE RESCUE TEAM.
THEN WE CAN HAVE OUR CHAT. FLAG THE DRIVER!
WAIT...
AMBULANCE
WHERE'S THE DRIVER?!
EMERGENCY

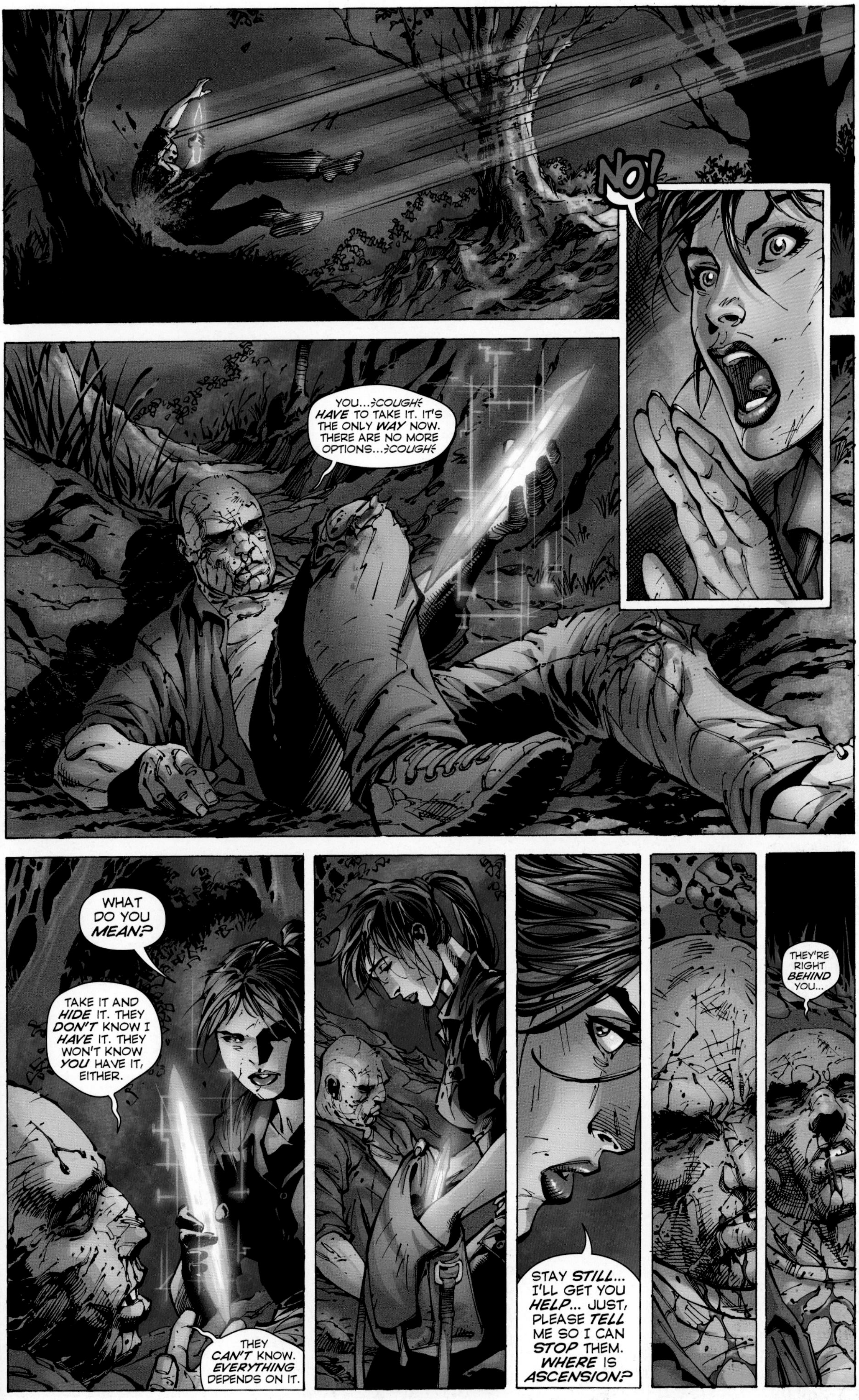
NO!
YOU... ⧽COUGH⧼ HAVE TO TAKE IT. IT'S THE ONLY WAY NOW. THERE ARE NO MORE OPTIONS... ⧽COUGH⧼
WHAT DO YOU MEAN?
TAKE IT AND HIDE IT. THEY DON'T KNOW I HAVE IT. THEY WON'T KNOW YOU HAVE IT, EITHER.
THEY CAN'T KNOW. EVERYTHING DEPENDS ON IT.
STAY STILL... I'LL GET YOU HELP... JUST, PLEASE TELL ME SO I CAN STOP THEM. WHERE IS ASCENSION?
THEY'RE RIGHT BEHIND YOU...

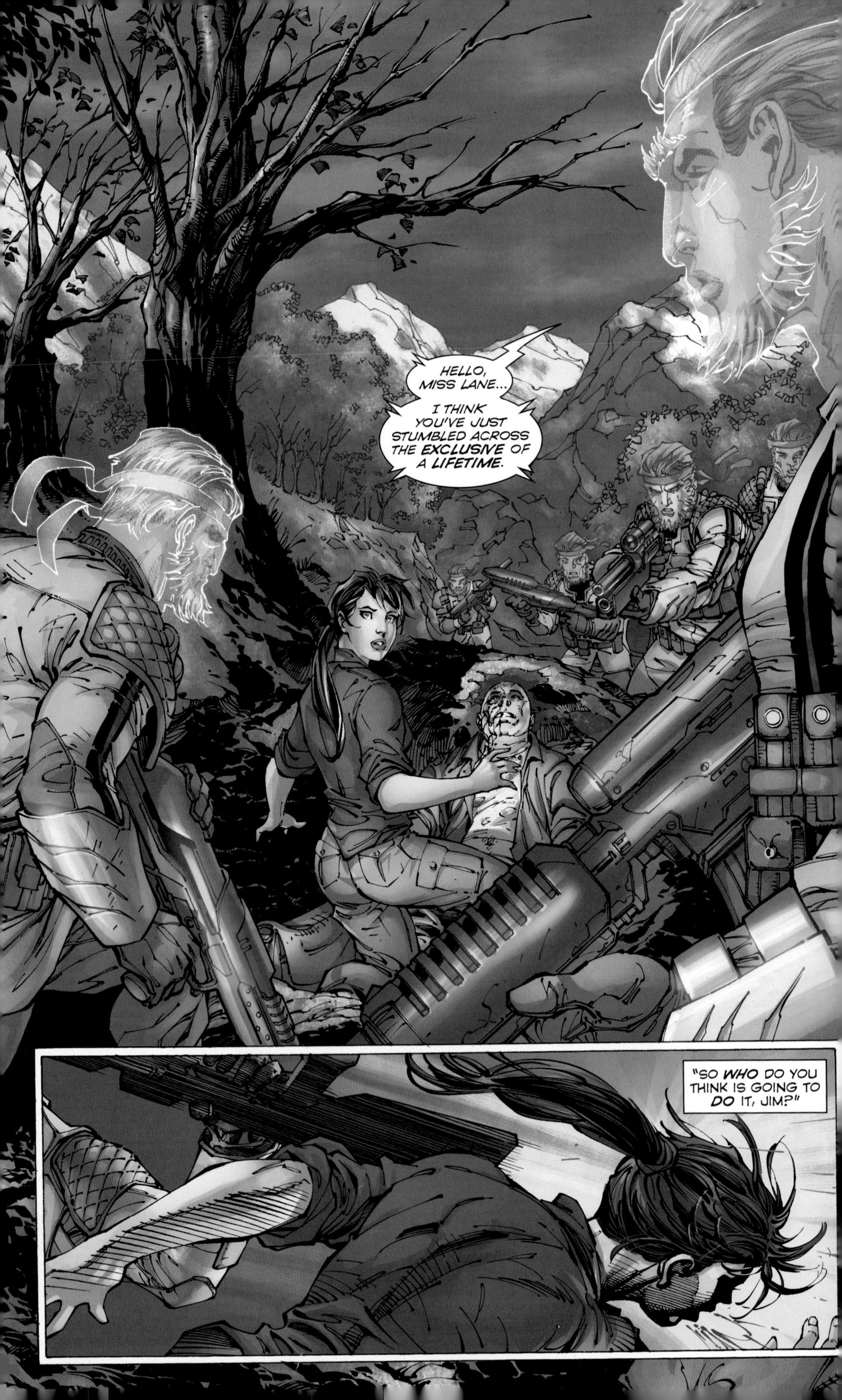
HELLO, MISS LANE... I THINK YOU'VE JUST STUMBLED ACROSS THE **EXCLUSIVE** OF A **LIFETIME**.
"SO ***WHO*** DO YOU THINK IS GOING TO ***DO*** IT, JIM?"

IF NOT *ME*, IF NOT SOME BIG BAD LIKE *BRAINIAC*, IF NOT A *LOVER*, THEN *WHO?*

AAARGH!

I'LL *TELL* YOU, JIM...

IF YOU PROMISE NOT TO TELL *ANYONE*. IF YOU'LL BE A REAL PAL AND KEEP IT *SECRET*.

...BECAUSE IT'LL BE *YOU*, JIM.

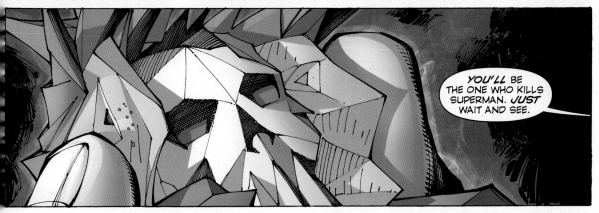

YOU'LL BE THE ONE WHO KILLS SUPERMAN. *JUST* WAIT AND SEE.

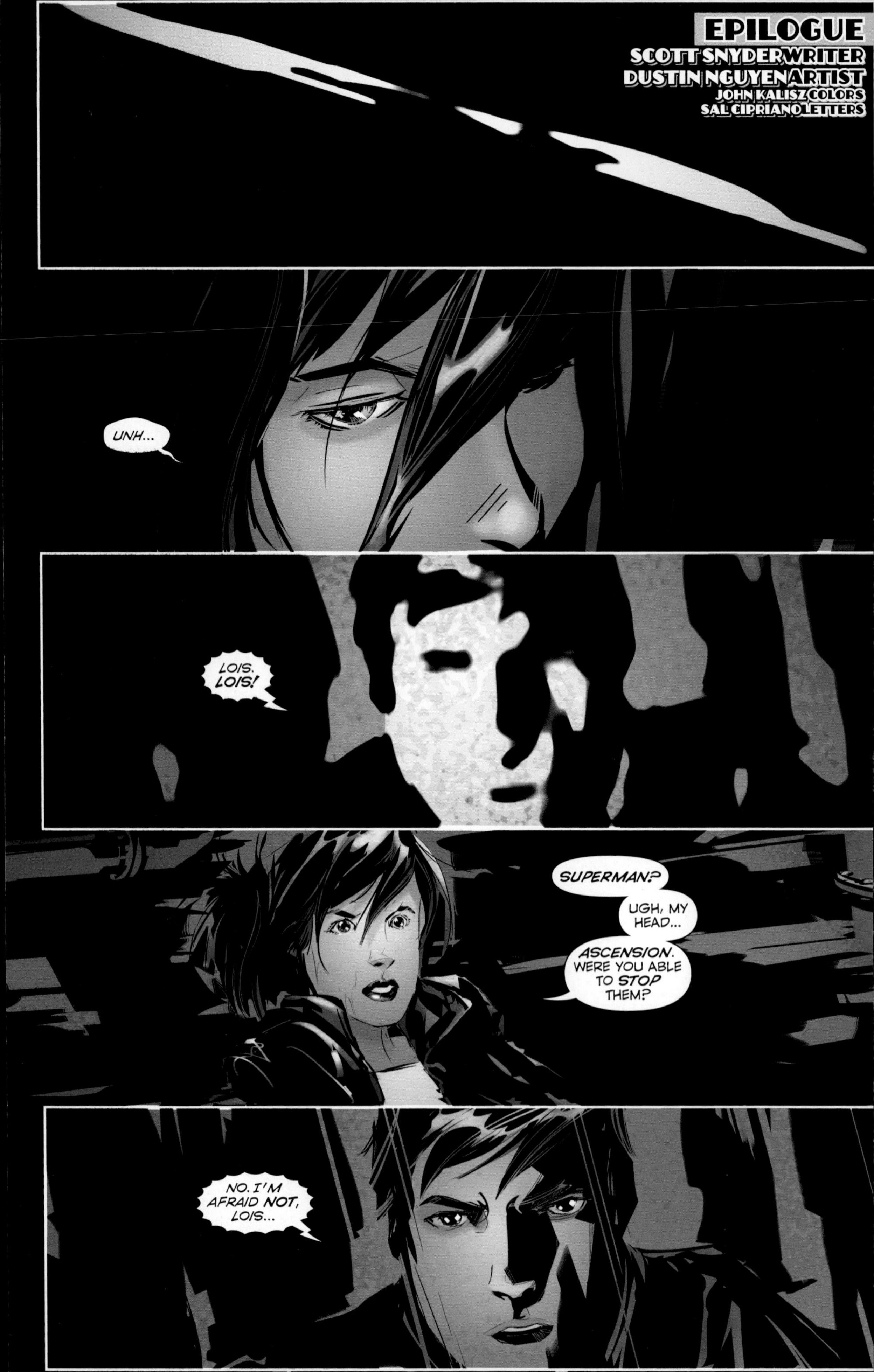
EPILOGUE
SCOTT SNYDER WRITER
DUSTIN NGUYEN ARTIST
JOHN KALISZ COLORS
SAL CIPRIANO LETTERS
UNH...
LOIS. LOIS!
SUPERMAN?
UGH, MY HEAD...
ASCENSION. WERE YOU ABLE TO STOP THEM?
NO. I'M AFRAID NOT, LOIS...

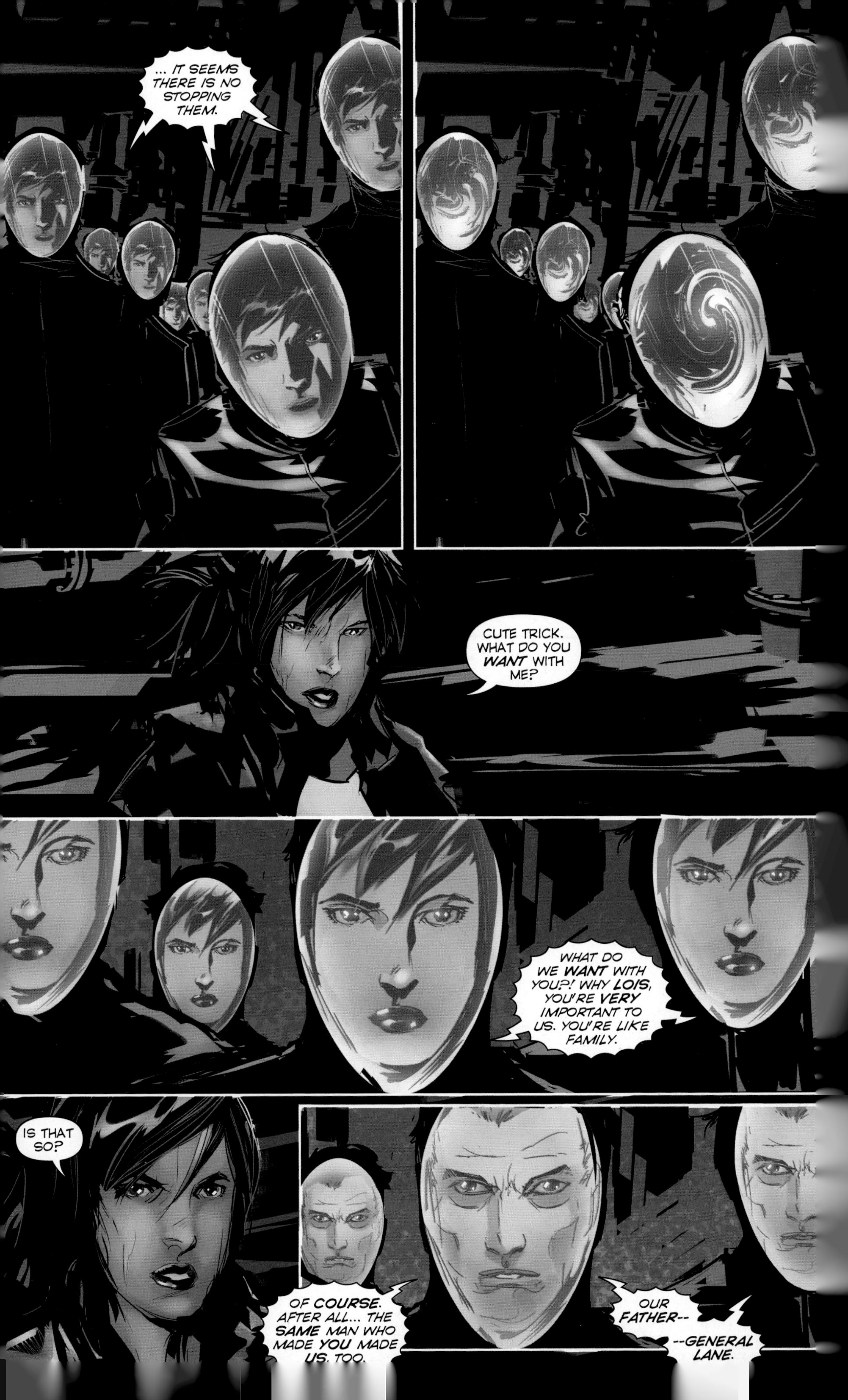
... IT SEEMS THERE IS NO STOPPING THEM.
CUTE TRICK. WHAT DO YOU WANT WITH ME?
WHAT DO WE WANT WITH YOU?! WHY LOIS, YOU'RE VERY IMPORTANT TO US. YOU'RE LIKE FAMILY.
IS THAT SO?
OF COURSE. AFTER ALL... THE SAME MAN WHO MADE YOU MADE US, TOO.
OUR FATHER--
--GENERAL LANE.

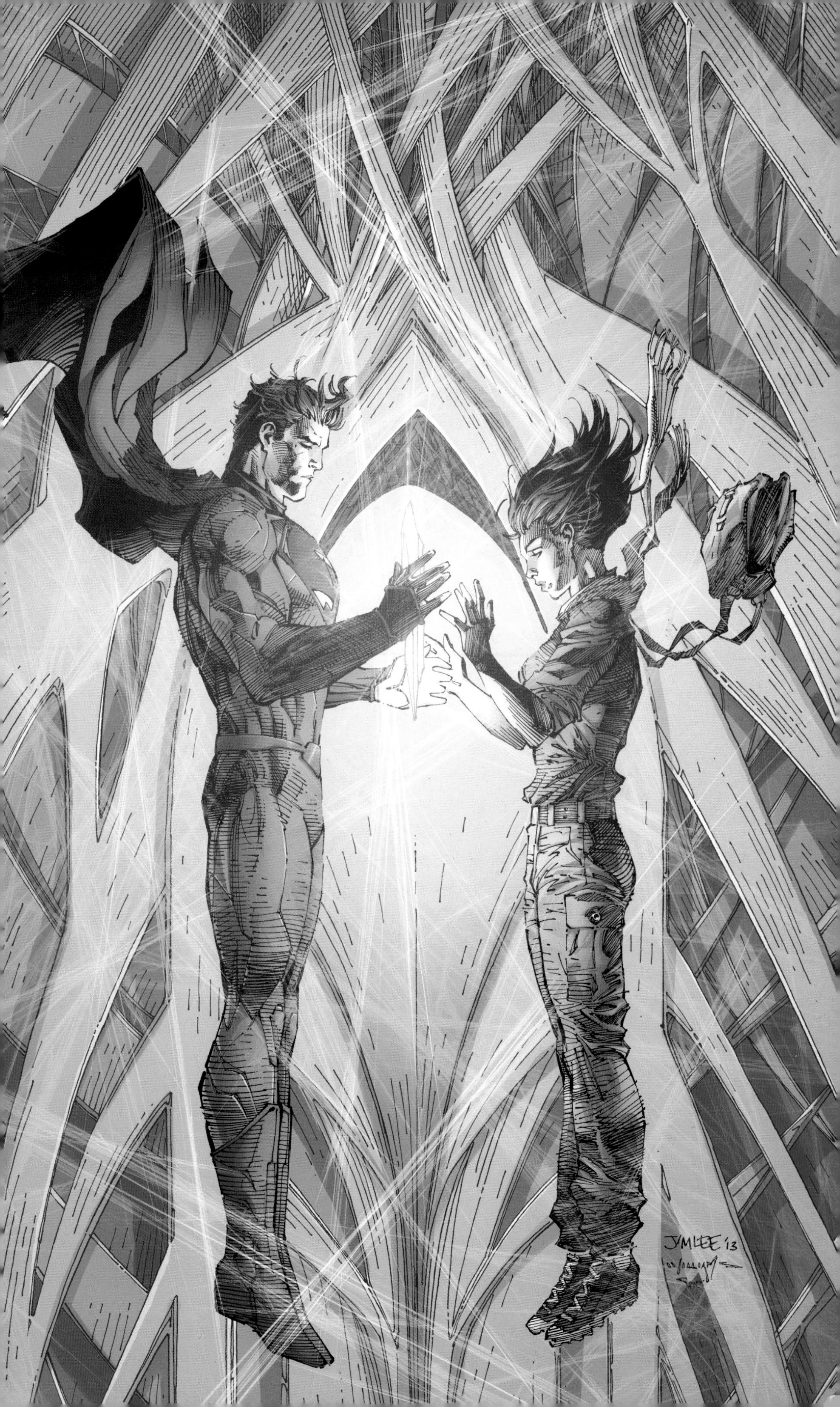
JYMLEE '13

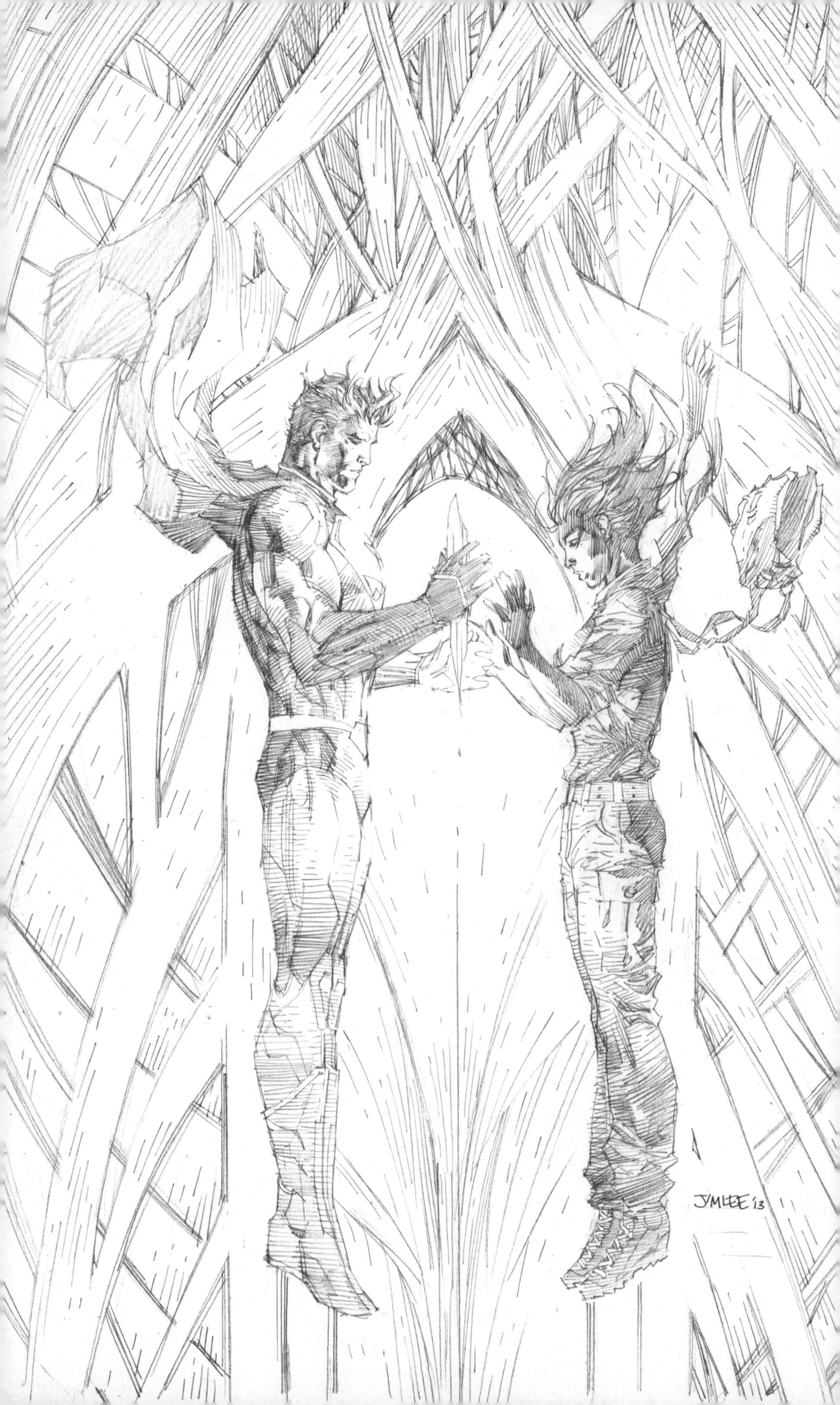

SMALLVILLE, KANSAS.
THEN.
NO MORE *HIDING*, KENT.
A PLACE BETWEEN
SCOTT SNYDER WRITER JIM LEE PENCILLER SCOTT WILLIAMS INKER ALEX SINCLAIR COLORIST
USTIN NGUYEN ARTIST, FLASHBACK SEQUENCE JOHN KALISZ COLORS, FLASHBACK SEQUENCE
SAL CIPRIANO LETTERING JIM LEE, SCOTT WILLIAMS, & ALEX SINCLAIR COVER

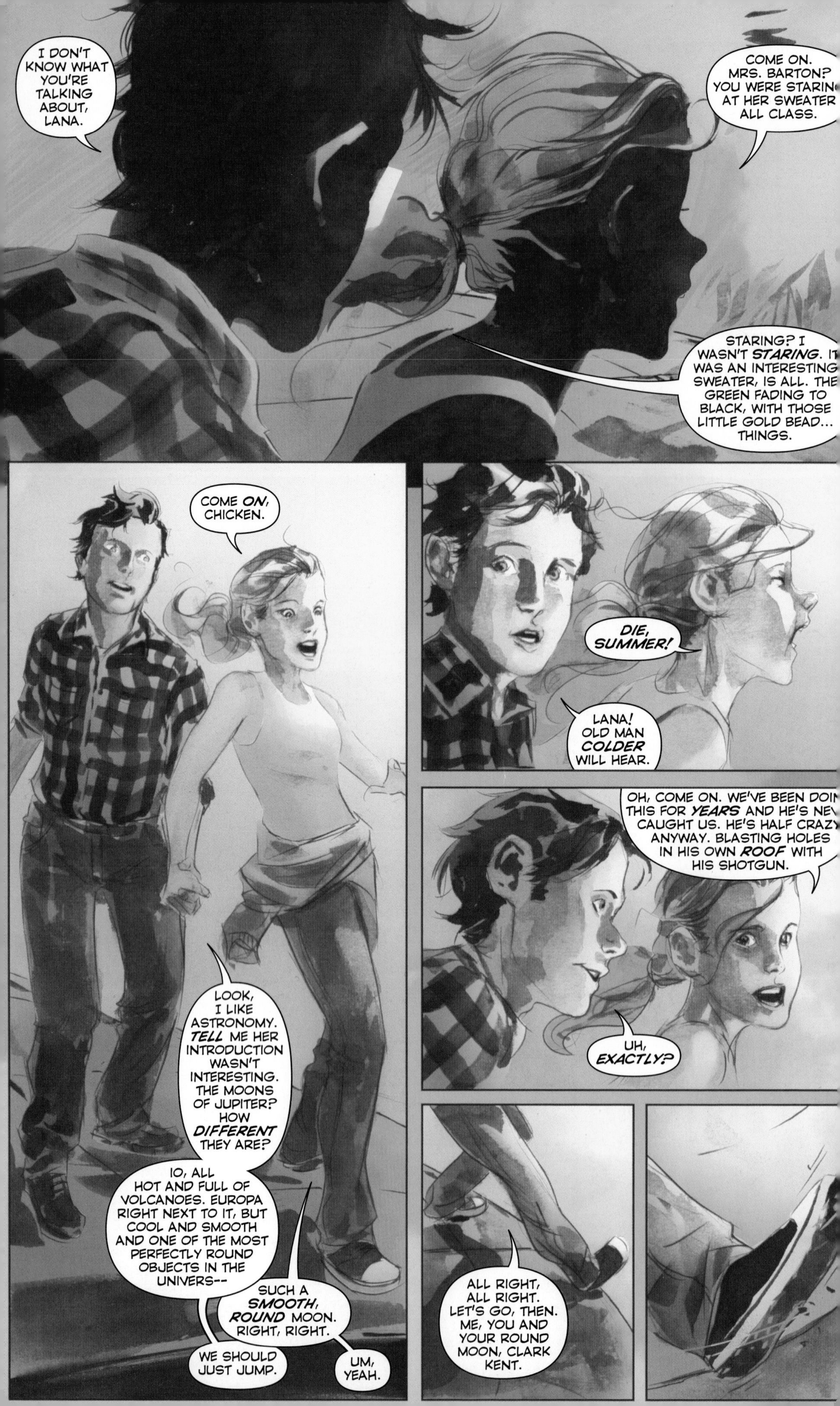
I DON'T KNOW WHAT YOU'RE TALKING ABOUT, LANA.
COME ON. MRS. BARTON? YOU WERE STARIN AT HER SWEATER ALL CLASS.
STARING? I WASN'T STARING. IT WAS AN INTERESTING SWEATER, IS ALL. THE GREEN FADING TO BLACK, WITH THOSE LITTLE GOLD BEAD... THINGS.
COME ON, CHICKEN.
LOOK, I LIKE ASTRONOMY. TELL ME HER INTRODUCTION WASN'T INTERESTING. THE MOONS OF JUPITER? HOW DIFFERENT THEY ARE?
IO, ALL HOT AND FULL OF VOLCANOES. EUROPA RIGHT NEXT TO IT, BUT COOL AND SMOOTH AND ONE OF THE MOST PERFECTLY ROUND OBJECTS IN THE UNIVERS--
SUCH A SMOOTH, ROUND MOON. RIGHT, RIGHT.
WE SHOULD JUST JUMP.
UM, YEAH.
DIE, SUMMER!
LANA! OLD MAN COLDER WILL HEAR.
OH, COME ON. WE'VE BEEN DOIN THIS FOR YEARS AND HE'S NEV CAUGHT US. HE'S HALF CRAZY ANYWAY. BLASTING HOLES IN HIS OWN ROOF WITH HIS SHOTGUN.
UH, EXACTLY?
ALL RIGHT, ALL RIGHT. LET'S GO, THEN. ME, YOU AND YOUR ROUND MOON, CLARK KENT.

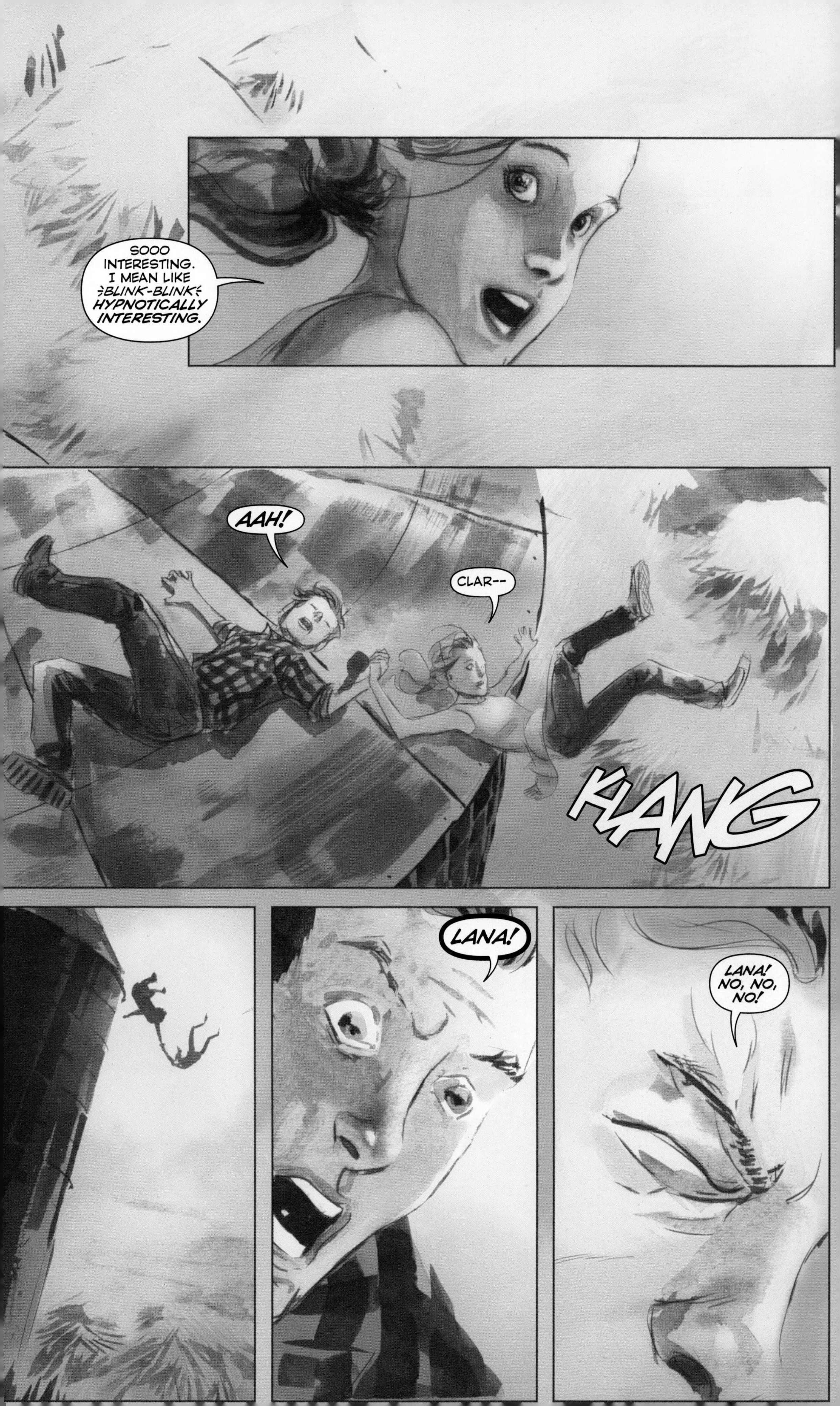
SOOO INTERESTING. I MEAN LIKE ⊰BLINK-BLINK⊱ HYPNOTICALLY INTERESTING.
AAH!
CLAR--
KLANG
LANA!
LANA! NO, NO, NO!

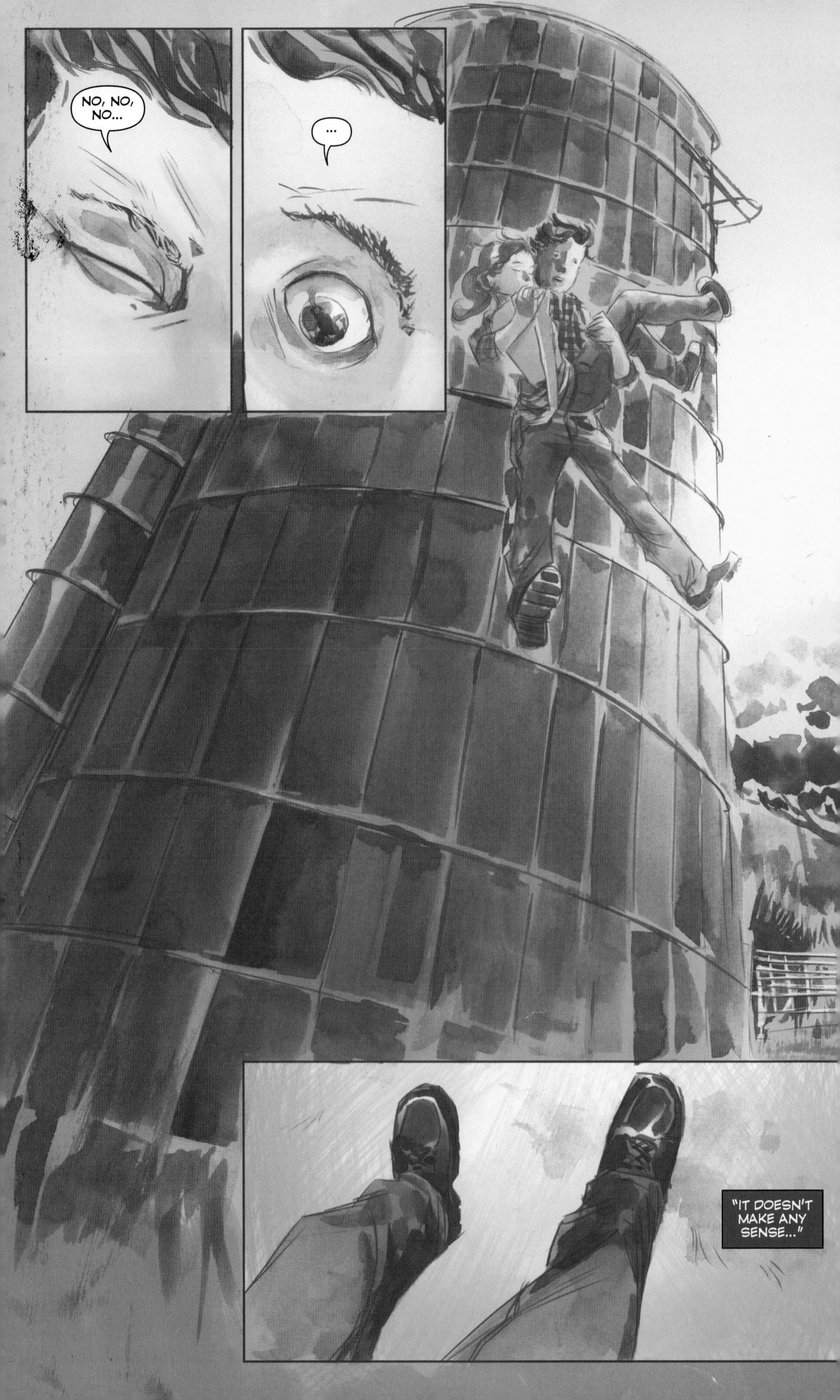
NO, NO, NO...
...
"IT DOESN'T MAKE ANY SENSE..."

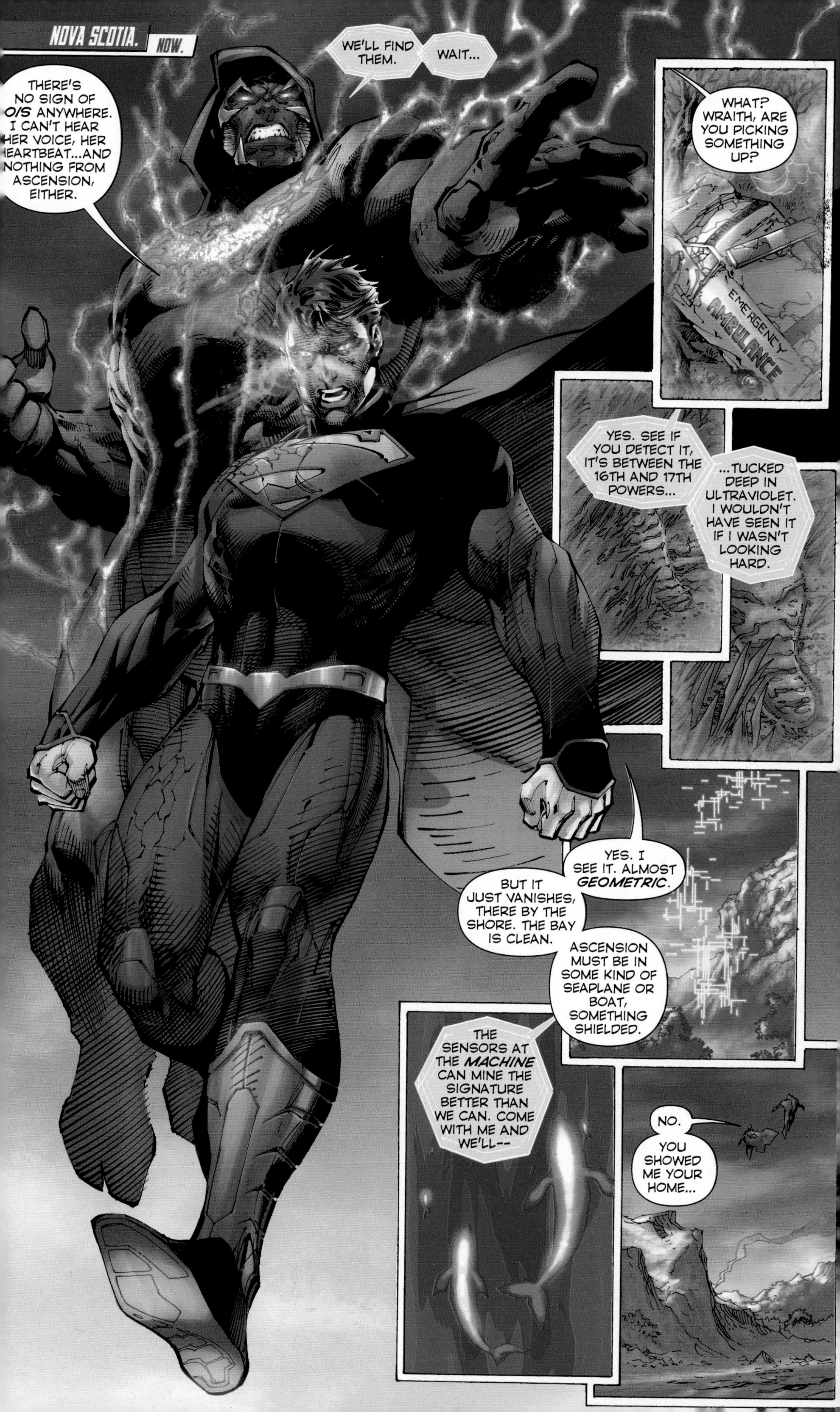
NOVA SCOTIA. NOW.
THERE'S NO SIGN OF LOIS ANYWHERE. I CAN'T HEAR HER VOICE, HER HEARTBEAT...AND NOTHING FROM ASCENSION, EITHER.
WE'LL FIND THEM.
WAIT...
WHAT? WRAITH, ARE YOU PICKING SOMETHING UP?
EMERGENCY
AMBULANCE
YES. SEE IF YOU DETECT IT, IT'S BETWEEN THE 16TH AND 17TH POWERS...
...TUCKED DEEP IN ULTRAVIOLET. I WOULDN'T HAVE SEEN IT IF I WASN'T LOOKING HARD.
YES. I SEE IT. ALMOST GEOMETRIC.
BUT IT JUST VANISHES, THERE BY THE SHORE. THE BAY IS CLEAN.
ASCENSION MUST BE IN SOME KIND OF SEAPLANE OR BOAT, SOMETHING SHIELDED.
THE SENSORS AT THE MACHINE CAN MINE THE SIGNATURE BETTER THAN WE CAN. COME WITH ME AND WE'LL--
NO.
YOU SHOWED ME YOUR HOME...

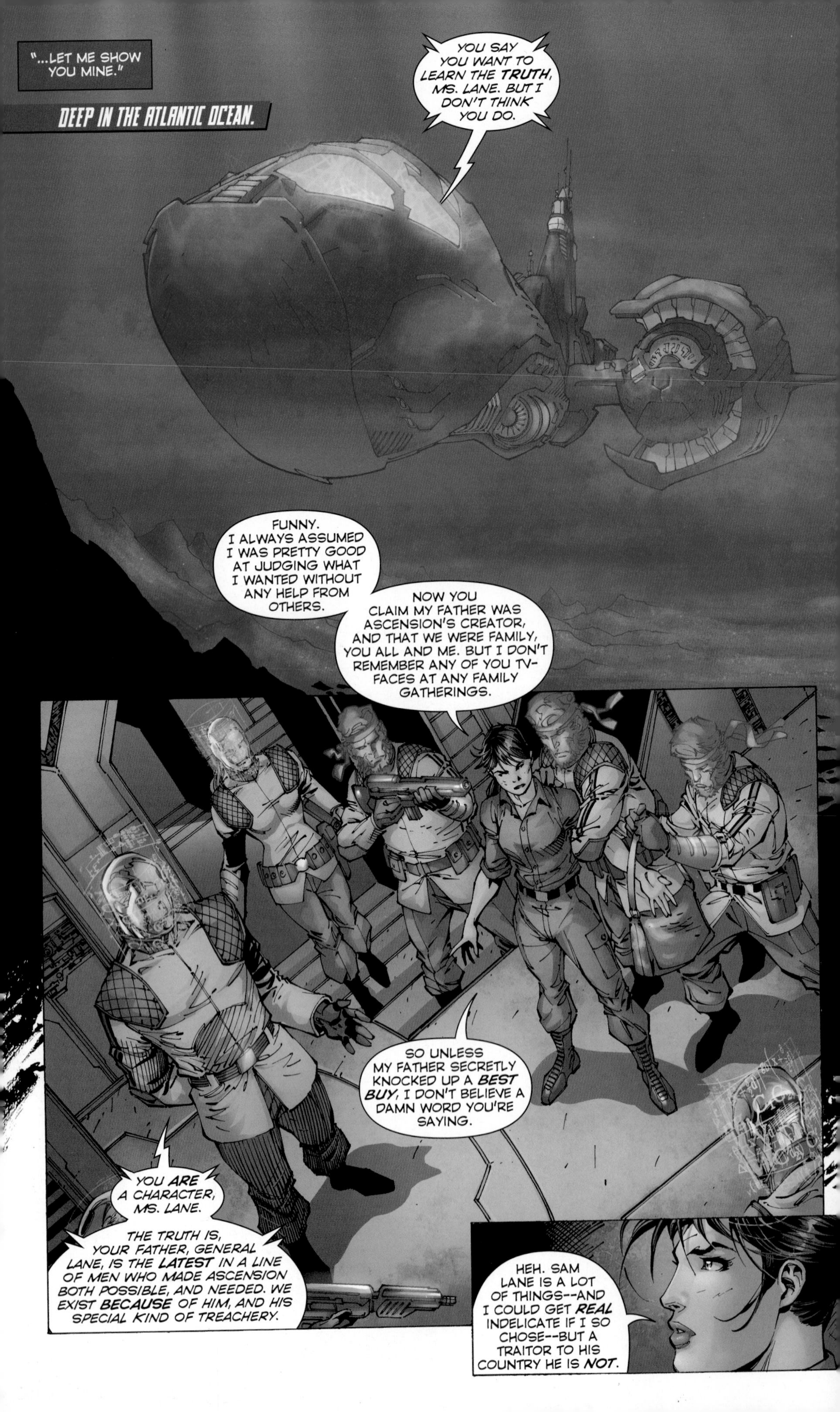
"...LET ME SHOW YOU MINE."
DEEP IN THE ATLANTIC OCEAN.
YOU SAY YOU WANT TO LEARN THE TRUTH, MS. LANE. BUT I DON'T THINK YOU DO.
FUNNY. I ALWAYS ASSUMED I WAS PRETTY GOOD AT JUDGING WHAT I WANTED WITHOUT ANY HELP FROM OTHERS.
NOW YOU CLAIM MY FATHER WAS ASCENSION'S CREATOR, AND THAT WE WERE FAMILY, YOU ALL AND ME. BUT I DON'T REMEMBER ANY OF YOU TV-FACES AT ANY FAMILY GATHERINGS.
SO UNLESS MY FATHER SECRETLY KNOCKED UP A BEST BUY, I DON'T BELIEVE A DAMN WORD YOU'RE SAYING.
YOU ARE A CHARACTER, MS. LANE.
THE TRUTH IS, YOUR FATHER, GENERAL LANE, IS THE LATEST IN A LINE OF MEN WHO MADE ASCENSION BOTH POSSIBLE, AND NEEDED. WE EXIST BECAUSE OF HIM, AND HIS SPECIAL KIND OF TREACHERY.
HEH. SAM LANE IS A LOT OF THINGS--AND I COULD GET REAL INDELICATE IF I SO CHOSE--BUT A TRAITOR TO HIS COUNTRY HE IS NOT.

OH, HE'S A TRAITOR. HE AND THE GENERALS BEFORE HIM, THE FACES YOU SEE HERE... LEONARDS, BANGLEY, GERUNS, ROGERS...

THEY'RE THE GREATEST TRAITORS IN MODERN HISTORY. EACH HAS TAKEN A TURN COMMANDING THE MOST TRAITOROUS ORGANIZATION ON THE PLANET--THE MACHINE.

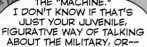

THE "MACHINE." I DON'T KNOW IF THAT'S JUST YOUR JUVENILE, FIGURATIVE WAY OF TALKING ABOUT THE MILITARY, OR--

I'VE KILLED A LOT OF PEOPLE MS. LANE.

HELL, I WAS GOING TO KILL YOU A MOMENT AGO, BUT I'VE DECIDED INSTEAD TO LEAVE YOU ALIVE TO TELL OUR STORY.

STILL, KEEP JOKING. FEEL FREE. MAYBE AFTER THE NEXT GOOD QUIP, I'LL BEAT YOU TO DEATH WITH YOUR FATHER'S FACE ON.

HOW'S THAT FOR FIGURATIVE?

RIGHT, THEN. THE MACHINE IS A SECRET BRANCH OF THE U.S. MILITARY. IT WAS FORMED IN 1938, WHEN AN ALIEN RACE FIRST MADE CONTACT WITH EARTH BY SENDING AN ENVOY. AN ENVOY WITH AN EQUATION EMBEDDED IN HIS SHIP.

NOW THIS EQUATION, IT WAS GEOLOGICAL IN NATURE. IT EXPLAINED, HOW TO EXPLOIT EARTH'S MINERALS FOR TECHNOLOGICAL ADVANCEMENT.

HOW TO USE GERMANIUM TO CREATE THE FIRST EFFECTIVE TRANSISTOR. HOW TO USE SILICATES FOR CONDUCTION.

SINCE 1938, THE MACHINE HAS BEEN USING THIS EQUATION --AND THE ALIEN--TO CHART A COURSE FOR THIS COUNTRY, AND MANKIND. I CREATED ASCENSION TO SET A NEW COURSE.

AND WHY SHOULD I BELIEVE A WORD YOU'RE SAYING? IF THIS IS SO TOP SECRET, HOW DO YOU KNOW WHAT IT IS?

HOW ABOUT YOU STOP HIDING BEHIND MY FATHER'S FACE AND SHOW YOUR DAMN CREDENTIALS?

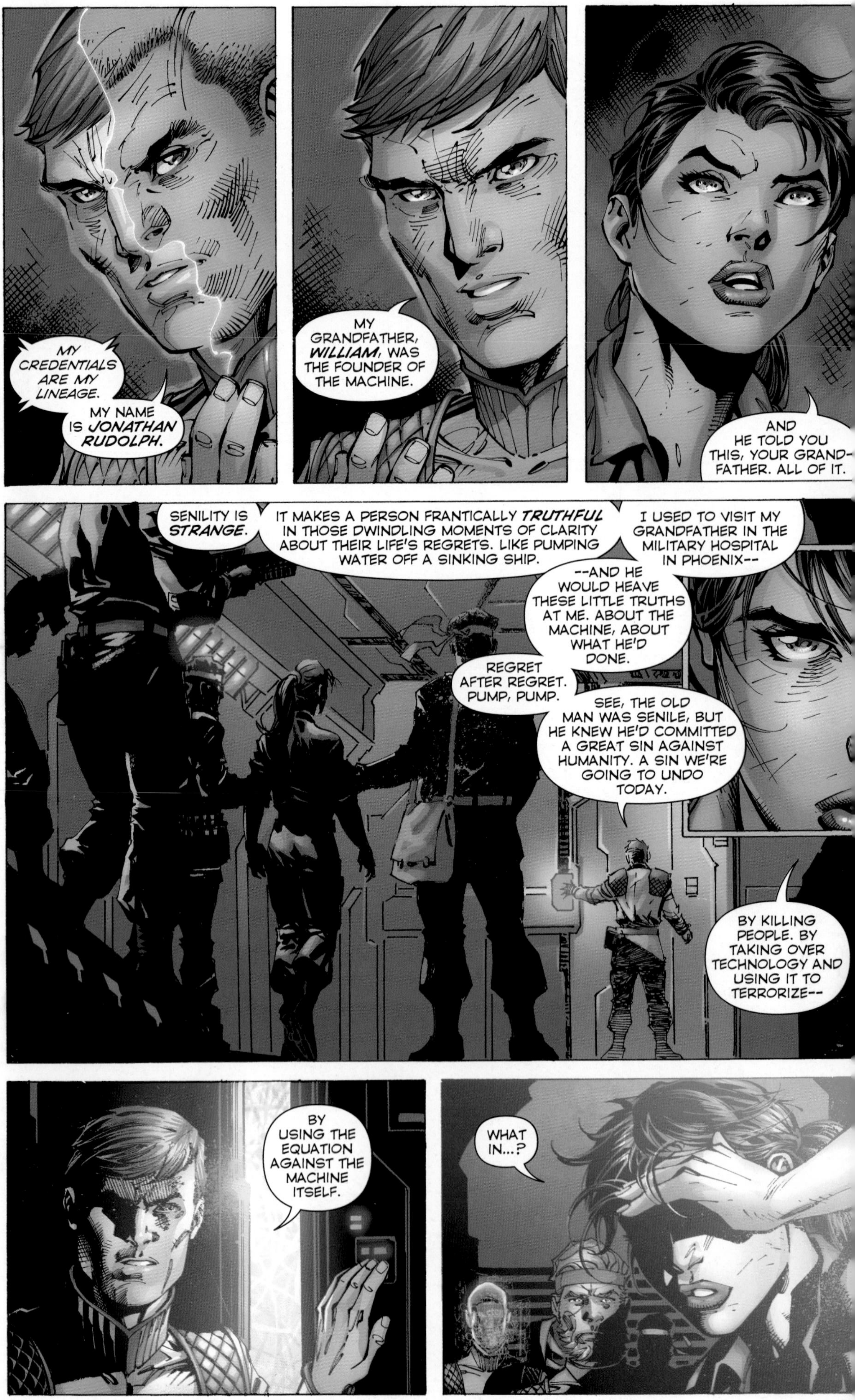

MY CREDENTIALS ARE MY LINEAGE.
MY NAME IS JONATHAN RUDOLPH.
MY GRANDFATHER, WILLIAM, WAS THE FOUNDER OF THE MACHINE.
AND HE TOLD YOU THIS, YOUR GRAND-FATHER. ALL OF IT.
SENILITY IS STRANGE.
IT MAKES A PERSON FRANTICALLY TRUTHFUL IN THOSE DWINDLING MOMENTS OF CLARITY ABOUT THEIR LIFE'S REGRETS. LIKE PUMPING WATER OFF A SINKING SHIP.
I USED TO VISIT MY GRANDFATHER IN THE MILITARY HOSPITAL IN PHOENIX--
--AND HE WOULD HEAVE THESE LITTLE TRUTHS AT ME. ABOUT THE MACHINE, ABOUT WHAT HE'D DONE.
REGRET AFTER REGRET. PUMP, PUMP.
SEE, THE OLD MAN WAS SENILE, BUT HE KNEW HE'D COMMITTED A GREAT SIN AGAINST HUMANITY. A SIN WE'RE GOING TO UNDO TODAY.
BY KILLING PEOPLE. BY TAKING OVER TECHNOLOGY AND USING IT TO TERRORIZE--
BY USING THE EQUATION AGAINST THE MACHINE ITSELF.
WHAT IN...?

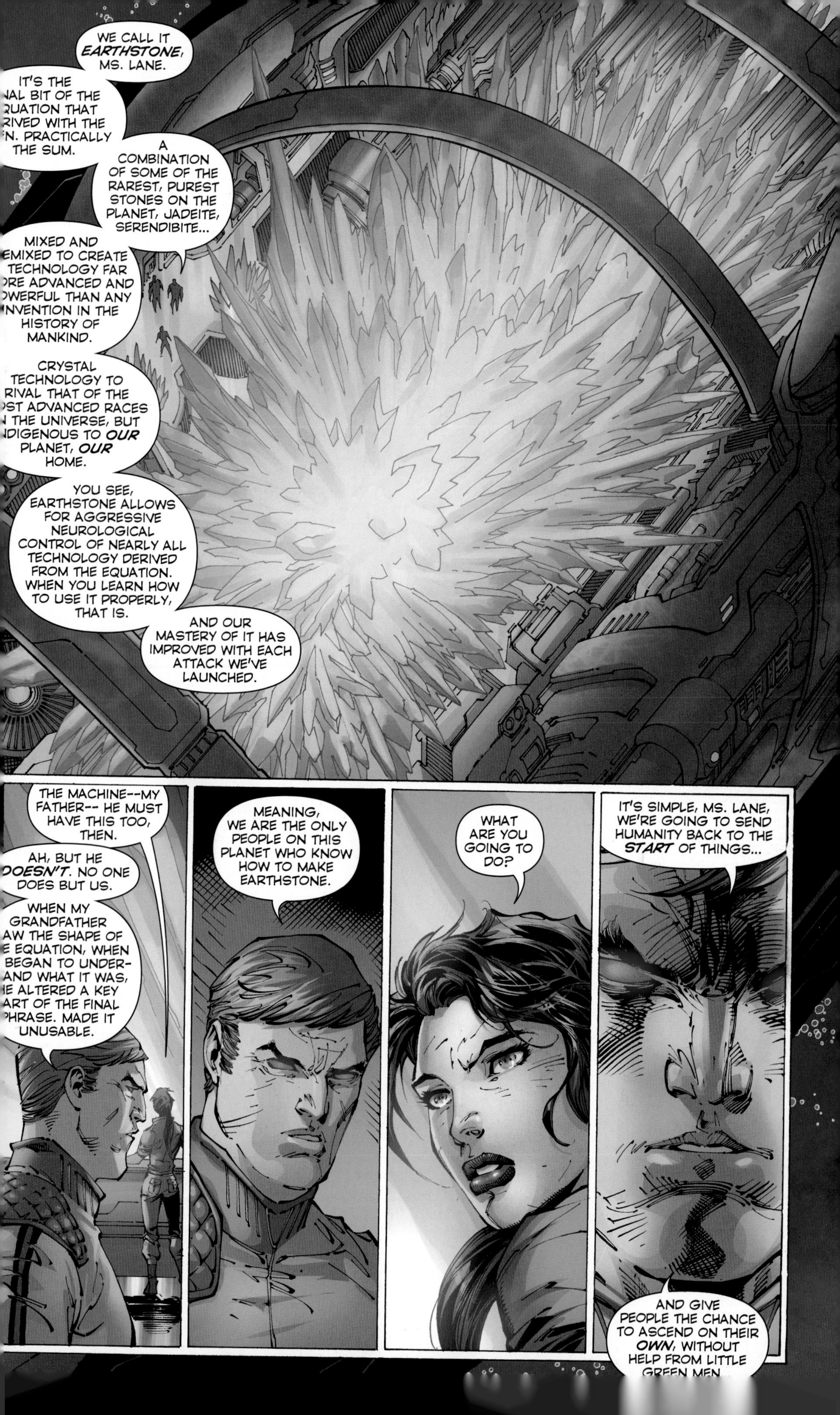
WE CALL IT *EARTHSTONE*, MS. LANE.
IT'S THE NAL BIT OF THE QUATION THAT RIVED WITH THE N. PRACTICALLY THE SUM.
A COMBINATION OF SOME OF THE RAREST, PUREST STONES ON THE PLANET, JADEITE, SERENDIBITE...
MIXED AND EMIXED TO CREATE TECHNOLOGY FAR ORE ADVANCED AND OWERFUL THAN ANY NVENTION IN THE HISTORY OF MANKIND.
CRYSTAL TECHNOLOGY TO RIVAL THAT OF THE OST ADVANCED RACES N THE UNIVERSE, BUT NDIGENOUS TO *OUR* PLANET, *OUR* HOME.
YOU SEE, EARTHSTONE ALLOWS FOR AGGRESSIVE NEUROLOGICAL CONTROL OF NEARLY ALL TECHNOLOGY DERIVED FROM THE EQUATION. WHEN YOU LEARN HOW TO USE IT PROPERLY, THAT IS.
AND OUR MASTERY OF IT HAS IMPROVED WITH EACH ATTACK WE'VE LAUNCHED.
THE MACHINE--MY FATHER-- HE MUST HAVE THIS TOO, THEN.
AH, BUT HE *DOESN'T*. NO ONE DOES BUT US.
WHEN MY GRANDFATHER AW THE SHAPE OF E EQUATION, WHEN BEGAN TO UNDER-AND WHAT IT WAS, IE ALTERED A KEY ART OF THE FINAL PHRASE. MADE IT UNUSABLE.
MEANING, WE ARE THE ONLY PEOPLE ON THIS PLANET WHO KNOW HOW TO MAKE EARTHSTONE.
WHAT ARE YOU GOING TO DO?
IT'S SIMPLE, MS. LANE, WE'RE GOING TO SEND HUMANITY BACK TO THE *START* OF THINGS...
AND GIVE PEOPLE THE CHANCE TO ASCEND ON THEIR *OWN*, WITHOUT HELP FROM LITTLE

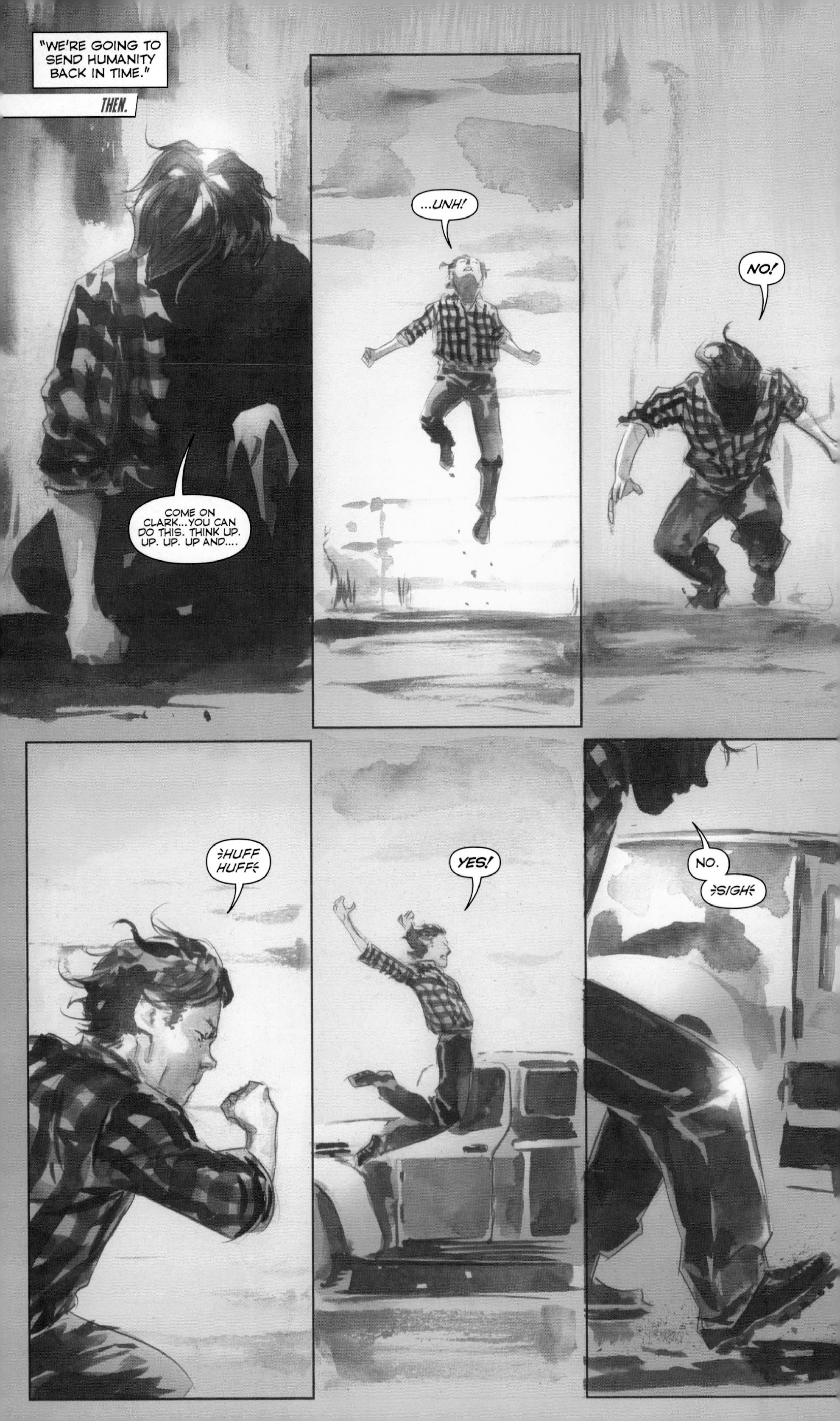
"WE'RE GOING TO SEND HUMANITY BACK IN TIME."
THEN.
COME ON CLARK...YOU CAN DO THIS. THINK UP. UP. UP. UP AND....
...UNH!
NO!
HUFF HUFF
YES!
NO.
SIGH

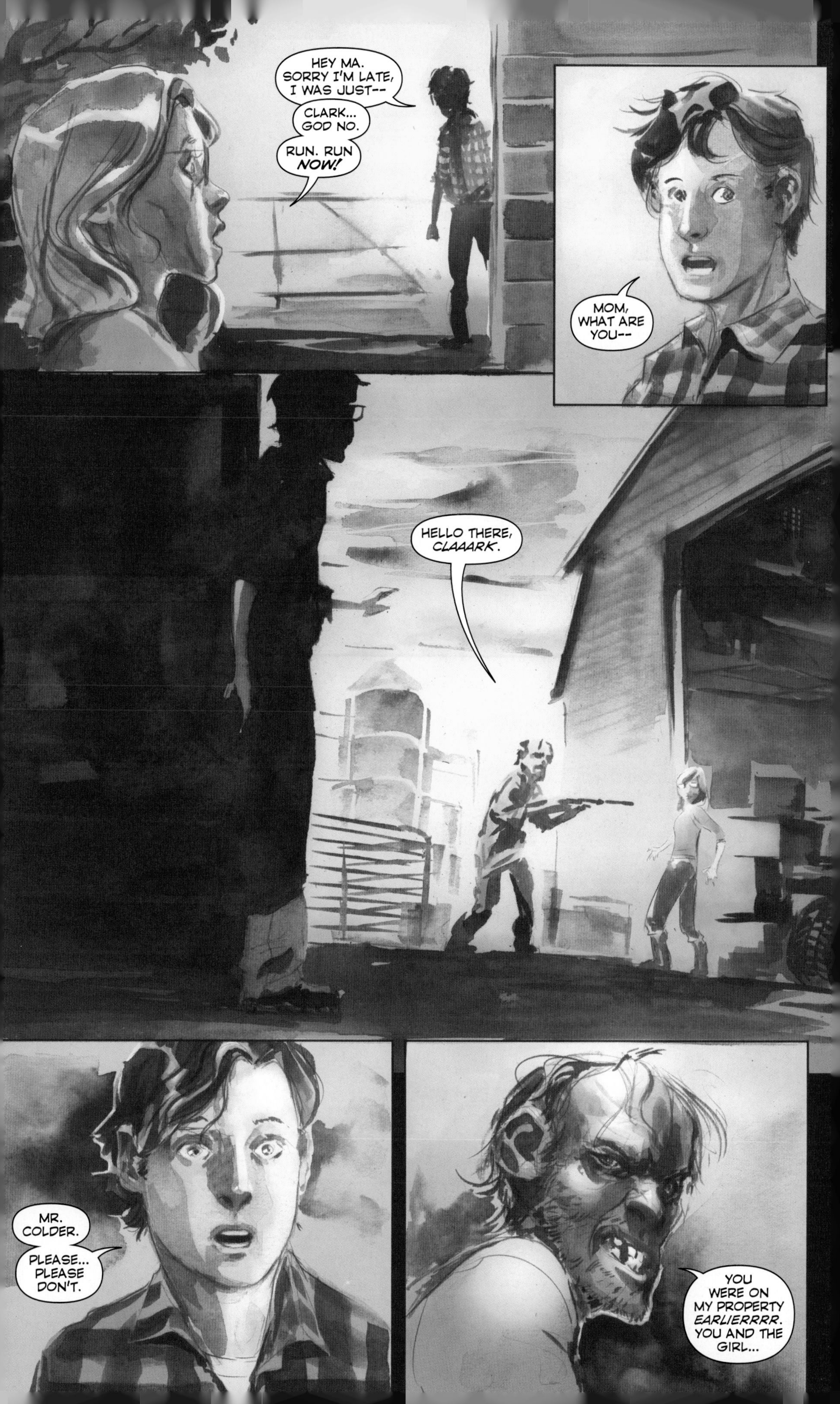
HEY MA. SORRY I'M LATE, I WAS JUST--
CLARK... GOD NO.
RUN. RUN *NOW!*
MOM, WHAT ARE YOU--
HELLO THERE, *CLAAARK*.
MR. COLDER.
PLEASE... PLEASE DON'T.
YOU WERE ON MY PROPERTY *EARLIERRRR*. YOU AND THE GIRL...

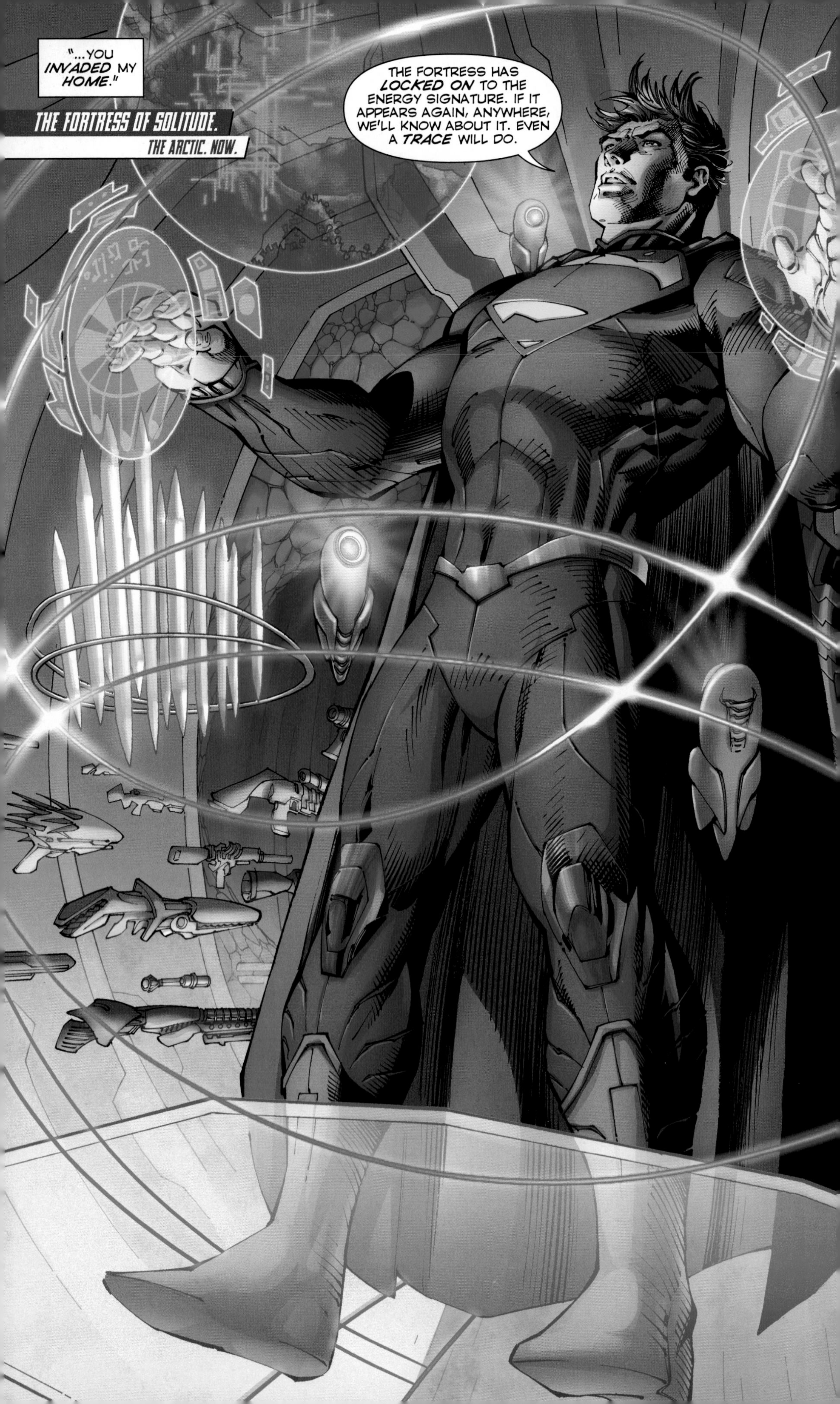
"...YOU INVADED MY HOME."
THE FORTRESS OF SOLITUDE.
THE ARCTIC. NOW.
THE FORTRESS HAS LOCKED ON TO THE ENERGY SIGNATURE. IF IT APPEARS AGAIN, ANYWHERE, WE'LL KNOW ABOUT IT. EVEN A TRACE WILL DO.

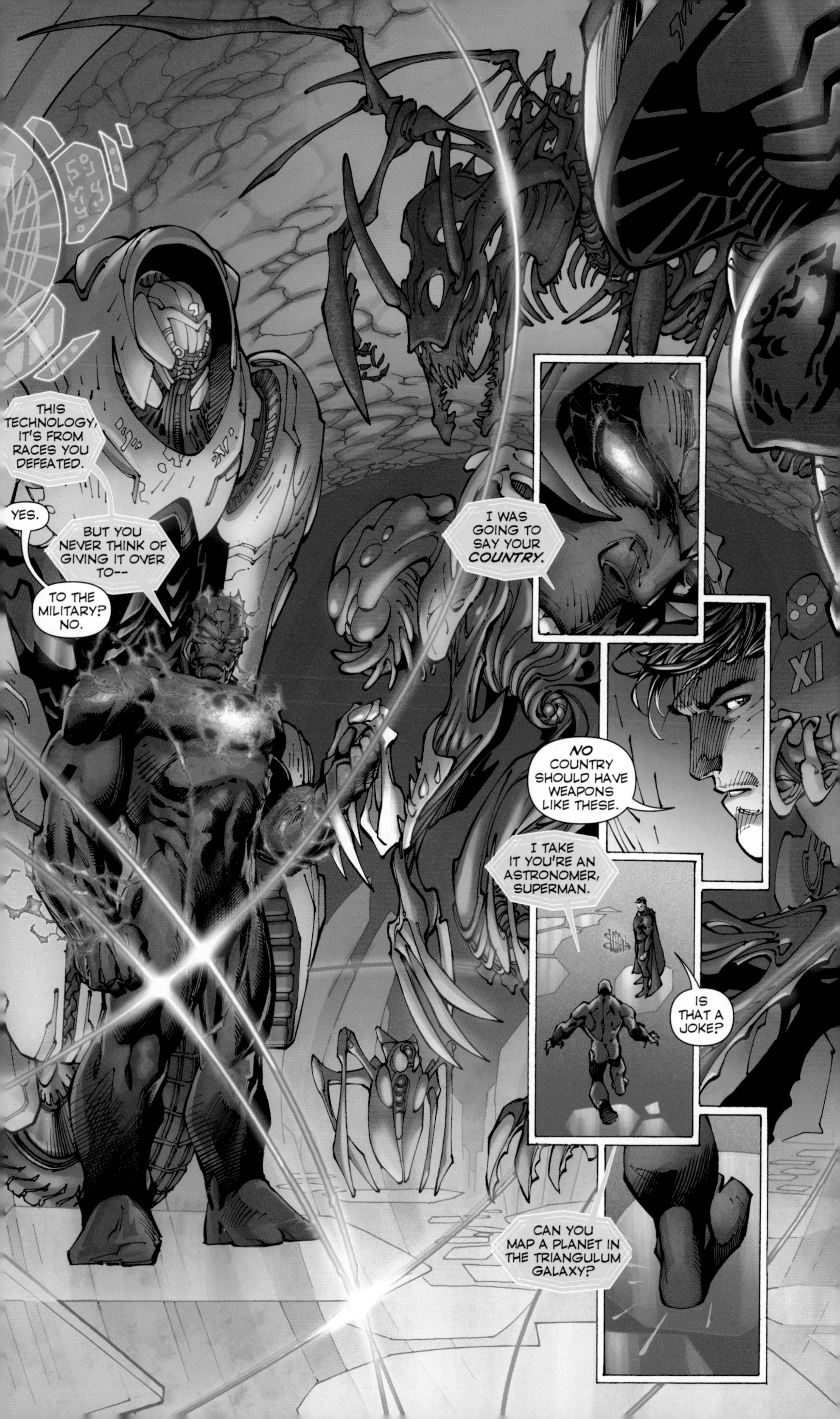
THIS TECHNOLOGY, IT'S FROM RACES YOU DEFEATED.
YES.
BUT YOU NEVER THINK OF GIVING IT OVER TO--
TO THE MILITARY? NO.
I WAS GOING TO SAY YOUR COUNTRY.
NO COUNTRY SHOULD HAVE WEAPONS LIKE THESE.
I TAKE IT YOU'RE AN ASTRONOMER, SUPERMAN.
IS THAT A JOKE?
CAN YOU MAP A PLANET IN THE TRIANGULUM GALAXY?

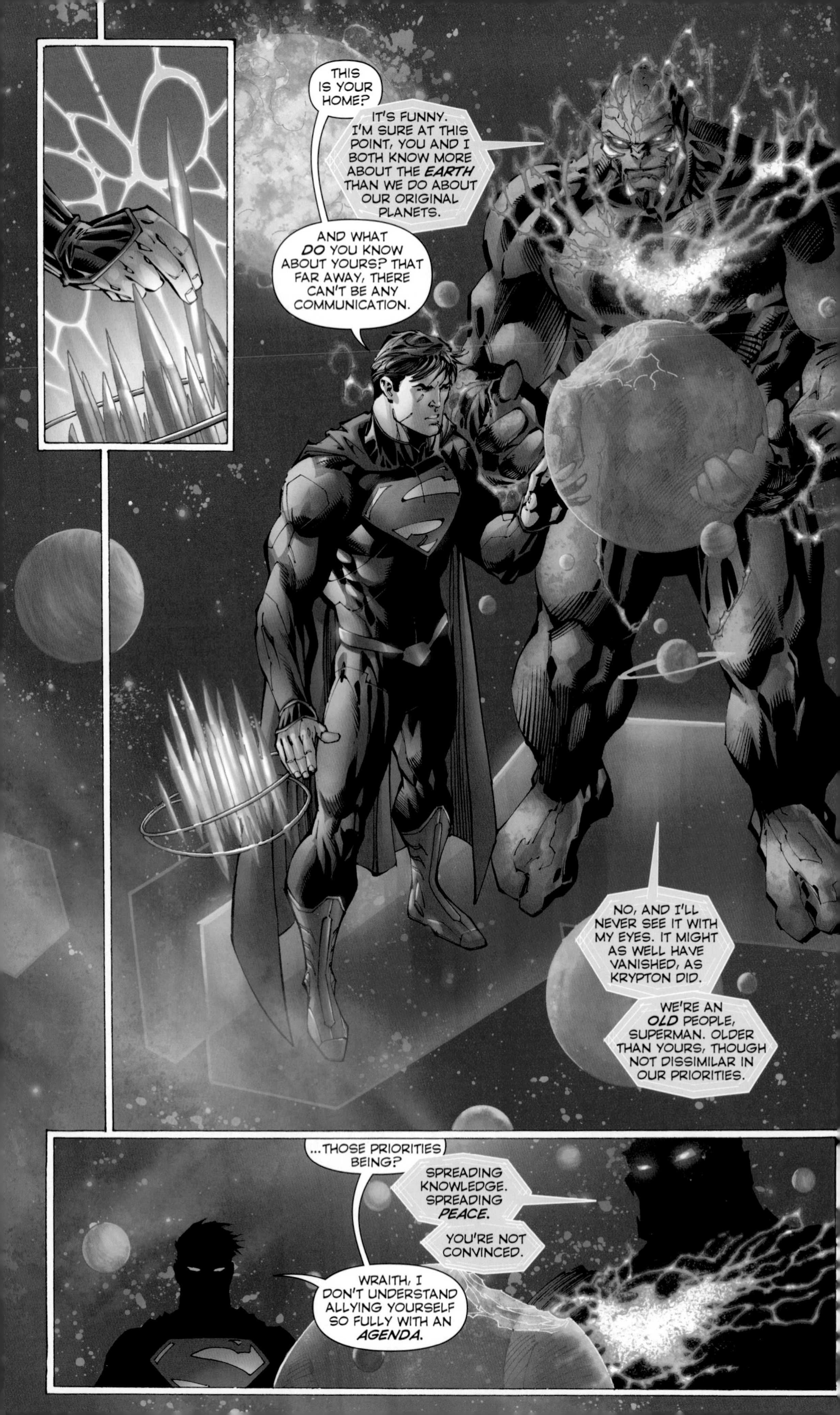
THIS IS YOUR HOME?
IT'S FUNNY. I'M SURE AT THIS POINT, YOU AND I BOTH KNOW MORE ABOUT THE EARTH THAN WE DO ABOUT OUR ORIGINAL PLANETS.
AND WHAT DO YOU KNOW ABOUT YOURS? THAT FAR AWAY, THERE CAN'T BE ANY COMMUNICATION.
NO, AND I'LL NEVER SEE IT WITH MY EYES. IT MIGHT AS WELL HAVE VANISHED, AS KRYPTON DID.
WE'RE AN OLD PEOPLE, SUPERMAN. OLDER THAN YOURS, THOUGH NOT DISSIMILAR IN OUR PRIORITIES.
...THOSE PRIORITIES BEING?
SPREADING KNOWLEDGE. SPREADING PEACE.
YOU'RE NOT CONVINCED.
WRAITH, I DON'T UNDERSTAND ALLYING YOURSELF SO FULLY WITH AN AGENDA.

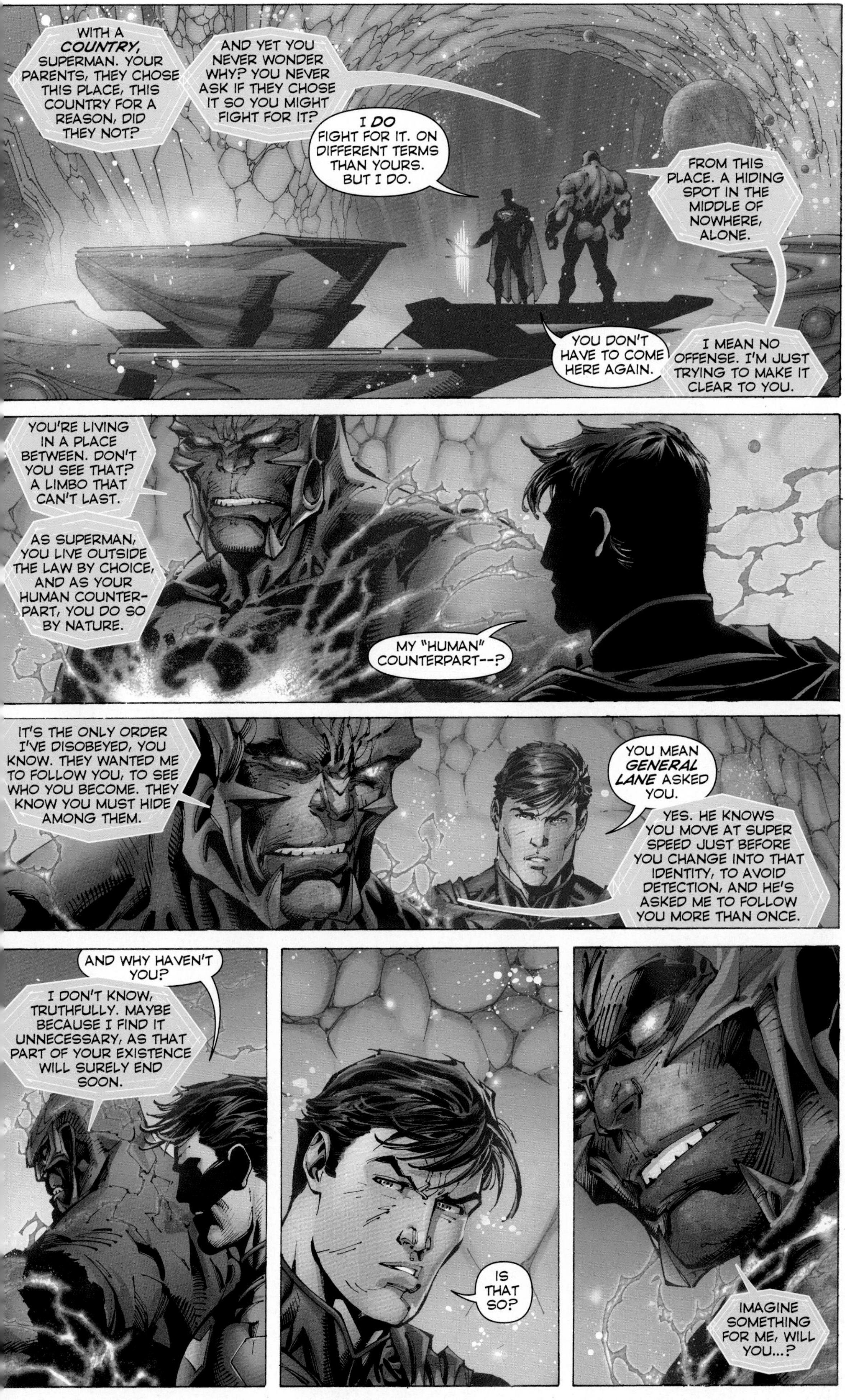
WITH A COUNTRY, SUPERMAN. YOUR PARENTS, THEY CHOSE THIS PLACE, THIS COUNTRY FOR A REASON, DID THEY NOT?
AND YET YOU NEVER WONDER WHY? YOU NEVER ASK IF THEY CHOSE IT SO YOU MIGHT FIGHT FOR IT?
I DO FIGHT FOR IT. ON DIFFERENT TERMS THAN YOURS. BUT I DO.
FROM THIS PLACE. A HIDING SPOT IN THE MIDDLE OF NOWHERE, ALONE.
YOU DON'T HAVE TO COME HERE AGAIN.
I MEAN NO OFFENSE. I'M JUST TRYING TO MAKE IT CLEAR TO YOU.
YOU'RE LIVING IN A PLACE BETWEEN. DON'T YOU SEE THAT? A LIMBO THAT CAN'T LAST.
AS SUPERMAN, YOU LIVE OUTSIDE THE LAW BY CHOICE, AND AS YOUR HUMAN COUNTER-PART, YOU DO SO BY NATURE.
MY "HUMAN" COUNTERPART--?
IT'S THE ONLY ORDER I'VE DISOBEYED, YOU KNOW. THEY WANTED ME TO FOLLOW YOU, TO SEE WHO YOU BECOME. THEY KNOW YOU MUST HIDE AMONG THEM.
YOU MEAN GENERAL LANE ASKED YOU.
YES. HE KNOWS YOU MOVE AT SUPER SPEED JUST BEFORE YOU CHANGE INTO THAT IDENTITY, TO AVOID DETECTION, AND HE'S ASKED ME TO FOLLOW YOU MORE THAN ONCE.
AND WHY HAVEN'T YOU?
I DON'T KNOW, TRUTHFULLY. MAYBE BECAUSE I FIND IT UNNECESSARY, AS THAT PART OF YOUR EXISTENCE WILL SURELY END SOON.
IS THAT SO?
IMAGINE SOMETHING FOR ME, WILL YOU...?

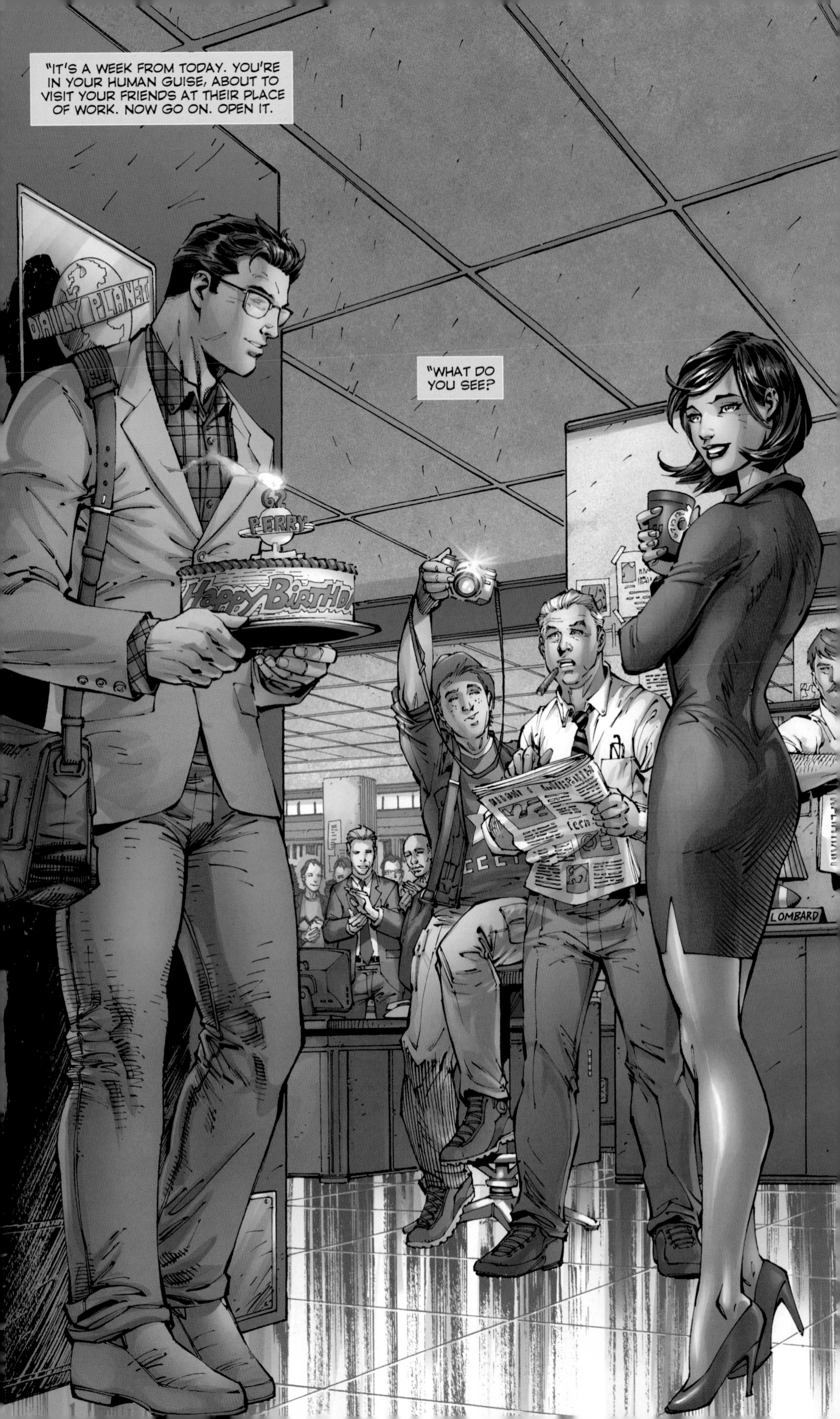
"IT'S A WEEK FROM TODAY. YOU'RE IN YOUR HUMAN GUISE, ABOUT TO VISIT YOUR FRIENDS AT THEIR PLACE OF WORK. NOW GO ON. OPEN IT.
"WHAT DO YOU SEE?
DAILY PLANET
62
PERRY
HAPPY BIRTHD
LOMBARD

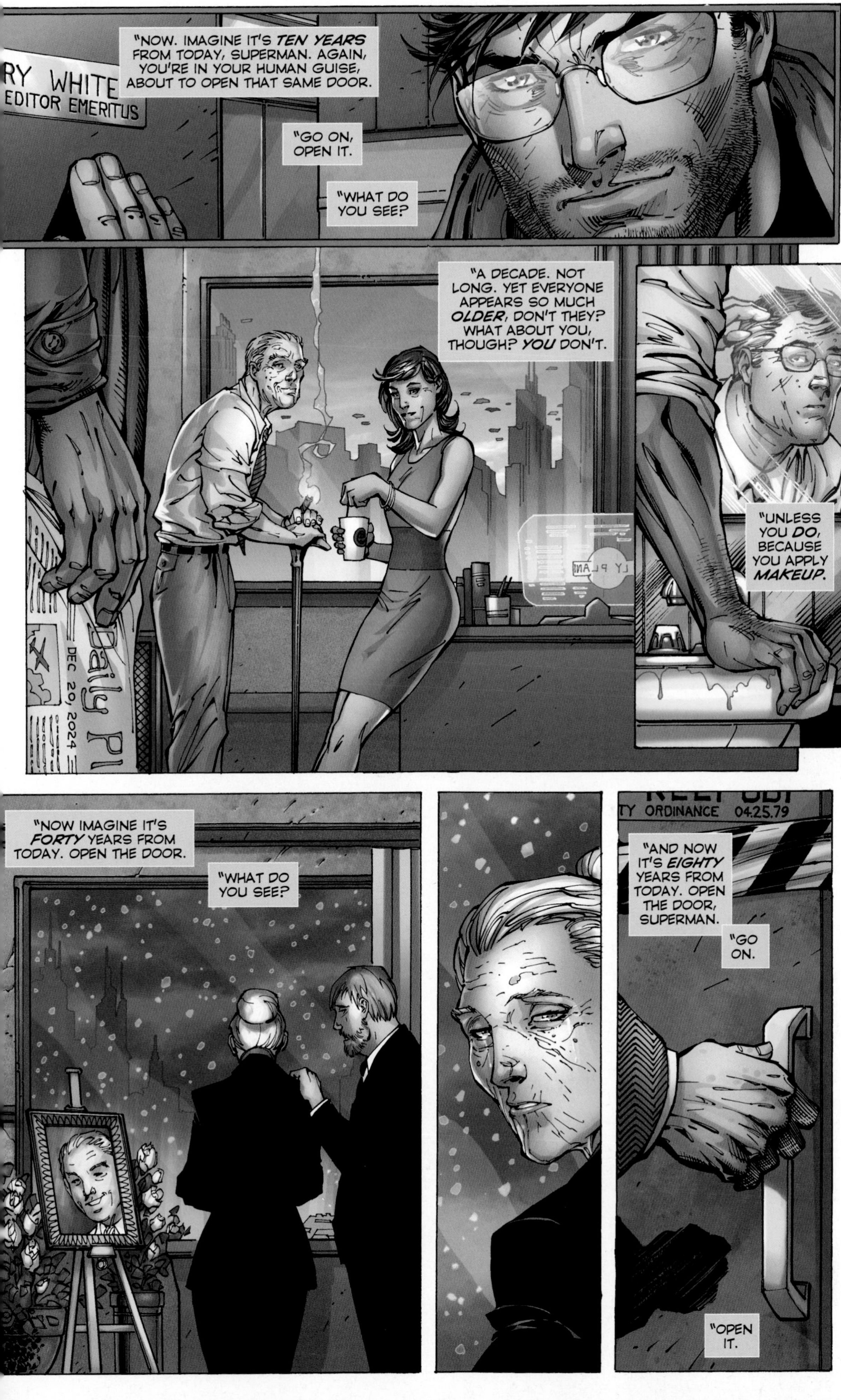

RY WHITE
EDITOR EMERITUS
"NOW. IMAGINE IT'S TEN YEARS FROM TODAY, SUPERMAN. AGAIN, YOU'RE IN YOUR HUMAN GUISE, ABOUT TO OPEN THAT SAME DOOR.
"GO ON, OPEN IT.
"WHAT DO YOU SEE?
"A DECADE. NOT LONG. YET EVERYONE APPEARS SO MUCH OLDER, DON'T THEY? WHAT ABOUT YOU, THOUGH? YOU DON'T.
"UNLESS YOU DO, BECAUSE YOU APPLY MAKEUP.
Daily Pl
DEC 20, 2024
"NOW IMAGINE IT'S FORTY YEARS FROM TODAY. OPEN THE DOOR.
"WHAT DO YOU SEE?
TY ORDINANCE 04.25.79
"AND NOW IT'S EIGHTY YEARS FROM TODAY. OPEN THE DOOR, SUPERMAN.
"GO ON.
"OPEN IT.

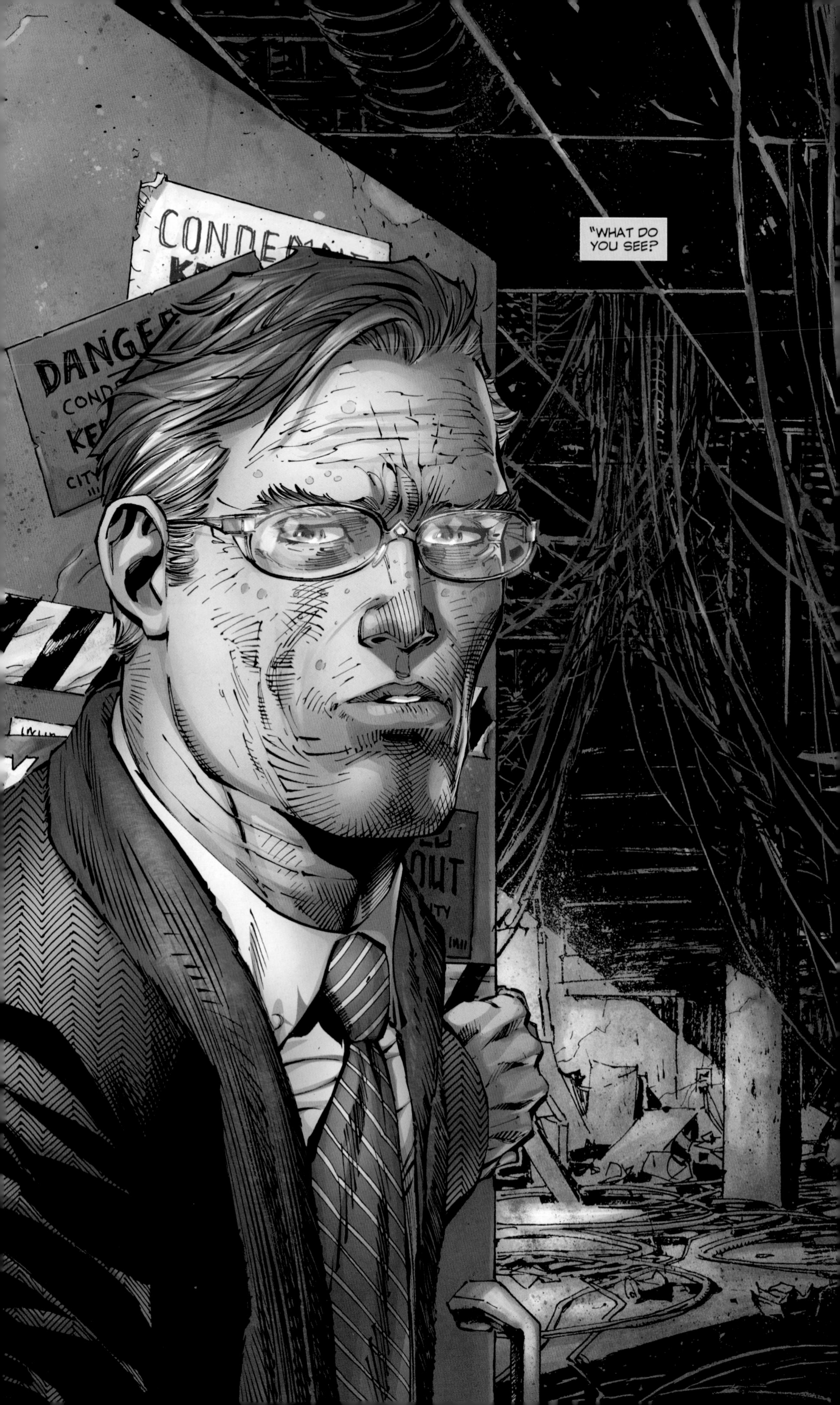
"WHAT DO YOU SEE?

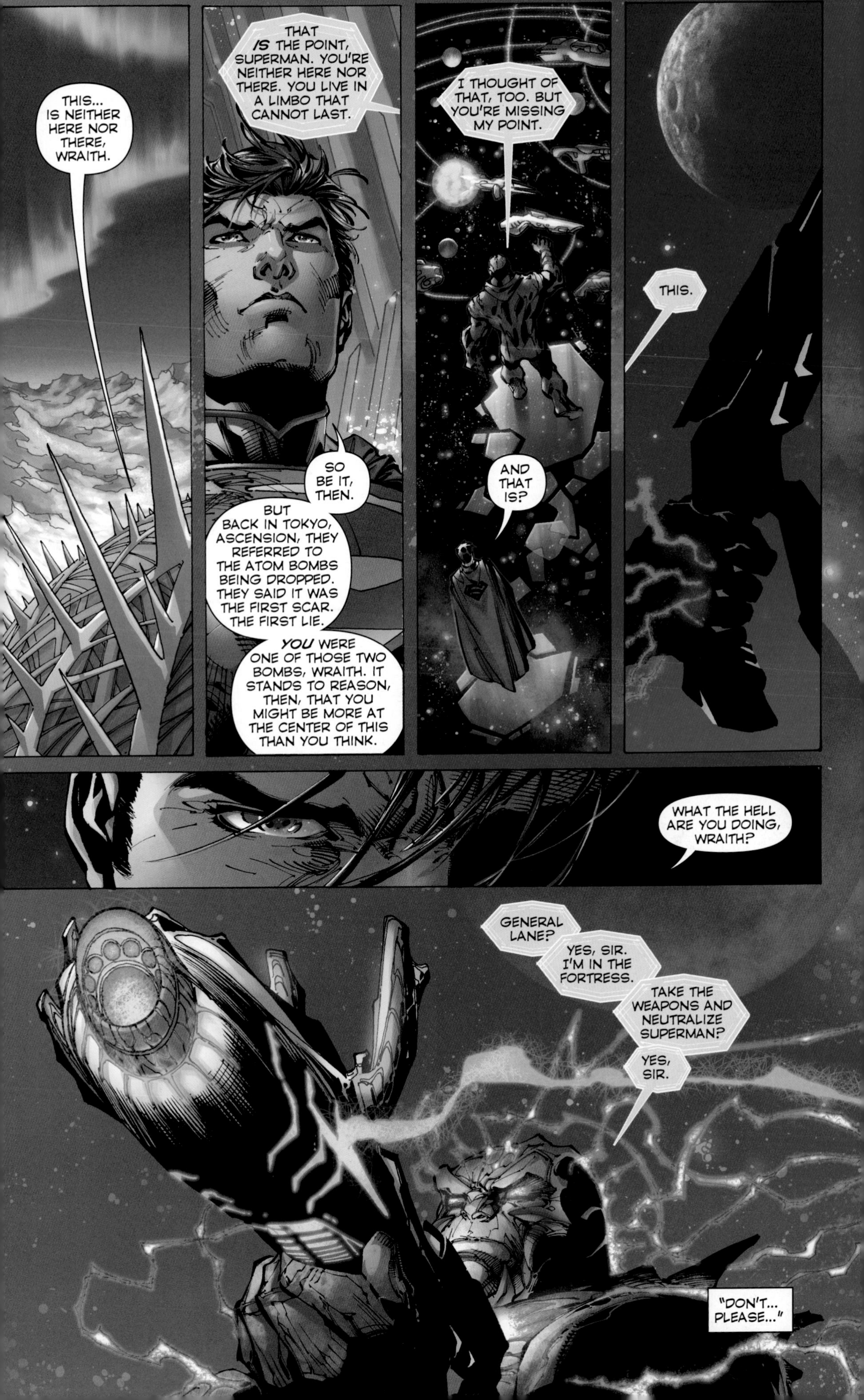
THIS... IS NEITHER HERE NOR THERE, WRAITH.
THAT *IS* THE POINT, SUPERMAN. YOU'RE NEITHER HERE NOR THERE. YOU LIVE IN A LIMBO THAT CANNOT LAST.
SO BE IT, THEN.
BUT BACK IN TOKYO, ASCENSION, THEY REFERRED TO THE ATOM BOMBS BEING DROPPED. THEY SAID IT WAS THE FIRST SCAR. THE FIRST LIE.
YOU WERE ONE OF THOSE TWO BOMBS, WRAITH. IT STANDS TO REASON, THEN, THAT YOU MIGHT BE MORE AT THE CENTER OF THIS THAN YOU THINK.
I THOUGHT OF THAT, TOO. BUT YOU'RE MISSING MY POINT.
AND THAT IS?
THIS.
WHAT THE HELL ARE YOU DOING, WRAITH?
GENERAL LANE?
YES, SIR. I'M IN THE FORTRESS.
TAKE THE WEAPONS AND NEUTRALIZE SUPERMAN?
YES, SIR.
"DON'T... PLEASE..."

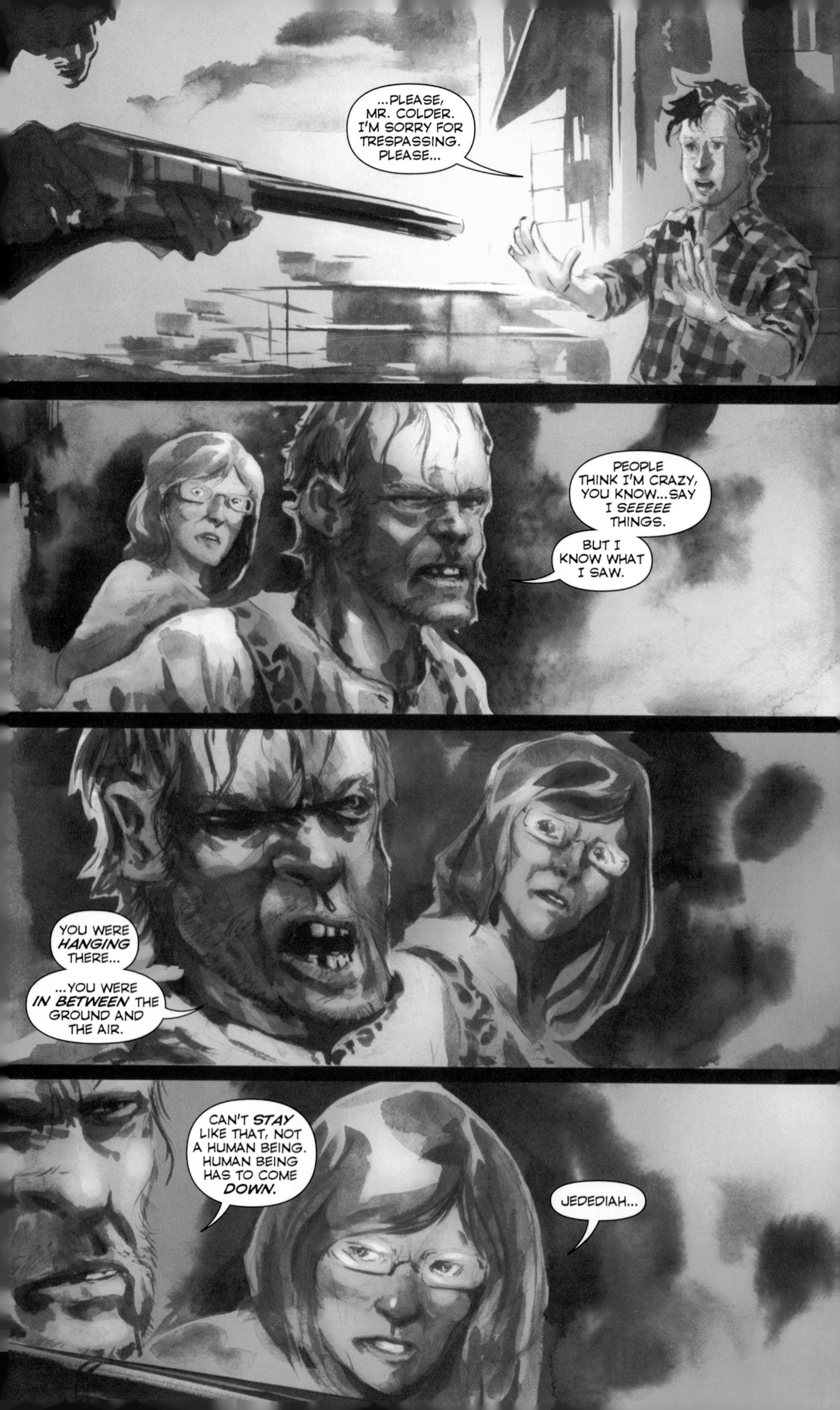
...PLEASE, MR. COLDER. I'M SORRY FOR TRESPASSING. PLEASE...
PEOPLE THINK I'M CRAZY, YOU KNOW...SAY I *SEEEEE* THINGS.
BUT I KNOW WHAT I SAW.
YOU WERE ***HANGING*** THERE...
...YOU WERE ***IN BETWEEN*** THE GROUND AND THE AIR.
CAN'T ***STAY*** LIKE THAT, NOT A HUMAN BEING. HUMAN BEING HAS TO COME ***DOWN.***
JEDEDIAH...

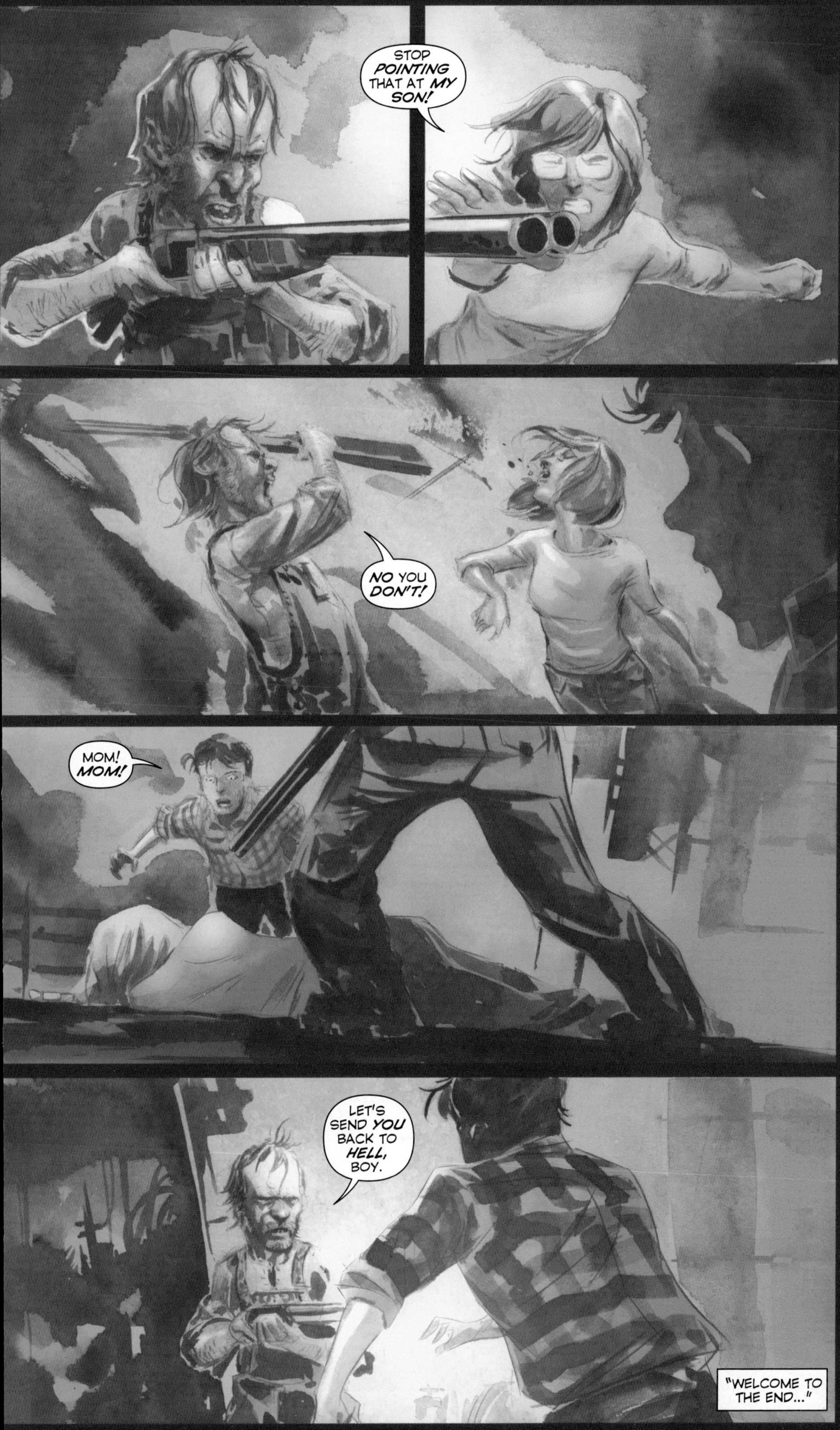
STOP POINTING THAT AT MY SON!
NO YOU DON'T!
MOM! MOM!
LET'S SEND YOU BACK TO HELL, BOY.
"WELCOME TO THE END..."

...OR SHOULD I SAY THE *START*. THE START OF THE *NEW* AGE. THE AGE OF *HUMAN* ACHIEVEMENT.

YOU'RE CRAZY.

HA. THAT MAY BE. BUT IT'S ONLY BECAUSE I SEE THE TRUTH, AND THAT TRUTH IS BLINDING.

SOON THE *WORLD* WILL BE BLINDED BY IT.

UNH!

GRAB HER! SHE'S GOT THE BAG!

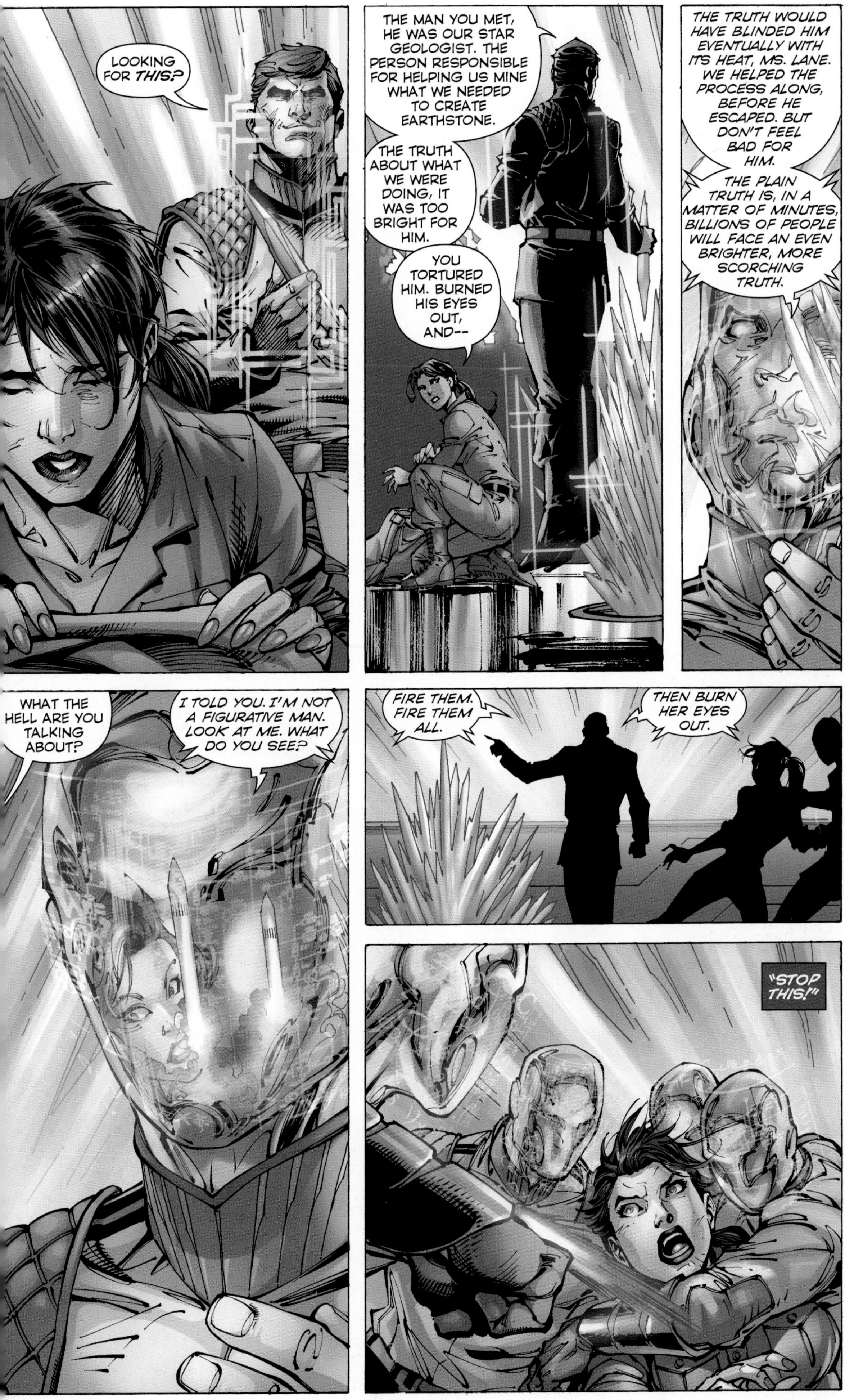
LOOKING FOR THIS?
THE MAN YOU MET, HE WAS OUR STAR GEOLOGIST. THE PERSON RESPONSIBLE FOR HELPING US MINE WHAT WE NEEDED TO CREATE EARTHSTONE.
THE TRUTH ABOUT WHAT WE WERE DOING, IT WAS TOO BRIGHT FOR HIM.
YOU TORTURED HIM. BURNED HIS EYES OUT, AND--
THE TRUTH WOULD HAVE BLINDED HIM EVENTUALLY WITH ITS HEAT, MS. LANE. WE HELPED THE PROCESS ALONG, BEFORE HE ESCAPED. BUT DON'T FEEL BAD FOR HIM.
THE PLAIN TRUTH IS, IN A MATTER OF MINUTES, BILLIONS OF PEOPLE WILL FACE AN EVEN BRIGHTER, MORE SCORCHING TRUTH.
WHAT THE HELL ARE YOU TALKING ABOUT?
I TOLD YOU. I'M NOT A FIGURATIVE MAN. LOOK AT ME. WHAT DO YOU SEE?
FIRE THEM. FIRE THEM ALL.
THEN BURN HER EYES OUT.
"STOP THIS!"

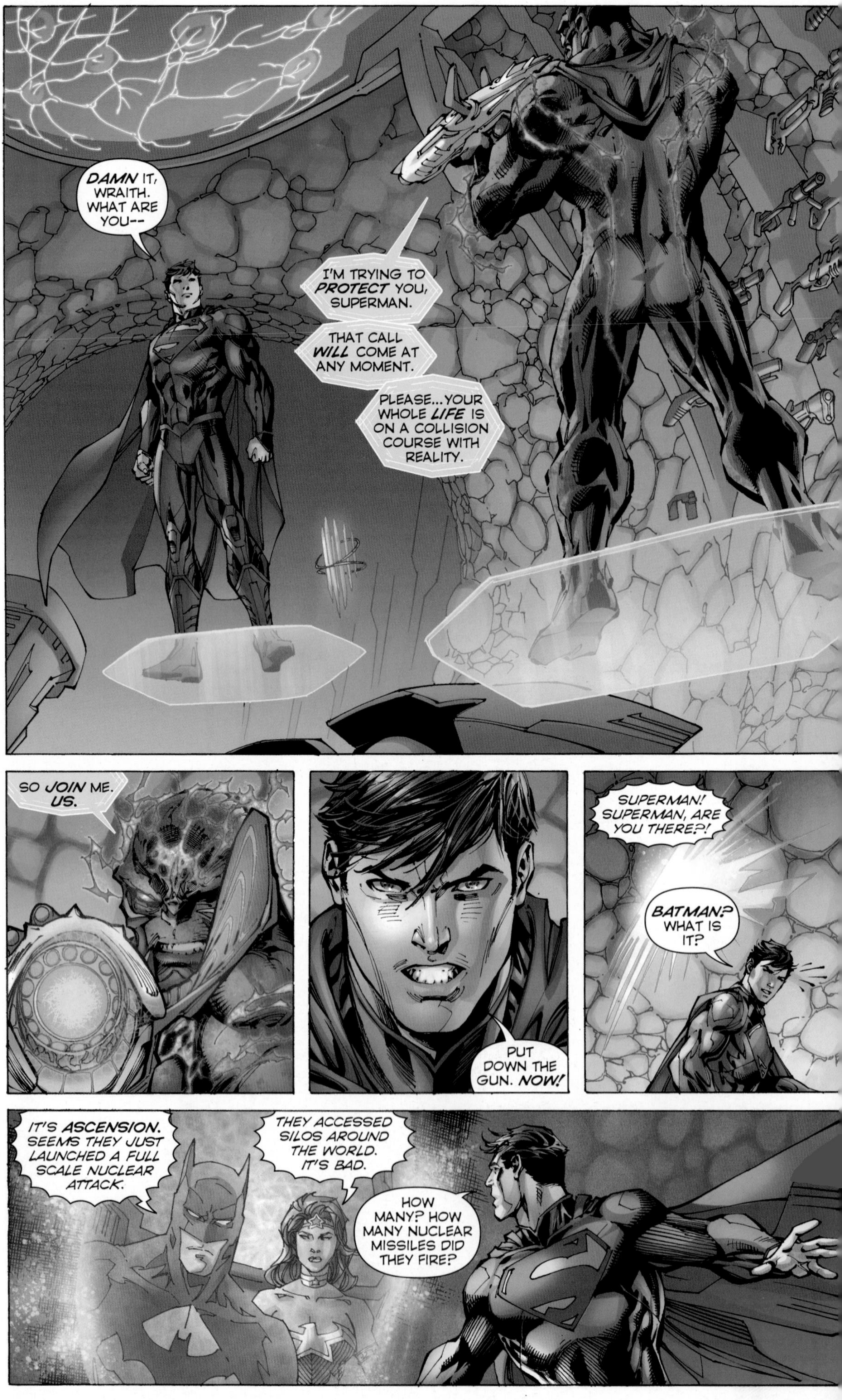
DAMN IT, WRAITH. WHAT ARE YOU--
I'M TRYING TO PROTECT YOU, SUPERMAN.
THAT CALL WILL COME AT ANY MOMENT.
PLEASE...YOUR WHOLE LIFE IS ON A COLLISION COURSE WITH REALITY.
SO JOIN ME. US.
PUT DOWN THE GUN. NOW!
SUPERMAN! SUPERMAN, ARE YOU THERE?!
BATMAN? WHAT IS IT?
IT'S ASCENSION. SEEMS THEY JUST LAUNCHED A FULL SCALE NUCLEAR ATTACK.
THEY ACCESSED SILOS AROUND THE WORLD. IT'S BAD.
HOW MANY? HOW MANY NUCLEAR MISSILES DID THEY FIRE?

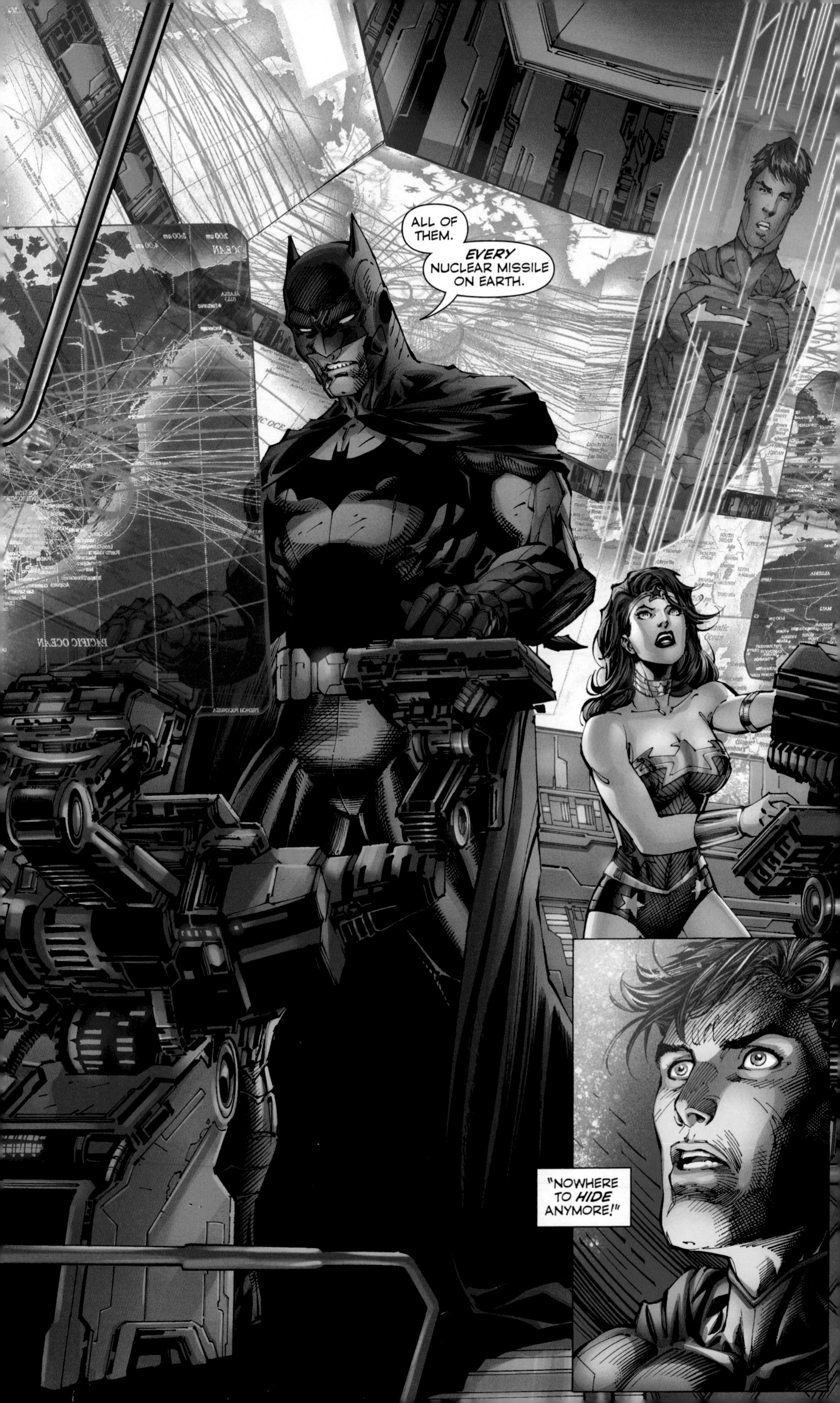
ALL OF THEM. EVERY NUCLEAR MISSILE ON EARTH.
"NOWHERE TO HIDE ANYMORE!"

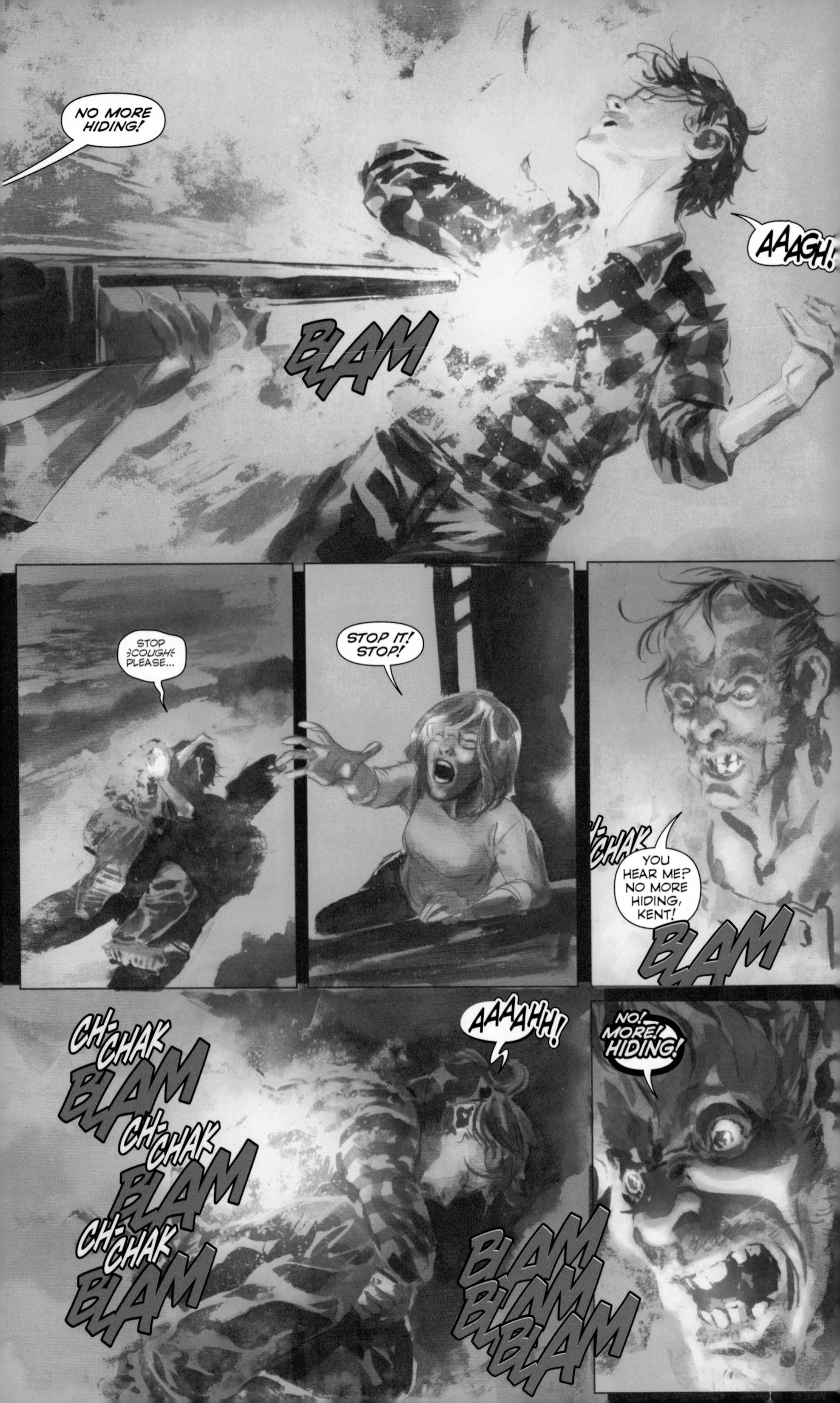

NO MORE HIDING!
AAAGH!
BLAM
STOP ⸗COUGH⸗ PLEASE...
STOP IT! STOP!
CH-CHAK
YOU HEAR ME? NO MORE HIDING, KENT!
BLAM
CH-CHAK
BLAM
CH-CHAK
BLAM
CH-CHAK
BLAM
AAAAHH!
BLAM
BLAM
BLAM
NO! MORE! HIDING!

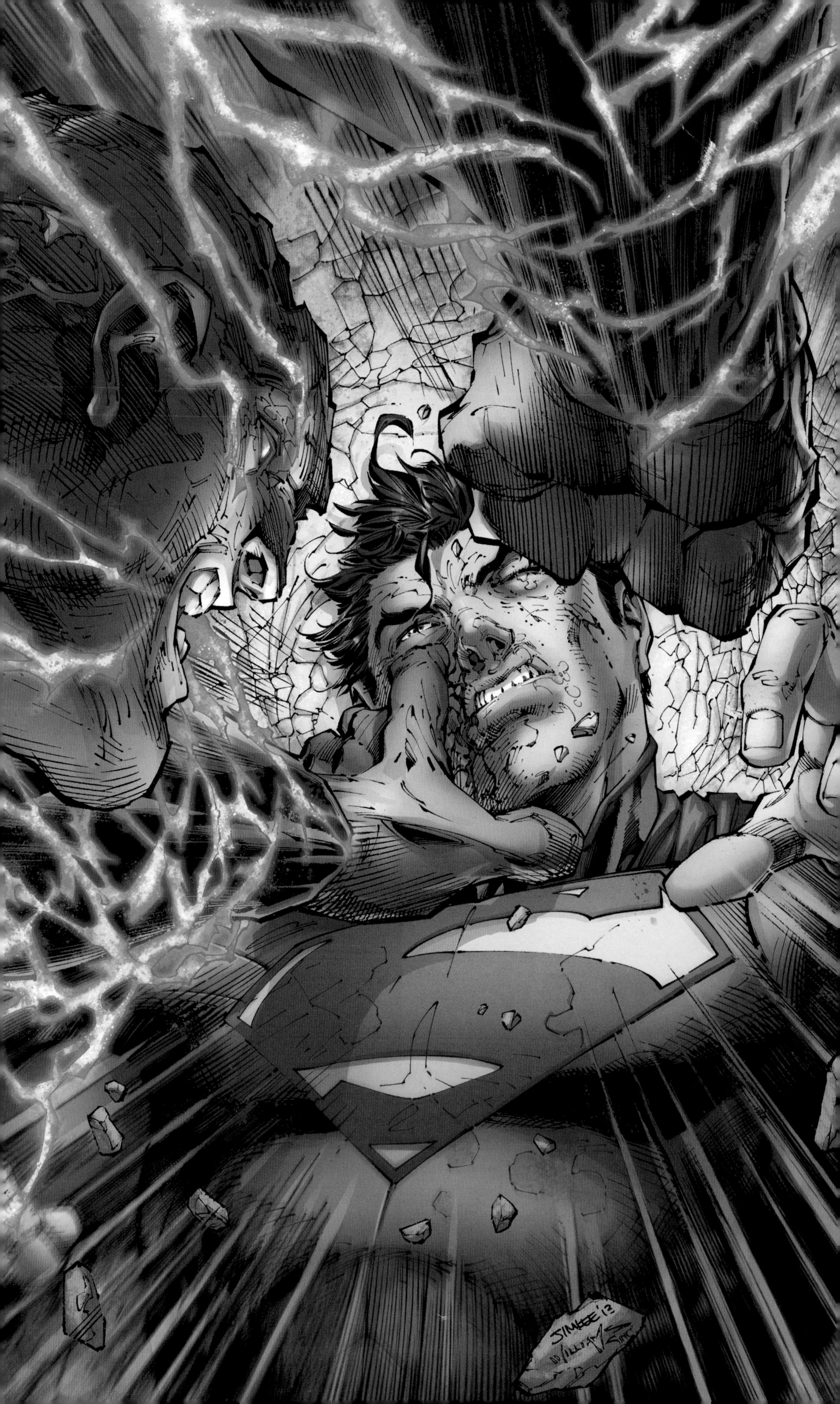

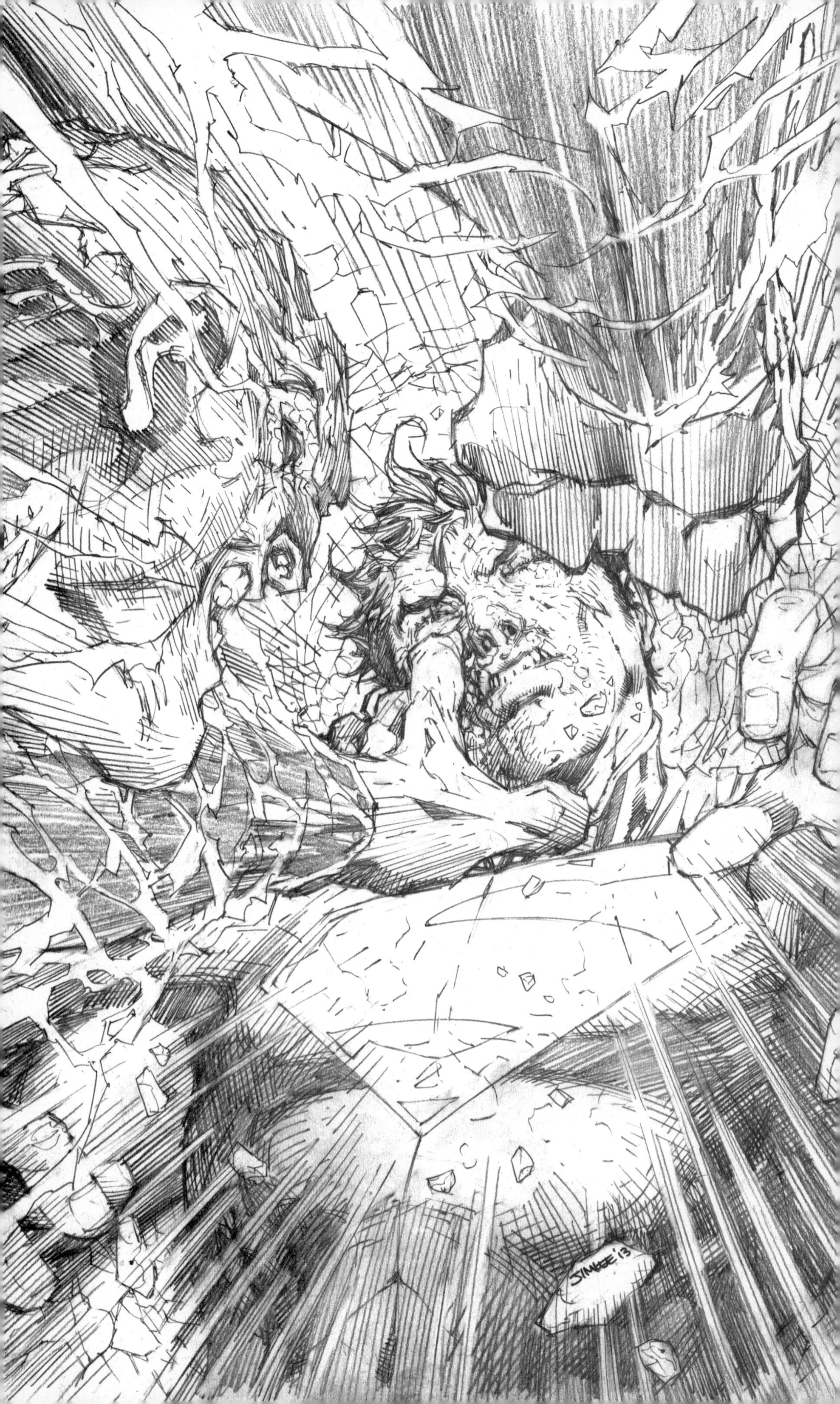

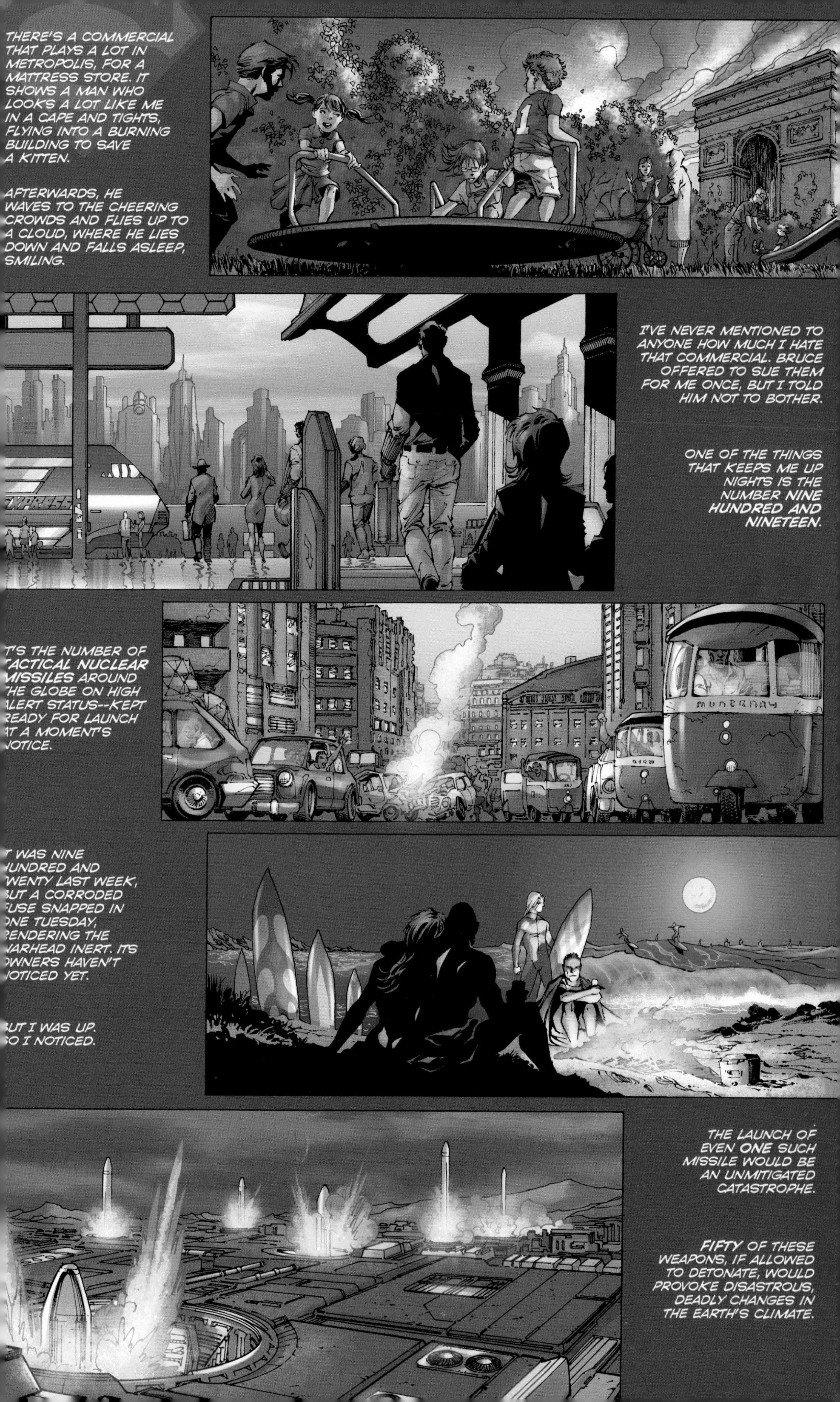
THERE'S A COMMERCIAL THAT PLAYS A LOT IN METROPOLIS, FOR A MATTRESS STORE. IT SHOWS A MAN WHO LOOKS A LOT LIKE ME IN A CAPE AND TIGHTS, FLYING INTO A BURNING BUILDING TO SAVE A KITTEN.
AFTERWARDS, HE WAVES TO THE CHEERING CROWDS AND FLIES UP TO A CLOUD, WHERE HE LIES DOWN AND FALLS ASLEEP, SMILING.
I'VE NEVER MENTIONED TO ANYONE HOW MUCH I HATE THAT COMMERCIAL. BRUCE OFFERED TO SUE THEM FOR ME ONCE, BUT I TOLD HIM NOT TO BOTHER.
ONE OF THE THINGS THAT KEEPS ME UP NIGHTS IS THE NUMBER NINE HUNDRED AND NINETEEN.
T'S THE NUMBER OF TACTICAL NUCLEAR MISSILES AROUND THE GLOBE ON HIGH ALERT STATUS--KEPT READY FOR LAUNCH AT A MOMENT'S NOTICE.
T WAS NINE HUNDRED AND WENTY LAST WEEK, BUT A CORRODED FUSE SNAPPED IN ONE TUESDAY, RENDERING THE WARHEAD INERT. ITS OWNERS HAVEN'T NOTICED YET.
UT I WAS UP. O I NOTICED.
THE LAUNCH OF EVEN ONE SUCH MISSILE WOULD BE AN UNMITIGATED CATASTROPHE.
FIFTY OF THESE WEAPONS, IF ALLOWED TO DETONATE, WOULD PROVOKE DISASTROUS, DEADLY CHANGES IN THE EARTH'S CLIMATE.

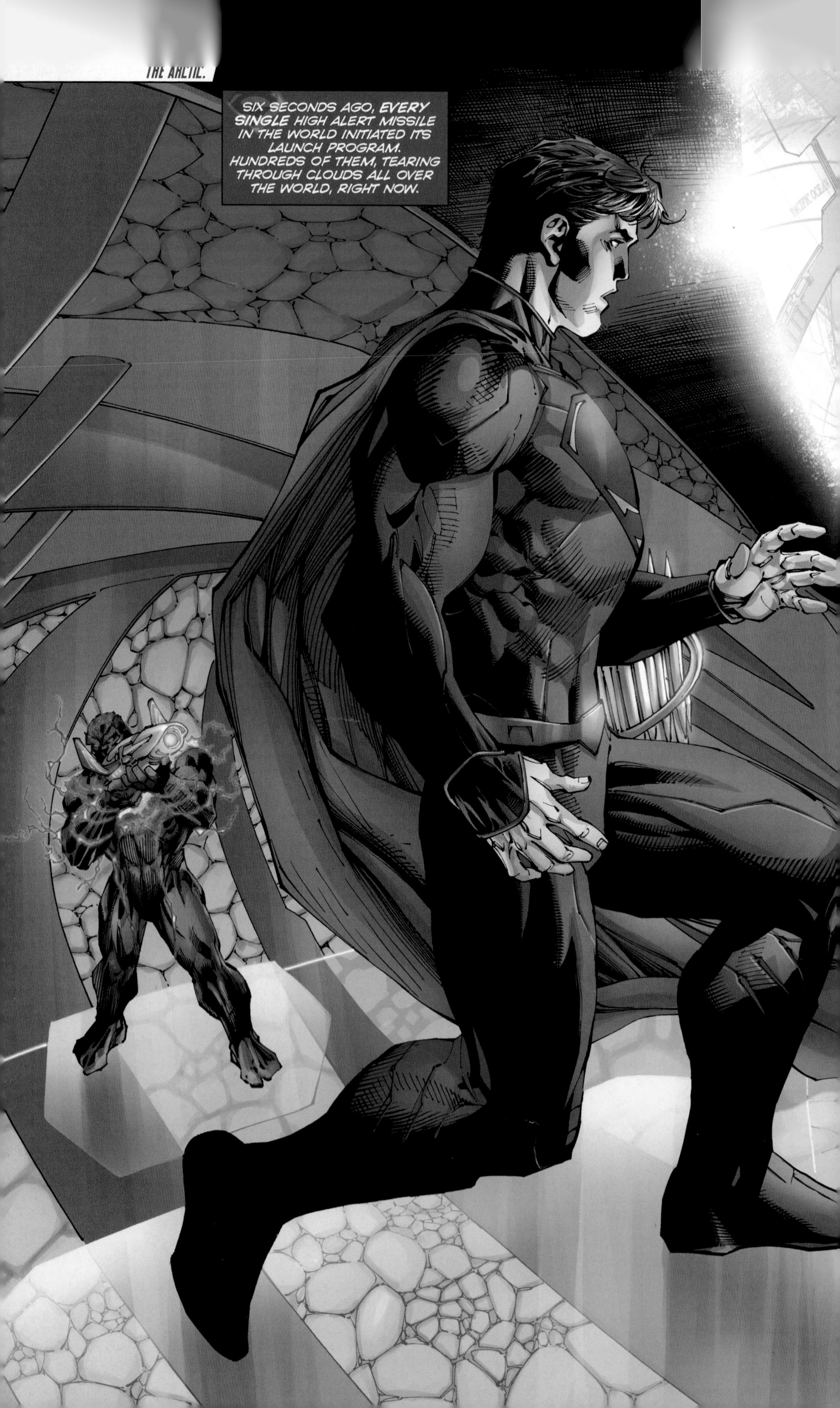
THE ARCTIC.
SIX SECONDS AGO, EVERY SINGLE HIGH ALERT MISSILE IN THE WORLD INITIATED ITS LAUNCH PROGRAM. HUNDREDS OF THEM, TEARING THROUGH CLOUDS ALL OVER THE WORLD, RIGHT NOW.

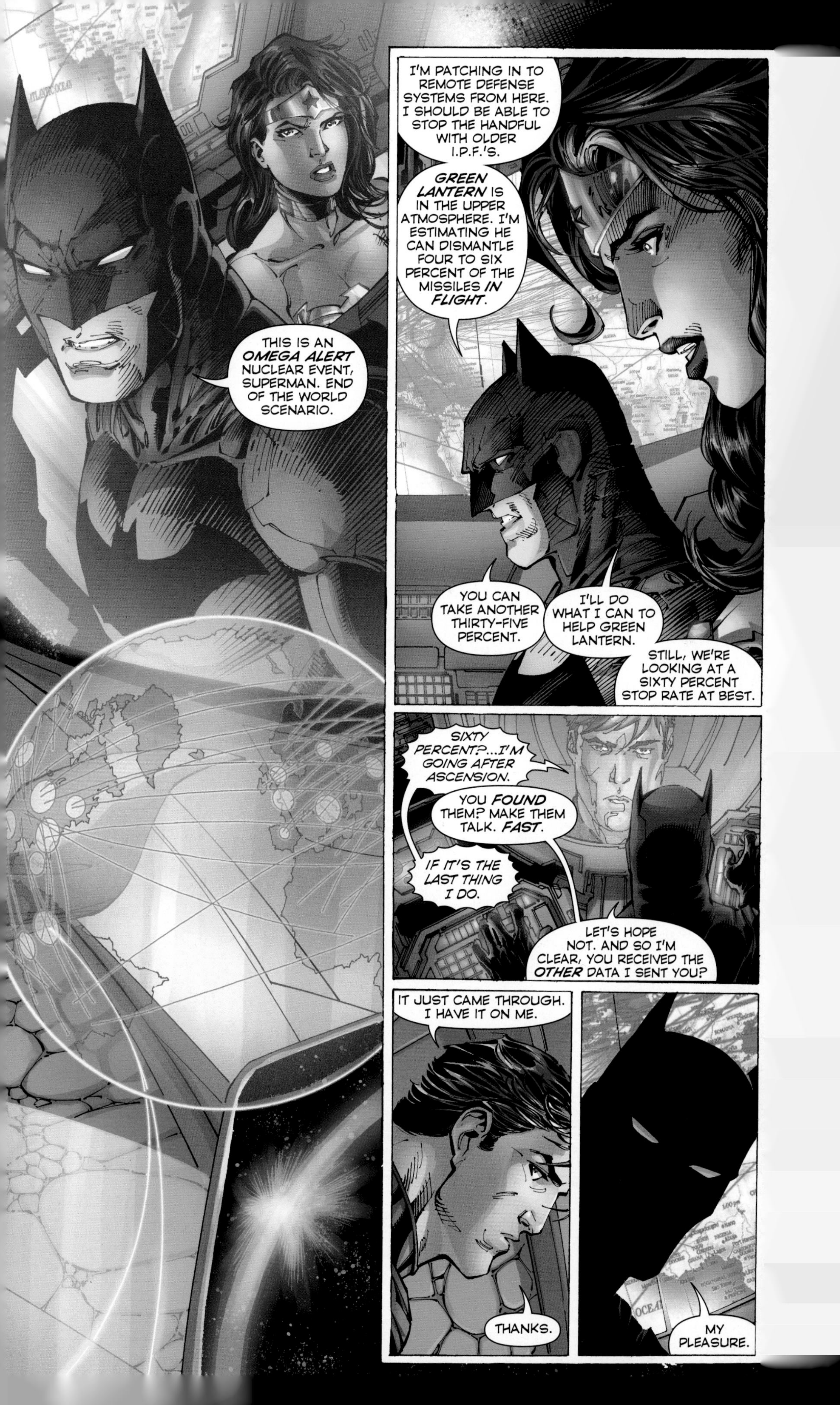
THIS IS AN OMEGA ALERT NUCLEAR EVENT, SUPERMAN. END OF THE WORLD SCENARIO.
I'M PATCHING IN TO REMOTE DEFENSE SYSTEMS FROM HERE. I SHOULD BE ABLE TO STOP THE HANDFUL WITH OLDER I.P.F.'S.
GREEN LANTERN IS IN THE UPPER ATMOSPHERE. I'M ESTIMATING HE CAN DISMANTLE FOUR TO SIX PERCENT OF THE MISSILES IN FLIGHT.
YOU CAN TAKE ANOTHER THIRTY-FIVE PERCENT.
I'LL DO WHAT I CAN TO HELP GREEN LANTERN.
STILL, WE'RE LOOKING AT A SIXTY PERCENT STOP RATE AT BEST.
SIXTY PERCENT?...I'M GOING AFTER ASCENSION.
YOU FOUND THEM? MAKE THEM TALK. FAST.
IF IT'S THE LAST THING I DO.
LET'S HOPE NOT. AND SO I'M CLEAR, YOU RECEIVED THE OTHER DATA I SENT YOU?
IT JUST CAME THROUGH. I HAVE IT ON ME.
THANKS.
MY PLEASURE.

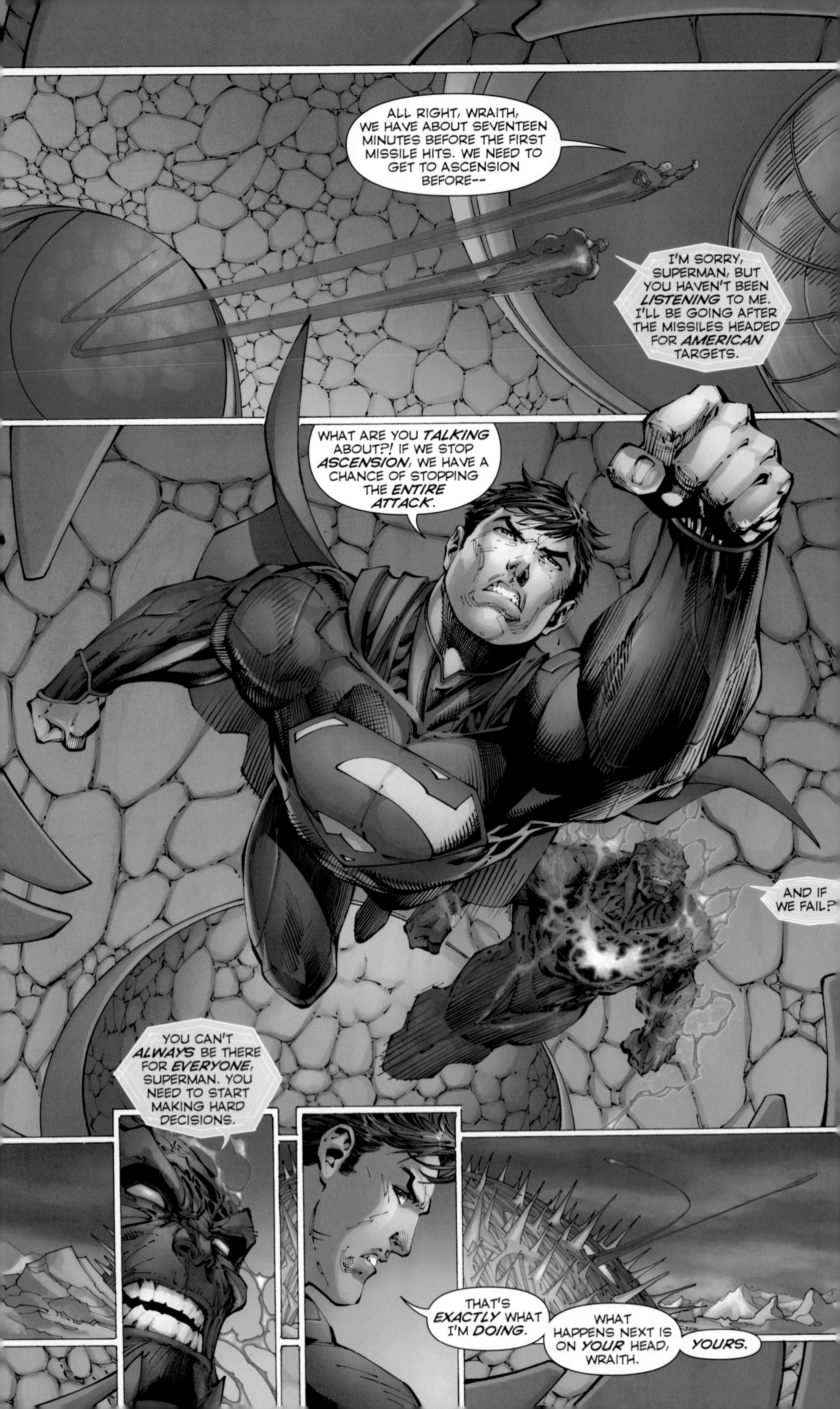
ALL RIGHT, WRAITH, WE HAVE ABOUT SEVENTEEN MINUTES BEFORE THE FIRST MISSILE HITS. WE NEED TO GET TO ASCENSION BEFORE--
I'M SORRY, SUPERMAN, BUT YOU HAVEN'T BEEN LISTENING TO ME. I'LL BE GOING AFTER THE MISSILES HEADED FOR AMERICAN TARGETS.
WHAT ARE YOU TALKING ABOUT?! IF WE STOP ASCENSION, WE HAVE A CHANCE OF STOPPING THE ENTIRE ATTACK.
AND IF WE FAIL?
YOU CAN'T ALWAYS BE THERE FOR EVERYONE, SUPERMAN. YOU NEED TO START MAKING HARD DECISIONS.
THAT'S EXACTLY WHAT I'M DOING.
WHAT HAPPENS NEXT IS ON YOUR HEAD, WRAITH.
YOURS.

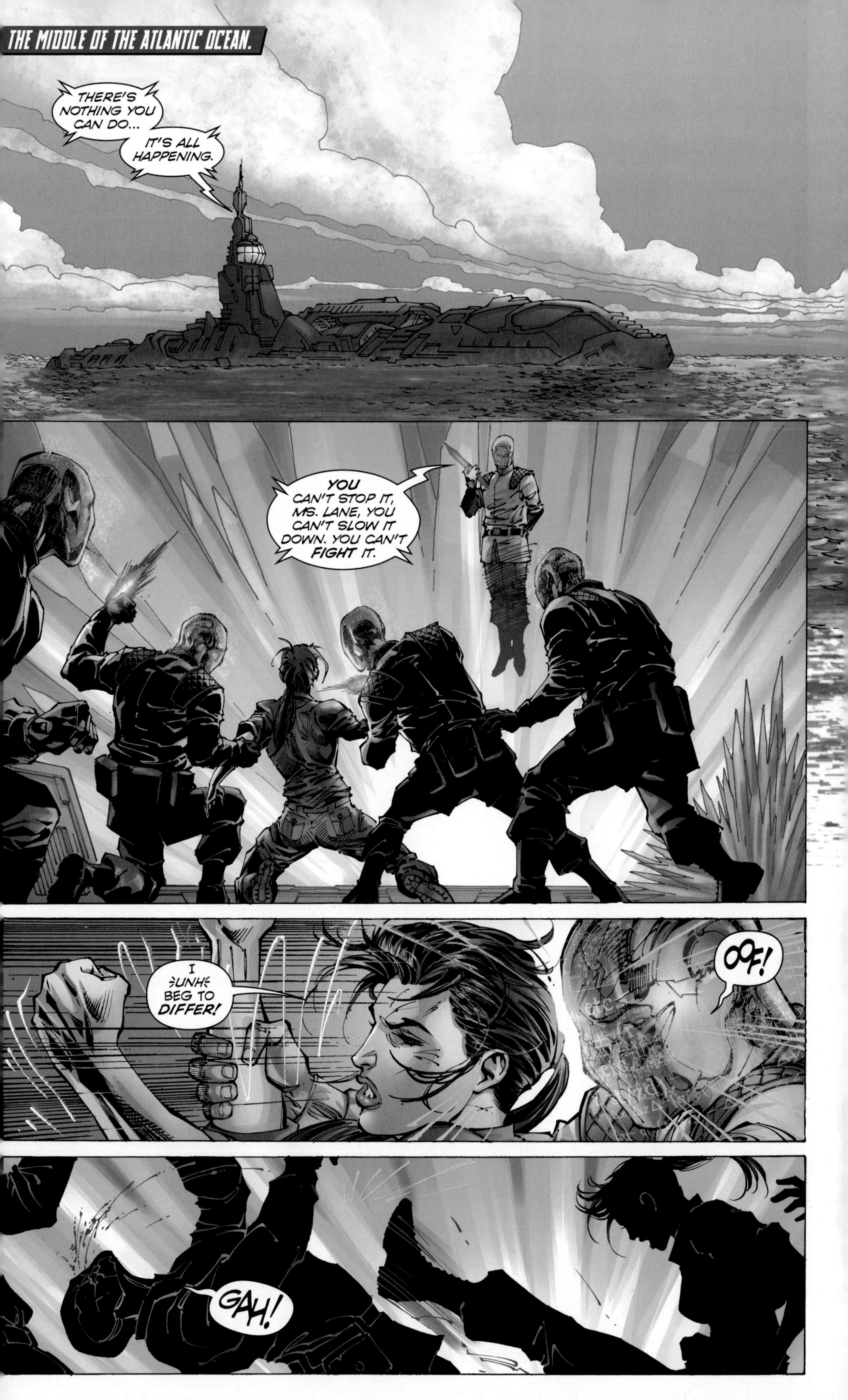
THE MIDDLE OF THE ATLANTIC OCEAN.
THERE'S NOTHING YOU CAN DO...
IT'S ALL HAPPENING.
YOU CAN'T STOP IT, MS. LANE, YOU CAN'T SLOW IT DOWN. YOU CAN'T FIGHT IT.
I UNH BEG TO DIFFER!
OOF!
GAH!

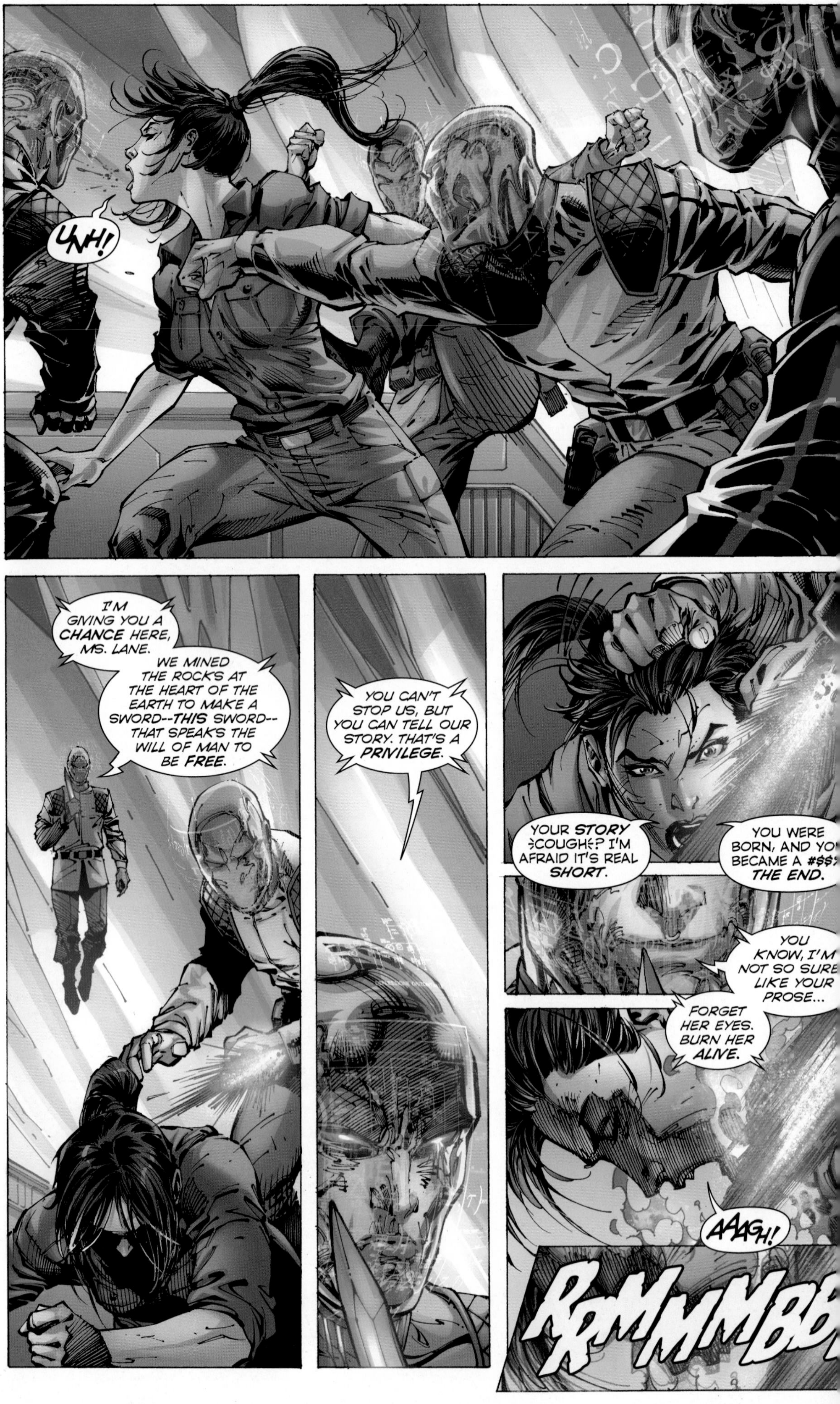
UNH!
I'M GIVING YOU A CHANCE HERE, MS. LANE.
WE MINED THE ROCKS AT THE HEART OF THE EARTH TO MAKE A SWORD--THIS SWORD--THAT SPEAKS THE WILL OF MAN TO BE FREE.
YOU CAN'T STOP US, BUT YOU CAN TELL OUR STORY. THAT'S A PRIVILEGE.
YOUR STORY ;COUGH;? I'M AFRAID IT'S REAL SHORT.
YOU WERE BORN, AND YO BECAME A #$$ THE END.
YOU KNOW, I'M NOT SO SURE LIKE YOUR PROSE...
FORGET HER EYES. BURN HER ALIVE.
AAAGH!
RRMMMBB

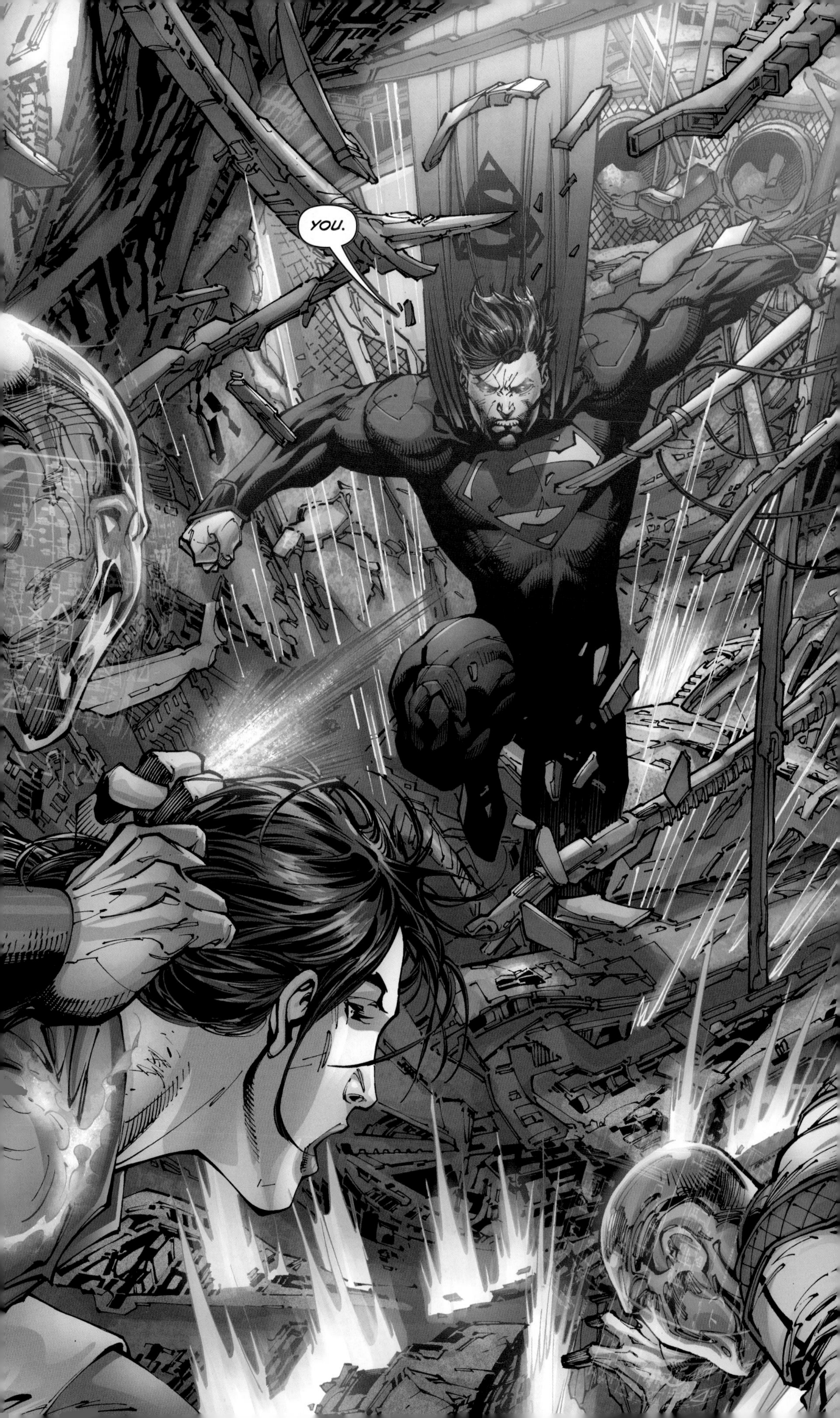
YOU.

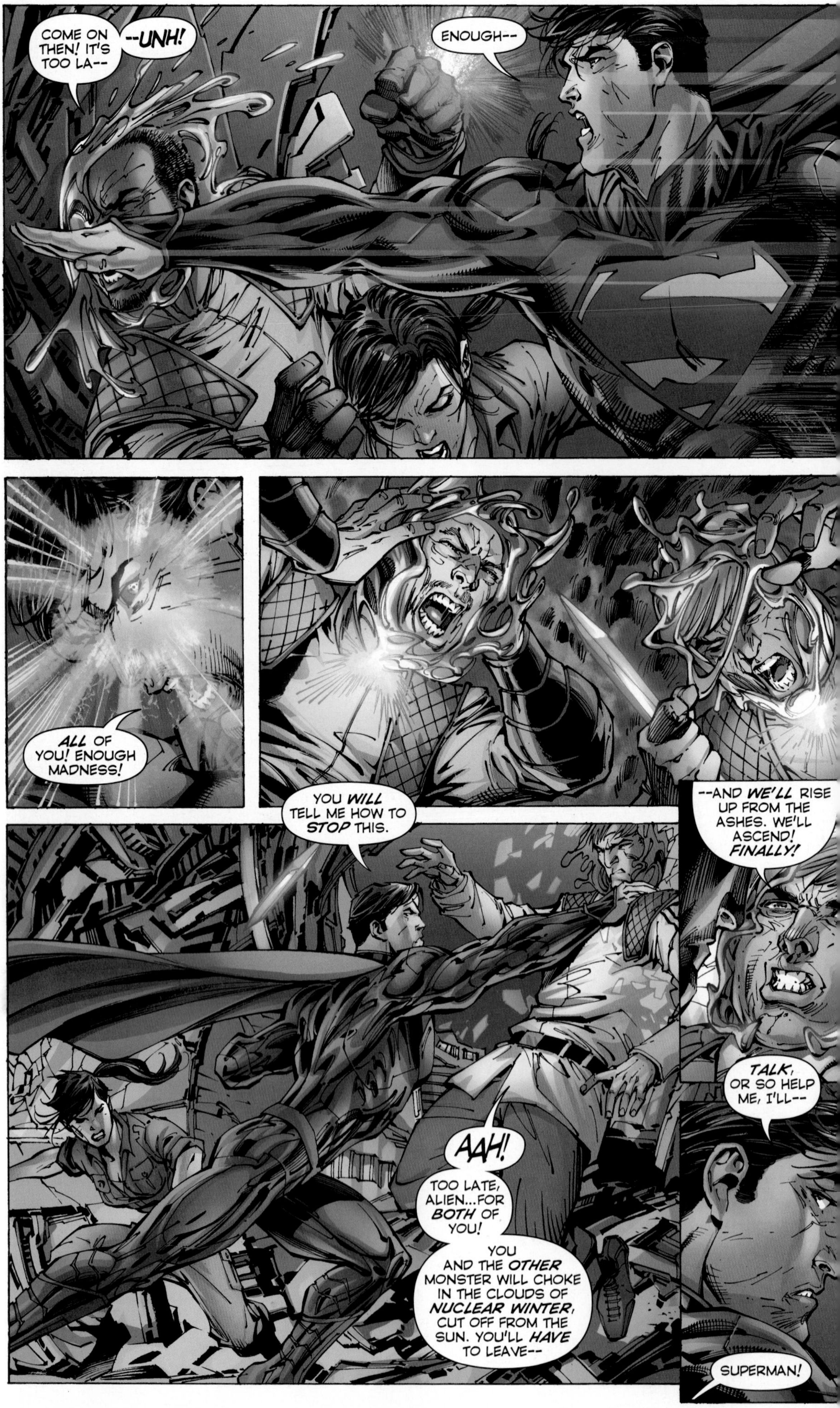

COME ON THEN! IT'S TOO LA--
--UNH!
ENOUGH--
ALL OF YOU! ENOUGH MADNESS!
YOU WILL TELL ME HOW TO STOP THIS.
AAH!
TOO LATE, ALIEN...FOR BOTH OF YOU!
YOU AND THE OTHER MONSTER WILL CHOKE IN THE CLOUDS OF NUCLEAR WINTER, CUT OFF FROM THE SUN. YOU'LL HAVE TO LEAVE--
--AND WE'LL RISE UP FROM THE ASHES. WE'LL ASCEND! FINALLY!
TALK, OR SO HELP ME, I'LL--
SUPERMAN!

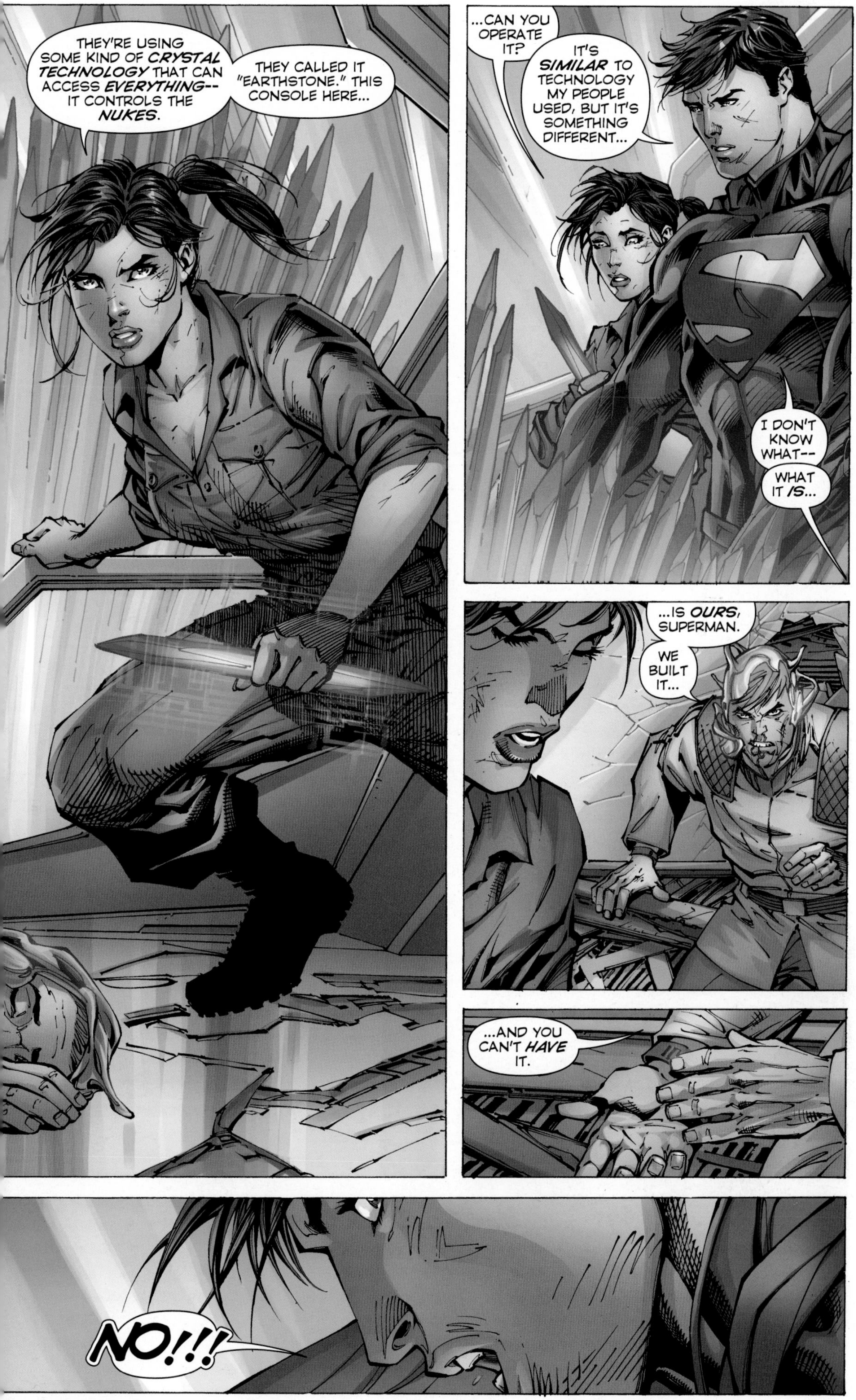

THEY'RE USING SOME KIND OF CRYSTAL TECHNOLOGY THAT CAN ACCESS EVERYTHING-- IT CONTROLS THE NUKES.
THEY CALLED IT "EARTHSTONE." THIS CONSOLE HERE...
...CAN YOU OPERATE IT?
IT'S SIMILAR TO TECHNOLOGY MY PEOPLE USED, BUT IT'S SOMETHING DIFFERENT...
I DON'T KNOW WHAT--
WHAT IT IS...
...IS OURS, SUPERMAN.
WE BUILT IT...
...AND YOU CAN'T HAVE IT.
NO!!!

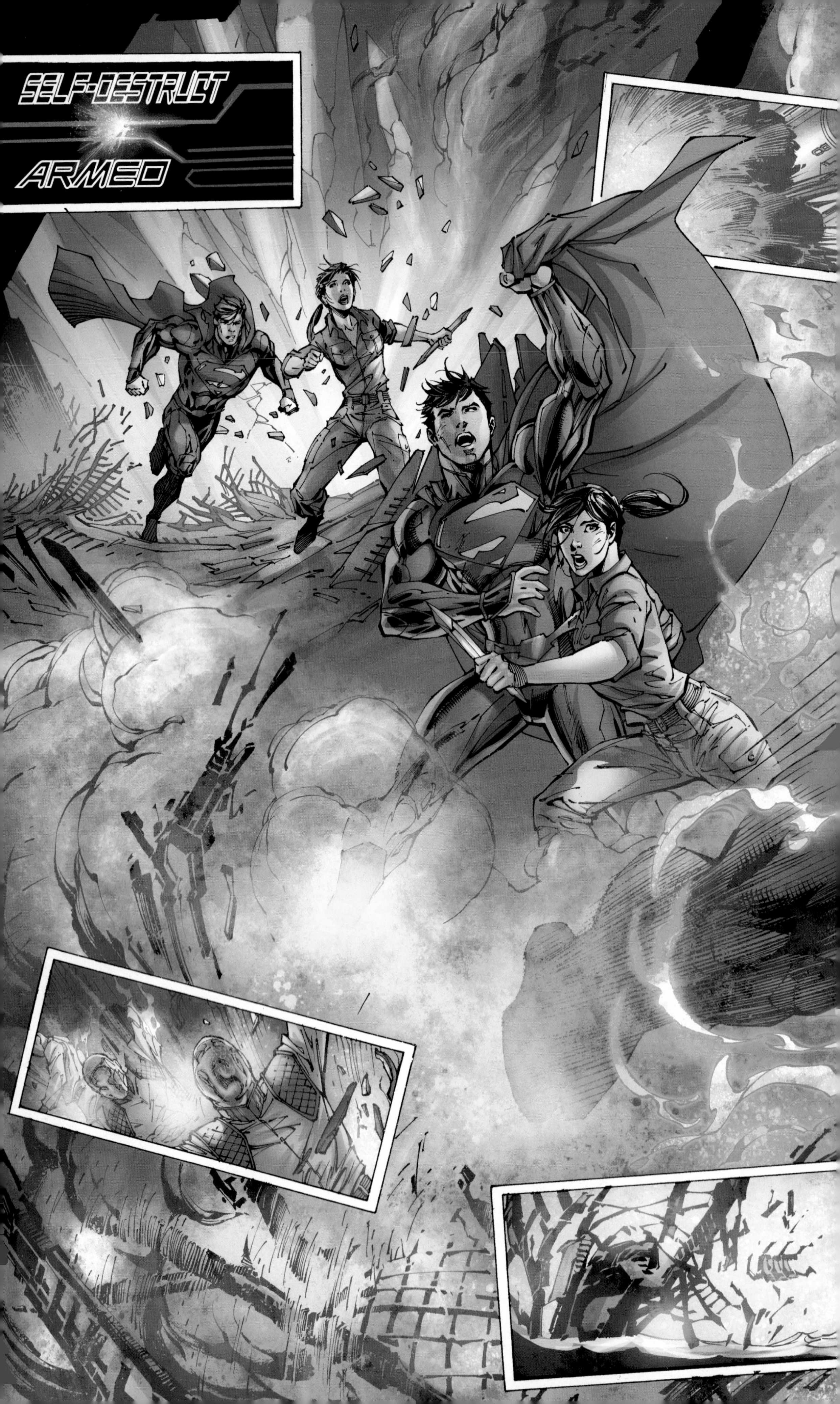
SELF-DESTRUCT
ARMED

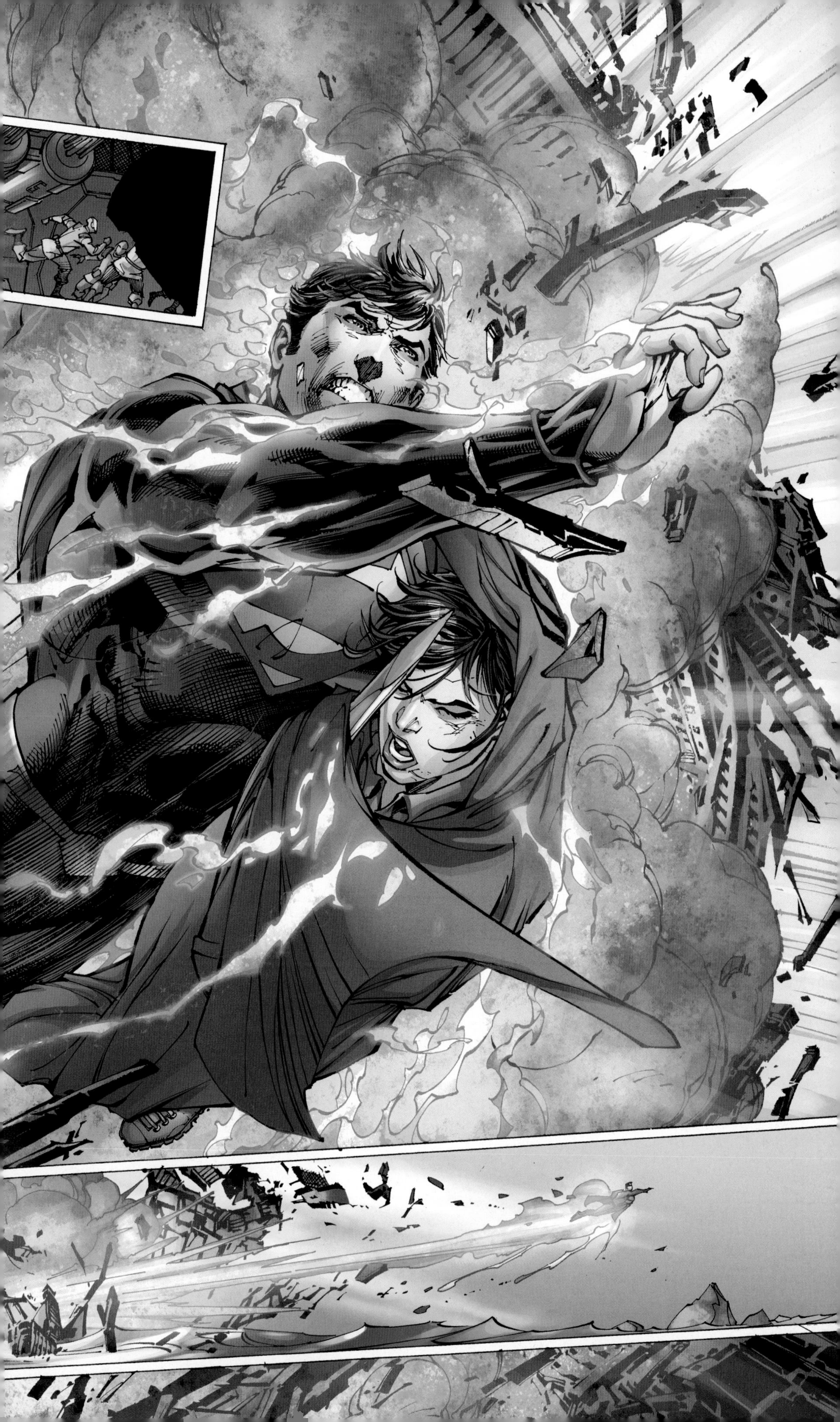

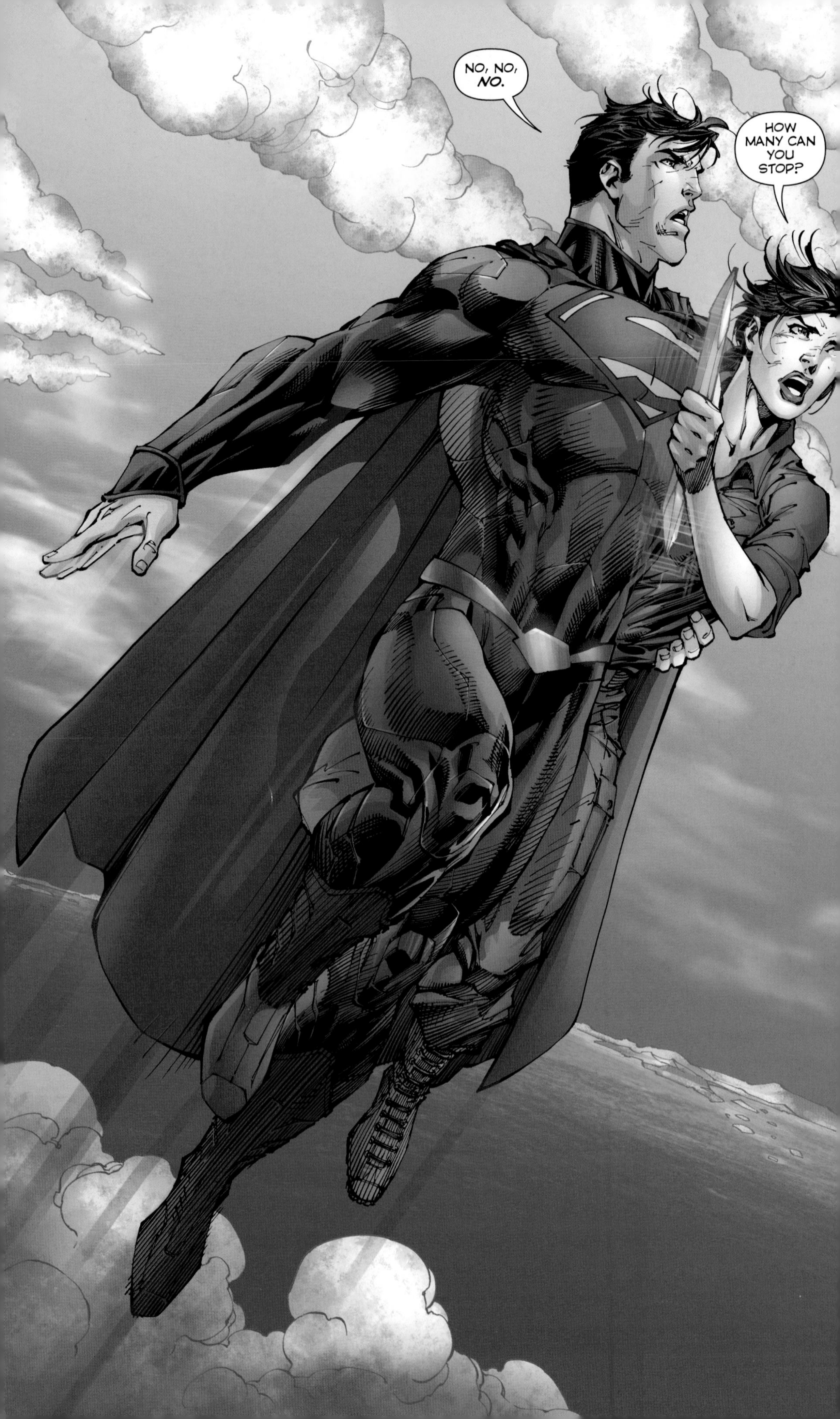
NO, NO, NO.
HOW MANY CAN YOU STOP?

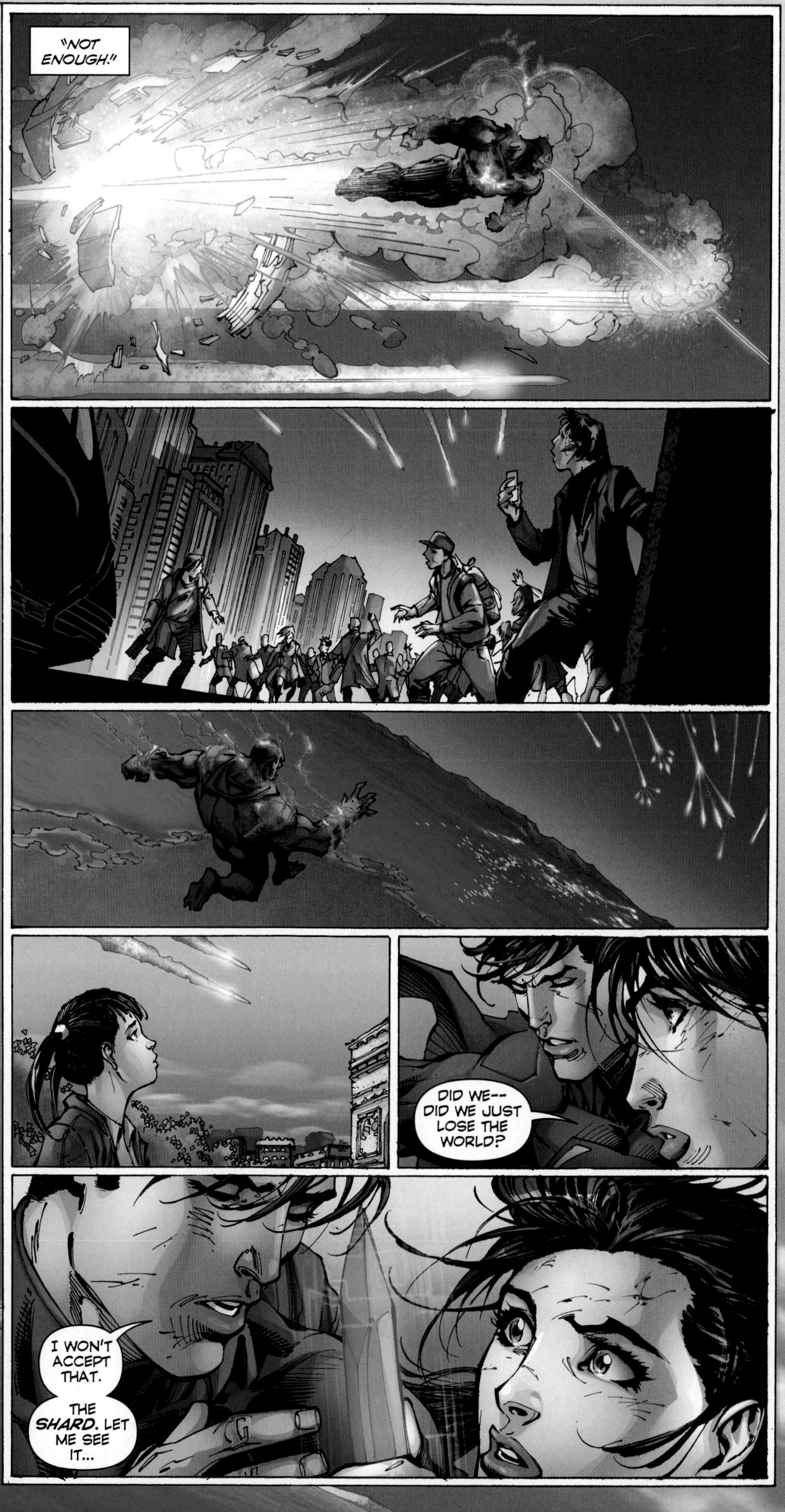
"NOT ENOUGH."
DID WE-- DID WE JUST LOSE THE WORLD?
I WON'T ACCEPT THAT.
THE SHARD. LET ME SEE IT...

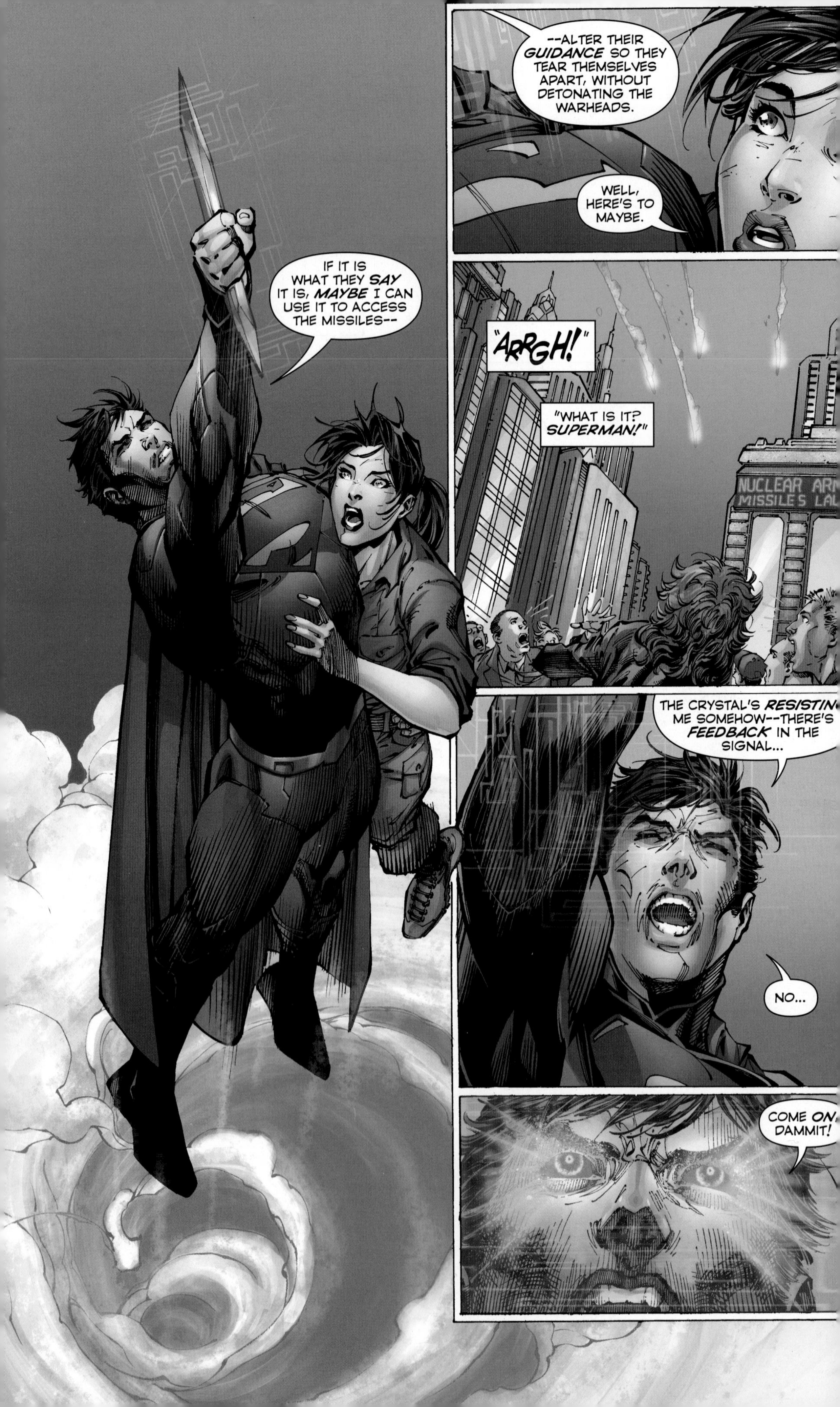

IF IT IS WHAT THEY SAY IT IS, MAYBE I CAN USE IT TO ACCESS THE MISSILES--
--ALTER THEIR GUIDANCE SO THEY TEAR THEMSELVES APART, WITHOUT DETONATING THE WARHEADS.
WELL, HERE'S TO MAYBE.
"ARRGH!"
"WHAT IS IT? SUPERMAN!"
NUCLEAR AR
MISSILES LA
THE CRYSTAL'S RESISTIN ME SOMEHOW--THERE'S FEEDBACK IN THE SIGNAL...
NO...
COME ON DAMMIT!

RAAAARGH!!

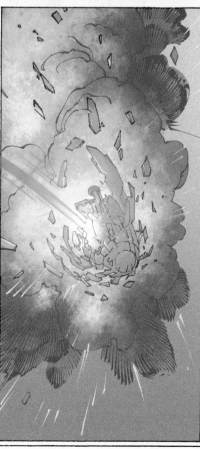

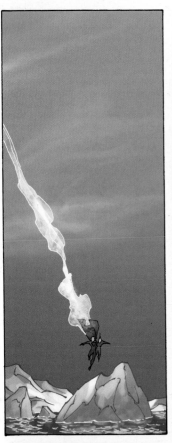

YOU JUST...SAVED THE WORLD.

YOU ≥COUGH≥ YOU DID, TOO.

SUPERMAN.

WELL DONE.

NOW I'M AFRAID I'M GOING TO HAVE TO ASK YOU TO HAND OVER THAT CRYSTAL. GENERAL LANE AND THE MACHINE NEED IT FOR STUDY.

YOU WANT EARTHSTONE? GO SCRAPE THE REST OF IT OFF THE OCEAN FLOOR. YOU'RE NOT TAKING THIS SHARD.

AND YOU CAN TELL MY FATHER AND THE MACHINE THAT IF THEY WANT SOMETHING TO STUDY, TRY THE PIECE I'M GOING TO WRITE ABOUT THEM--AND ABOUT YOU, YOU STOOGE.

WELL THEN, HERE WE ARE. FOR WHAT IT'S WORTH, I'M SORRY.

I TOLD YOU IT WOULD COME TO THIS.

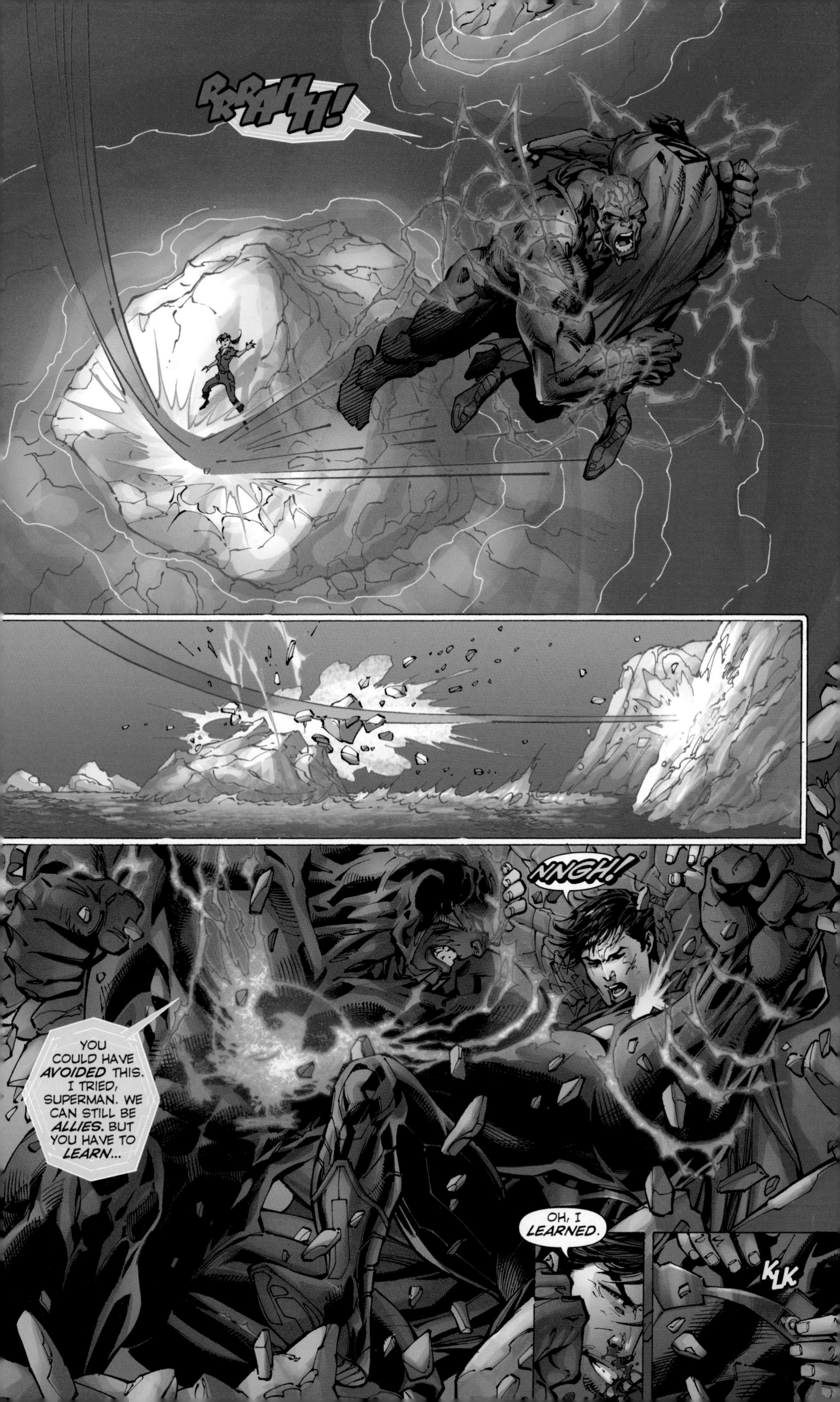
RRRAHHH!
NNGH!
YOU COULD HAVE AVOIDED THIS. I TRIED, SUPERMAN. WE CAN STILL BE ALLIES. BUT YOU HAVE TO LEARN...
OH, I LEARNED.
KLK

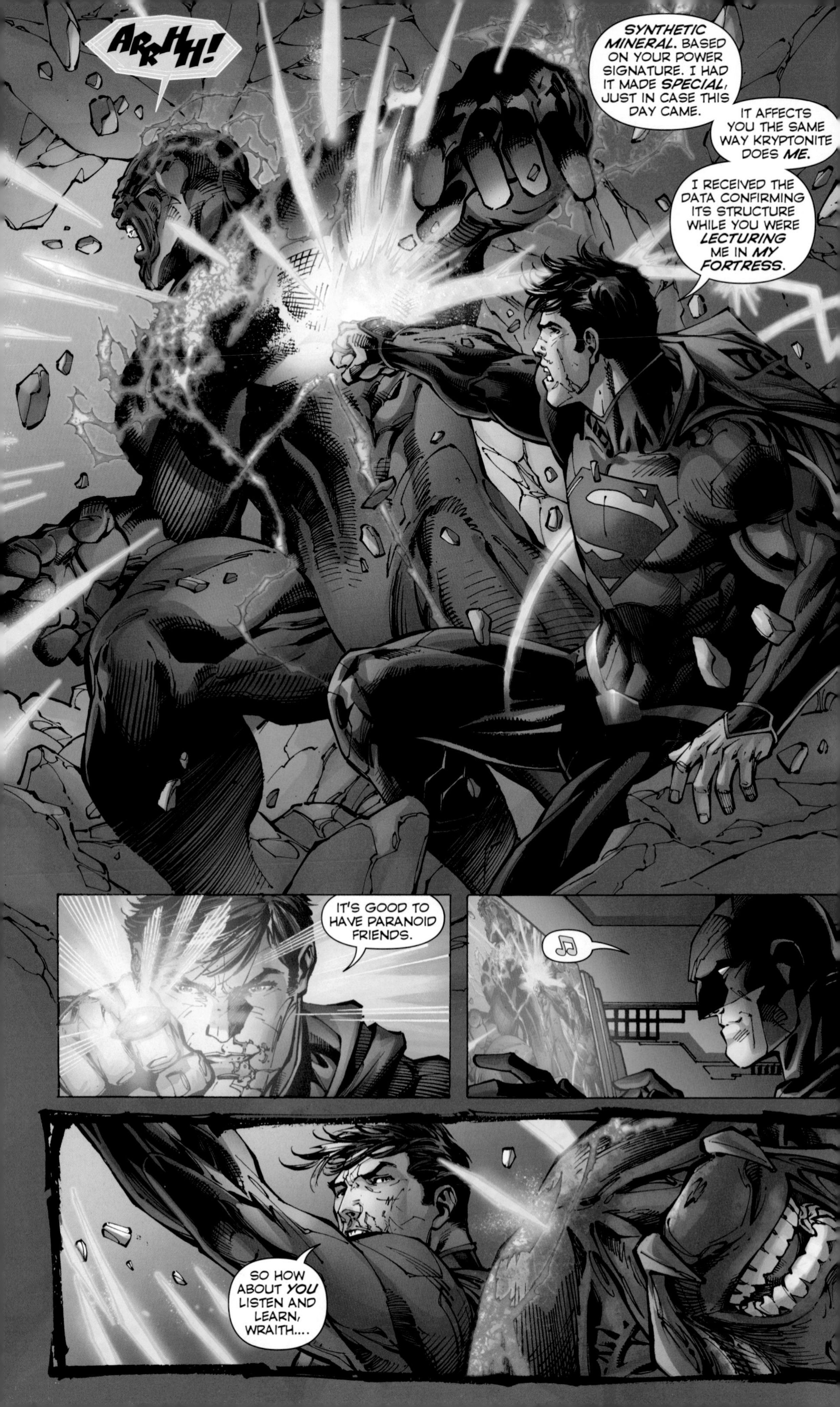

ARRHH!
SYNTHETIC MINERAL. BASED ON YOUR POWER SIGNATURE. I HAD IT MADE SPECIAL, JUST IN CASE THIS DAY CAME.
IT AFFECTS YOU THE SAME WAY KRYPTONITE DOES ME.
I RECEIVED THE DATA CONFIRMING ITS STRUCTURE WHILE YOU WERE LECTURING ME IN MY FORTRESS.
IT'S GOOD TO HAVE PARANOID FRIENDS.
♫
SO HOW ABOUT YOU LISTEN AND LEARN, WRAITH....

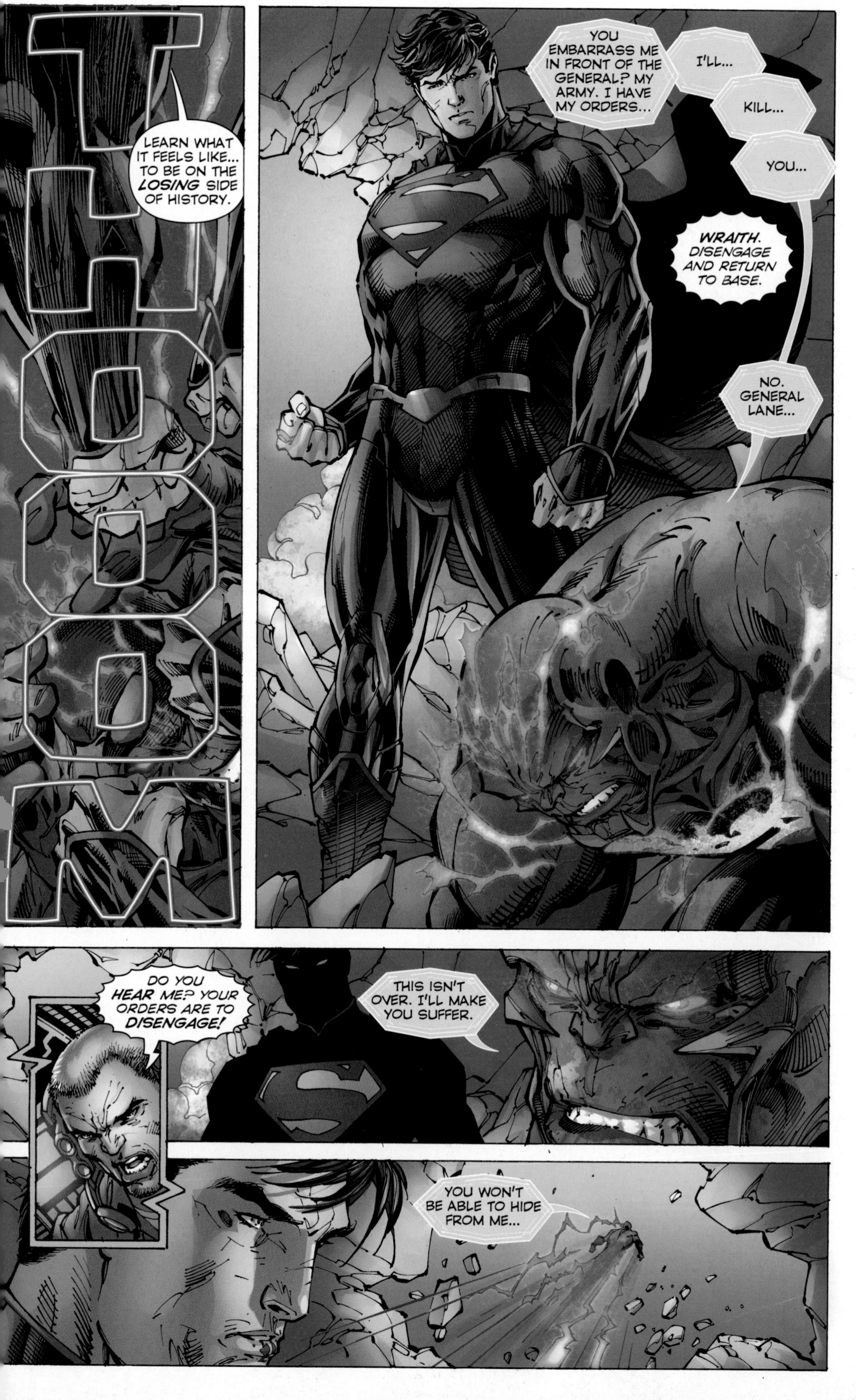
THOOOM
LEARN WHAT IT FEELS LIKE... TO BE ON THE LOSING SIDE OF HISTORY.
YOU EMBARRASS ME IN FRONT OF THE GENERAL? MY ARMY. I HAVE MY ORDERS...
I'LL...
KILL...
YOU...
WRAITH. DISENGAGE AND RETURN TO BASE.
NO. GENERAL LANE...
DO YOU HEAR ME? YOUR ORDERS ARE TO DISENGAGE!
THIS ISN'T OVER. I'LL MAKE YOU SUFFER.
YOU WON'T BE ABLE TO HIDE FROM ME...

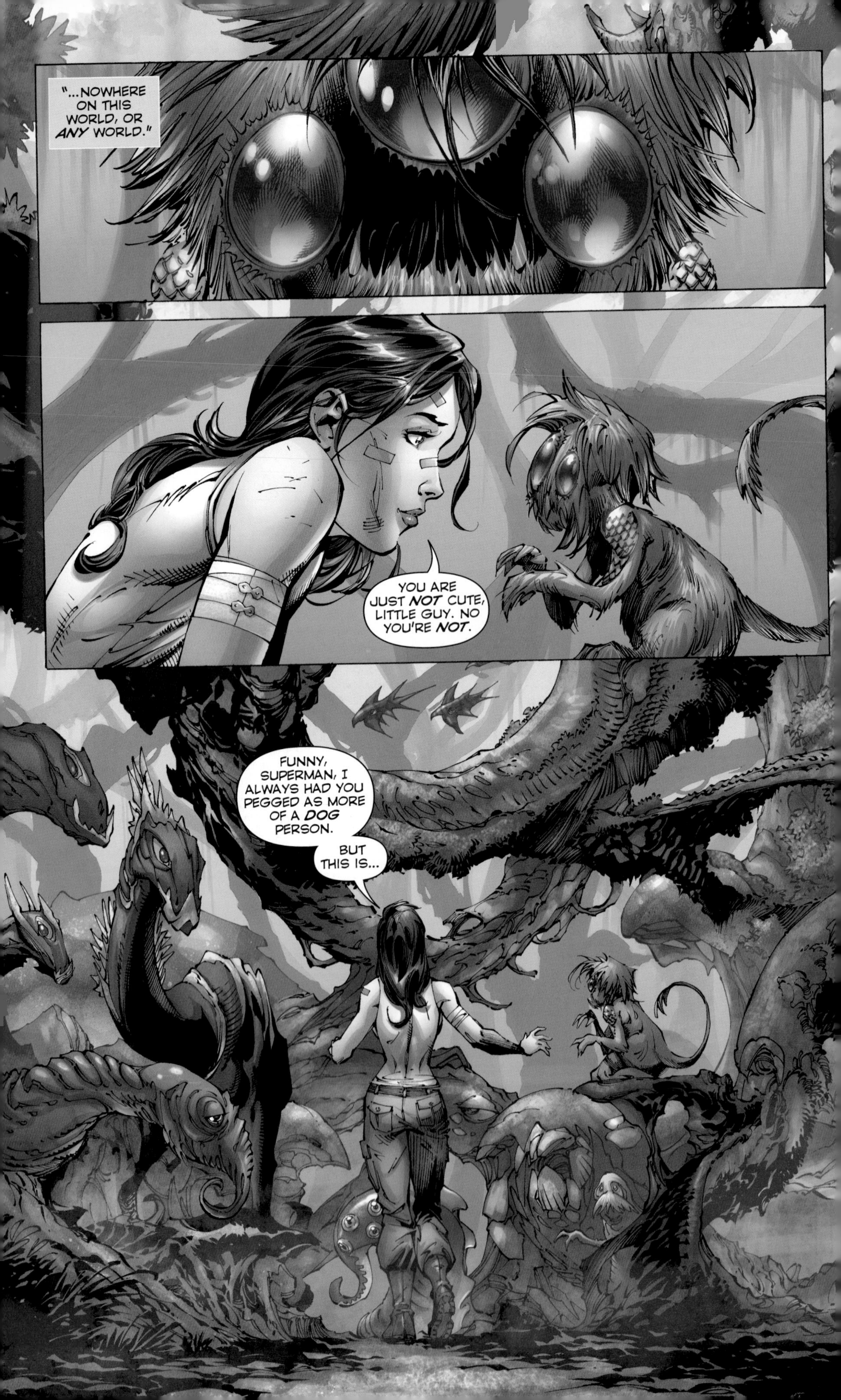
"...NOWHERE ON THIS WORLD, OR ANY WORLD."
YOU ARE JUST NOT CUTE, LITTLE GUY. NO YOU'RE NOT.
FUNNY, SUPERMAN, I ALWAYS HAD YOU PEGGED AS MORE OF A DOG PERSON.
BUT THIS IS...

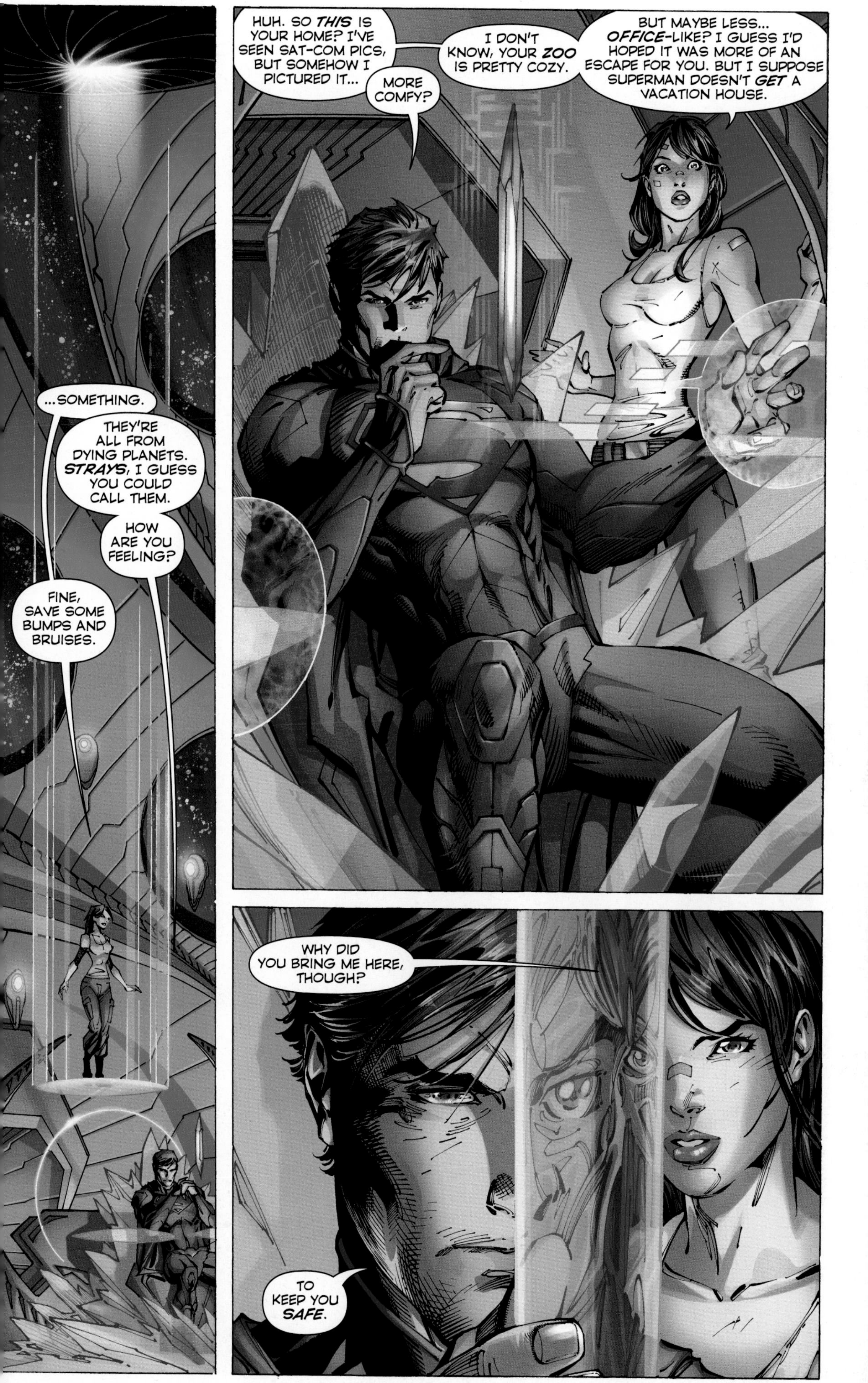

HUH. SO THIS IS YOUR HOME? I'VE SEEN SAT-COM PICS, BUT SOMEHOW I PICTURED IT...
MORE COMFY?
I DON'T KNOW, YOUR ZOO IS PRETTY COZY.
BUT MAYBE LESS... OFFICE-LIKE? I GUESS I'D HOPED IT WAS MORE OF AN ESCAPE FOR YOU. BUT I SUPPOSE SUPERMAN DOESN'T GET A VACATION HOUSE.
...SOMETHING.
THEY'RE ALL FROM DYING PLANETS. STRAYS, I GUESS YOU COULD CALL THEM.
HOW ARE YOU FEELING?
FINE, SAVE SOME BUMPS AND BRUISES.
WHY DID YOU BRING ME HERE, THOUGH?
TO KEEP YOU SAFE.

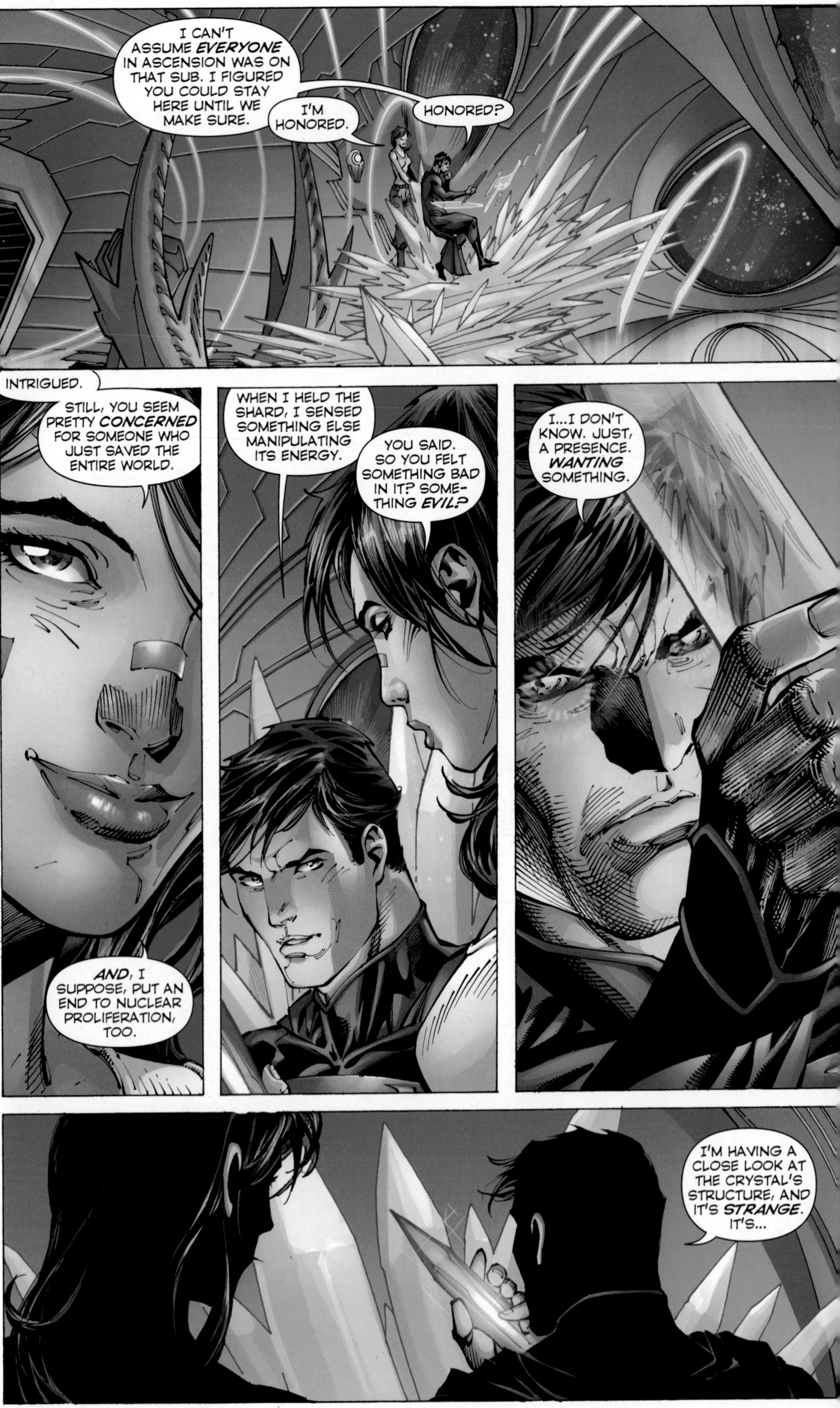
I CAN'T ASSUME EVERYONE IN ASCENSION WAS ON THAT SUB. I FIGURED YOU COULD STAY HERE UNTIL WE MAKE SURE.
I'M HONORED.
HONORED?
INTRIGUED.
STILL, YOU SEEM PRETTY CONCERNED FOR SOMEONE WHO JUST SAVED THE ENTIRE WORLD.
AND, I SUPPOSE, PUT AN END TO NUCLEAR PROLIFERATION, TOO.
WHEN I HELD THE SHARD, I SENSED SOMETHING ELSE MANIPULATING ITS ENERGY.
YOU SAID. SO YOU FELT SOMETHING BAD IN IT? SOME-THING EVIL?
I...I DON'T KNOW. JUST, A PRESENCE. WANTING SOMETHING.
I'M HAVING A CLOSE LOOK AT THE CRYSTAL'S STRUCTURE, AND IT'S STRANGE. IT'S...

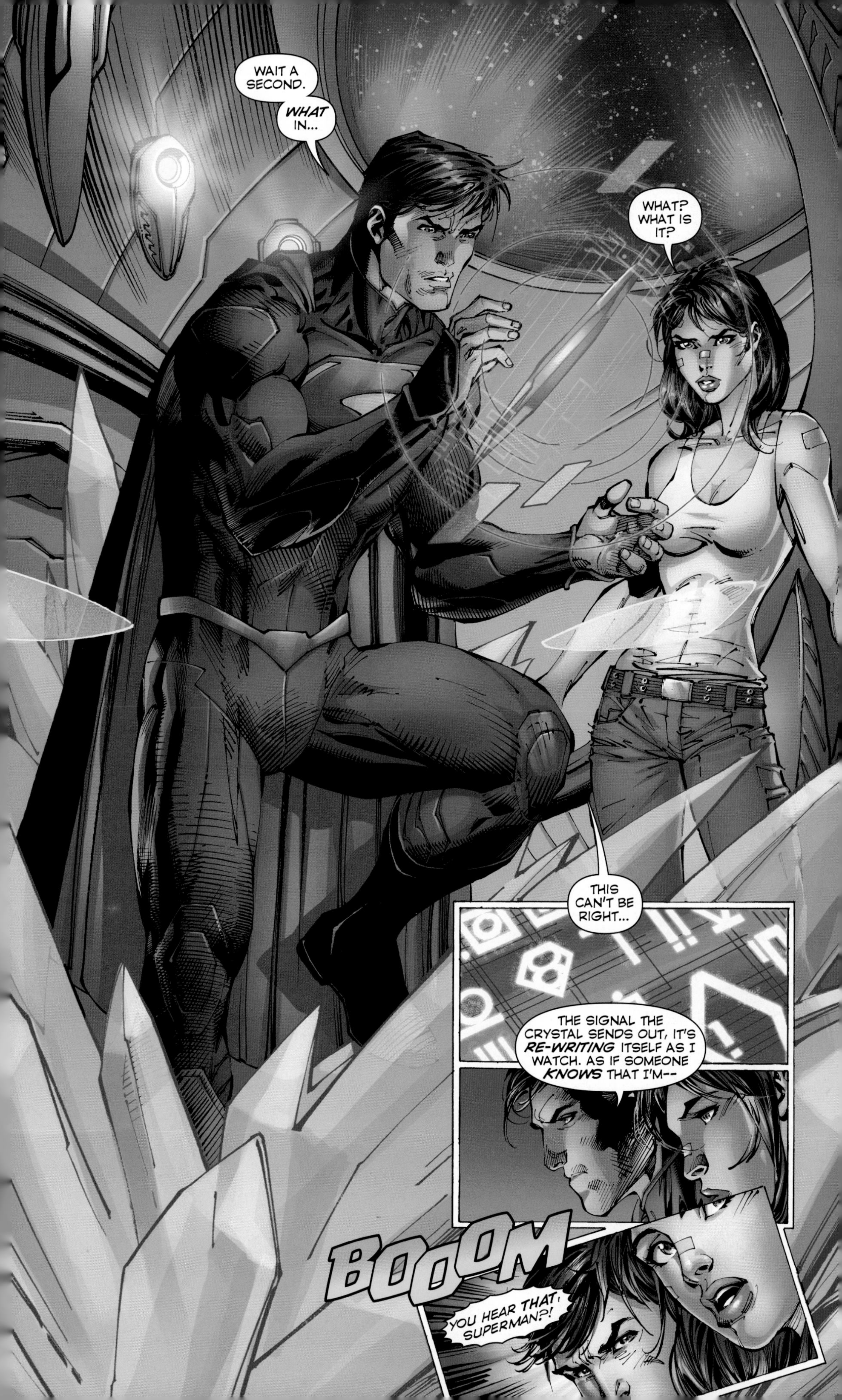
WAIT A SECOND.
WHAT IN...
WHAT? WHAT IS IT?
THIS CAN'T BE RIGHT...
THE SIGNAL THE CRYSTAL SENDS OUT, IT'S RE-WRITING ITSELF AS I WATCH. AS IF SOMEONE KNOWS THAT I'M--
BOOOM
YOU HEAR THAT, SUPERMAN?!

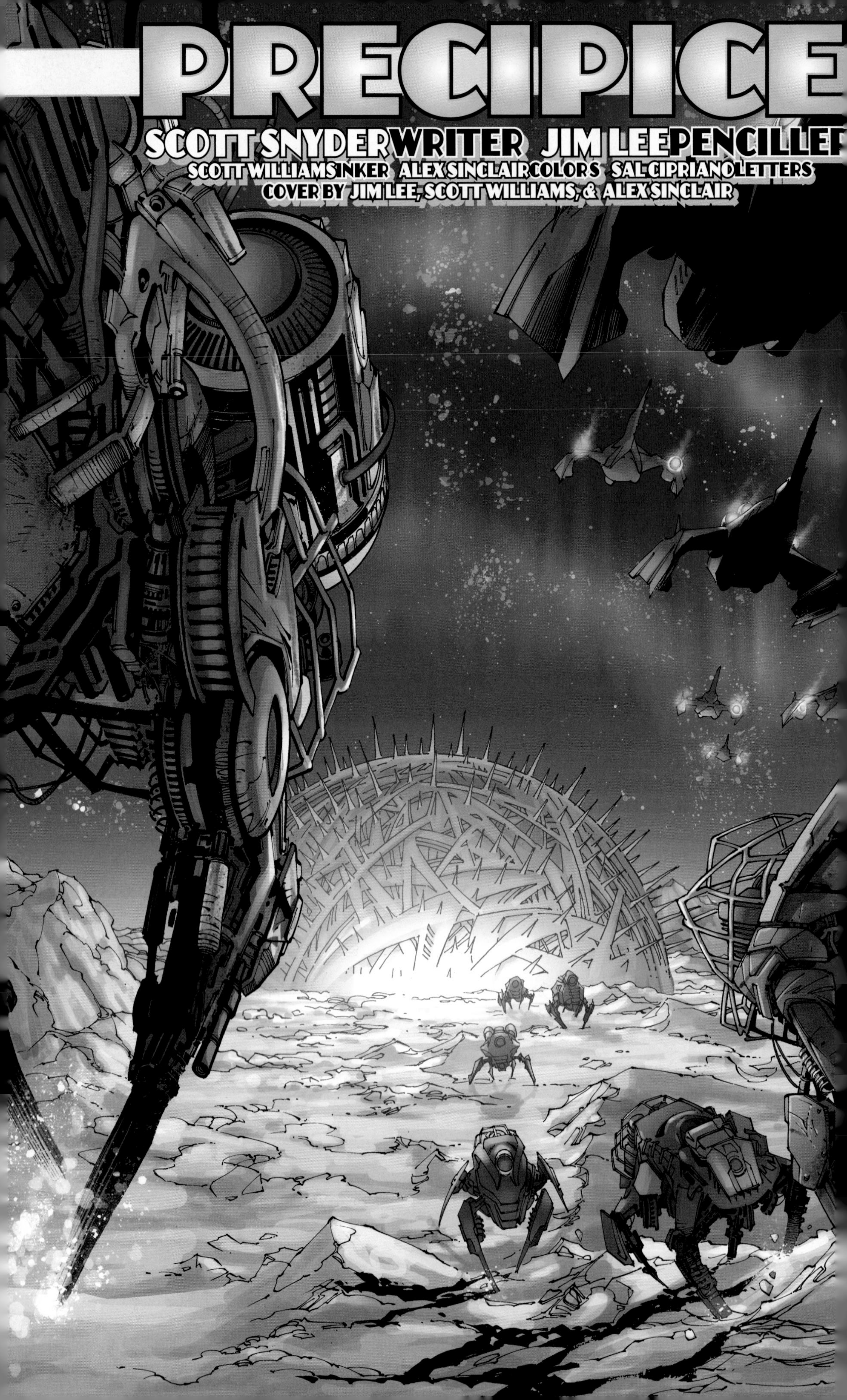
PRECIPICE
SCOTT SNYDER WRITER JIM LEE PENCILLE
SCOTT WILLIAMS INKER ALEX SINCLAIR COLORS SAL CIPRIANO LETTERS
COVER BY JIM LEE, SCOTT WILLIAMS, & ALEX SINCLAIR

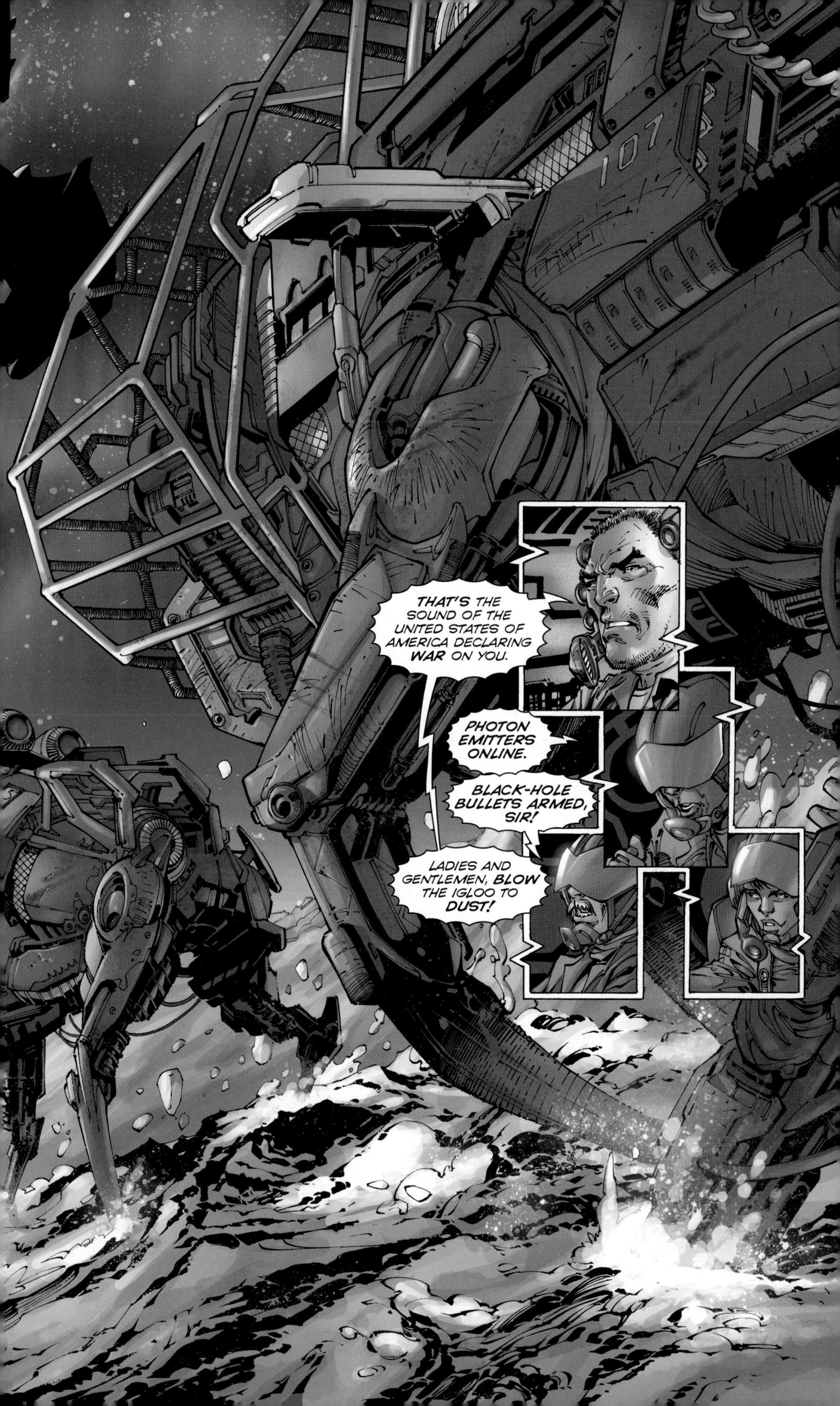
THAT'S THE SOUND OF THE UNITED STATES OF AMERICA DECLARING WAR ON YOU.
PHOTON EMITTERS ONLINE.
BLACK-HOLE BULLETS ARMED, SIR!
LADIES AND GENTLEMEN, BLOW THE IGLOO TO DUST!
107

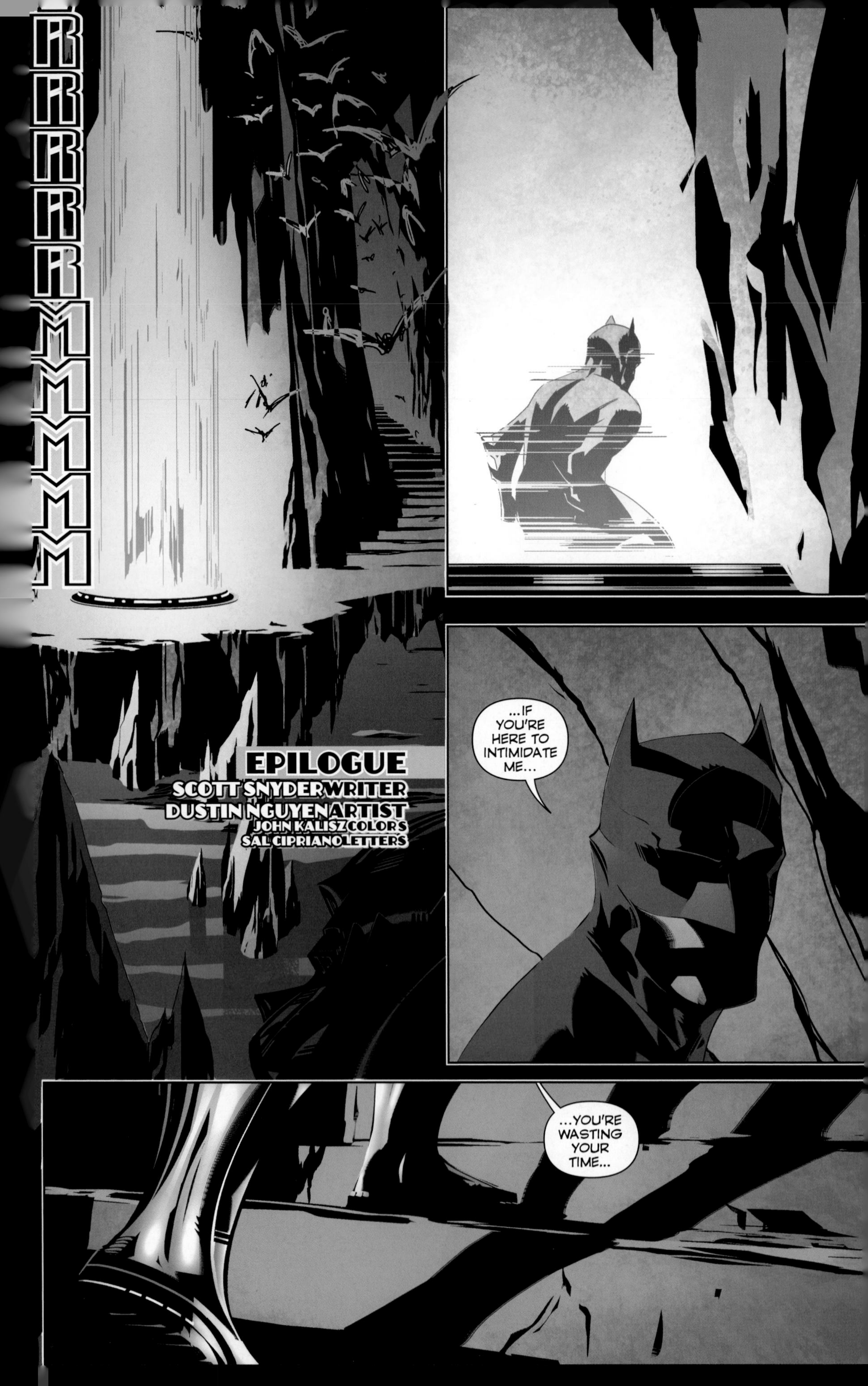
RRRRRMMMMMM
EPILOGUE
SCOTT SNYDER WRITER
DUSTIN NGUYEN ARTIST
JOHN KALISZ COLORS
SAL CIPRIANO LETTERS
...IF YOU'RE HERE TO INTIMIDATE ME...
...YOU'RE WASTING YOUR TIME...

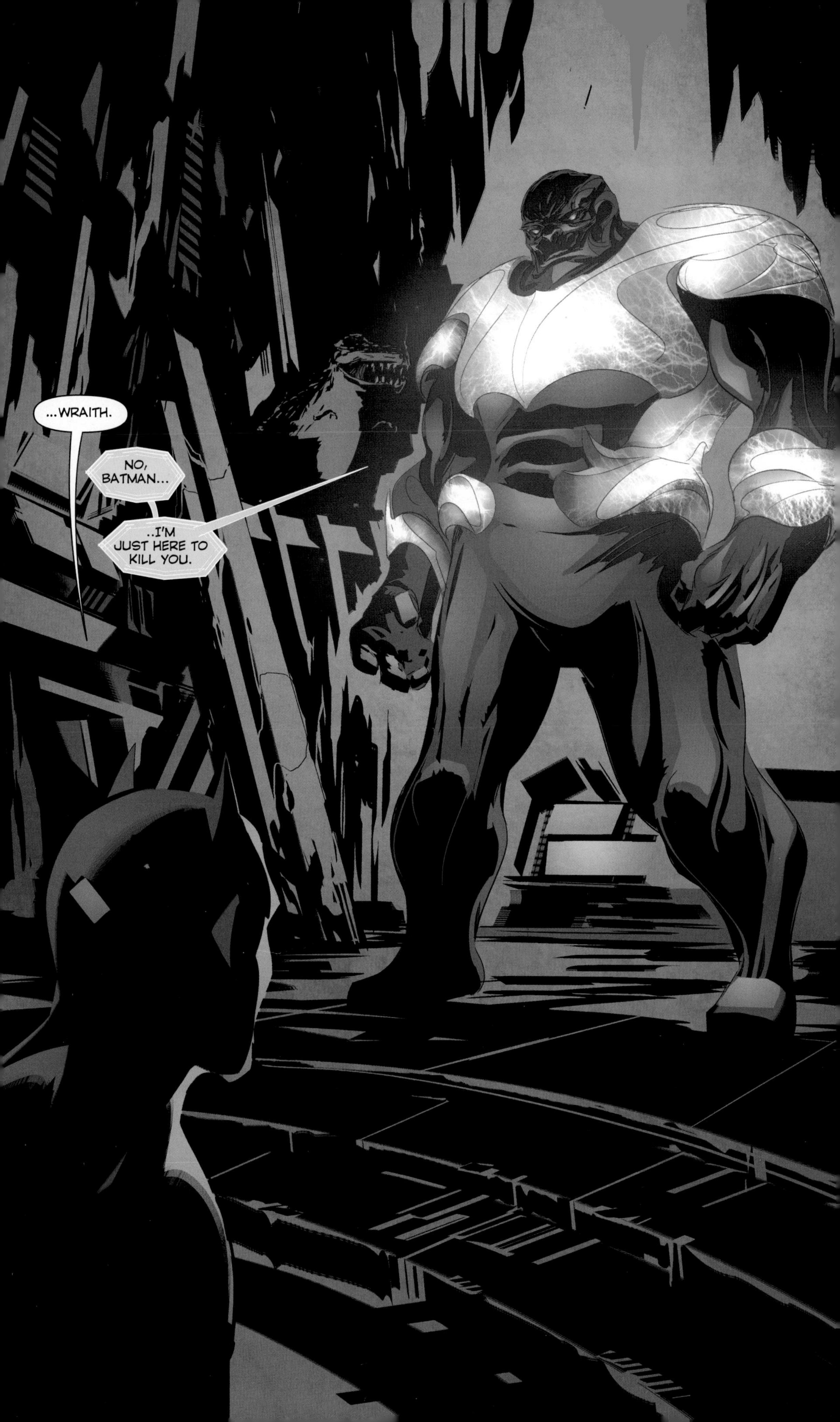
...WRAITH.
NO, BATMAN...
..I'M JUST HERE TO KILL YOU.

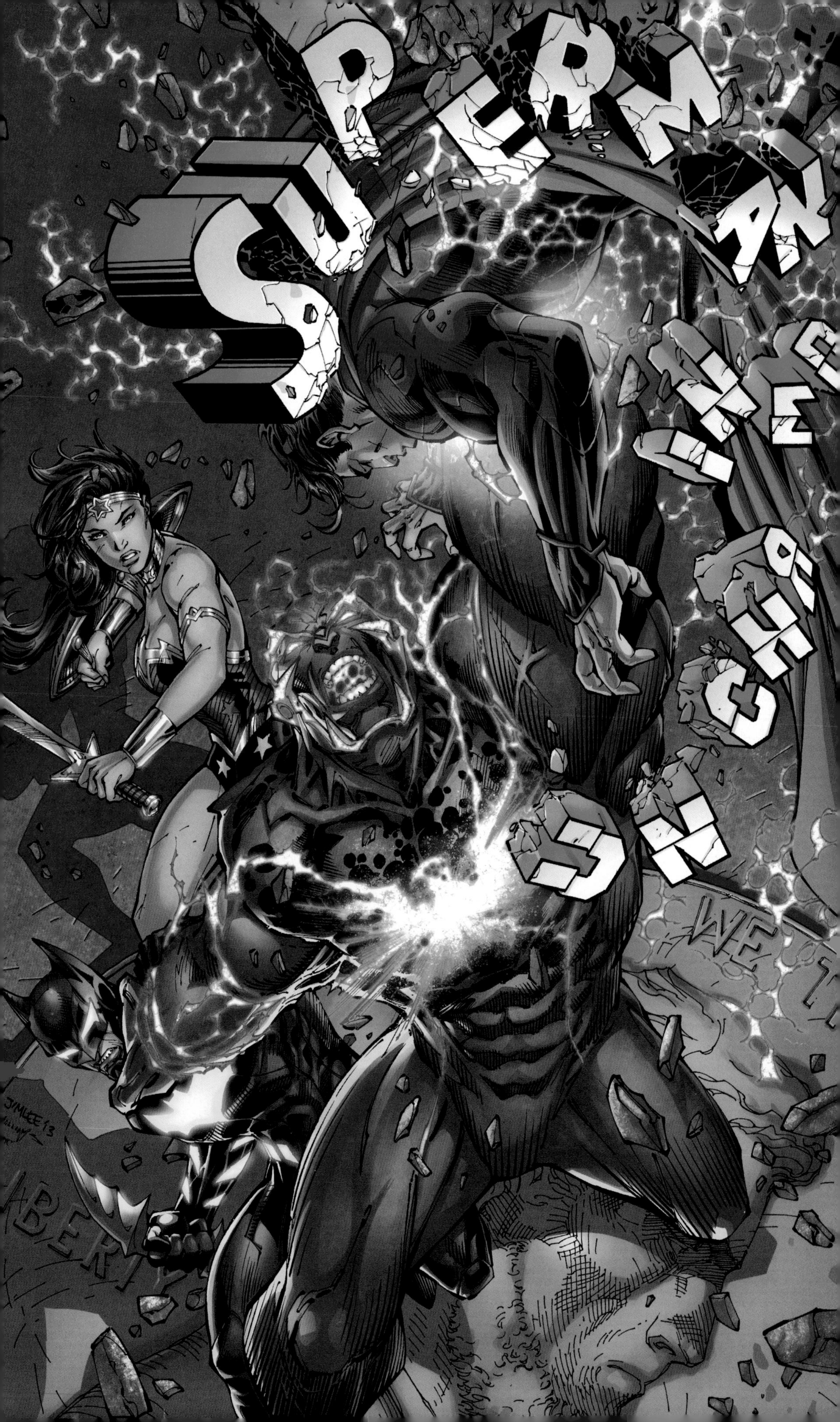
SUPERMAN
JIMLEE 13

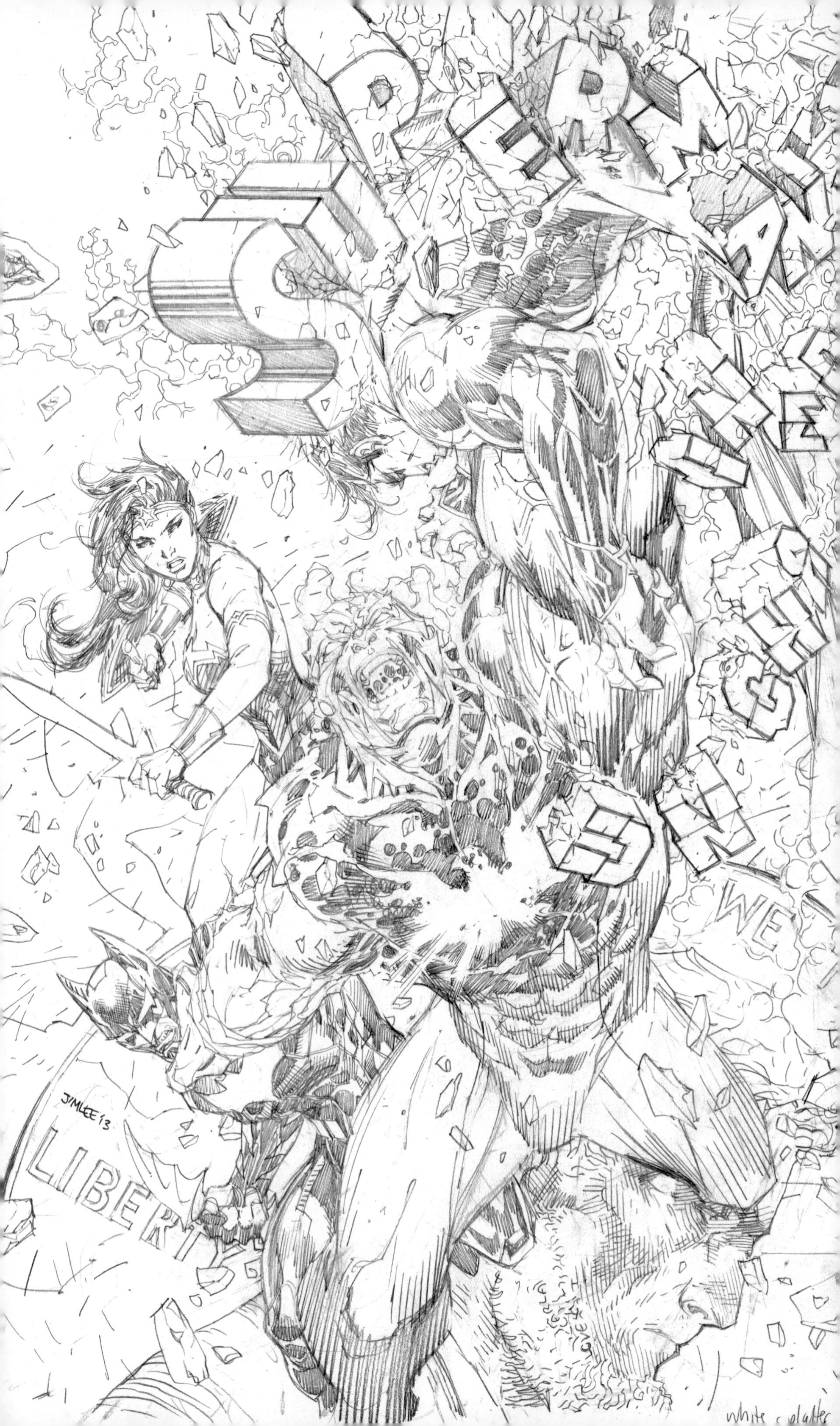

WE
JIMLEE '13
LIBER

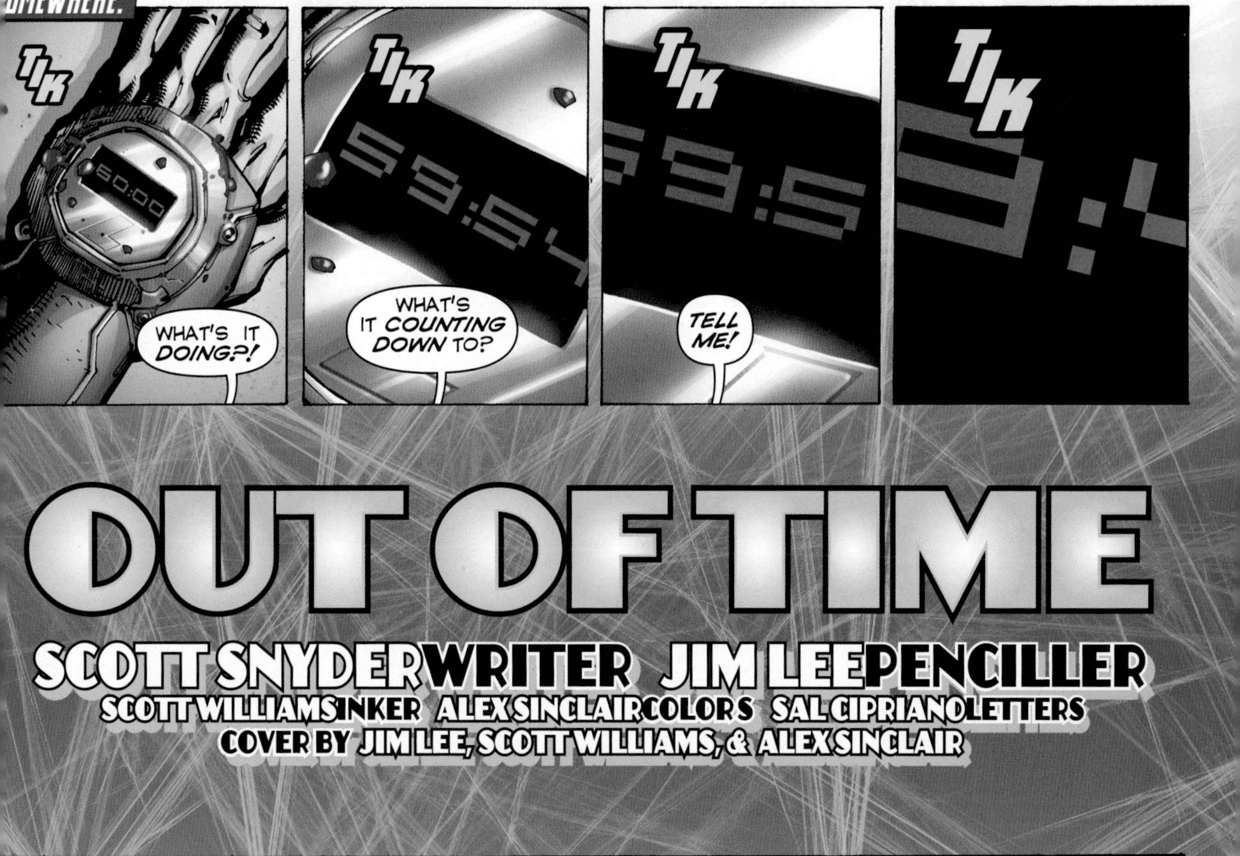
SOMEWHERE.
TIK
60:00
WHAT'S IT DOING?!
TIK
WHAT'S IT COUNTING DOWN TO?
TIK
TELL ME!
TIK

OUT OF TIME

SCOTT SNYDER WRITER JIM LEE PENCILLER

SCOTT WILLIAMS INKER ALEX SINCLAIR COLORS SAL CIPRIANO LETTERS

COVER BY JIM LEE, SCOTT WILLIAMS, & ALEX SINCLAIR

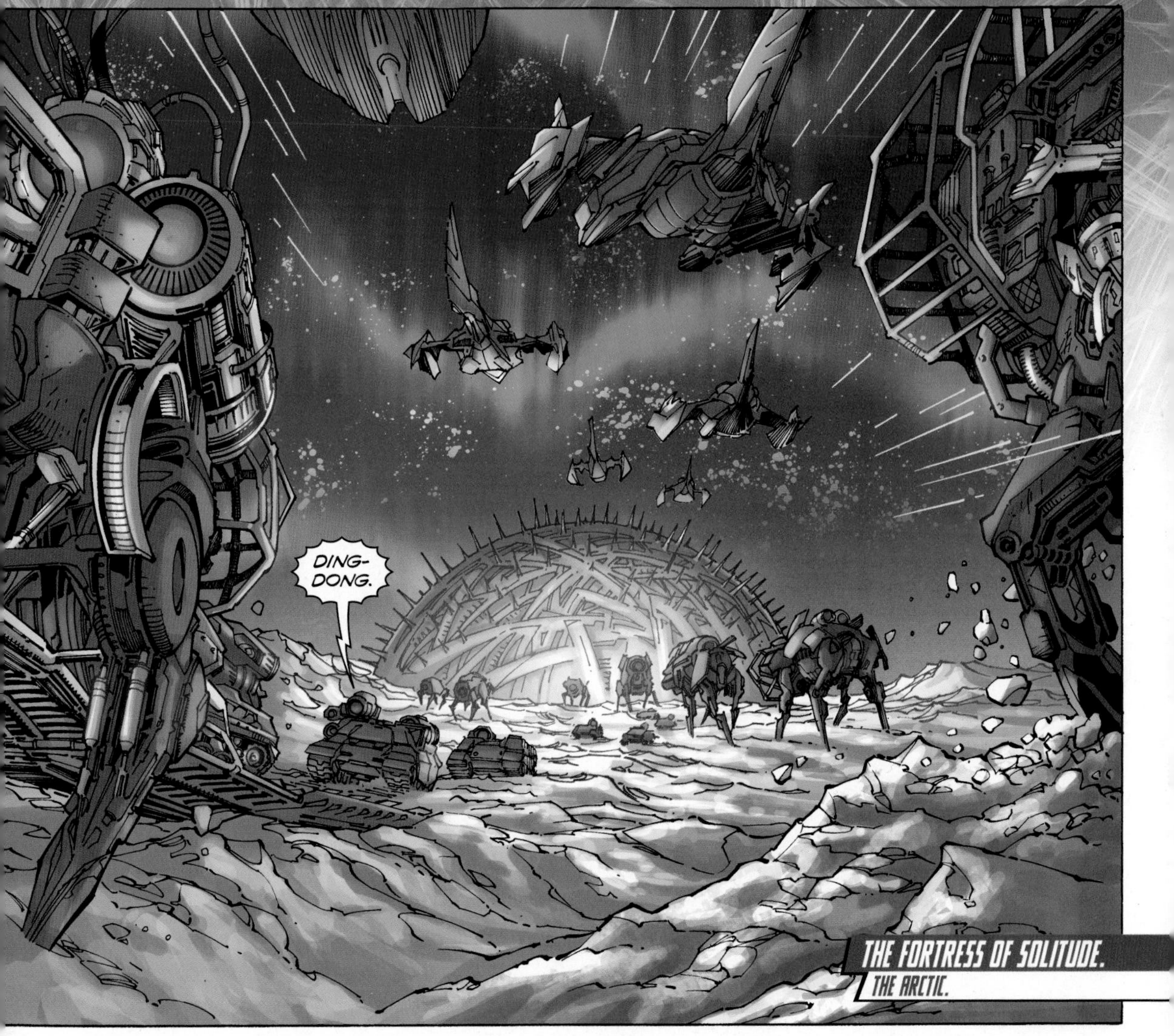
DING-DONG.
THE FORTRESS OF SOLITUDE.
THE ARCTIC.

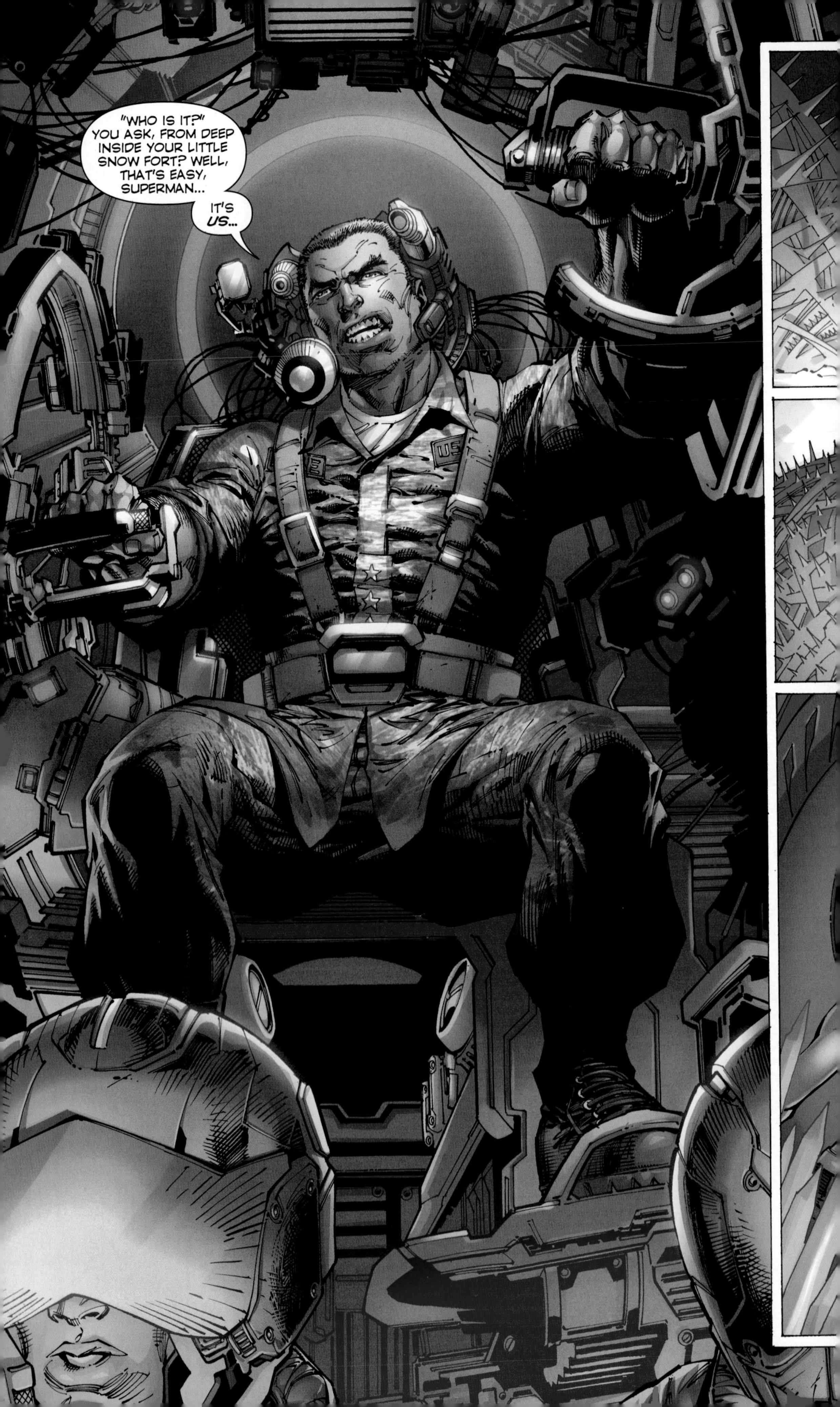
"WHO IS IT?" YOU ASK, FROM DEEP INSIDE YOUR LITTLE SNOW FORT? WELL, THAT'S EASY, SUPERMAN...
IT'S *US*...

"THE *DOGS* OF *WAR*...

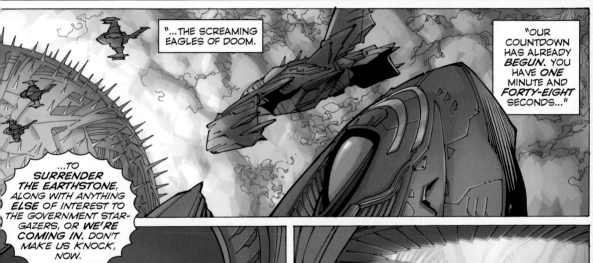

"...THE SCREAMING EAGLES OF DOOM.

"OUR COUNTDOWN HAS ALREADY *BEGUN*. YOU HAVE *ONE* MINUTE AND *FORTY-EIGHT* SECONDS..."

...TO *SURRENDER THE EARTHSTONE*, ALONG WITH ANYTHING *ELSE* OF INTEREST TO THE GOVERNMENT STAR-GAZERS, OR *WE'RE COMING IN*. DON'T MAKE US KNOCK, NOW.

SUPERMAN, I *KNOW* MY FATHER. HE'LL DESTROY THIS WHOLE PLACE. YOU NEED TO--

NO, LOIS.

I *WON'T* GIVE HIM WHAT'S IN HERE.

YOU'RE JUST GOING TO LET HIM TAKE YOU DOWN? YOU CAN'T WIN.

MAYBE, MAYBE NOT. BUT I HAVE TO TRY.

"DYING HERE, IN YOUR HOME, IS ALL THAT'S LEFT FOR YOU."

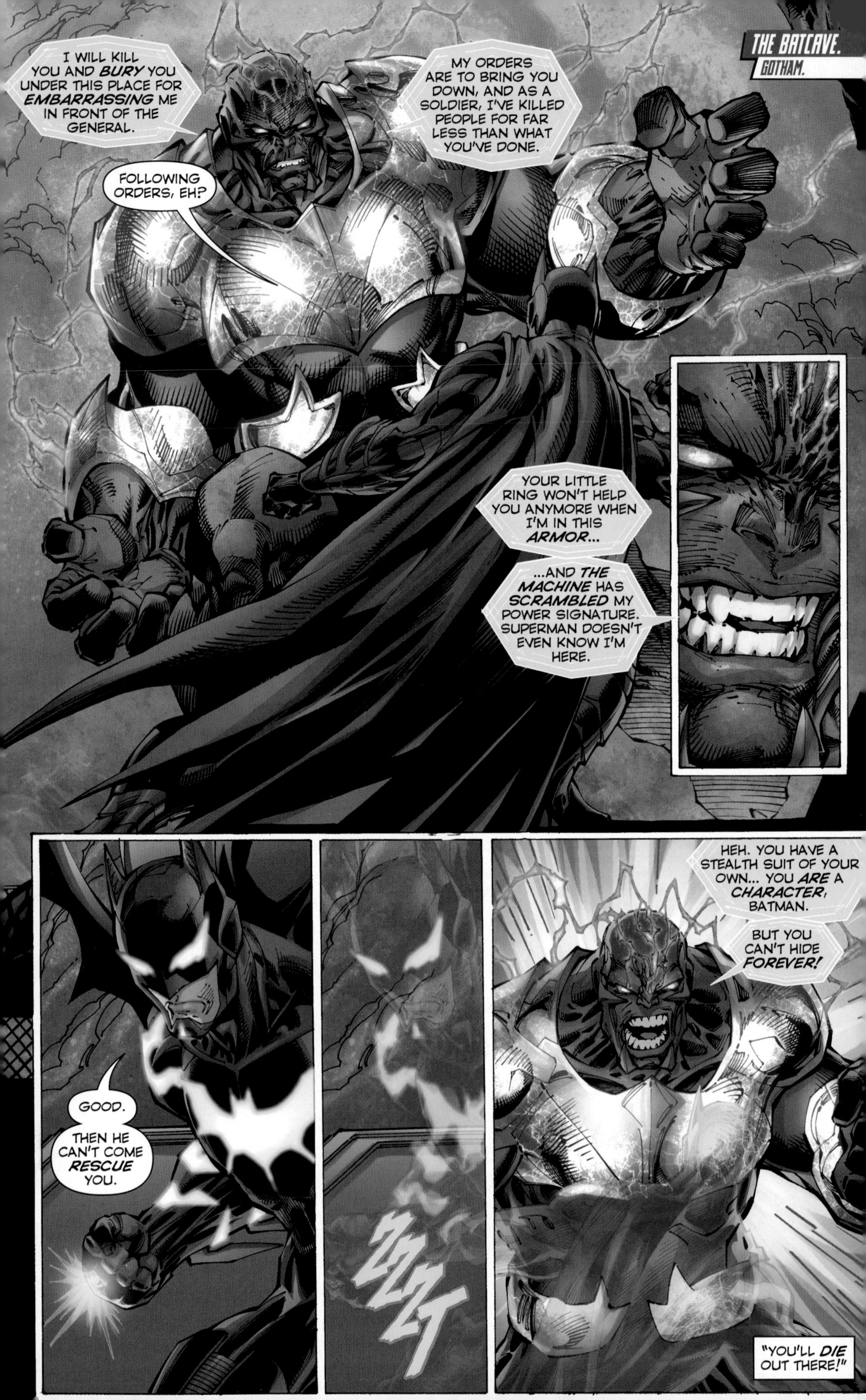

THE BATCAVE. GOTHAM.
I WILL KILL YOU AND BURY YOU UNDER THIS PLACE FOR EMBARRASSING ME IN FRONT OF THE GENERAL.
MY ORDERS ARE TO BRING YOU DOWN, AND AS A SOLDIER, I'VE KILLED PEOPLE FOR FAR LESS THAN WHAT YOU'VE DONE.
FOLLOWING ORDERS, EH?
YOUR LITTLE RING WON'T HELP YOU ANYMORE WHEN I'M IN THIS ARMOR...
...AND THE MACHINE HAS SCRAMBLED MY POWER SIGNATURE. SUPERMAN DOESN'T EVEN KNOW I'M HERE.
GOOD.
THEN HE CAN'T COME RESCUE YOU.
ZZZT
HEH. YOU HAVE A STEALTH SUIT OF YOUR OWN... YOU ARE A CHARACTER, BATMAN.
BUT YOU CAN'T HIDE FOREVER!
"YOU'LL DIE OUT THERE!"

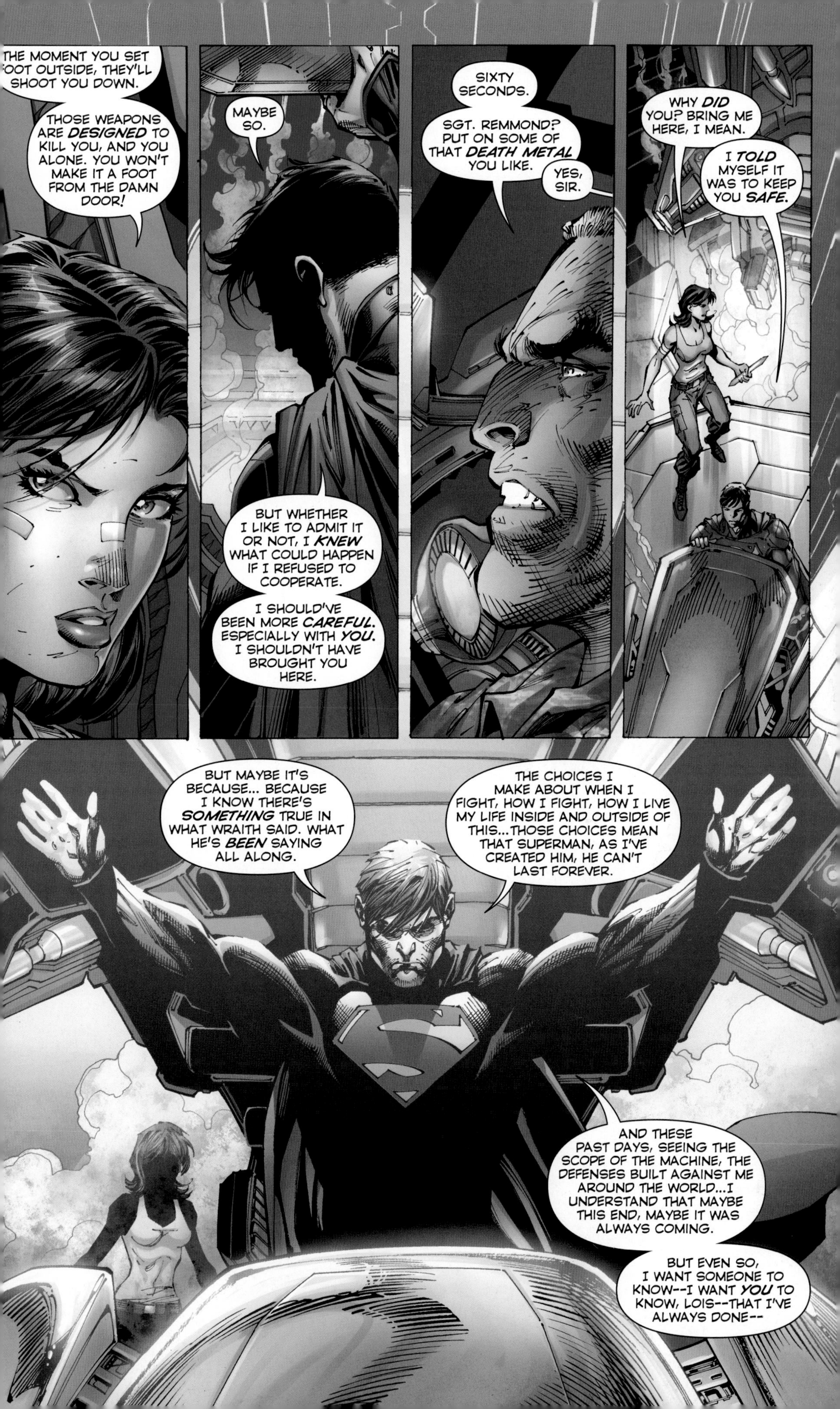

THE MOMENT YOU SET FOOT OUTSIDE, THEY'LL SHOOT YOU DOWN.
THOSE WEAPONS ARE *DESIGNED* TO KILL YOU, AND YOU ALONE. YOU WON'T MAKE IT A FOOT FROM THE DAMN DOOR!
MAYBE SO.
BUT WHETHER I LIKE TO ADMIT IT OR NOT, I *KNEW* WHAT COULD HAPPEN IF I REFUSED TO COOPERATE.
I SHOULD'VE BEEN MORE *CAREFUL.* ESPECIALLY WITH *YOU.* I SHOULDN'T HAVE BROUGHT YOU HERE.
SIXTY SECONDS.
SGT. REMMOND? PUT ON SOME OF THAT *DEATH METAL* YOU LIKE.
YES, SIR.
WHY *DID* YOU? BRING ME HERE, I MEAN.
I *TOLD* MYSELF IT WAS TO KEEP YOU *SAFE.*
BUT MAYBE IT'S BECAUSE... BECAUSE I KNOW THERE'S *SOMETHING* TRUE IN WHAT WRAITH SAID. WHAT HE'S *BEEN* SAYING ALL ALONG.
THE CHOICES I MAKE ABOUT WHEN I FIGHT, HOW I FIGHT, HOW I LIVE MY LIFE INSIDE AND OUTSIDE OF THIS...THOSE CHOICES MEAN THAT SUPERMAN, AS I'VE CREATED HIM, HE CAN'T LAST FOREVER.
AND THESE PAST DAYS, SEEING THE SCOPE OF THE MACHINE, THE DEFENSES BUILT AGAINST ME AROUND THE WORLD...I UNDERSTAND THAT MAYBE THIS END, MAYBE IT WAS ALWAYS COMING.
BUT EVEN SO, I WANT SOMEONE TO KNOW--I WANT *YOU* TO KNOW, LOIS--THAT I'VE ALWAYS DONE--

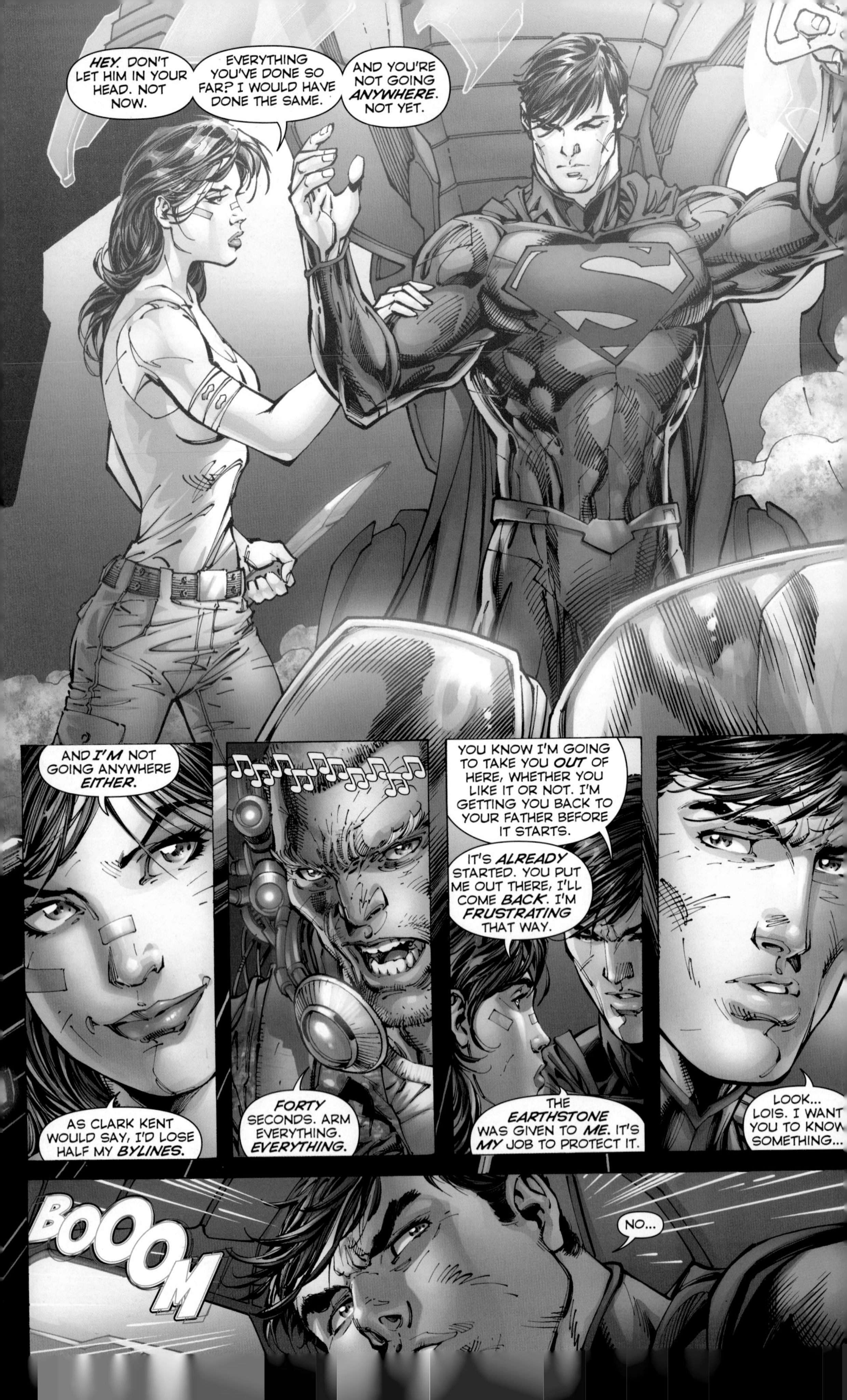
HEY. DON'T LET HIM IN YOUR HEAD. NOT NOW.
EVERYTHING YOU'VE DONE SO FAR? I WOULD HAVE DONE THE SAME.
AND YOU'RE NOT GOING ANYWHERE. NOT YET.
AND I'M NOT GOING ANYWHERE EITHER.
AS CLARK KENT WOULD SAY, I'D LOSE HALF MY BYLINES.
FORTY SECONDS. ARM EVERYTHING. EVERYTHING.
YOU KNOW I'M GOING TO TAKE YOU OUT OF HERE, WHETHER YOU LIKE IT OR NOT. I'M GETTING YOU BACK TO YOUR FATHER BEFORE IT STARTS.
IT'S ALREADY STARTED. YOU PUT ME OUT THERE, I'LL COME BACK. I'M FRUSTRATING THAT WAY.
THE EARTHSTONE WAS GIVEN TO ME. IT'S MY JOB TO PROTECT IT.
LOOK... LOIS. I WANT YOU TO KNOW SOMETHING...
BOOOM
NO...

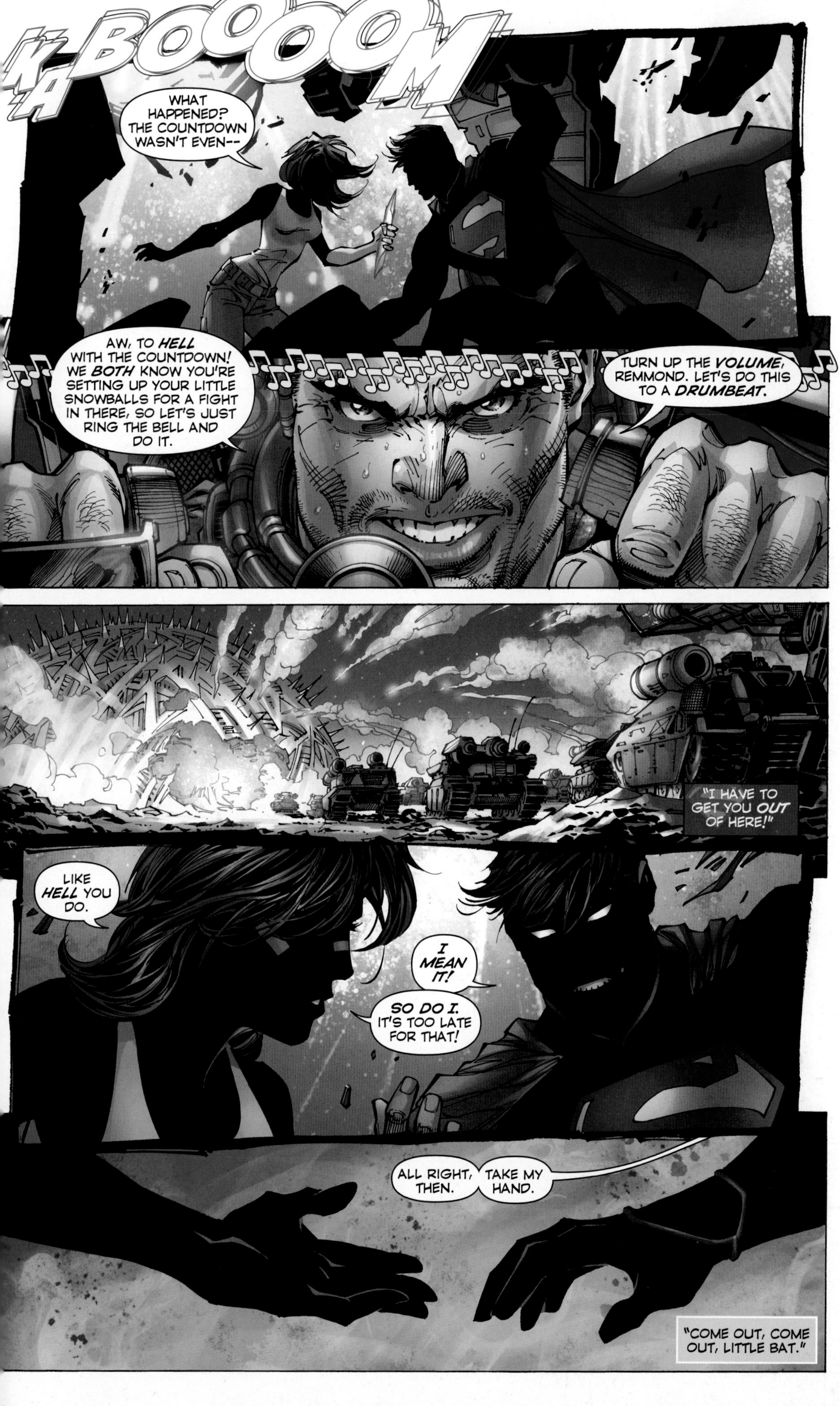
KA-BOOOOOM
WHAT HAPPENED? THE COUNTDOWN WASN'T EVEN--
AW, TO HELL WITH THE COUNTDOWN! WE BOTH KNOW YOU'RE SETTING UP YOUR LITTLE SNOWBALLS FOR A FIGHT IN THERE, SO LET'S JUST RING THE BELL AND DO IT.
TURN UP THE VOLUME, REMMOND. LET'S DO THIS TO A DRUMBEAT.
"I HAVE TO GET YOU OUT OF HERE!"
LIKE HELL YOU DO.
I MEAN IT!
SO DO I. IT'S TOO LATE FOR THAT!
ALL RIGHT, THEN.
TAKE MY HAND.
"COME OUT, COME OUT, LITTLE BAT."

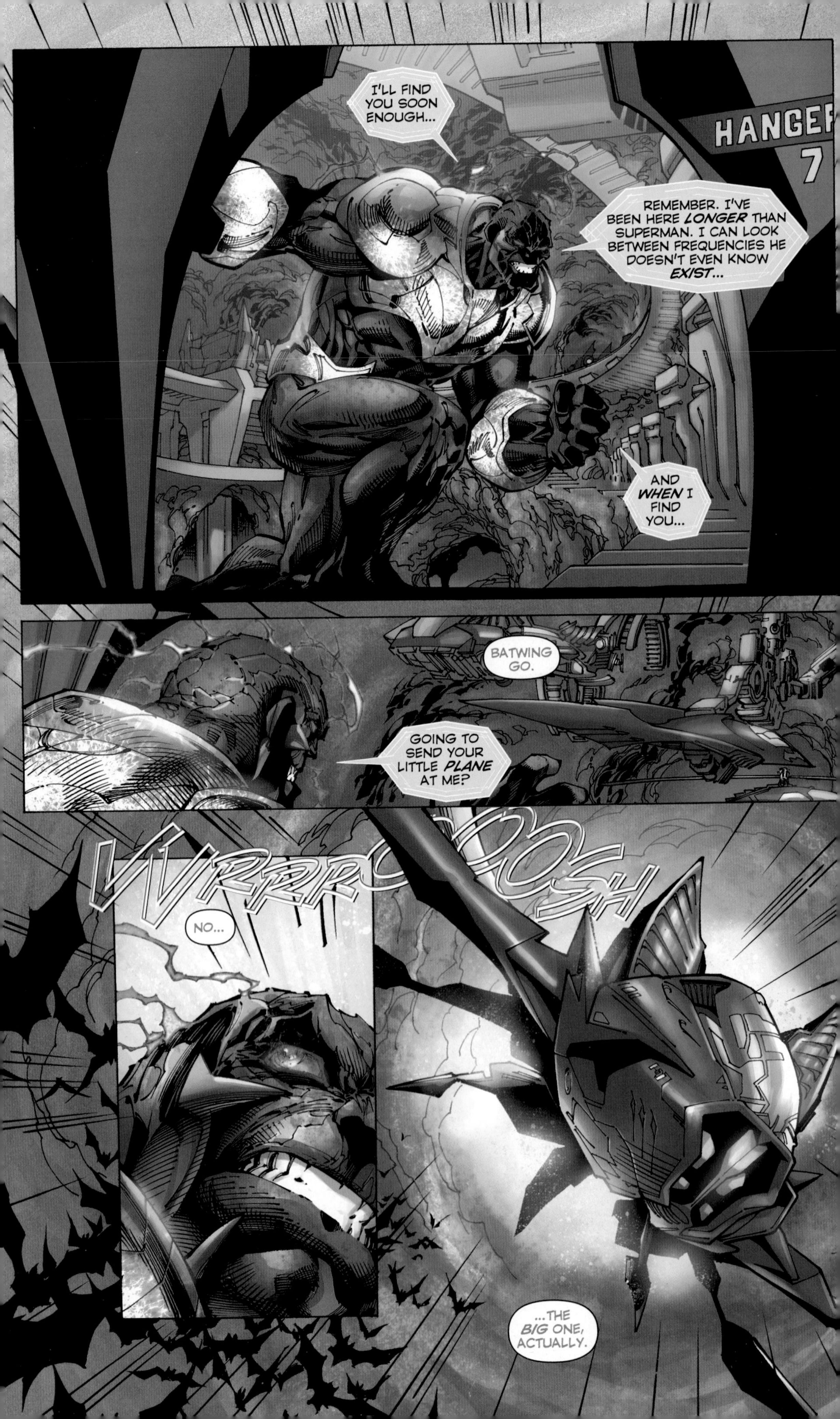

HANGER 7
I'LL FIND YOU SOON ENOUGH...
REMEMBER. I'VE BEEN HERE *LONGER* THAN SUPERMAN. I CAN LOOK BETWEEN FREQUENCIES HE DOESN'T EVEN KNOW *EXIST*...
AND *WHEN* I FIND YOU...
BATWING GO.
GOING TO SEND YOUR LITTLE *PLANE* AT ME?
VVRRROOOOSH
NO...
...THE *BIG* ONE, ACTUALLY.

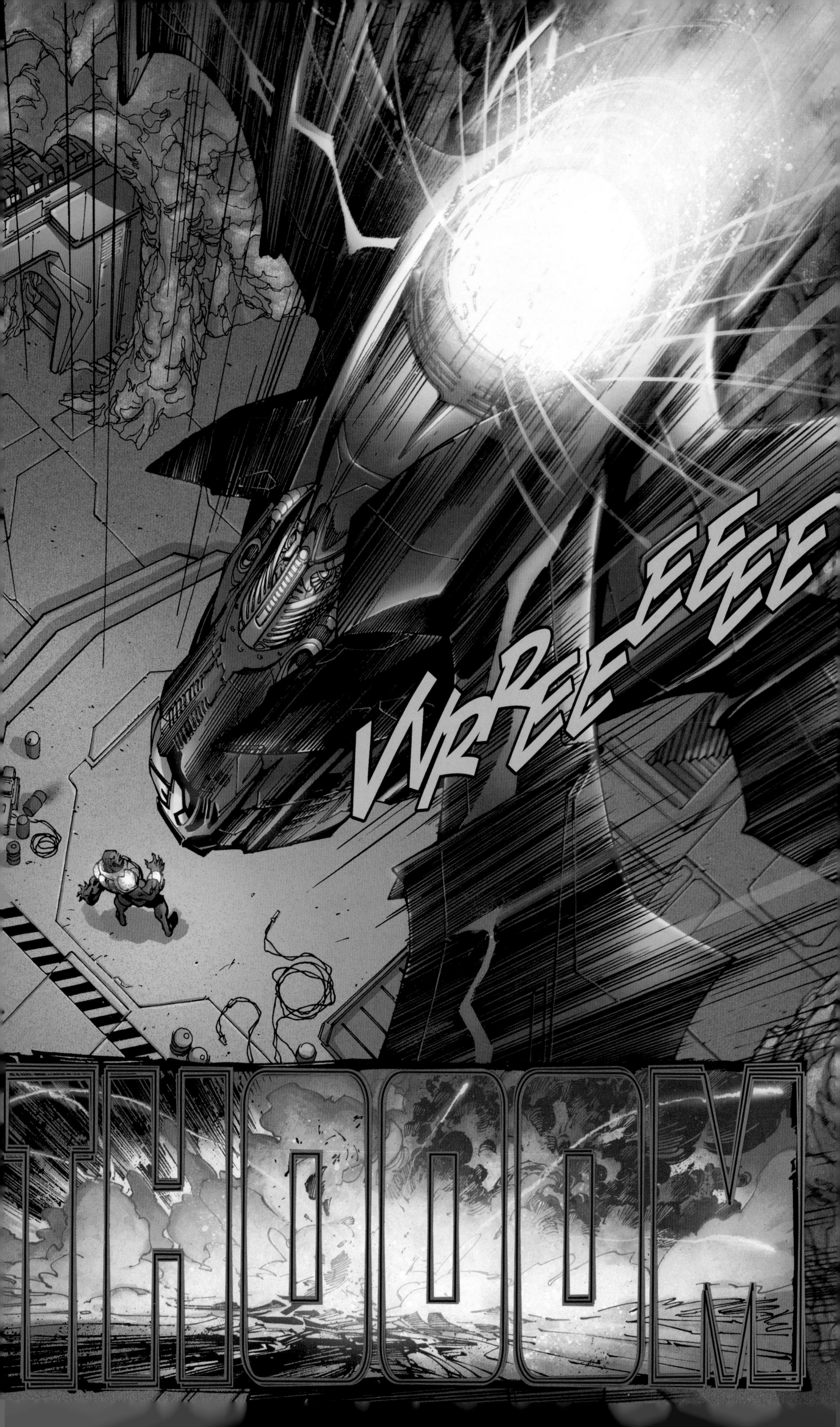
VVREEEEEEEE
THOOOM

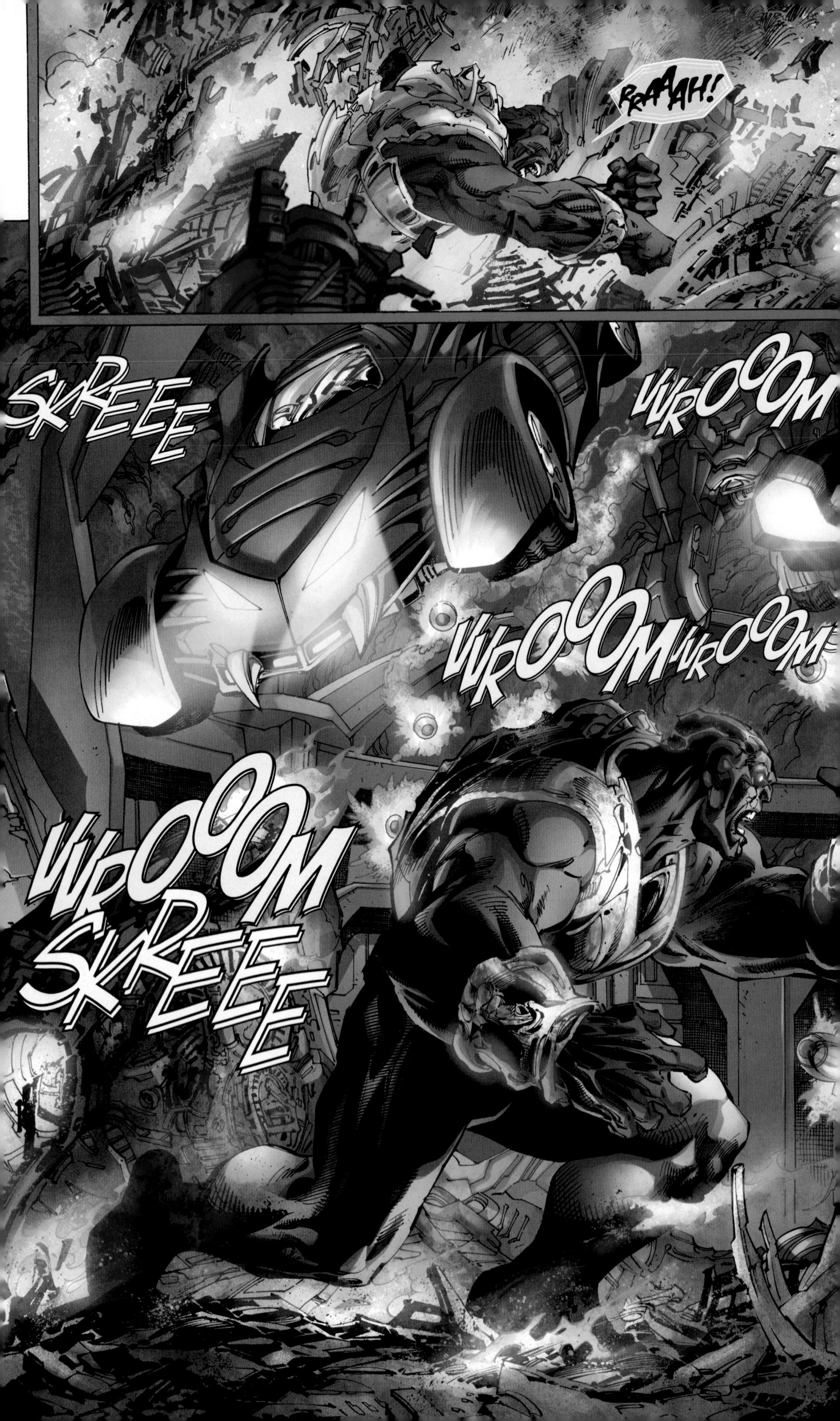
RRAAAH!
SKREEEE
VVROOOM
VVROOOOM VROOOOM
VVROOOOM
SKREEEE

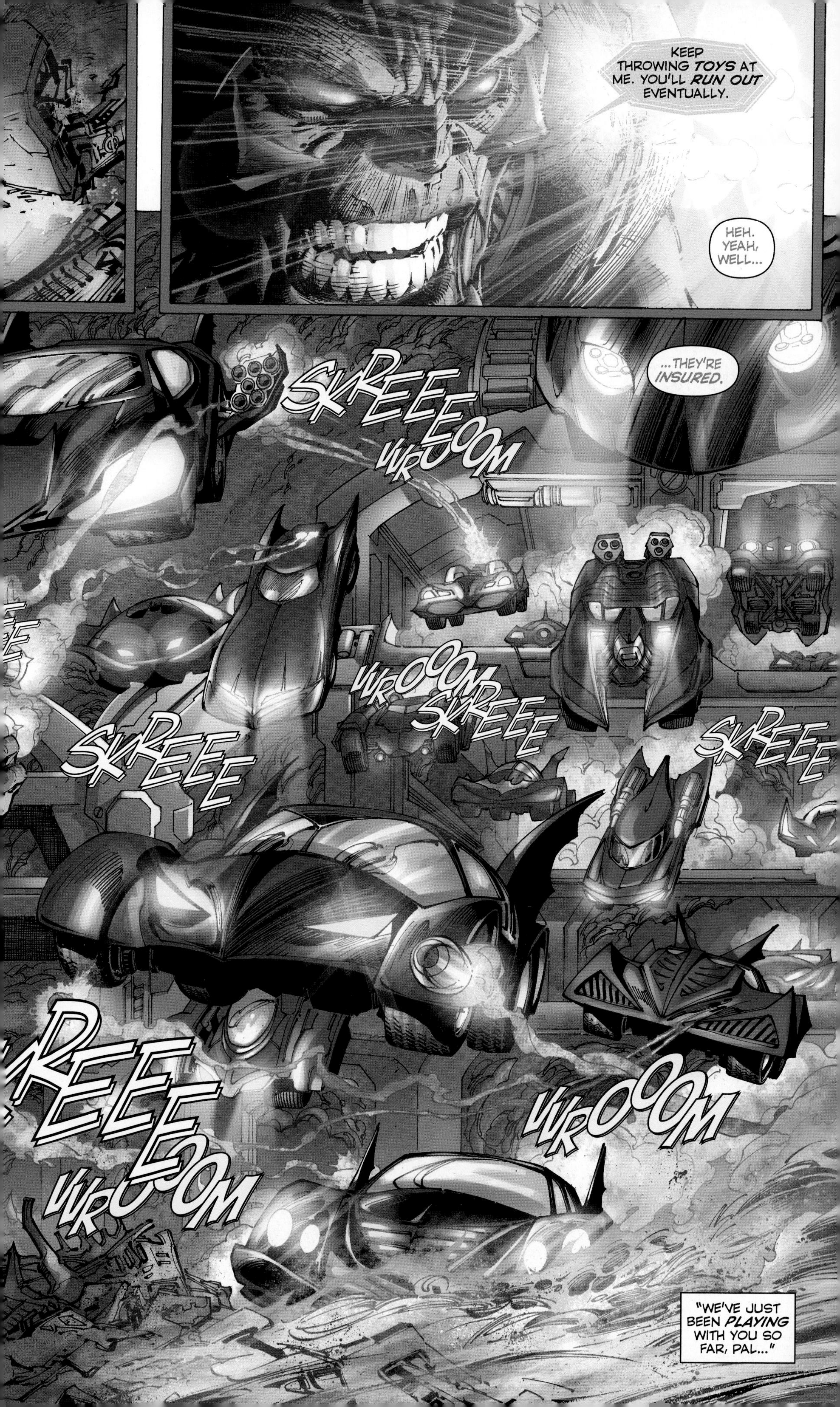
KEEP THROWING TOYS AT ME. YOU'LL RUN OUT EVENTUALLY.
HEH. YEAH, WELL...
...THEY'RE INSURED.
SKREEEEE
VVROOOM
VVROOOM
SKREEEE
SKREEEE
SKREEEE
REEEEE
VVROOOM
VVROOOM
"WE'VE JUST BEEN PLAYING WITH YOU SO FAR, PAL..."

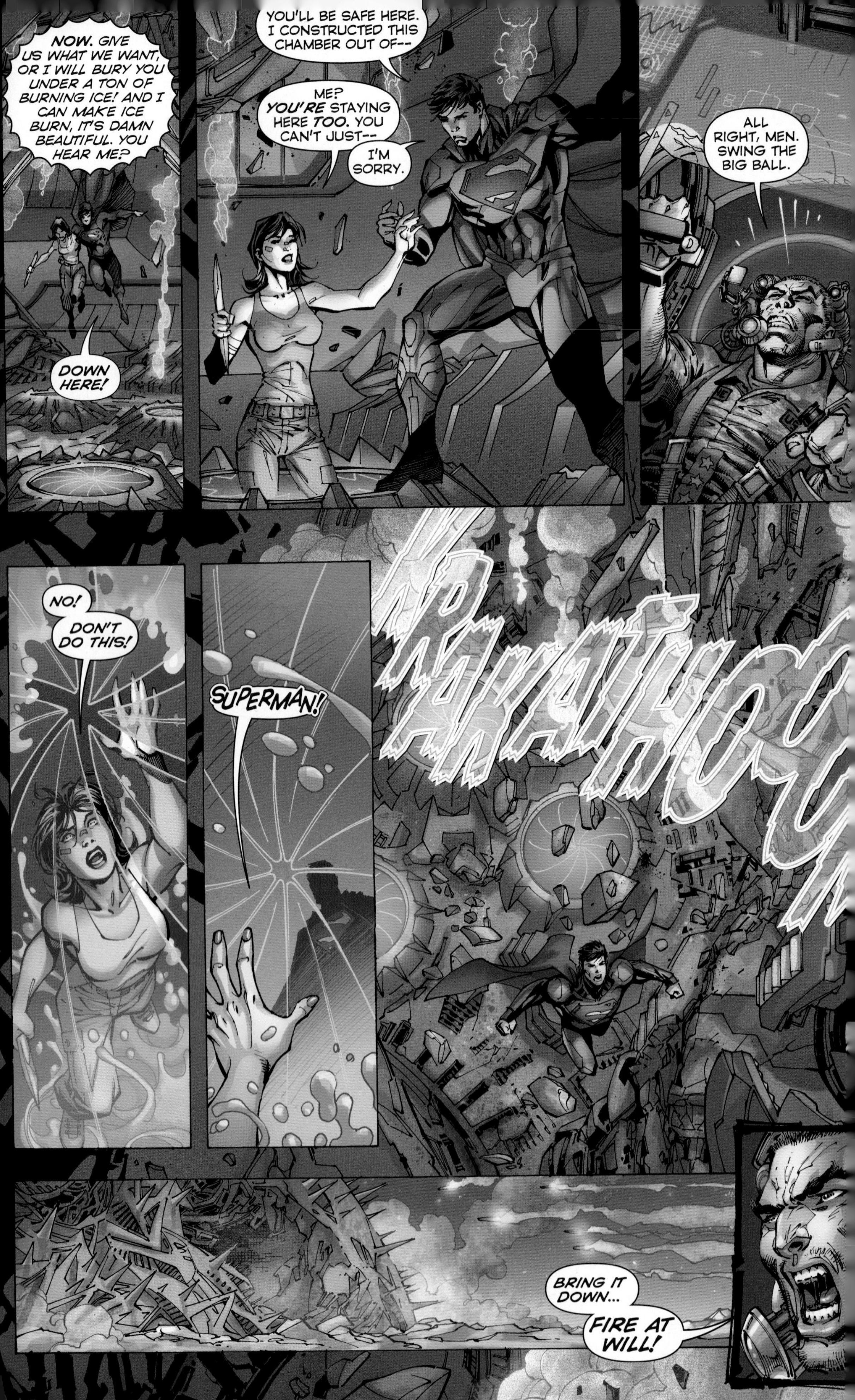
NOW. GIVE US WHAT WE WANT, OR I WILL BURY YOU UNDER A TON OF BURNING ICE! AND I CAN MAKE ICE BURN, IT'S DAMN BEAUTIFUL. YOU HEAR ME?
DOWN HERE!
YOU'LL BE SAFE HERE. I CONSTRUCTED THIS CHAMBER OUT OF--
ME? YOU'RE STAYING HERE TOO. YOU CAN'T JUST--
I'M SORRY.
ALL RIGHT, MEN. SWING THE BIG BALL.
NO! DON'T DO THIS!
SUPERMAN!
BRING IT DOWN...
FIRE AT WILL!

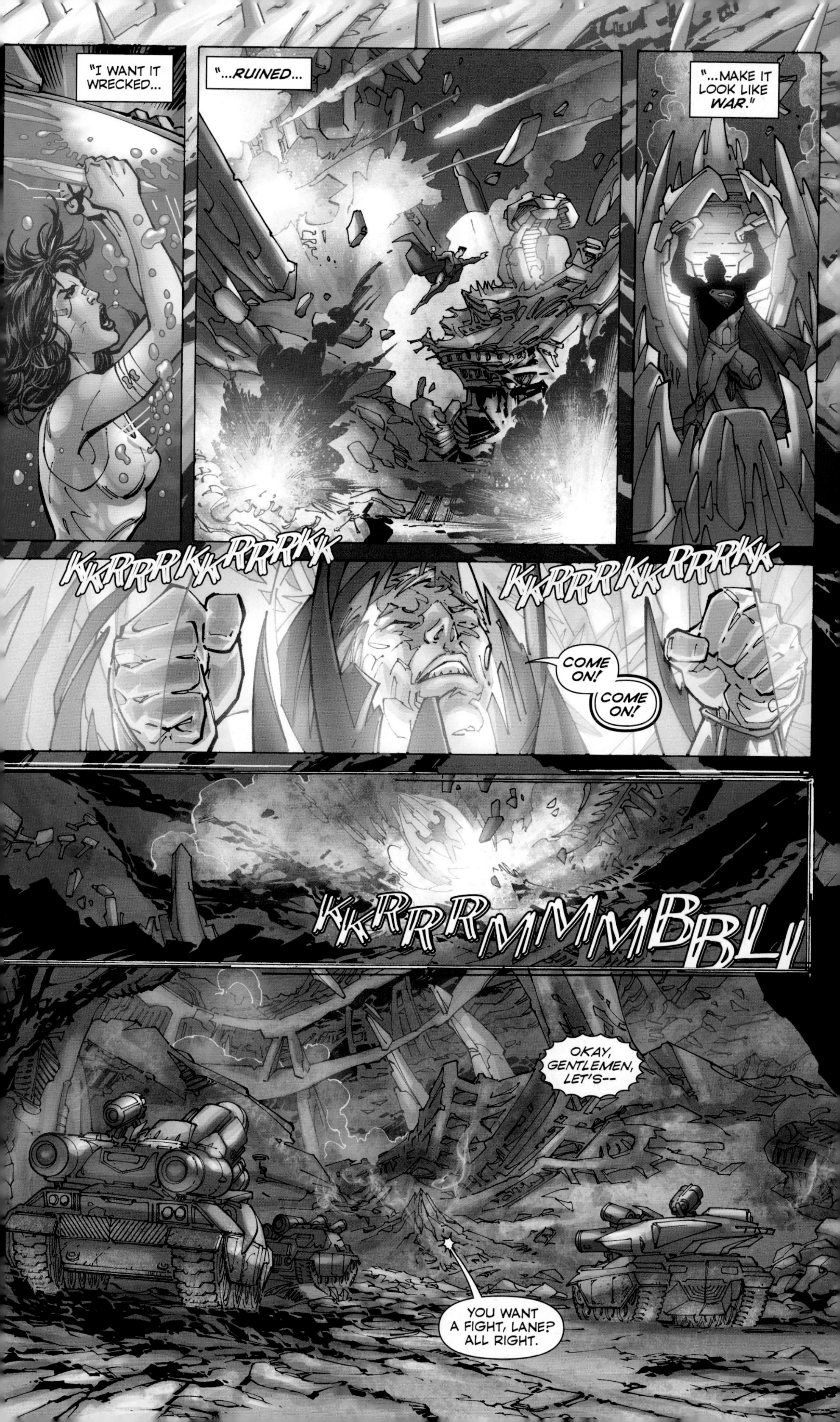
"I WANT IT WRECKED...
"...RUINED...
"...MAKE IT LOOK LIKE WAR."
KKRRRRKKRRRRKK
KKRRRRKKRRRRKK
COME ON!
COME ON!
KKRRRRMMMMBBLI
OKAY, GENTLEMEN, LET'S--
YOU WANT A FIGHT, LANE? ALL RIGHT.

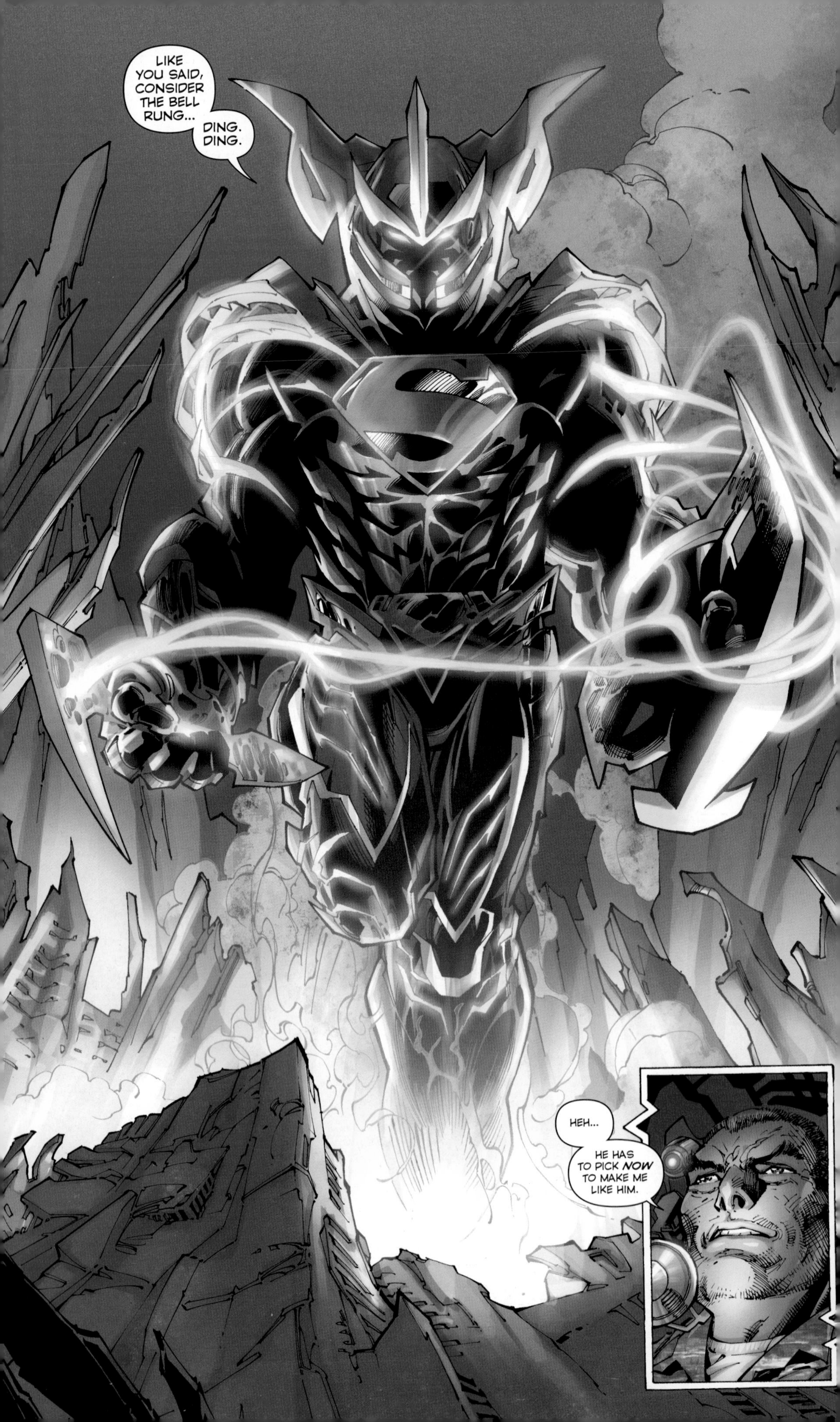
LIKE YOU SAID, CONSIDER THE BELL RUNG...
DING. DING.
HEH...
HE HAS TO PICK *NOW* TO MAKE ME LIKE HIM.

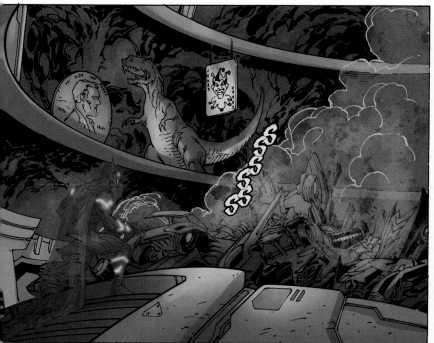

I'M DONE *LOOKING* FOR YOU...

...HOW ABOUT I JUST COOK THE AIR?

ZZZTT

UNH!

NOW...

...LET'S SEE YOU *FLY,* LITTLE BAT.

THWMP

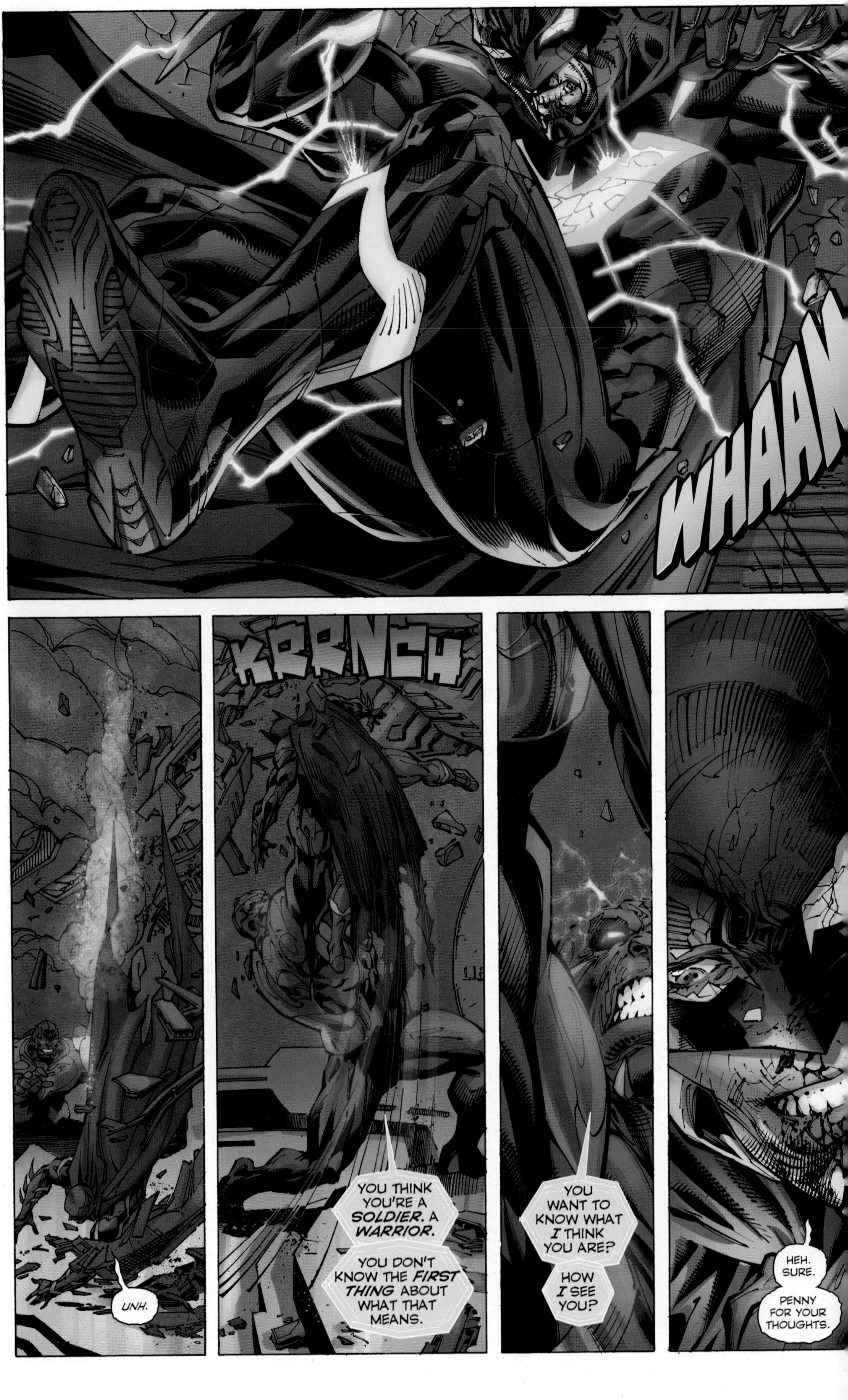

WHAAM
KRRNCH
UNH.
YOU THINK YOU'RE A SOLDIER. A WARRIOR.
YOU DON'T KNOW THE FIRST THING ABOUT WHAT THAT MEANS.
YOU WANT TO KNOW WHAT I THINK YOU ARE?
HOW I SEE YOU?
HEH. SURE.
PENNY FOR YOUR THOUGHTS.

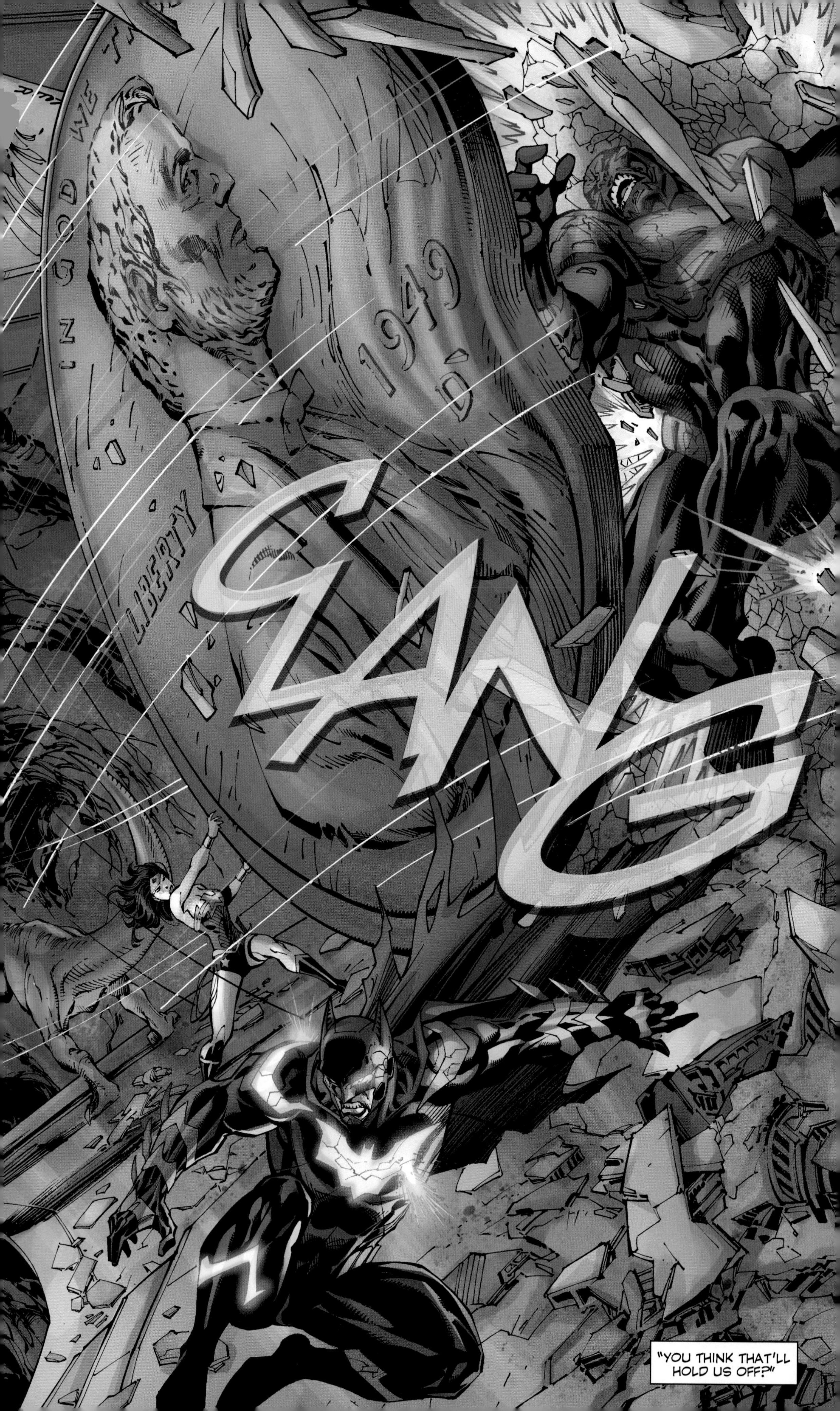
IN GOD WE TRUST
LIBERTY
1949
D
CLANG
"YOU THINK THAT'LL HOLD US OFF?"

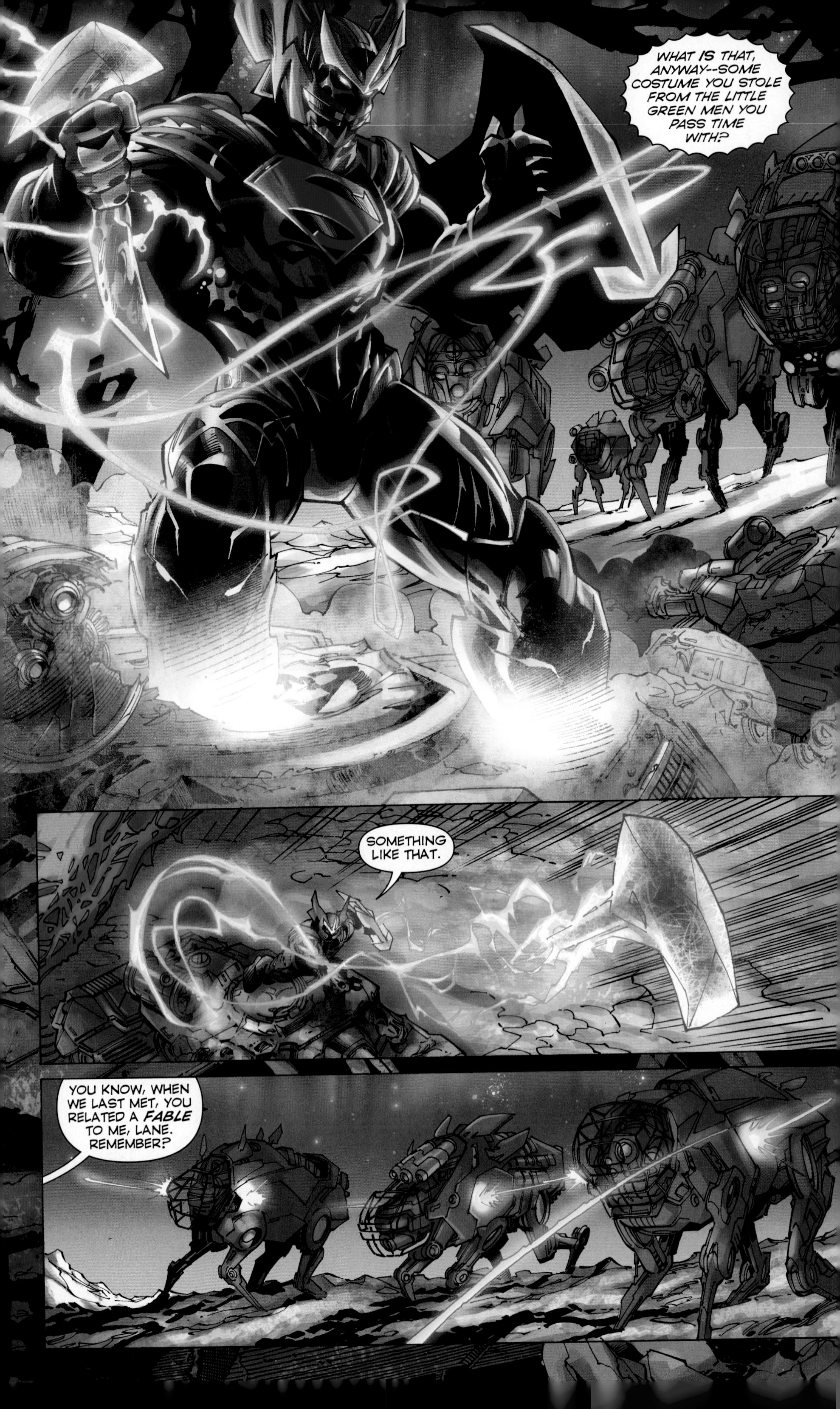
WHAT *IS* THAT, ANYWAY--SOME COSTUME YOU STOLE FROM THE LITTLE GREEN MEN YOU PASS TIME WITH?
SOMETHING LIKE THAT.
YOU KNOW, WHEN WE LAST MET, YOU RELATED A *FABLE* TO ME, LANE. REMEMBER?

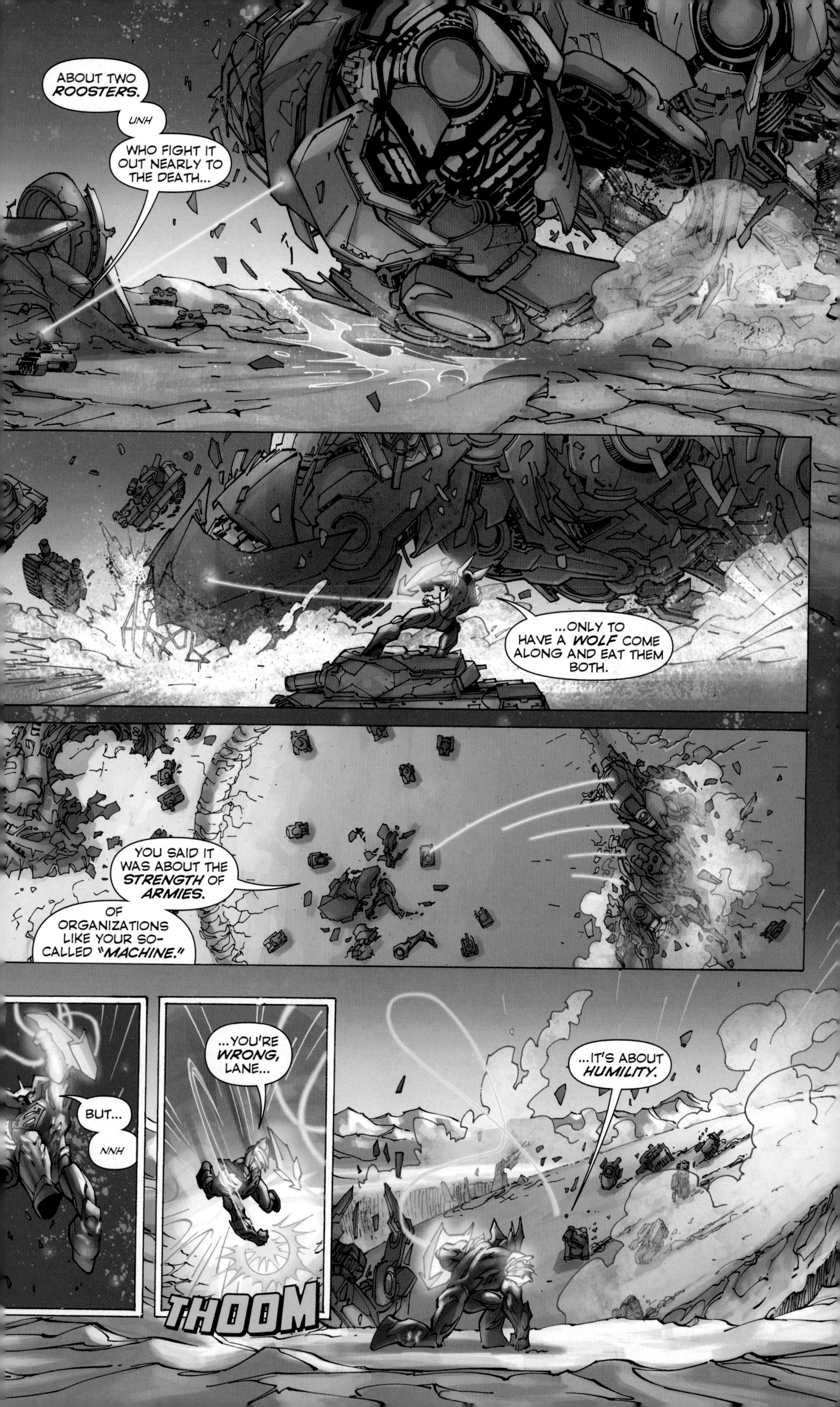
ABOUT TWO ROOSTERS.
UNH
WHO FIGHT IT OUT NEARLY TO THE DEATH...
...ONLY TO HAVE A WOLF COME ALONG AND EAT THEM BOTH.
YOU SAID IT WAS ABOUT THE STRENGTH OF ARMIES.
OF ORGANIZATIONS LIKE YOUR SO-CALLED "MACHINE."
BUT...
NNH
...YOU'RE WRONG, LANE...
THOOM
...IT'S ABOUT HUMILITY.

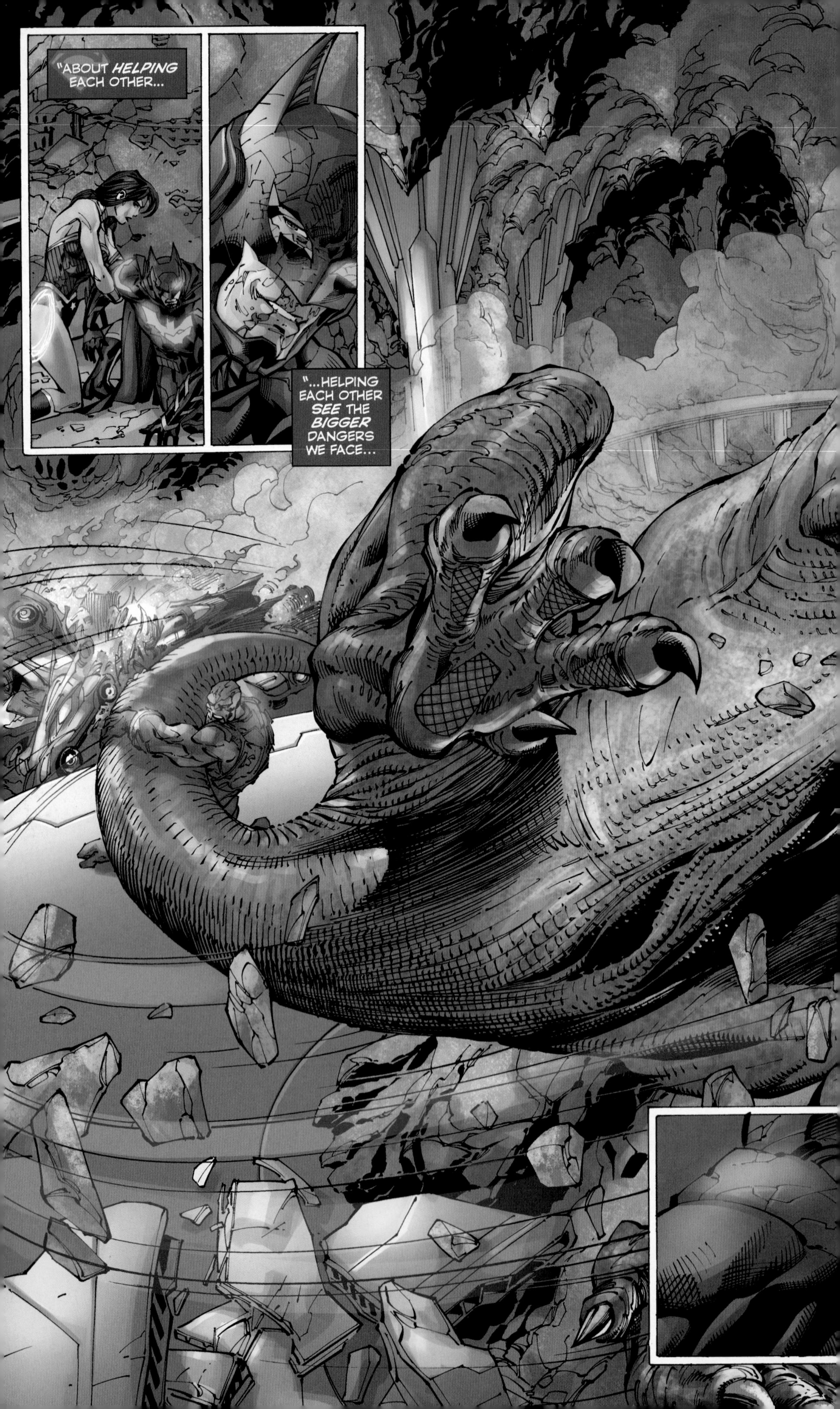
"ABOUT HELPING EACH OTHER...
"...HELPING EACH OTHER SEE THE BIGGER DANGERS WE FACE...

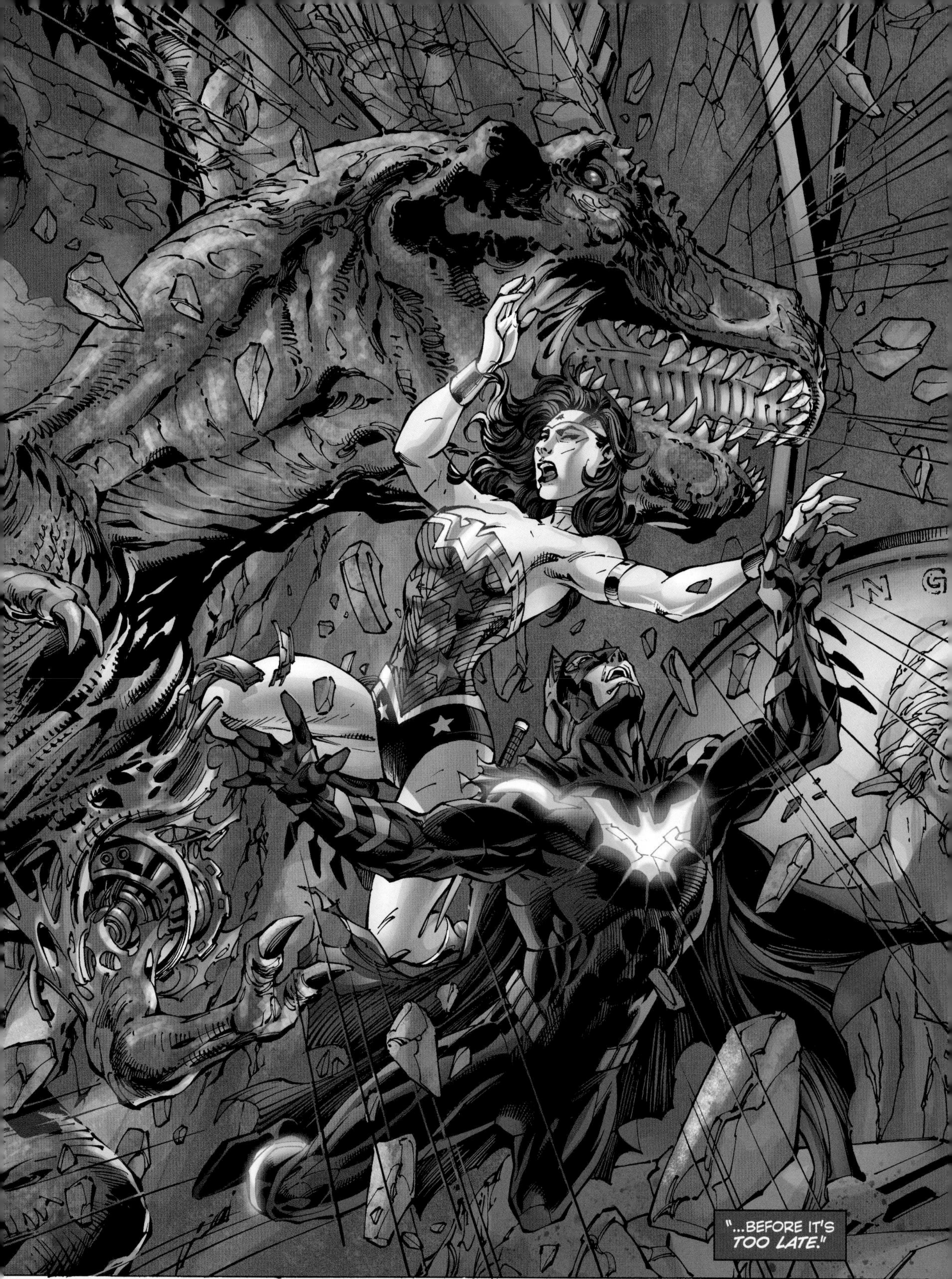
"...BEFORE IT'S
TOO LATE."

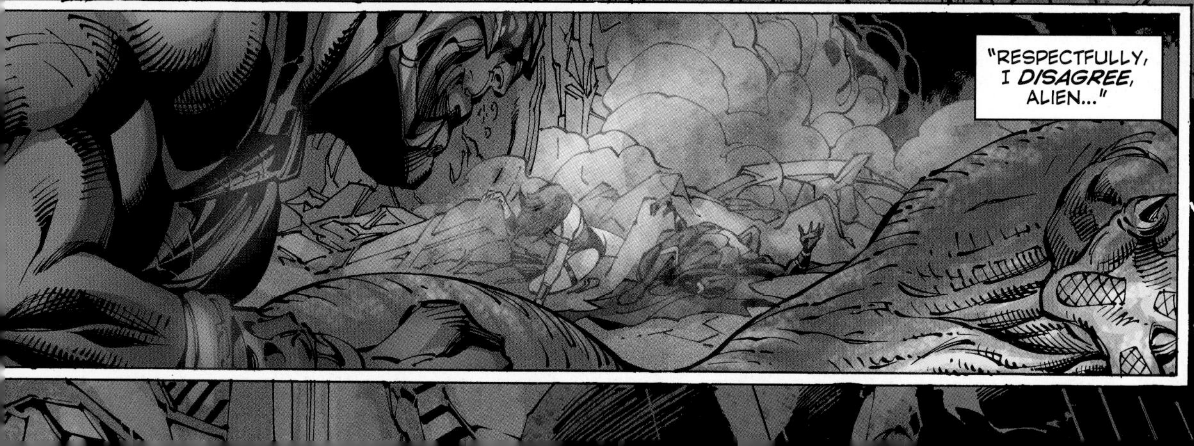
"RESPECTFULLY,
I DISAGREE,
ALIEN..."

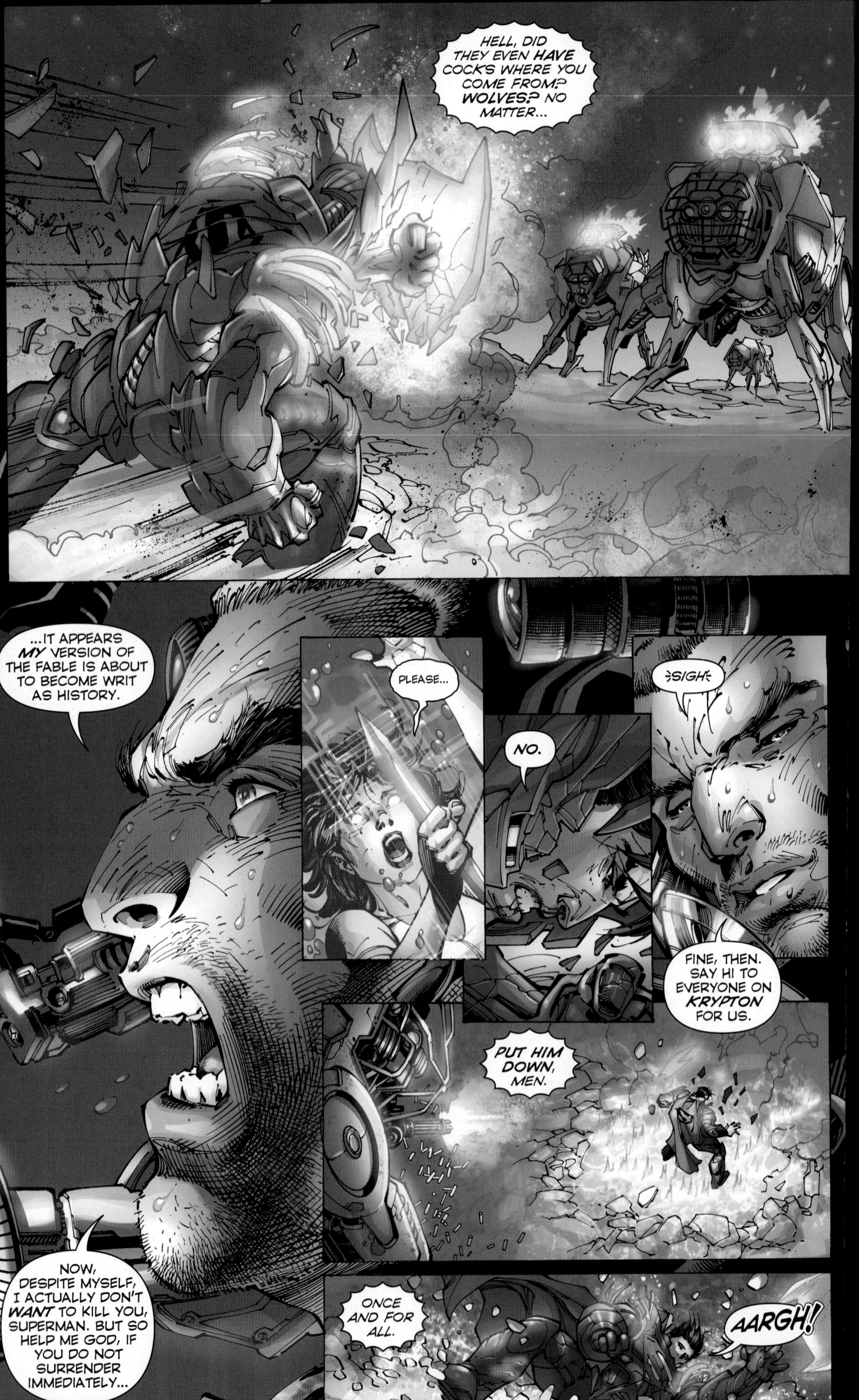
HELL, DID THEY EVEN HAVE COCKS WHERE YOU COME FROM? WOLVES? NO MATTER...
...IT APPEARS MY VERSION OF THE FABLE IS ABOUT TO BECOME WRIT AS HISTORY.
NOW, DESPITE MYSELF, I ACTUALLY DON'T WANT TO KILL YOU, SUPERMAN. BUT SO HELP ME GOD, IF YOU DO NOT SURRENDER IMMEDIATELY...
PLEASE...
NO.
SIGH
FINE, THEN. SAY HI TO EVERYONE ON KRYPTON FOR US.
PUT HIM DOWN, MEN.
ONCE AND FOR ALL.
AARGH!

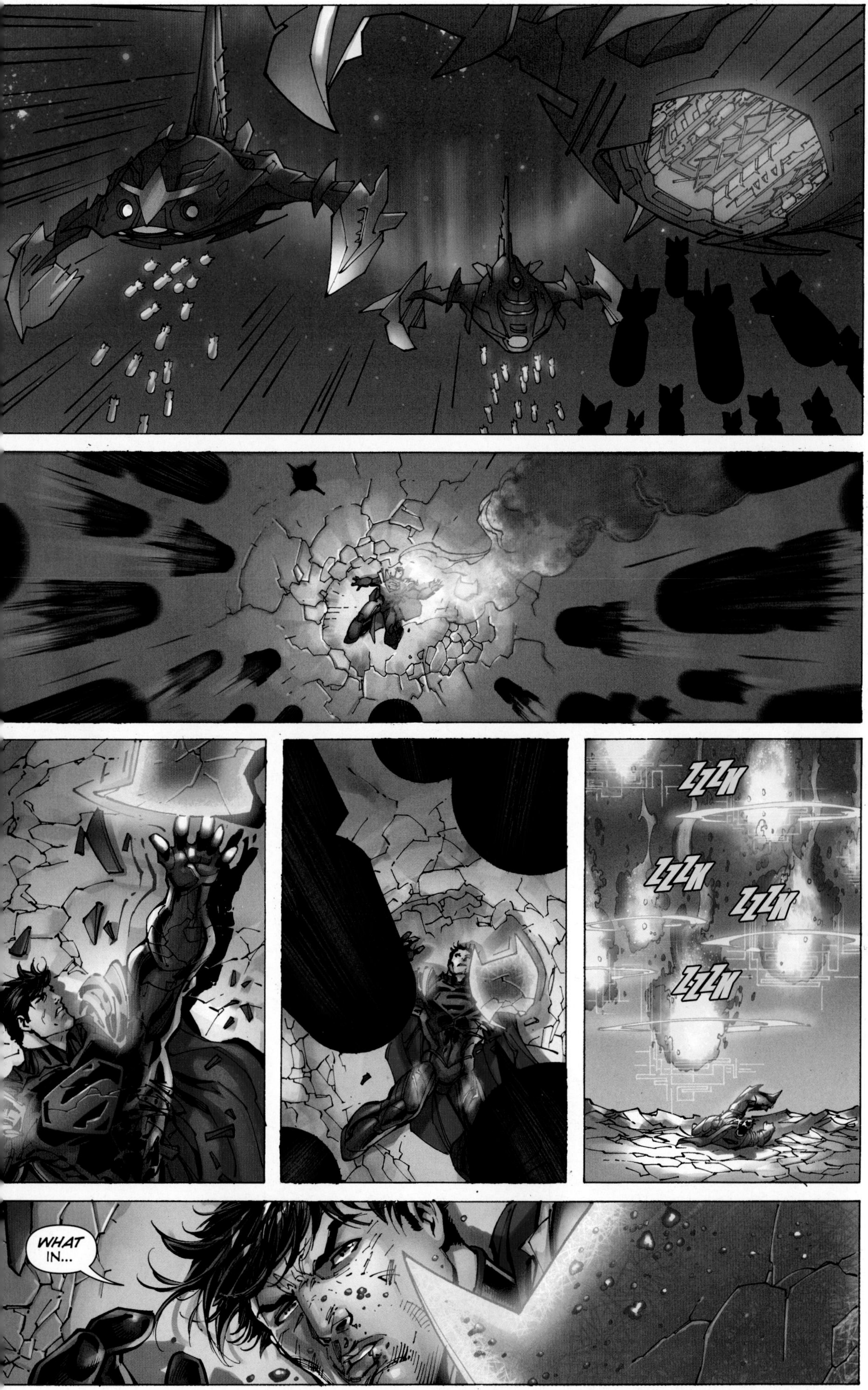
ZZZK
ZZZK
ZZZK
ZZZK
WHAT IN...

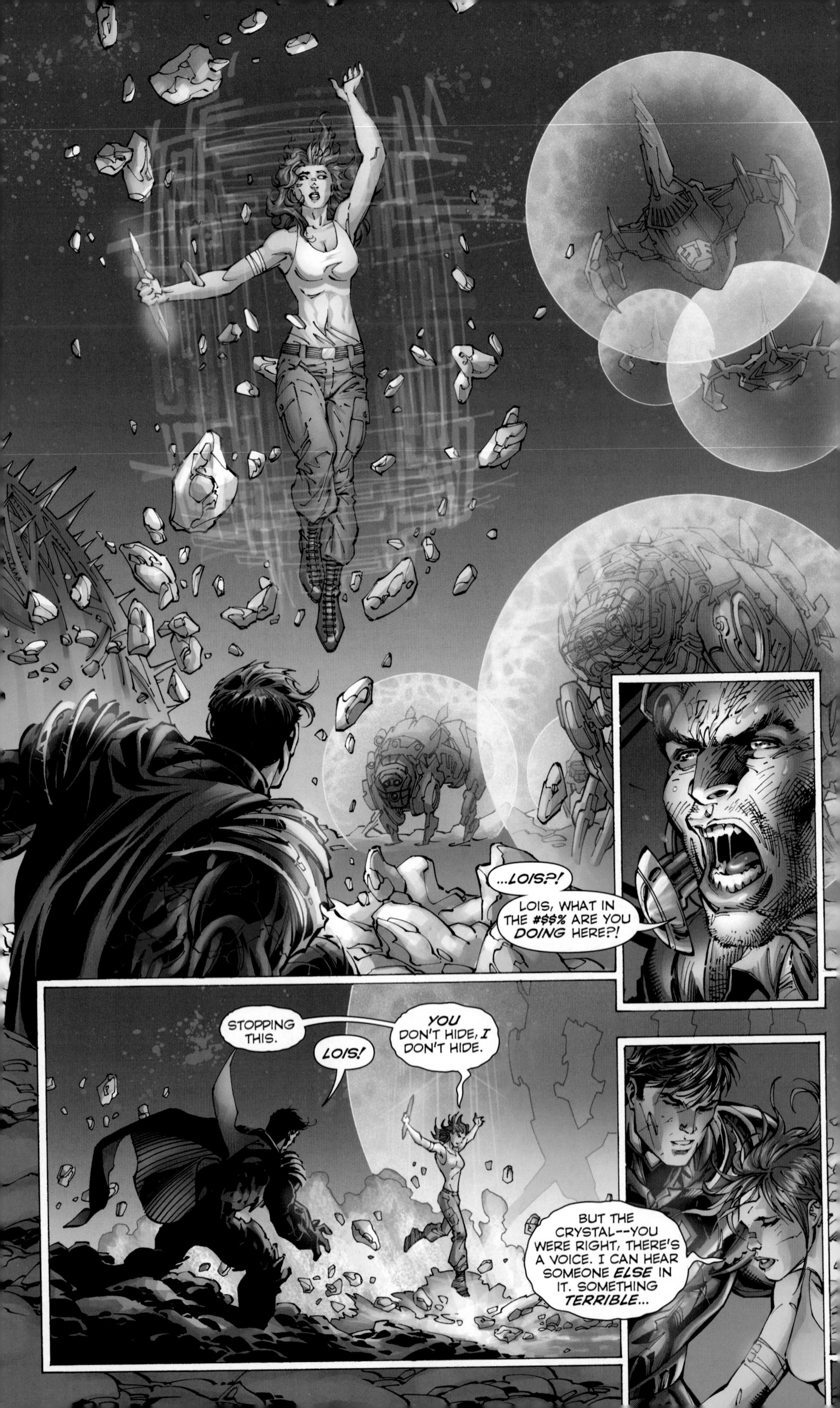

...LOIS?!
LOIS, WHAT IN THE #$$% ARE YOU DOING HERE?!
STOPPING THIS.
LOIS!
YOU DON'T HIDE, I DON'T HIDE.
BUT THE CRYSTAL--YOU WERE RIGHT, THERE'S A VOICE. I CAN HEAR SOMEONE ELSE IN IT. SOMETHING TERRIBLE...

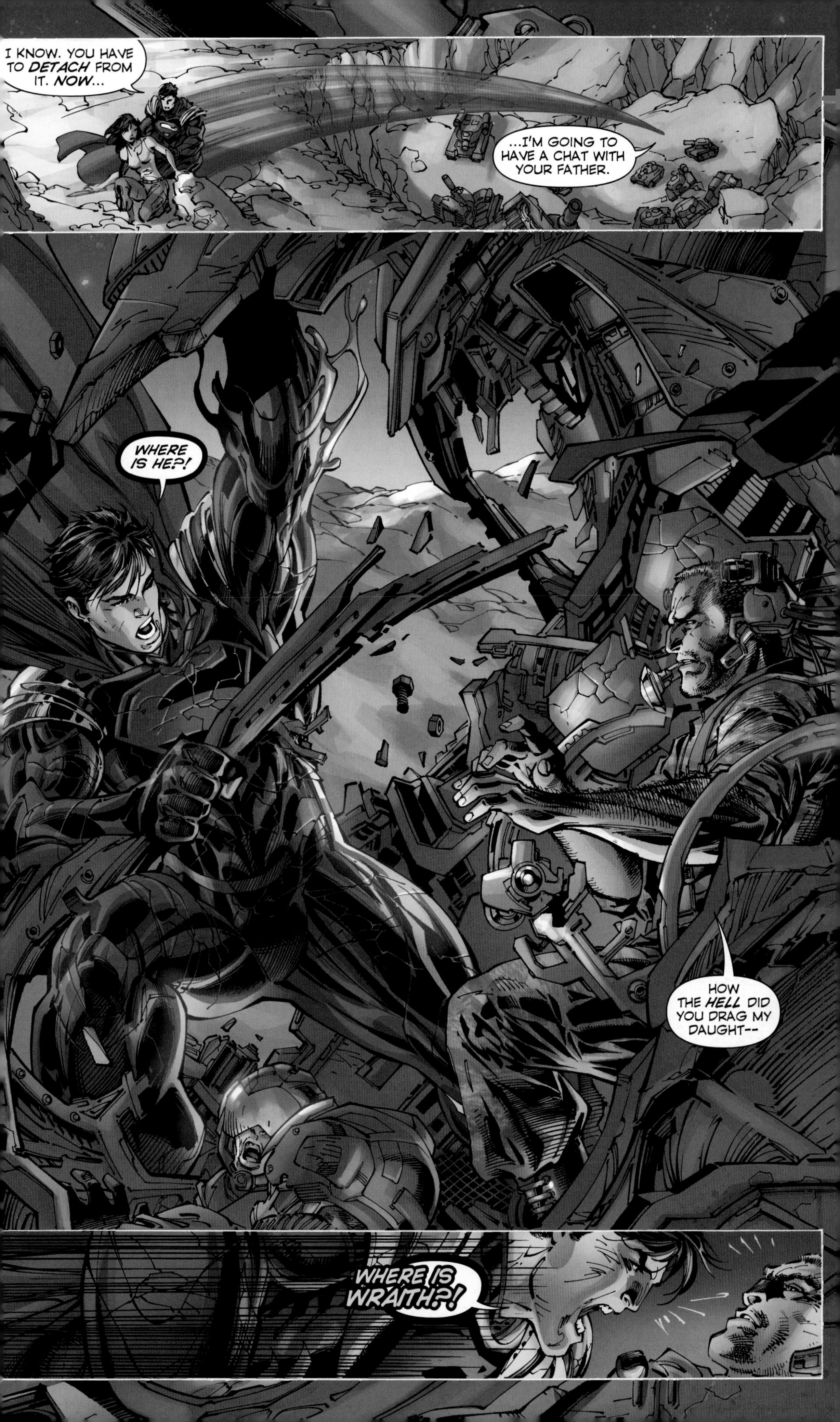
I KNOW. YOU HAVE TO DETACH FROM IT. NOW...
...I'M GOING TO HAVE A CHAT WITH YOUR FATHER.
WHERE IS HE?!
HOW THE HELL DID YOU DRAG MY DAUGHT--
WHERE IS WRAITH?!

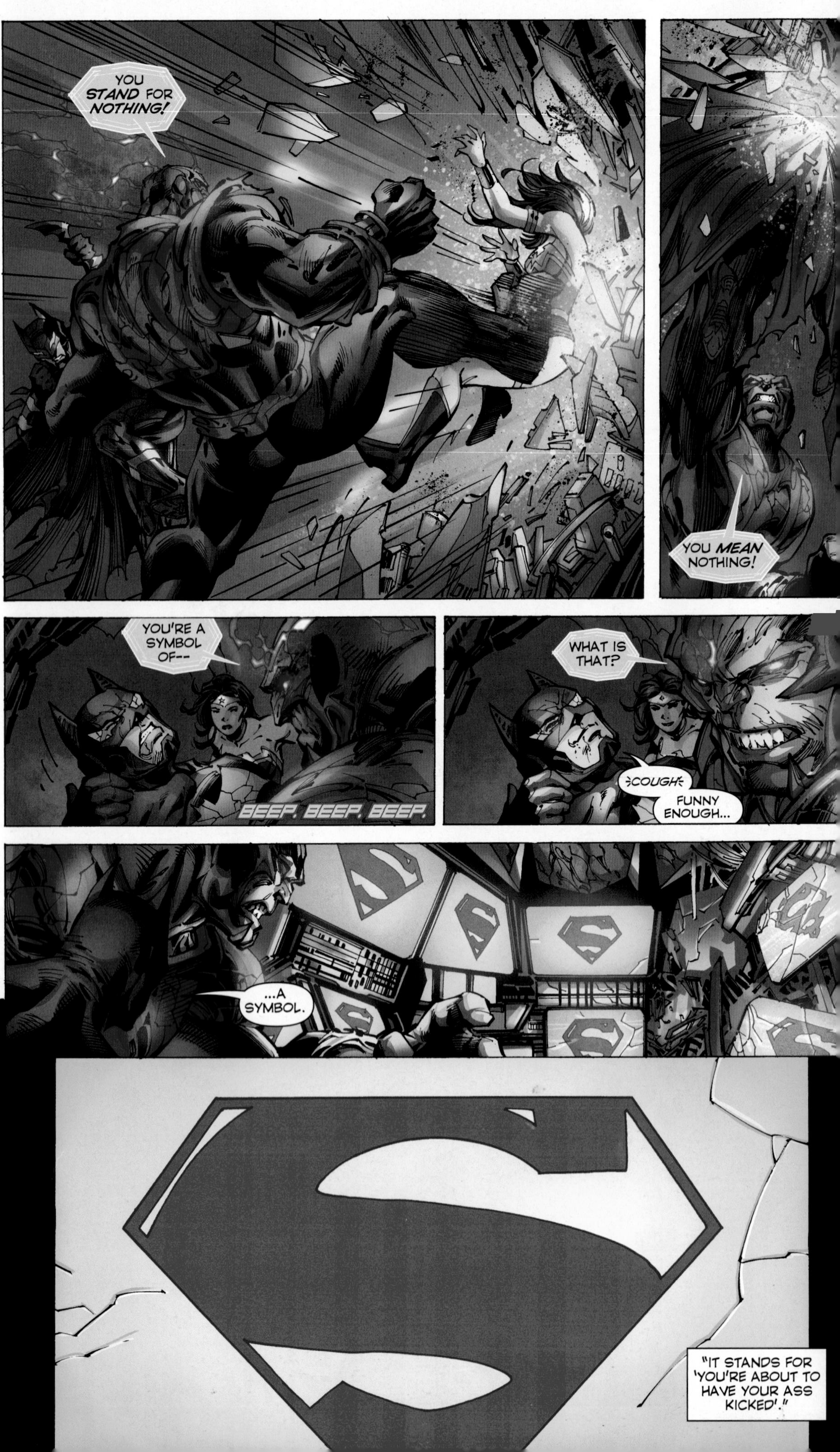

YOU STAND FOR NOTHING!
YOU MEAN NOTHING!
YOU'RE A SYMBOL OF--
BEEP. BEEP. BEEP.
WHAT IS THAT?
COUGH
FUNNY ENOUGH...
...A SYMBOL.
"IT STANDS FOR 'YOU'RE ABOUT TO HAVE YOUR ASS KICKED'."

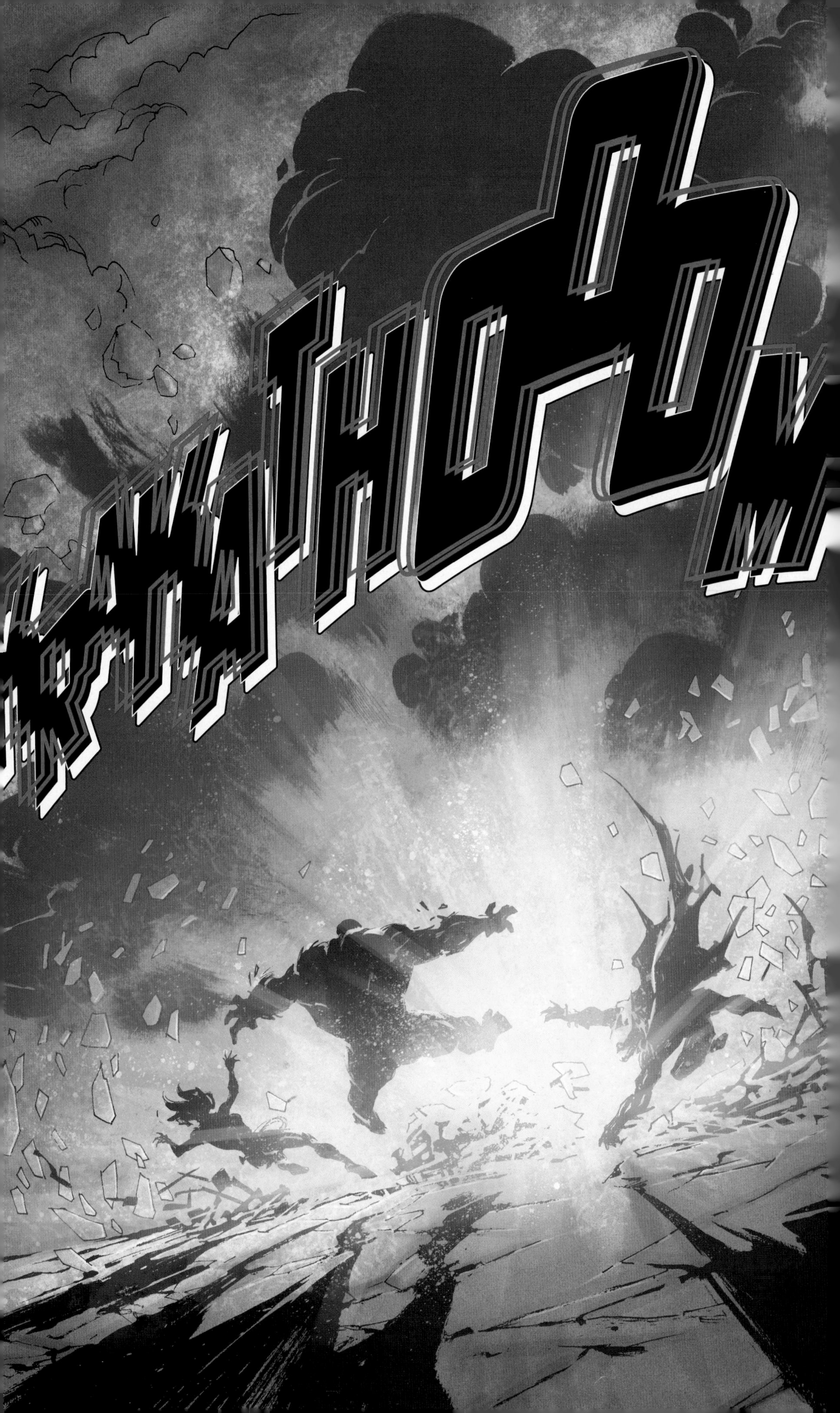
THOOM

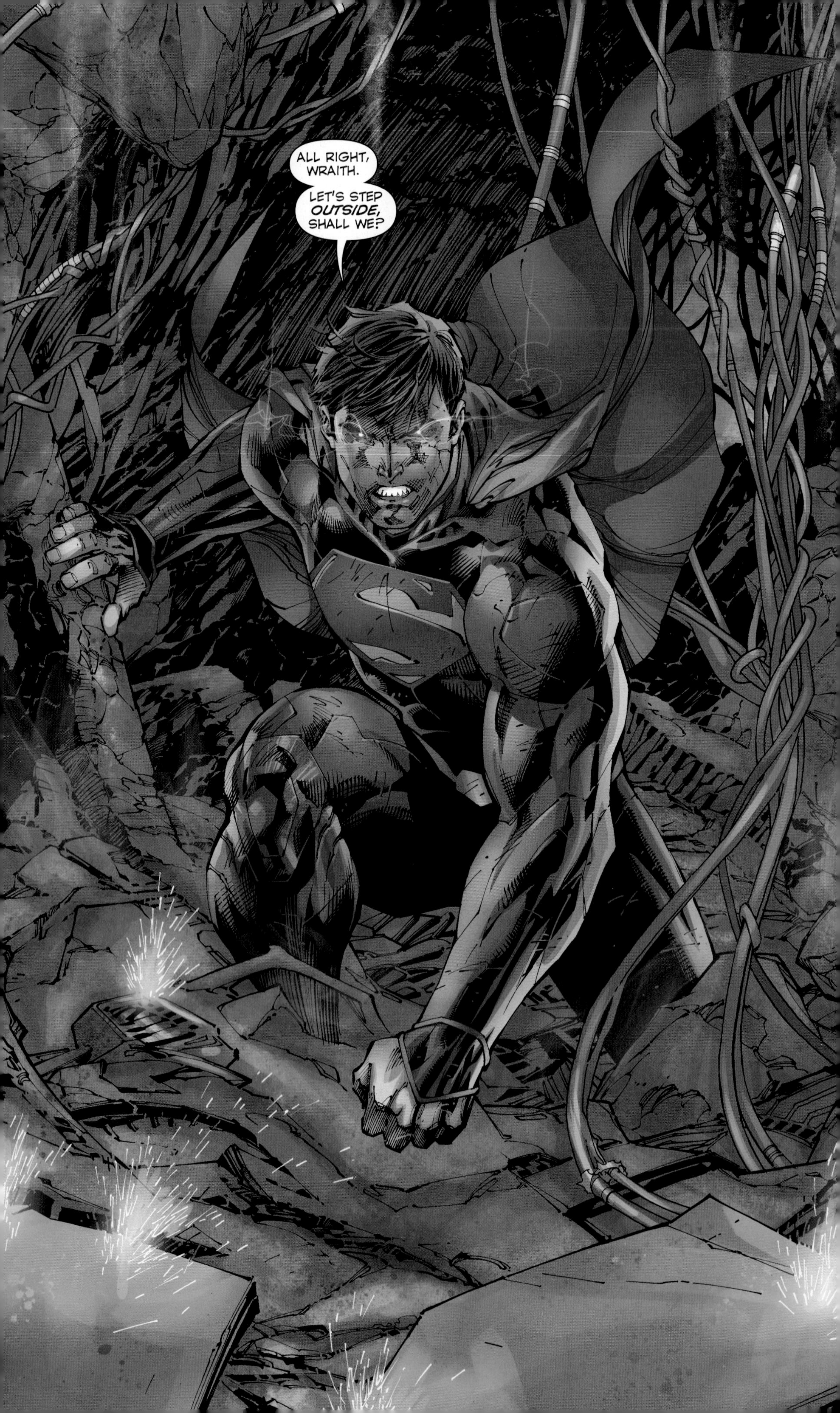
ALL RIGHT, WRAITH.
LET'S STEP *OUTSIDE*, SHALL WE?

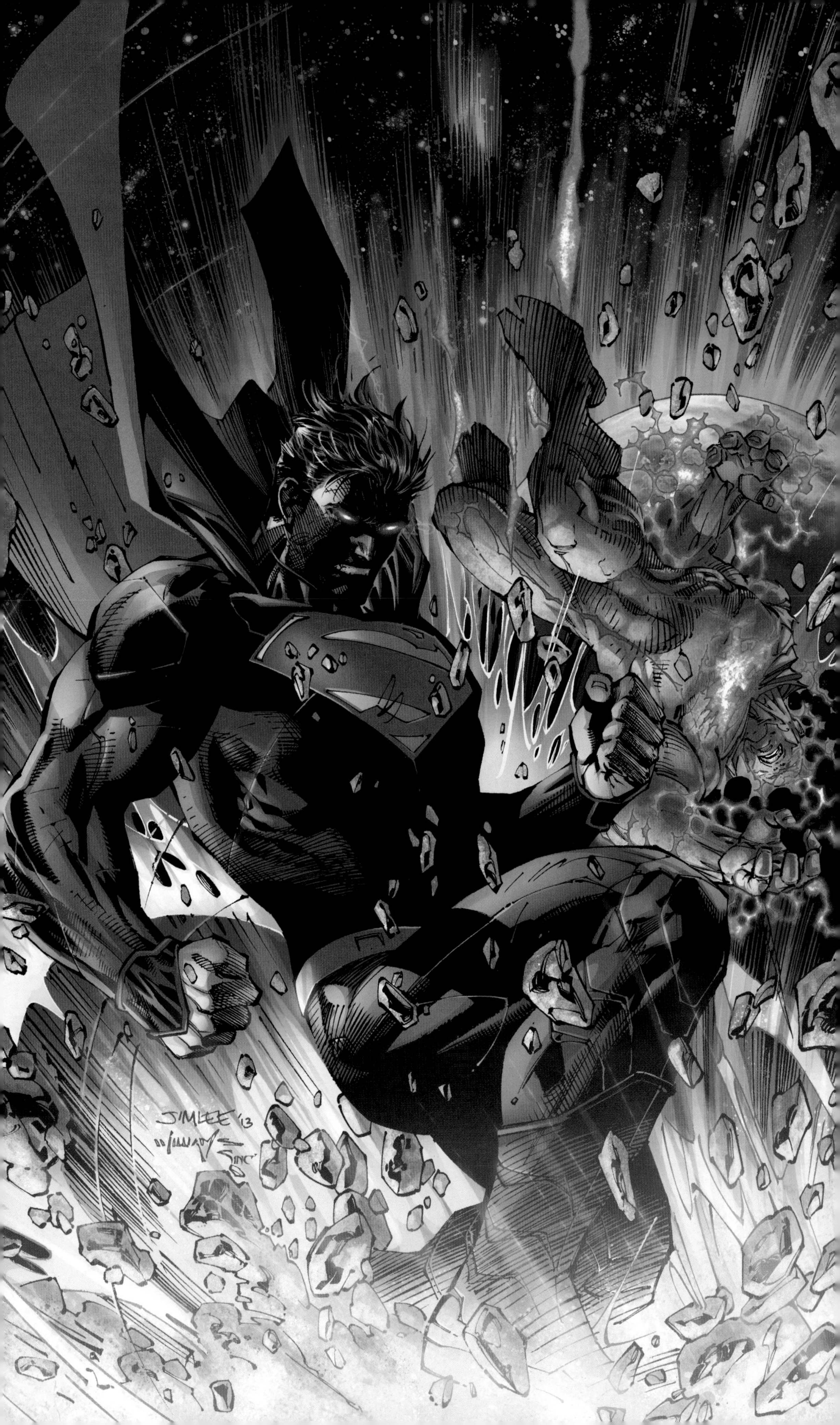
JIMLEE '13

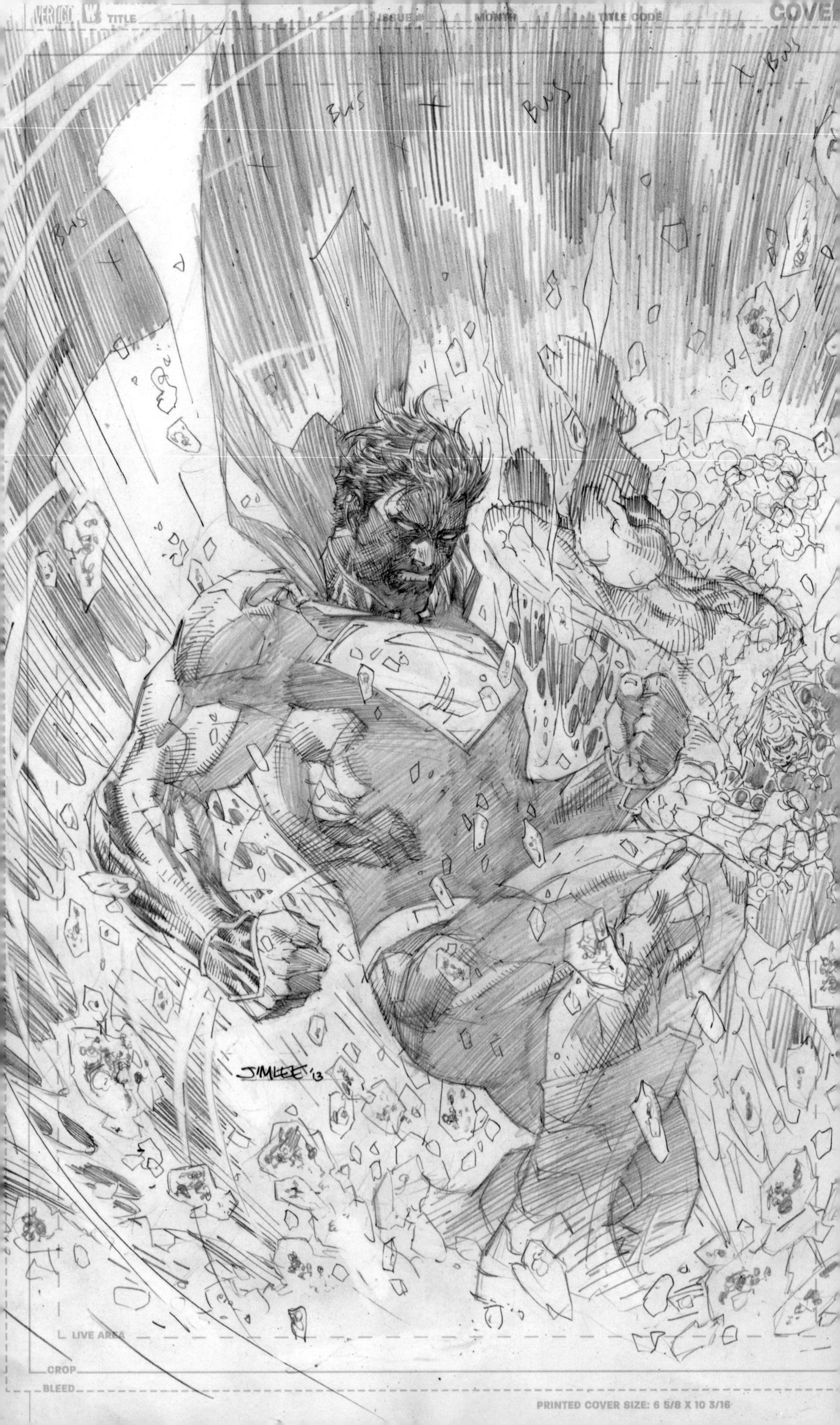
TITLE
ISSUE #
MONTH
TITLE CODE
COVER
JIM LEE '13
LIVE AREA
CROP
BLEED
PRINTED COVER SIZE: 6 5/8 X 10 3/16

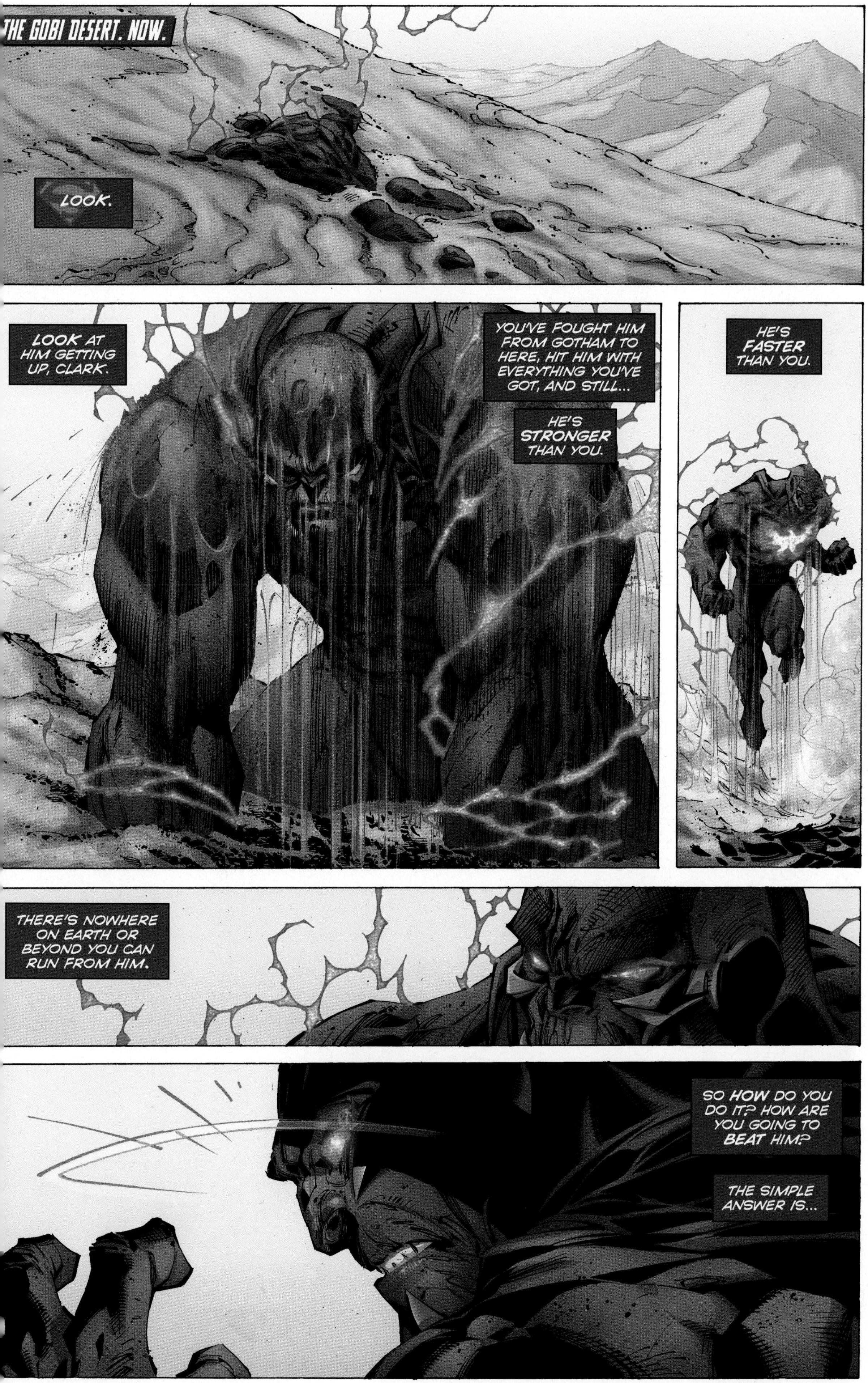

THE GOBI DESERT. NOW.
LOOK.
LOOK AT HIM GETTING UP, CLARK.
YOU'VE FOUGHT HIM FROM GOTHAM TO HERE, HIT HIM WITH EVERYTHING YOU'VE GOT, AND STILL...
HE'S STRONGER THAN YOU.
HE'S FASTER THAN YOU.
THERE'S NOWHERE ON EARTH OR BEYOND YOU CAN RUN FROM HIM.
SO HOW DO YOU DO IT? HOW ARE YOU GOING TO BEAT HIM?
THE SIMPLE ANSWER IS...

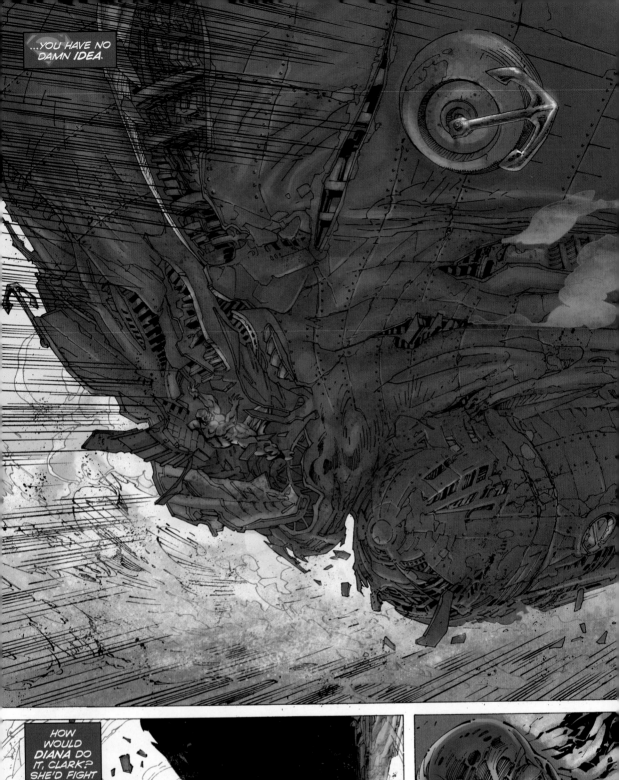

...YOU HAVE NO DAMN *IDEA*.

HOW WOULD *DIANA* DO IT, CLARK? SHE'D FIGHT THROUGH. UNLEASH THE WARRIOR.

THAT LOOKS HEAVY, SUPERMAN...

LET ME TAKE IT OFF YOUR HANDS.

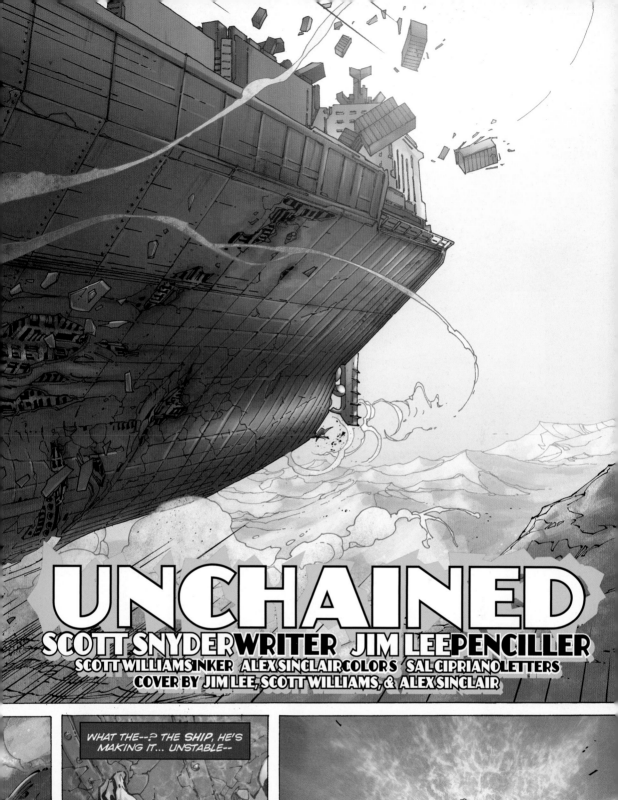

UNCHAINED

SCOTT SNYDER WRITER   **JIM LEE** PENCILLER

SCOTT WILLIAMS INKER   **ALEX SINCLAIR** COLORS   **SAL CIPRIANO** LETTERS
COVER BY JIM LEE, SCOTT WILLIAMS, & ALEX SINCLAIR

WHAT THE--? THE *SHIP*, HE'S MAKING IT... UNSTABLE--

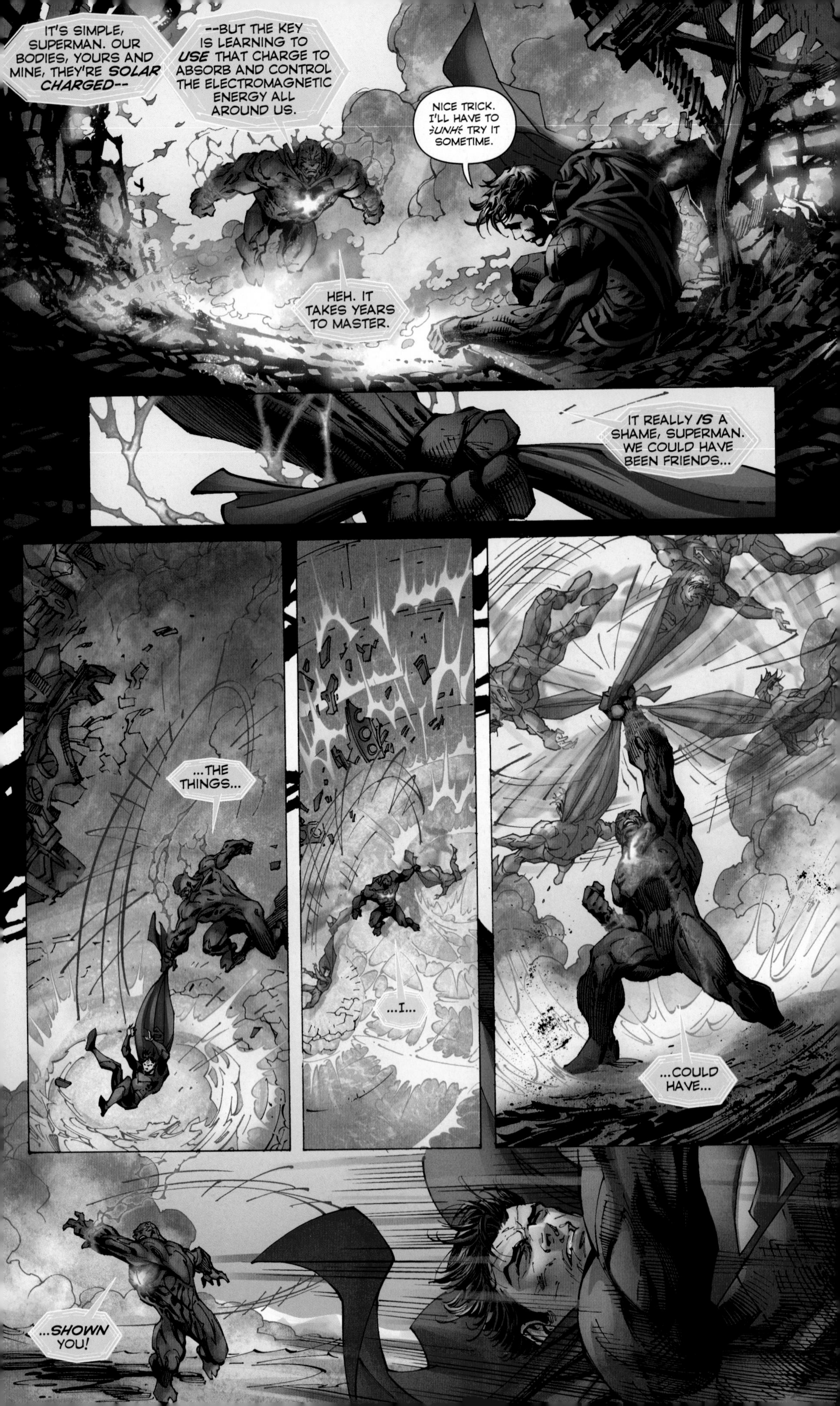

IT'S SIMPLE, SUPERMAN. OUR BODIES, YOURS AND MINE, THEY'RE SOLAR CHARGED--
--BUT THE KEY IS LEARNING TO USE THAT CHARGE TO ABSORB AND CONTROL THE ELECTROMAGNETIC ENERGY ALL AROUND US.
NICE TRICK. I'LL HAVE TO UNH TRY IT SOMETIME.
HEH. IT TAKES YEARS TO MASTER.
IT REALLY IS A SHAME, SUPERMAN. WE COULD HAVE BEEN FRIENDS...
...THE THINGS...
...I...
...COULD HAVE...
...SHOWN YOU!

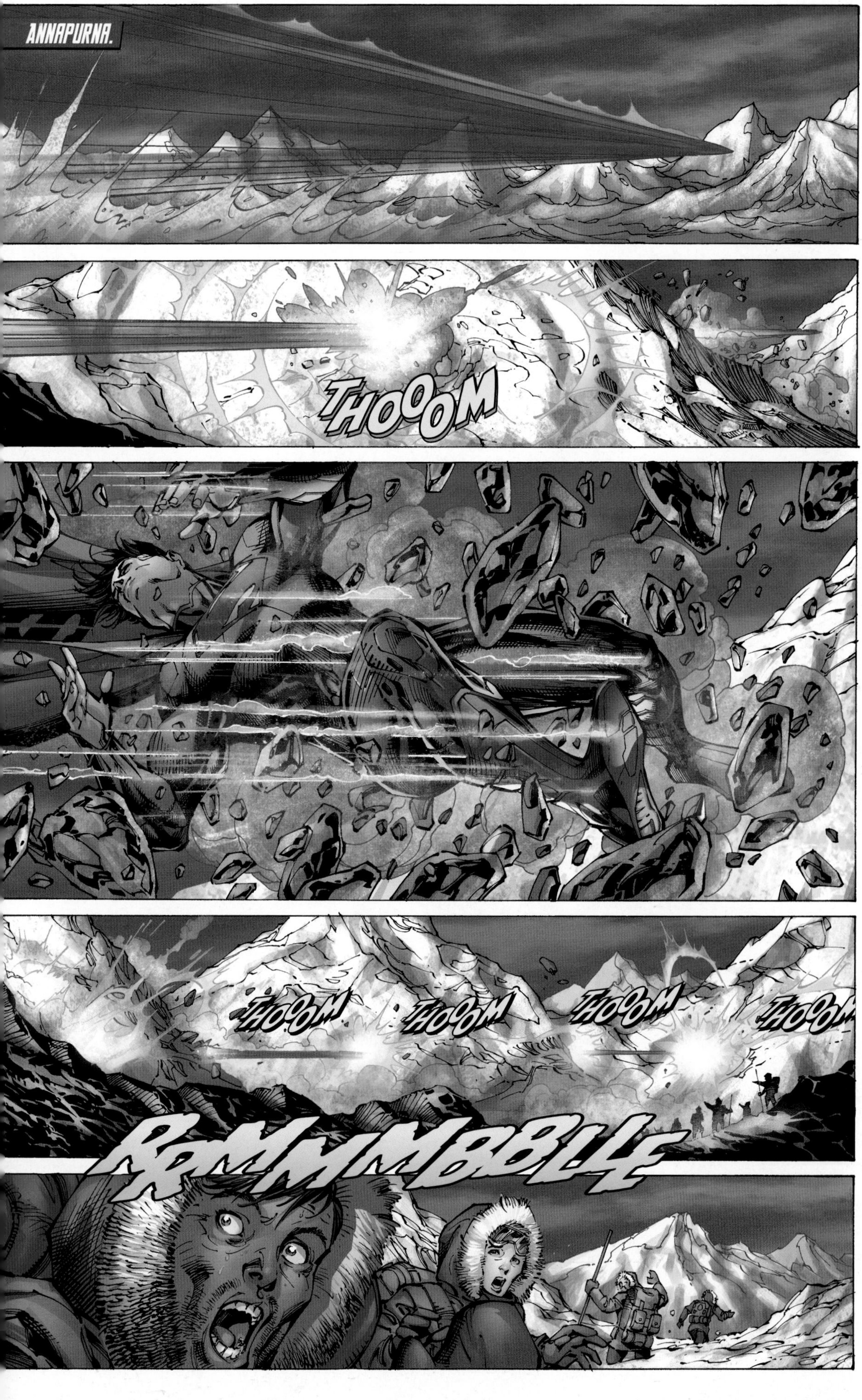
ANNAPURNA.
THOOOM
THOOOM
THOOOM
THOOOM
THOOOM
RRMMMBBLLE

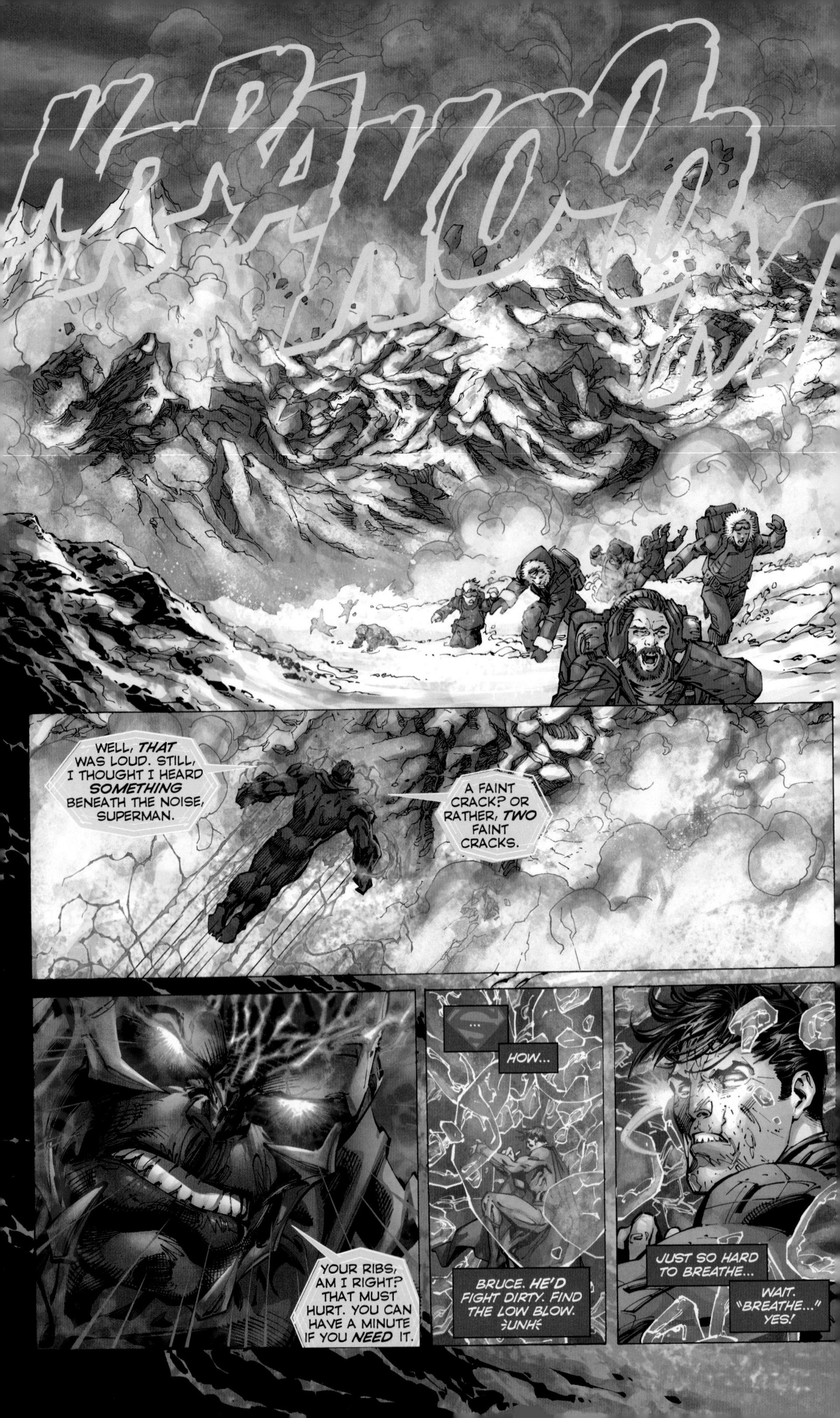

WELL, THAT WAS LOUD. STILL, I THOUGHT I HEARD SOMETHING BENEATH THE NOISE, SUPERMAN.
A FAINT CRACK? OR RATHER, TWO FAINT CRACKS.
YOUR RIBS, AM I RIGHT? THAT MUST HURT. YOU CAN HAVE A MINUTE IF YOU NEED IT.
...
HOW...
BRUCE. HE'D FIGHT DIRTY. FIND THE LOW BLOW. UNH
JUST SO HARD TO BREATHE...
WAIT. "BREATHE..." YES!

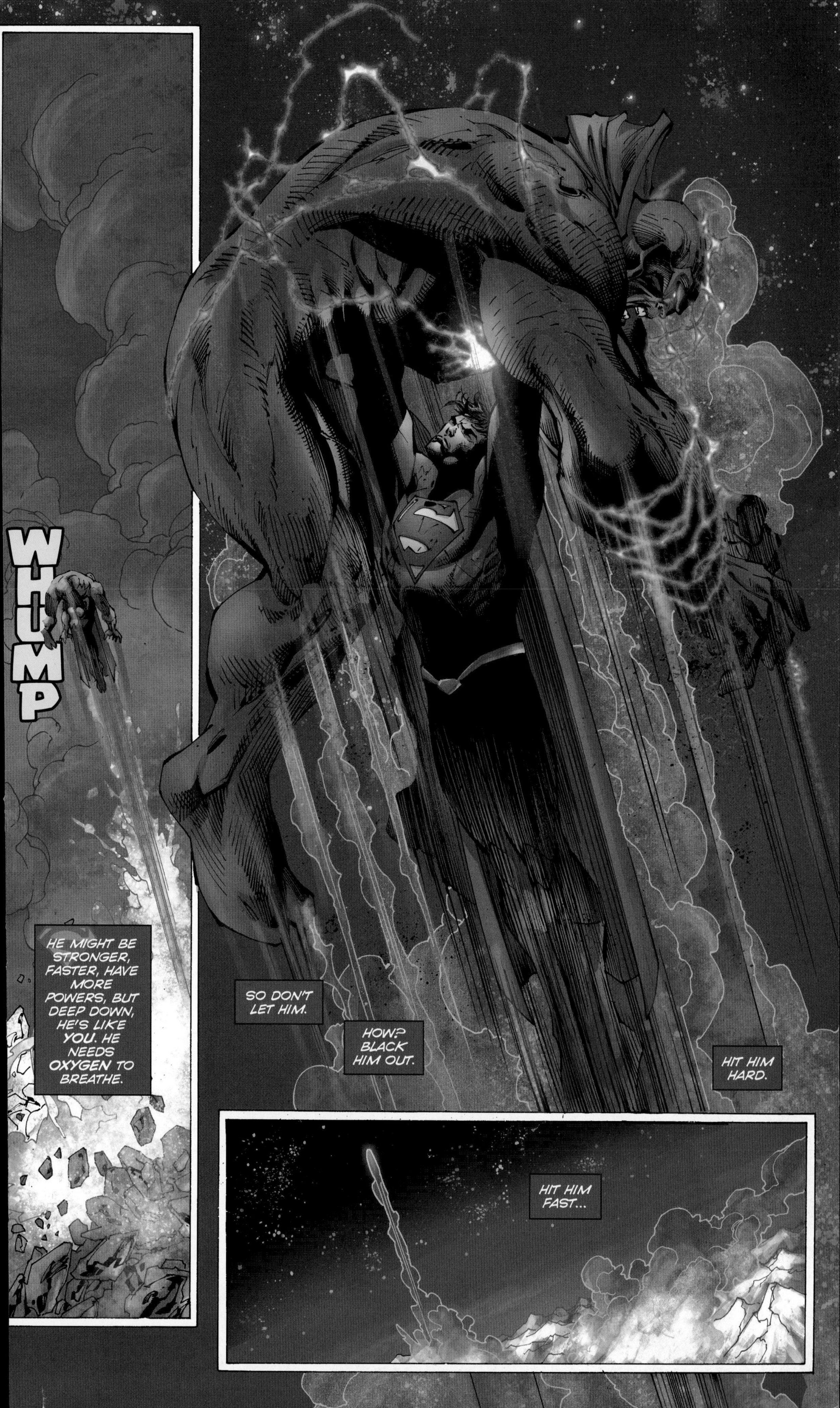
WHUMP
HE MIGHT BE STRONGER, FASTER, HAVE MORE POWERS, BUT DEEP DOWN, HE'S LIKE YOU. HE NEEDS OXYGEN TO BREATHE.
SO DON'T LET HIM.
HOW? BLACK HIM OUT.
HIT HIM HARD.
HIT HIM FAST...

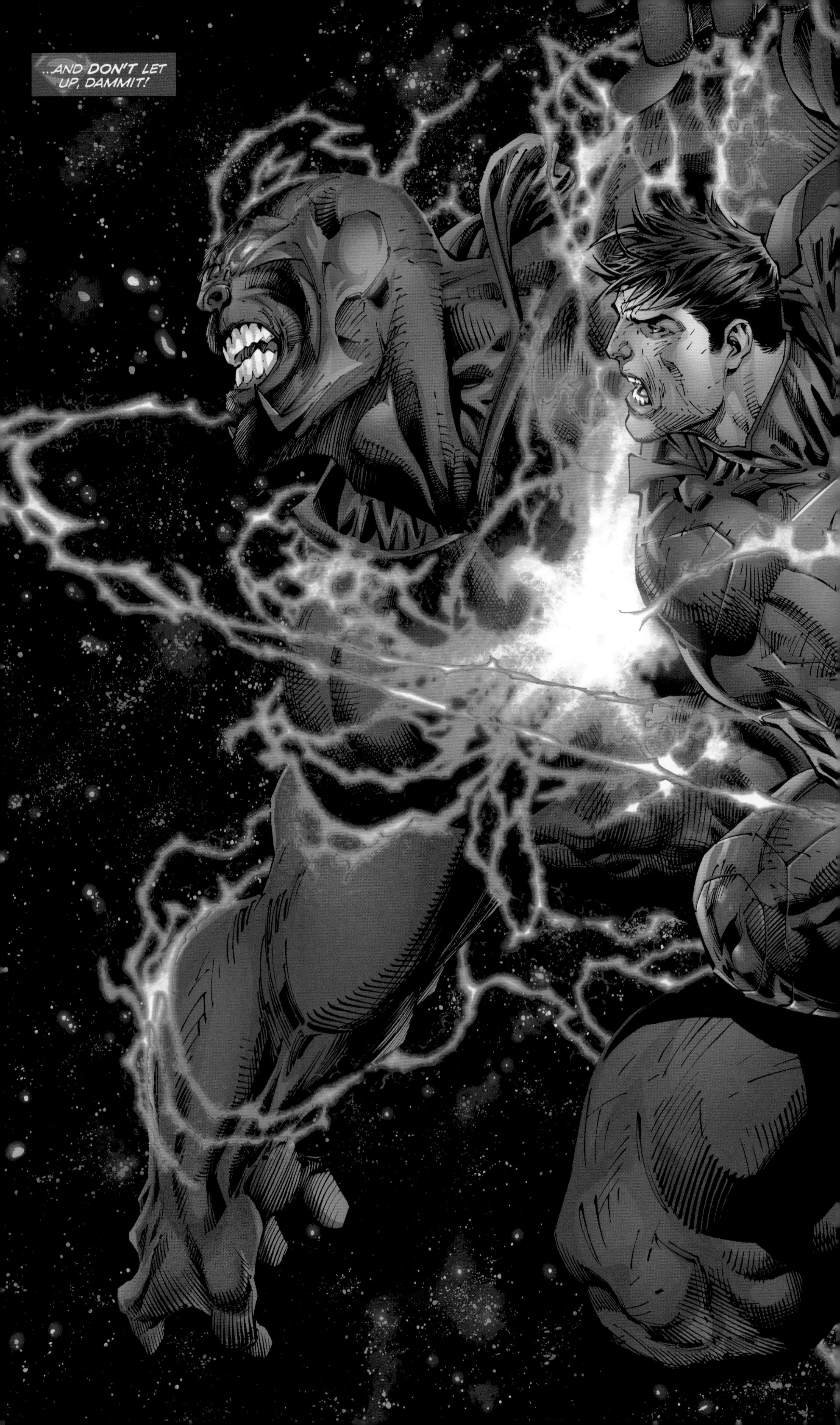
...AND DON'T LET UP, DAMMIT!

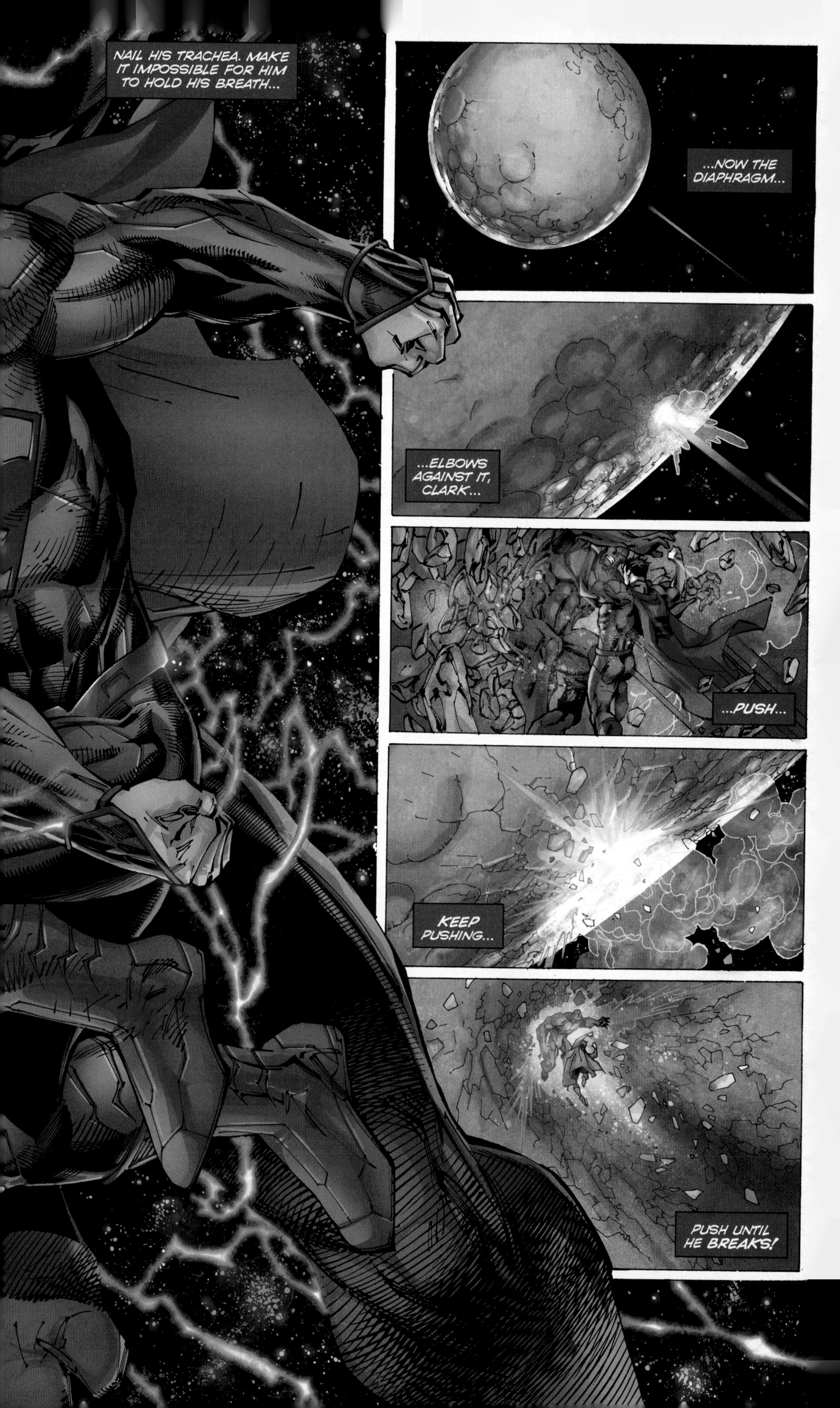
NAIL HIS TRACHEA. MAKE IT IMPOSSIBLE FOR HIM TO HOLD HIS BREATH...
...NOW THE DIAPHRAGM...
...ELBOWS AGAINST IT, CLARK...
...PUSH...
KEEP PUSHING...
PUSH UNTIL HE BREAKS!

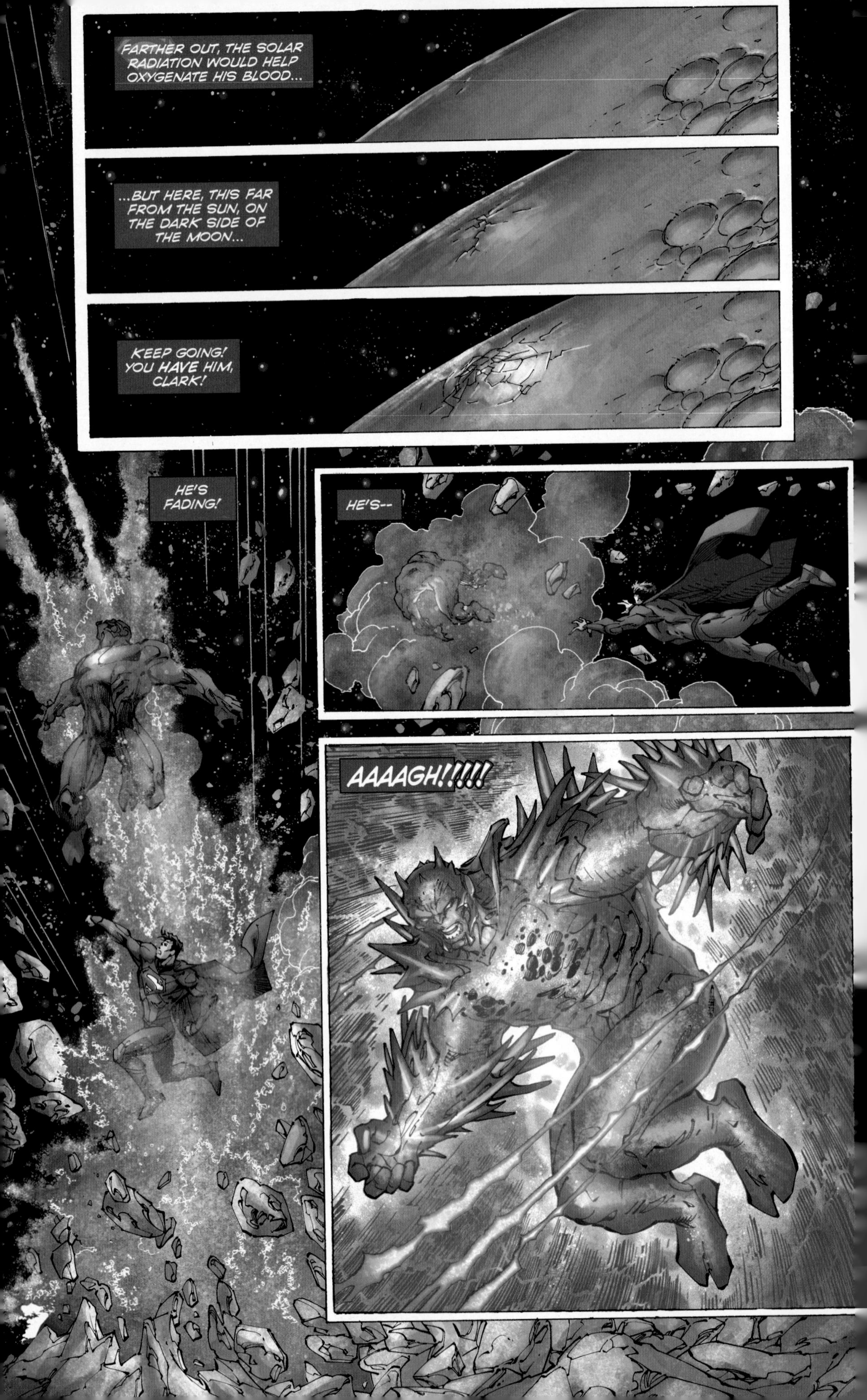

FARTHER OUT, THE SOLAR RADIATION WOULD HELP OXYGENATE HIS BLOOD...
...BUT HERE, THIS FAR FROM THE SUN, ON THE DARK SIDE OF THE MOON...
KEEP GOING! YOU HAVE HIM, CLARK!
HE'S FADING!
HE'S--
AAAAGH!!!!!

HOW...?

...HIS ENERGY SIGNATURE, HE'S MANIPULATING IT...

...SIMULATING THE RADIOACTIVITY OF...

KRYPTONITE.

;GASP;

"NICE TRICK."

"I'LL HAVE TO TRY IT SOMETIME."

LIKE NOW.

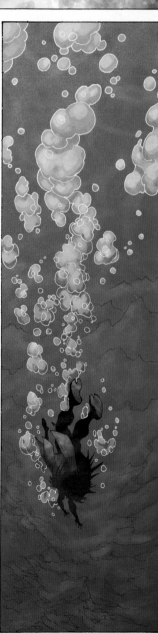

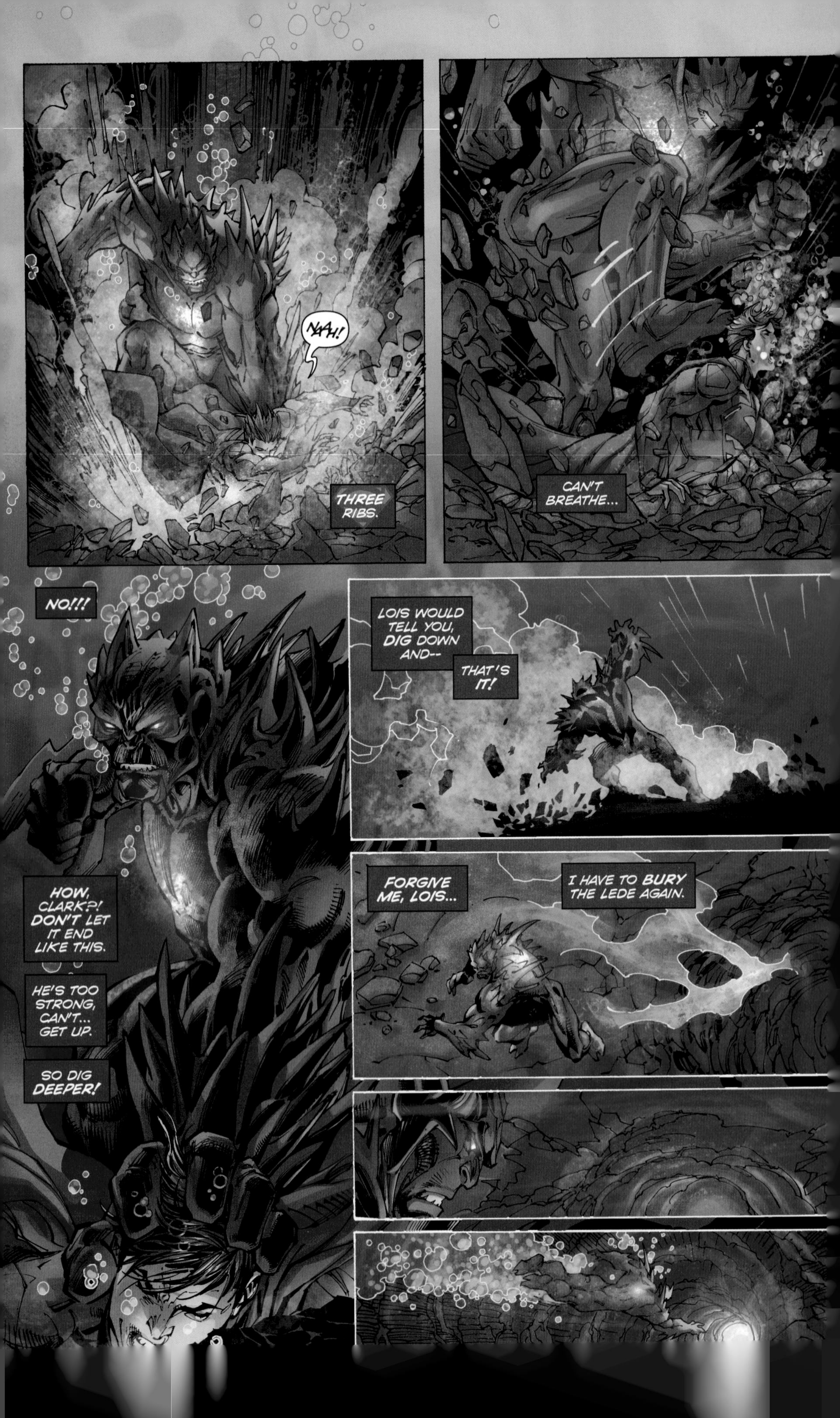
NYAAH!
THREE RIBS.
CAN'T BREATHE...
NO!!!
LOIS WOULD TELL YOU, DIG DOWN AND--
THAT'S IT!
HOW, CLARK?! DON'T LET IT END LIKE THIS.
HE'S TOO STRONG, CAN'T... GET UP.
SO DIG DEEPER!
FORGIVE ME, LOIS...
I HAVE TO BURY THE LEDE AGAIN.

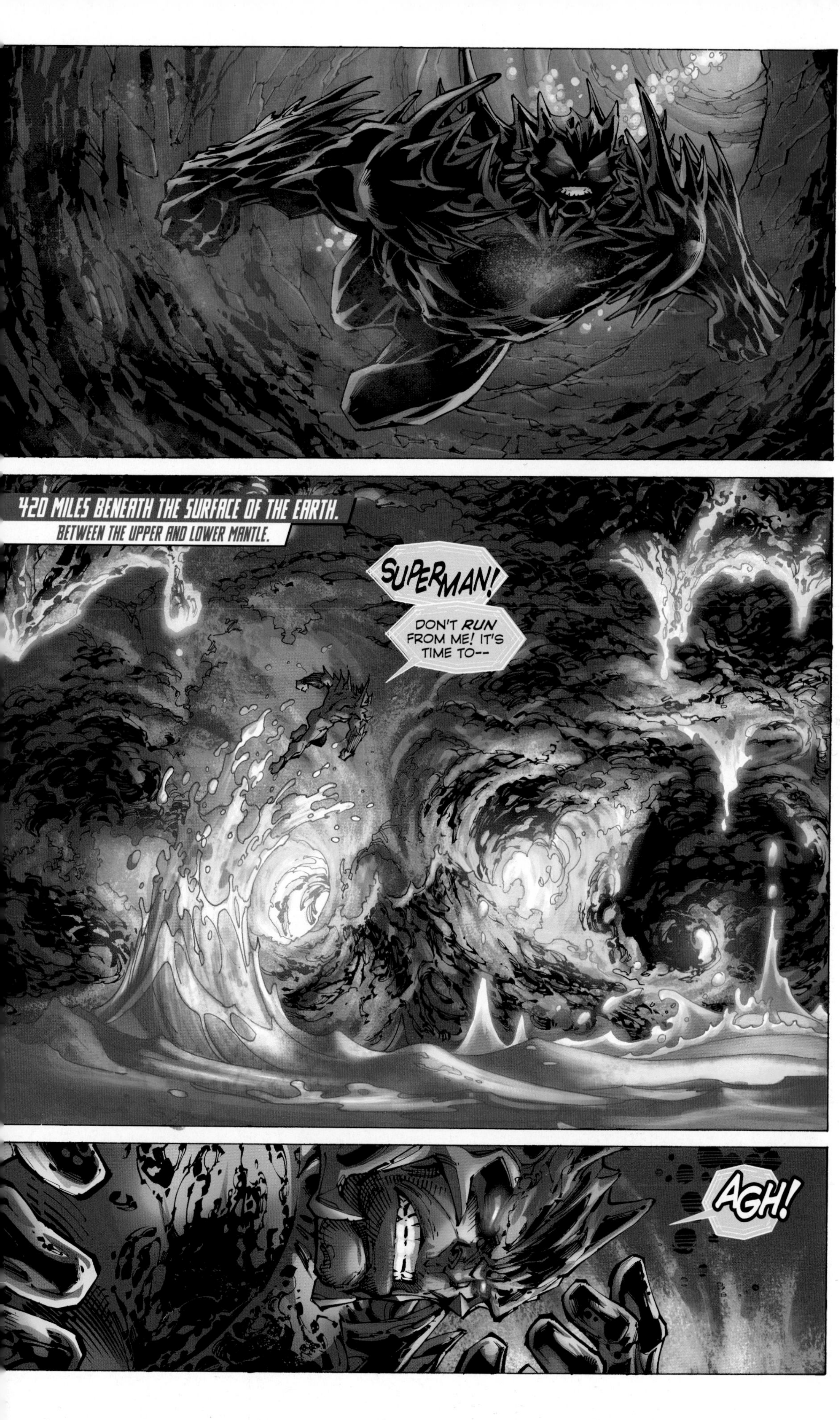
420 MILES BENEATH THE SURFACE OF THE EARTH.
BETWEEN THE UPPER AND LOWER MANTLE.
SUPERMAN!
DON'T RUN FROM ME! IT'S TIME TO--
AGH!

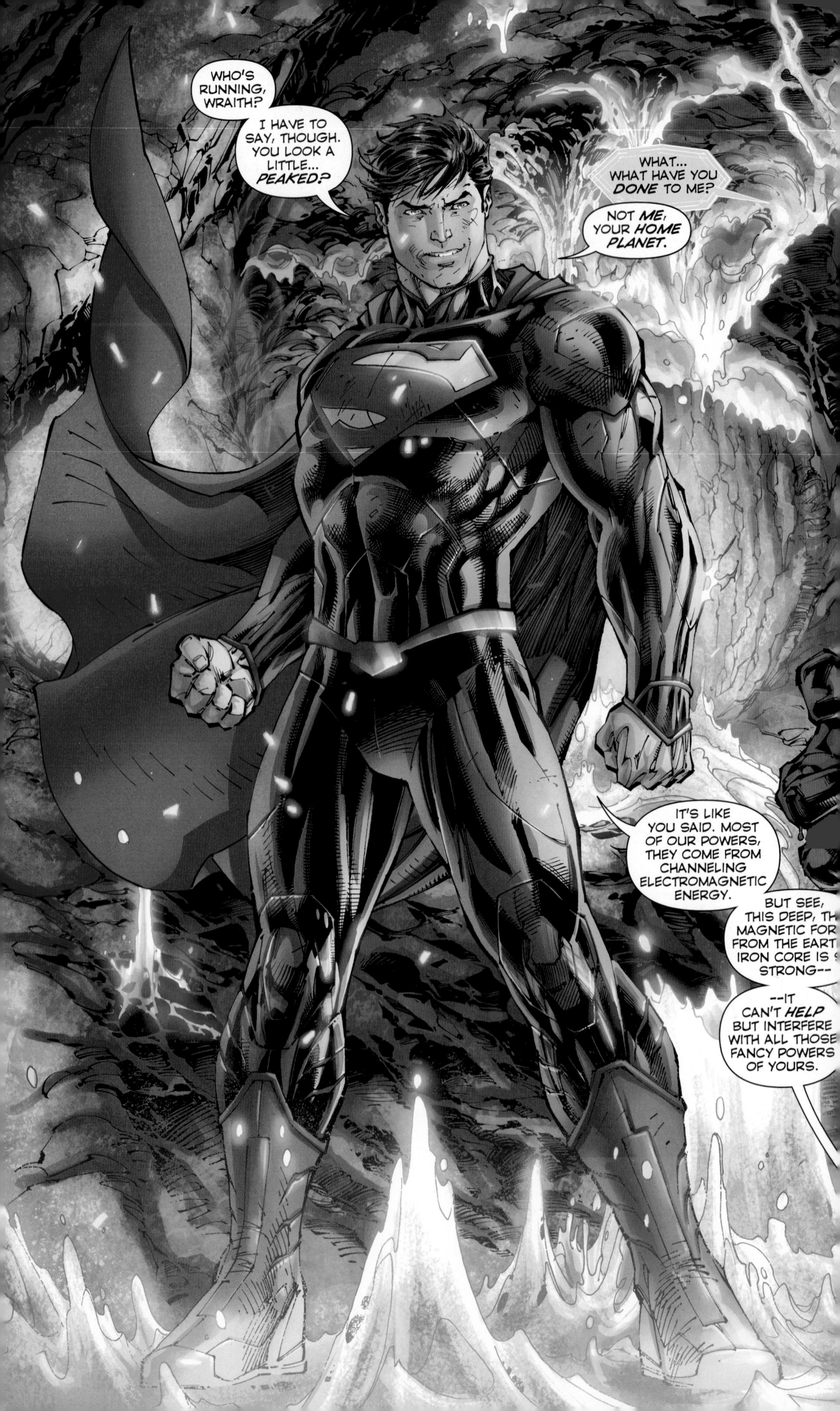
WHO'S RUNNING, WRAITH?
I HAVE TO SAY, THOUGH. YOU LOOK A LITTLE... PEAKED?
WHAT... WHAT HAVE YOU DONE TO ME?
NOT ME, YOUR HOME PLANET.
IT'S LIKE YOU SAID. MOST OF OUR POWERS, THEY COME FROM CHANNELING ELECTROMAGNETIC ENERGY.
BUT SEE, THIS DEEP, TH MAGNETIC FOR FROM THE EART IRON CORE IS STRONG--
--IT CAN'T HELP BUT INTERFERE WITH ALL THOSE FANCY POWERS OF YOURS.

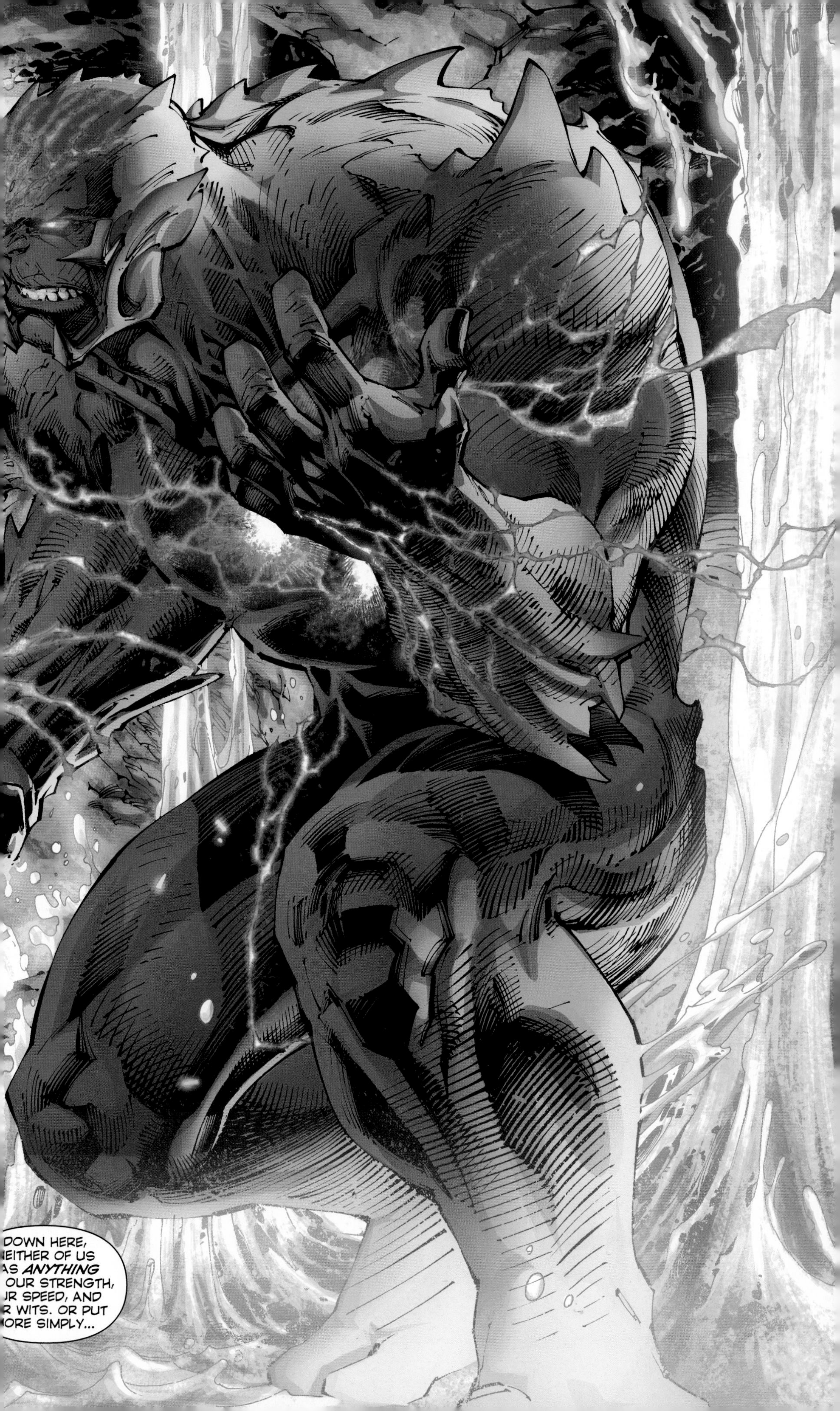
DOWN HERE, NEITHER OF US AS ANYTHING OUR STRENGTH, R SPEED, AND R WITS. OR PUT ORE SIMPLY...

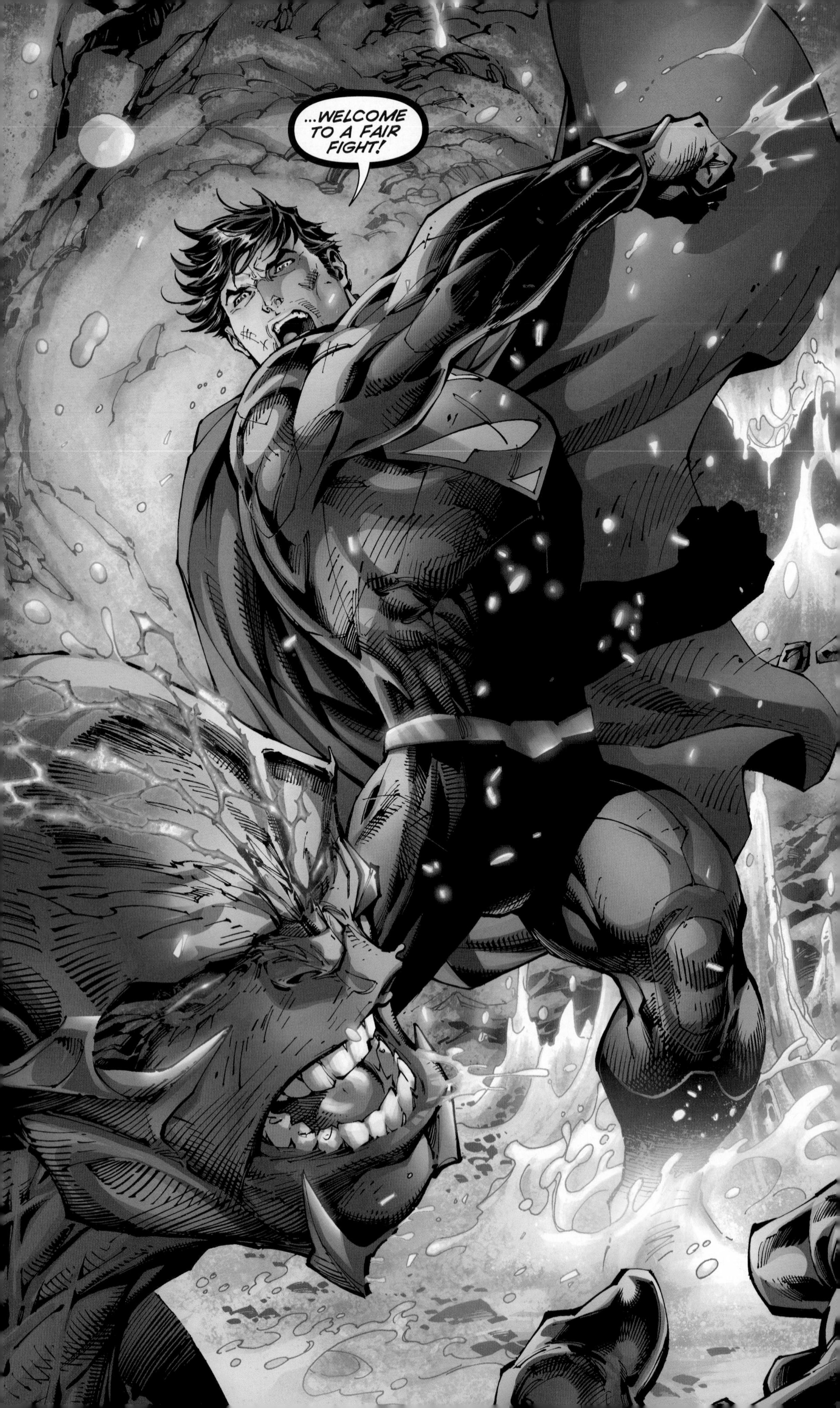
...WELCOME TO A FAIR FIGHT!

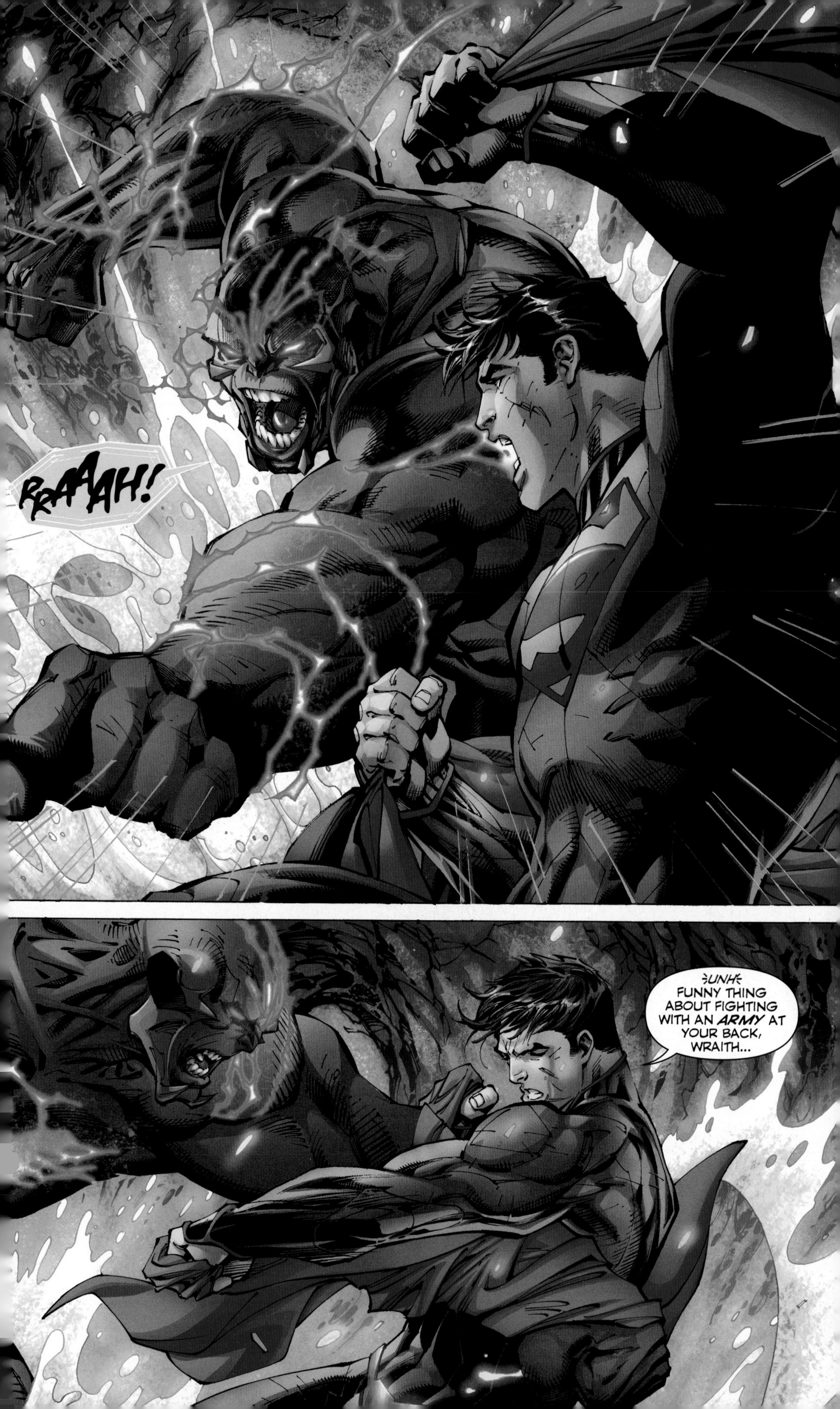
RRAAAAH!
UNH FUNNY THING ABOUT FIGHTING WITH AN ARMY AT YOUR BACK, WRAITH...

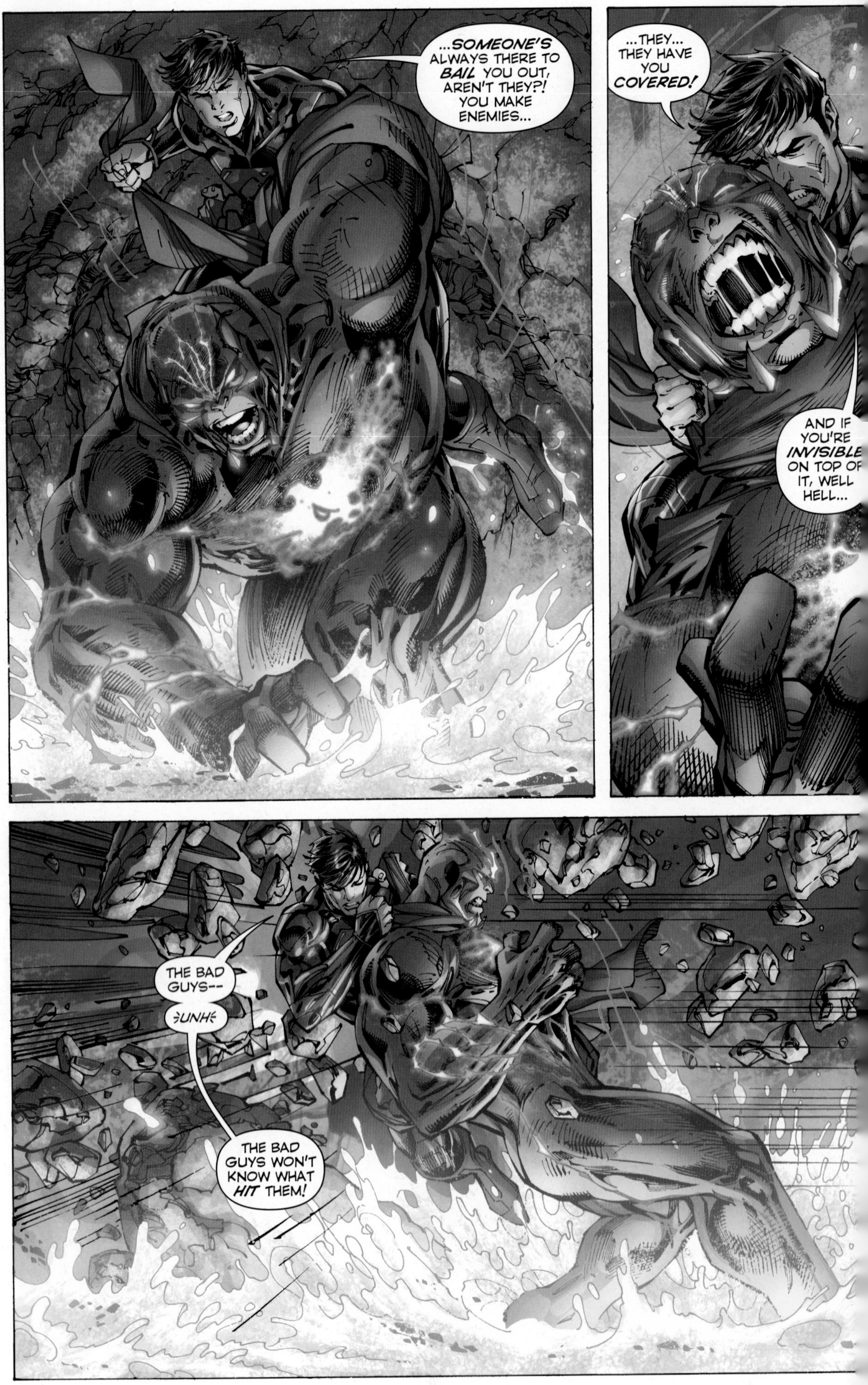

...SOMEONE'S ALWAYS THERE TO BAIL YOU OUT, AREN'T THEY?! YOU MAKE ENEMIES...
...THEY... THEY HAVE YOU COVERED!
AND IF YOU'RE INVISIBLE ON TOP OF IT, WELL HELL...
THE BAD GUYS--
UNH
THE BAD GUYS WON'T KNOW WHAT HIT THEM!

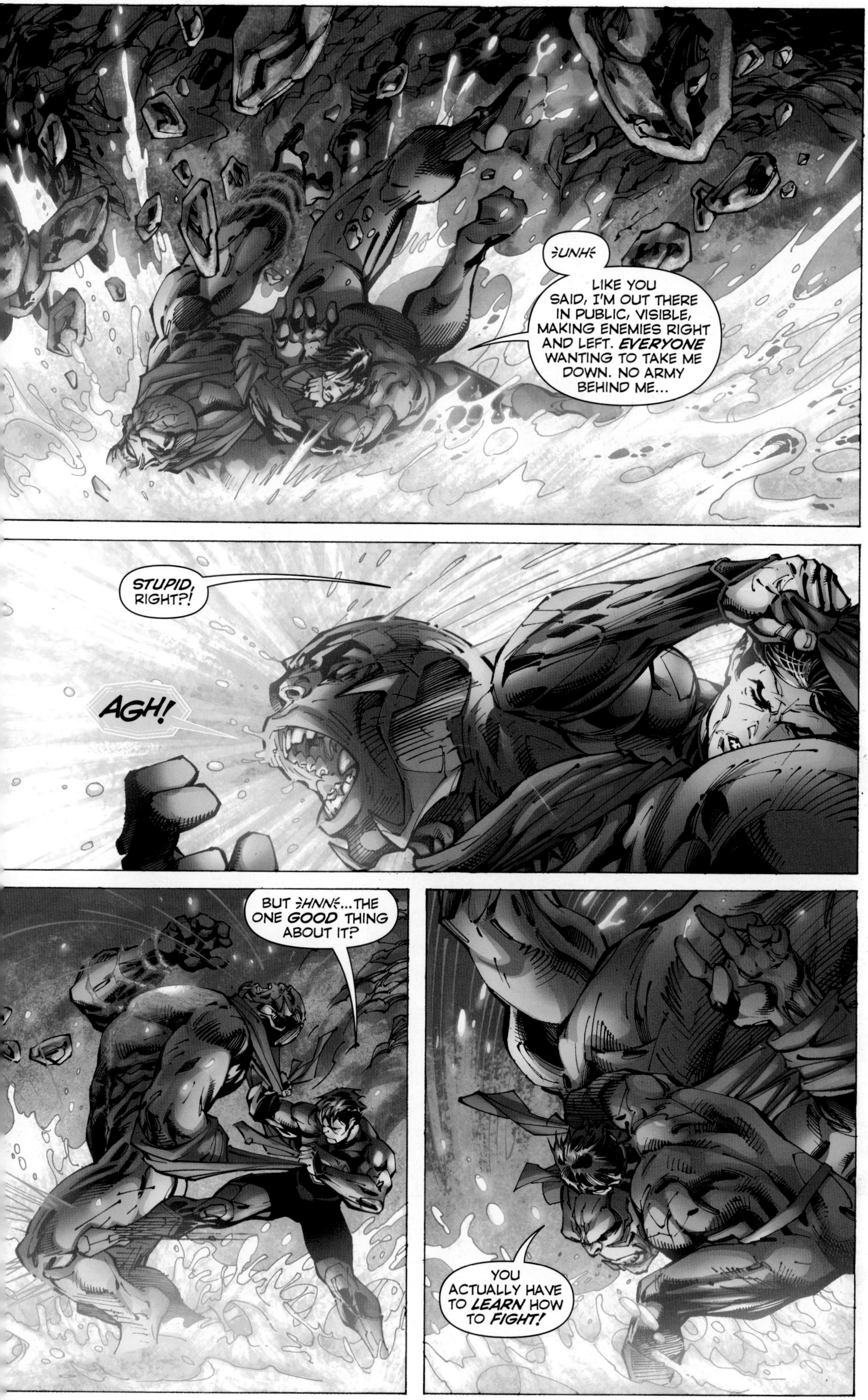

UNH
LIKE YOU SAID, I'M OUT THERE IN PUBLIC, VISIBLE, MAKING ENEMIES RIGHT AND LEFT. EVERYONE WANTING TO TAKE ME DOWN. NO ARMY BEHIND ME...
STUPID, RIGHT?!
AGH!
BUT HNN...THE ONE GOOD THING ABOUT IT?
YOU ACTUALLY HAVE TO LEARN HOW TO FIGHT!

AAAGH!

HH!

NOW *TELL* ME! WHAT'S *BURIED* IN THAT *SIGNAL?!*

THE *EARTHSTONE!* WHO'S *BEHIND* IT?! *TALK!!*

I DON'T KNOW WHAT ⸢COUGH⸣ WHAT YOU'RE *TALKING* ABOUT.

TO THINK, THOUGH, THAT I THOUGHT WE COULD BE FRIENDS...ALLIES, WHEN ALL *YOU* ARE IS--

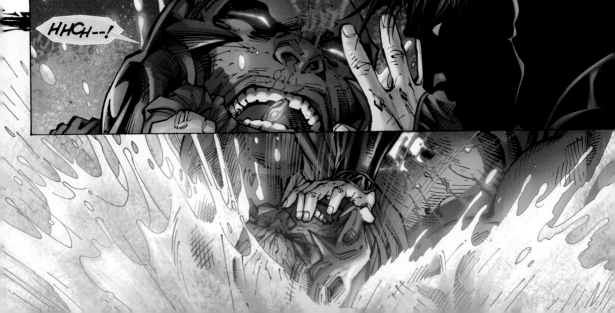

HHCH--!

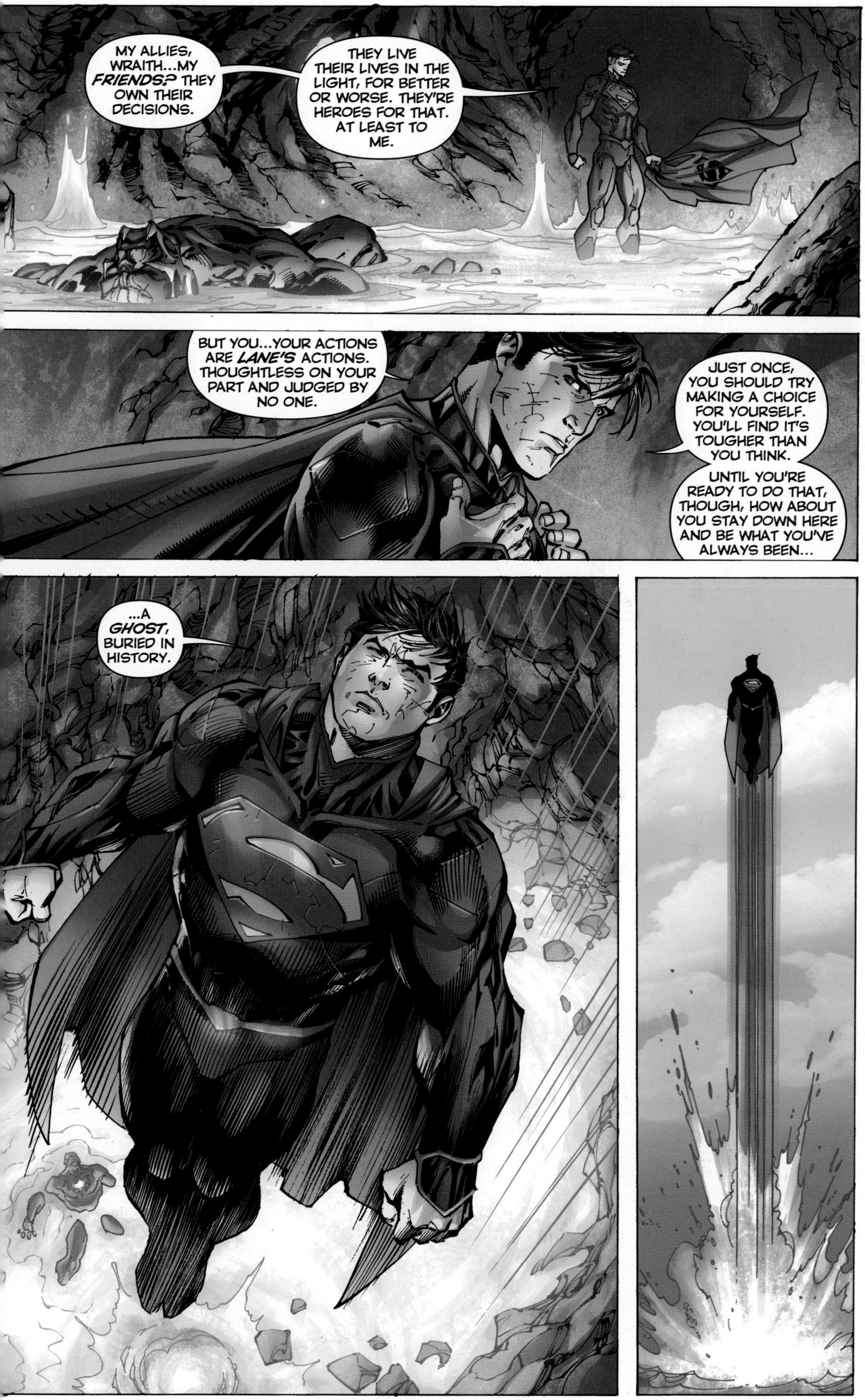
MY ALLIES, WRAITH...MY FRIENDS? THEY OWN THEIR DECISIONS.
THEY LIVE THEIR LIVES IN THE LIGHT, FOR BETTER OR WORSE. THEY'RE HEROES FOR THAT. AT LEAST TO ME.
BUT YOU...YOUR ACTIONS ARE LANE'S ACTIONS. THOUGHTLESS ON YOUR PART AND JUDGED BY NO ONE.
JUST ONCE, YOU SHOULD TRY MAKING A CHOICE FOR YOURSELF. YOU'LL FIND IT'S TOUGHER THAN YOU THINK.
UNTIL YOU'RE READY TO DO THAT, THOUGH, HOW ABOUT YOU STAY DOWN HERE AND BE WHAT YOU'VE ALWAYS BEEN...
...A GHOST, BURIED IN HISTORY.

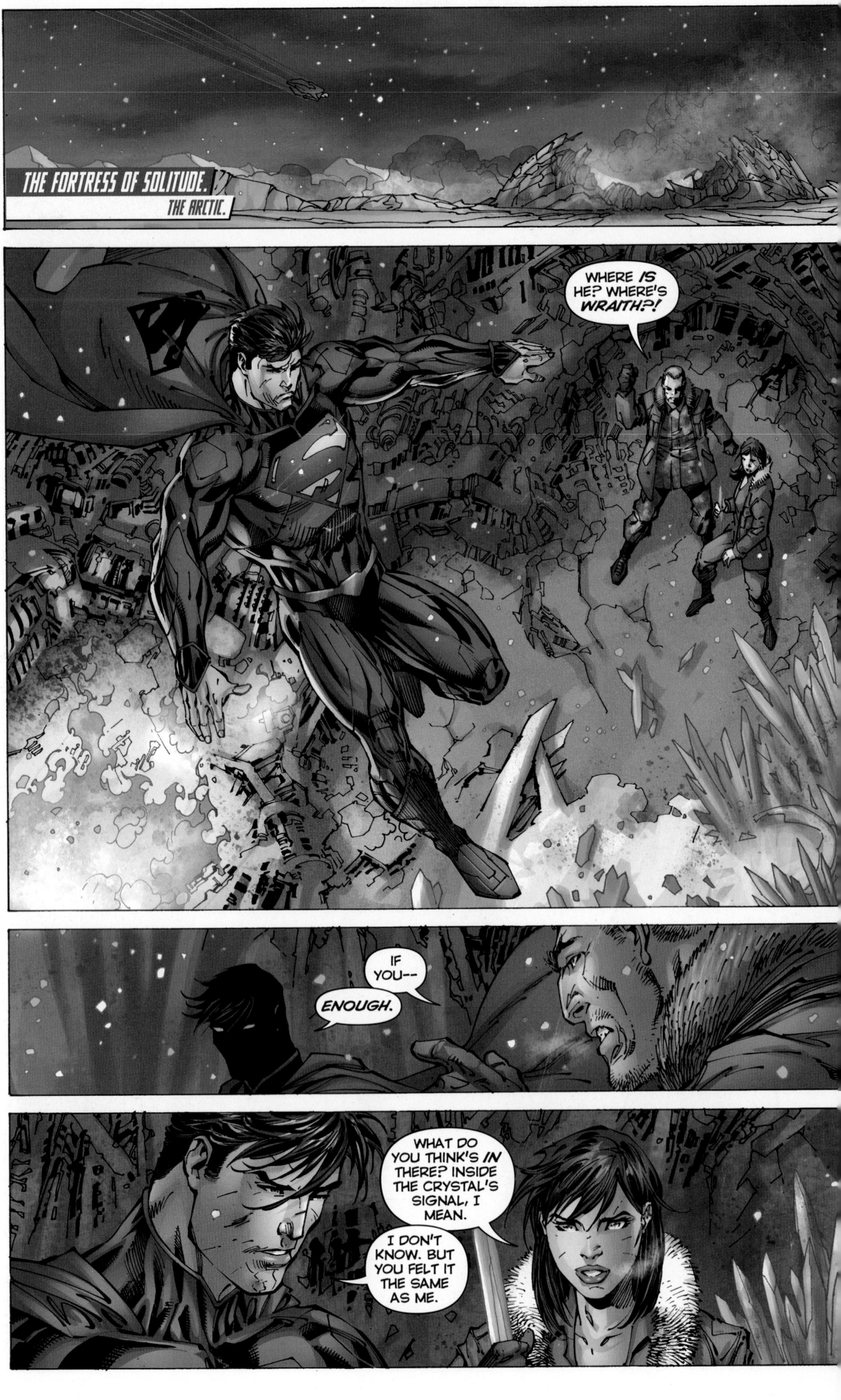

THE FORTRESS OF SOLITUDE.
THE ARCTIC.
WHERE *IS* HE? WHERE'S *WRAITH*?!
IF YOU--
ENOUGH.
WHAT DO YOU THINK'S *IN* THERE? INSIDE THE CRYSTAL'S SIGNAL, I MEAN.
I DON'T KNOW. BUT YOU FELT IT THE SAME AS ME.

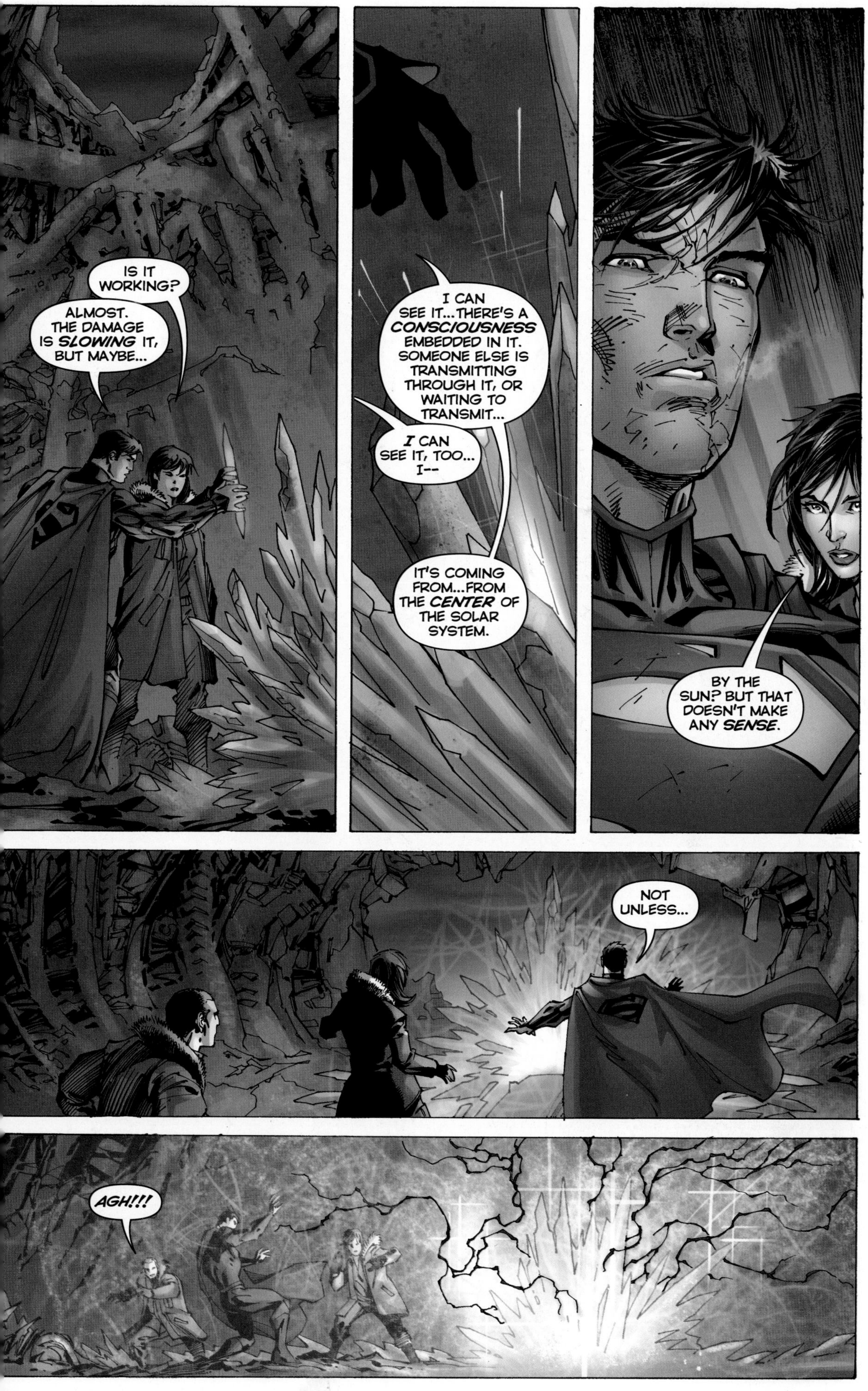
IS IT WORKING?
ALMOST. THE DAMAGE IS SLOWING IT, BUT MAYBE...
I CAN SEE IT...THERE'S A CONSCIOUSNESS EMBEDDED IN IT. SOMEONE ELSE IS TRANSMITTING THROUGH IT, OR WAITING TO TRANSMIT...
I CAN SEE IT, TOO... I--
IT'S COMING FROM...FROM THE CENTER OF THE SOLAR SYSTEM.
BY THE SUN? BUT THAT DOESN'T MAKE ANY SENSE.
NOT UNLESS...
AGH!!!

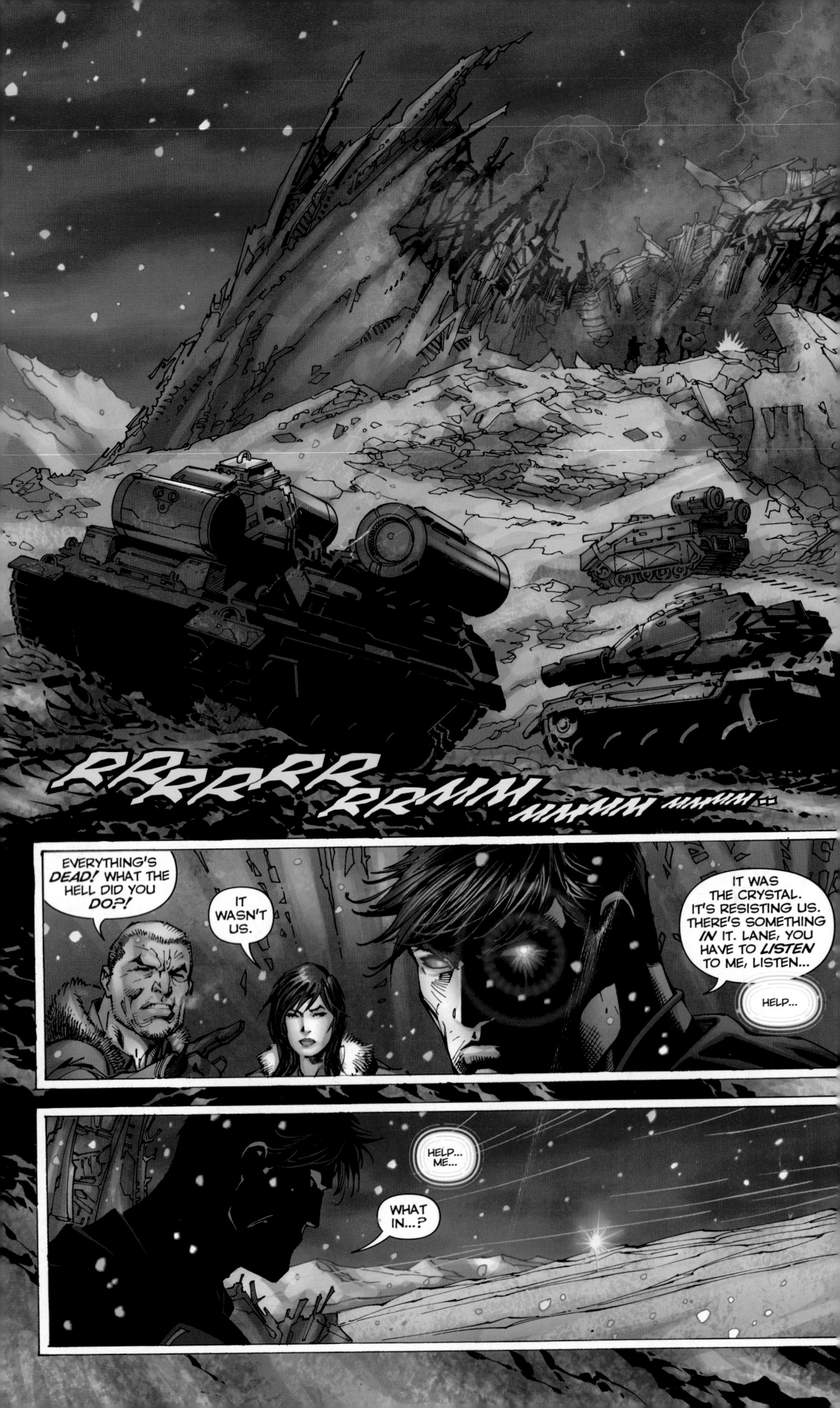

RRRRRRR RRMMM MMMMM MMMM
EVERYTHING'S DEAD! WHAT THE HELL DID YOU DO?!
IT WASN'T US.
IT WAS THE CRYSTAL. IT'S RESISTING US. THERE'S SOMETHING IN IT. LANE, YOU HAVE TO LISTEN TO ME, LISTEN...
HELP...
HELP... ME...
WHAT IN...?

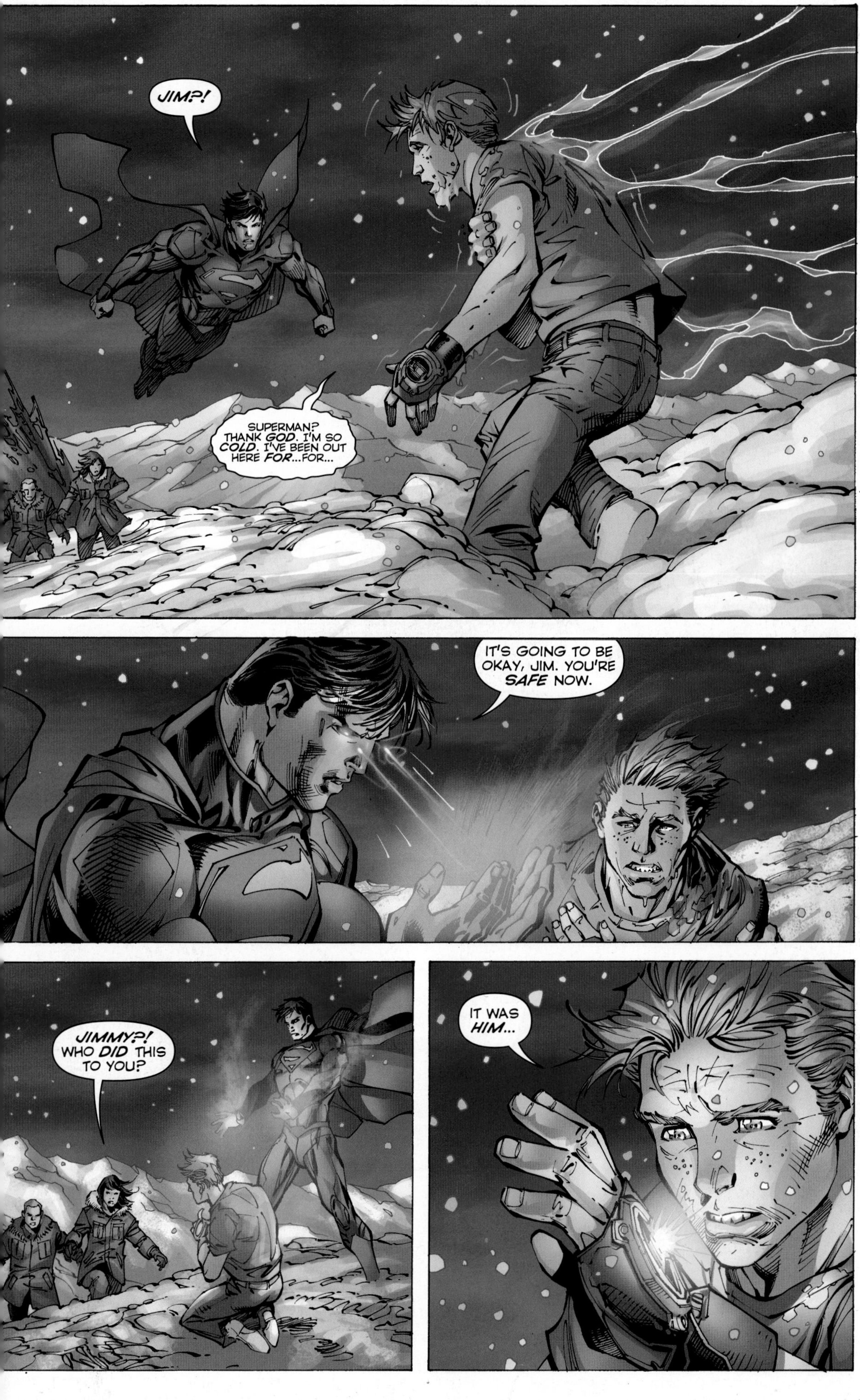
JIM?!
SUPERMAN? THANK GOD. I'M SO COLD. I'VE BEEN OUT HERE FOR...FOR...
IT'S GOING TO BE OKAY, JIM. YOU'RE SAFE NOW.
JIMMY?! WHO DID THIS TO YOU?
IT WAS HIM...

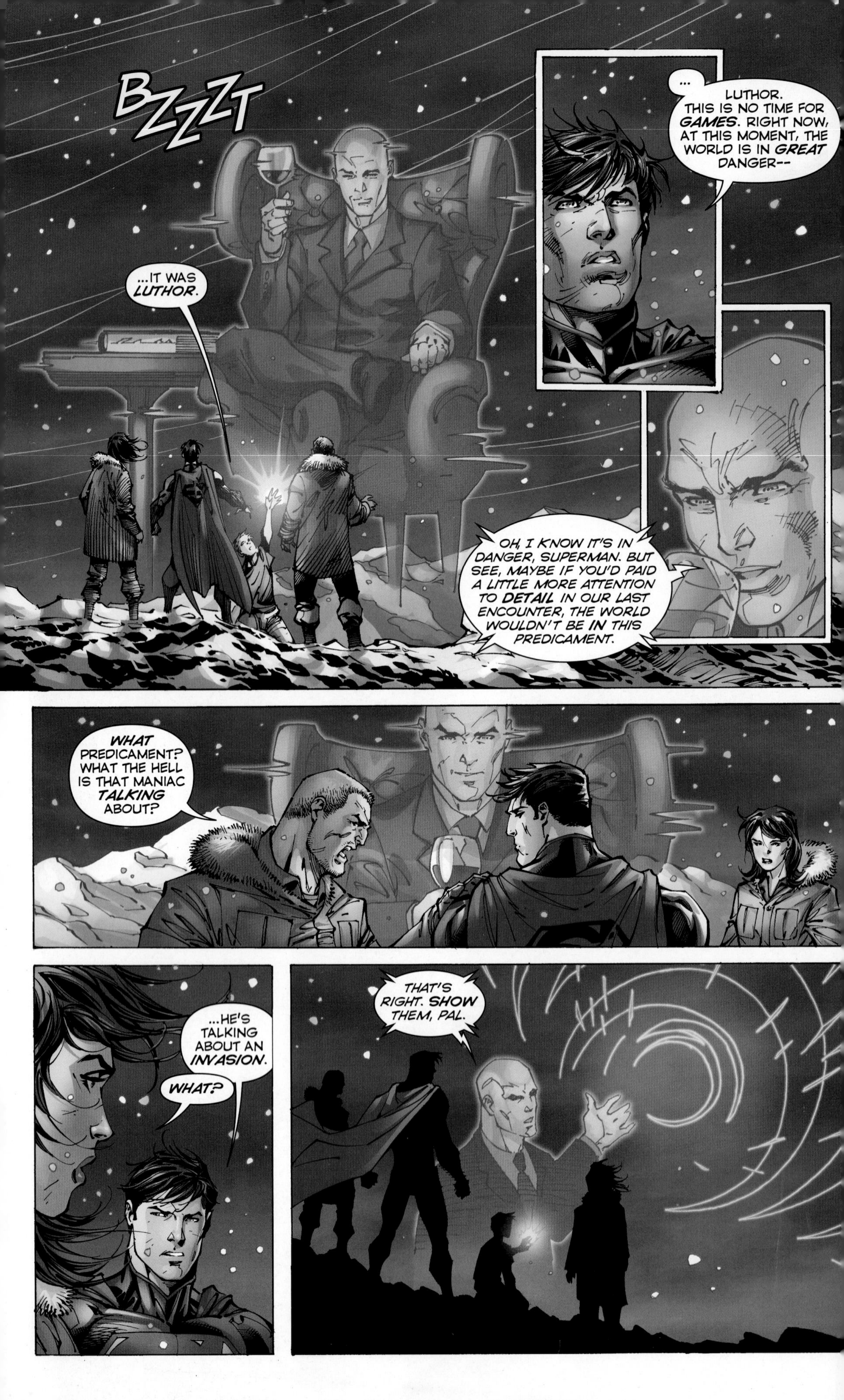
BZZZZT
...IT WAS LUTHOR.
...
LUTHOR. THIS IS NO TIME FOR GAMES. RIGHT NOW, AT THIS MOMENT, THE WORLD IS IN GREAT DANGER--
OH, I KNOW IT'S IN DANGER, SUPERMAN. BUT SEE, MAYBE IF YOU'D PAID A LITTLE MORE ATTENTION TO DETAIL IN OUR LAST ENCOUNTER, THE WORLD WOULDN'T BE IN THIS PREDICAMENT.
WHAT PREDICAMENT? WHAT THE HELL IS THAT MANIAC TALKING ABOUT?
...HE'S TALKING ABOUT AN INVASION.
WHAT?
THAT'S RIGHT. SHOW THEM, PAL.

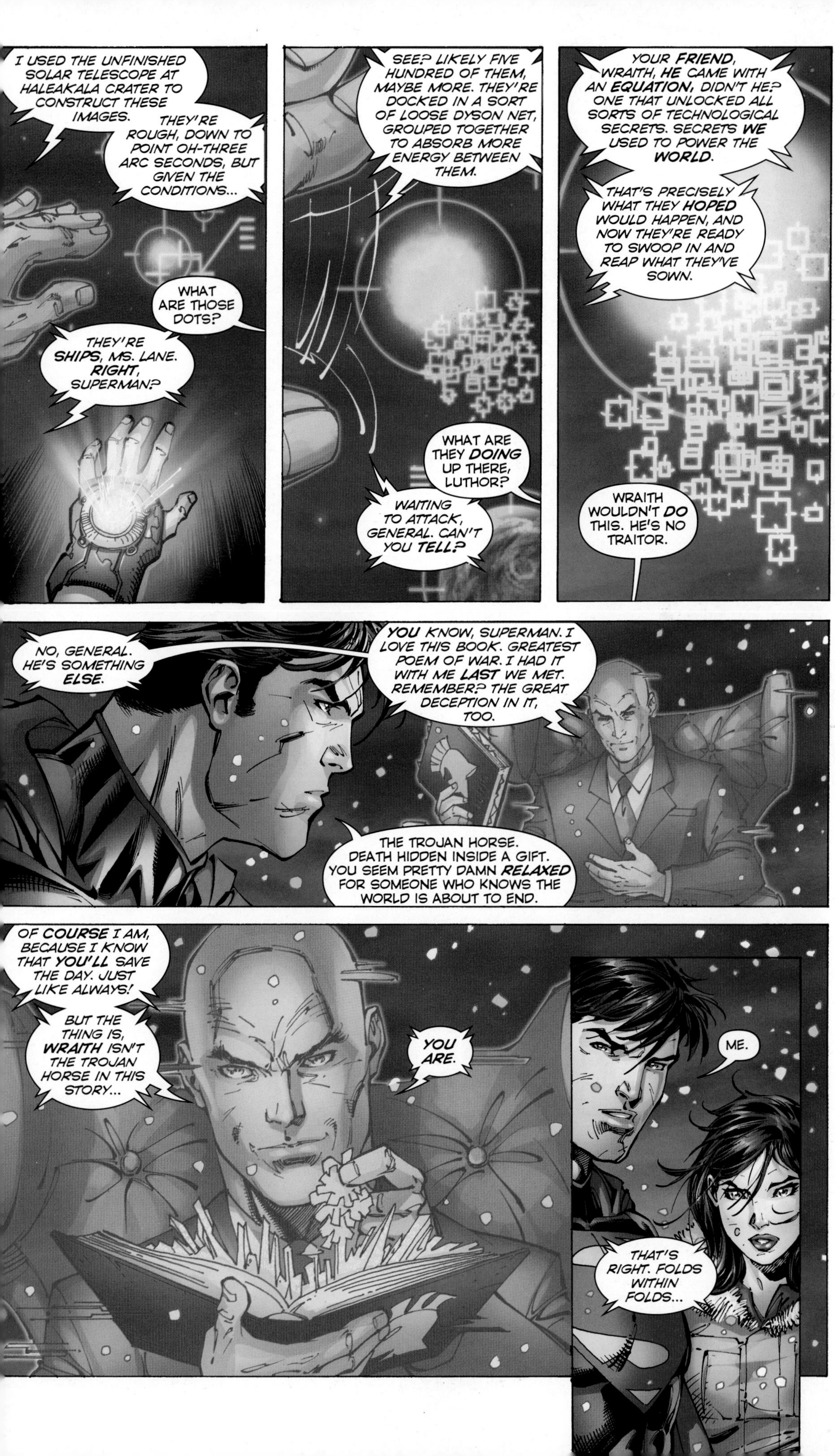
I USED THE UNFINISHED SOLAR TELESCOPE AT HALEAKALA CRATER TO CONSTRUCT THESE IMAGES.
THEY'RE ROUGH, DOWN TO POINT OH-THREE ARC SECONDS, BUT GIVEN THE CONDITIONS...
WHAT ARE THOSE DOTS?
THEY'RE SHIPS, MS. LANE. RIGHT, SUPERMAN?
SEE? LIKELY FIVE HUNDRED OF THEM, MAYBE MORE. THEY'RE DOCKED IN A SORT OF LOOSE DYSON NET, GROUPED TOGETHER TO ABSORB MORE ENERGY BETWEEN THEM.
WHAT ARE THEY DOING UP THERE, LUTHOR?
WAITING TO ATTACK, GENERAL. CAN'T YOU TELL?
YOUR FRIEND, WRAITH, HE CAME WITH AN EQUATION, DIDN'T HE? ONE THAT UNLOCKED ALL SORTS OF TECHNOLOGICAL SECRETS. SECRETS WE USED TO POWER THE WORLD.
THAT'S PRECISELY WHAT THEY HOPED WOULD HAPPEN, AND NOW THEY'RE READY TO SWOOP IN AND REAP WHAT THEY'VE SOWN.
WRAITH WOULDN'T DO THIS. HE'S NO TRAITOR.
NO, GENERAL. HE'S SOMETHING ELSE.
YOU KNOW, SUPERMAN. I LOVE THIS BOOK. GREATEST POEM OF WAR. I HAD IT WITH ME LAST WE MET. REMEMBER? THE GREAT DECEPTION IN IT, TOO.
THE TROJAN HORSE. DEATH HIDDEN INSIDE A GIFT. YOU SEEM PRETTY DAMN RELAXED FOR SOMEONE WHO KNOWS THE WORLD IS ABOUT TO END.
OF COURSE I AM, BECAUSE I KNOW THAT YOU'LL SAVE THE DAY. JUST LIKE ALWAYS!
BUT THE THING IS, WRAITH ISN'T THE TROJAN HORSE IN THIS STORY...
YOU ARE.
ME.
THAT'S RIGHT. FOLDS WITHIN FOLDS...

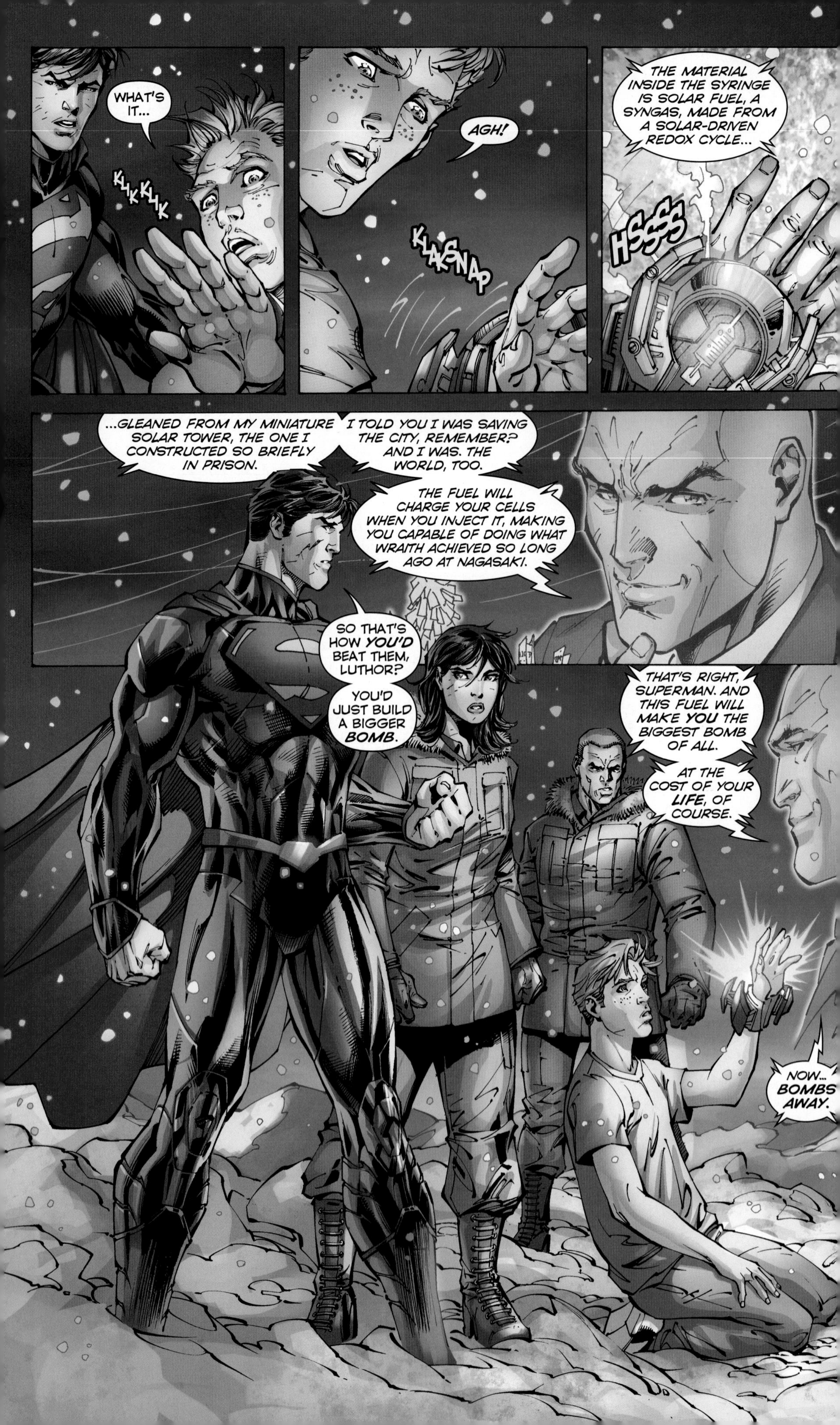

WHAT'S IT...
KLAK KLAK
AGH!
KLAKSNAP
THE MATERIAL INSIDE THE SYRINGE IS SOLAR FUEL, A SYNGAS, MADE FROM A SOLAR-DRIVEN REDOX CYCLE...
HSSSS
...GLEANED FROM MY MINIATURE SOLAR TOWER, THE ONE I CONSTRUCTED SO BRIEFLY IN PRISON.
I TOLD YOU I WAS SAVING THE CITY, REMEMBER? AND I WAS. THE WORLD, TOO.
THE FUEL WILL CHARGE YOUR CELLS WHEN YOU INJECT IT, MAKING YOU CAPABLE OF DOING WHAT WRAITH ACHIEVED SO LONG AGO AT NAGASAKI.
SO THAT'S HOW YOU'D BEAT THEM, LUTHOR?
YOU'D JUST BUILD A BIGGER BOMB.
THAT'S RIGHT, SUPERMAN. AND THIS FUEL WILL MAKE YOU THE BIGGEST BOMB OF ALL.
AT THE COST OF YOUR LIFE, OF COURSE.
NOW... BOMBS AWAY.

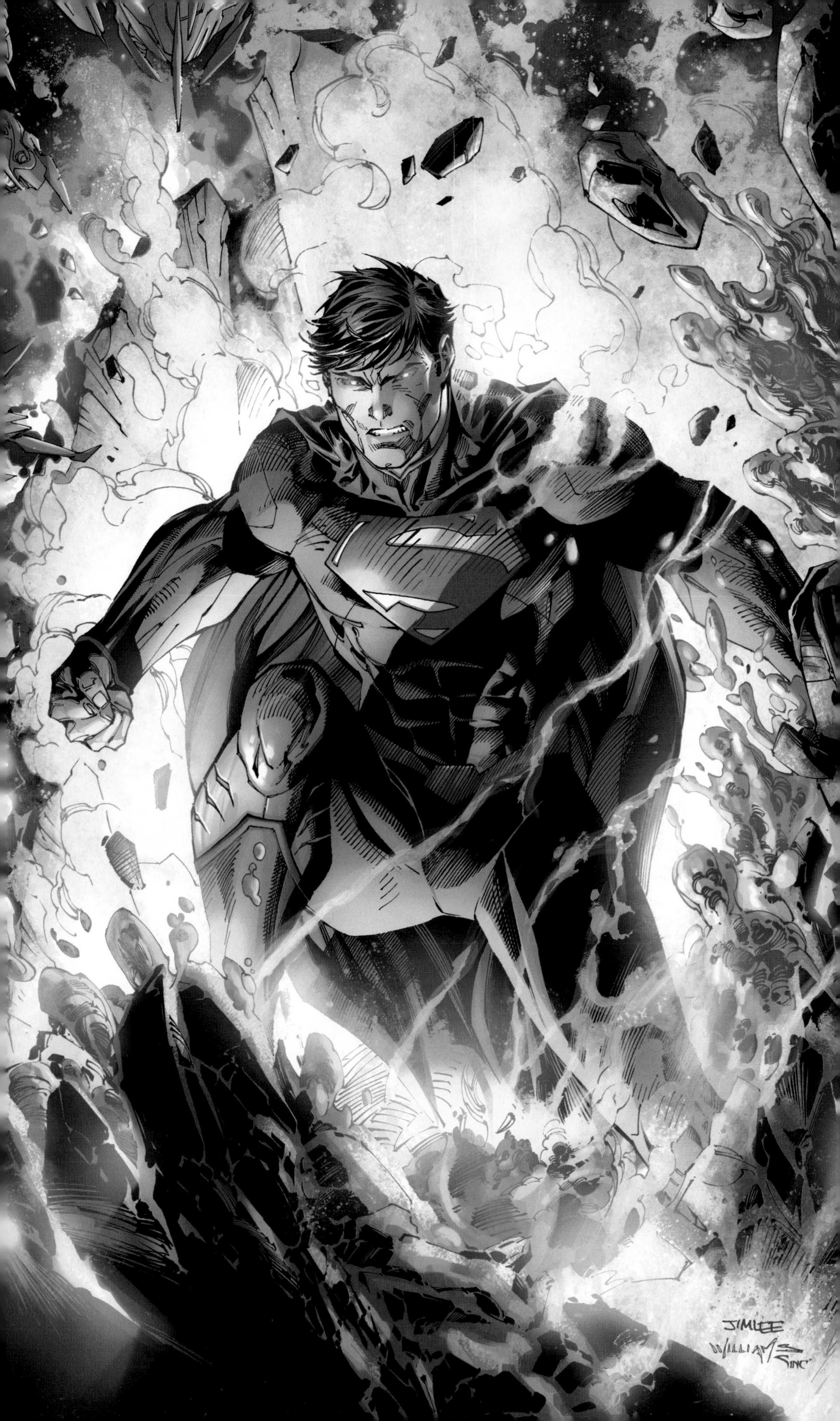

SUPERMAN UNCHAINED 9 COVER

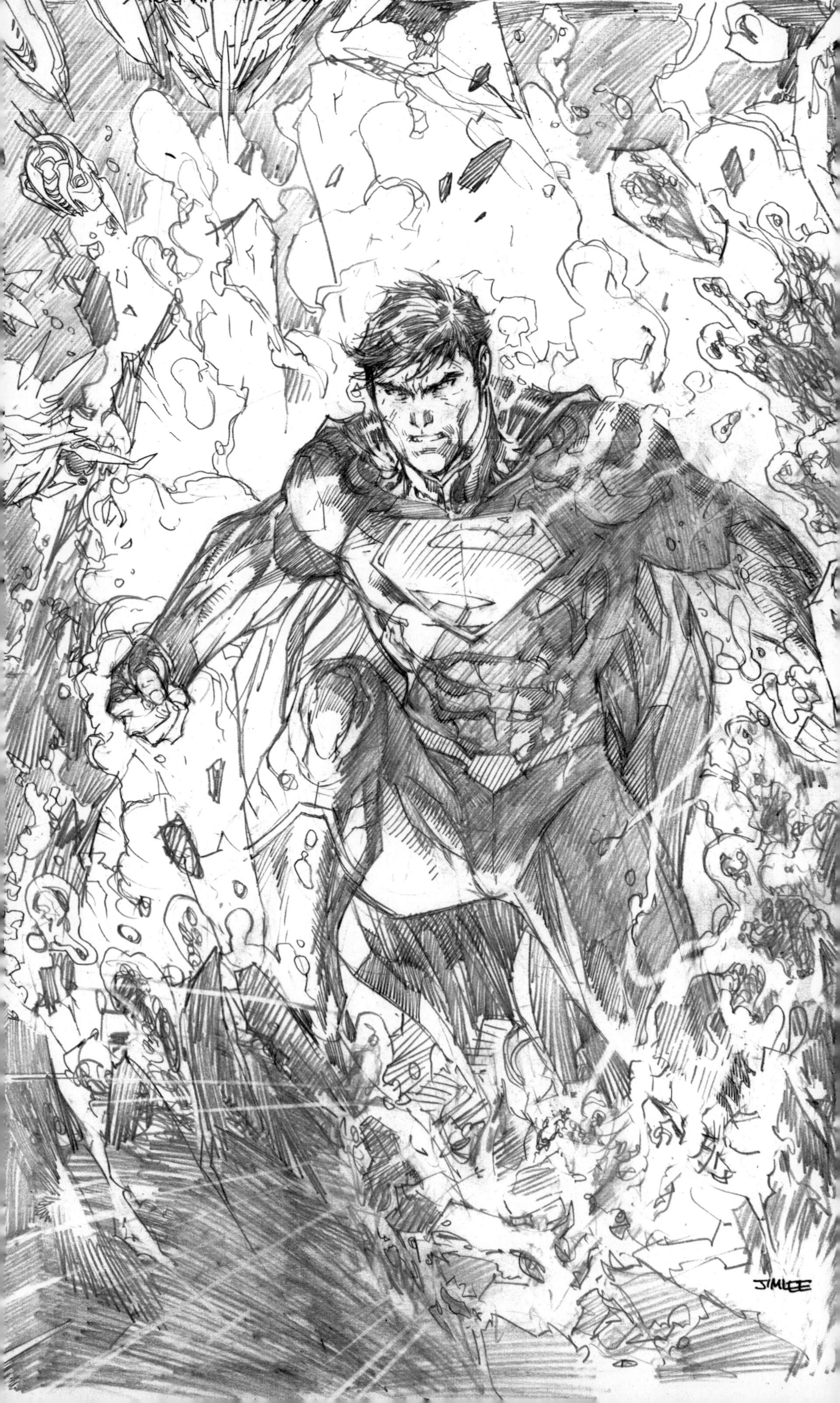
JIMLEE

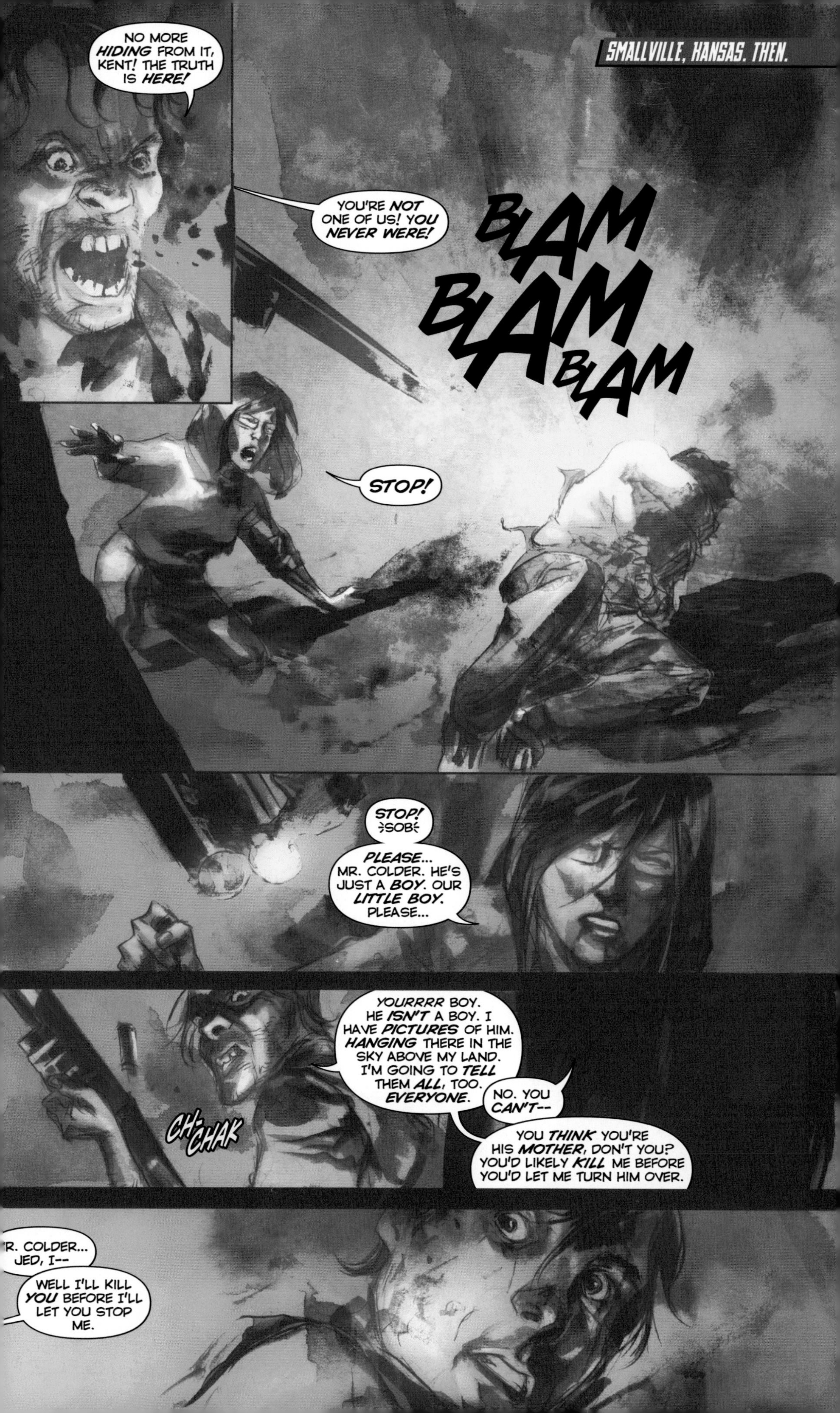
SMALLVILLE, KANSAS. THEN.
NO MORE HIDING FROM IT, KENT! THE TRUTH IS HERE!
YOU'RE NOT ONE OF US! YOU NEVER WERE!
BLAM BLAM BLAM BLAM
STOP!
STOP! SOB PLEASE... MR. COLDER. HE'S JUST A BOY. OUR LITTLE BOY. PLEASE...
YOURRRR BOY. HE ISN'T A BOY. I HAVE PICTURES OF HIM. HANGING THERE IN THE SKY ABOVE MY LAND. I'M GOING TO TELL THEM ALL, TOO. EVERYONE.
NO. YOU CAN'T--
CH-CHAK
YOU THINK YOU'RE HIS MOTHER, DON'T YOU? YOU'D LIKELY KILL ME BEFORE YOU'D LET ME TURN HIM OVER.
R. COLDER... JED, I--
WELL I'LL KILL YOU BEFORE I'LL LET YOU STOP ME.

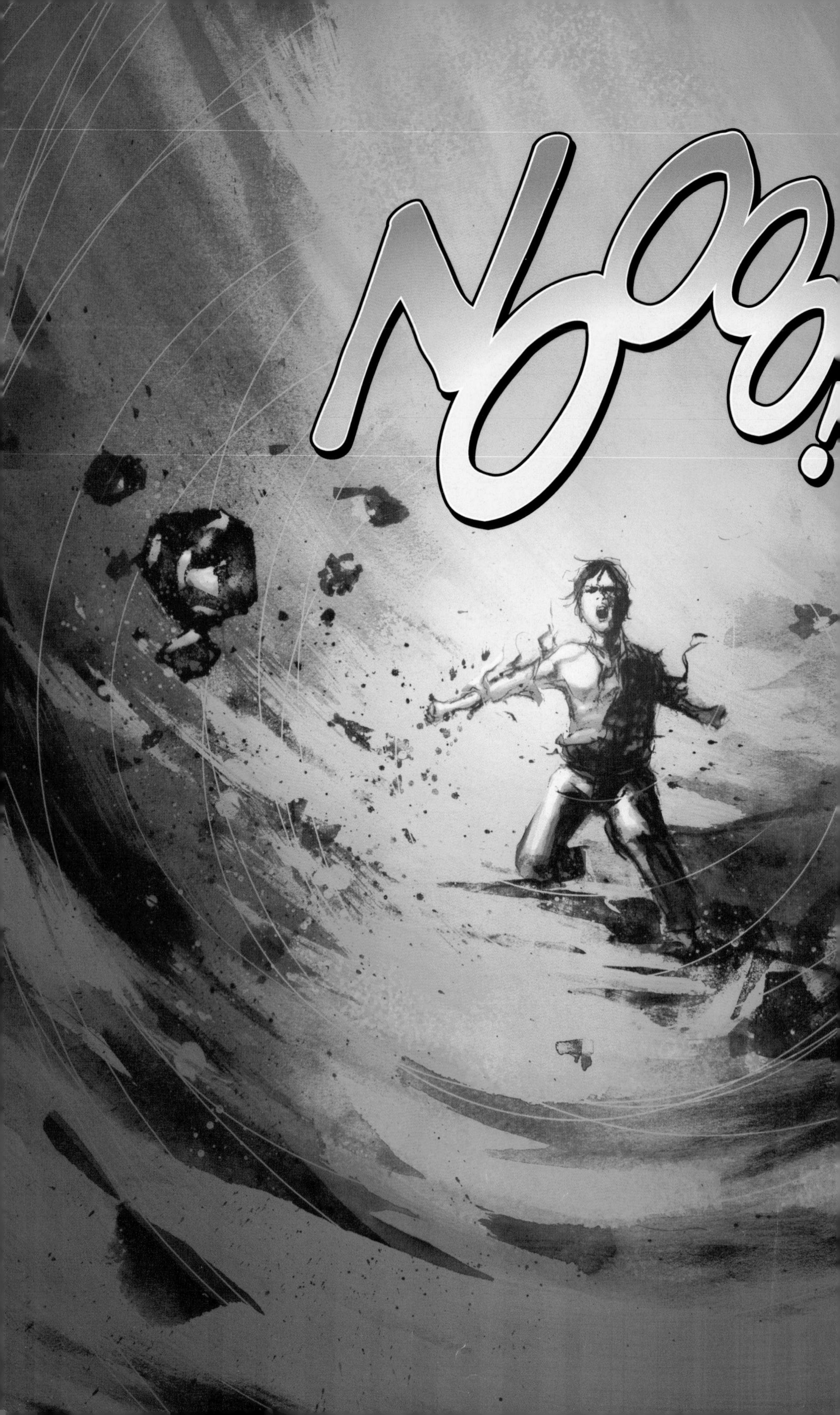
NOOO!

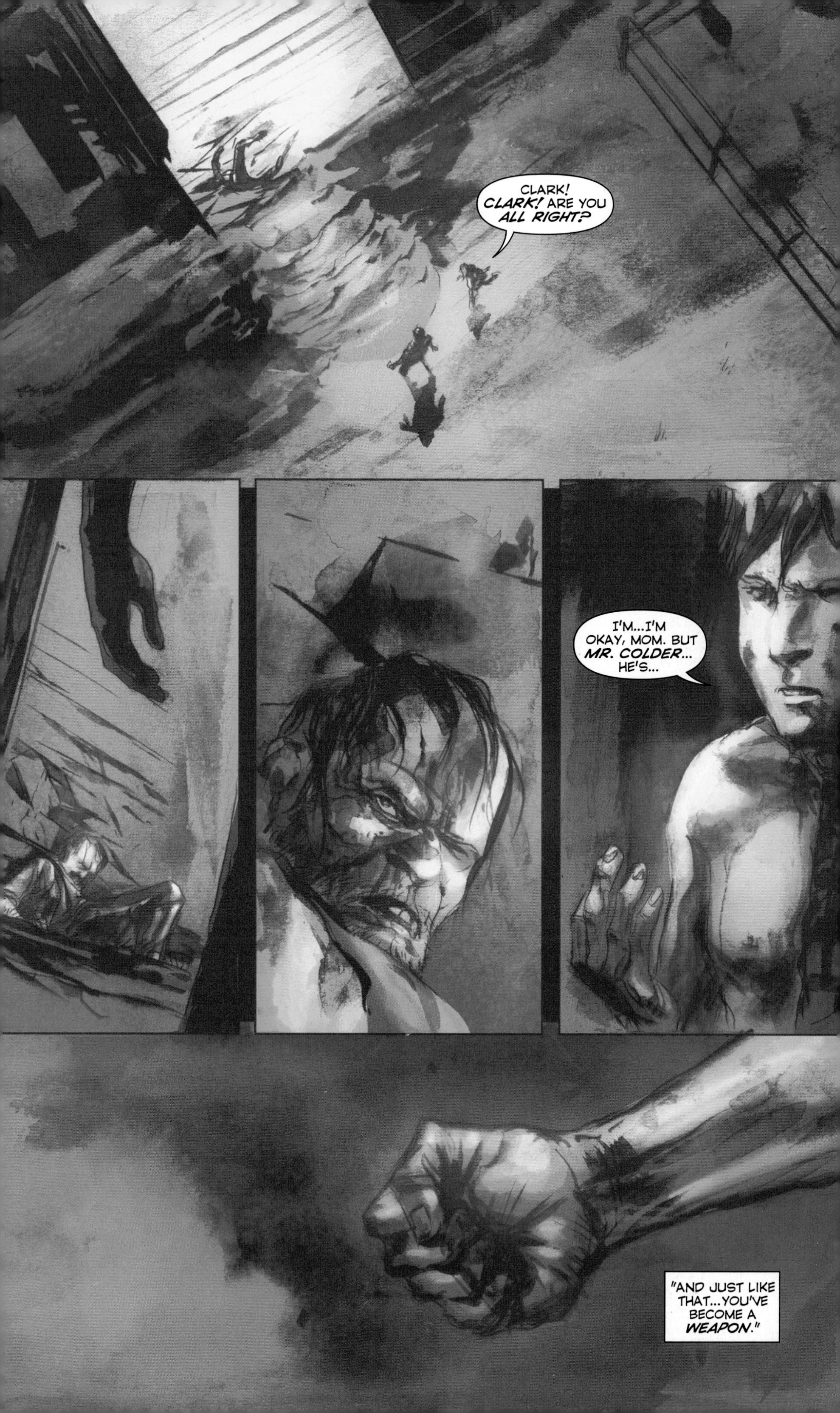
CLARK! CLARK! ARE YOU ALL RIGHT?
I'M...I'M OKAY, MOM. BUT MR. COLDER... HE'S...
"AND JUST LIKE THAT...YOU'VE BECOME A WEAPON."

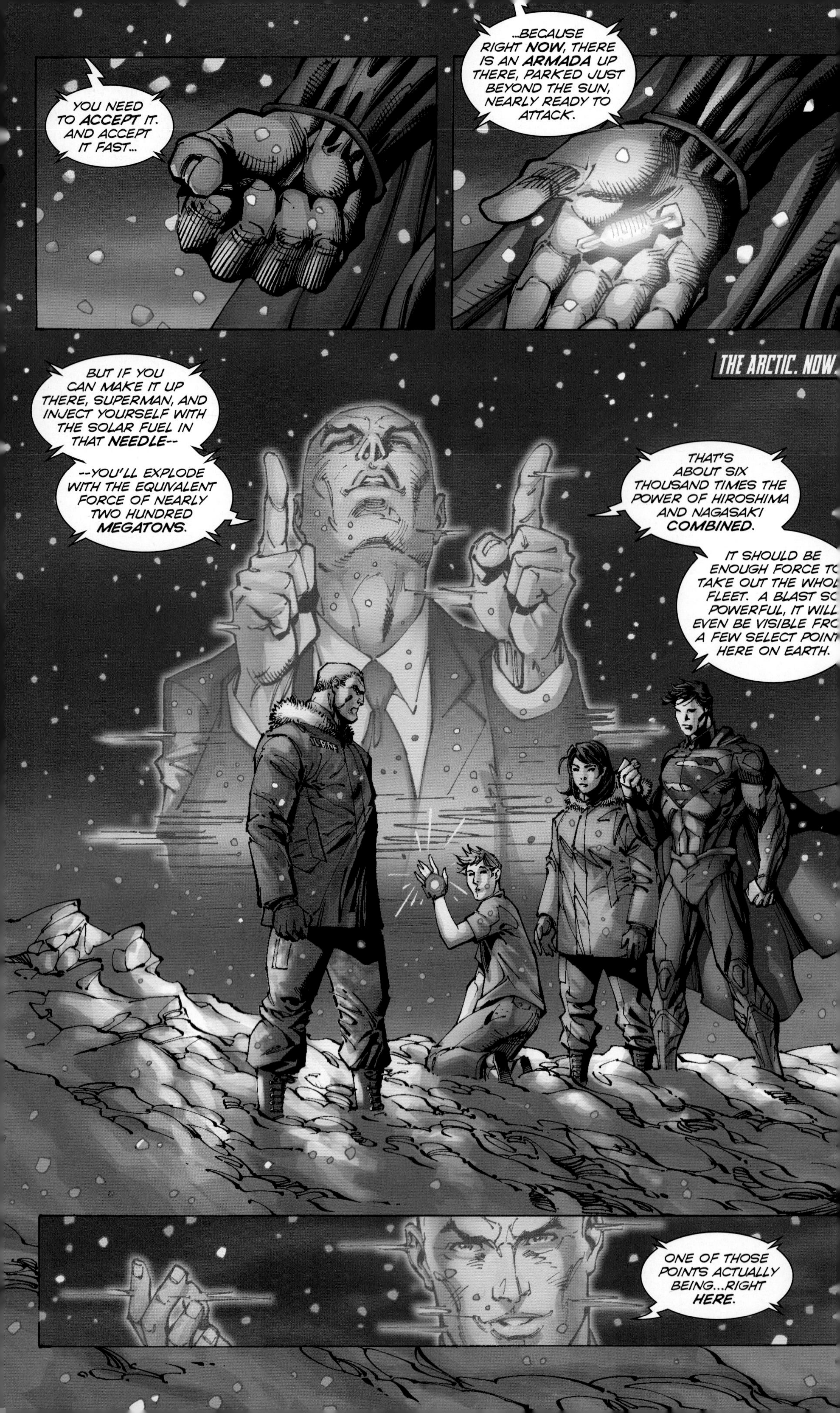
YOU NEED TO ACCEPT IT. AND ACCEPT IT FAST...
...BECAUSE RIGHT NOW, THERE IS AN ARMADA UP THERE, PARKED JUST BEYOND THE SUN, NEARLY READY TO ATTACK.
THE ARCTIC. NOW.
BUT IF YOU CAN MAKE IT UP THERE, SUPERMAN, AND INJECT YOURSELF WITH THE SOLAR FUEL IN THAT NEEDLE--
--YOU'LL EXPLODE WITH THE EQUIVALENT FORCE OF NEARLY TWO HUNDRED MEGATONS.
THAT'S ABOUT SIX THOUSAND TIMES THE POWER OF HIROSHIMA AND NAGASAKI COMBINED.
IT SHOULD BE ENOUGH FORCE TO TAKE OUT THE WHOLE FLEET. A BLAST SO POWERFUL, IT WILL EVEN BE VISIBLE FROM A FEW SELECT POINTS HERE ON EARTH.
ONE OF THOSE POINTS ACTUALLY BEING...RIGHT HERE.

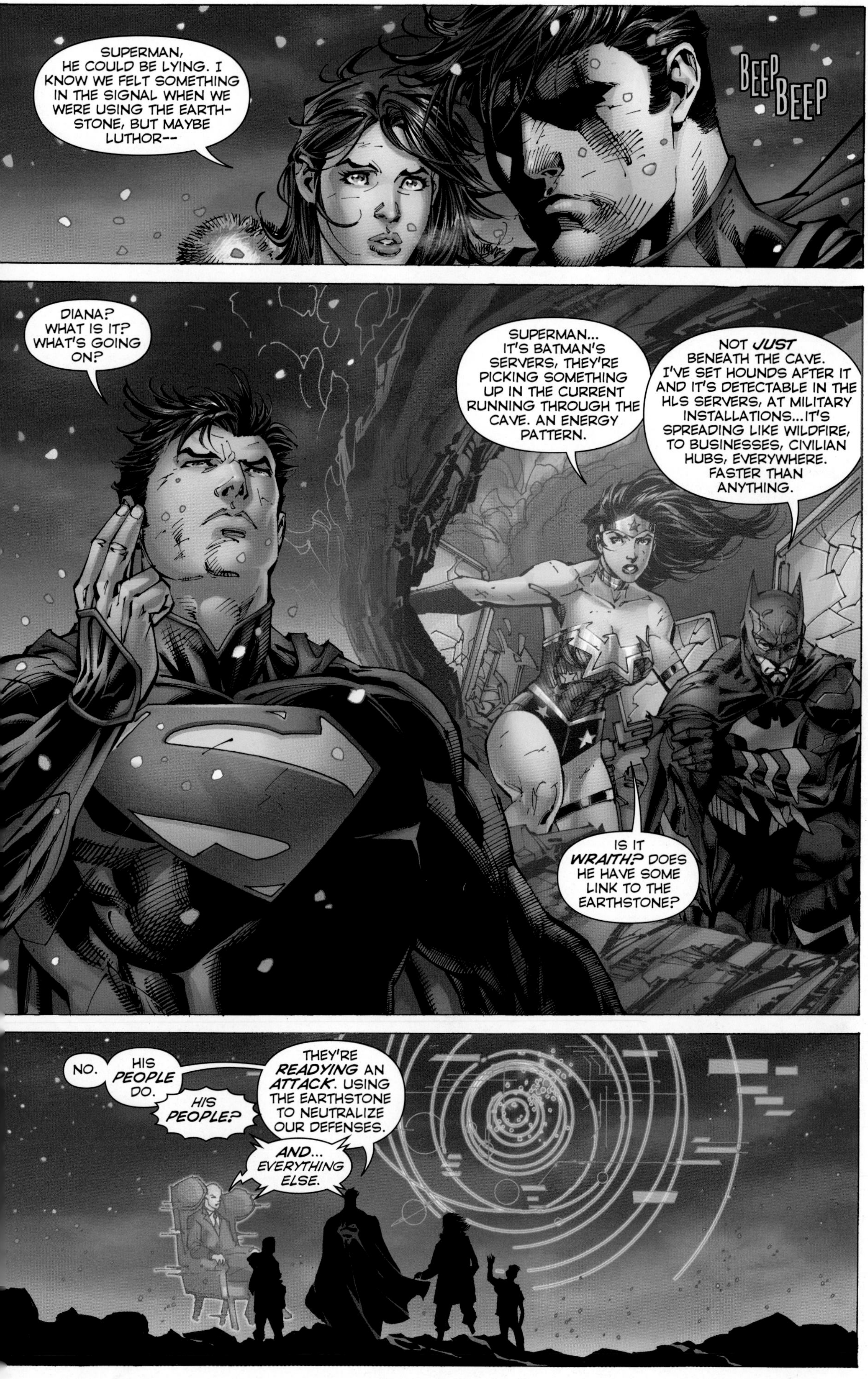

SUPERMAN, HE COULD BE LYING. I KNOW WE FELT SOMETHING IN THE SIGNAL WHEN WE WERE USING THE EARTH-STONE, BUT MAYBE LUTHOR--
BEEP BEEP
DIANA? WHAT IS IT? WHAT'S GOING ON?
SUPERMAN... IT'S BATMAN'S SERVERS, THEY'RE PICKING SOMETHING UP IN THE CURRENT RUNNING THROUGH THE CAVE. AN ENERGY PATTERN.
NOT *JUST* BENEATH THE CAVE. I'VE SET HOUNDS AFTER IT AND IT'S DETECTABLE IN THE HLS SERVERS, AT MILITARY INSTALLATIONS...IT'S SPREADING LIKE WILDFIRE, TO BUSINESSES, CIVILIAN HUBS, EVERYWHERE. FASTER THAN ANYTHING.
IS IT *WRAITH?* DOES HE HAVE SOME LINK TO THE EARTHSTONE?
NO.
HIS *PEOPLE* DO.
HIS PEOPLE?
THEY'RE *READYING* AN *ATTACK*. USING THE EARTHSTONE TO NEUTRALIZE OUR DEFENSES.
AND... EVERYTHING ELSE.

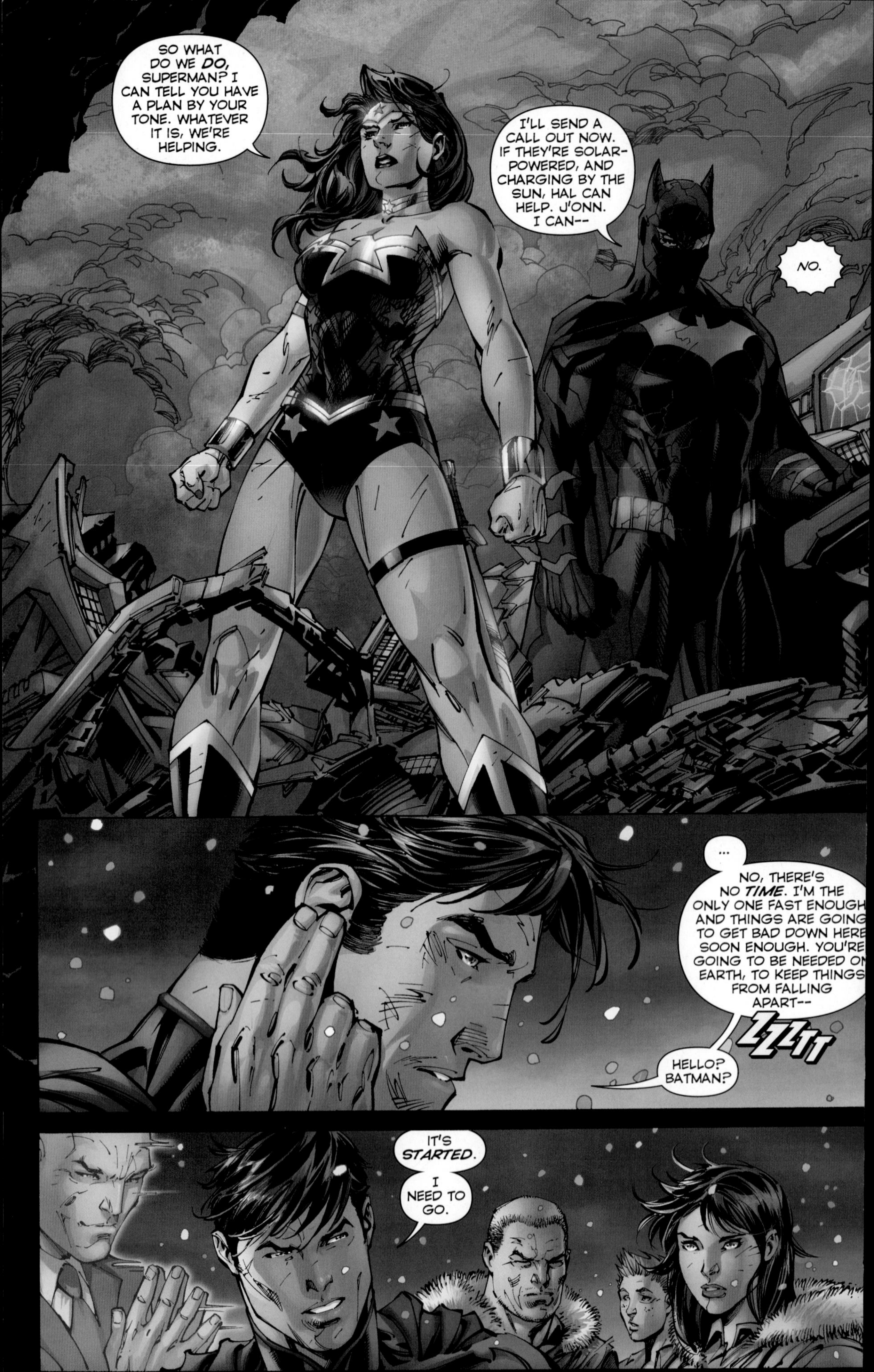

SO WHAT DO WE *DO*, SUPERMAN? I CAN TELL YOU HAVE A PLAN BY YOUR TONE. WHATEVER IT IS, WE'RE HELPING.
I'LL SEND A CALL OUT NOW. IF THEY'RE SOLAR-POWERED, AND CHARGING BY THE SUN, HAL CAN HELP. J'ONN. I CAN--
NO.
...
NO, THERE'S NO *TIME*. I'M THE ONLY ONE FAST ENOUGH AND THINGS ARE GOING TO GET BAD DOWN HERE SOON ENOUGH. YOU'RE GOING TO BE NEEDED ON EARTH, TO KEEP THINGS FROM FALLING APART--
ZZZTT
HELLO? BATMAN?
IT'S *STARTED*.
I NEED TO GO.

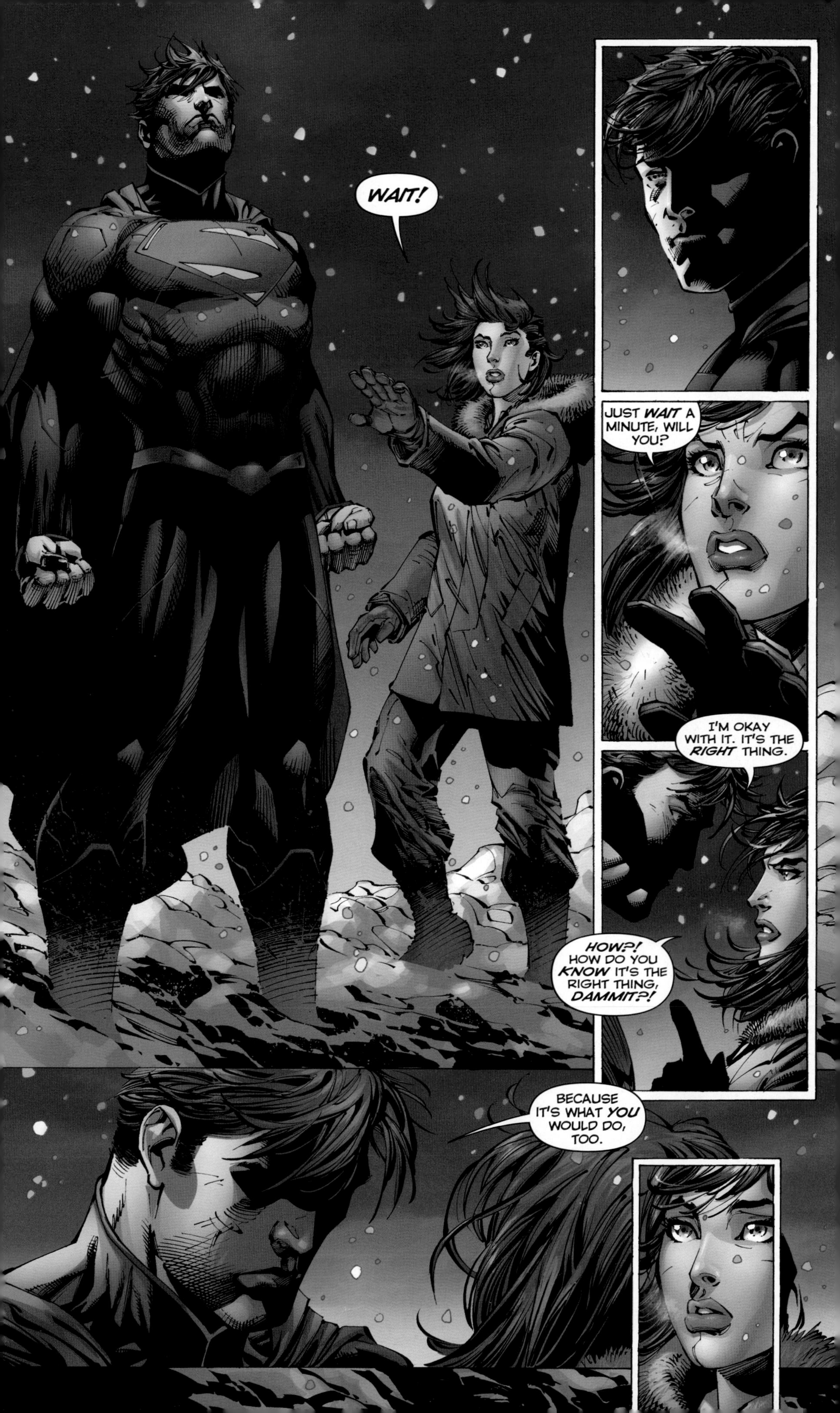
WAIT!
JUST WAIT A MINUTE, WILL YOU?
I'M OKAY WITH IT. IT'S THE RIGHT THING.
HOW?! HOW DO YOU KNOW IT'S THE RIGHT THING, DAMMIT?!
BECAUSE IT'S WHAT YOU WOULD DO, TOO.

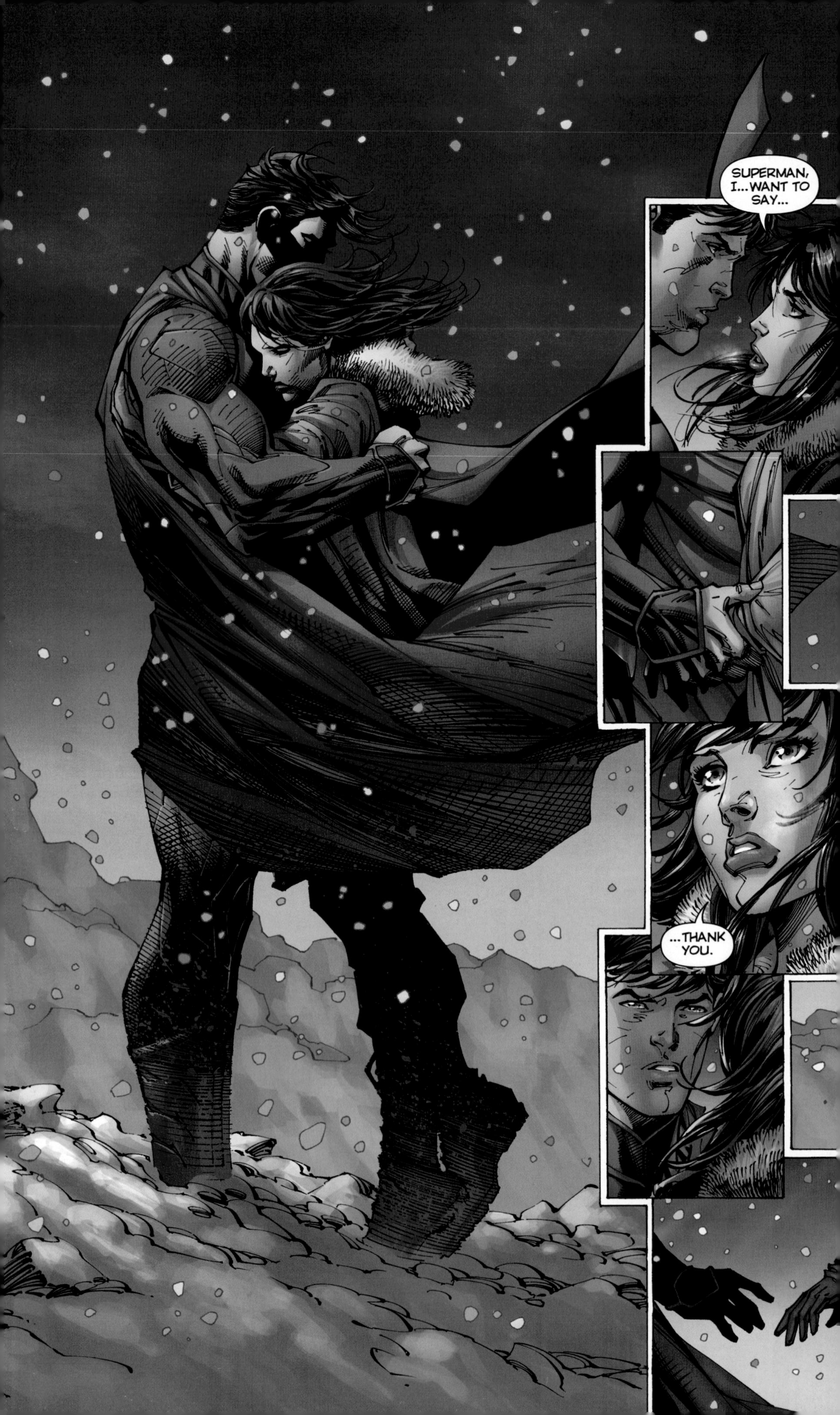
SUPERMAN, I...WANT TO SAY...
...THANK YOU.

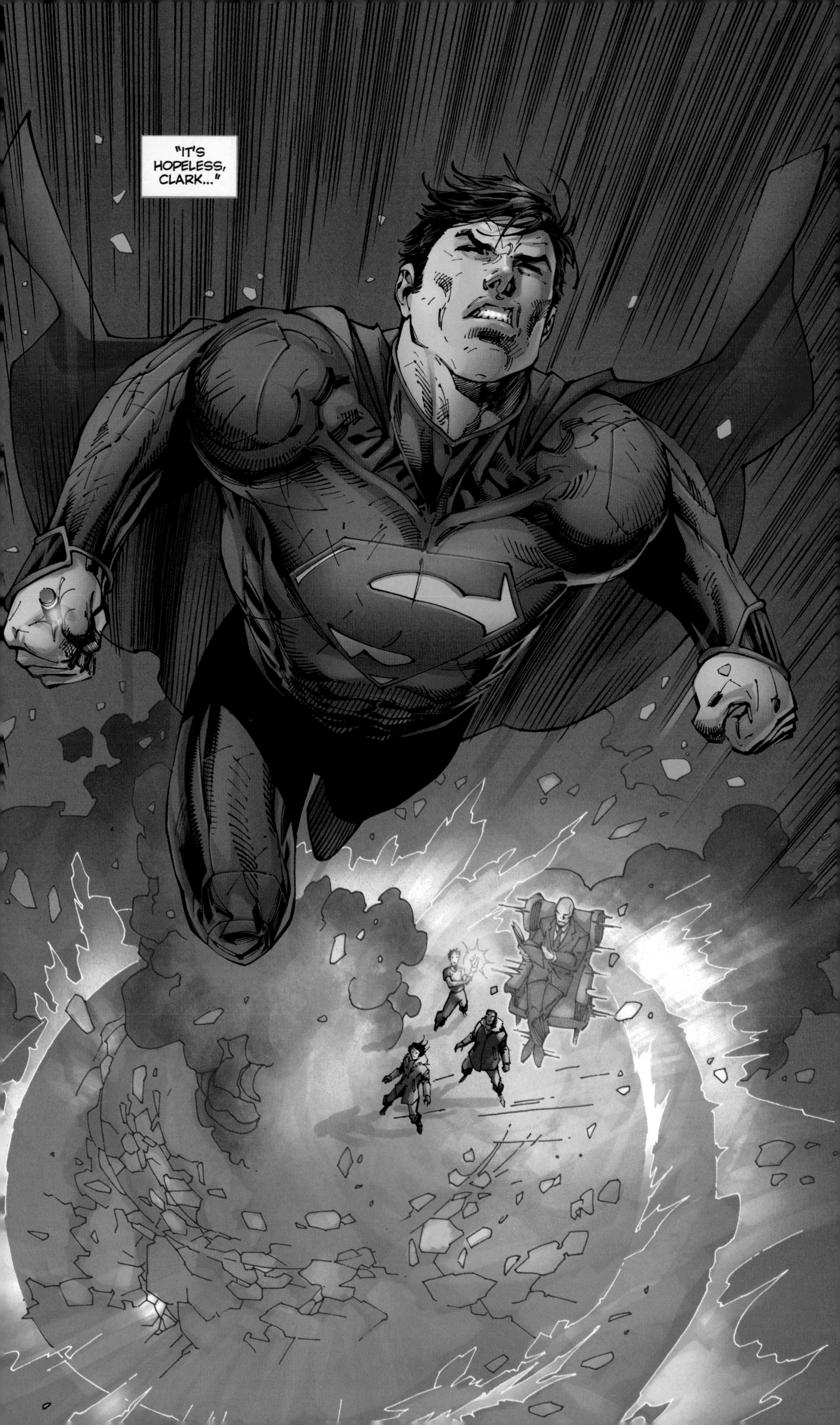
"IT'S HOPELESS, CLARK..."

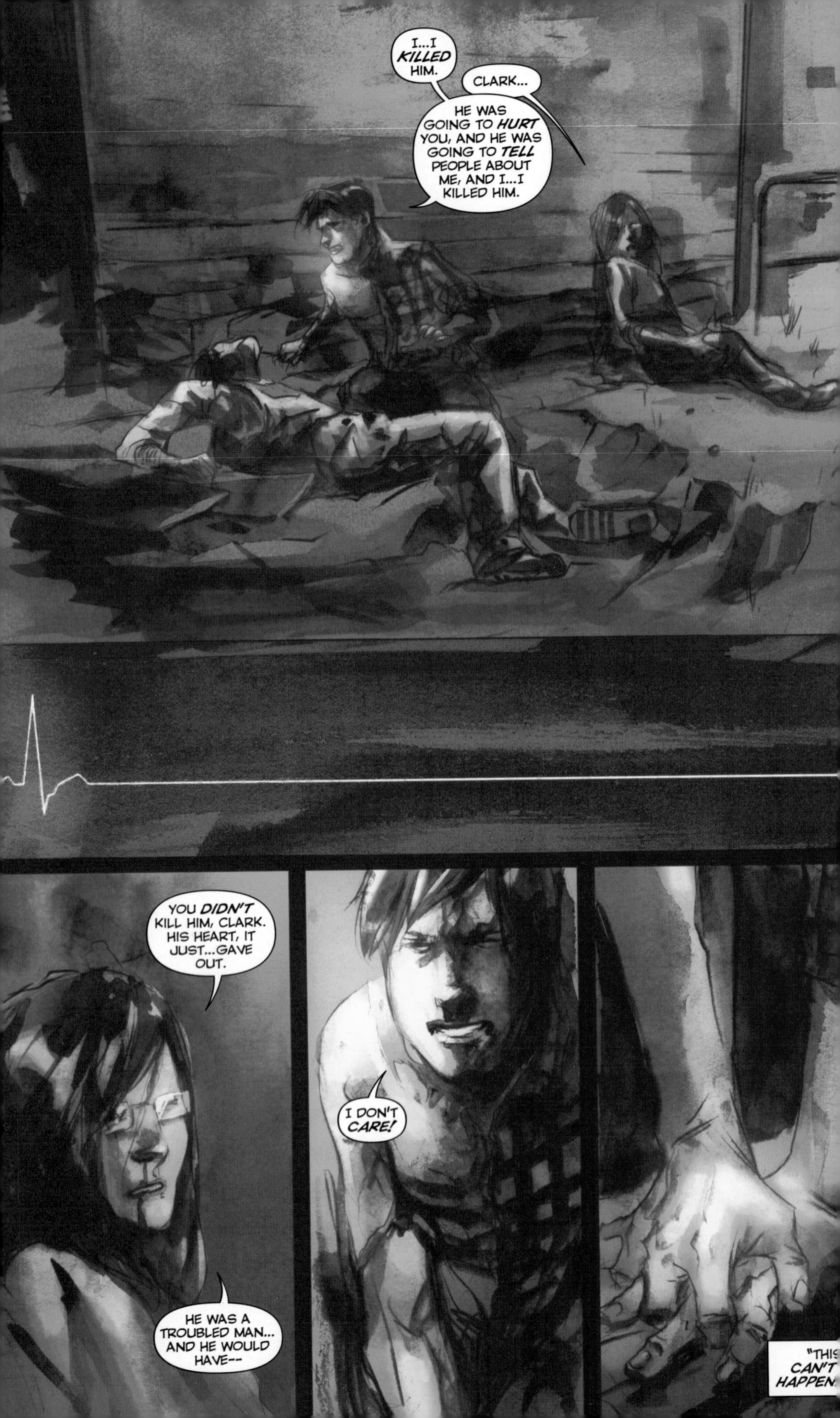
I...I *KILLED* HIM.
CLARK...
HE WAS GOING TO *HURT* YOU, AND HE WAS GOING TO *TELL* PEOPLE ABOUT ME, AND I...I KILLED HIM.
YOU *DIDN'T* KILL HIM, CLARK. HIS HEART, IT JUST...GAVE OUT.
HE WAS A TROUBLED MAN... AND HE WOULD HAVE--
I DON'T *CARE!*
"THIS *CAN'T* HAPPEN.

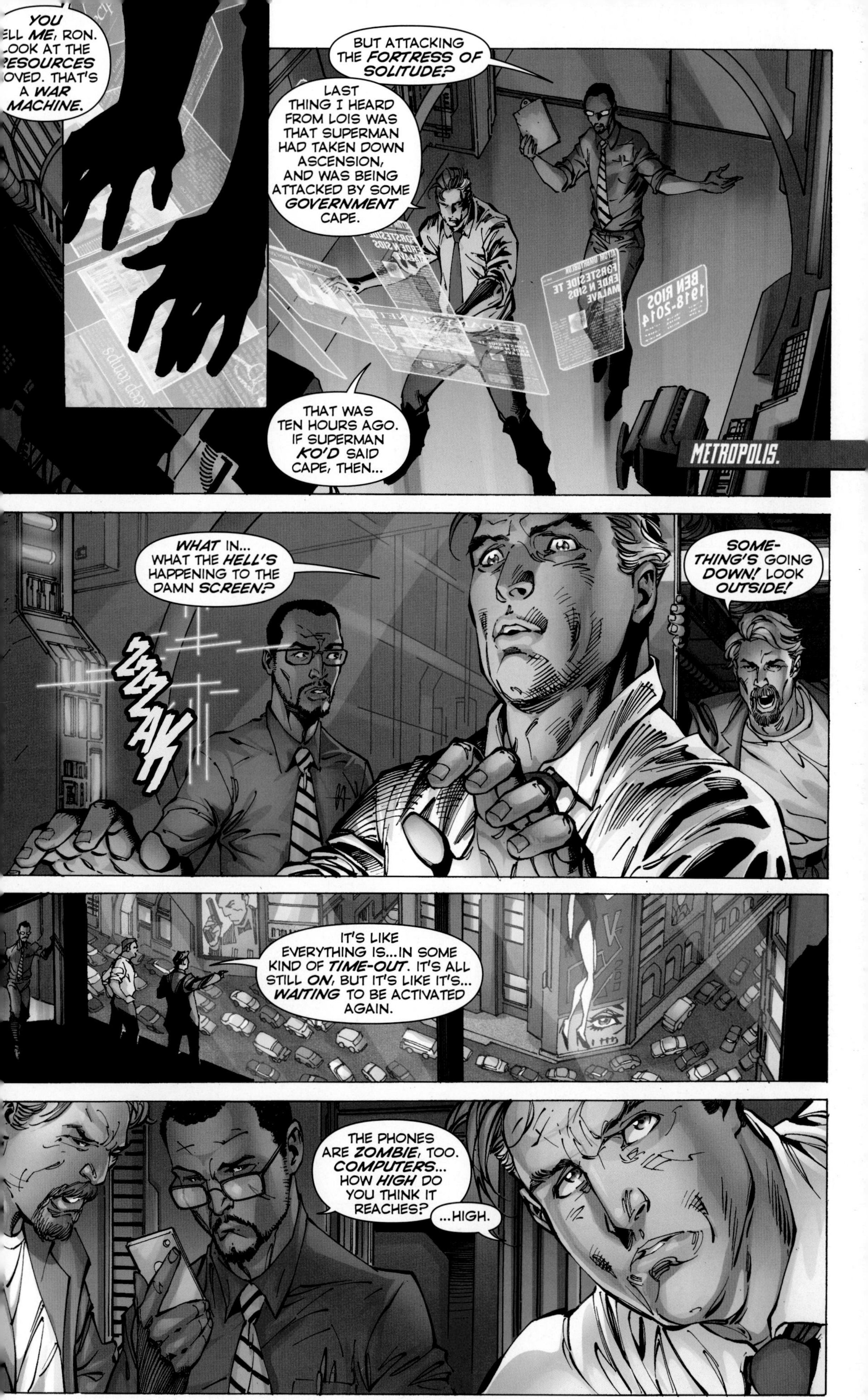

YOU ...ELL ME, RON. ...OOK AT THE ...ESOURCES ...OVED. THAT'S A WAR MACHINE.
BUT ATTACKING THE FORTRESS OF SOLITUDE?
LAST THING I HEARD FROM LOIS WAS THAT SUPERMAN HAD TAKEN DOWN ASCENSION, AND WAS BEING ATTACKED BY SOME GOVERNMENT CAPE.
THAT WAS TEN HOURS AGO. IF SUPERMAN KO'D SAID CAPE, THEN...
METROPOLIS.
WHAT IN... WHAT THE HELL'S HAPPENING TO THE DAMN SCREEN?
ZZZZAK
SOME-THING'S GOING DOWN! LOOK OUTSIDE!
IT'S LIKE EVERYTHING IS...IN SOME KIND OF TIME-OUT. IT'S ALL STILL ON, BUT IT'S LIKE IT'S... WAITING TO BE ACTIVATED AGAIN.
THE PHONES ARE ZOMBIE, TOO. COMPUTERS... HOW HIGH DO YOU THINK IT REACHES?
...HIGH.

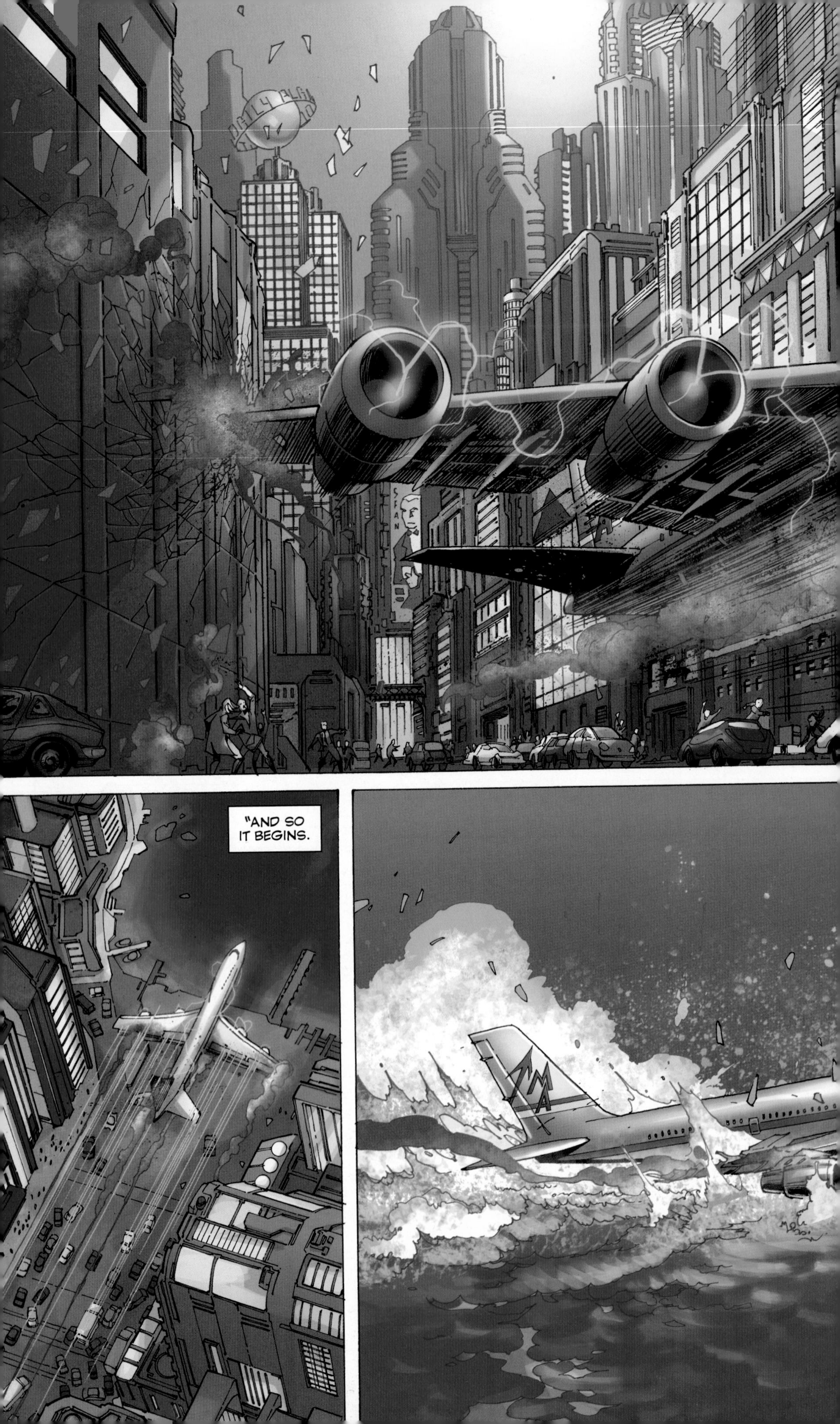
"AND SO IT BEGINS.

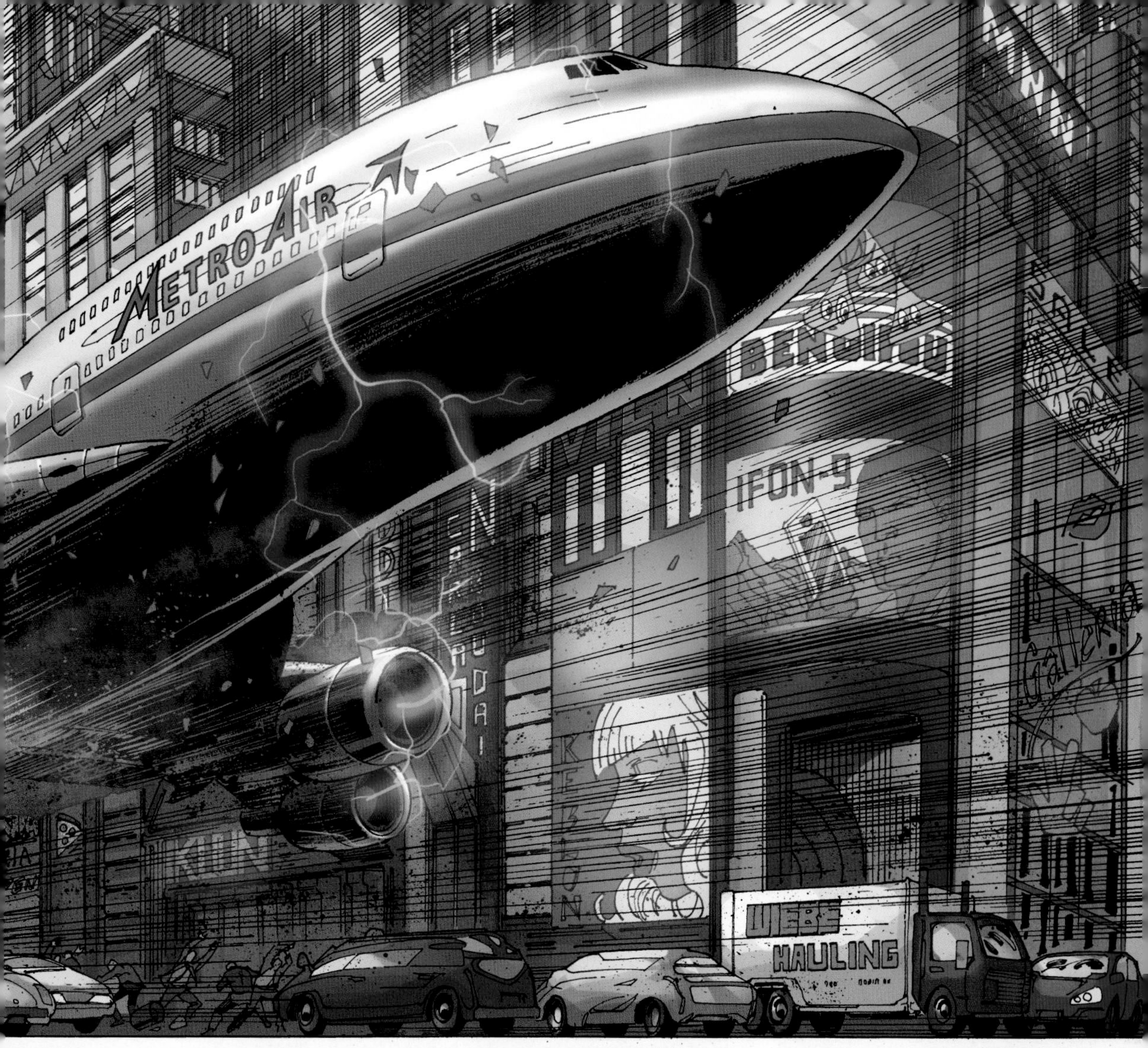
METRO AIR
IFON-9
WEBB
HAULING

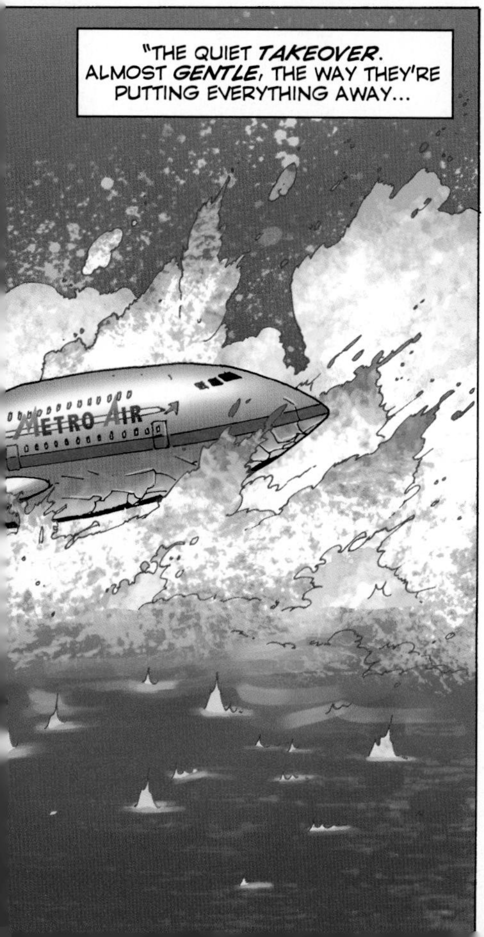
"THE QUIET *TAKEOVER*. ALMOST *GENTLE*, THE WAY THEY'RE PUTTING EVERYTHING AWAY...
METRO AIR

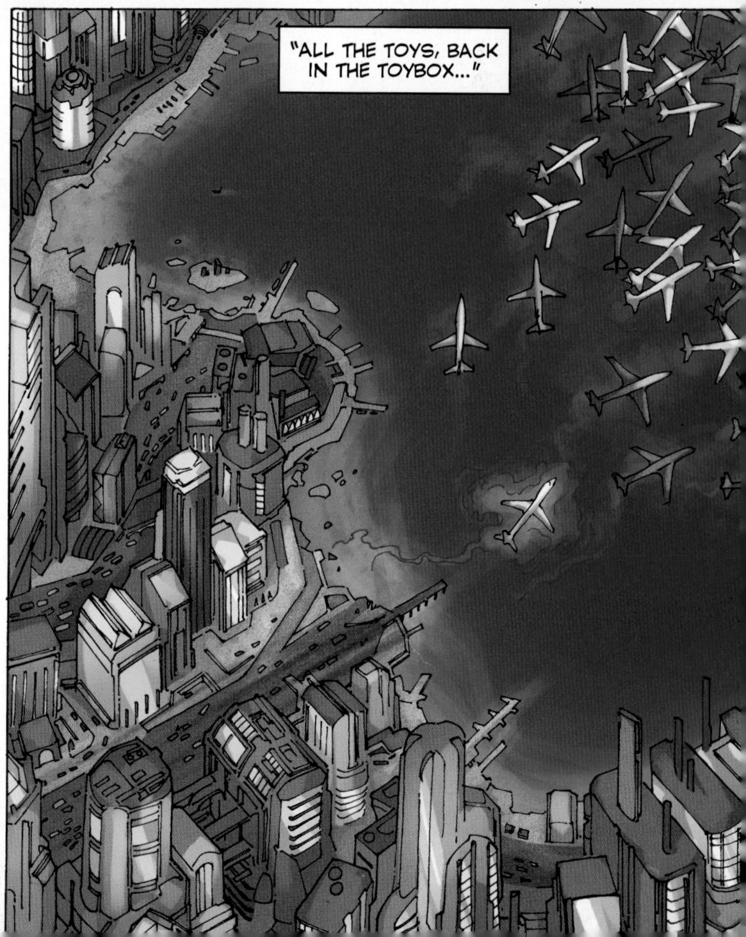
"ALL THE TOYS, BACK IN THE TOYBOX..."

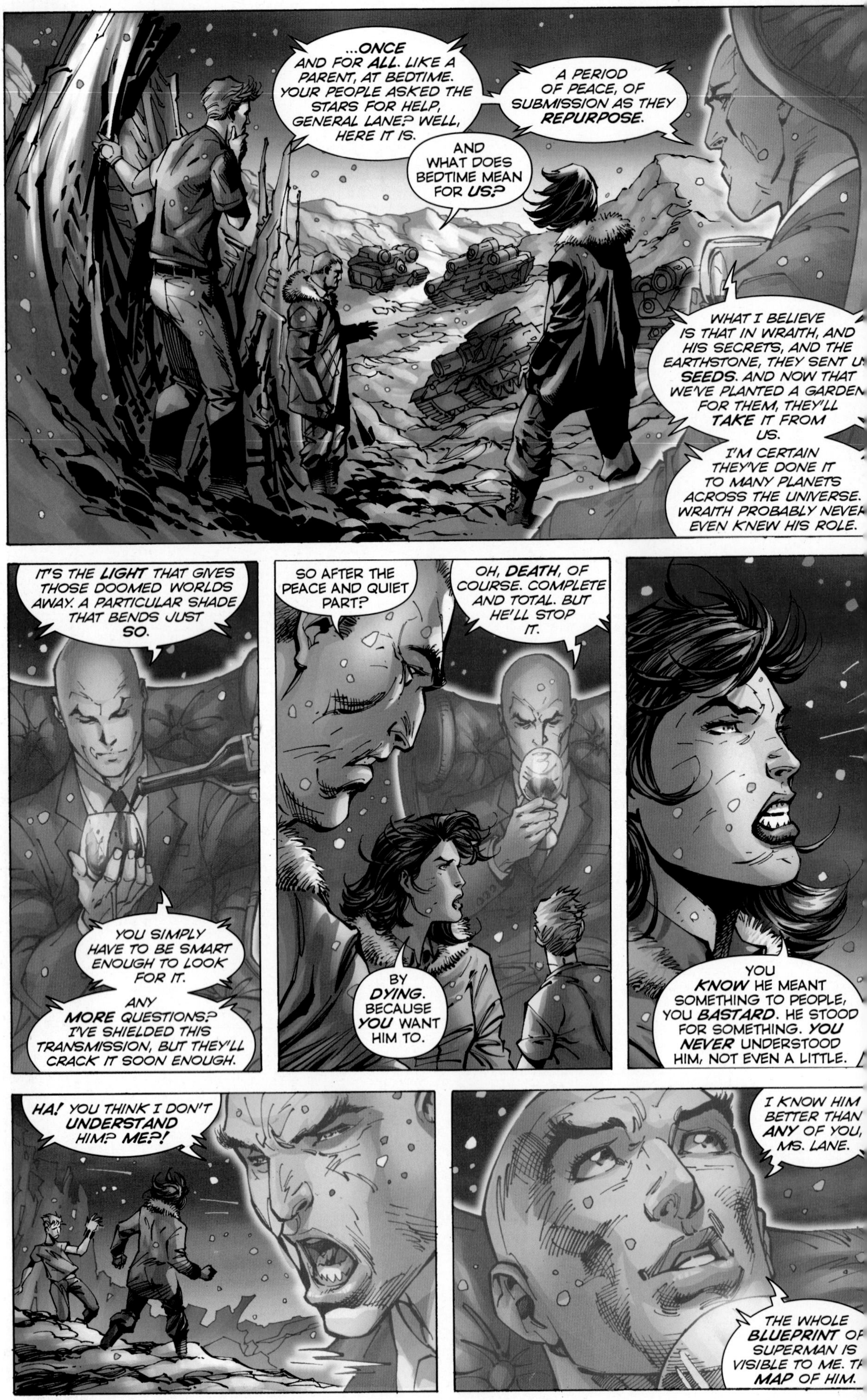
...ONCE AND FOR ALL. LIKE A PARENT, AT BEDTIME. YOUR PEOPLE ASKED THE STARS FOR HELP, GENERAL LANE? WELL, HERE IT IS.
A PERIOD OF PEACE, OF SUBMISSION AS THEY REPURPOSE.
AND WHAT DOES BEDTIME MEAN FOR US?
WHAT I BELIEVE IS THAT IN WRAITH, AND HIS SECRETS, AND THE EARTHSTONE, THEY SENT U SEEDS. AND NOW THAT WE'VE PLANTED A GARDEN FOR THEM, THEY'LL TAKE IT FROM US.
I'M CERTAIN THEY'VE DONE IT TO MANY PLANETS ACROSS THE UNIVERSE. WRAITH PROBABLY NEVER EVEN KNEW HIS ROLE.
IT'S THE LIGHT THAT GIVES THOSE DOOMED WORLDS AWAY. A PARTICULAR SHADE THAT BENDS JUST SO.
YOU SIMPLY HAVE TO BE SMART ENOUGH TO LOOK FOR IT.
ANY MORE QUESTIONS? I'VE SHIELDED THIS TRANSMISSION, BUT THEY'LL CRACK IT SOON ENOUGH.
SO AFTER THE PEACE AND QUIET PART?
OH, DEATH, OF COURSE. COMPLETE AND TOTAL. BUT HE'LL STOP IT.
BY DYING. BECAUSE YOU WANT HIM TO.
YOU KNOW HE MEANT SOMETHING TO PEOPLE, YOU BASTARD. HE STOOD FOR SOMETHING. YOU NEVER UNDERSTOOD HIM, NOT EVEN A LITTLE.
HA! YOU THINK I DON'T UNDERSTAND HIM? ME?!
I KNOW HIM BETTER THAN ANY OF YOU, MS. LANE.
THE WHOLE BLUEPRINT OF SUPERMAN IS VISIBLE TO ME. TH MAP OF HIM.

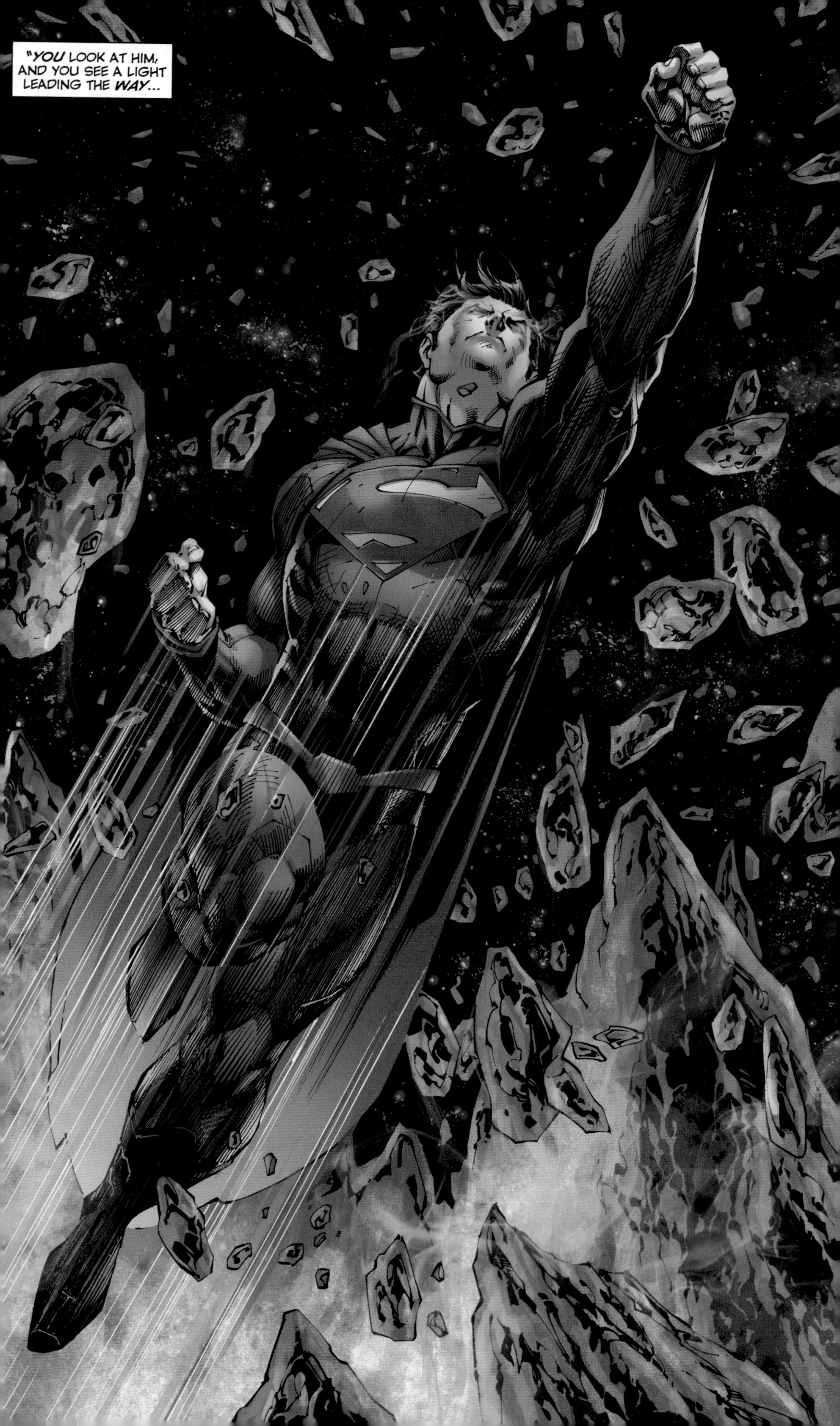
"YOU LOOK AT HIM, AND YOU SEE A LIGHT LEADING THE WAY...

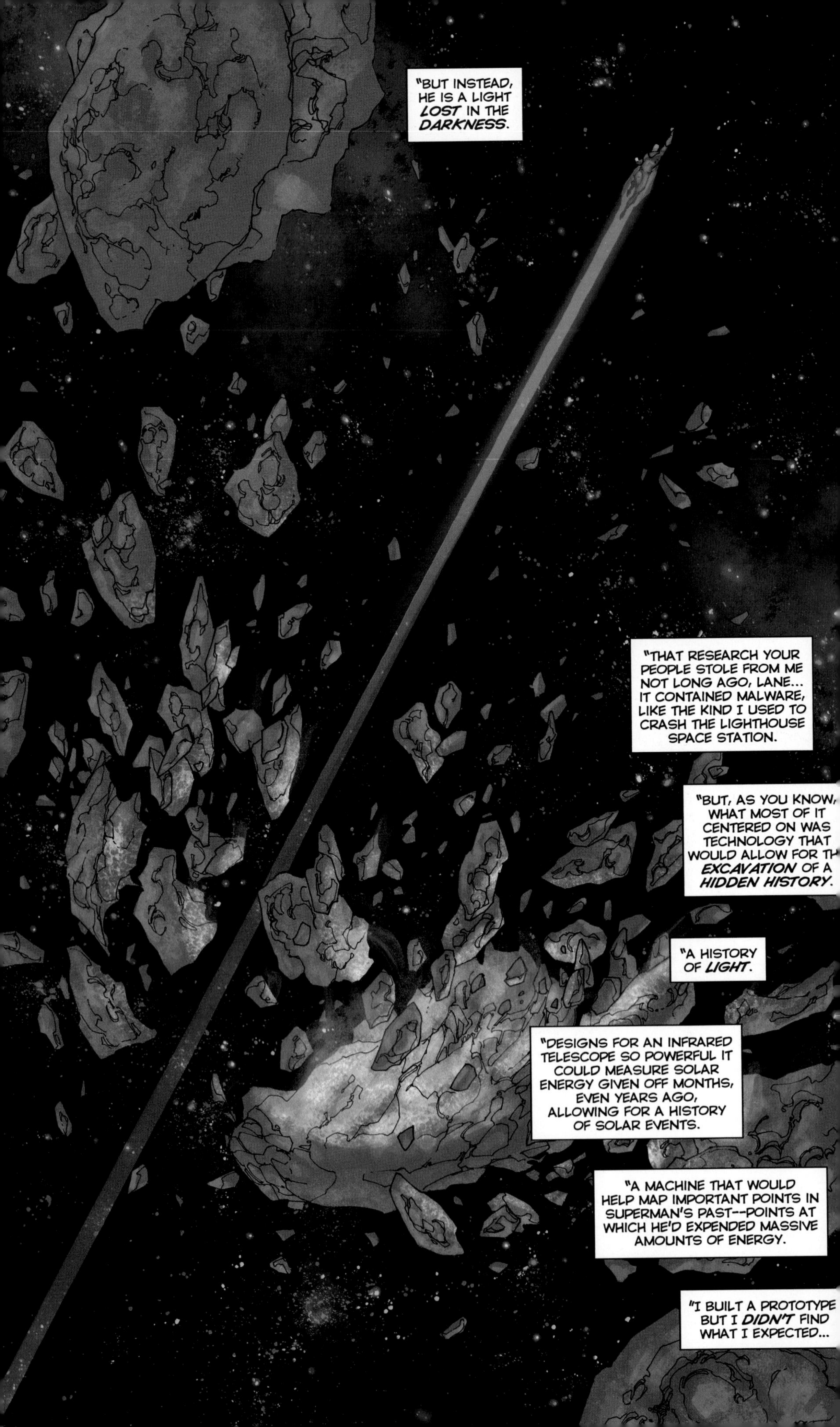
"BUT INSTEAD, HE IS A LIGHT *LOST* IN THE *DARKNESS*.
"THAT RESEARCH YOUR PEOPLE STOLE FROM ME NOT LONG AGO, LANE... IT CONTAINED MALWARE, LIKE THE KIND I USED TO CRASH THE LIGHTHOUSE SPACE STATION.
"BUT, AS YOU KNOW, WHAT MOST OF IT CENTERED ON WAS TECHNOLOGY THAT WOULD ALLOW FOR THE *EXCAVATION* OF A *HIDDEN HISTORY*.
"A HISTORY OF *LIGHT*.
"DESIGNS FOR AN INFRARED TELESCOPE SO POWERFUL IT COULD MEASURE SOLAR ENERGY GIVEN OFF MONTHS, EVEN YEARS AGO, ALLOWING FOR A HISTORY OF SOLAR EVENTS.
"A MACHINE THAT WOULD HELP MAP IMPORTANT POINTS IN SUPERMAN'S PAST--POINTS AT WHICH HE'D EXPENDED MASSIVE AMOUNTS OF ENERGY.
"I BUILT A PROTOTYPE BUT I *DIDN'T* FIND WHAT I EXPECTED...

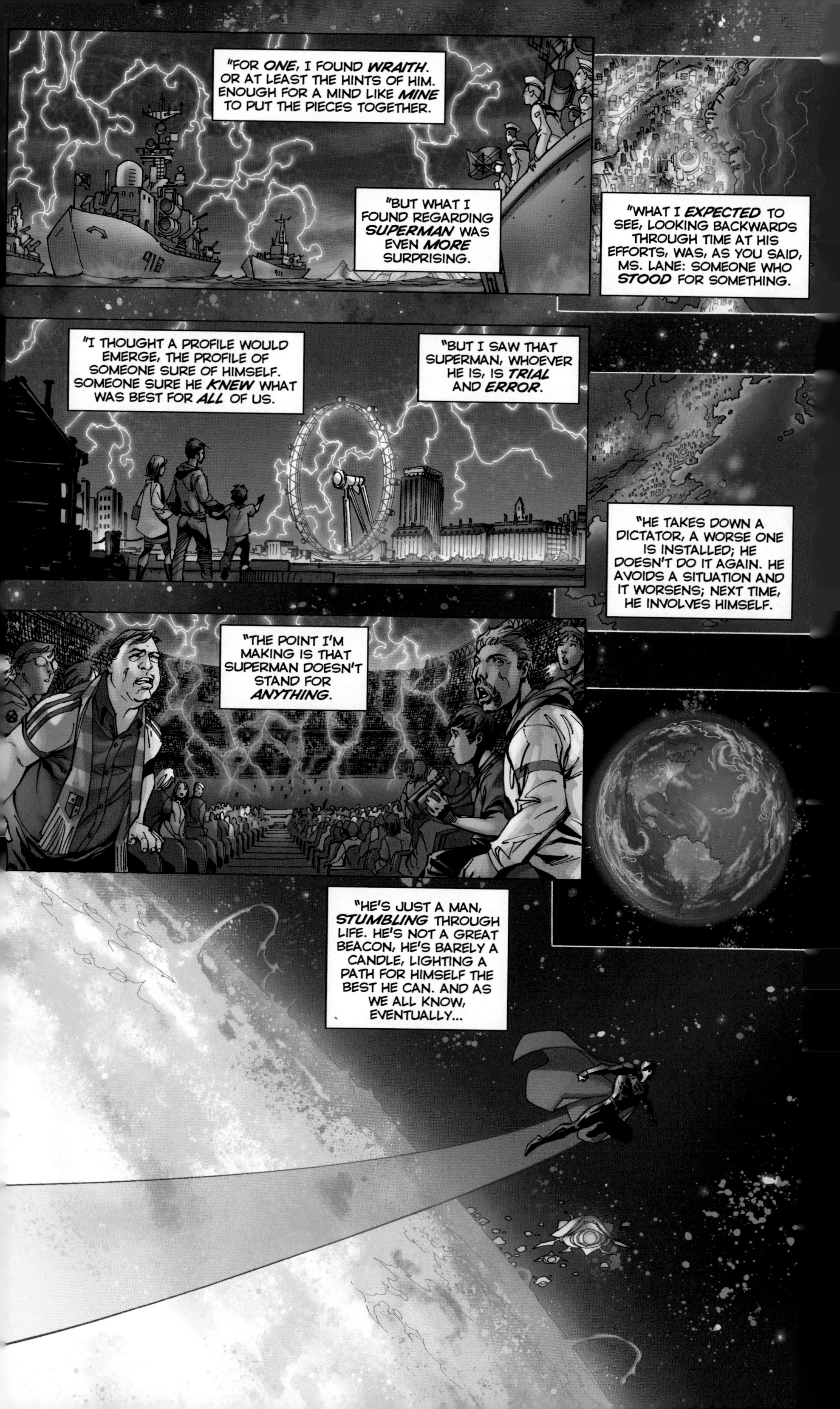

"FOR ONE, I FOUND WRAITH. OR AT LEAST THE HINTS OF HIM. ENOUGH FOR A MIND LIKE MINE TO PUT THE PIECES TOGETHER.
"BUT WHAT I FOUND REGARDING SUPERMAN WAS EVEN MORE SURPRISING.
"WHAT I EXPECTED TO SEE, LOOKING BACKWARDS THROUGH TIME AT HIS EFFORTS, WAS, AS YOU SAID, MS. LANE: SOMEONE WHO STOOD FOR SOMETHING.
"I THOUGHT A PROFILE WOULD EMERGE, THE PROFILE OF SOMEONE SURE OF HIMSELF. SOMEONE SURE HE KNEW WHAT WAS BEST FOR ALL OF US.
"BUT I SAW THAT SUPERMAN, WHOEVER HE IS, IS TRIAL AND ERROR.
"HE TAKES DOWN A DICTATOR, A WORSE ONE IS INSTALLED; HE DOESN'T DO IT AGAIN. HE AVOIDS A SITUATION AND IT WORSENS; NEXT TIME, HE INVOLVES HIMSELF.
"THE POINT I'M MAKING IS THAT SUPERMAN DOESN'T STAND FOR ANYTHING.
"HE'S JUST A MAN, STUMBLING THROUGH LIFE. HE'S NOT A GREAT BEACON, HE'S BARELY A CANDLE, LIGHTING A PATH FOR HIMSELF THE BEST HE CAN. AND AS WE ALL KNOW, EVENTUALLY...

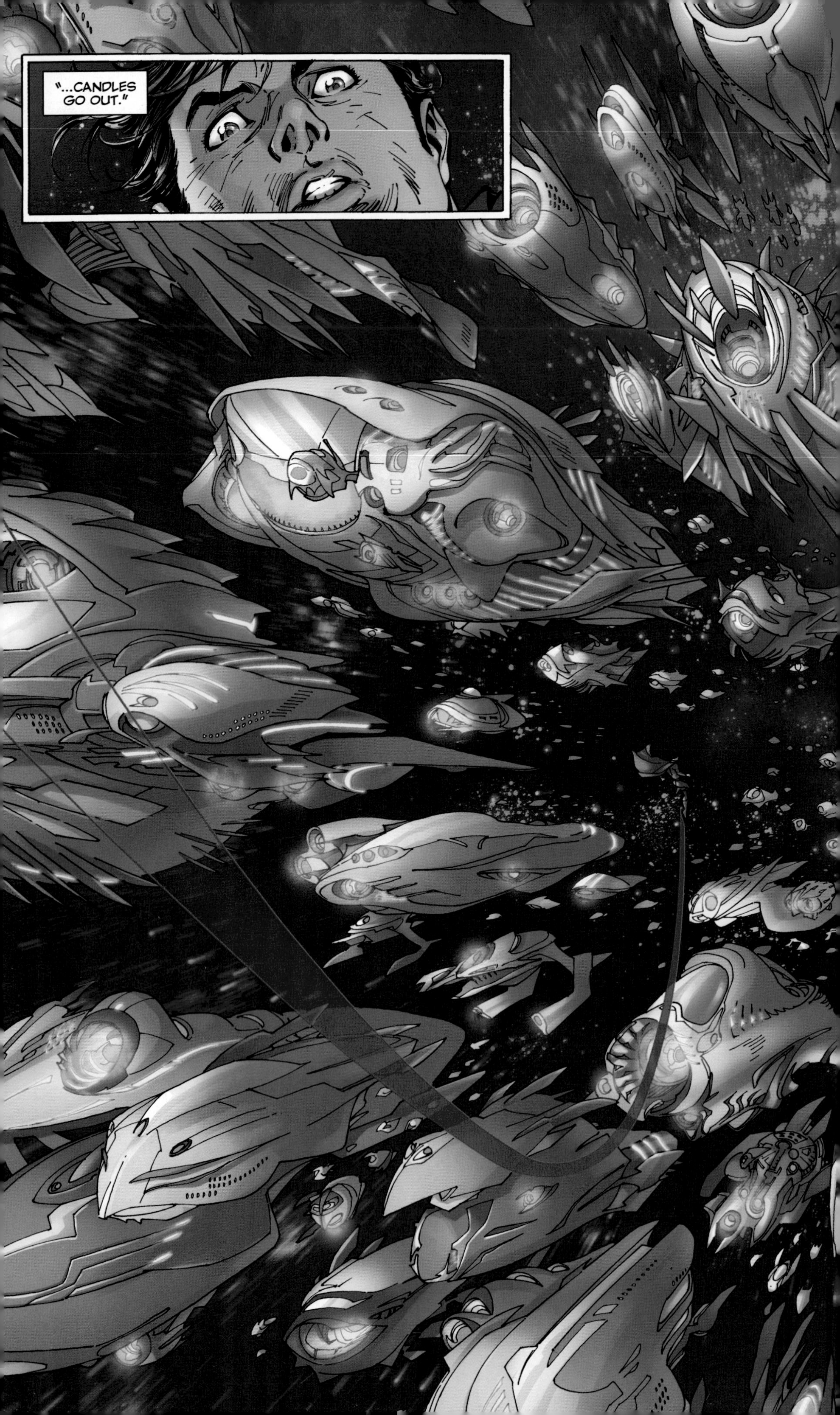
"...CANDLES GO OUT."

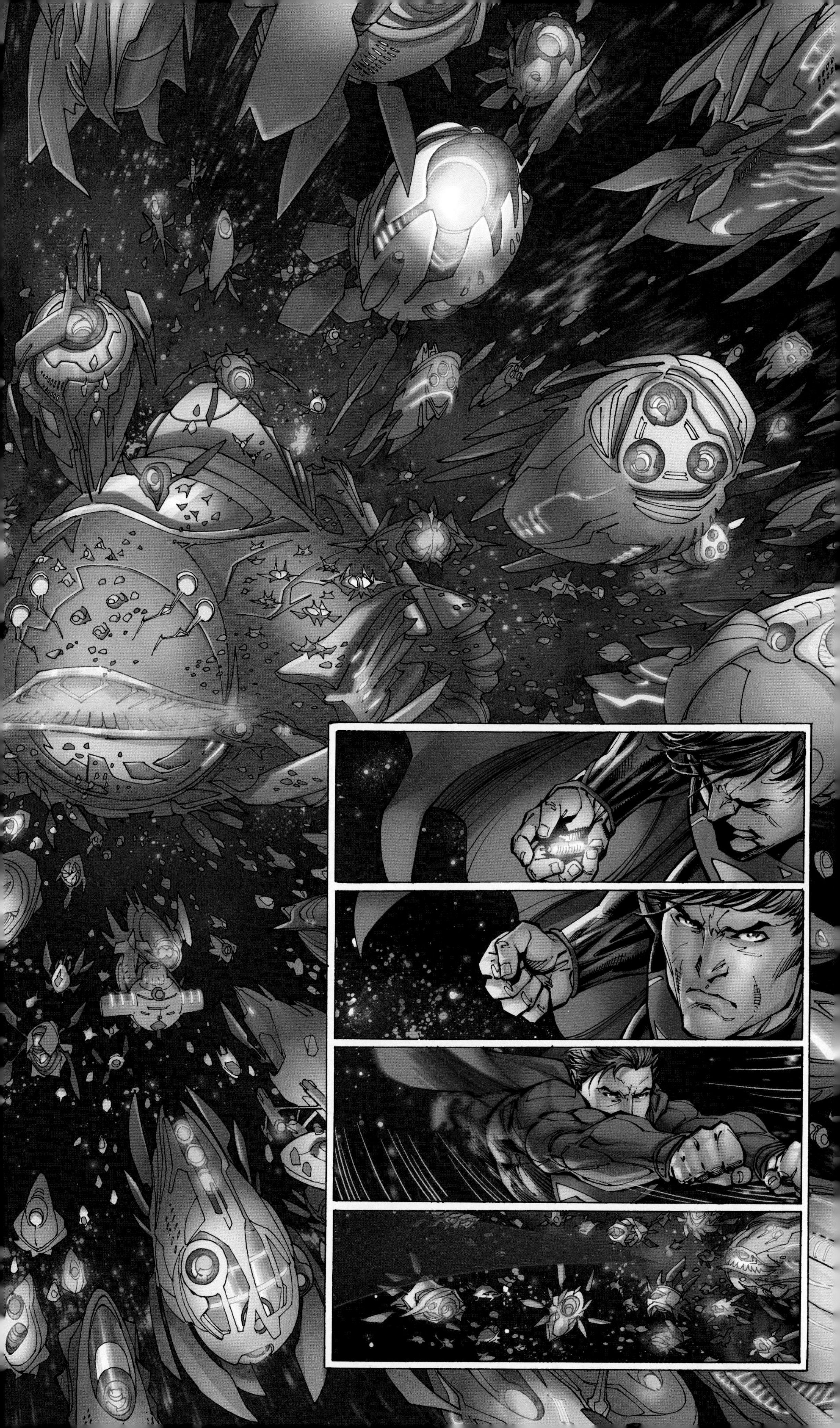

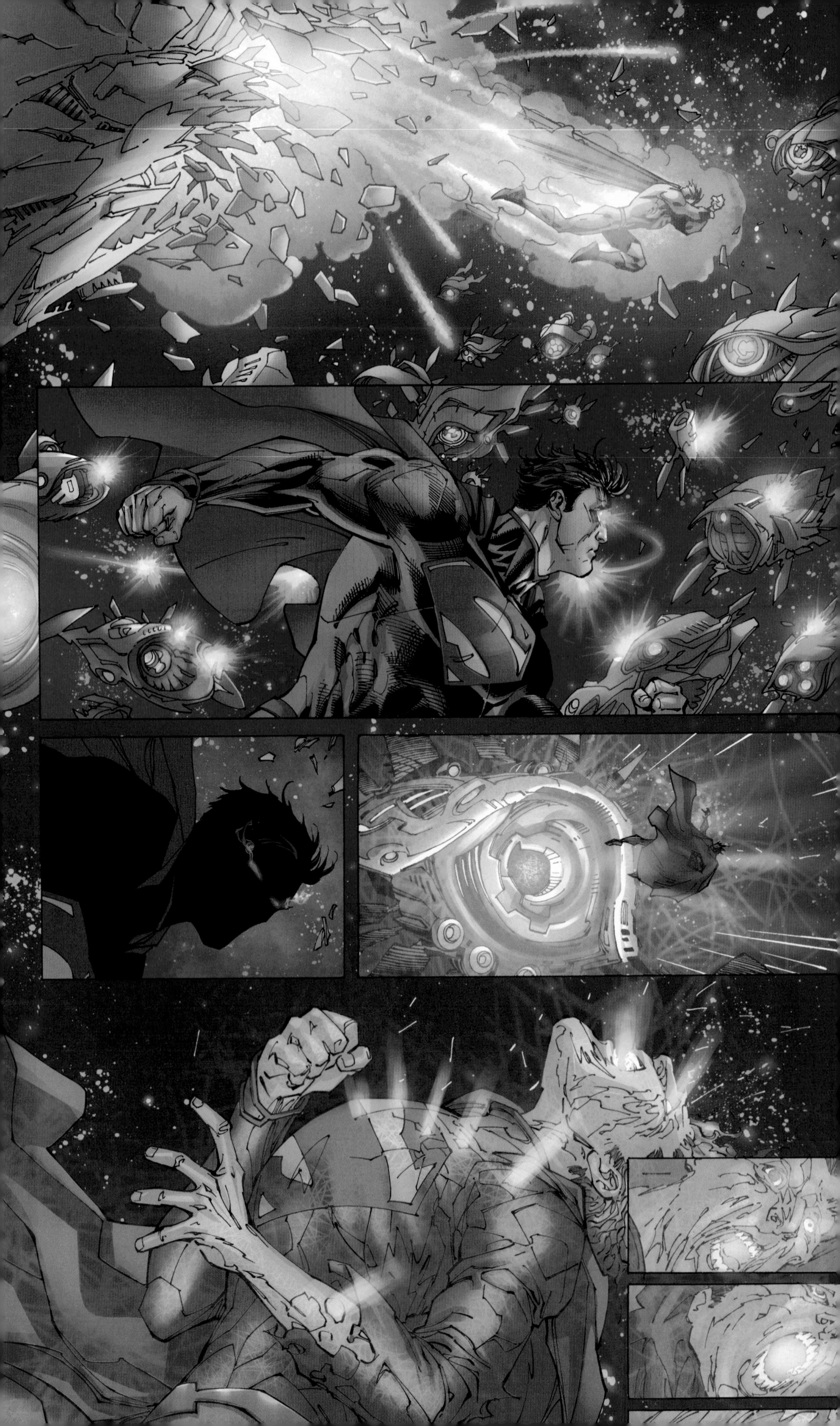

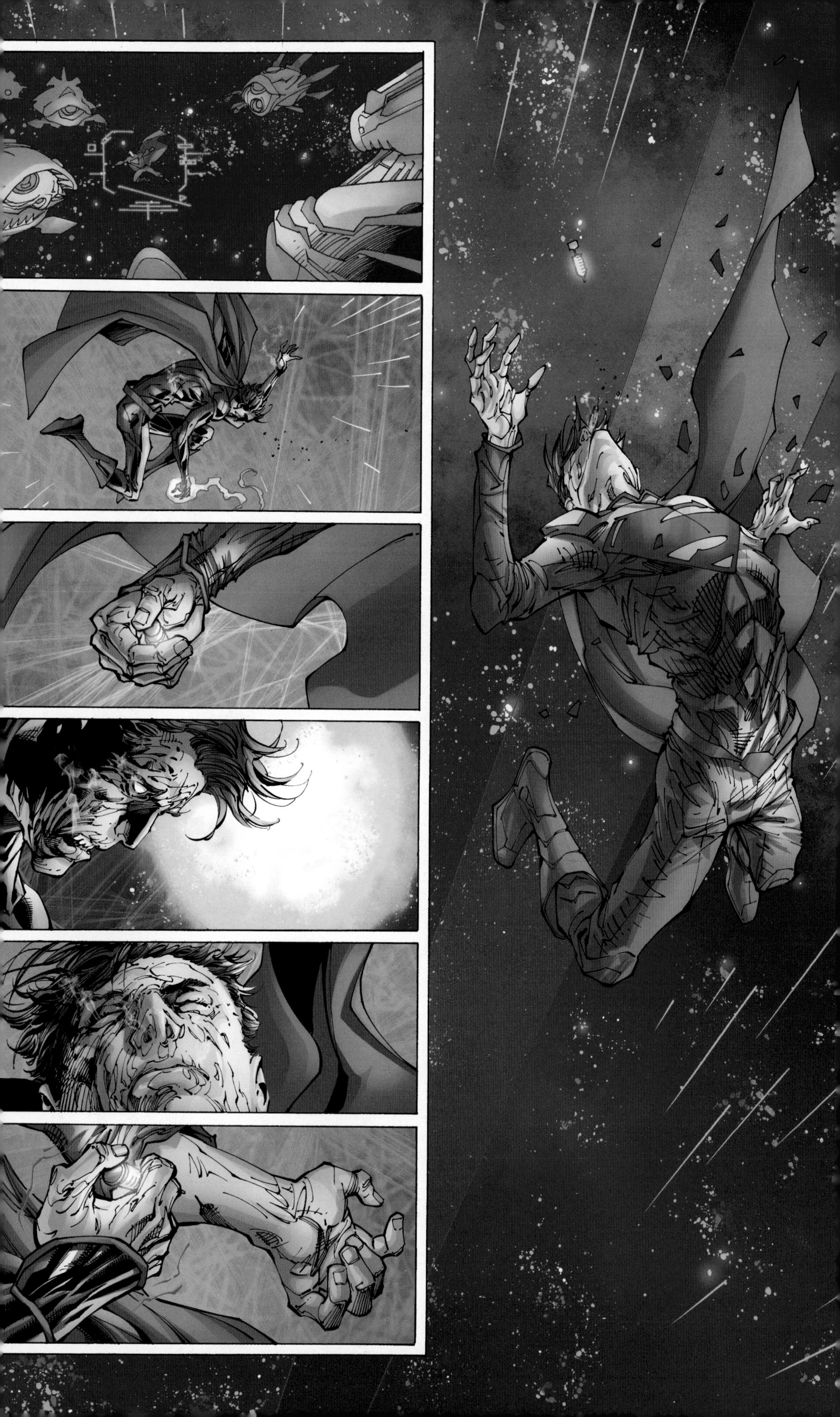

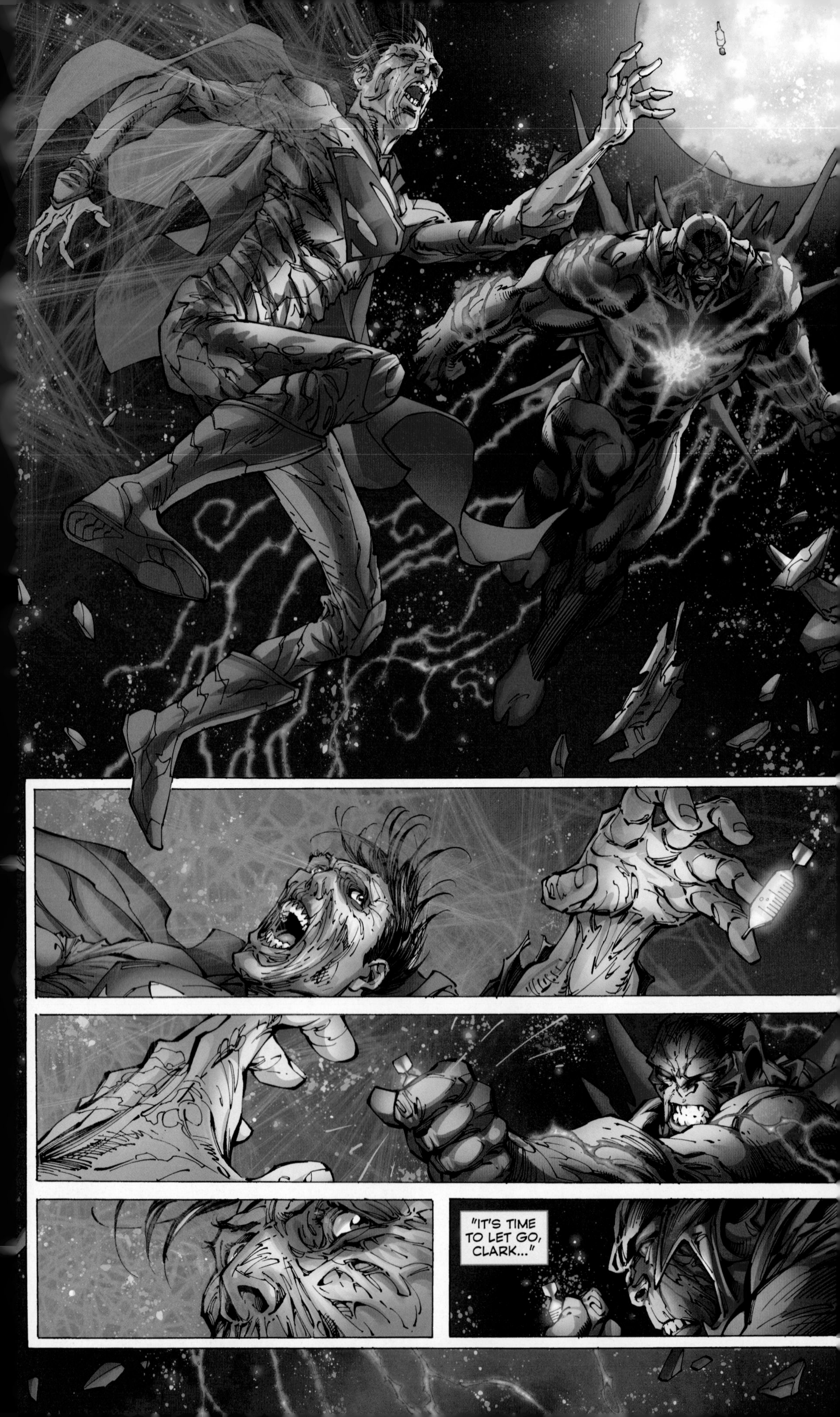
"IT'S TIME TO LET GO, CLARK..."

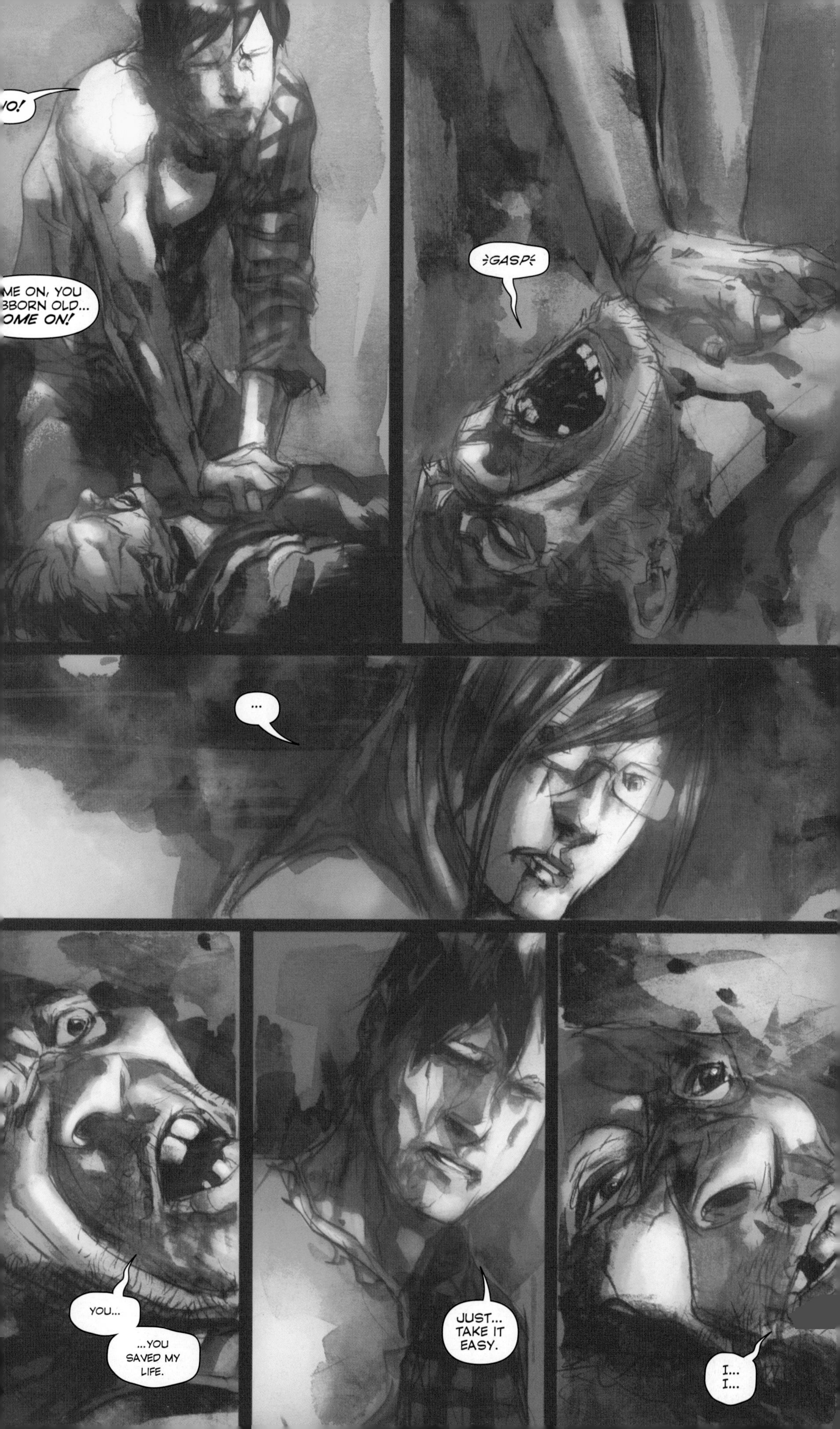

IO!
ME ON, YOU
BBORN OLD...
OME ON!
GASP
...
YOU...
...YOU SAVED MY LIFE.
JUST... TAKE IT EASY.
I... I...

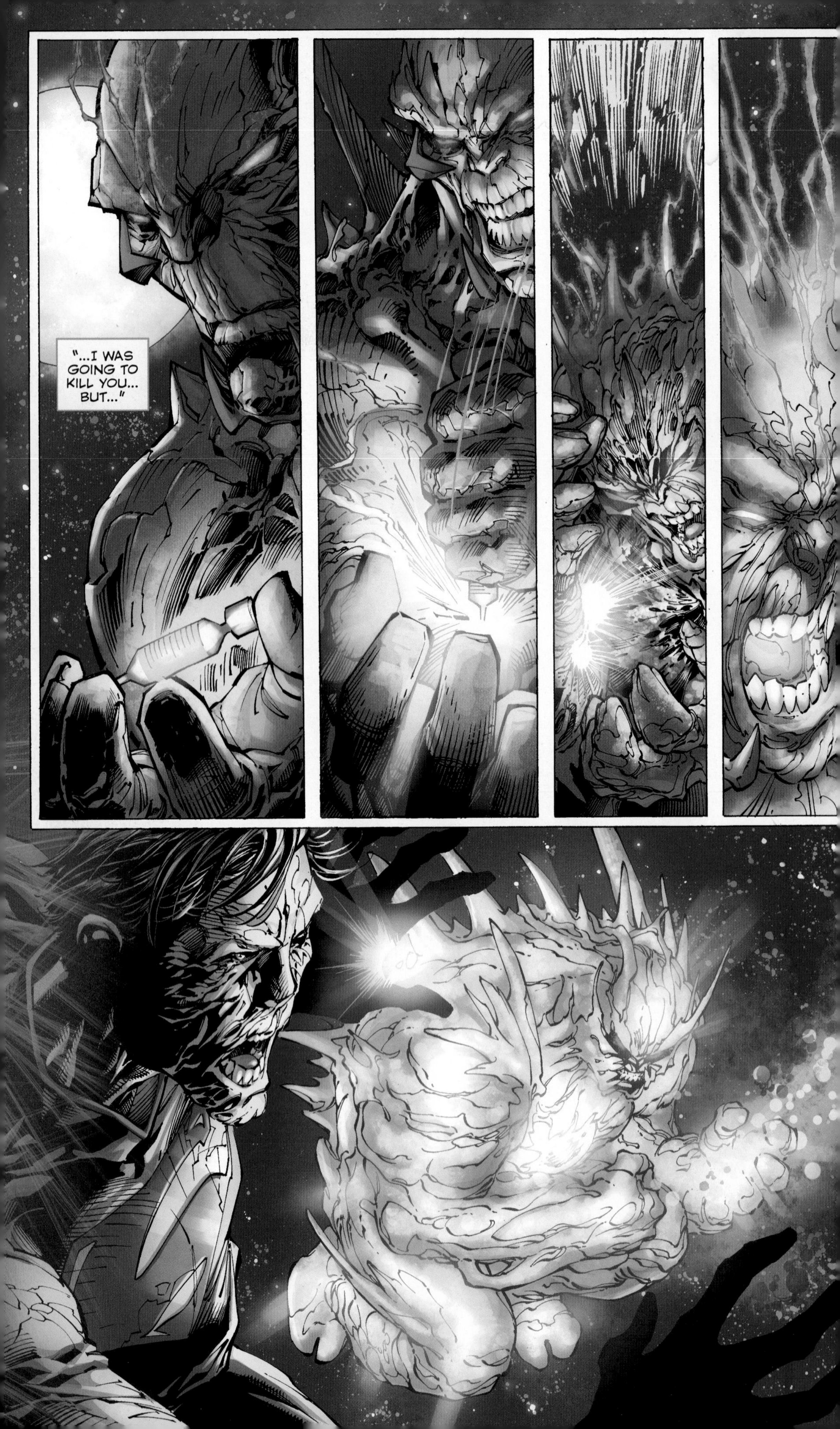
"...I WAS GOING TO KILL YOU... BUT..."

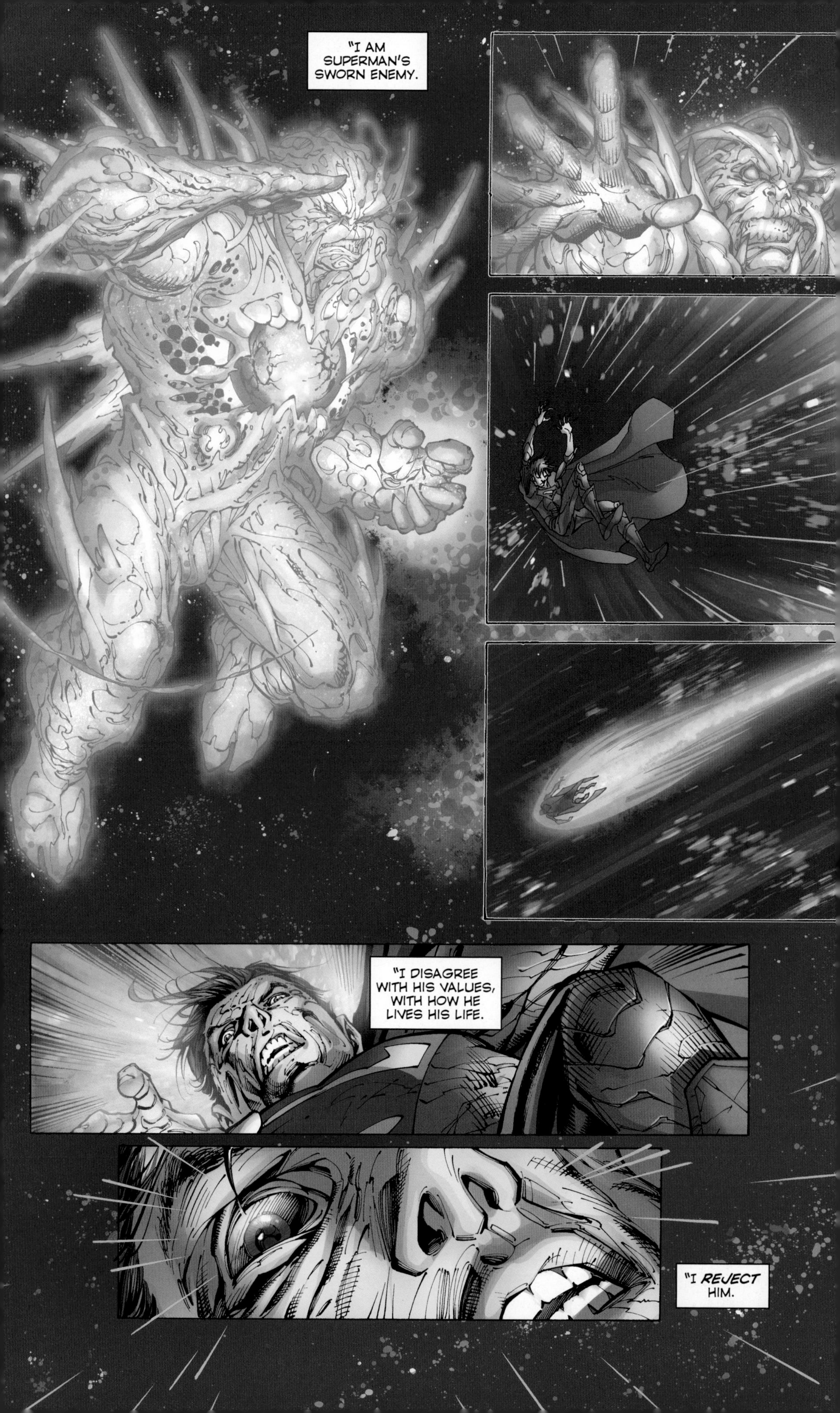
"I AM SUPERMAN'S SWORN ENEMY.
"I DISAGREE WITH HIS VALUES, WITH HOW HE LIVES HIS LIFE.
"I *REJECT* HIM.

"EVEN NOW, AT THE END, I AM GLAD HE'S GONE.

"BUT I'LL SAY THIS, BY WAY OF A GOODBYE.

"YEARS AGO, BACK WHEN THE WORLD WAS ON THE BRINK OF WAR, WE SENT A MESSAGE INTO SPACE.

"AN EQUATION THAT WAS MORE *EMOTIONAL* THAN MATHEMATICAL. AN EQUATION THAT ADDED U TO MORE THAN THE SUM C ITS PARTS--NONSENSICAL BUT *ASPIRATIONAL*.

"AN EQUATION THAT CALLED OUT, AND SAID 'HELP US BE BETTER.'

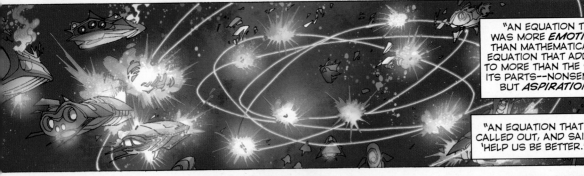

"WE SHOULD NEVER HAVE TURNED TO THE STARS FOR GUIDANCE. IF THERE IS AN ANSWER, IT'S HERE ON EARTH WITH *US*.

"FOR YEARS, I THOUGHT SUPERMAN WAS TRYING TO *BE* THE ANSWER TO THAT INFERNAL EQUATION. AND I *HATED* HIM FOR IT.

"BUT I SEE NOW WHAT HIS ACTIONS SAY--THERE *IS* NO ANSWER. FIGURE IT OUT FOR *YOURSELF* HOW TO BE BETTER, AS HE IS TRYING TO DO...

"AND PERHAPS, NOV AT THE END, I CAN ADMIT THAT IN BEIN THE *FARTHEST* THIN FROM AN ANSWER T THAT EQUATION...

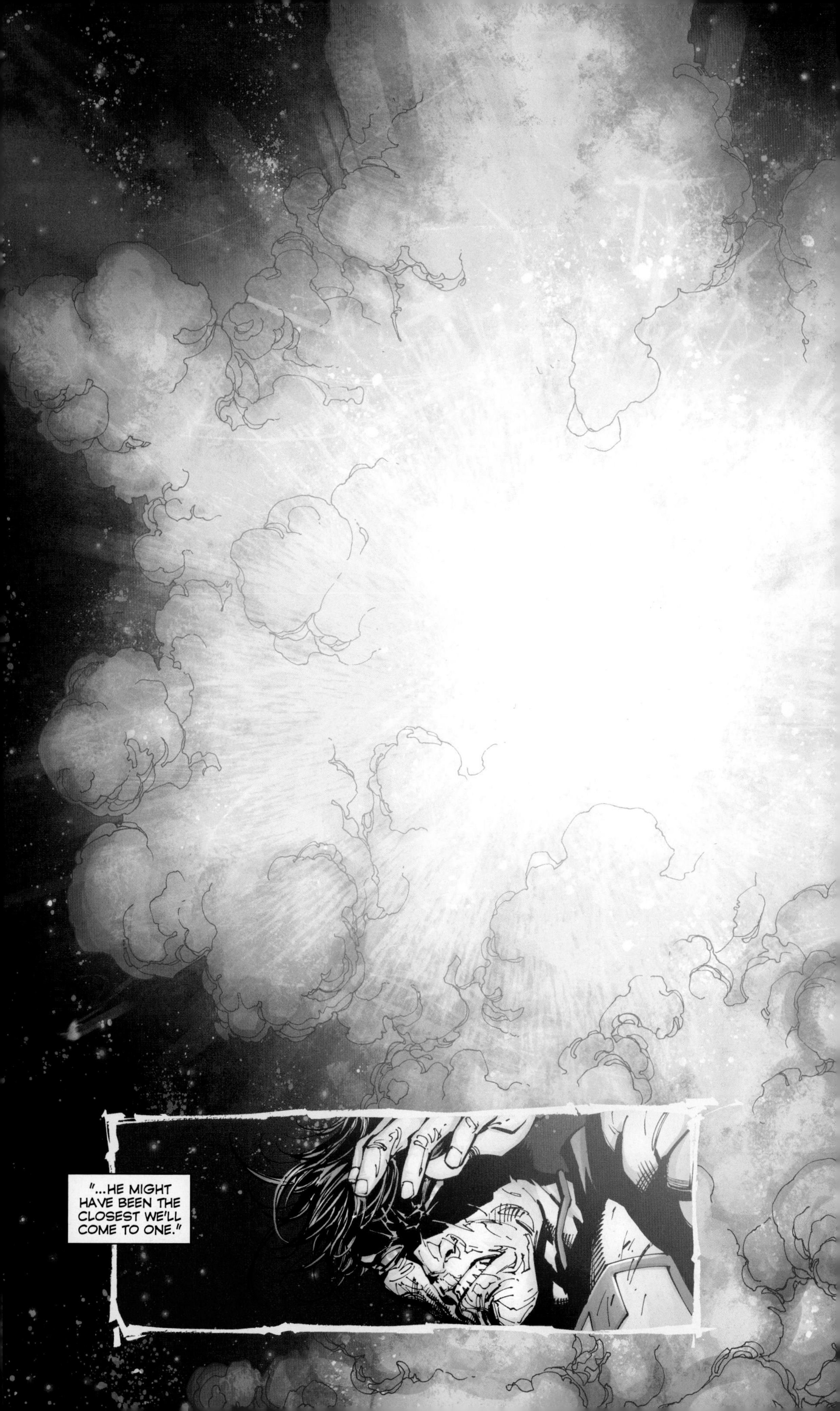
"...HE MIGHT HAVE BEEN THE CLOSEST WE'LL COME TO ONE."

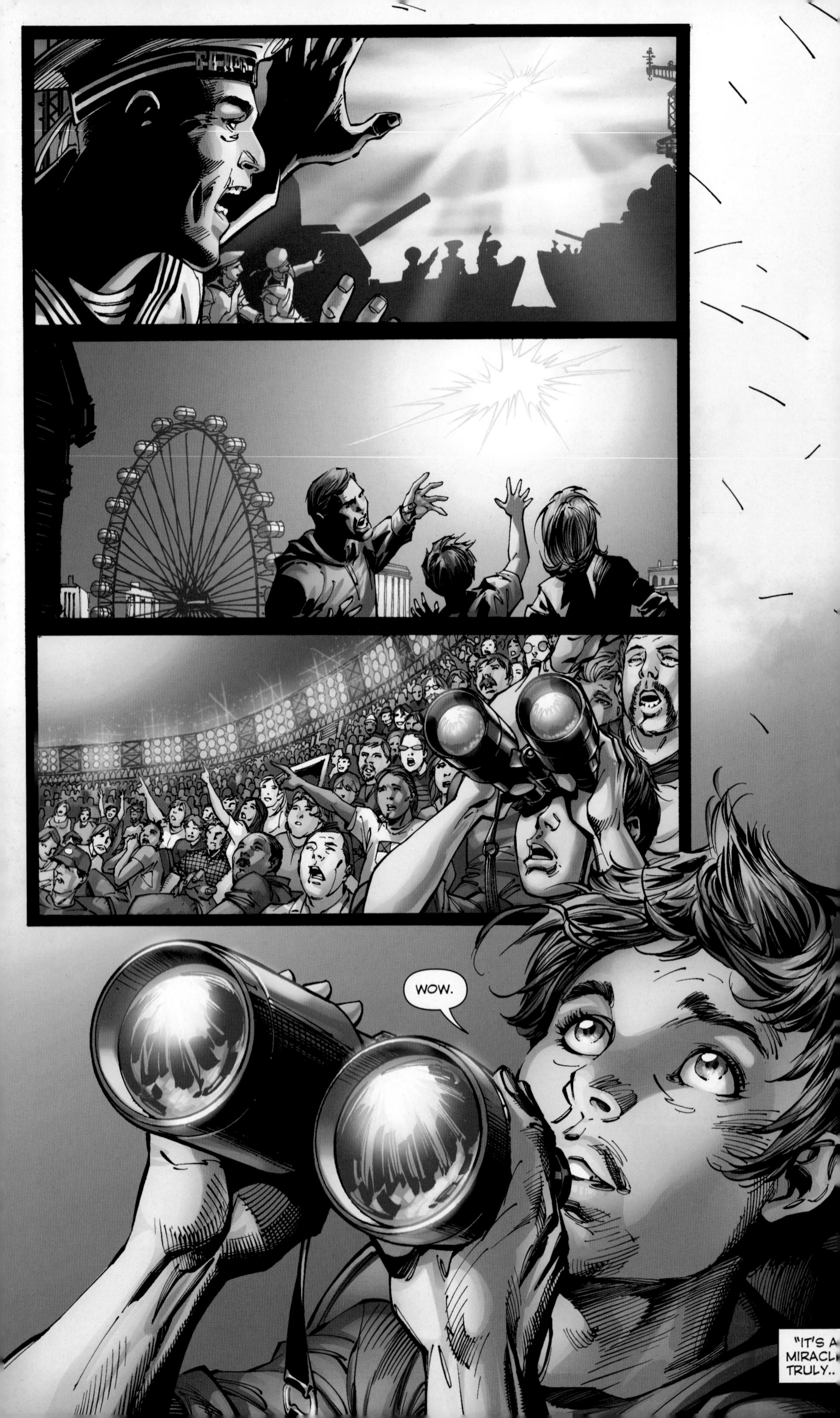
WOW.
"IT'S A
MIRACL
TRULY..

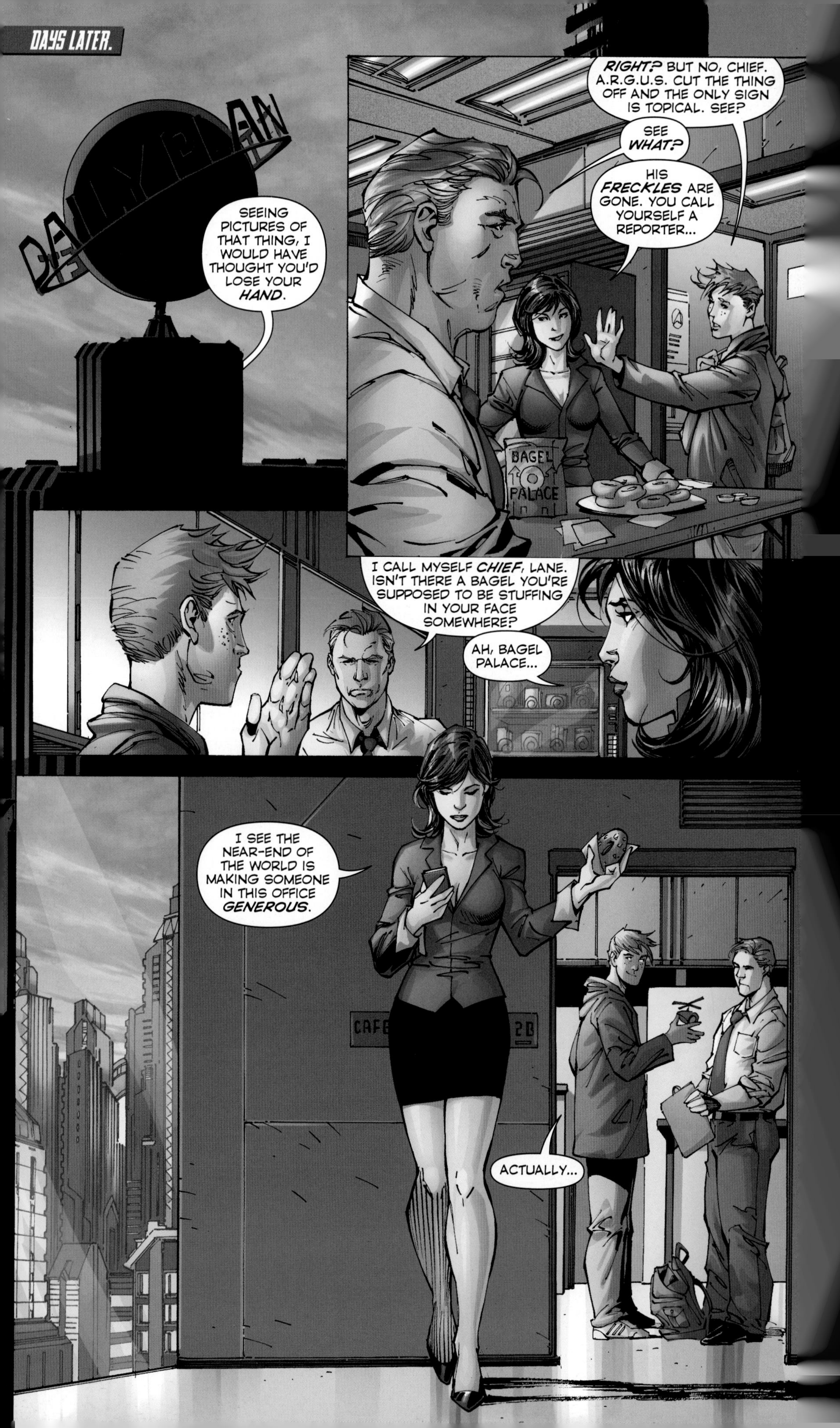
DAYS LATER.
DAILY PLANET
SEEING PICTURES OF THAT THING, I WOULD HAVE THOUGHT YOU'D LOSE YOUR HAND.
RIGHT? BUT NO, CHIEF. A.R.G.U.S. CUT THE THING OFF AND THE ONLY SIGN IS TOPICAL. SEE?
SEE WHAT?
HIS FRECKLES ARE GONE. YOU CALL YOURSELF A REPORTER...
BAGEL PALACE
I CALL MYSELF CHIEF, LANE. ISN'T THERE A BAGEL YOU'RE SUPPOSED TO BE STUFFING IN YOUR FACE SOMEWHERE?
AH, BAGEL PALACE...
I SEE THE NEAR-END OF THE WORLD IS MAKING SOMEONE IN THIS OFFICE GENEROUS.
ACTUALLY...

"...NOT SOMEONE IN THE *OFFICE*, EXACTLY."

RING

SMALLVILLE

I'LL PUT SOMETHING UP SOON. I'M ALMOST DONE WITH A HUMAN-INTEREST THING, "SURVIVORS OF FLIGHT 493"--

GREAT, GREAT. AFTER ALL, I ALREADY COVERED "ALIEN ARMADA DESTROYED, SUPERMAN RECAPTURES LUTHOR."

BUT SURE, GO WITH THAT.

YOU HAV 'TIL I FINISH MASSIVE, MU BAGEL TO *SOMETH* UP.

IT'S *CORN*, ACTUALLY. I'M EATI TO *SPITE* YOU FOR HAVING ANYTHING

BUT...IT FELT GOOD TO BE THERE, YES. I GUESS I'LL PLAY IT BY *EAR*.

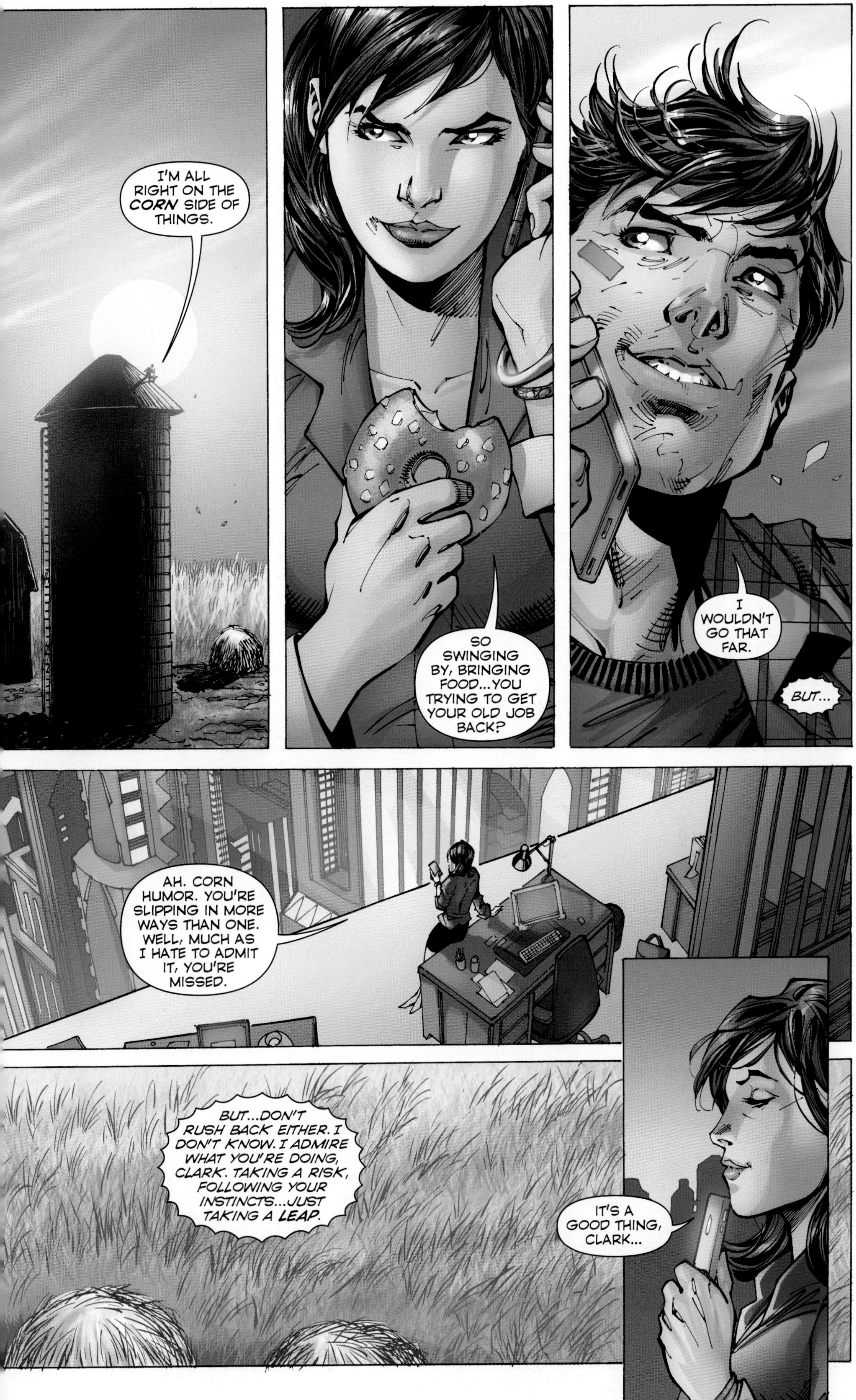
I'M ALL RIGHT ON THE CORN SIDE OF THINGS.
SO SWINGING BY, BRINGING FOOD...YOU TRYING TO GET YOUR OLD JOB BACK?
I WOULDN'T GO THAT FAR.
BUT...
AH. CORN HUMOR. YOU'RE SLIPPING IN MORE WAYS THAN ONE. WELL, MUCH AS I HATE TO ADMIT IT, YOU'RE MISSED.
BUT...DON'T RUSH BACK EITHER. I DON'T KNOW. I ADMIRE WHAT YOU'RE DOING, CLARK. TAKING A RISK, FOLLOWING YOUR INSTINCTS...JUST TAKING A LEAP.
IT'S A GOOD THING, CLARK...

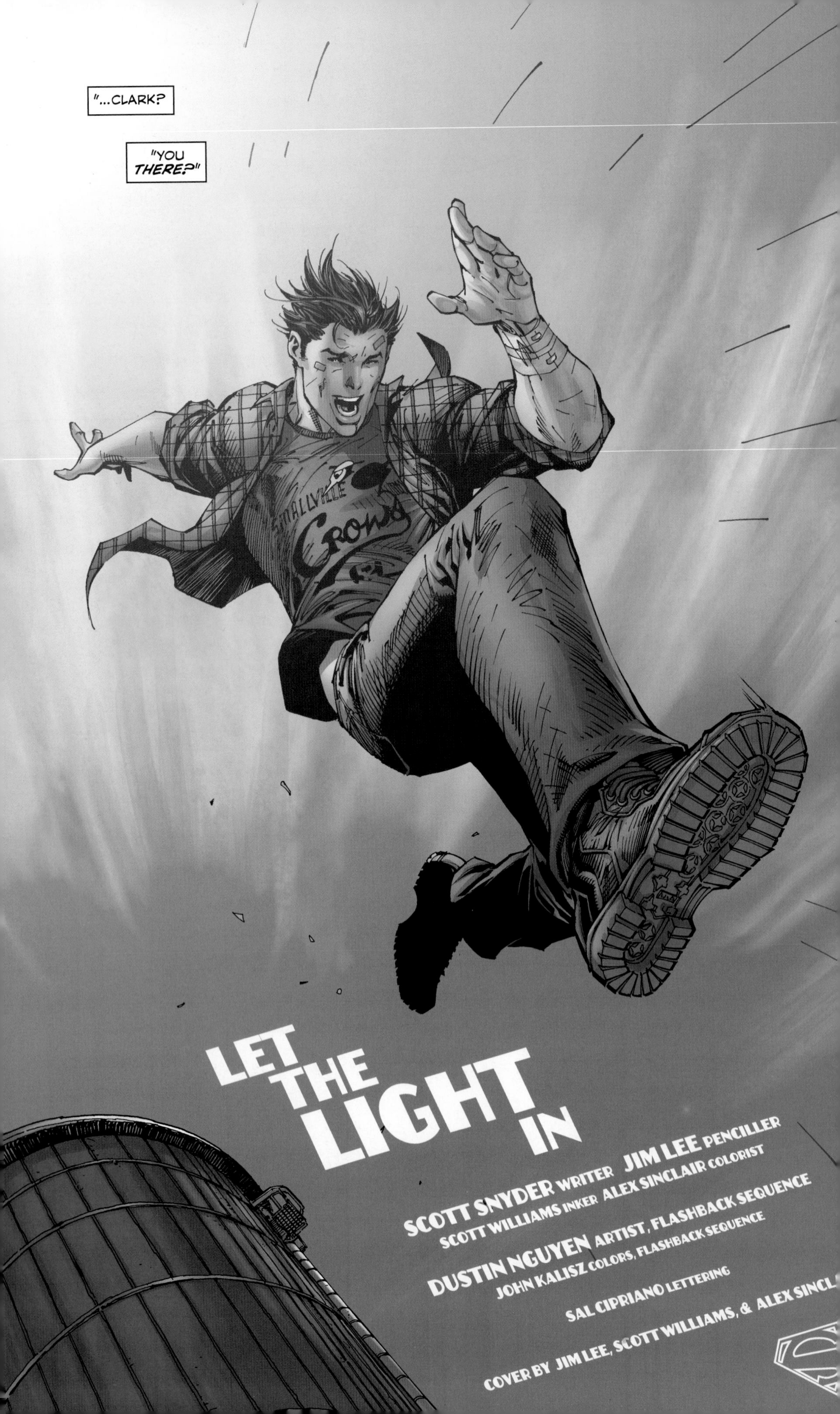
"...CLARK?
"YOU THERE?"
LET THE LIGHT IN
SCOTT SNYDER WRITER JIM LEE PENCILLER
SCOTT WILLIAMS INKER ALEX SINCLAIR COLORIST
DUSTIN NGUYEN ARTIST, FLASHBACK SEQUENCE
JOHN KALISZ COLORS, FLASHBACK SEQUENCE
SAL CIPRIANO LETTERING
COVER BY JIM LEE, SCOTT WILLIAMS, & ALEX SINCL

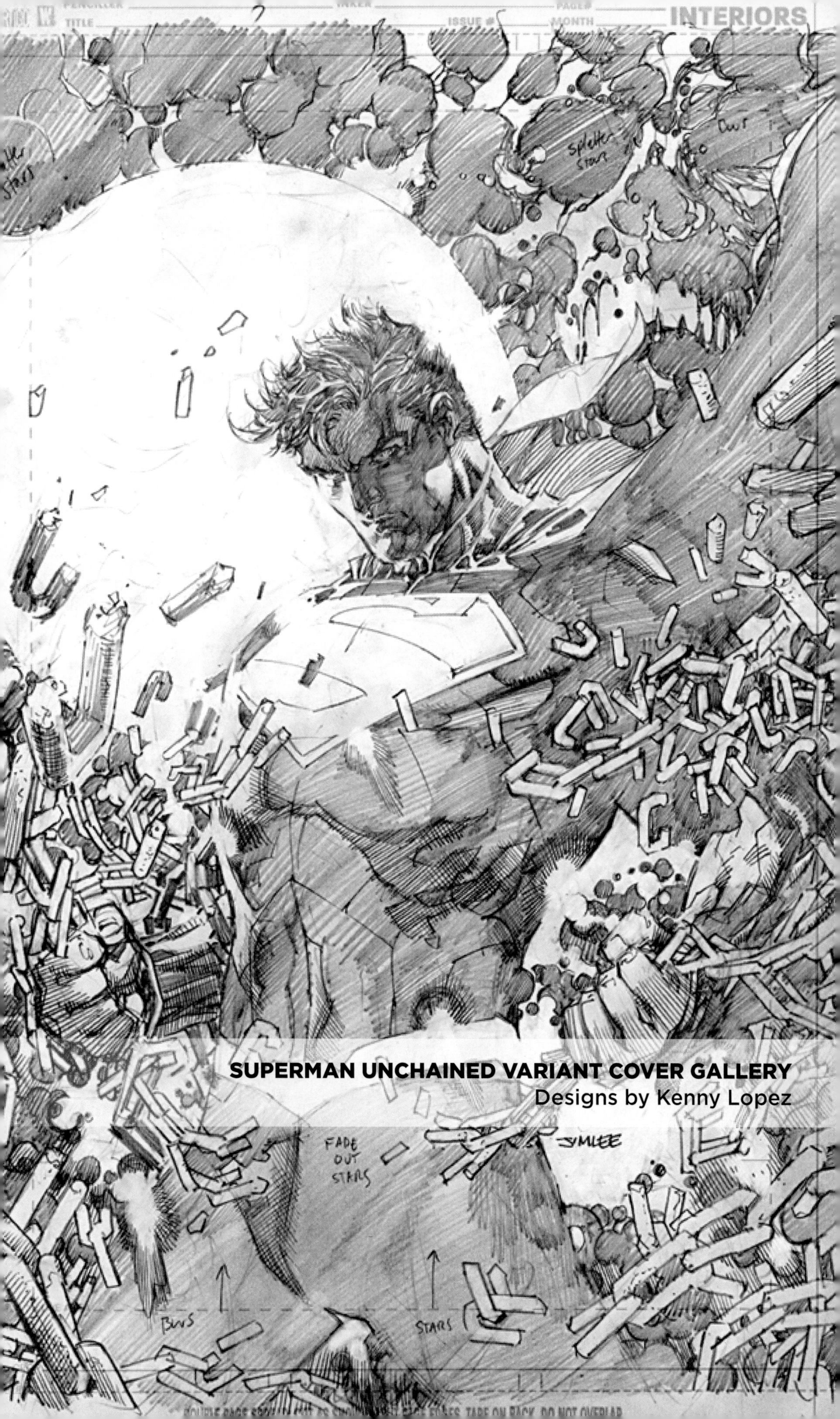
INTERIORS
Splatter Stars
FADE OUT STARS
JIMLEE
STARS

SUPERMAN UNCHAINED VARIANT COVER GALLERY

Designs by Kenny Lopez

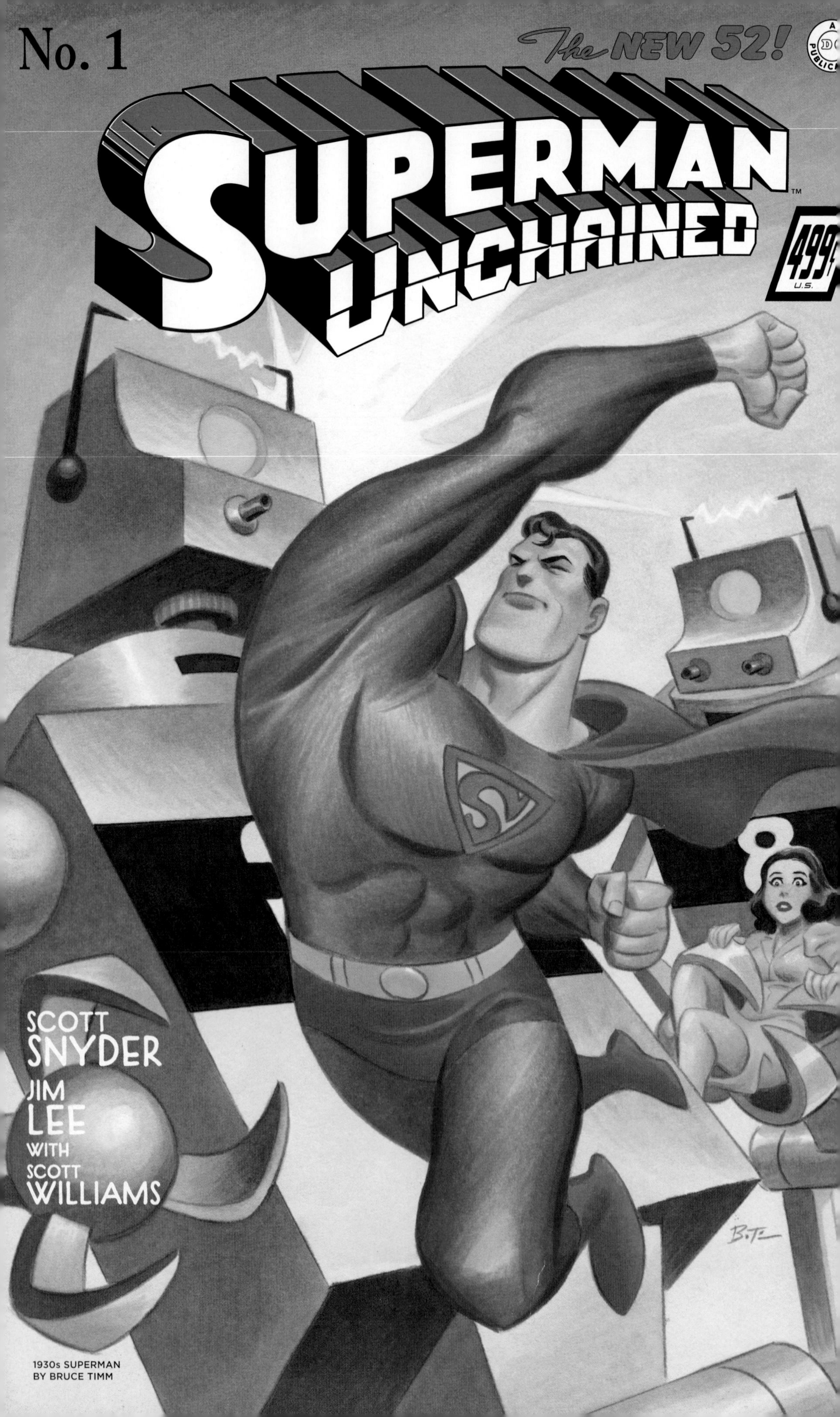
No. 1
The NEW 52!
SUPERMAN
UNCHAINED
SCOTT SNYDER
JIM LEE
WITH
SCOTT WILLIAMS
1930s SUPERMAN BY BRUCE TIMM

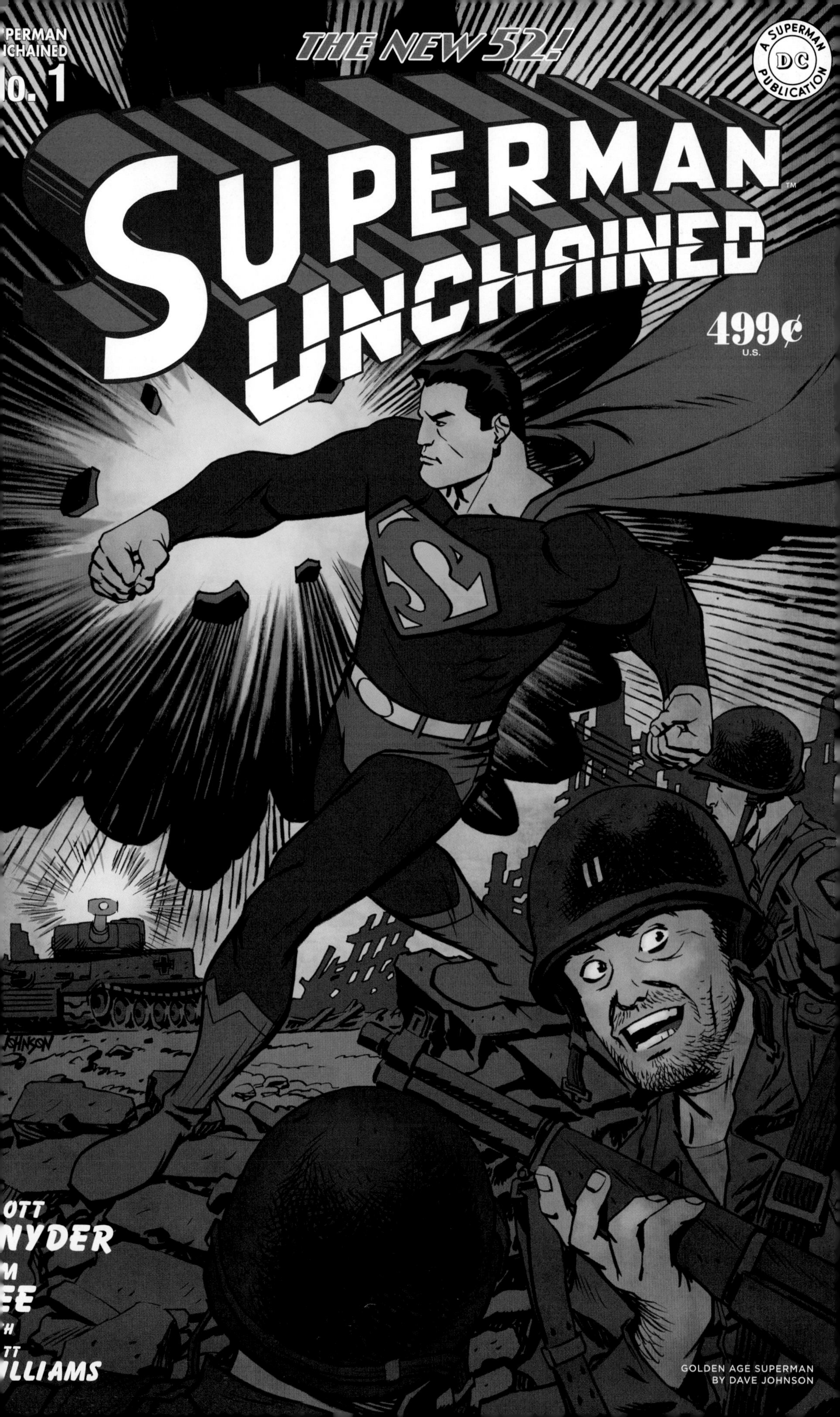

PERMAN
CHAINED
o. 1
THE NEW 52!
A SUPERMAN DC PUBLICATION
SUPERMAN
UNCHAINED
499¢
U.S.
JOHNSON
OTT
NYDER
EE
TT
LLIAMS
GOLDEN AGE SUPERMAN
BY DAVE JOHNSON

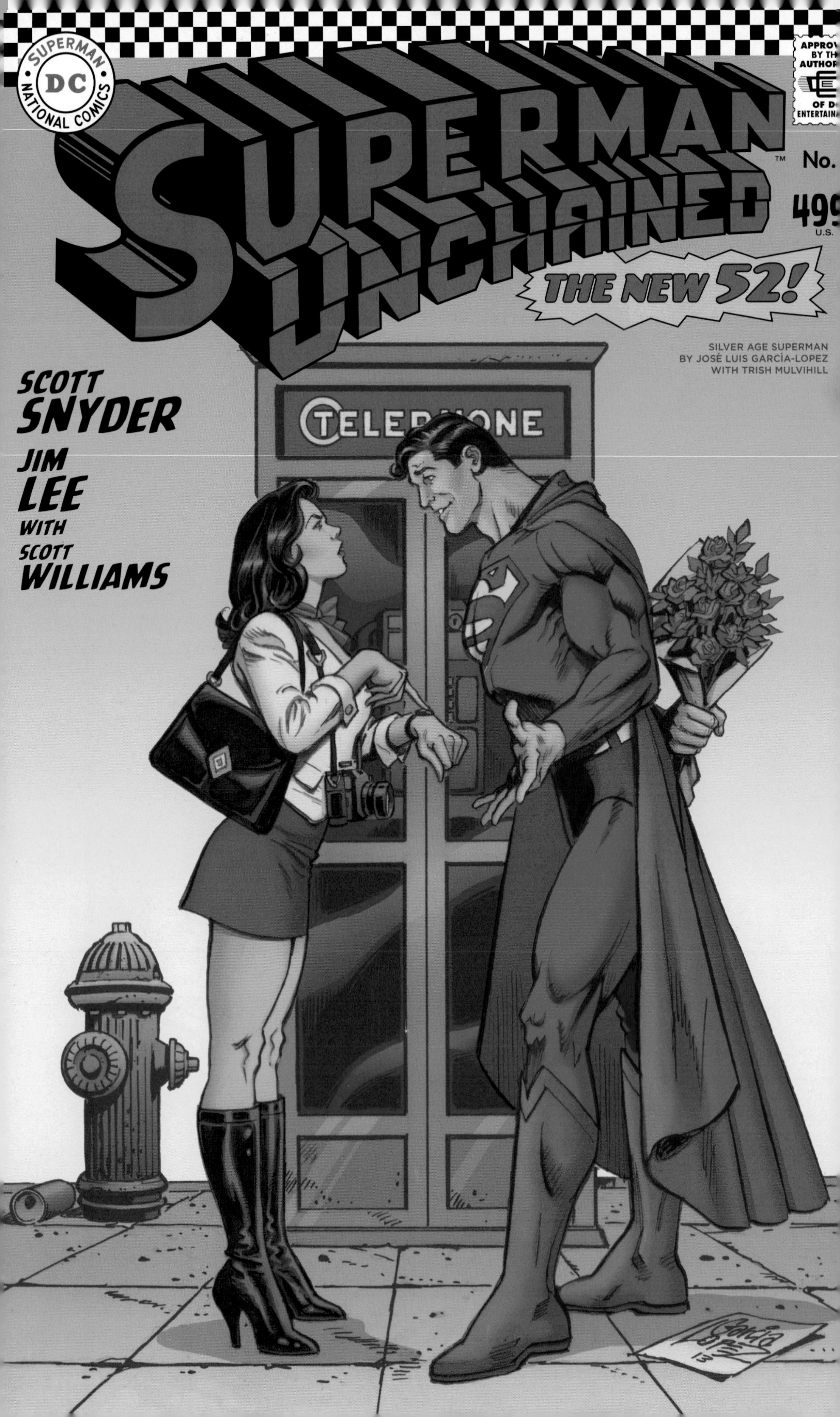

SUPERMAN
DC
NATIONAL COMICS
SUPERMAN UNCHAINED
No.
U.S.
THE NEW 52!
SILVER AGE SUPERMAN
BY JOSÉ LUIS GARCÍA-LOPEZ
WITH TRISH MULVIHILL
SCOTT SNYDER
JIM LEE
WITH
SCOTT WILLIAMS
TELEPHONE

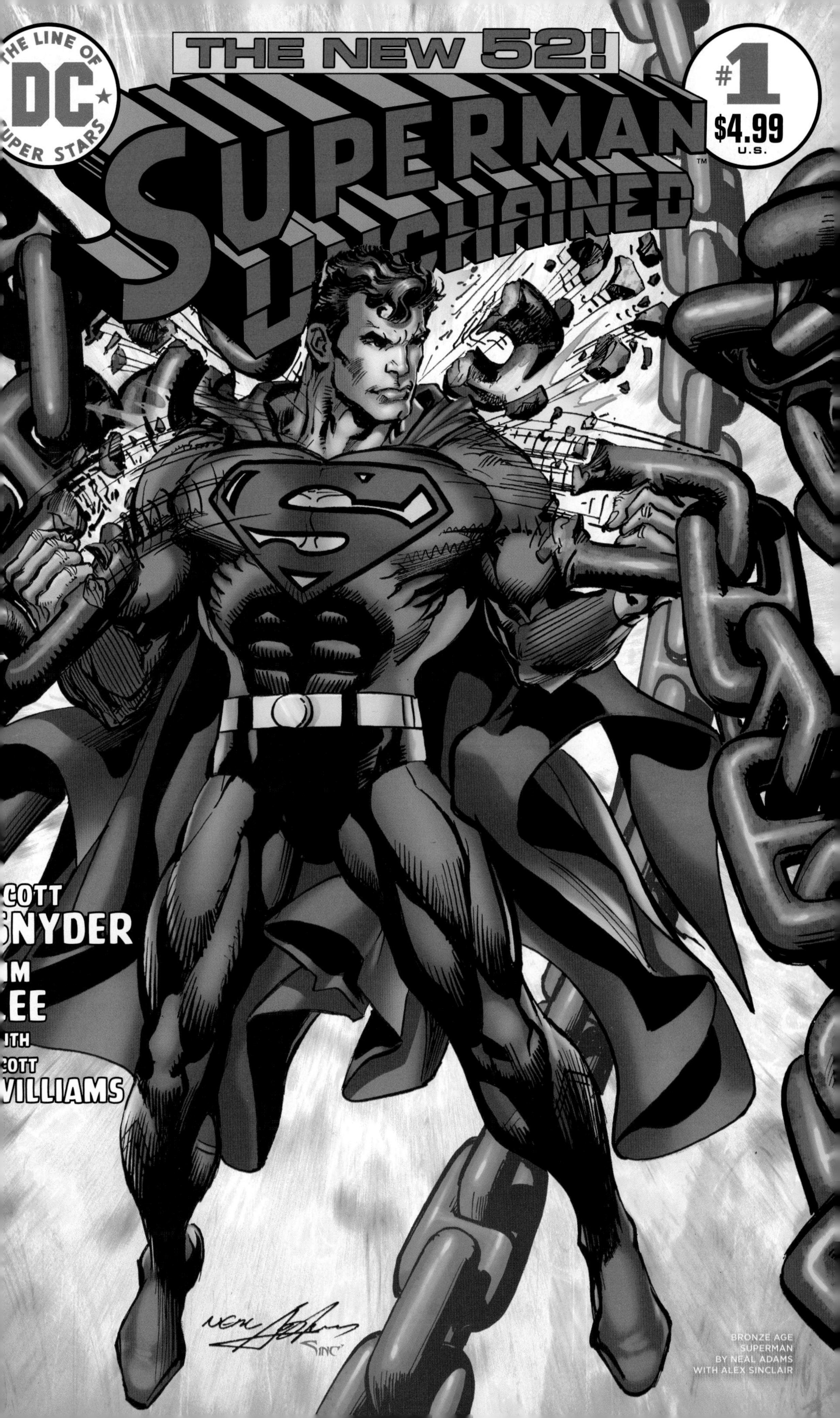
THE LINE OF DC SUPER STARS
THE NEW 52!
#1
$4.99
U.S.
SUPERMAN
UNCHAINED
COTT
SNYDER
M
EE
ITH
COTT
WILLIAMS
BRONZE AGE
SUPERMAN
BY NEAL ADAMS
WITH ALEX SINCLAIR

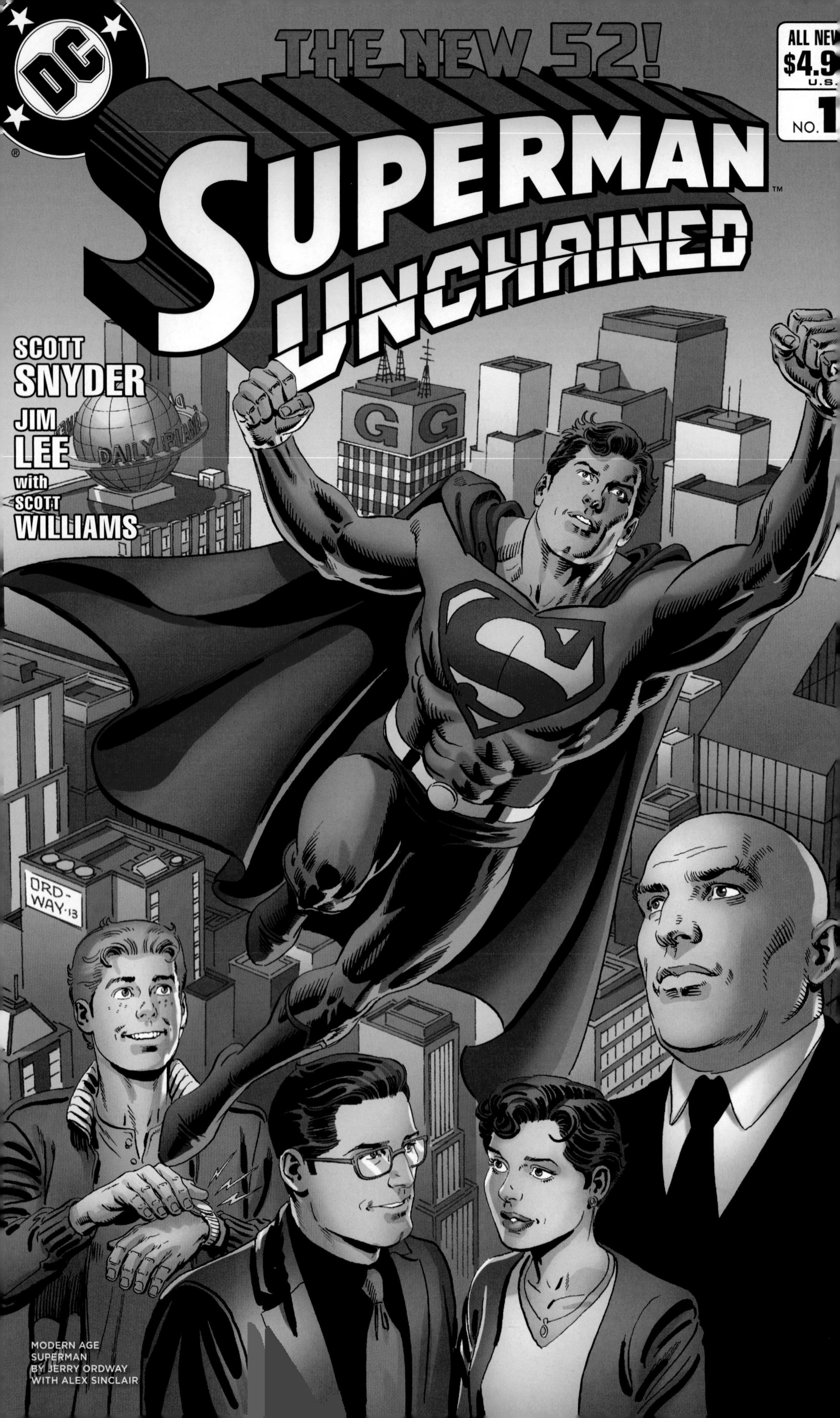
DC
THE NEW 52!
ALL NEW
$4.9
U.S.
NO. 1
SUPERMAN
UNCHAINED
SCOTT SNYDER
JIM LEE
with SCOTT WILLIAMS
DAILY PLANET
ORD-WAY ·13
MODERN AGE
SUPERMAN
BY JERRY ORDWAY
WITH ALEX SINCLAIR

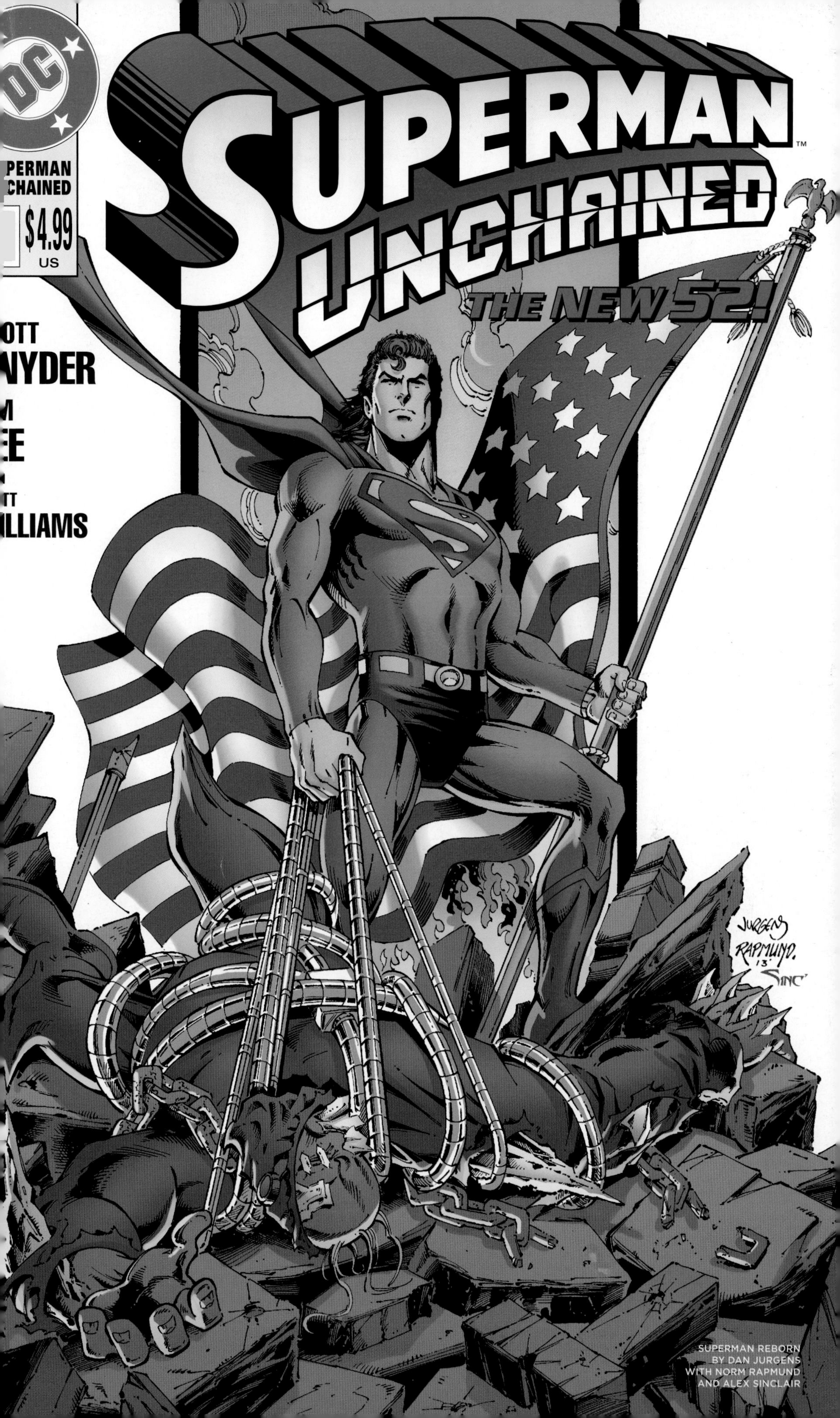

SUPERMAN UNCHAINED
THE NEW 52!
PERMAN
CHAINED
$4.99
US
OTT
NYDER
M
E
TT
LLIAMS
JURGENS
RAPMUND
'13
SINC
SUPERMAN REBORN
BY DAN JURGENS
WITH NORM RAPMUND
AND ALEX SINCLAIR

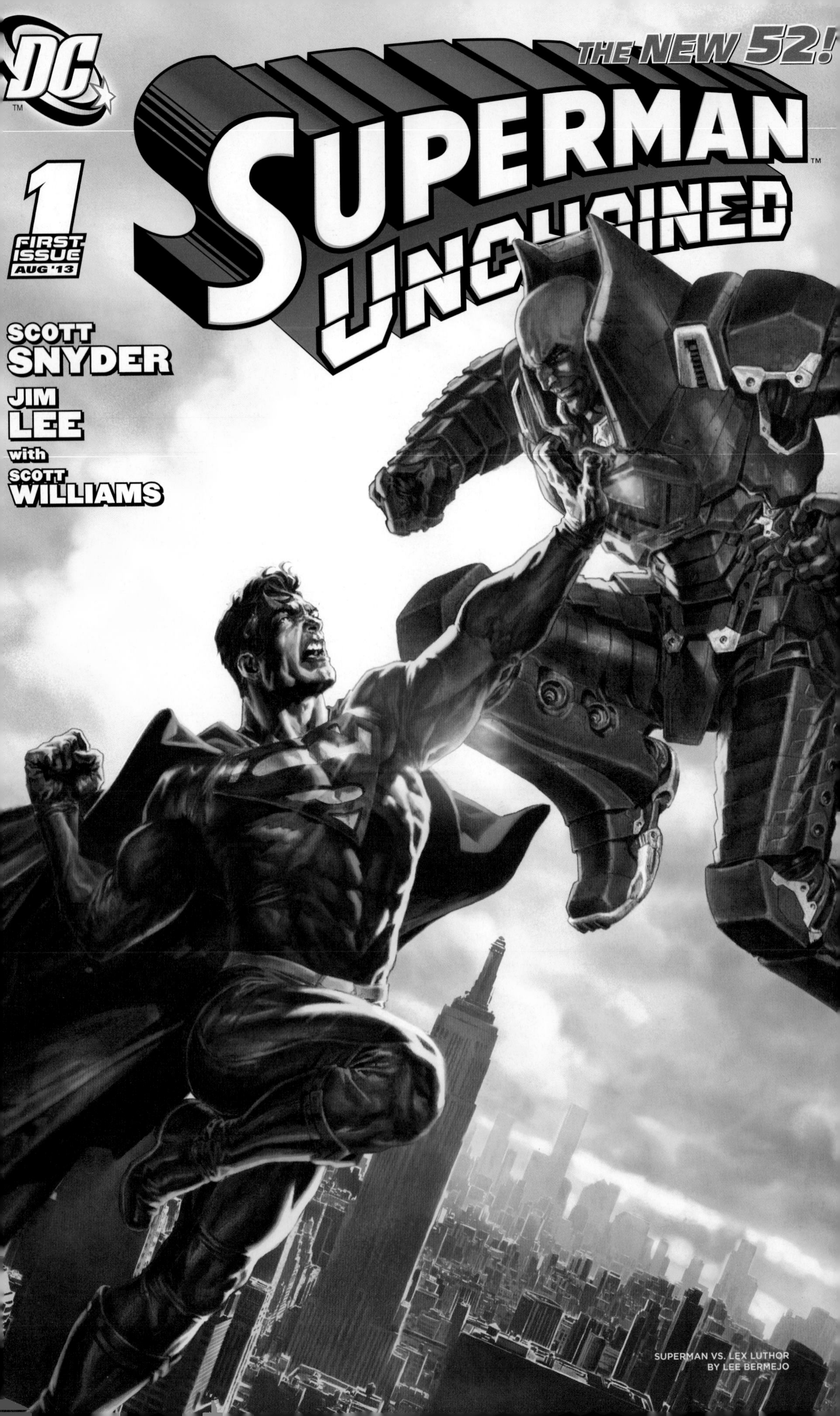

DC
THE NEW 52!
SUPERMAN
UNCHAINED
1
FIRST ISSUE
AUG '13
SCOTT SNYDER
JIM LEE
with
SCOTT WILLIAMS

SUPERMAN VS. LEX LUTHOR
BY LEE BERMEJO

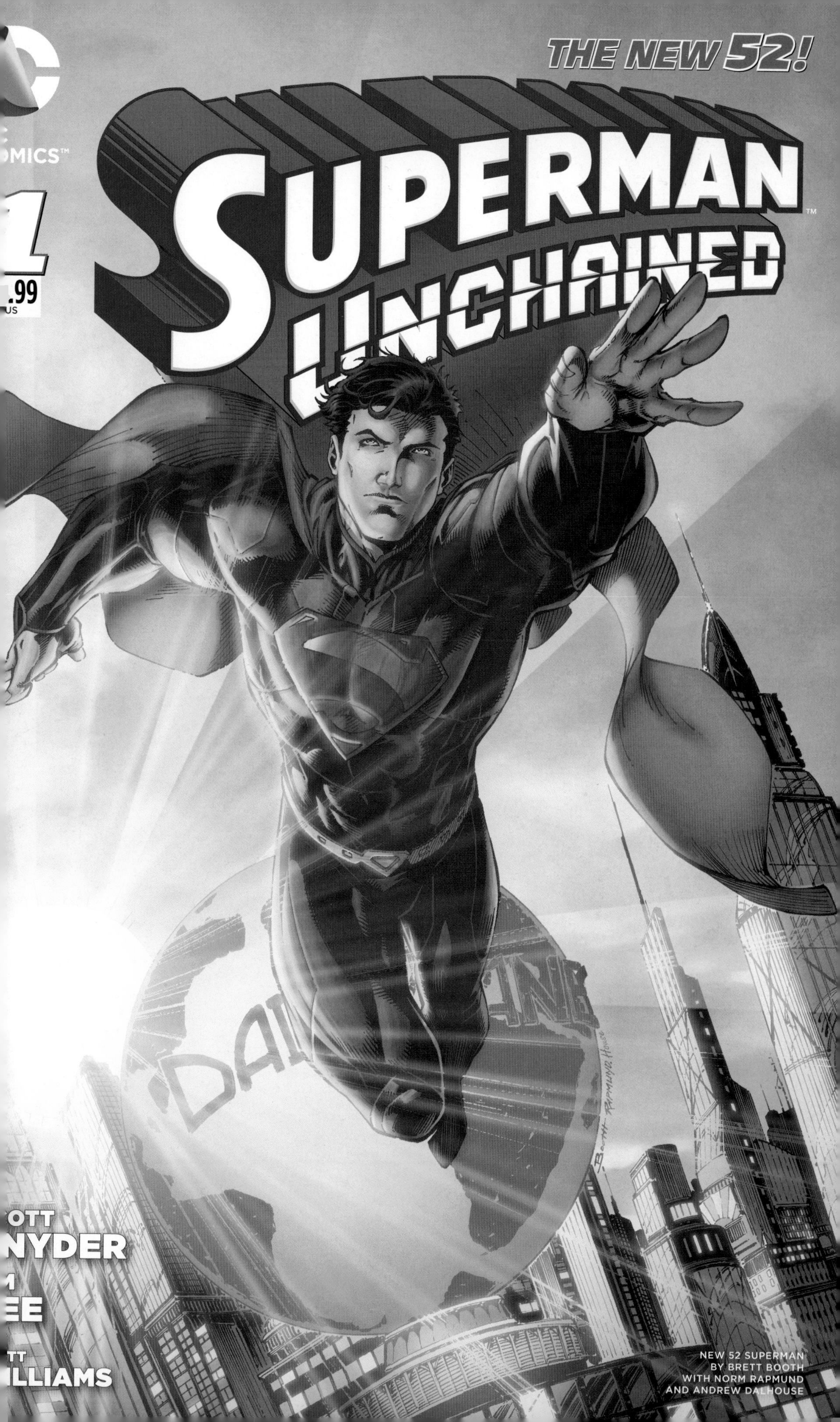
THE NEW 52!
SUPERMAN
UNCHAINED
1
.99
US
OMICS
OTT
NYDER
EE
TT
LLIAMS
NEW 52 SUPERMAN
BY BRETT BOOTH
WITH NORM RAPMUND
AND ANDREW DALHOUSE

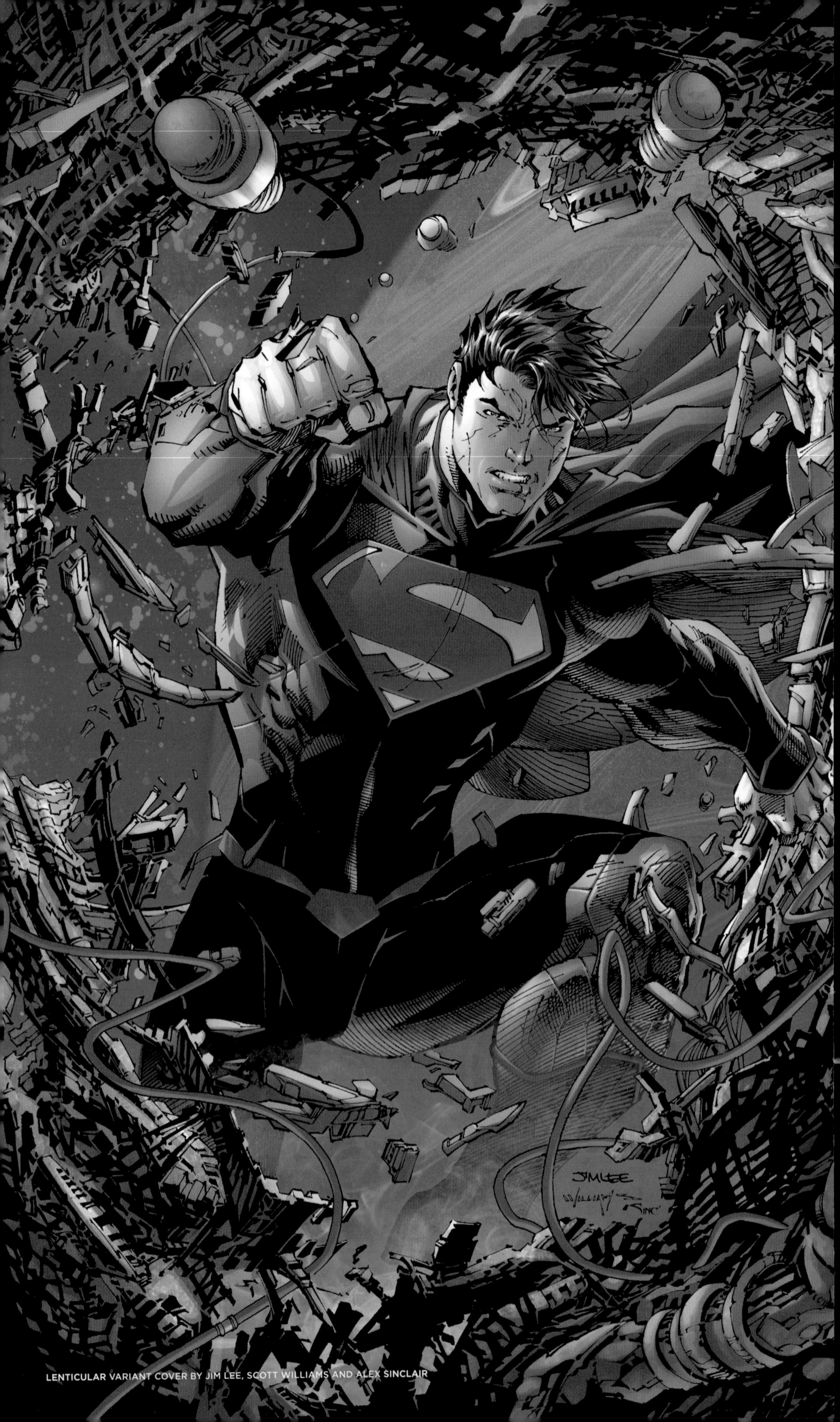

LENTICULAR VARIANT COVER BY JIM LEE, SCOTT WILLIAMS AND ALEX SINCLAIR

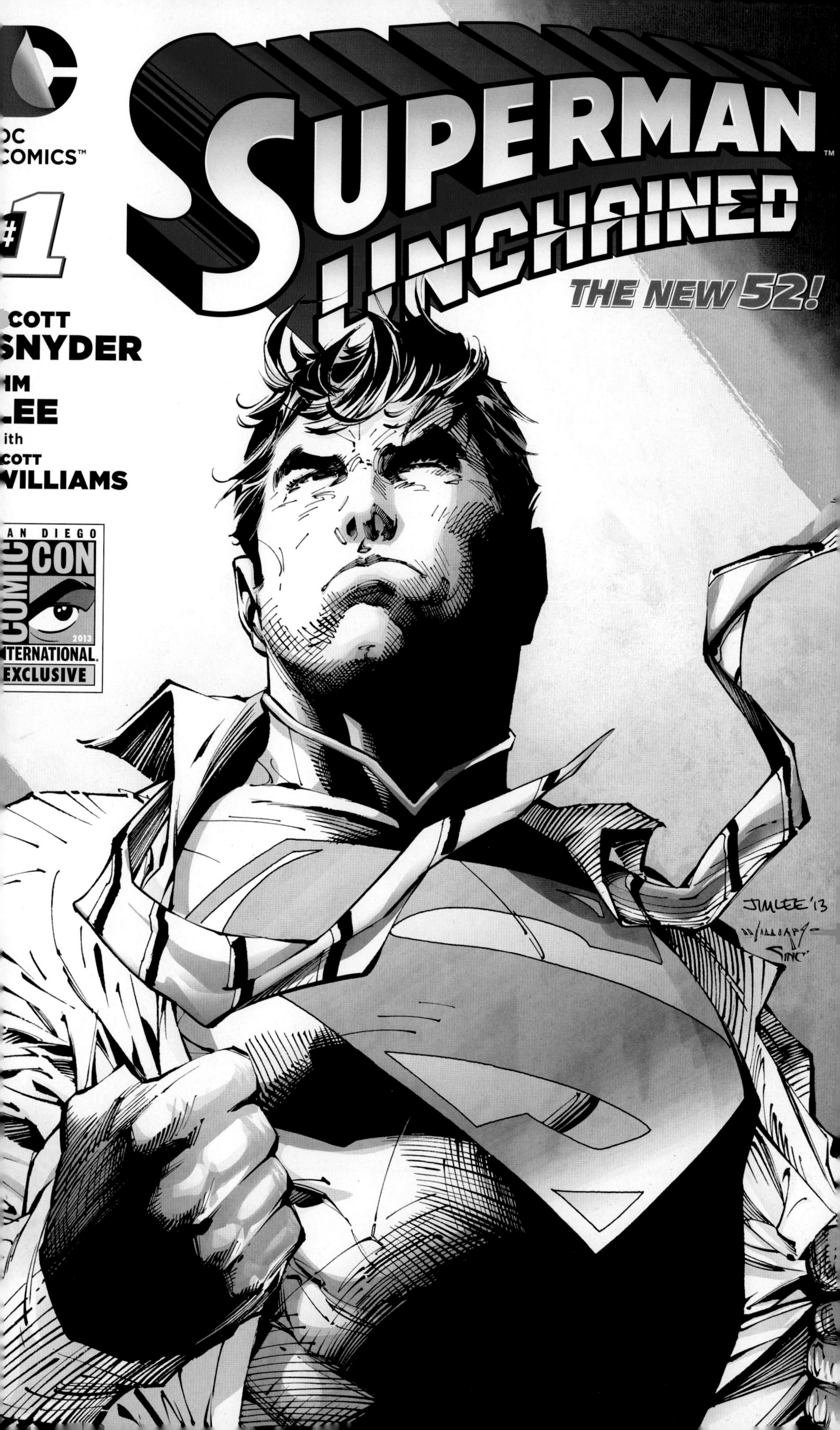

COMICS™
SUPERMAN™
UNCHAINED
THE NEW 52!
#1
COTT
SNYDER
IM
LEE
ith
COTT
WILLIAMS
AN DIEGO
COMIC CON
2013
NTERNATIONAL
EXCLUSIVE
JIMLEE '13

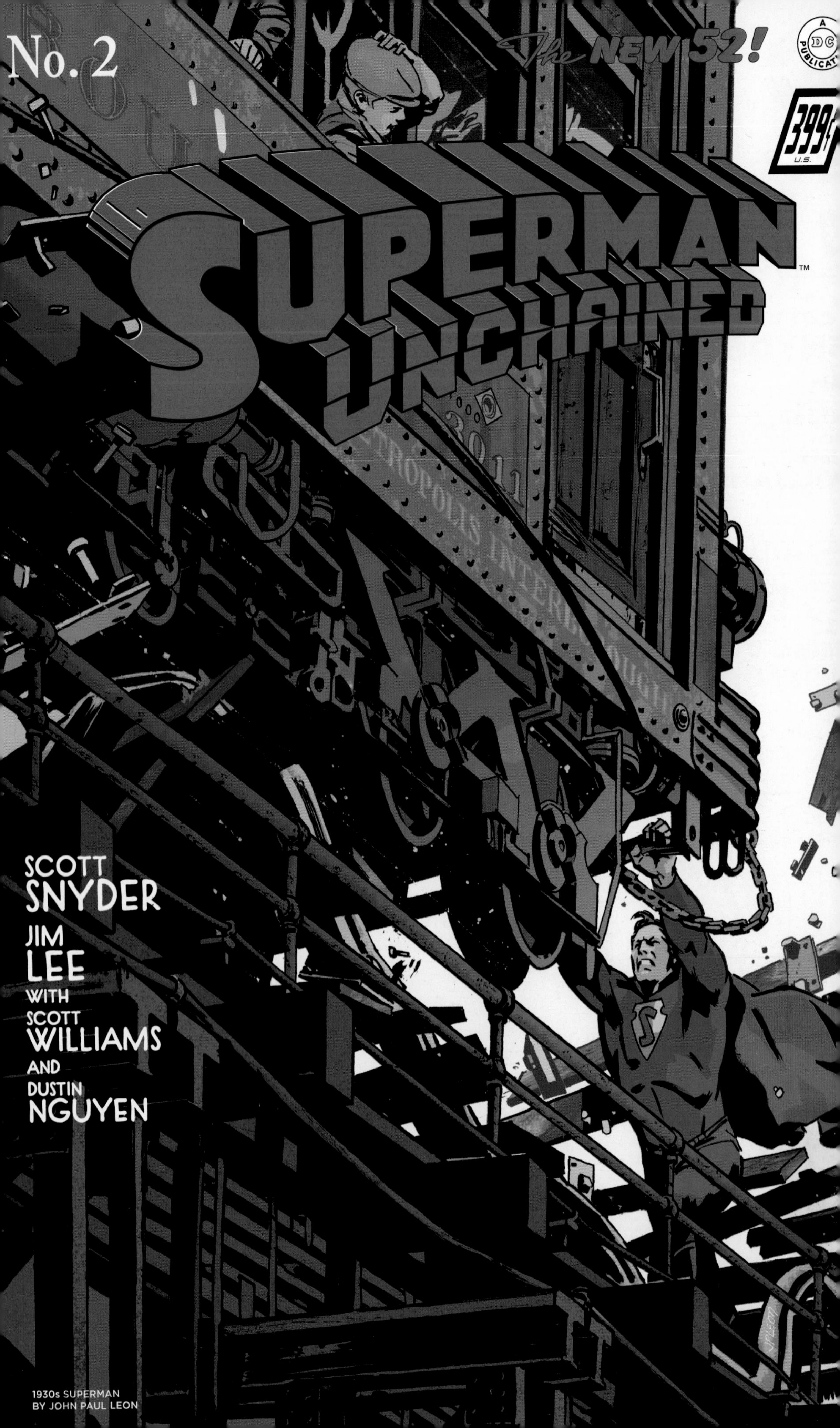
No. 2
The NEW 52!
A DC PUBLICATION
399¢ U.S.
SUPERMAN UNCHAINED™
SCOTT SNYDER
JIM LEE
WITH
SCOTT WILLIAMS
AND
DUSTIN NGUYEN

1930s SUPERMAN
BY JOHN PAUL LEON

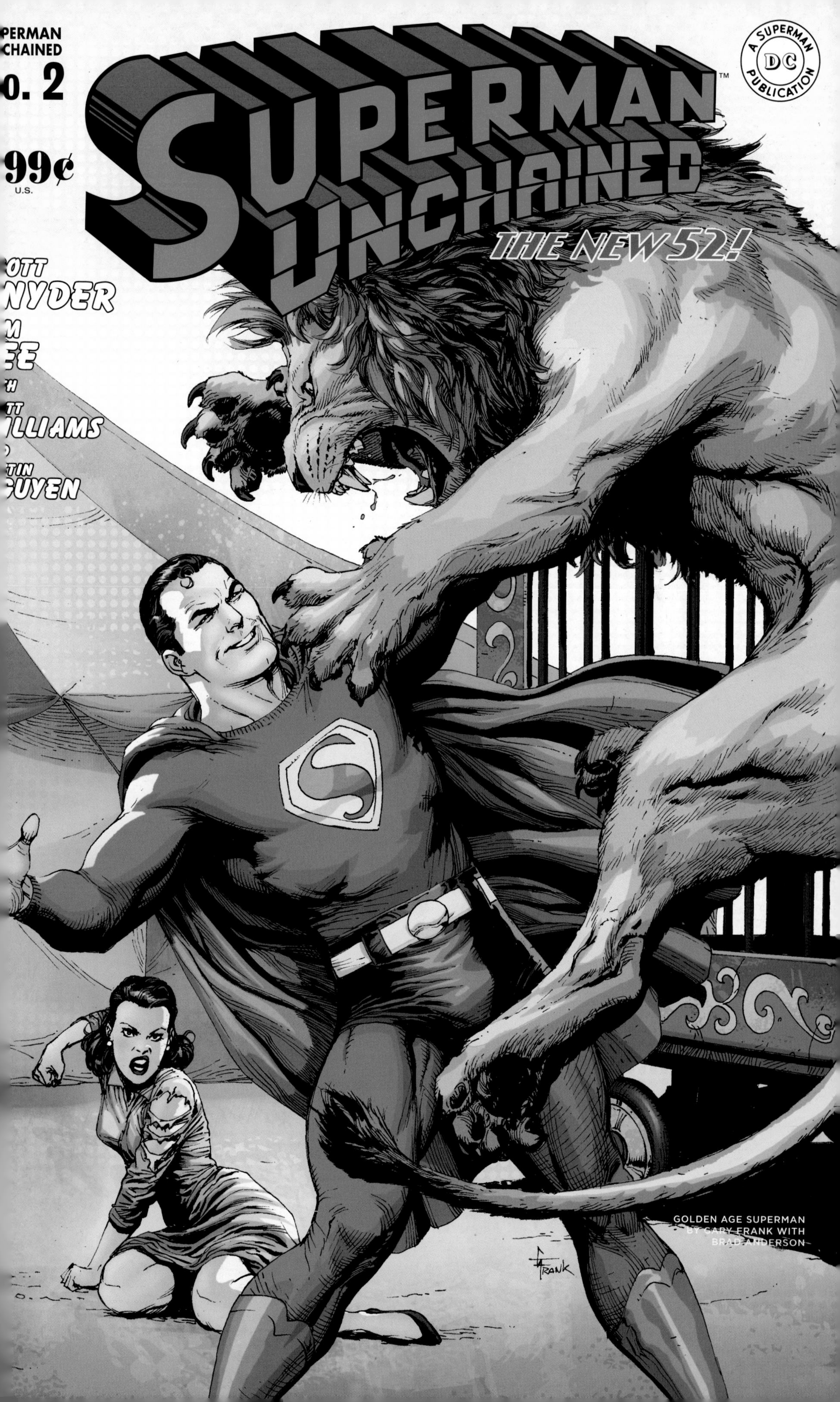
PERMAN
CHAINED
o. 2
99¢
U.S.
SUPERMAN
UNCHAINED
THE NEW 52!
A SUPERMAN DC PUBLICATION
OTT
NYDER
EE
LLIAMS
GUYEN
GOLDEN AGE SUPERMAN
BY GARY FRANK WITH
BRAD ANDERSON
FRANK

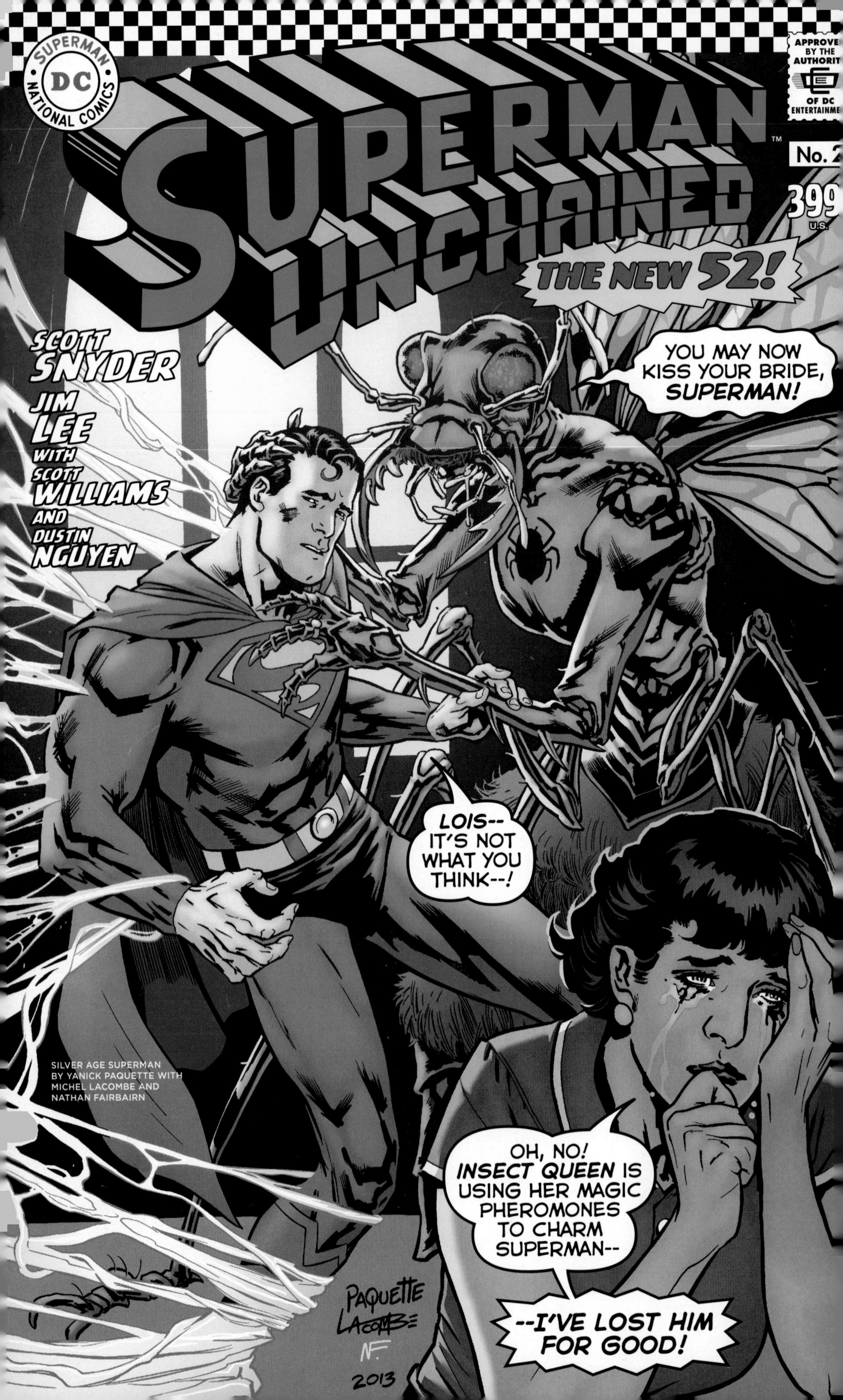

SUPERMAN DC NATIONAL COMICS
APPROVED BY THE AUTHORITY OF DC ENTERTAINMENT
SUPERMAN UNCHAINED
No. 2
399 U.S.
THE NEW 52!
SCOTT SNYDER
JIM LEE
WITH
SCOTT WILLIAMS
AND
DUSTIN NGUYEN
YOU MAY NOW KISS YOUR BRIDE, SUPERMAN!
LOIS-- IT'S NOT WHAT YOU THINK--!
SILVER AGE SUPERMAN BY YANICK PAQUETTE WITH MICHEL LACOMBE AND NATHAN FAIRBAIRN
OH, NO! INSECT QUEEN IS USING HER MAGIC PHEROMONES TO CHARM SUPERMAN--
--I'VE LOST HIM FOR GOOD!
PAQUETTE LACOMBE NF. 2013

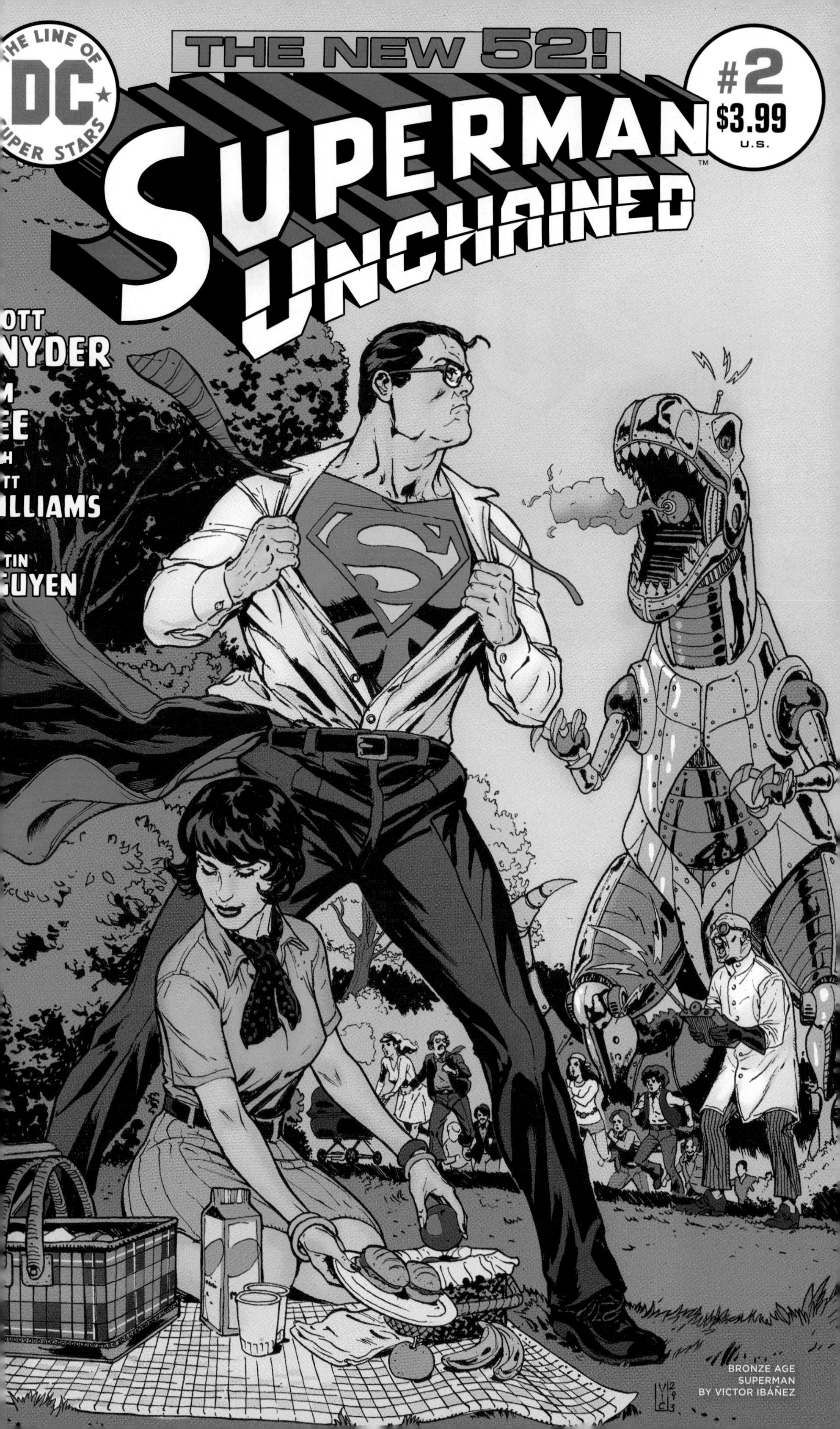
THE LINE OF DC SUPER STARS
THE NEW 52!
#2
$3.99
U.S.
SUPERMAN
UNCHAINED
OTT
NYDER
M
EE
H
TT
LLIAMS
TIN
GUYEN
BRONZE AGE
SUPERMAN
BY VICTOR IBÁÑEZ

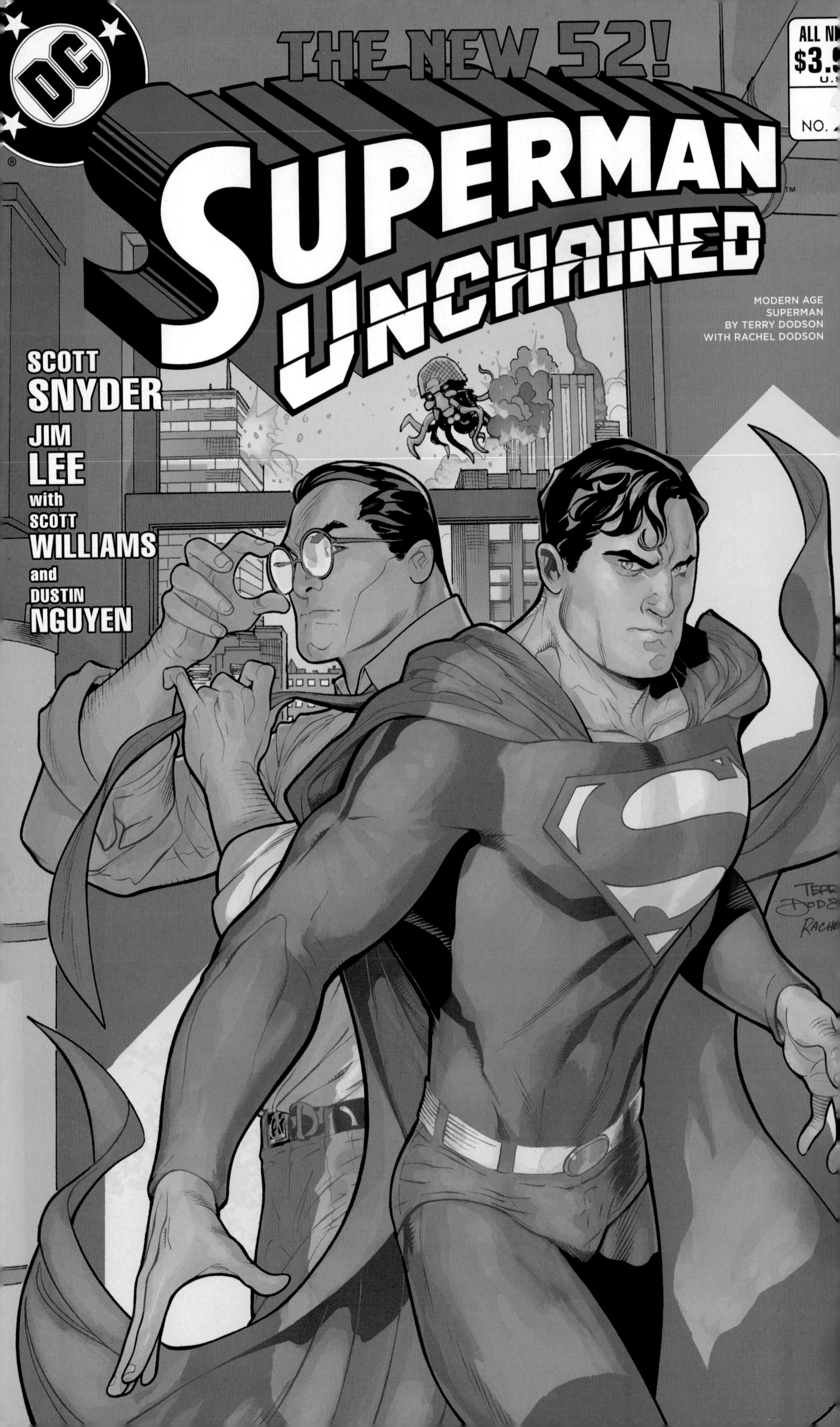
THE NEW 52!
ALL N
$3.9
NO.
SUPERMAN
UNCHAINED
MODERN AGE
SUPERMAN
BY TERRY DODSON
WITH RACHEL DODSON
SCOTT
SNYDER
JIM
LEE
with
SCOTT
WILLIAMS
and
DUSTIN
NGUYEN

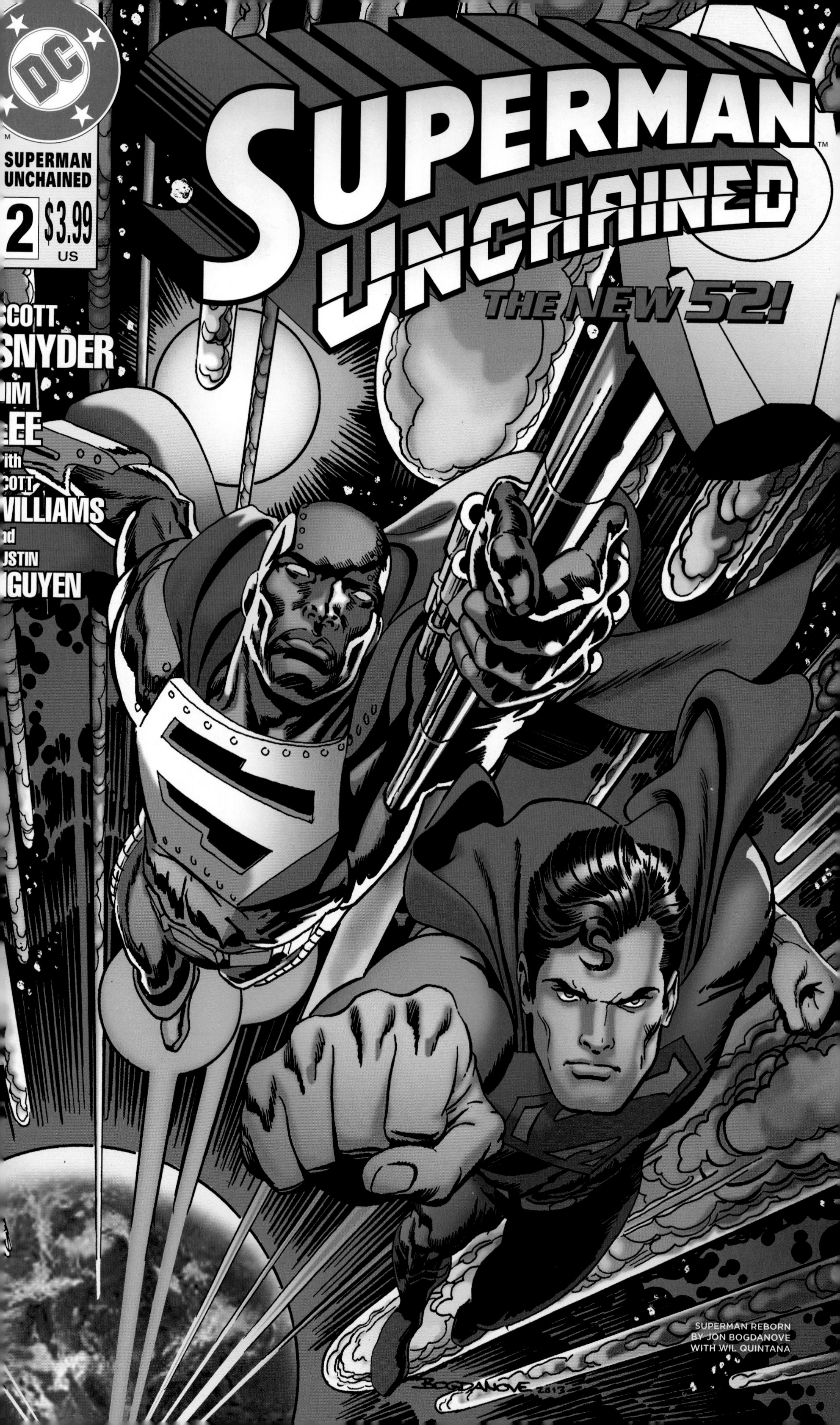
DC
SUPERMAN
UNCHAINED
2 $3.99
US
SUPERMAN UNCHAINED
THE NEW 52!
COTT
SNYDER
IM
EE
ith
COTT
WILLIAMS
d
USTIN
GUYEN
BOGDANOVE 2013
SUPERMAN REBORN
BY JON BOGDANOVE
WITH WIL QUINTANA

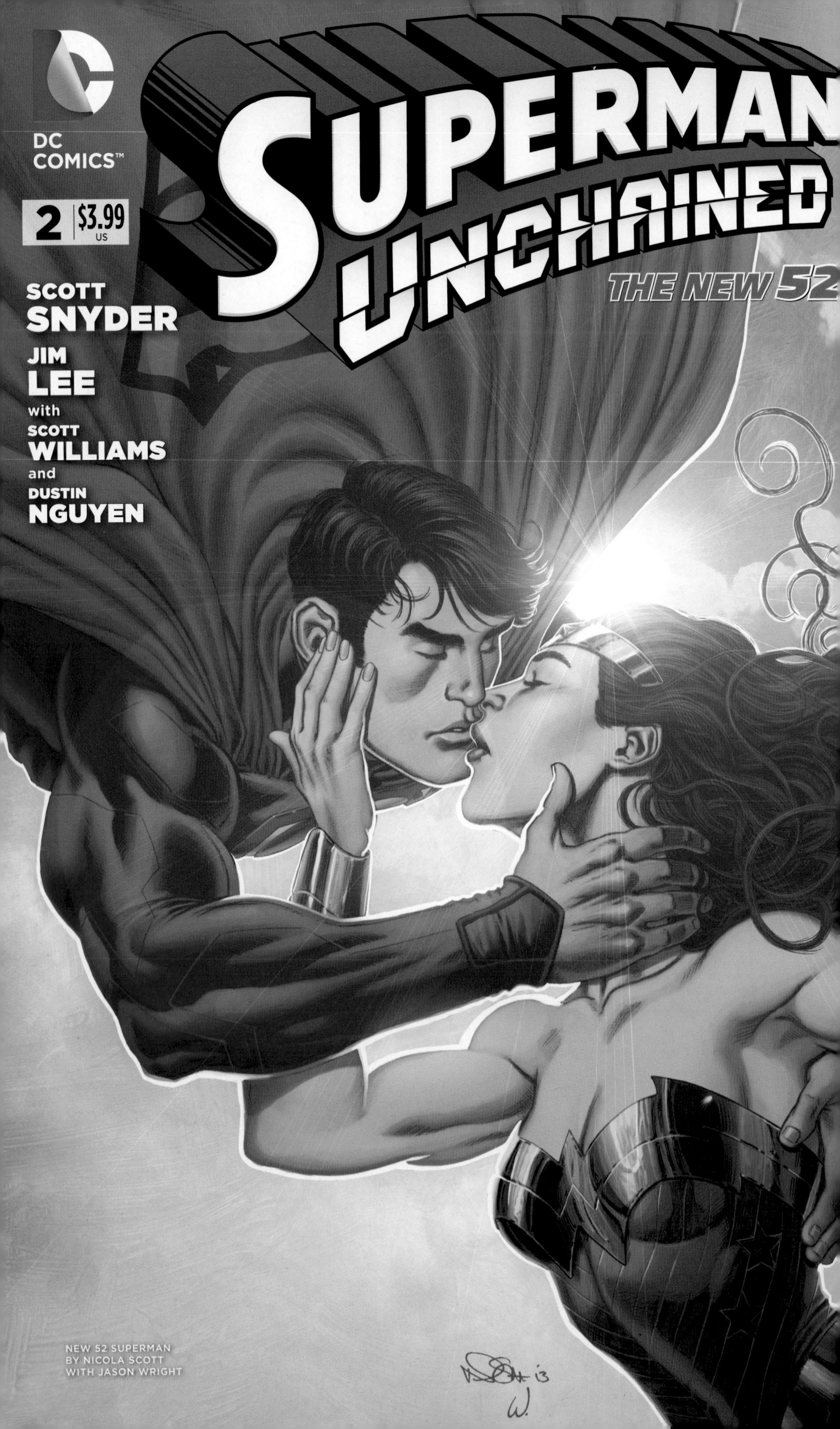
DC COMICS™
2 $3.99 US
SUPERMAN UNCHAINED
THE NEW 52
SCOTT SNYDER
JIM LEE
with
SCOTT WILLIAMS
and
DUSTIN NGUYEN
NEW 52 SUPERMAN
BY NICOLA SCOTT
WITH JASON WRIGHT

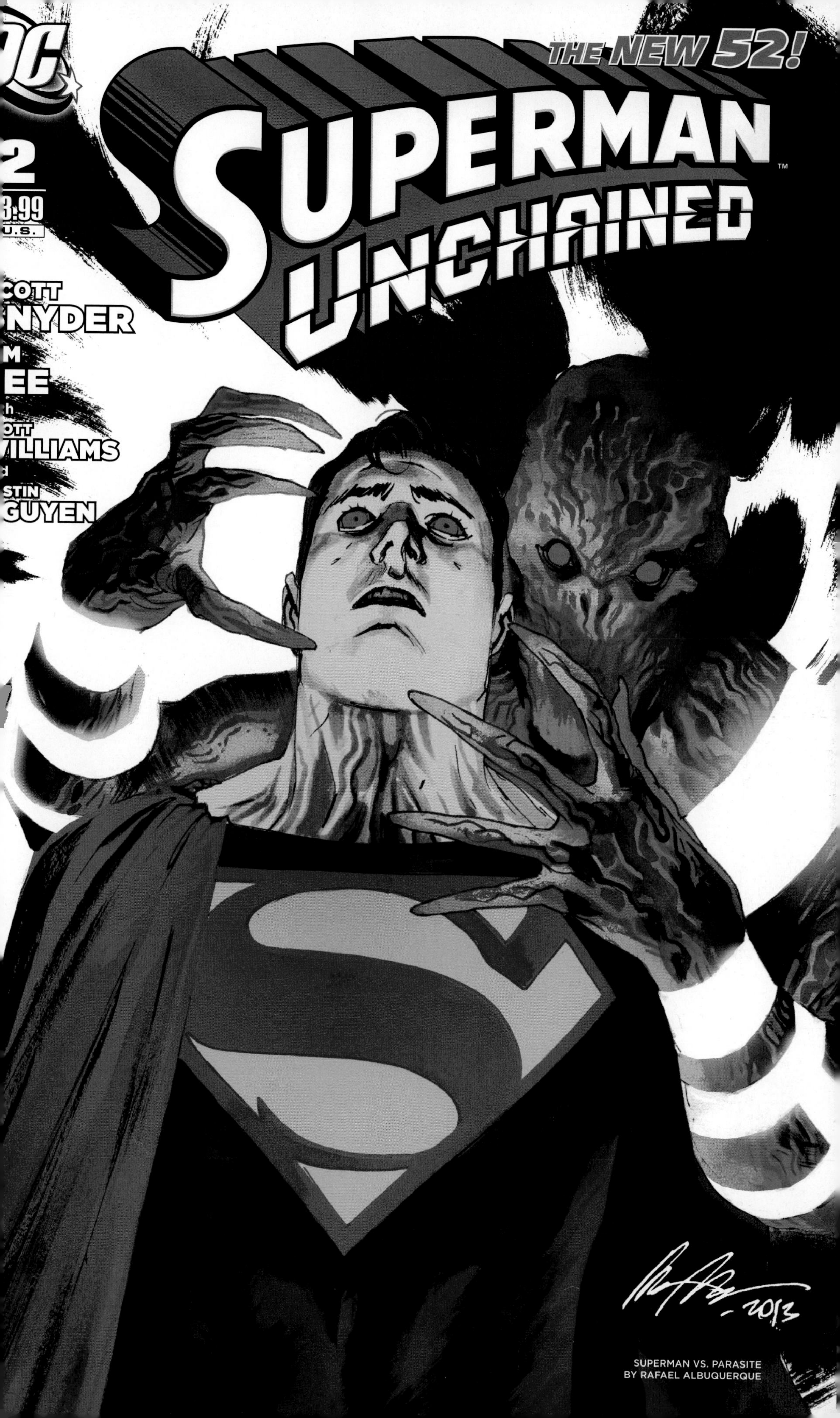
THE NEW 52!
SUPERMAN
UNCHAINED
2
3.99
U.S.
COTT
NYDER
M
EE
h
OTT
VILLIAMS
d
STIN
GUYEN
- 2013
SUPERMAN VS. PARASITE
BY RAFAEL ALBUQUERQUE

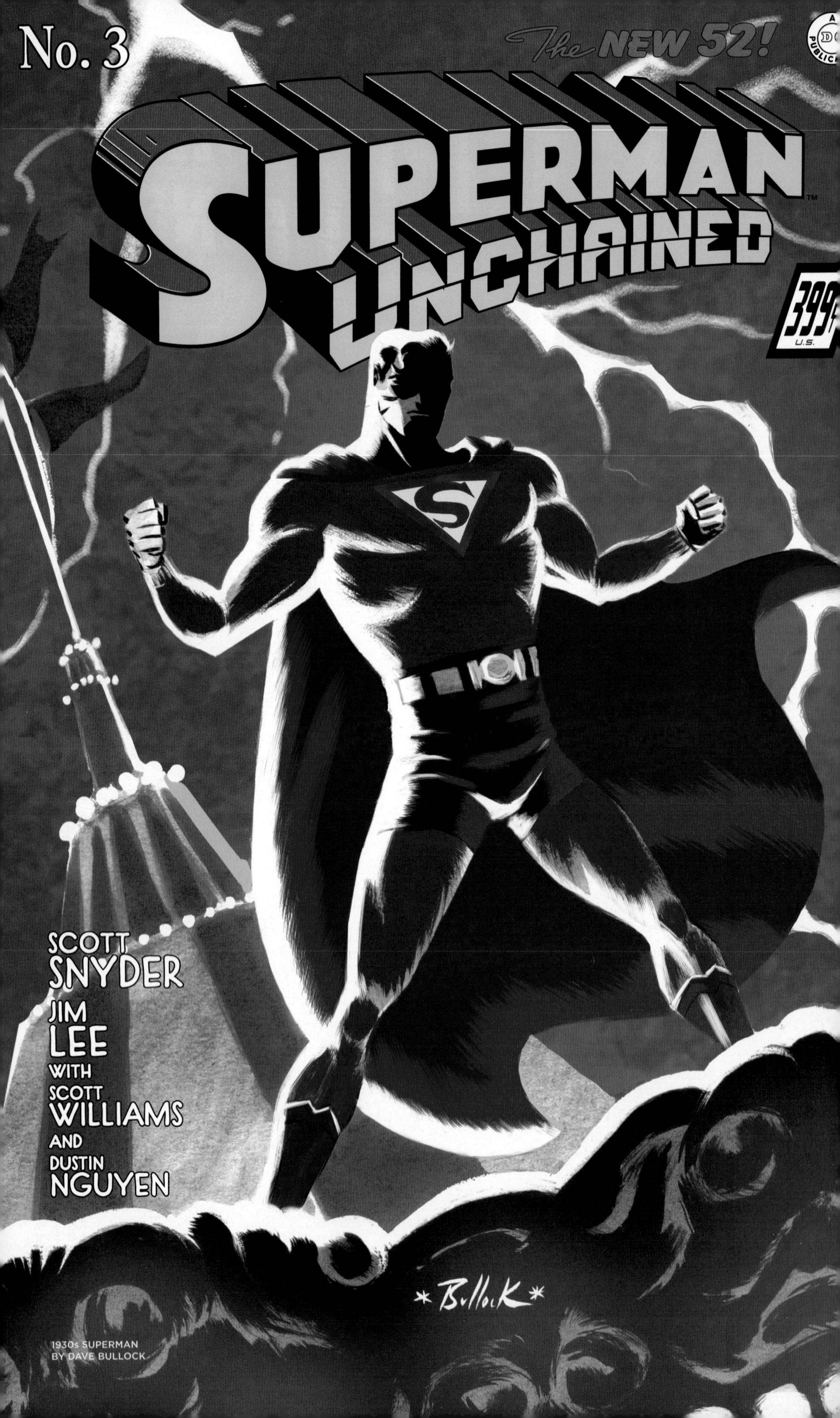
No. 3
The NEW 52!
SUPERMAN UNCHAINED
399 U.S.
SCOTT SNYDER
JIM LEE
WITH
SCOTT WILLIAMS
AND
DUSTIN NGUYEN
Bullock
1930s SUPERMAN
BY DAVE BULLOCK

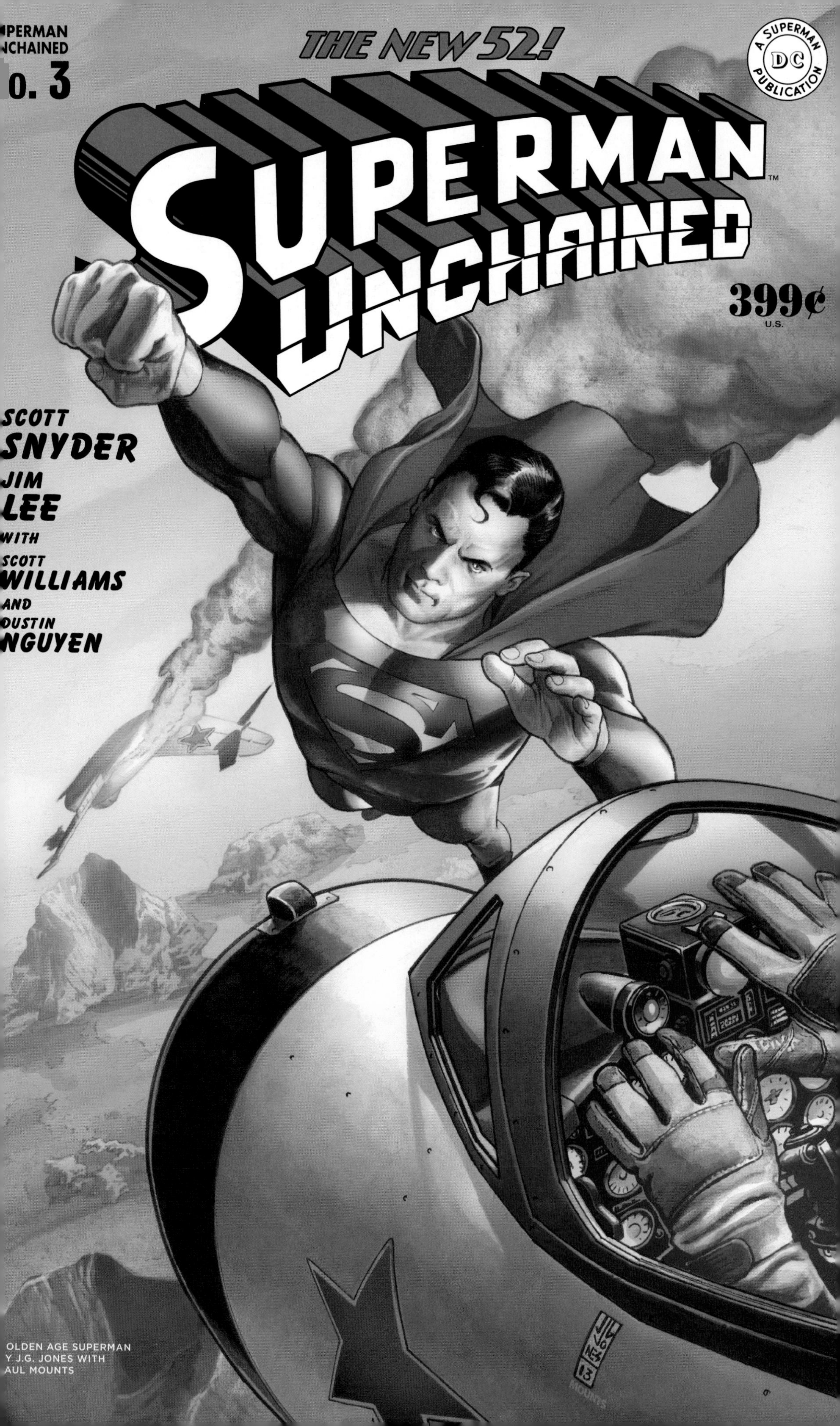

PERMAN
NCHAINED
O. 3
THE NEW 52!
A SUPERMAN DC PUBLICATION
SUPERMAN™
UNCHAINED
399¢
U.S.
SCOTT
SNYDER
JIM
LEE
WITH
SCOTT
WILLIAMS
AND
DUSTIN
NGUYEN
J.G. JONES 13
MOUNTS

OLDEN AGE SUPERMAN
Y J.G. JONES WITH
AUL MOUNTS

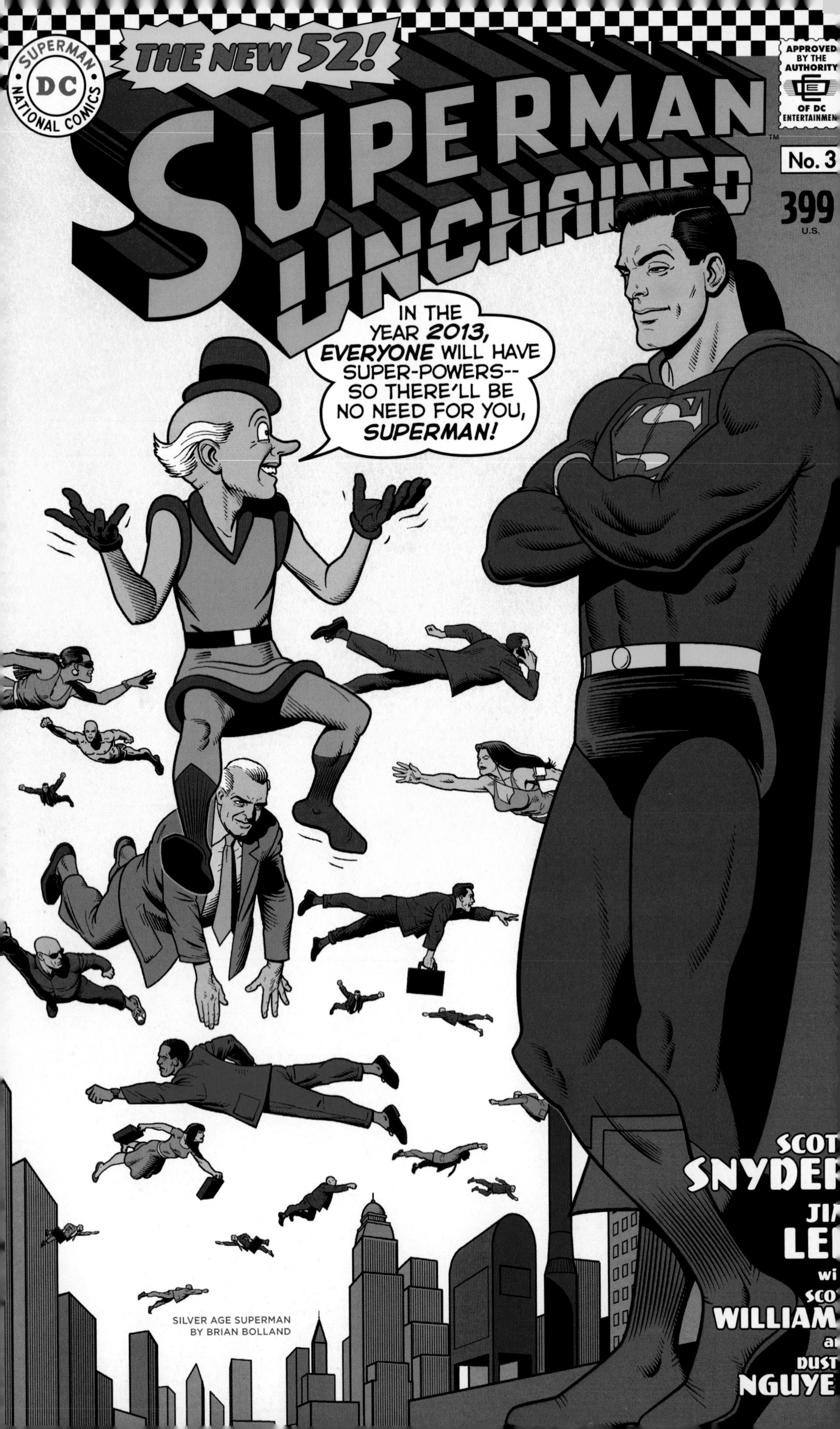
SUPERMAN DC NATIONAL COMICS
THE NEW 52!
APPROVED BY THE AUTHORITY OF DC ENTERTAINMENT
SUPERMAN UNCHAINED
No. 3
399 U.S.
IN THE YEAR 2013, EVERYONE WILL HAVE SUPER-POWERS-- SO THERE'LL BE NO NEED FOR YOU, SUPERMAN!
SILVER AGE SUPERMAN BY BRIAN BOLLAND
SCOT
SNYDE
JI
LE
wi
SCO
WILLIAM
a
DUST
NGUYE

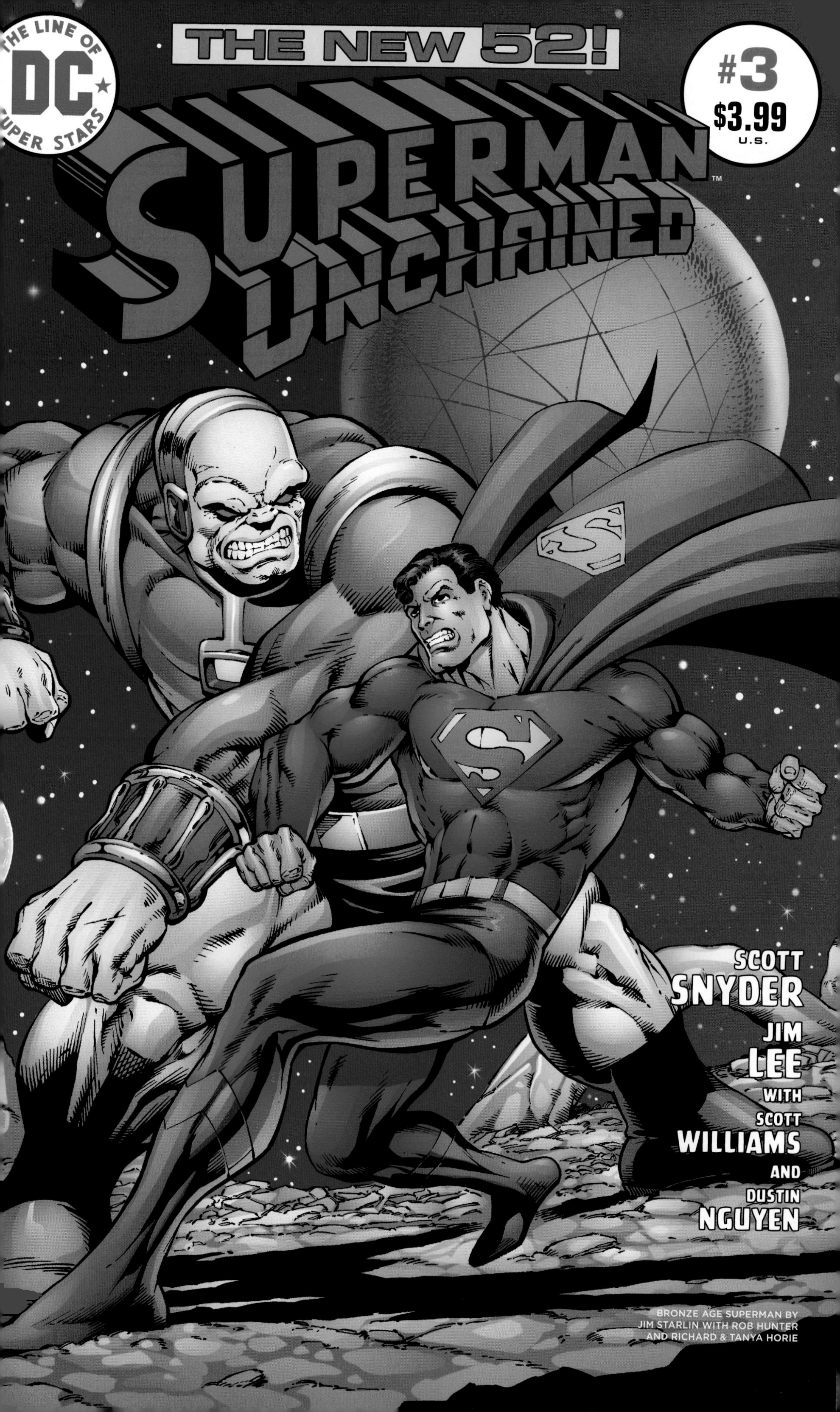
THE LINE OF DC SUPER STARS
THE NEW 52!
#3
$3.99
U.S.
SUPERMAN
UNCHAINED
SCOTT SNYDER
JIM LEE
WITH
SCOTT WILLIAMS
AND
DUSTIN NGUYEN
BRONZE AGE SUPERMAN BY
JIM STARLIN WITH ROB HUNTER
AND RICHARD & TANYA HORIE

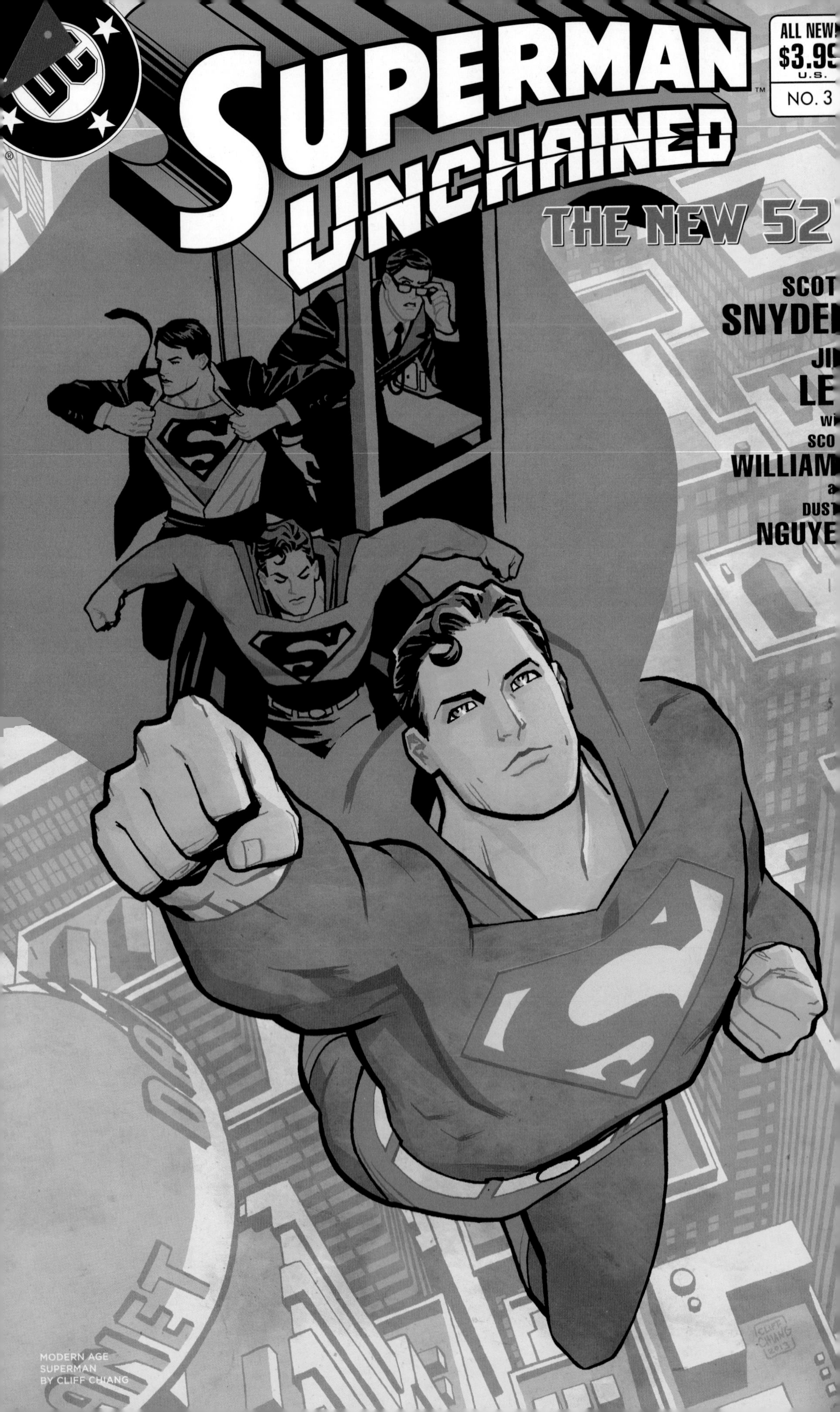
DC
SUPERMAN
UNCHAINED
ALL NEW!
$3.99
U.S.
NO. 3
THE NEW 52
SCOT
SNYDE
JI
LE
SCO
WILLIAM
DUST
NGUYE
CLIFF CHIANG 2013
MODERN AGE SUPERMAN BY CLIFF CHIANG

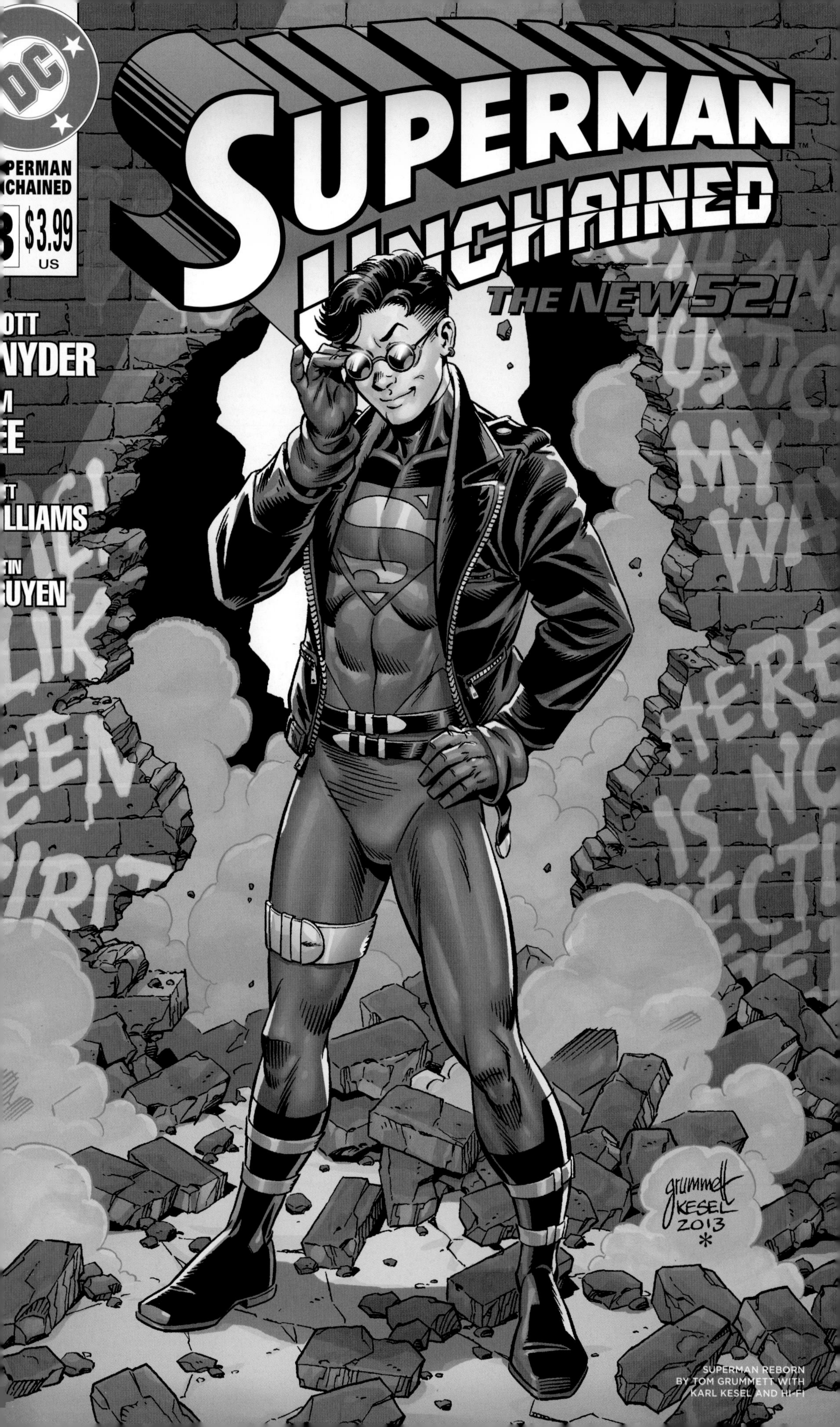
SUPERMAN
UNCHAINED
THE NEW 52!
PERMAN
CHAINED
$3.99
US
OTT
NYDER
LLIAMS
UYEN
grummett
KESEL
2013

SUPERMAN REBORN
BY TOM GRUMMETT WITH
KARL KESEL AND HI-FI

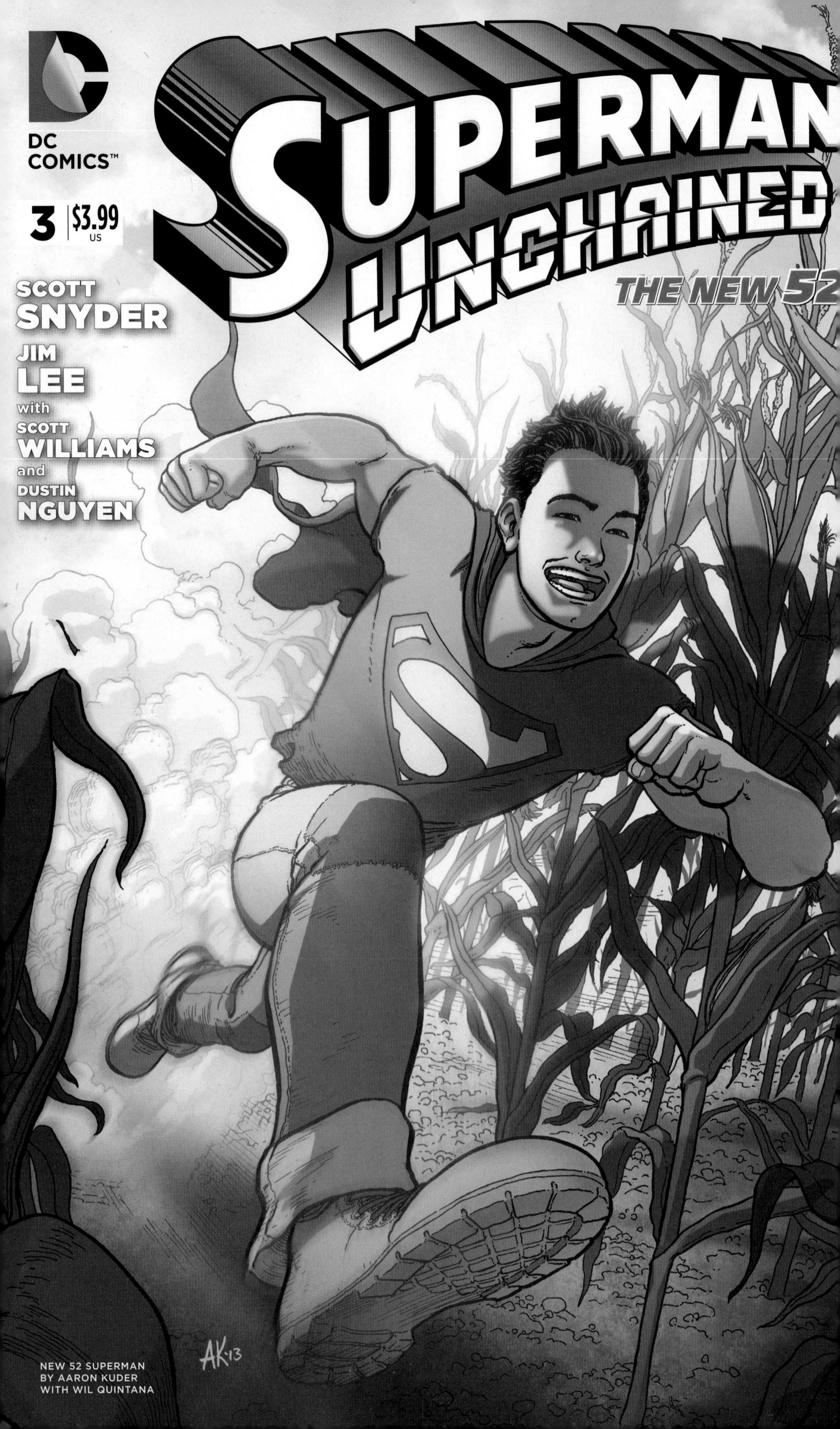
DC COMICS™
3 $3.99 US
SUPERMAN UNCHAINED
THE NEW 52
SCOTT SNYDER
JIM LEE
with
SCOTT WILLIAMS
and
DUSTIN NGUYEN
AK'13
NEW 52 SUPERMAN
BY AARON KUDER
WITH WIL QUINTANA

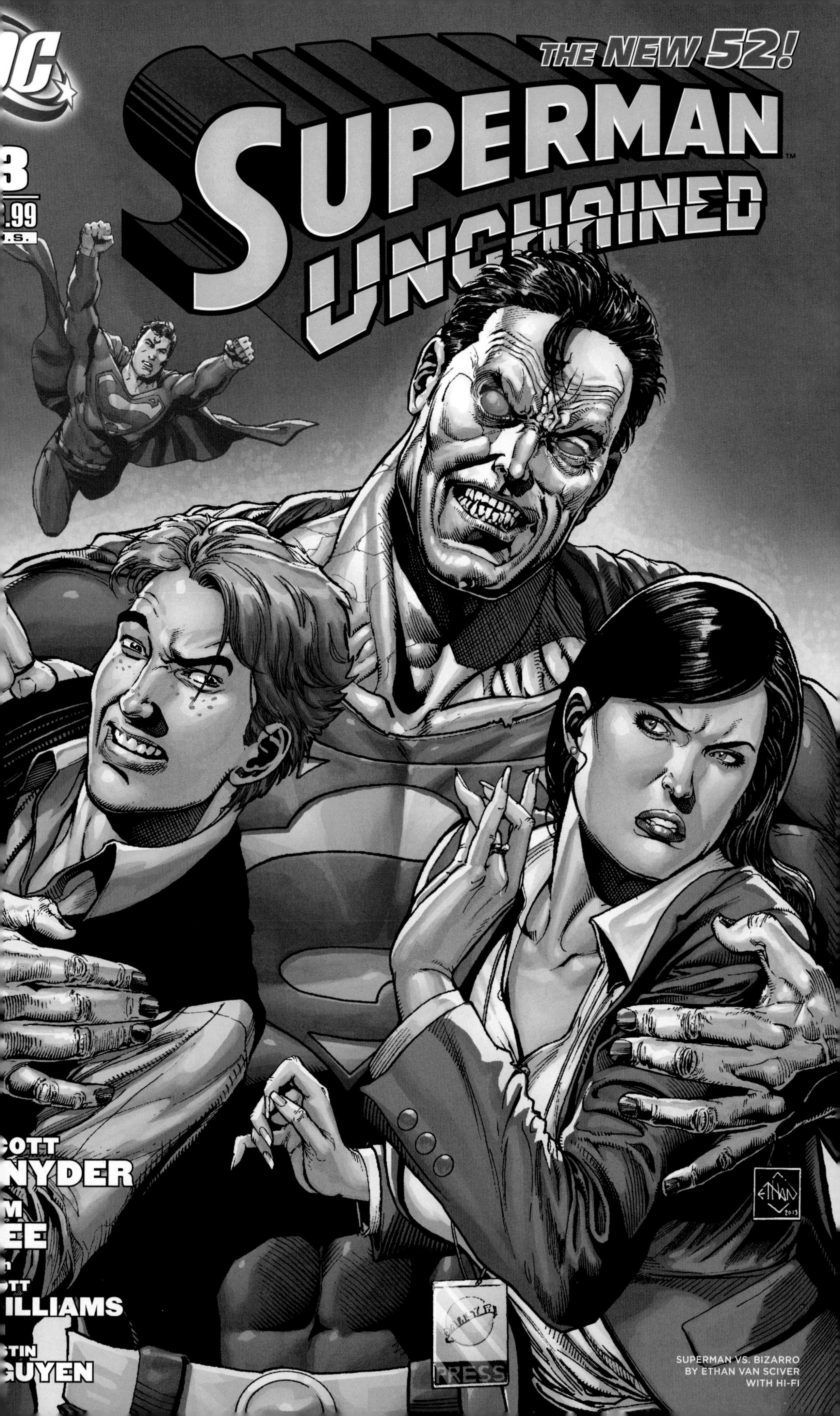
THE NEW 52!
SUPERMAN
UNCHAINED
3
.99
.S.
OTT
NYDER
M
EE
TT
ILLIAMS
TIN
GUYEN
SUPERMAN VS. BIZARRO
BY ETHAN VAN SCIVER
WITH HI-FI

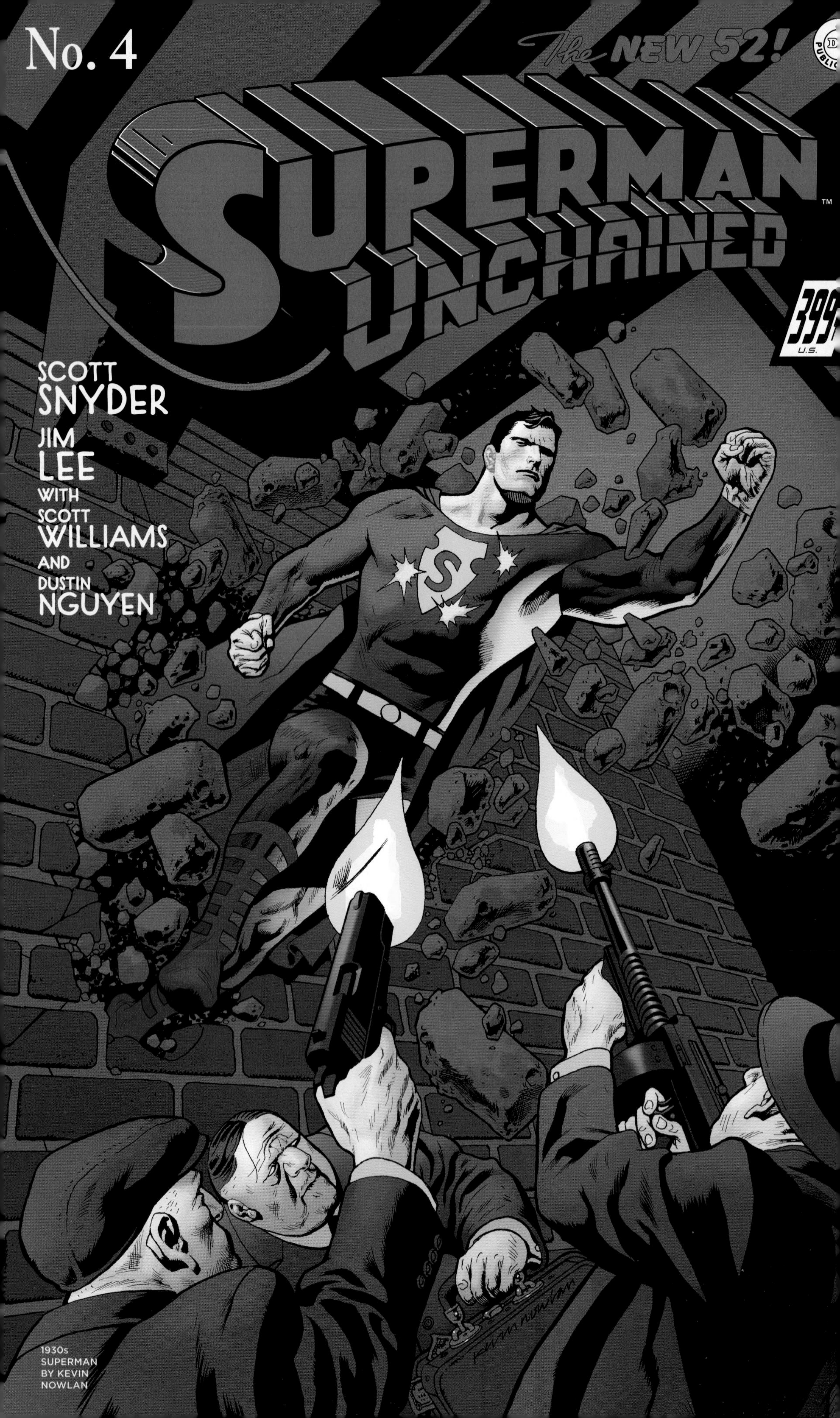
No. 4
The NEW 52!
SUPERMAN
UNCHAINED
399 U.S.
SCOTT SNYDER
JIM LEE
WITH
SCOTT WILLIAMS
AND
DUSTIN NGUYEN
1930s SUPERMAN BY KEVIN NOWLAN

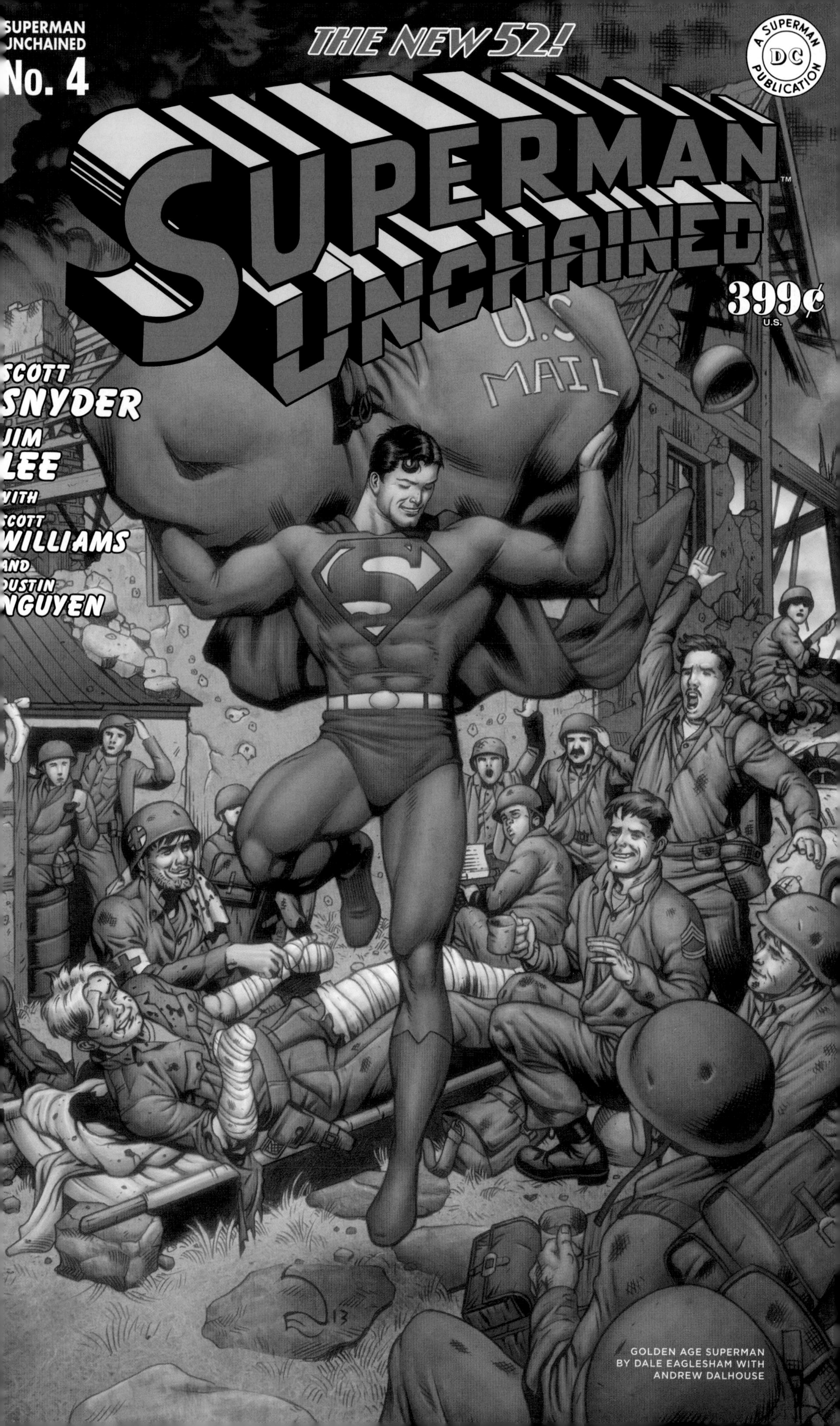
SUPERMAN UNCHAINED
No. 4
THE NEW 52!
A SUPERMAN DC PUBLICATION
SUPERMAN UNCHAINED™
399¢ U.S.
U.S. MAIL
SCOTT SNYDER
JIM LEE
WITH
SCOTT WILLIAMS
AND
DUSTIN NGUYEN
GOLDEN AGE SUPERMAN
BY DALE EAGLESHAM WITH
ANDREW DALHOUSE

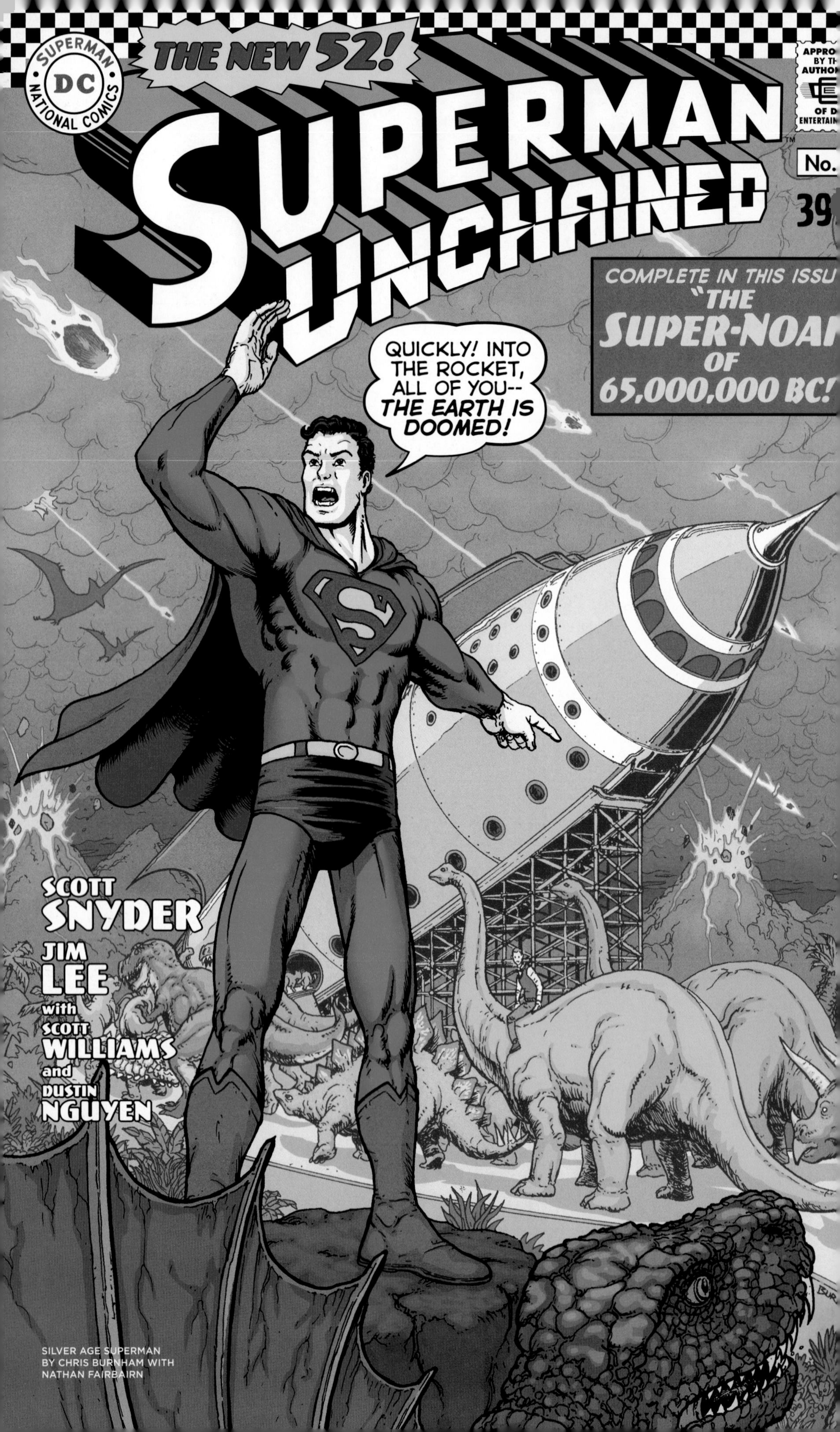
SUPERMAN DC NATIONAL COMICS
THE NEW 52!
SUPERMAN UNCHAINED
No.
39
COMPLETE IN THIS ISSU
"THE SUPER-NOA
OF 65,000,000 BC!
QUICKLY! INTO THE ROCKET, ALL OF YOU-- THE EARTH IS DOOMED!
SCOTT SNYDER
JIM LEE
with SCOTT WILLIAMS
and DUSTIN NGUYEN
SILVER AGE SUPERMAN
BY CHRIS BURNHAM WITH
NATHAN FAIRBAIRN

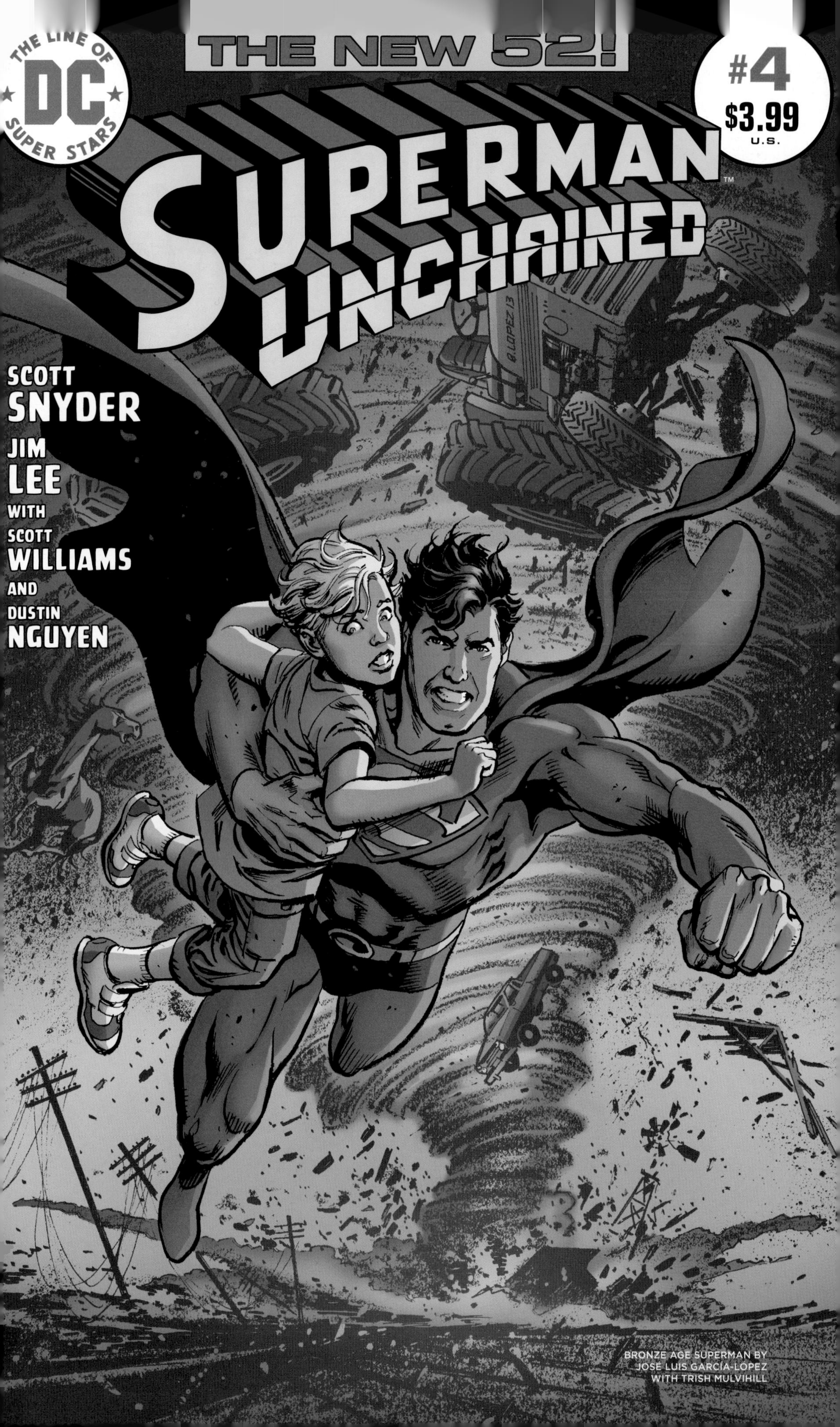
THE LINE OF DC SUPER STARS
THE NEW 52!
#4
$3.99 U.S.
SUPERMAN UNCHAINED
SCOTT SNYDER
JIM LEE
WITH SCOTT WILLIAMS
AND DUSTIN NGUYEN
BRONZE AGE SUPERMAN BY
JOSÉ LUIS GARCÍA-LOPEZ
WITH TRISH MULVIHILL

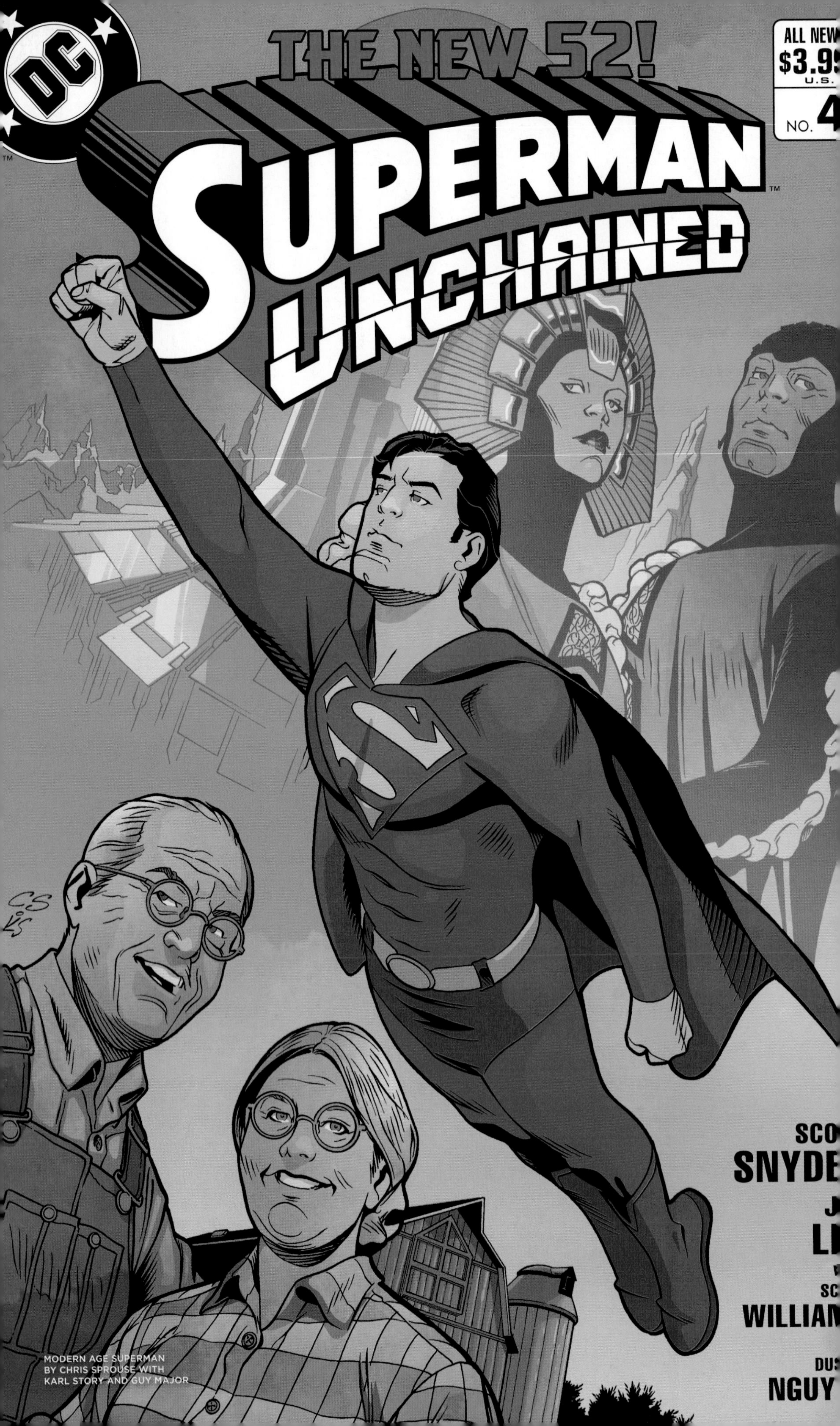
DC
THE NEW 52!
ALL NEW
$3.9
U.S.
NO. 4
SUPERMAN
UNCHAINED
CS
KS
SCO
SNYDE
J
L
SC
WILLIAM
DU
NGUY

MODERN AGE SUPERMAN
BY CHRIS SPROUSE WITH
KARL STORY AND GUY MAJOR

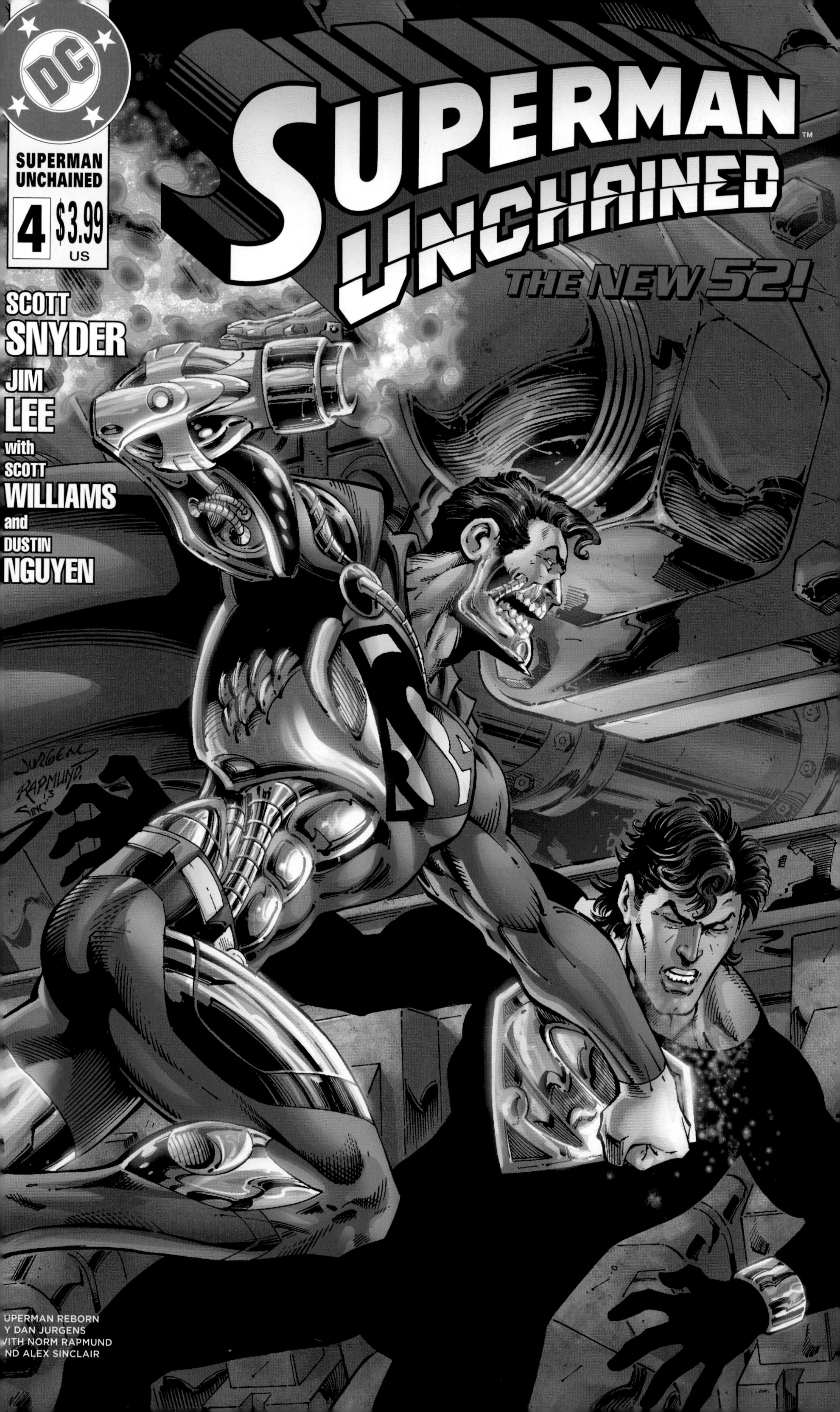
DC
SUPERMAN UNCHAINED
4 $3.99 US
SUPERMAN™
UNCHAINED
THE NEW 52!
SCOTT SNYDER
JIM LEE
with SCOTT WILLIAMS
and DUSTIN NGUYEN
UPERMAN REBORN
Y DAN JURGENS
VITH NORM RAPMUND
ND ALEX SINCLAIR

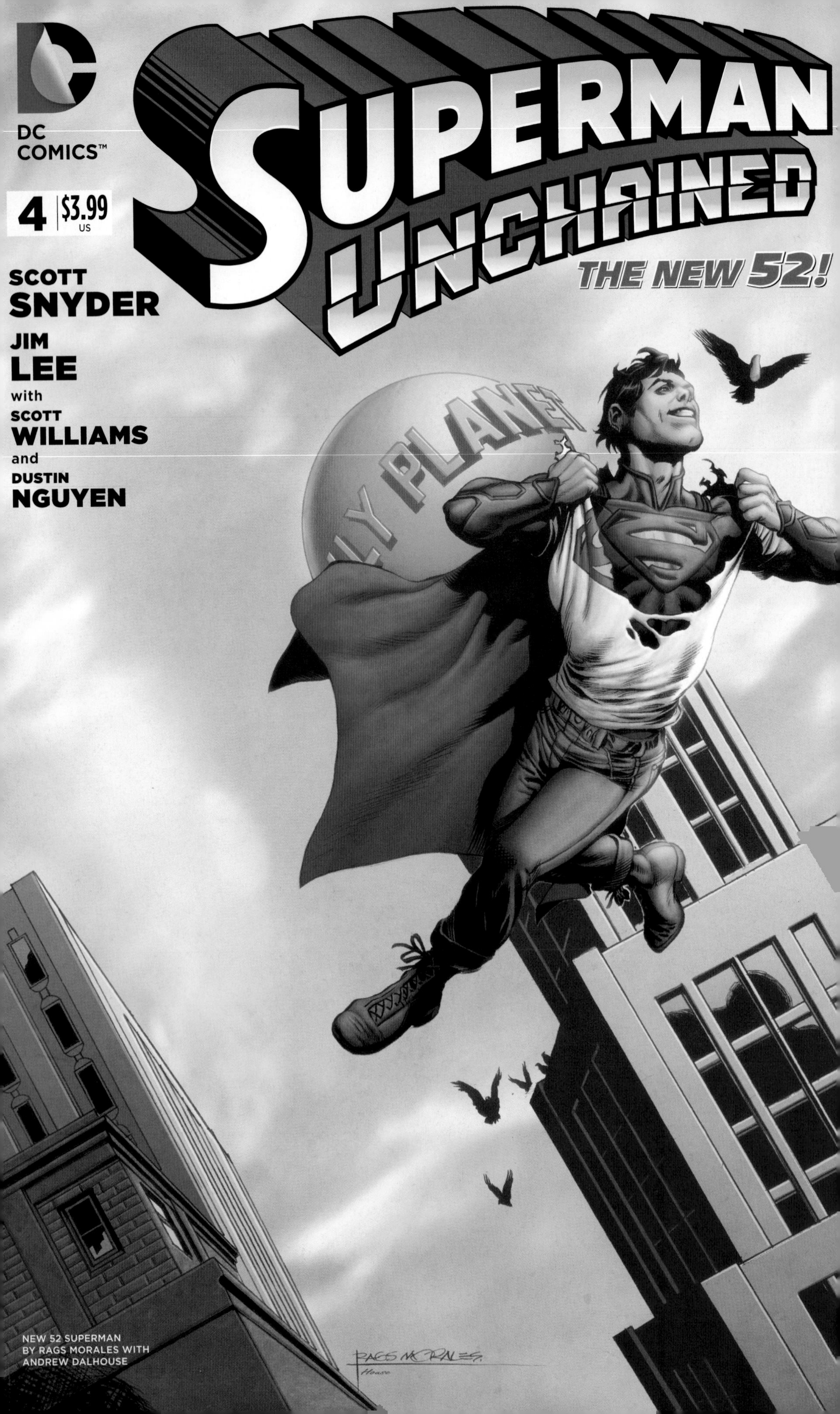
DC COMICS™
4 $3.99 US
SUPERMAN UNCHAINED
THE NEW 52!
SCOTT SNYDER
JIM LEE
with
SCOTT WILLIAMS
and
DUSTIN NGUYEN
DAILY PLANET
NEW 52 SUPERMAN
BY RAGS MORALES WITH
ANDREW DALHOUSE
RAGS MORALES

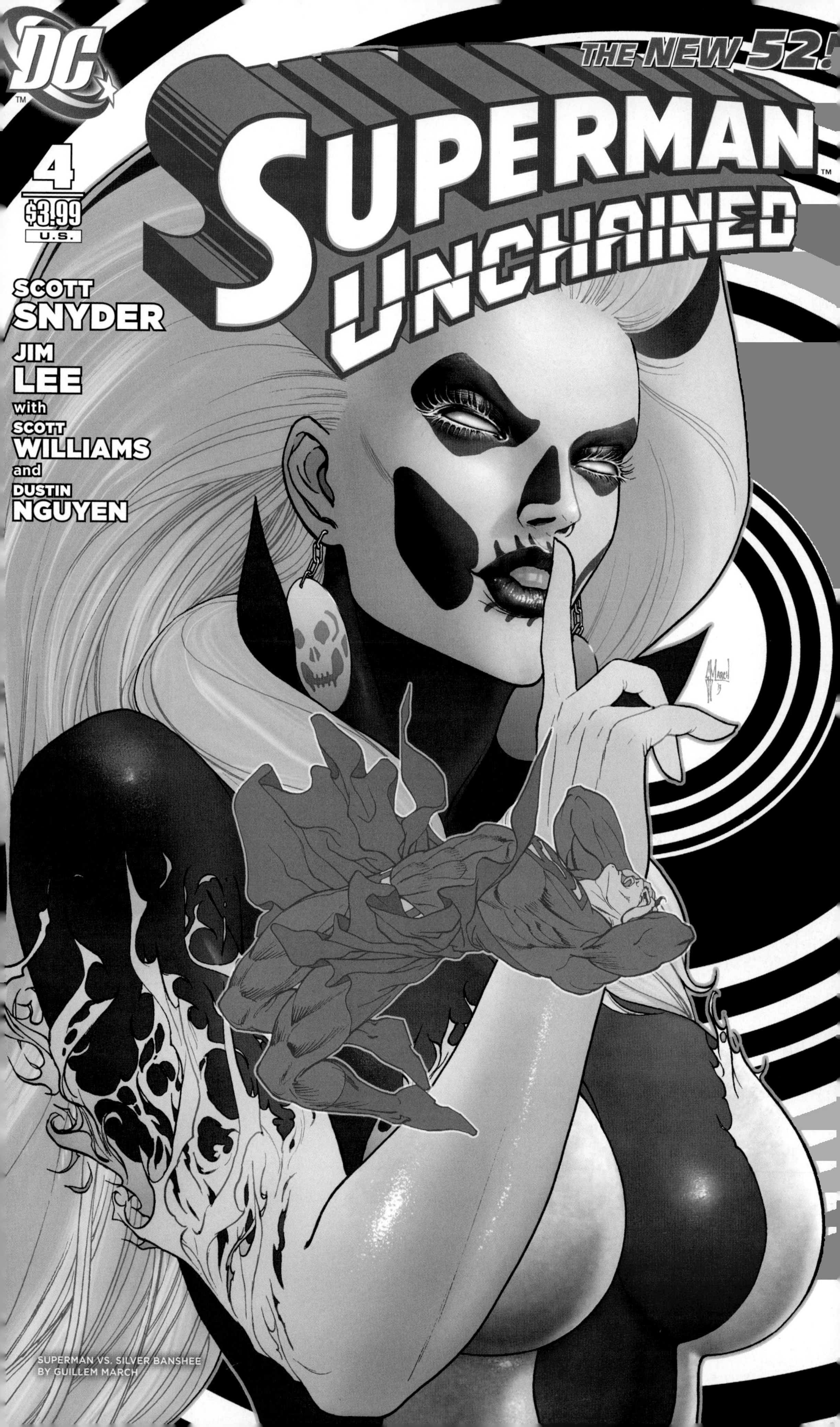
DC
THE NEW 52!
SUPERMAN
UNCHAINED
4
$3.99
U.S.
SCOTT
SNYDER
JIM
LEE
with
SCOTT
WILLIAMS
and
DUSTIN
NGUYEN
SUPERMAN VS. SILVER BANSHEE
BY GUILLEM MARCH

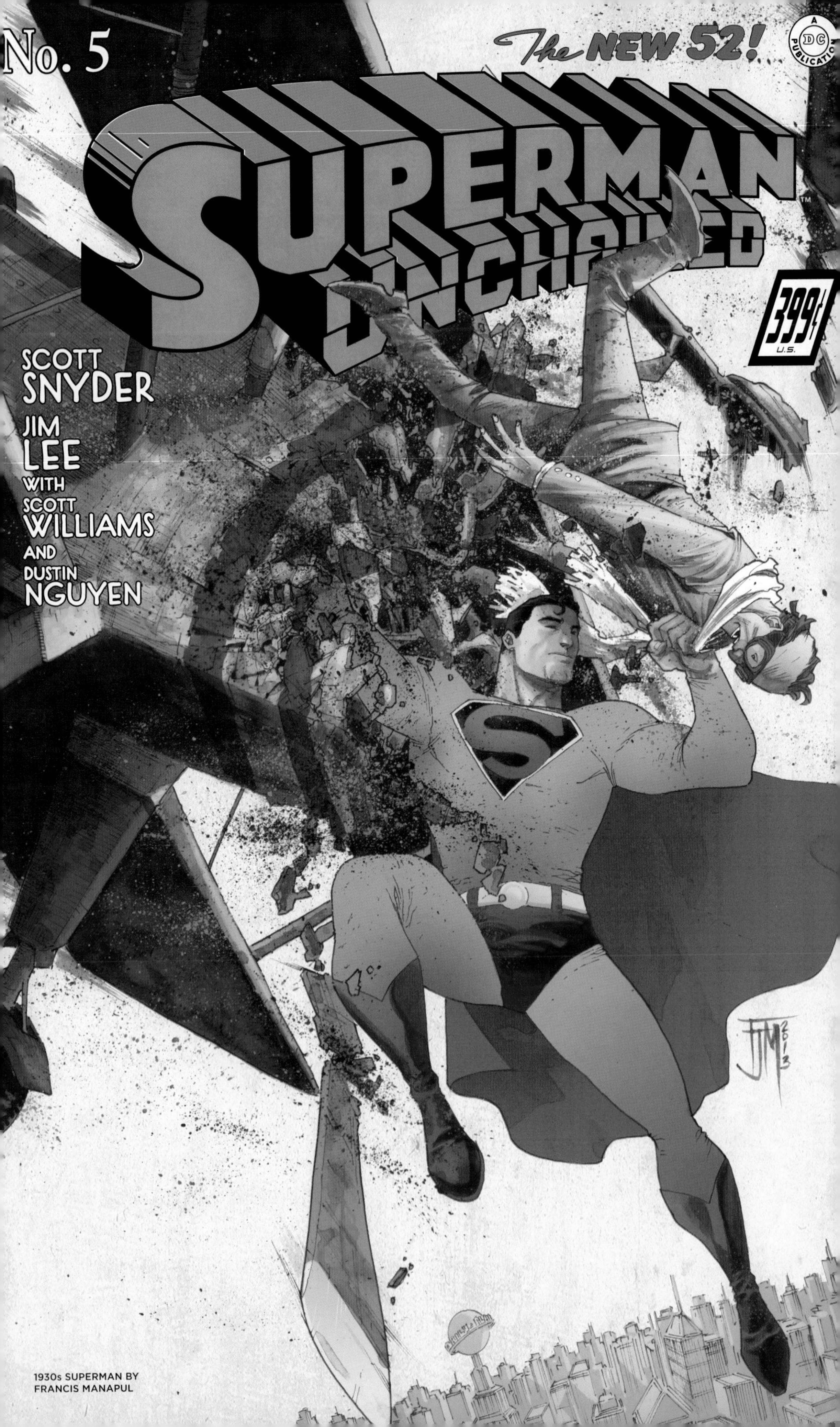
No. 5
The NEW 52!
A DC PUBLICATION
SUPERMAN
UNCHAINED
™
399¢ U.S.
SCOTT SNYDER
JIM LEE
WITH
SCOTT WILLIAMS
AND
DUSTIN NGUYEN
1930s SUPERMAN BY
FRANCIS MANAPUL

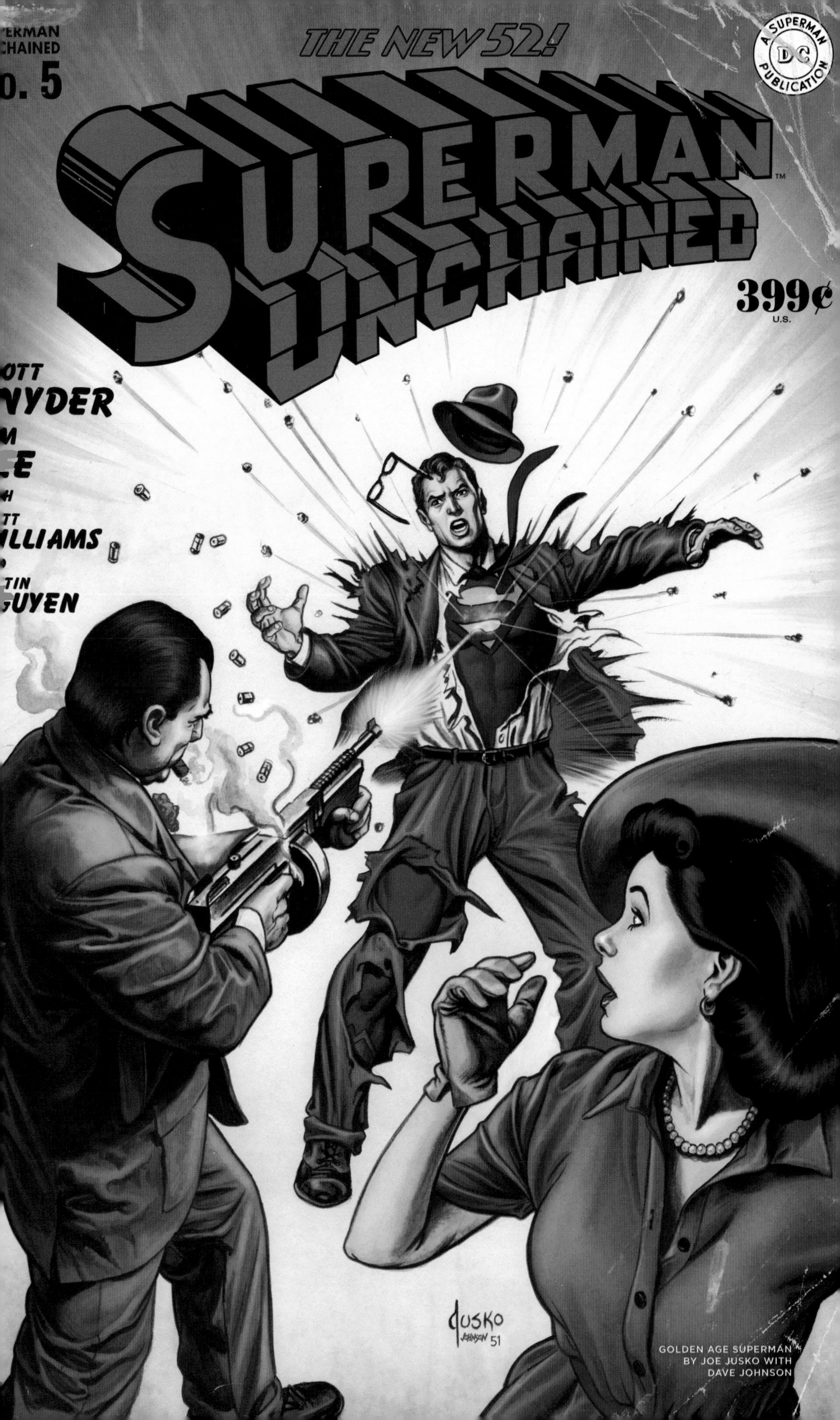

ERMAN
CHAINED
o. 5
THE NEW 52!
A SUPERMAN DC PUBLICATION
SUPERMAN
UNCHAINED
399¢
U.S.
OTT
NYDER
M
LE
H
TT
LLIAMS
TIN
GUYEN
JUSKO
JOHNSON 51
GOLDEN AGE SUPERMAN
BY JOE JUSKO WITH
DAVE JOHNSON

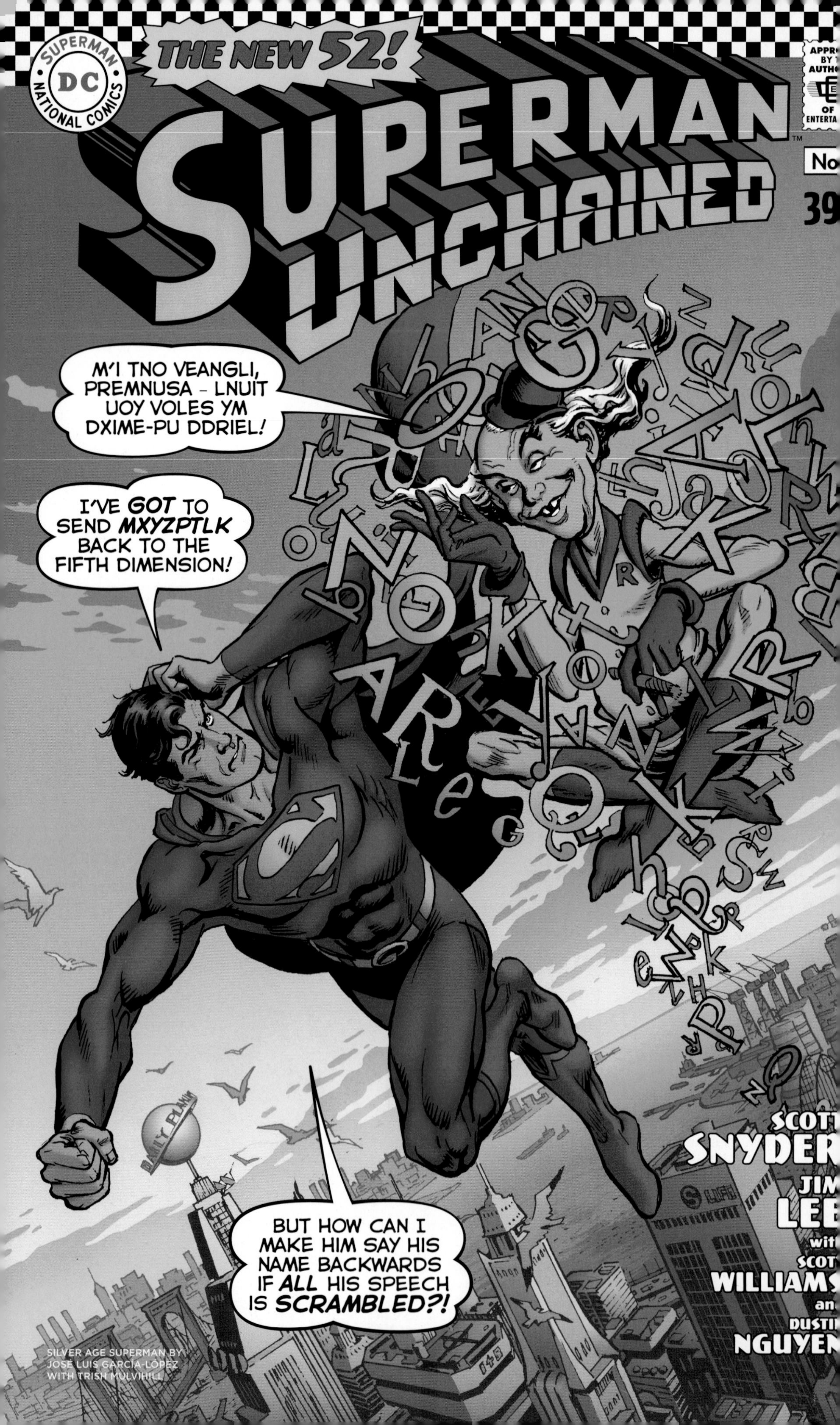
SUPERMAN DC NATIONAL COMICS
THE NEW 52!
SUPERMAN UNCHAINED
M'I TNO VEANGLI, PREMNUSA - LNUIT UOY VOLES YM DXIME-PU DDRIEL!
I'VE GOT TO SEND MXYZPTLK BACK TO THE FIFTH DIMENSION!
BUT HOW CAN I MAKE HIM SAY HIS NAME BACKWARDS IF ALL HIS SPEECH IS SCRAMBLED?!
SNYDER
WILLIAMS
NGUYEN

SILVER AGE SUPERMAN BY JOSÉ LUIS GARCÍA-LÓPEZ WITH TRISH MULVIHILL

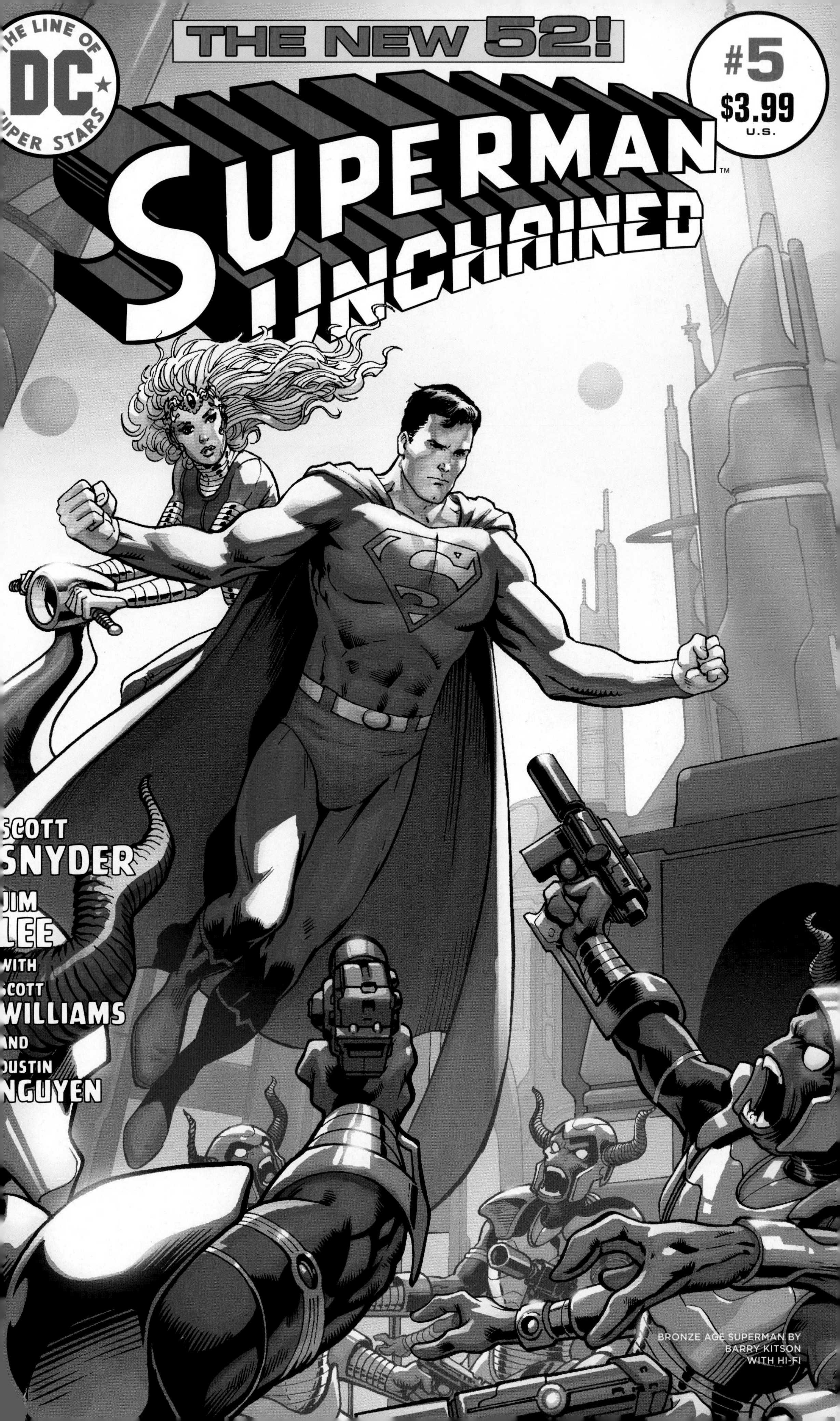
THE LINE OF DC SUPER STARS
THE NEW 52!
#5
$3.99
U.S.
SUPERMAN™
UNCHAINED
SCOTT
SNYDER
JIM
LEE
WITH
SCOTT
WILLIAMS
AND
DUSTIN
NGUYEN
BRONZE AGE SUPERMAN BY
BARRY KITSON
WITH HI-FI

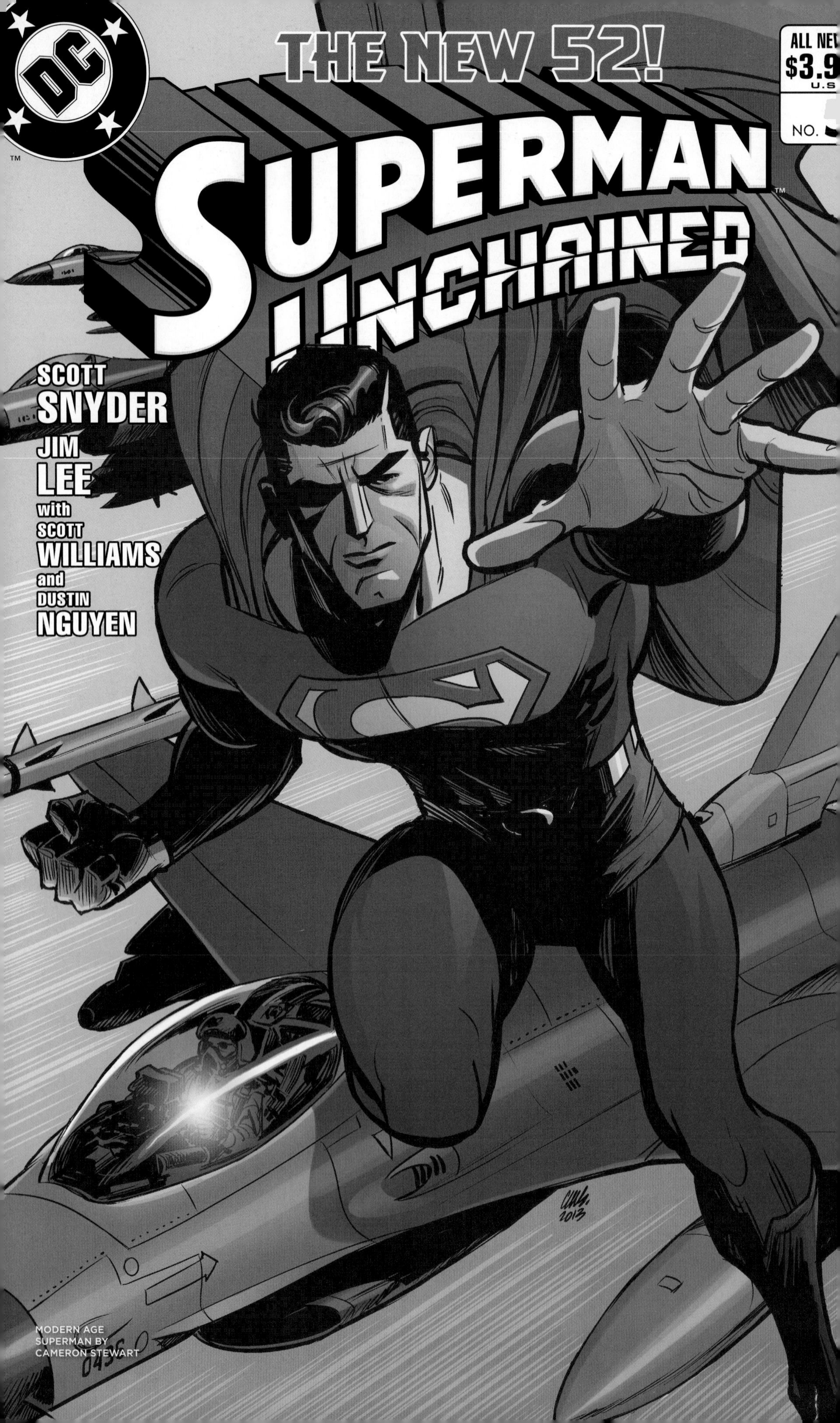
THE NEW 52!
ALL NEW
$3.9
U.S
NO.
DC
SUPERMAN UNCHAINED
SCOTT SNYDER
JIM LEE
with
SCOTT WILLIAMS
and
DUSTIN NGUYEN
MODERN AGE SUPERMAN BY CAMERON STEWART

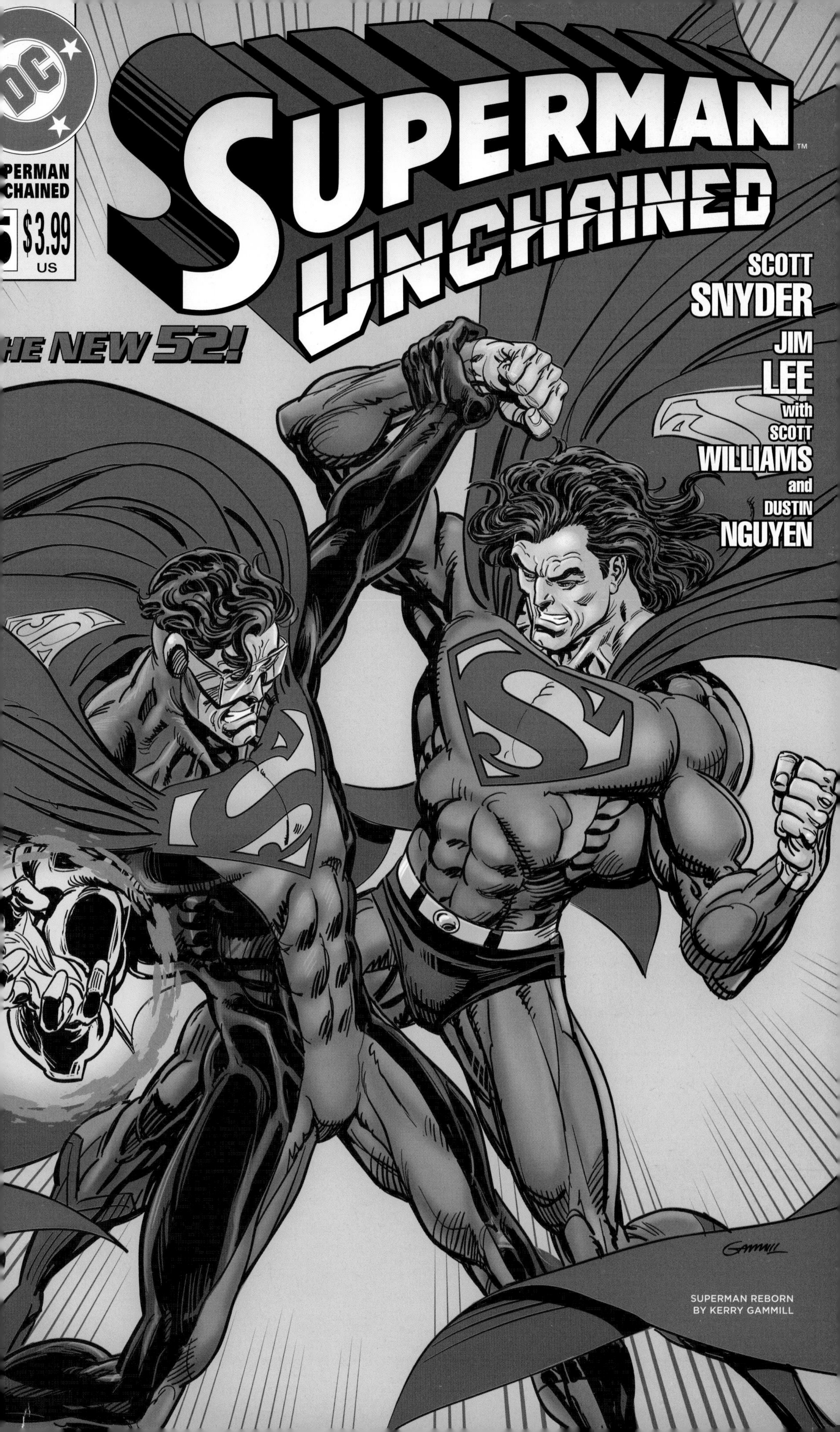

SUPERMAN™
UNCHAINED
PERMAN
CHAINED
$3.99
US
HE NEW 52!
SCOTT
SNYDER
JIM
LEE
with
SCOTT
WILLIAMS
and
DUSTIN
NGUYEN
GAMMILL
SUPERMAN REBORN
BY KERRY GAMMILL

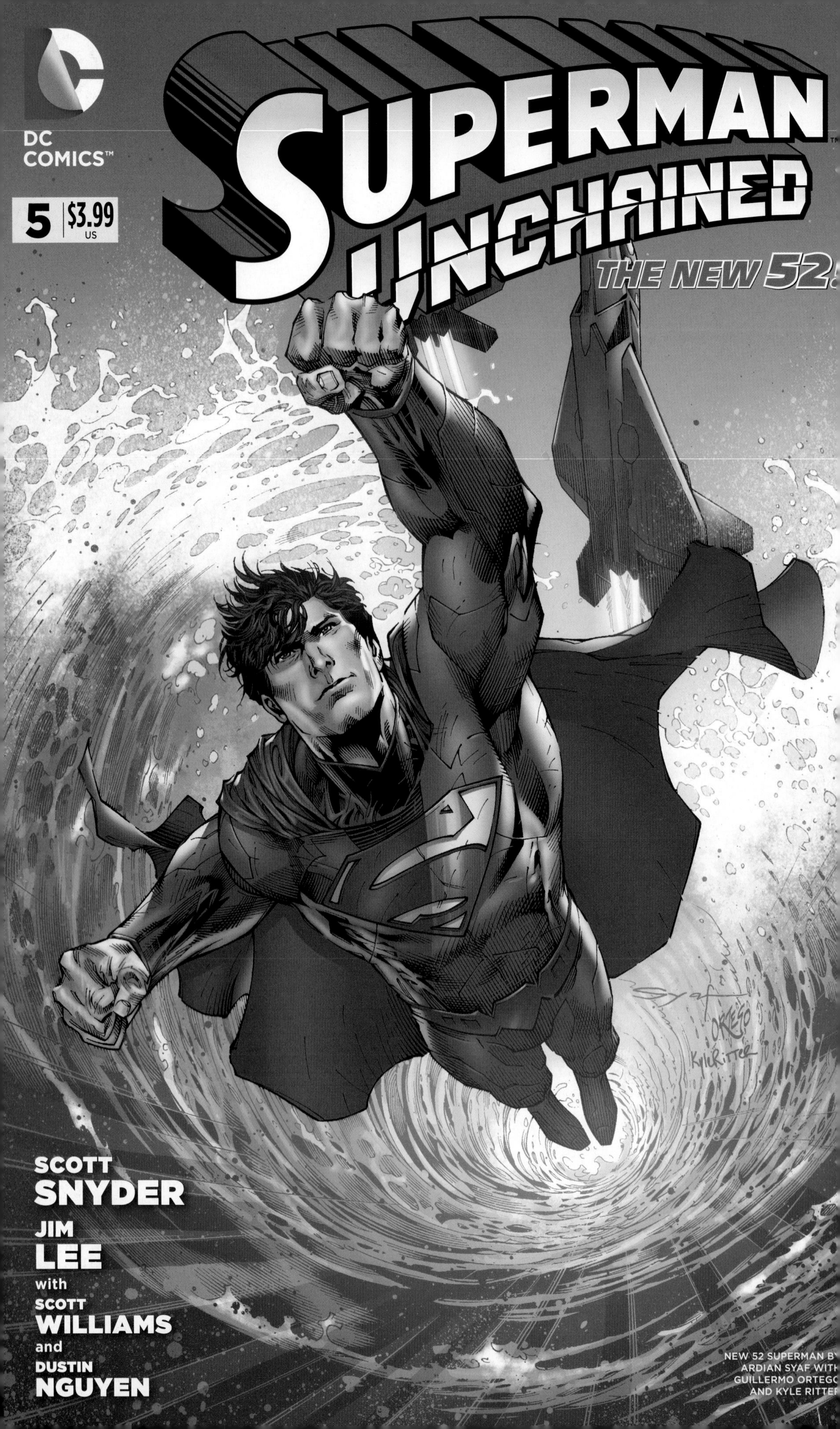
DC COMICS™
5 $3.99 US
SUPERMAN UNCHAINED
THE NEW 52!
SCOTT SNYDER
JIM LEE
with
SCOTT WILLIAMS
and
DUSTIN NGUYEN
NEW 52 SUPERMAN BY ARDIAN SYAF WITH GUILLERMO ORTEGO AND KYLE RITTER

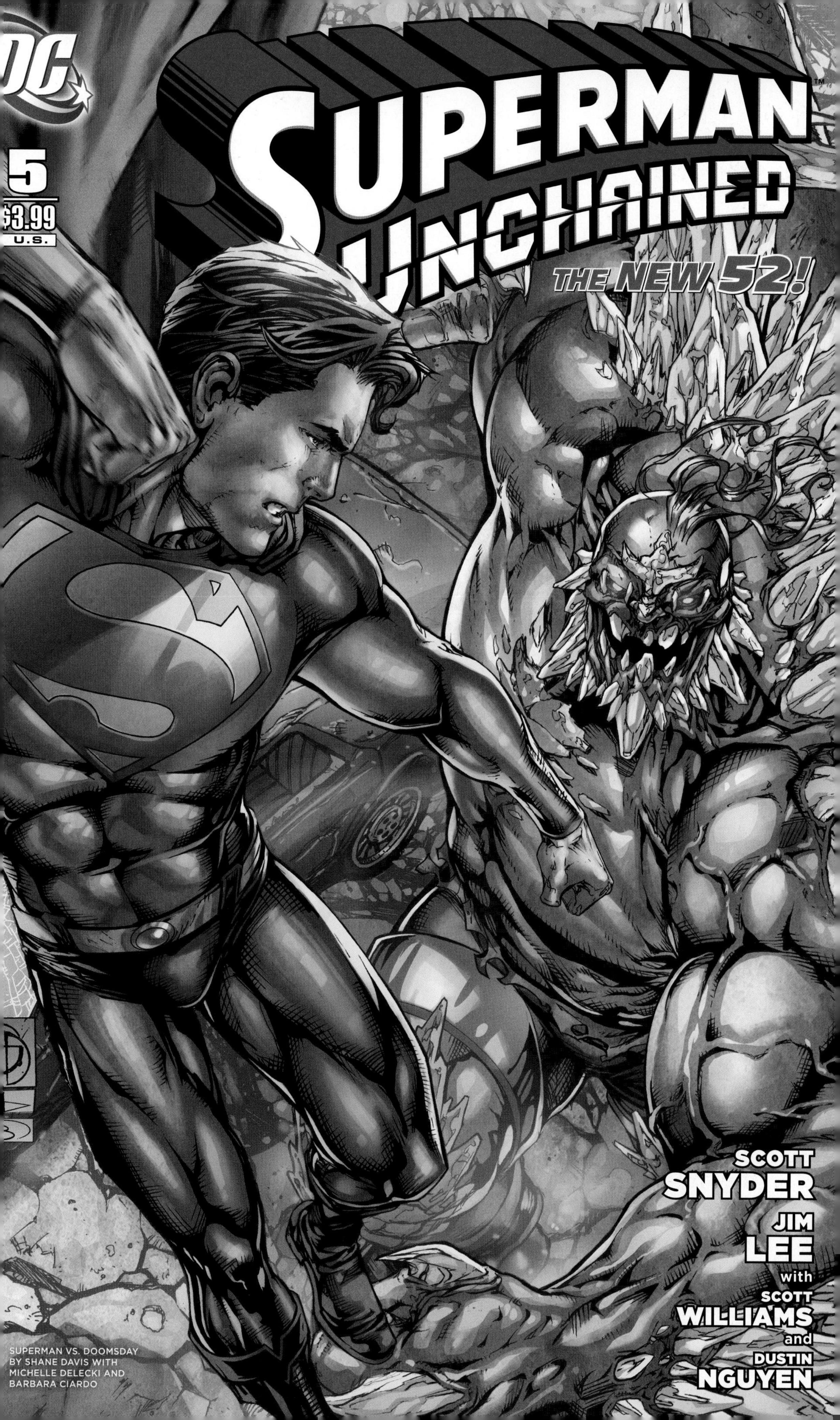
DC
SUPERMAN UNCHAINED
5
$3.99 U.S.
THE NEW 52!
SCOTT SNYDER
JIM LEE
with
SCOTT WILLIAMS
and
DUSTIN NGUYEN
SUPERMAN VS. DOOMSDAY BY SHANE DAVIS WITH MICHELLE DELECKI AND BARBARA CIARDO

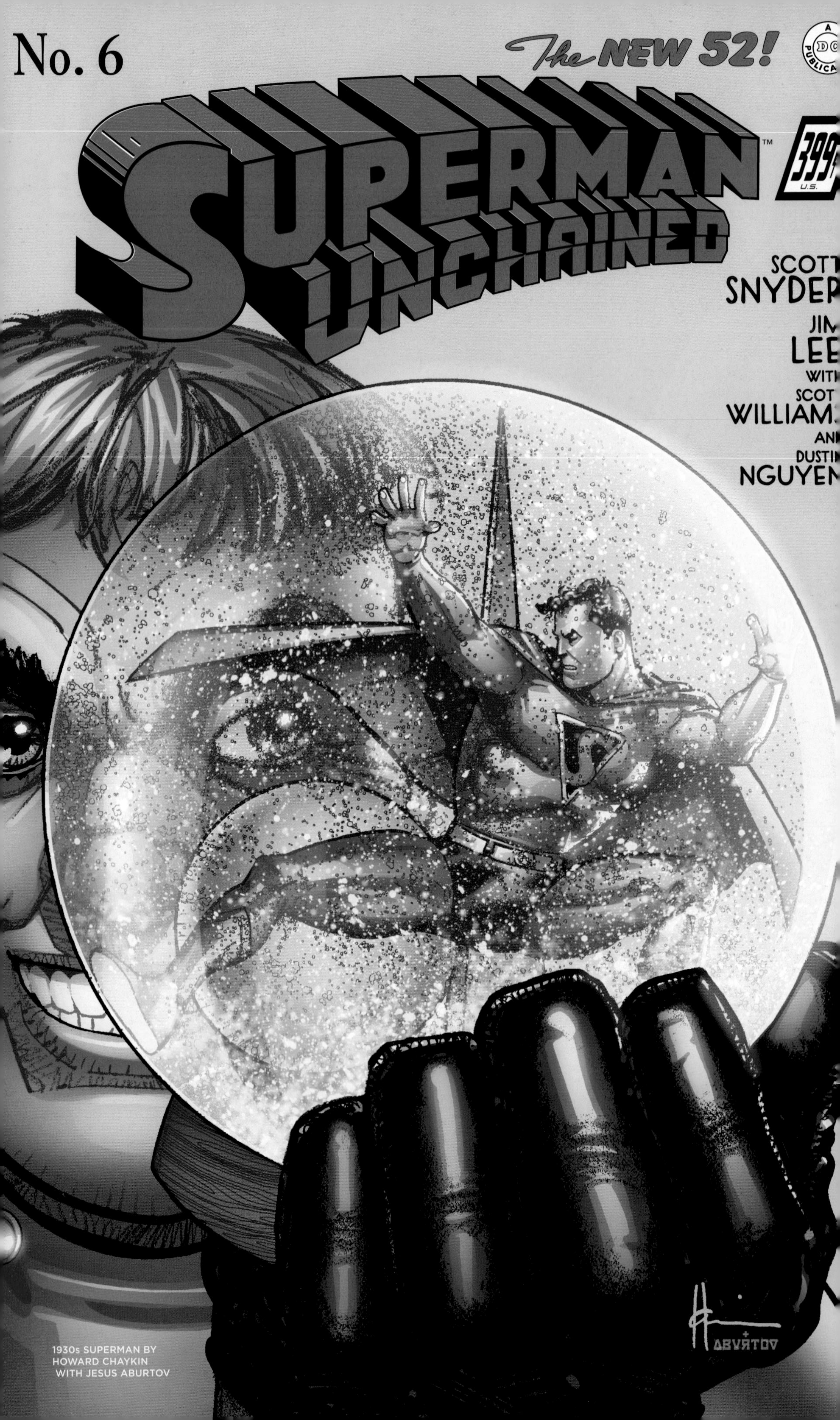
No. 6
The NEW 52!
A DC PUBLICATION
SUPERMAN UNCHAINED
$3.99 U.S.
SCOTT SNYDER
JIM LEE
WITH
SCOTT WILLIAMS
AND
DUSTIN NGUYEN
1930s SUPERMAN BY
HOWARD CHAYKIN
WITH JESUS ABURTOV
ABURTOV

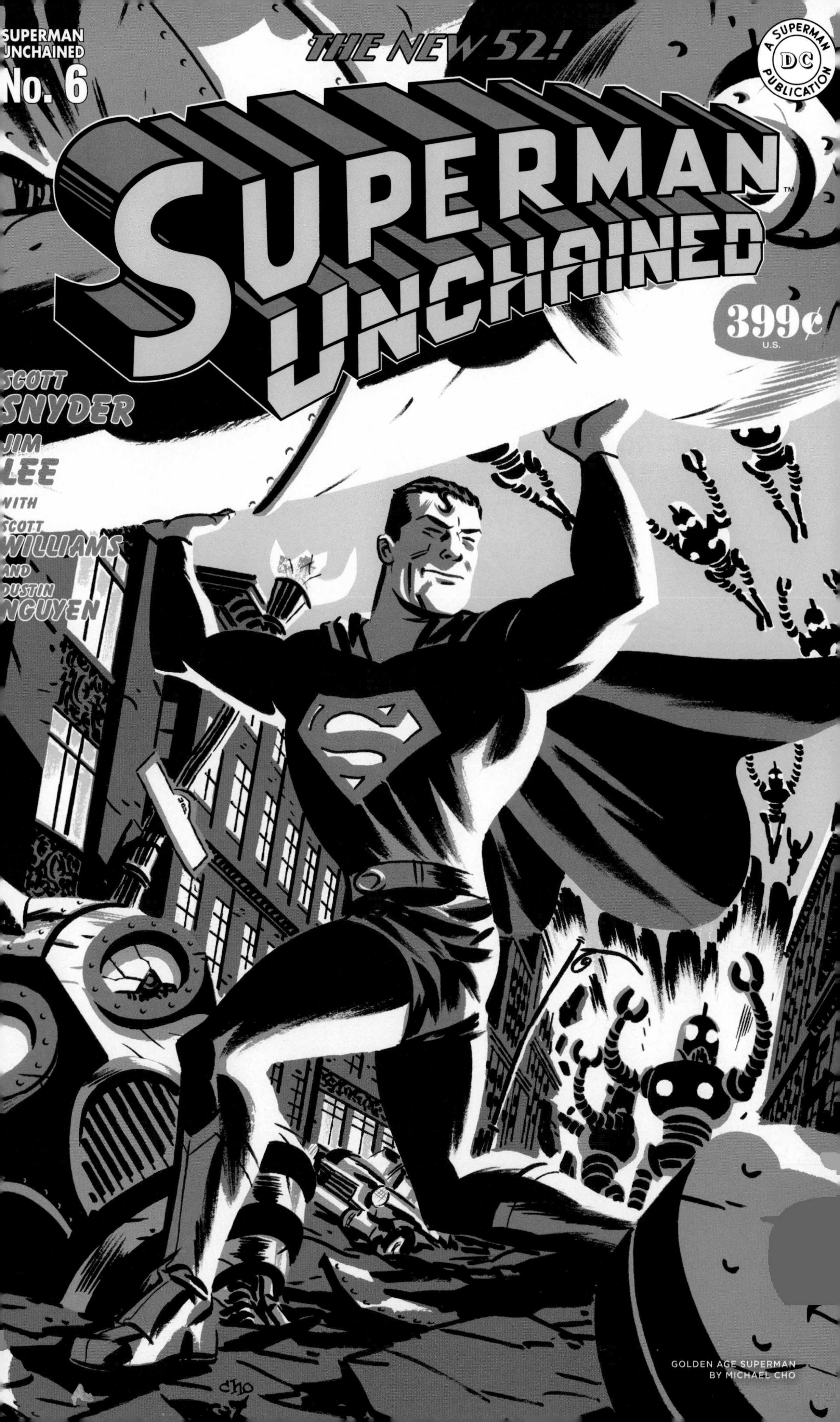
SUPERMAN UNCHAINED
No. 6
THE NEW 52!
A SUPERMAN DC PUBLICATION
SUPERMAN™
UNCHAINED
399¢ U.S.
SCOTT SNYDER
JIM LEE
WITH
SCOTT WILLIAMS
AND
DUSTIN NGUYEN
CHO
GOLDEN AGE SUPERMAN
BY MICHAEL CHO

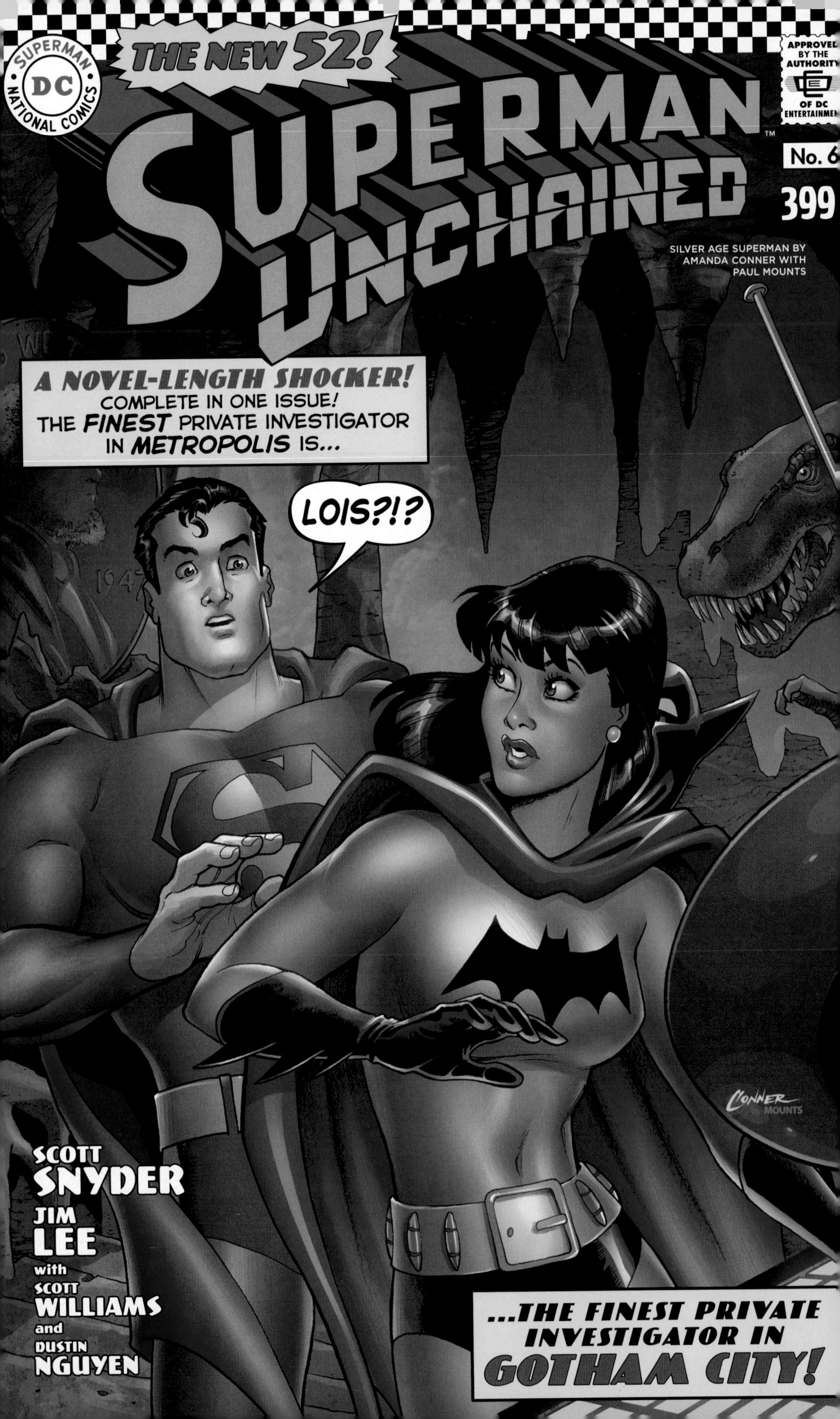

SUPERMAN DC NATIONAL COMICS
THE NEW 52!
APPROVED BY THE AUTHORITY OF DC ENTERTAINMENT
SUPERMAN UNCHAINED
No. 6
399
SILVER AGE SUPERMAN BY AMANDA CONNER WITH PAUL MOUNTS
A NOVEL-LENGTH SHOCKER!
COMPLETE IN ONE ISSUE!
THE FINEST PRIVATE INVESTIGATOR IN METROPOLIS IS...
LOIS?!?
...THE FINEST PRIVATE INVESTIGATOR IN GOTHAM CITY!
SCOTT SNYDER
JIM LEE
with SCOTT WILLIAMS and DUSTIN NGUYEN
CONNER MOUNTS

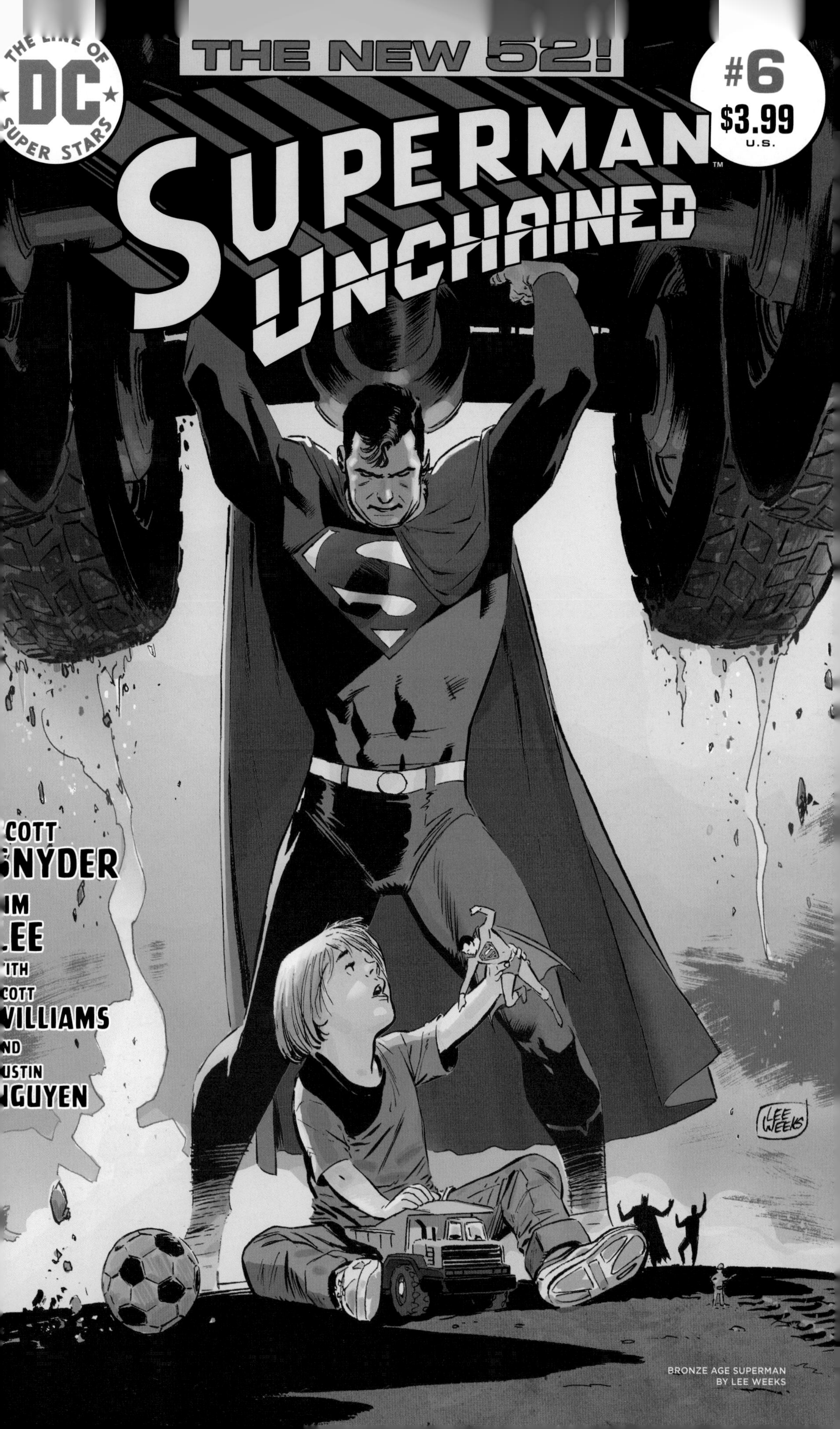
THE LINE OF DC SUPER STARS
THE NEW 52!
#6
$3.99
U.S.
SUPERMAN UNCHAINED
COTT
SNYDER
IM
LEE
ITH
COTT
WILLIAMS
ND
USTIN
NGUYEN
LEE WEEKS

BRONZE AGE SUPERMAN
BY LEE WEEKS

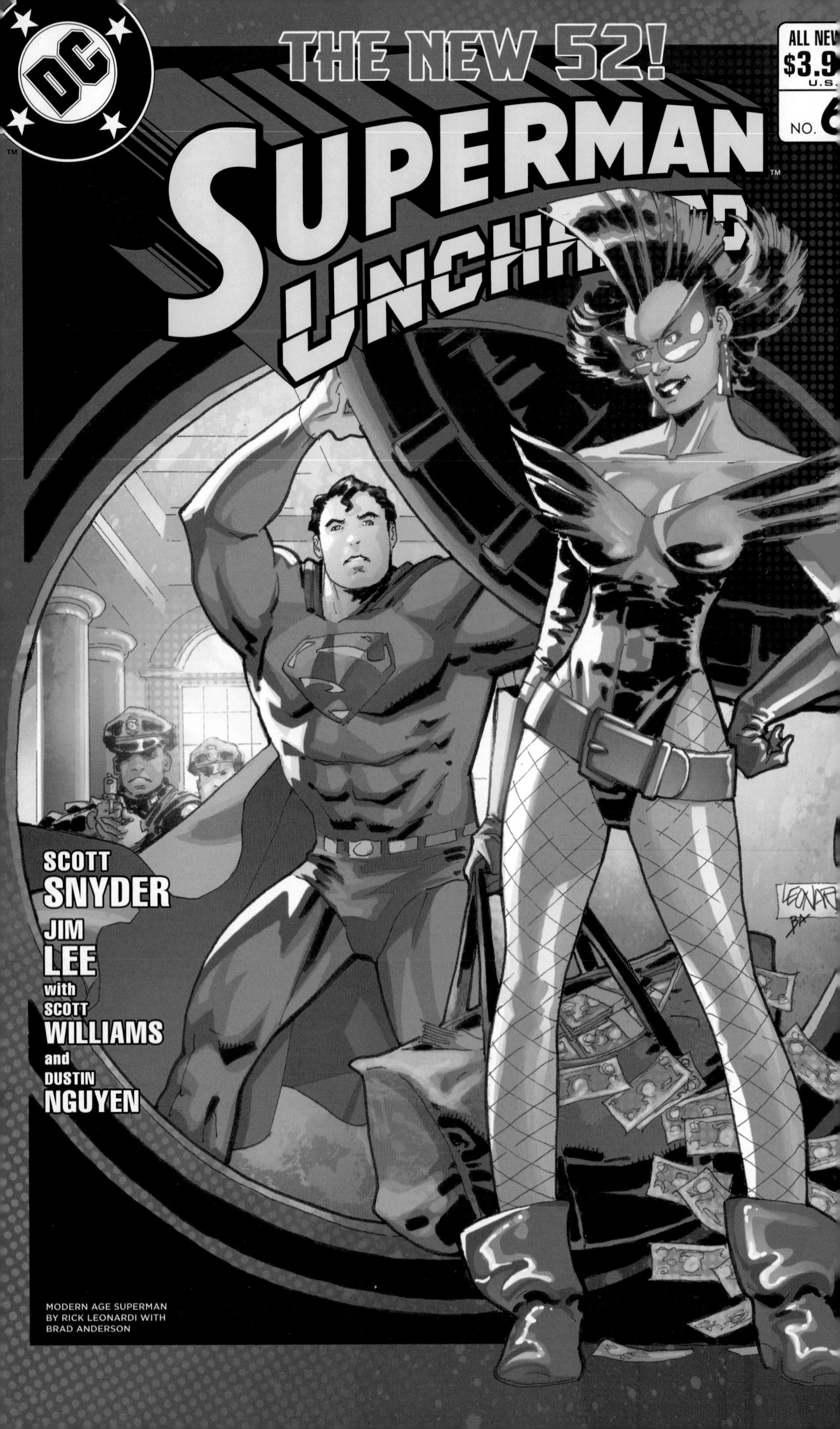
DC
THE NEW 52!
ALL NEW
$3.9
U.S.
NO. 6
SUPERMAN
UNCHAINED
SCOTT
SNYDER
JIM
LEE
with
SCOTT
WILLIAMS
and
DUSTIN
NGUYEN
MODERN AGE SUPERMAN
BY RICK LEONARDI WITH
BRAD ANDERSON

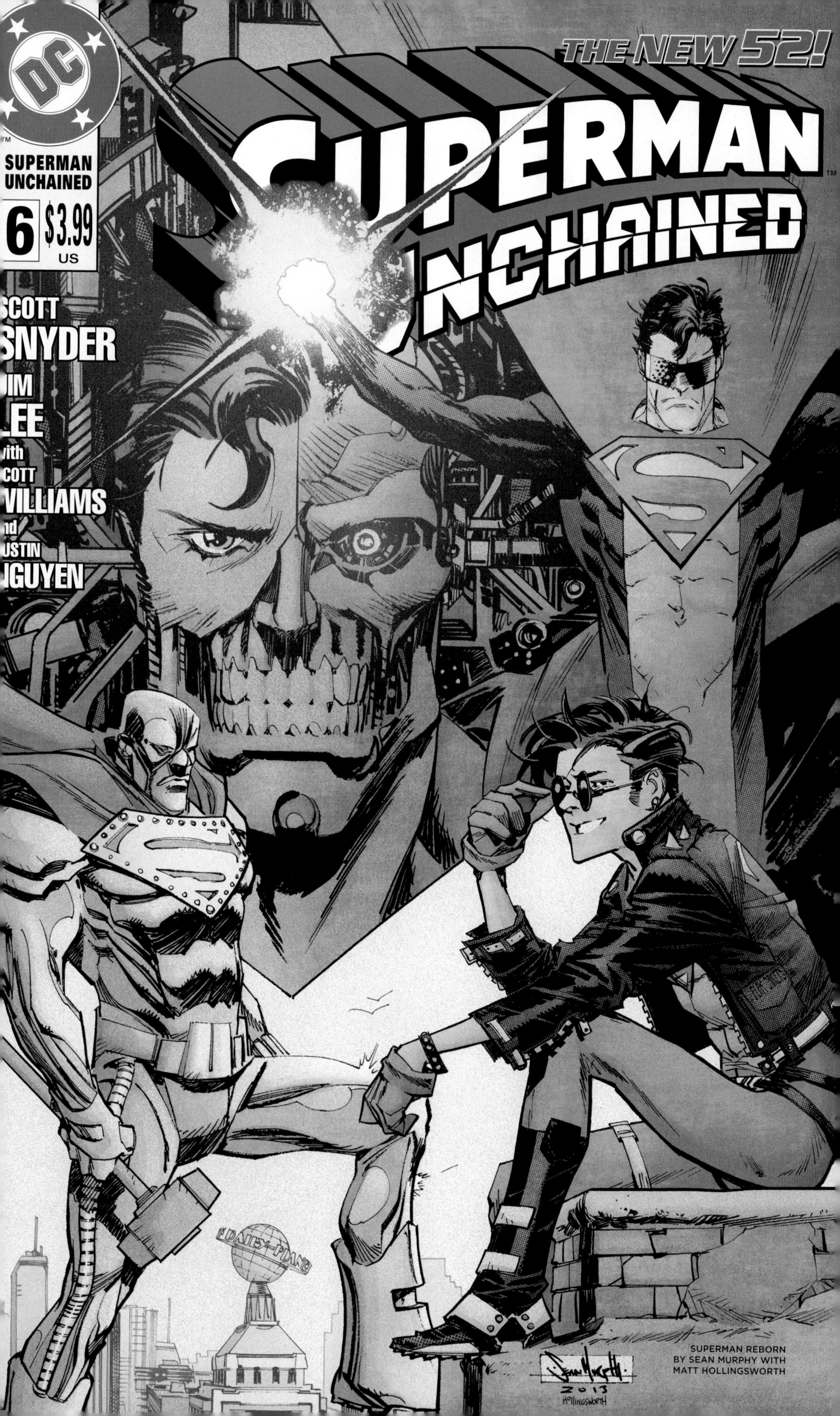
THE NEW 52!
SUPERMAN UNCHAINED
SUPERMAN UNCHAINED
6 $3.99 US
SCOTT SNYDER
JIM LEE
with SCOTT WILLIAMS and DUSTIN NGUYEN
DAILY PLANET

SUPERMAN REBORN
BY SEAN MURPHY WITH
MATT HOLLINGSWORTH

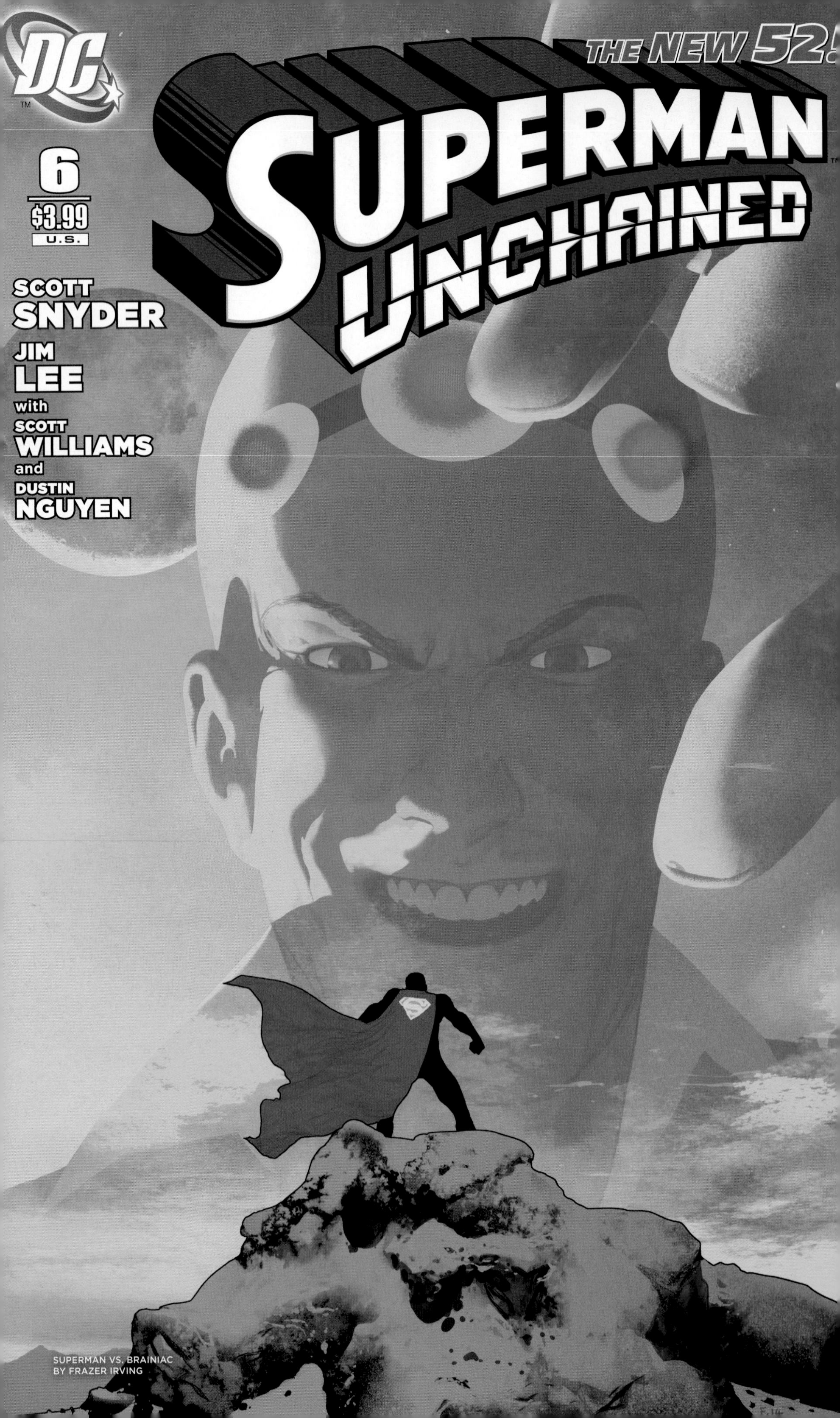

THE NEW 52!
SUPERMAN UNCHAINED
6
$3.99 U.S.
SCOTT SNYDER
JIM LEE
with
SCOTT WILLIAMS
and
DUSTIN NGUYEN
SUPERMAN VS. BRAINIAC
BY FRAZER IRVING

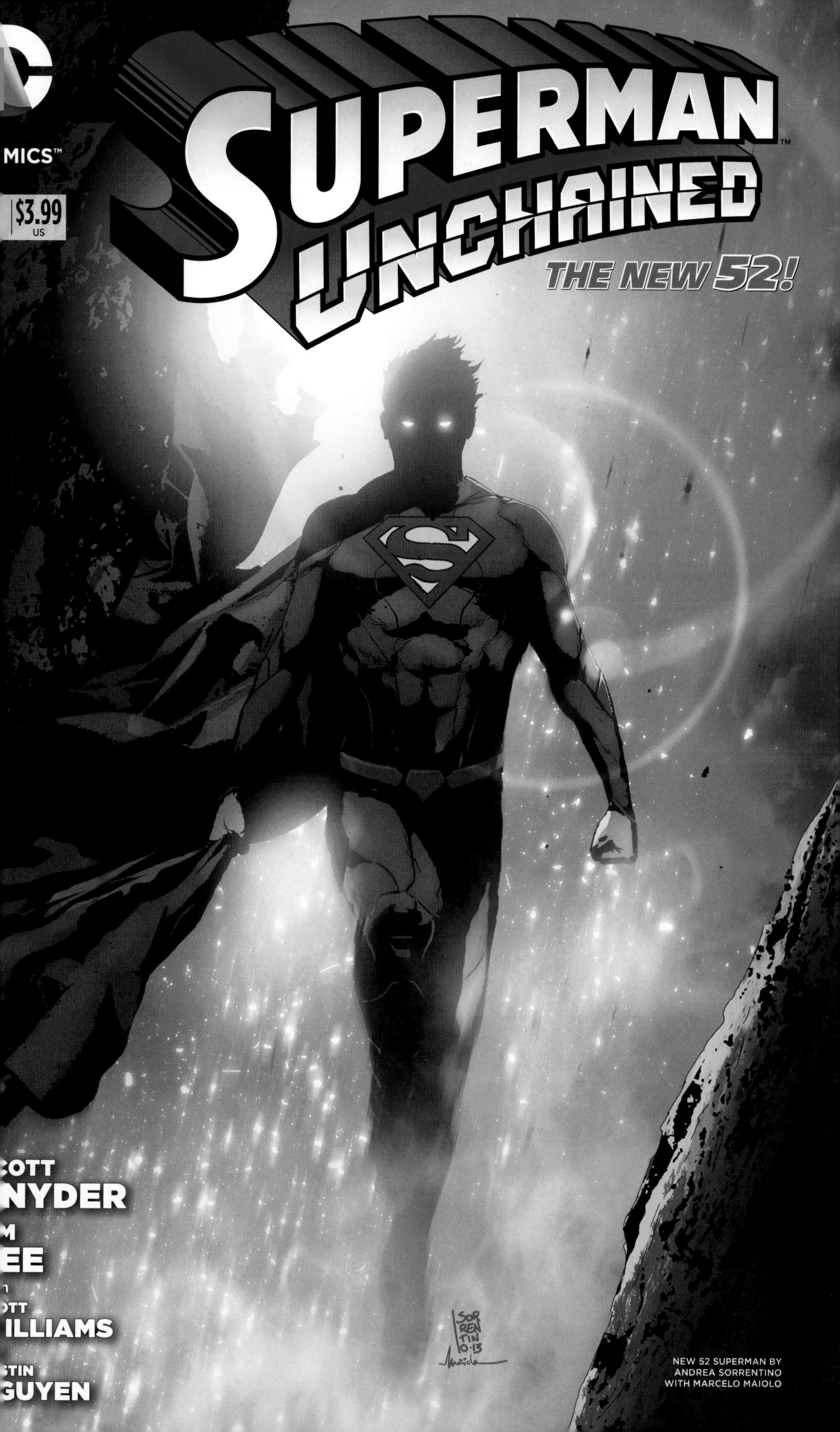
MICS™
$3.99
US
SUPERMAN™
UNCHAINED
THE NEW 52!
OTT
NYDER
M
EE
OTT
ILLIAMS
STIN
GUYEN
SOR
REN
TIN
10·13
NEW 52 SUPERMAN BY
ANDREA SORRENTINO
WITH MARCELO MAIOLO

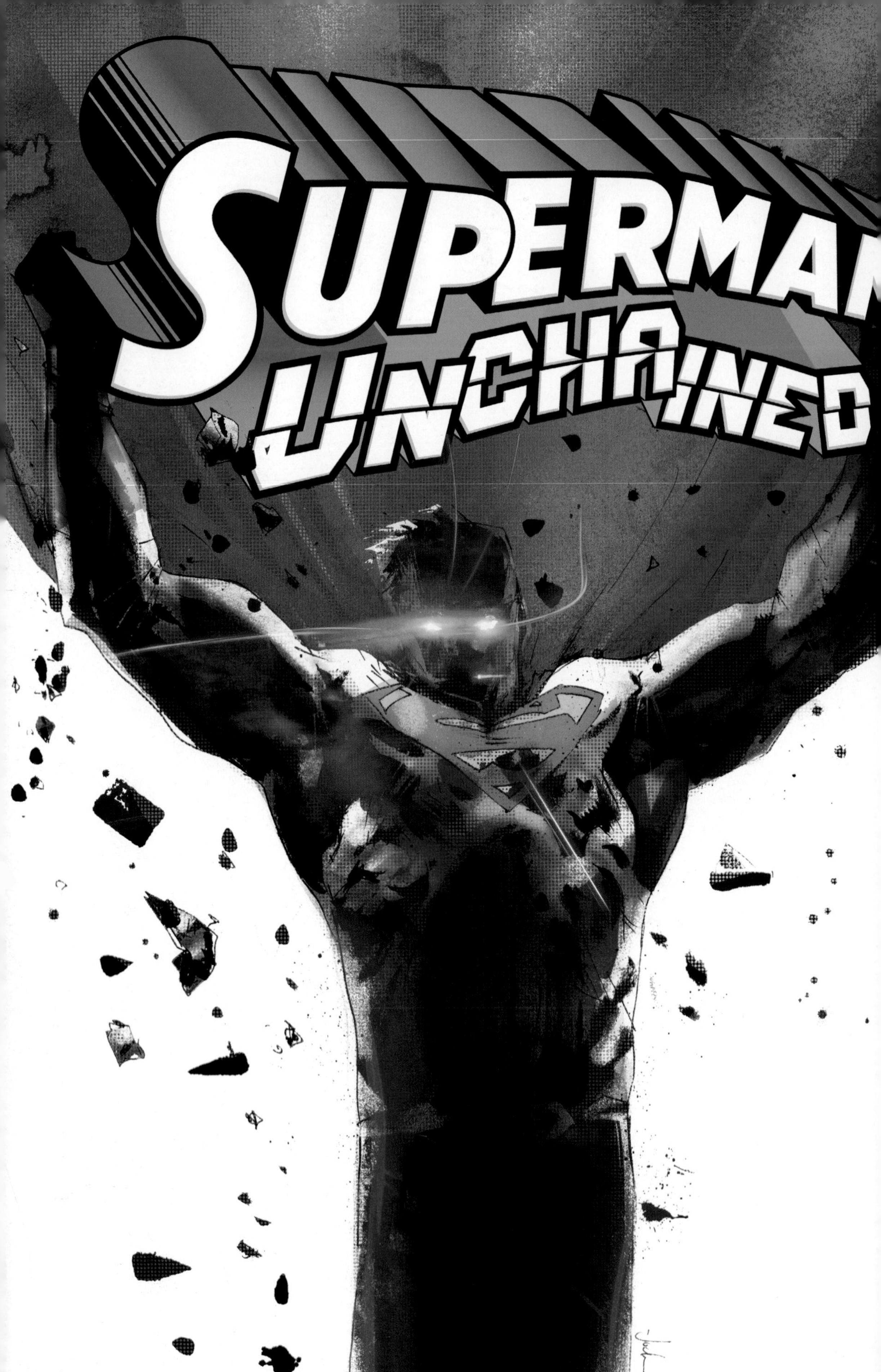
SUPERMAN
UNCHAINED

ART BY JOCK

ART BY ANDY KUBERT AND BRAD ANDERSON

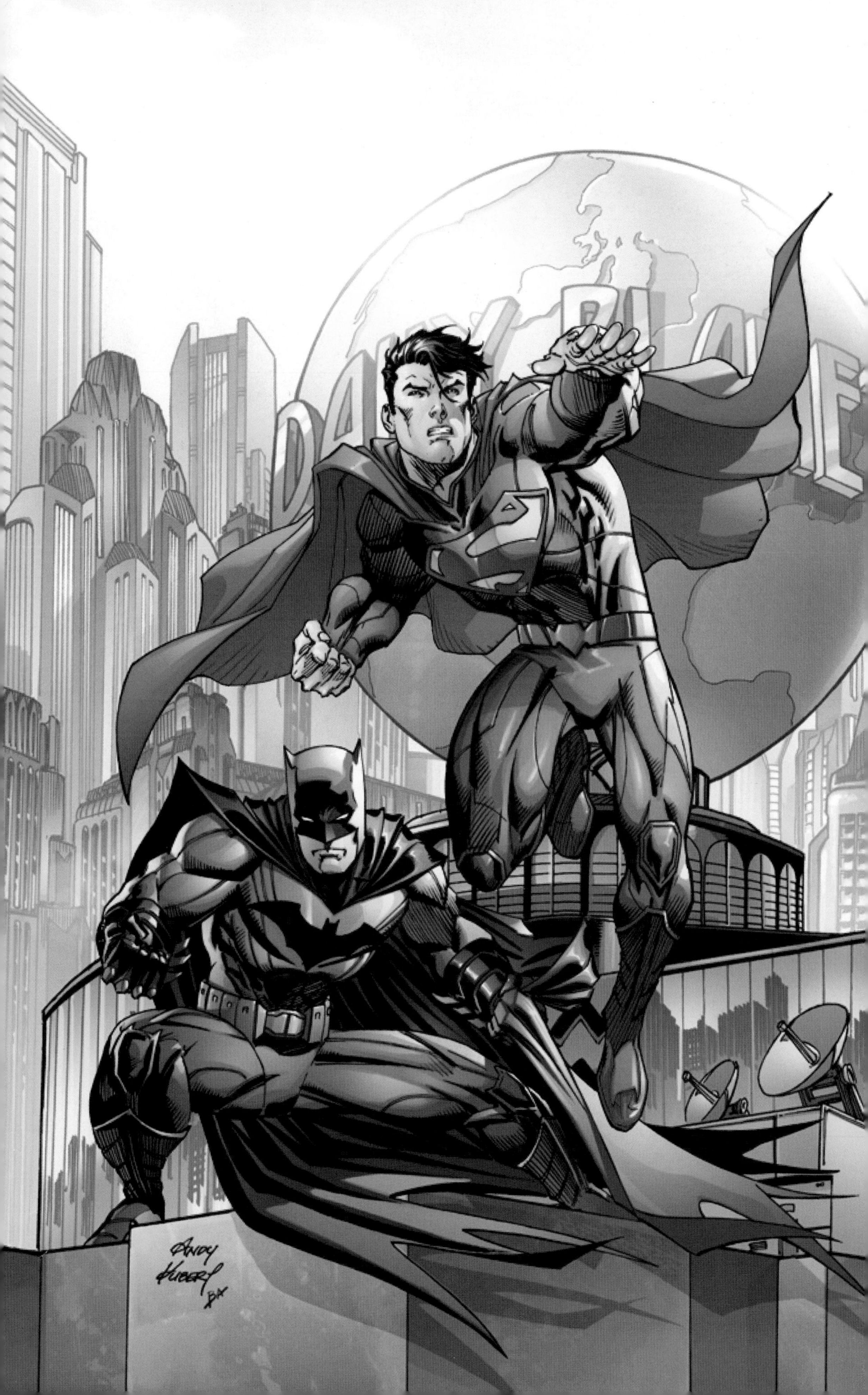

ART BY DUSTIN NGUYEN

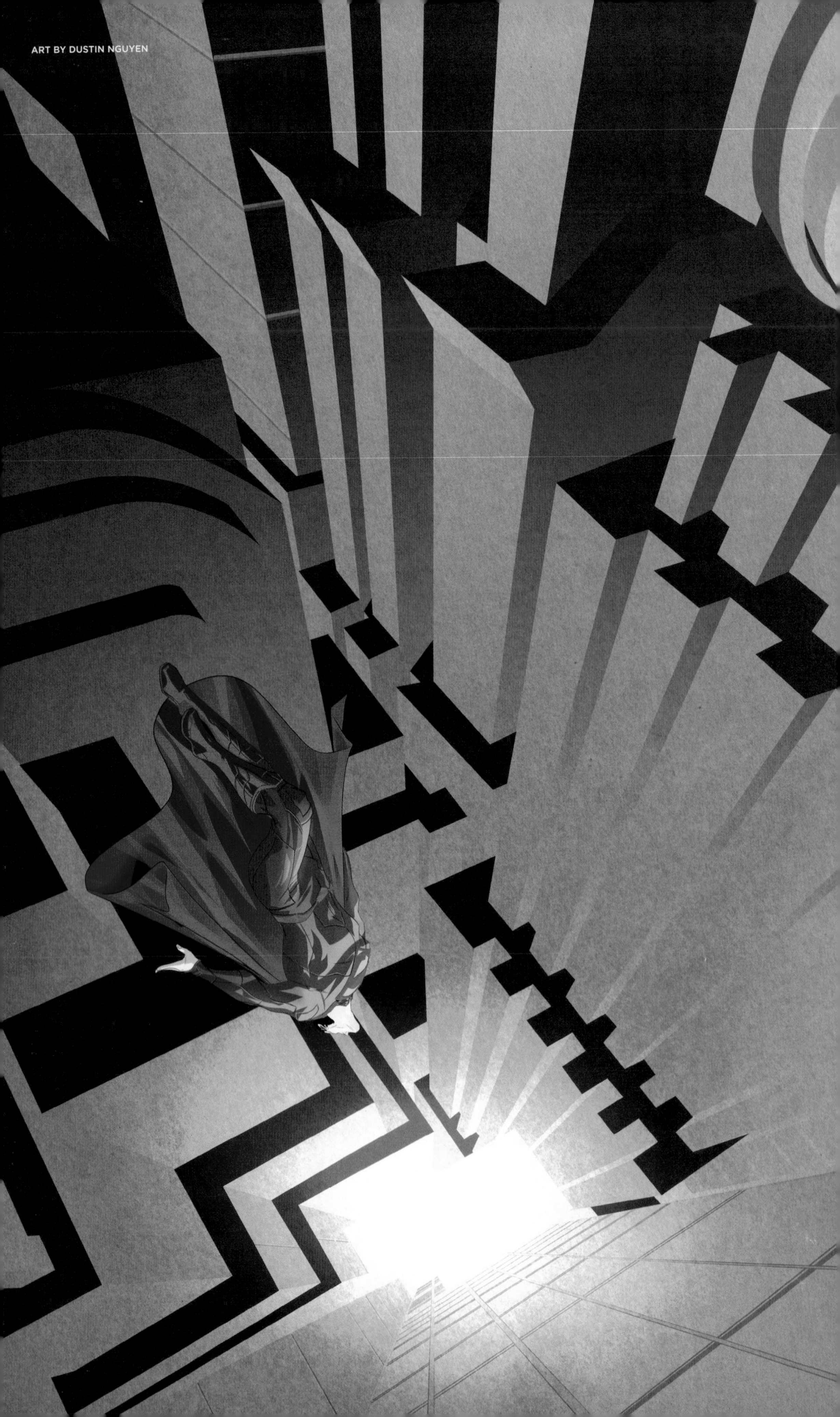

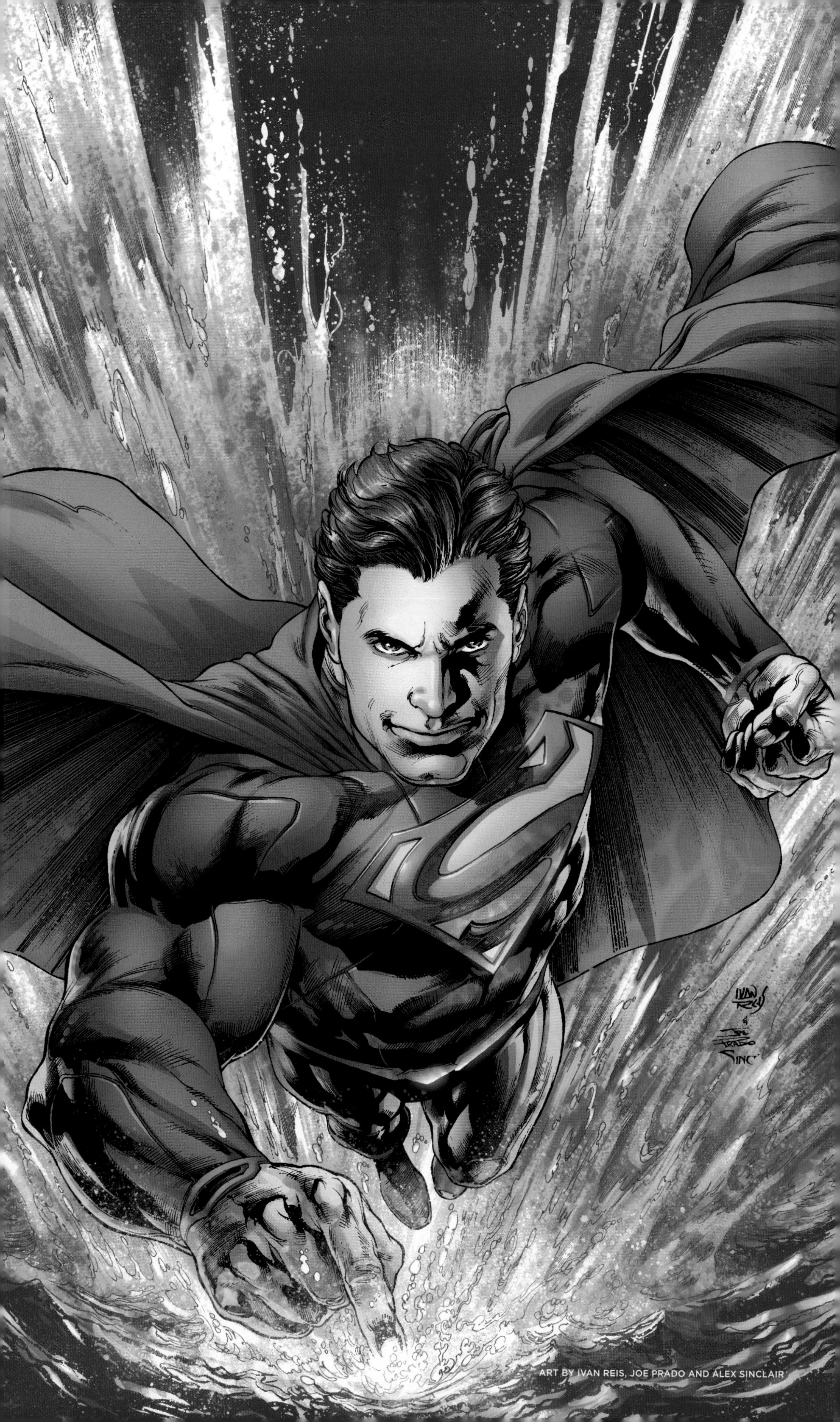
ART BY IVAN REIS, JOE PRADO AND ALEX SINCLAIR

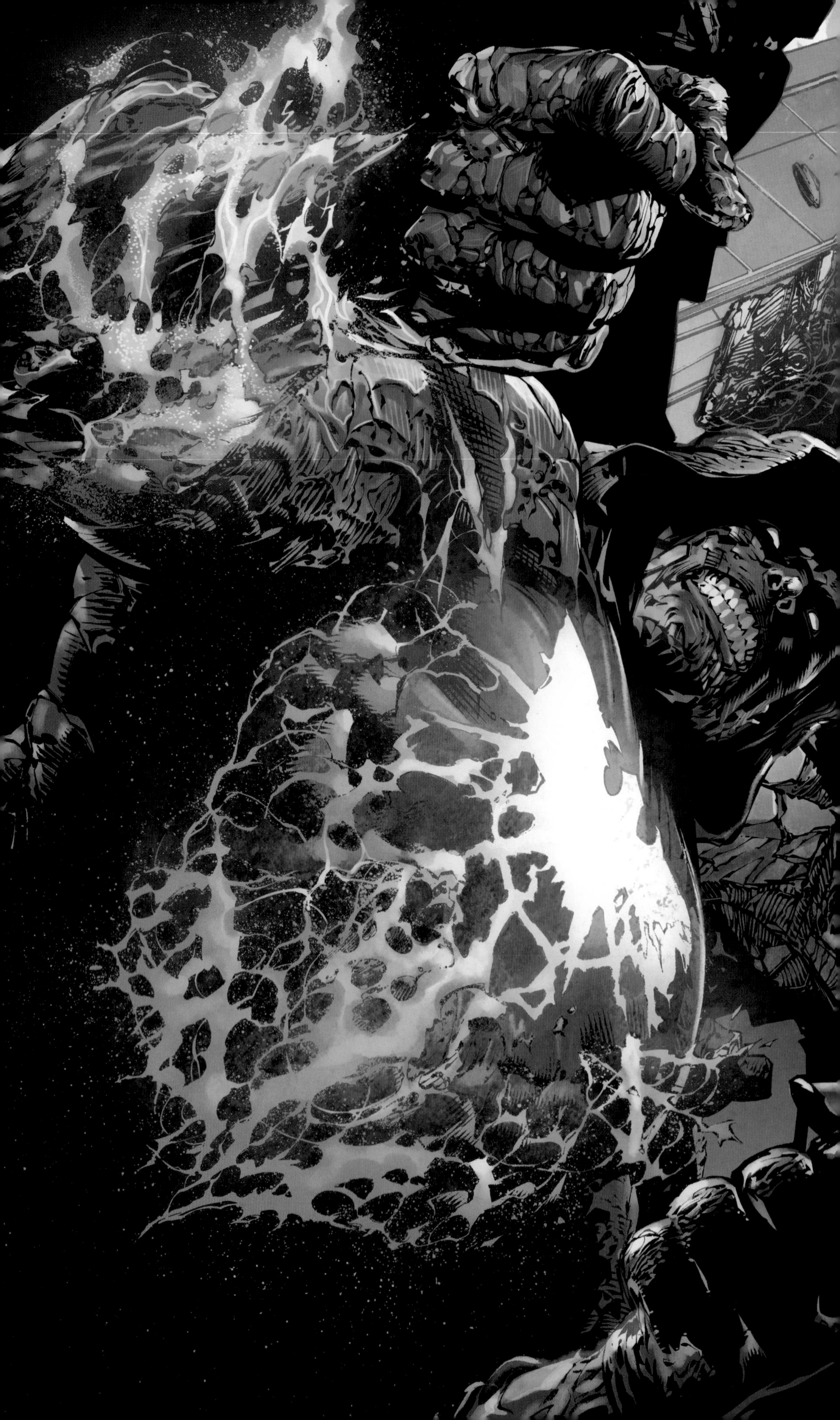

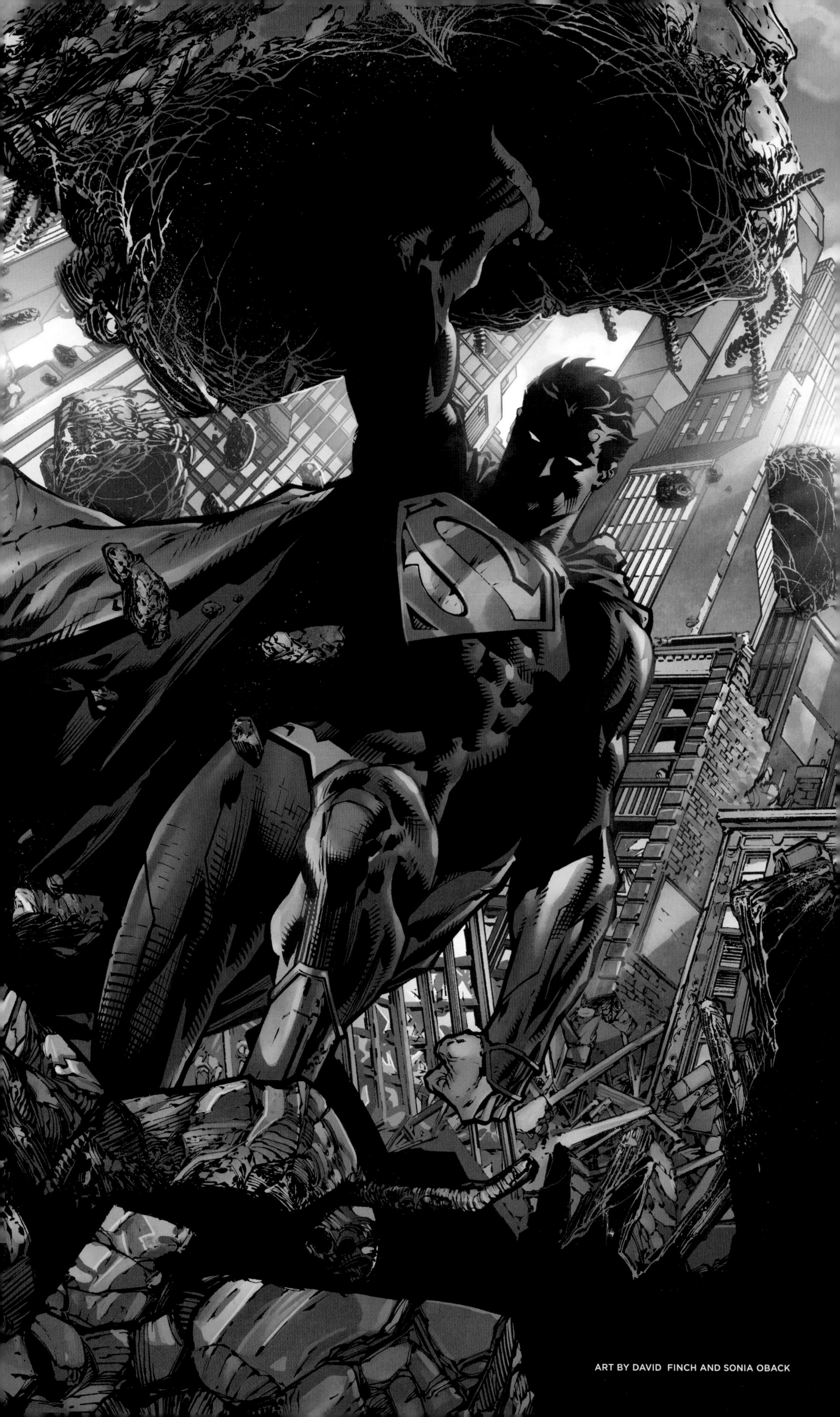

ART BY DAVID FINCH AND SONIA OBACK

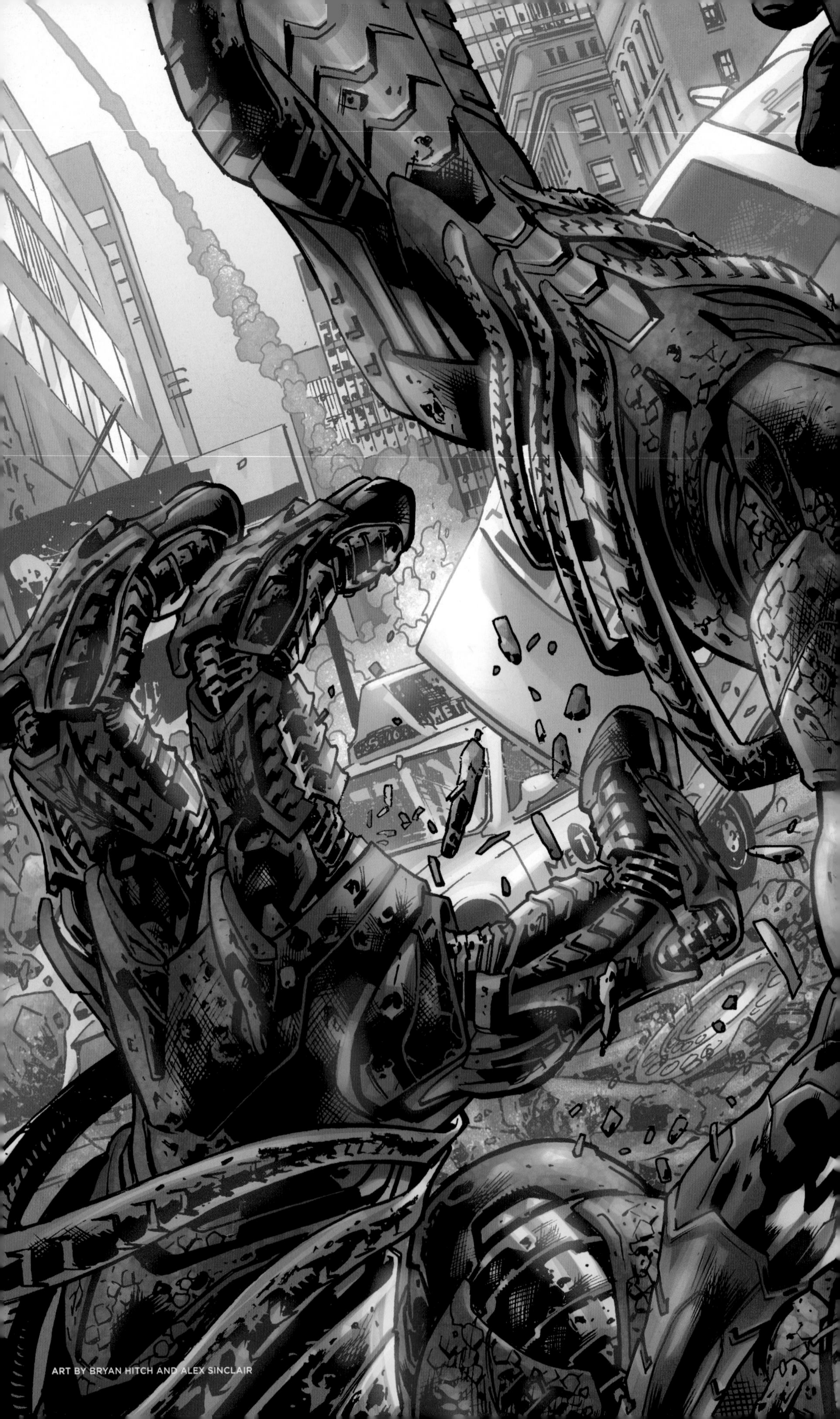

ART BY BRYAN HITCH AND ALEX SINCLAIR

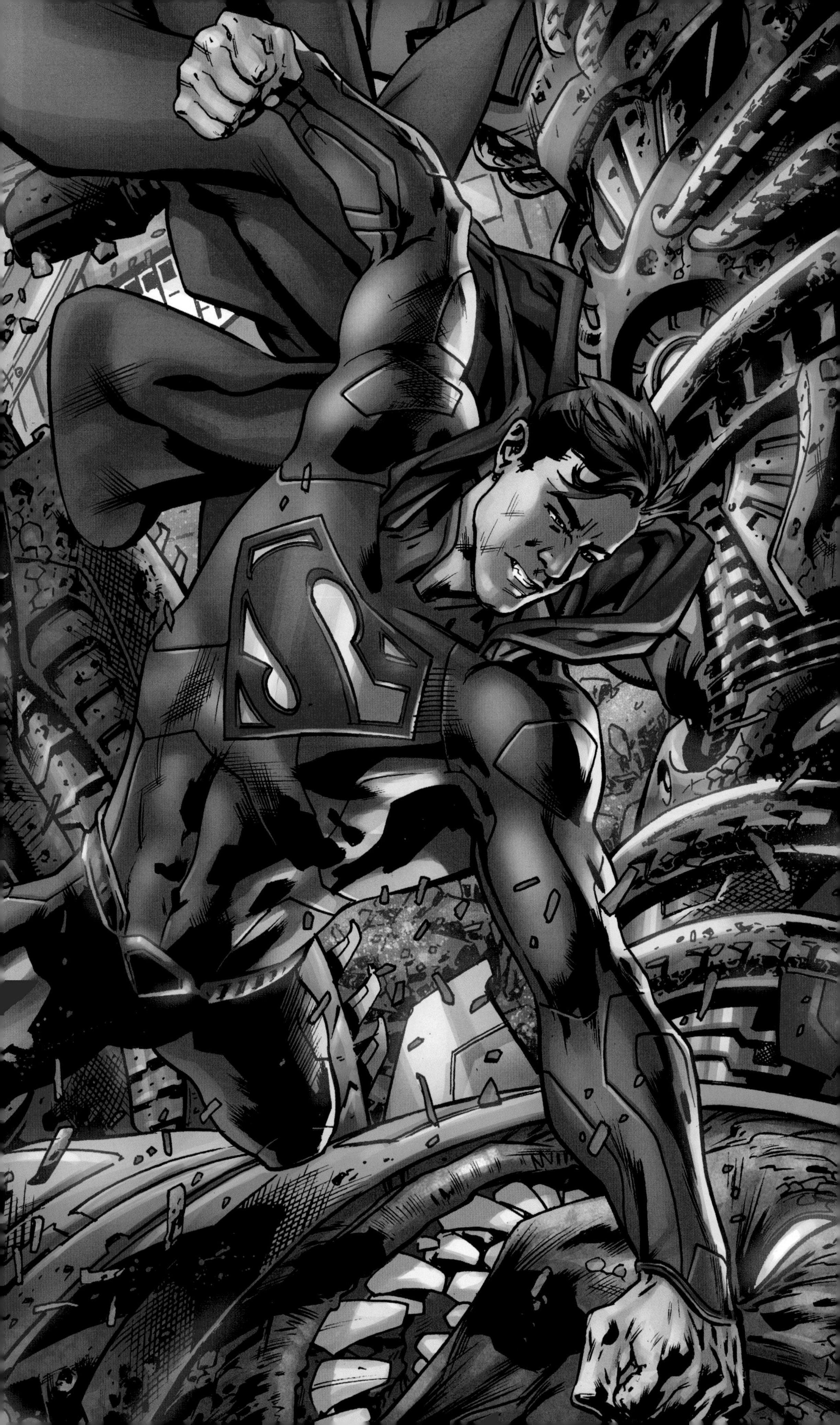

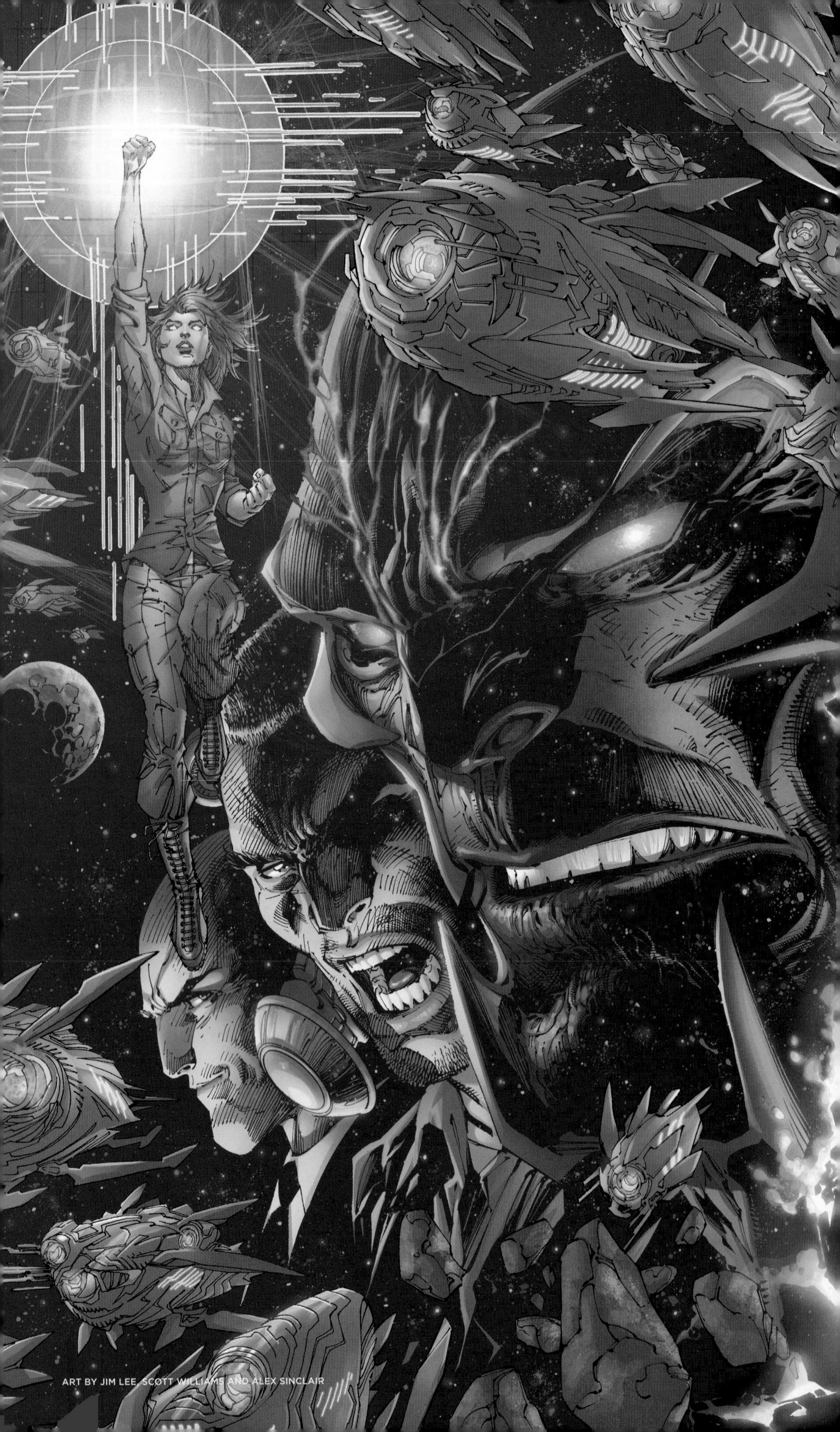

ART BY JIM LEE, SCOTT WILLIAMS AND ALEX SINCLAIR

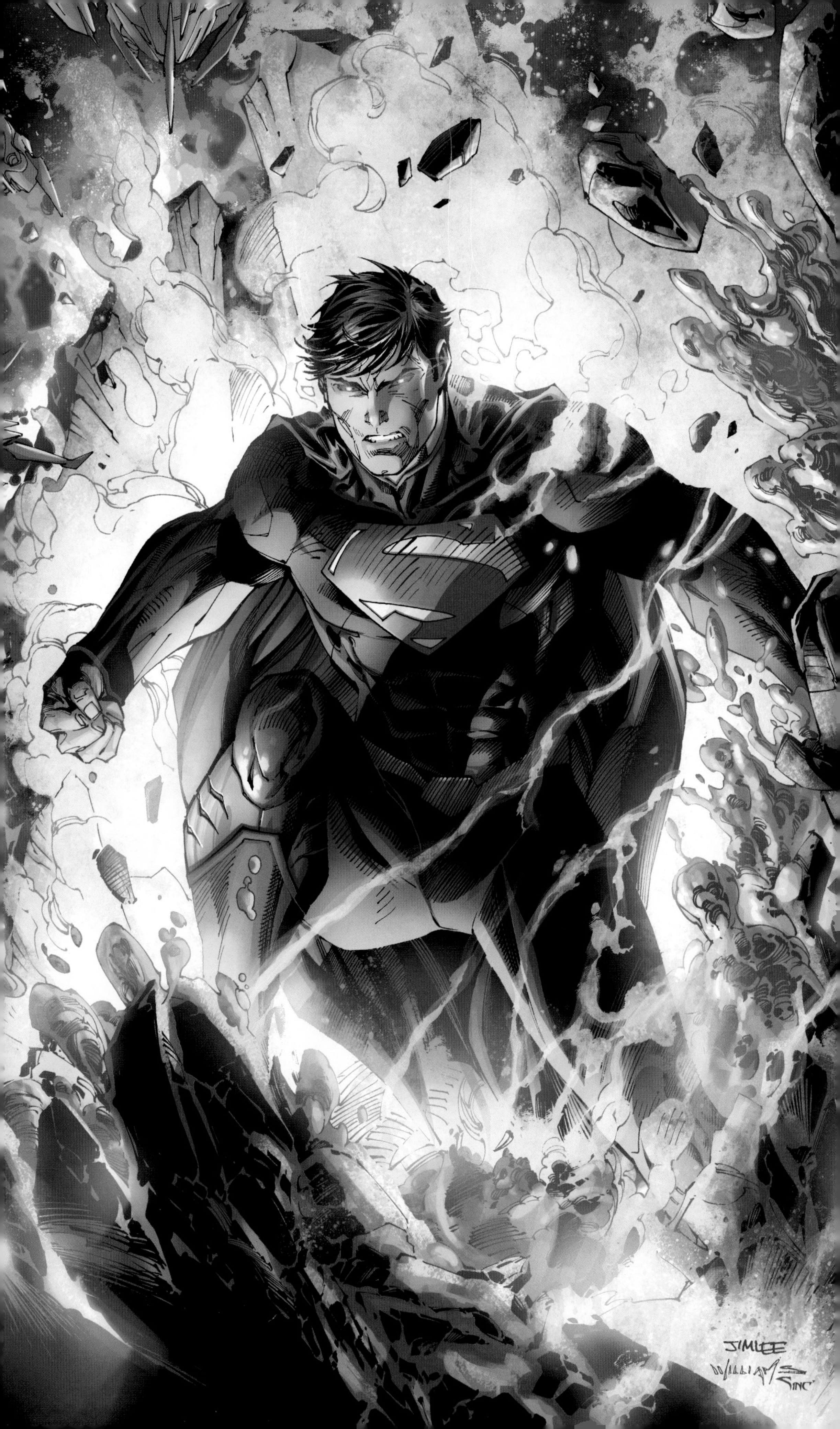
JIMLEE

SUPERMAN UNCHAINED

PAGE 1

The scene – we're in a modest home in Nagasaki, the morning of the city's atomic destruction. A young boy is drawing a picture as his mother and father discuss the rumors of a doomsday weapon that may or may not have wiped out Hiroshima three days prior.

1.
A chalk drawing of the sun. A child's drawing, colored in yellow.

> AIKA (OFF-PANEL): <The fury from the skies, though...>

> AIKA (OFF-PANEL): <...They say the fury was unlike anything before.>

2.
Now we see the scene. In the fore, ICHIRU, 7, on the floor, drawing a picture with chalk on paper as his parents, HIDEKI (early 30s) and AIKA (same, early 30s) talk in the background. They sit at a small table, eating modest breakfasts – cracked bowls of nori and rice.

> CAPTION: Nagasaki. August 9th, 1945.

> AIKA: < And if such a weapon exists, Hideki, no city will be safe. We could move, still. To your cousin's.>

> HIDEKI: <My cousin makes paste and lives in a shelter, Aika. Stop it.>

3.
But now ICHURU looks up, like he hears something...

> HIDEKI: <Ichuru, come eat before lessons.>

> ICHURU: <...coming.>

4.
CUT TO: A SLIVER of a CLOSE-UP of the propeller of "BOCKSCAR" the B-29 BOMBER that delivered "FAT MAN" to its drop site over Nagasaki. It's thousands of feet up, approaching the city.

5.
Now we're back in the room: AIKA and HIDEKI in the fore, talking to each other, not noticing ICHIRU walking toward the door to their home in the background, back to them, and us.

> AIKA: <Look, I'm simply saying that if the reports are true, then -->

> HIDEKI: <No one knows what's true right now, Aika. Maybe it was a bomb. Maybe it was many bombs. Maybe it was an angel of death. He flew down from the heavens and burned Hiroshima to the ground. The point is, we don't know.>

6.
ICHIRU out on the porch of their home, in the busy commercial district of Nagasaki. The streets are bustling with people going about their day – it's morning. Already that morning there have been two air-raid scares, so people are tired, nervous. He is raising a dingy set of BINOCULARS to his eyes.

> HIDEKI: <And until we do, I ask you to stop talking about it in front the boy. You'll scare him.>

PAGES 2-3

Jim, I thought doing this sequence through a series of circular views of the binoculars, as seen by ICHIRU, could be a cool, emotionally gripping way of doing it - constrained, claustrophobic, really experiencing it with ICHIRU.

The idea would be to follow the circular panels across the spread - to read a row horizontally across pages 2 and 3, then go to the next row, read horizontally again, then the same for the final row.

The dead space behind the circular panels we could leave black, or color as sky, or anything you think.

I think this could be something different from us that underscores the story in an evocative way here.

PAGE 2-3 CONTINUED...

1.
CIRCULAR PANEL. The SKY. A CLOUD. We're looking with ICHIRU through the binoculars at the sky for this sequence. Love it to have the unstable jerky feel of that.

AIKA CAPTION: <"Maybe he should be scared. Maybe we should all be—">

HIDEKI CAPTION: <"Hold on. Ichuru? Ichuru what is it? Birds? The ducks should be returning any day now.">

ICHURU: < "No, father. Not birds."

2.
CIRCULAR PANEL. From the cloud, a PLANE emerges. It's BOCKSCAR, right over the city.

ICHURU CAPTION: <"It's a plane. Just one.">

AIKA CAPTION: <"Plane!? Did you say a plane, Ichuru?">

HIDEKI CAPTION: < "Calm down, Aika. If it's only one, it's nothing. A scout. You know that. Ichuru, now come eat.">

3.
CIRCULAR PANEL. We see a dark shape drop from the plane... BOCKSCAR has just dropped the bomb, FAT MAN. But the shape could be a little blurry, uncertain.

ICHURU CAPTION: < "Father!">

4.
CIRCULAR PANEL. The SKY – ICHIRU is frantically searching for whatever just dropped. Maybe movement lines, blur – we're searching for the bomb with him.

HIDEKI CAPTION: <"What? What is it!?">

HIDEKI: <"What did you see, son?">

5.
CIRCULAR PANEL. He finds it – clearly it's a BOMB.

ICHURU CAPTION < "I think it's... it was a --">

AIKA CAPTION: < "Is it a bomb? A bomb? Hideki!">

6.
CIRCULAR PANEL. But then the BOMB breaks open, revealing what seems to be a human shape...

ICHURU CAPTION: <No, momma! It's not a bomb...">

HIDEKI CAPTION: "Well, what then?">

7.
CIRCULAR PANEL. A MAN inside – the man is in silhouette, but seems to cut a similar profile to SUPERMAN, if a little bigger.

ICHURU CAPTION < "It's... it's a man!">

8.
CIRCULAR PANEL. BLURRY, as the BINOCULARS readjust.

HIDEKI CAPTION < "A man? Falling? Give me those...>

ICHURU CAPTION: <"No, wait! Let me!">

9.
CIRCULAR PANEL. Now we're CLOSER on the MAN, his eyes are burning red! Looking right at us, like an angry SUPERMAN.

ICHURU CAPTION < "I see him. But...">

HIDEKI CAPTION < "But what?">

ICHURU CAPTION < "But it's not a man at all.">

SUPERMAN UNCHAINED

PAGE 2-3 CONTINUED...

10.
CIRCULAR PANEL. The MAN'S whole body is heating up, his eyes blazing red - clearly, he's about to cause some kind of bio-electric explosion.

ICHURU CAPTION < "It's... it's him. It's--">

11.
WHITE, from a blast. The BINOCULAR LENSES crack and bubble with heat. We're being slammed by the blast.

12.
WHITE, fading to BLACK, to transition to...

PAGE 4

1.
...Space. We're looking at black, starlit space.

CAPTION: Now.

SUPERMAN V.O.: We had a game in the summers, when I was growing up called the "tall leap."

2.
A red/blue STREAK races into the panel, headed down, to the left on a diagonal tack. SUPERMAN rocketing towards Earth.

SUPERMAN V.O.: There was a farm near Pete Ross's place, owned by a man named Jed Tall. He was the only farmer in Smallville who still used old-fashioned haystacks instead of bales. The big mountains of hay left out in the sun on planks to dry.

3.
SUPERMAN'S fists, heating up, as he reenters the atmosphere. His eyes behind them, determined.

SUPERMAN V.O.: He'd harvest late, in August, so Lana, Pete and I would go to his farm one night around then, and we'd climb to the top of his silo, and we'd jump, thirty feet down, into the stack below.

4.
We're behind him now - we see the earth in the distance, in front of him; he's barreling toward an object falling toward earth ahead of him. This object is actually a prototypical AMERICAN SPACE STATION. Something brand new the government hasn't yet revealed to the public. We can see the basic idea of it here, about five hundred yards ahead of SUPERMAN, but the sheer size of the thing isn't clear to us yet.

SUPERMAN V.O.: "The Tall Leap."

SUPERMAN V.O.: I think of that sometimes, when I'm coming back in from out there. How similar reentry feels to that fall from Jed Tall's silo. How fast the world suddenly goes from being an image in the darkness, this vision of blue and green, glowing in the blackness, to oceans and trees.

SUPERMAN V.O.: Falling from that silo, the fields you saw from the sky rushing toward you, taking on detail and texture, becoming real. All of it happening so fast...

PAGES 5-6

SPLASH - BOOM! SUPERMAN crashing through the SPACE STATION like a missile. The SPACE STATION is huge, the size of a small city block! But this image is all about SUPER-MAN. The first time we see him, in all his glory. As he just smashed through the SPACE STATION (I was thinking he smashed through its propulsion system, to slow it down), he could be covered in fire, coolant, anything you think will make the most incredibly heroic and memorable image possible. (Fire could be pretty awesome, though!:))

As for the SPACE STATION itself, it's high-tech, super-modern, and it has heavy defenses. Shields for asteroid hits. Lasers to cut thickest metal, even missiles to destroy detritus. I imagine it has multiple titanium arms that extend from its core when it needs - all of which will be fighting SUPERMAN in a sec. It's going to be attacking him with everything it's got.

SUPERMAN V.O.: ... you had to remind yourself to brace for hit.

PAGE 5-6 CONTINUED...

[NOTE: Jim, the story SUPERMAN just told will be a bit of a recurring theme – that notion of the ideal vs. the reality. Something seen from above, or through memory, something ideal versus the reality of the thing, good or bad. The conflicts of moving from one to the other, how they don't always match up, for example when Superman...[redacted]

PAGE 7

1.
SUPERMAN, turning to face/fly back up towards the plunging SPACE STATION as it now racing toward him, no longer propelled by its thrusters, but by gravity. He looks badass. Like he's going to go to war with this thing – he could still be somewhat on fire here, too.

> SUPERMAN V.O.: The U.S.S Intrepid... [here Superman explains that this space station is an American prototype of a new sort. It's made to repair satellites and so it has all sorts of tools for that.

He also explains how it's the seventh thing to fall from space in the last hour. Each thing before was a satellite, weaponized and aimed to crash into and blow up US military bases. He'll make a joke about Chicken Little, the sky seems to be falling today. In fact, even now, as he's stopping this one, he's getting word that an eighth object – another satellite – has fallen from the sky over Southeast Asia. The narration will run through the next couple of panels.]

2.
SUPERMAN now bracing himself against a sealed PORTAL into the SPACE STATION.

3.
SUPERMAN tosses the doors away, revealing TWO ASTRONAUTS inside the SPACE STATION. They're wearing jumpsuits, but not full gear. They're strapped into their seats, terrified. They have clear oxygen masks over their mouths and noses.

> ASTRONAUT 1: Superman, thank God! The whole station just suddenly went crazy!

> ASTRONAUT 2: It's like it... I don't know, like it has a mind of its own! It's gone rogue! Help us, please!

4.
SUPERMAN, looking badass as he has them now by their jumpsuits. Eyes could be still steaming or red if you like, Jim!

> SUPERMAN: Trust me.

5.
And flings them out into the air! The idea here, Jim, is that he is getting them out of the way the only way he can, so he can demolish this SPACE STATION, which he knows will soon start fighting with him to the death. SUPERMAN is watching them fall.

PAGE 8-10

FIGHT SEQEUNCE!

PAGE 8

1.
WHAM! The GIANT TITANIUM CLAW of the SPACE STATION grabs SUPERMAN around the neck and face.

Again, I'll use narration here to explain the INTREPID'S defenses, and to show SUPERMAN'S thinking as he figures out how to bring it down.

2.
SUPERMAN smashes the arm and FIRES his HEAT VISION, but...

3.
An ENERGY SHIELD pops up around the whole core of the SPACE STATION, protecting it.

4.
3 more ARMS clamp down on SUPERMAN!

PAGES 8-10 CONTINUED...

5.
Now the SPACE STATION releases dozens of TINY REPAIR BOTS at SUPERMAN. Like a swarm of little DRONES.

PAGE 9

1.
The DRONES swarm SUPERMAN, covering him – or Jim, if you prefer, each could be firing a laser at him, so like dozens of lasers all hitting him at once...whichever you prefer.

The bottom line is – these drones are making it impossible for SUPERMAN to concentrate or focus on destroying the STATION itself, and he's running out of time, the ground is rushing up at them!

2.
DRONES attacking him as he stares at the SPACE STATION, trying to figure out how to get past its shields. The SHIELDS cover its core, making it impossible to take down.

3.
His eyes radiate – Jim, he's using his X-RAY VISION here, but intensifying it. So anything you think that would suggest that, go for it! The idea is that the shields can't protect against X-RAYS – they're radiation, not a blast of heat or cold. SUPERMAN has outsmarted the SPACE STATION'S COMPUTER.

4.
Small - CLOSE on his eyes, X-RAYS intensifying.

5.
The SPACE STATION starts to flicker, spark. SHIELD dissipating. The DRONES, too.

PAGE 10

1.
SUPERMAN flies down to save the falling ASTRONAUTS, the earth rushing toward them all so fast!

2.
SUPERMAN grabs the ASTRONAUTS...

3.
And then, holding the ASTRONAUTS in one hand, protecting them, he raises his other arm and wham, braces against the plummeting hunk of metal that was the SPACE STATION. The ground below is filled with SOLDIERS watching now, cheering SUPERMAN.

4.
He puts the ASTRONAUTS down. SOLDIERS are already helping them.

    SFX: BEEP. BEEP.

    SUPERMAN: Jimmy? What is it?

    JIMMY (in SUPERMAN'S ear): Clark, you'll never guess what's going down with Superman right now. We're hearing it on the wire here at the Planet.

5.
We see SUPERMAN flying away from the POV of the ASTRONAUTS/SOLDIERS. SUPER-MAN salutes them as he exits.

    JIMMY: They're saying someone sabotaged a bunch of satellites, wired them to explode or something and aimed them at U.S. targets all over the world. They're saying it was Ascension.

    SUPERMAN: The North Koreans wouldn't....

    JIMMY: But with tensions the way they've been lately over the missile shield. Why, you think it was someone else? Who?

JIM LEE

SUPERMAN UNCHAINED

PAGE 11

1.
The scene – we're inside a HYPER MODERN POLICE HELICOPTER (it's Metropolis!) that was transporting 4 PRISONERS to the MAW, the prison at the edge of Metropolis by the falls. But – the 4 PRISONERS have overrun the 5 GUARDS and are desperately fighting with them, leaving the controls of the COPTER unmanned – the situation is dire – this COPTER is diving, twisting...

I imagine this angle as though we're in LUTHOR'S POV – he's sitting strapped into the final seat in the back of the COPTER. So we're looking forward with him at the action in the COPTER, from the back.

> PRISONER 1: Dammit, Luthor, grab the controls! This is our chance to get out of here!

2.
REVERSE ANGLE – We're looking at PRISONER (LEX!), sitting strapped into the final back seat, working on a book – the book is the ILIAD.

His face is hidden behind the book.

> LEX: In a minute.

3.
Small - DETAIL LEX is folding an intricate corner of a book page – the book is the ILIAD. It's like he's folding origami with his fingernail.

> LEX: I'm almost...done.

4.
We're outside the COPTER, seeing the situation. The 'COPTER is damaged, already missing a pontoon, its blades smoking...it twists wildly, diving at an impossible angle.

> PRISONER 1 (OP): Are you out of your damn mind? We're turning over! You don't take those controls and we're all going to--

5.
Inside with the PRISONERS as WHUMP - something (someone) grabs the 'COPTER.

6.
Small - LEX smiles, though we can't see his full face.

PAGE 12

1.
Of course, it's SUPERMAN, carrying the HELICOPTER. He has it upside down, as he caught it from the bottom. We see the MAW and all here.

2.
Moments later, he has lowered it onto the platform of the PRISON, where GUARDS wait, armed and angry. He lowered it onto the platform upside down, though, as the pontoons are smashed, the propellers too.

Jim, any choreography here you think would be really fun and funny, go for it. Like if we see SUPERMAN from LEX'S POV, upside down, too.

3.
SUPERMAN approaches LEX, who is hanging upside down, still working on his book. We still haven't seen his face.

4.
SUPERMAN using a finger to move the book up, revealing LEX'S upside-down face.

5.
SUPERMAN'S face or eyes, seen upside down by LEX.

> SUPERMAN: What are you up to, Luthor?

6.
LUTHOR, upside-down face.

> LUTHOR: Saving the city, you?

SUPERMAN UNCHAINED

PAGE 13

1.
Both, facing each other in profile.

SUPERMAN: The eight objects that fell from space today, seven satellites and the Intrepid space station. All were weaponized and programmed to explode using malware strangely similar to the kind you described in your doctorate research.

LEX: Well, I'm flattered you've been reading my old schoolwork, Superman, but I'm afraid all that research was stolen years ago. The theft was well documented. Have you looked into that cyber terrorist group that's been making such a name for itself lately?

2.

SUPERMAN: Ascension. But this is too big for them, Luthor. You know it.

LUTHOR: (sigh) All right then, so tell me. Why would I do this, in your opinion? Drop space junk from the sky?

SUPERMAN: I don't know yet. But my guess? To show that you can. That you can still affect the world. That you're still here, just before the doors slam shut on you.

3.
LUTHOR, smirking.

LUTHOR: The doors... Heh.

LUTHOR: Want to see something?

4.
Big - LUTHOR opens his book, revealing a glorious FOLDED PAPER MODEL OF METROPOLIS of his own making, like an intricate pop-up book setup. Rising from the center of the city is the SOLAR TREE we'll see when we see the model itself, the solar tower. All paper.

LUTHOR: Five thousand and twenty-three folds. Not perfect, but the trip from Death Valley was bumpy. I was serious about saving the city, Superman.

[Here LEX will explain the solar tower, Jim. The one he will build as part of his good behavior.]

5.
SUPERMAN closes the book on the paper city.

SUPERMAN: Only for you, Luthor, could being transferred to a supermax be considered growth.

6.
LEX, as SUPERMAN walks away.

LUTHOR: Well, everyone has to start somewhere.

[Superman saying he'll connect Luthor to this somehow...]

JIMMY: "I am the evil empire..."

PAGE 14

Jim, the idea with this scene is that CLARK is in his new self-rented office - we haven't seen it yet, so it's yours to design. It's in Metropolis' downtown, and within walking distance of the Daily Planet; in fact, I was hoping we could have the Planet in view, through the window - not across the street, as that feels a little weird of CLARK, but a few blocks down, so the Planet building is visible at the end of the avenue or something. The building CLARK is in I imagine is art deco. It's the old HQ of an old greeting card company - which will be something LOIS will tease him on. The notion that the cards made here were full of perfect sentiments, vs. the reality. The accusation against SUPERMAN in our story is essentially is that he's irrelevant as he strives to embody the ideal, without compromise, without living a human life in the trenches, doing the dirty work needed to be done to make some shred of those ideals a reality. So there's a lot of ideal vs. reality. The ideal as silly, as unattainable, as naïve in the story - like the narration at the start - the way the real world rushes up to hit you in the face so fast, LUTHOR pointing out that he's reshaping the city, an actual progressive human achievement vs. what SUPERMAN does.

PAGE 14 CONTINUED...

As for the offices, they're just rented office space, cubicles divided. I imagine that there could be other people renting other cubicles, but I'd rather he be alone in this scene with Jimmy. It could be as simple as the dividers between cubicles being ceiling tall.

I'd just like the simplicity of the offices here to contrast with the modern, higher-tech offices of the PLANET.

As for CLARK'S little space itself, it's a small cubicle with a big view of the city's gleaming downtown. On the corkboard by his head, a pennant for the SMALLVILLE CROWS. And on his desk, a small picture of his parents' farm.

For CLARK'S look, I know he's been in T-shirts and hoodies in "SUPERMAN" but I'd like to go for a more mature look. Obviously, he's the same guy, age-wise and everything, but since he's on his own, I think it makes sense to have him dress a little more adult, out of pride. So, a buttondown and cords is what I was thinking. Business casual. He's typing on a cool, modern tablet/laptop.

He's seated, typing.

JIMMY OLSEN is behind him, fidgeting as he eats a bagel for lunch. He has brought CLARK lunch, too - it sits uneaten on CLARK'S desk.

Also - JIMMY is playing with a HIGH-TECH CAMERA with a propeller - it's flying around the office.

1.
CLARK in his new office, with JIMMY. He's typing, busy, while JIM plays with a HIGH-TECH CAMERA with a propeller - it's flying around the office. JIM is controlling it with a remote.

    JIMMY:...It's true, isn't it? I am.

    CLARK: You're not the evil empire, Jim.

    JIM: I even have droids! Look at this thing. Edge gave it to me to practice with. He wants me to be his star paparazzo. More than that, like a super paparazzo sent back from the future to destroy—

    CLARK: Careful with that.

2.
A shot of the office building from outside, locating it for us.

    JIM: You know he sent me to the hotel where Bruce Wayne was staying to get pictures of him working out, shirtless, yesterday, right?

    JIM: I barely made it inside the lobby before Wayne made me, didn't say anything, just pointed at me. Man, have you seen the guns on that guy?

    CLARK: He pads his jackets.

    JIM: Really?

    CLARK: What about the photo you had on page one last week? Of the construction strikers. The little girl in front.

3.
CLARK turns to JIM, earnest, even as the FLYING CAMERA hovers.

    JIM: In the hard hat? I know, I just...the way things are lately, I admire it, Clark, what you did. Sticking it to the Planet that way.

    CLARK: I didn't leave the Planet to stick it to anyone, Jim. It's just that right now, the kinds of stories that matter to me as a reporter - the human angle pieces, stories that see the big events through lived experience - there isn't a big place for them at the Planet.

    CLARK: But the truth is, I still love the Planet, what it stands for at heart.

PAGE 14 CONTINUED...

5.
CLARK, smiling, taking his bag of breakfast JIM brought. The CORN BAGEL is YELLOW!

CLARK: Besides, as a rule, envoys from evil empires don't bring breakfast.

JIM: It's Bagel Palace. New place. Fifty kinds of bagels. Fifty. They have a corn bagel. I thought of you.

CLARK: It's yellow. I'm flattered.

JIM: So what are you working on?

PAGE 15

1.
Small - CLARK picking up his phone.

CLARK: Story on the Intrepid crash. I managed to get an interview with one of the astronauts last night. Posted it precisely two minutes ago. "Seven minutes of--"
SFX [CLAR'S CELL]: BEEP BEEP.

CLARK: Hang on.

2.
A shot of LOIS LANE, at the bustling Planet offices, on her Bluetooth to CLARK as she's looking over layouts of the paper on a big touch screen - go as modern as you want, Jim - want it to look cool, like we're seeing her through the photos of the news if we can at times.

LOIS: "Seven minutes of terror?" You're slipping, Smallville.

CLARK (VIA PHONE): I see. Because I buried my lede?

LOIS: Well, for starters.

3.
CLARK, standing now, looking out the window at the Planet. JIMMY (if you put him in any of these panels, Jim, is clearly uncomfortable she's calling while he's there). He's grabbing the CAMERA out of the sky.

CLARK: Not every story Superman is involved in needs him in the title, Lois.

JIM (whispering) Lois?! Clark, I'm not here, OK? Clark?

4.
LOIS, moving the layout of the paper around.

LOIS: Maybe not, but--

PERRY (OFF PANEL): Lois!

LOIS: Hang on. Yeah, Chief.

5.
PERRY talking to LOIS as she gestures to the layout of the paper on screen/glass.

PERRY: The story you just posted is five hundred words over count. How am I supposed to--

LOIS: Five hundred hundred and eleven. It's fine, I already made space. I moved this ad, see?

PERRY: Moved the ad.

LOIS: Come on, Chief. It's for men's tortoise shell glasses. It should be in the Style section. Which is where I put it. No, actually, scratch that. Anywhere but the Style section. No offense, Clark.

PAGE 16

Jim, I see this page as a rapid-fire conversation between CLARK and LOIS. It's fun, and a little tense, so it while it's a lot of dialogue, it should be a fun back-and-forth but I'll leave the layouts totally up to you based on the conversation. Just gave bare bones direction as to who's the focus of each panel.

1.
CLARK. JIMMY is peeking out the window carrying the flying camera.

PERRY (VIA PHONE): You're talking to Kent? Tell him when he's done with his walkabout, he can—

LOIS(VIA PHONE): Yeah, yeah, Chief. Done.

LOIS(VIA PHONE): Now, where was I?

CLARK: I'm slipping.

LOIS (VIA PHONE): You are.

2.
LOIS.

CLARK (VIA PHONE): Because I didn't go on about Ascension.

LOIS: Partly.

CLARK (VIA PHONE): I don't believe it was them.

LOIS: What you believe isn't what's likely. And what's likely should be printed. Otherwise you're writing opinion, Smallville. But yes, this one seems above Ascension's pay grade. Who are you thinking? Luthor?

CLARK (VIA PHONE): I was... But honestly, now I'm not so sure.

3.
CLARK.

LOIS (VIA PHONE): Eight highly defended, protected celestial bodies suddenly fall from the sky, aimed at military installations. I don't know, but it feels...

CLARK: ...Like the start of something bigger, I know.

LOIS (VIA PHONE): I've been trying to get my father all morning. He's been holed up at some base in the southwest the last year though. Impossible to--

PERRY (VIA PHONE): Lois! You moved the glasses ad to the obituaries. They paid good money!

4.

LOIS: I got to go. Tell Olsen to bring me back a poppy and cream cheese. You know they have--

CLARK (VIA PHONE): Corn bagels, yes. I'm flattered.

LOIS: But why I called. Your facts are wrong. You wrote that Superman stopped seven of the eight objects that fell from the sky, letting one crash into an unmanned military installation near Vigan City in the Philippines.

CLARK (VIA PHONE): And...

5.
CLARK, concerned, looking at aerial views of a military installation just sent by LOIS.

LOIS (VIA PHONE): And... Superman stopped all eight objects from crashing. See for yourself. I just sent you the pics. See?

LOIS (VIA PHONE): Smallville? Clark?

CLARK: I'm here. I should go.

LOIS (VIA PHONE): [need Parting line]

PAGE 17

1.
SUPERMAN'S eyes, flaring up – he's using his heat vision like a flare.

2.
Large - SUPERMAN moving through the water like he's flying, bubbles trailing, scanning the sea floor for the wreckage of the SATELLITE that crashed somewhere. BTW - I think it could be cool to have SUPERMAN fly through the water, like he's above water – he doesn't have to swim. He just flies slower. Love for this to feel really otherworldly, Jim, like a world only SUPERMAN could see this way. Here's a sonar-engendered CGI of an underwater mountain range.

The SUPERMAN V.O. here will be straightforward, about how none of this adds up. He knows where Diana was, Hal... There's no one who could have stopped the falling satellite but him. So who was it? And Lois was right, the whole thing feels like the start of something bigger, something more ominous....

3.
SUPERMAN moving through the ocean, flying, looking...

4.
Until he sees.... The WRECKAGE of the 8th SATELLITE. Underwater sand billowing up around him as he stops.

PAGE 18

1.
He investigates and finds...

2.
A HAND IMPRINT on a piece of the wreckage.

3.
SUPERMAN senses something behind him.

4.
TORPEDOES coming at him from a distant SUB.

5.
A barrage of TORPEDOES coming hits him (and the wreckage) BOOM! BOOM! Underwater explosions envelop him.

PAGE 19

1.
The bubbles/smoke clears and SUPERMAN is looking badass.

2.
On the SUB, on the bridge, the CAPTAIN is looking shocked and pale as are the OFFICERS – looking at the screen, they just realized they accidentally fired on SUPERMAN.

OFFICER: Is that....Superman?

CAPTAIN: Call home.

3.
GENERAL LANE, in a command center. Clearly the nerve center of a major military base. Highest tech. Go to town, Jim! Behind him is a big window.

A COLONEL is coming up behind him to talk.

COLONEL: General Lane. We just got word from the Dakota, sir. They were destroying the satellite wreckage as you asked, and... well, they may have fired on Superman.

LANE: May have?

COLONEL: Did.

LANE: And Superman?

COLONEL: Isn't happy, sir.

SUPERMAN UNCHAINED

PAGE 19 CONTINUED...

4.
COLONEL and LANE – LANE looking tough, unfazed.

    LANE: Patch me through to the Dakota. I'll talk to him.

    COLONEL: The captain, he thinks Superman may have been investigating the wreckage.

    LANE: What did Superman see?

    COLONEL: As far as we know, nothing. But if we're wrong...

    LANE: If we're wrong...

5.
LANE goes to the window and looks down at...

    LANE: ...Then I'll deal with it.

    COLONEL: He's not one to back down, sir.

    LANE: Neither am I. But the fact is, Superman can dig all he wants.

PAGE 20

Jim, I Was thinking this page could be a tour of this cool, underground base, while LANE is talking. We see what's coming in the story, the scope of this thing... Cool?

1.
The window behind LANE looks down on... a vast, underground military base, but one with a fake sky, that lights the roads, the barracks, allows for grass, trees... I was thinking there could even be a pond.

    LANE CONT.: "This place, all of it..."

2.
More views - we see that we're clearly underground somewhere – a huge cavern blasted/cut in deep rock. But there's a false sky overhead, rounded panels that give the place light – not corny, just pale blue manmade sunlight light. And beneath that sky is a MILITARY BASE. Barracks. An obstacle course. Small vehicles to drive. Essentially, we're in an underground military town. Again, not like a false prop town or base, but a working base. There's nothing illusory about this place to WRAITH. There's a library. There's a basketball court – essentially, it's a base designed for soldiers who can live there without leaving for months. They don't want much traffic to the surface, so it's pretty much sustainable. There could even be gardens or crops fields if you want. Up for anything here.

    LANE CONT.: "It's deeper than he'll dig. But even if he does figure out the truth..."

3.
At the end of the town/base, as we move through, we see a rock wall. And built into the rock is a heavy door, not unlike the door to the FORTRESS of SOLITUDE. But it's more modern and functional here.

    LANE CONT.: "...And we have to deal with him, we will. Or rather, he will. And if what the Kryptonian wants is war...we'll bring it to his doorstep. Because the fact of the matter is..."

SPLASH – We're on the other side of the door. The trick is not giving away... [redacted] What WRAITH looks like here, Jim. I imagine him as still pretty silhouetted, hovering, eyes glowing red so it's very clear this is the same guy from the opening 3 pages. This is shot of WRAITH in a room testing his power. He floats, powerful looking, in a bright room, with eyes glowing red.

As for the room, one thing I'm going to be playing with is the notion of [redacted] Anyway, here, [redacted]

    LANE CONT: "...America has its own Superman, and has for seventy years."

                 TO BE CONTINUED.

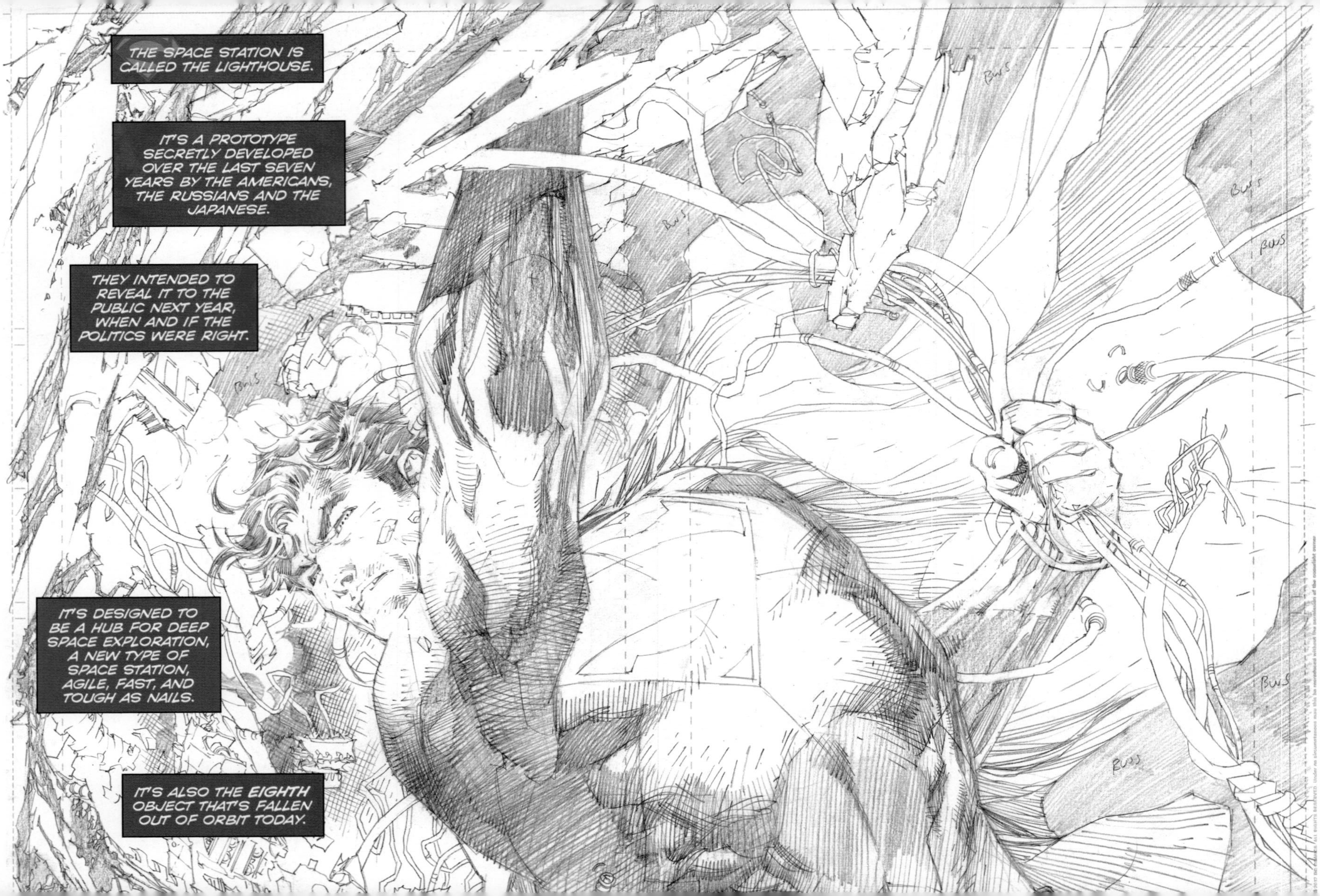
THE SPACE STATION IS CALLED THE LIGHTHOUSE.
IT'S A PROTOTYPE SECRETLY DEVELOPED OVER THE LAST SEVEN YEARS BY THE AMERICANS, THE RUSSIANS AND THE JAPANESE.
THEY INTENDED TO REVEAL IT TO THE PUBLIC NEXT YEAR, WHEN AND IF THE POLITICS WERE RIGHT.
IT'S DESIGNED TO BE A HUB FOR DEEP SPACE EXPLORATION, A NEW TYPE OF SPACE STATION, AGILE, FAST, AND TOUGH AS NAILS.
IT'S ALSO THE EIGHTH OBJECT THAT'S FALLEN OUT OF ORBIT TODAY.

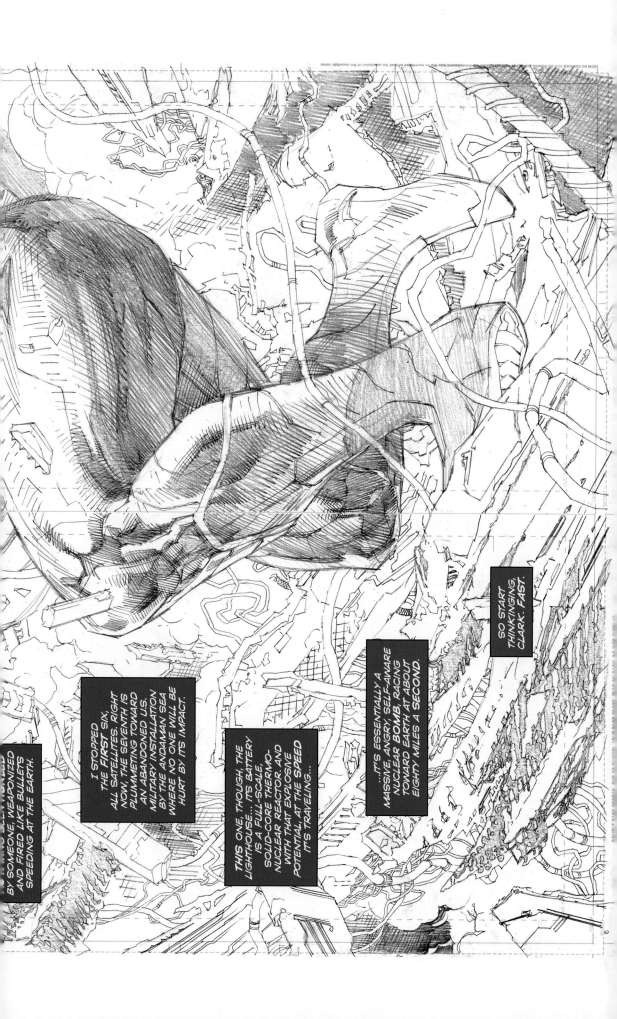

...BY SOMEONE, WEAPONIZED AND FIRED LIKE BULLETS SPEEDING AT THE EARTH.

I STOPPED THE FIRST SIX, ALL SATELLITES. RIGHT NOW, THE SEVENTH IS PLUMMETING TOWARD AN ABANDONED U.S. MILITARY INSTALLATION BY THE ANDAMAN SEA WHERE NO ONE WILL BE HURT BY ITS IMPACT.

THIS ONE, THOUGH, THE LIGHTHOUSE... ITS BATTERY IS A FULL-SCALE, SOLID-CORE THERMO-NUCLEAR REACTOR. AND WITH THAT EXPLOSIVE POTENTIAL, AT THE SPEED IT'S TRAVELING...

...IT'S ESSENTIALLY A MASSIVE, ANGRY, SELF-AWARE NUCLEAR BOMB RACING TOWARD EARTH AT ABOUT EIGHTY MILES A SECOND.

SO START THINKINGING, CLARK. FAST.

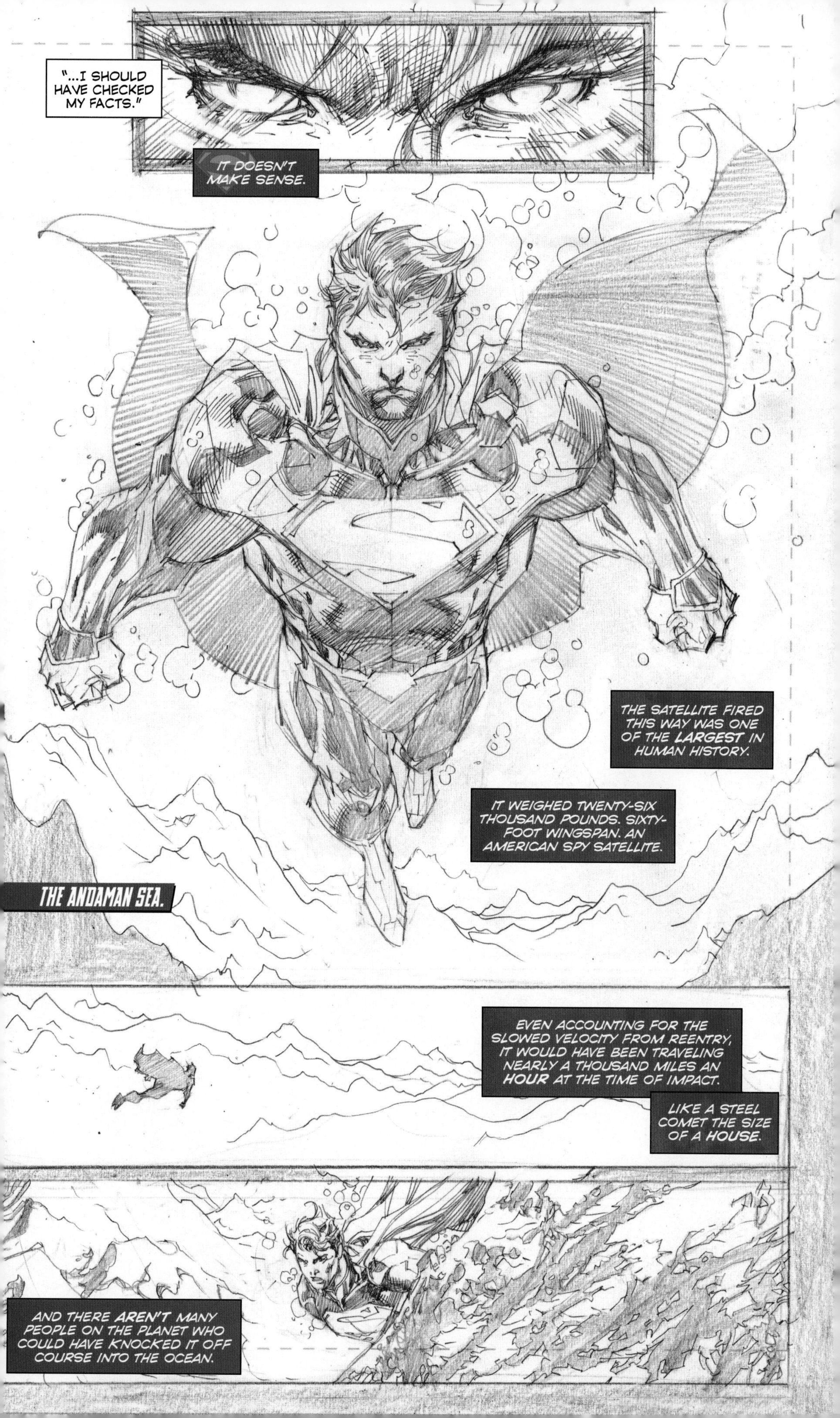

"...I SHOULD HAVE CHECKED MY FACTS."
IT DOESN'T MAKE SENSE.
THE SATELLITE FIRED THIS WAY WAS ONE OF THE LARGEST IN HUMAN HISTORY.
IT WEIGHED TWENTY-SIX THOUSAND POUNDS. SIXTY-FOOT WINGSPAN. AN AMERICAN SPY SATELLITE.
THE ANDAMAN SEA.
EVEN ACCOUNTING FOR THE SLOWED VELOCITY FROM REENTRY, IT WOULD HAVE BEEN TRAVELING NEARLY A THOUSAND MILES AN HOUR AT THE TIME OF IMPACT.
LIKE A STEEL COMET THE SIZE OF A HOUSE.
AND THERE AREN'T MANY PEOPLE ON THE PLANET WHO COULD HAVE KNOCKED IT OFF COURSE INTO THE OCEAN.

"BUT IF HE DOES, SIR--"

"IF HE DOES, HE'LL LEARN WE HAVE ALL SORTS OF WEAPONS HE'S NEVER SEEN BEFORE."

"STILL, IF HE FINDS OUT THE TRUTH ABOUT--"

...HE *WON'T* FIND THIS PLACE.

"COLONEL, THE TRUTH ABOUT THIS PLACE IS IN FACT OUR *GREATEST* WEAPON AGAINST HIM."

"BECAUSE SUPERMAN MAY BE STRONG, AND HE MAY BE FAST, AND HE MAY HAVE HIS LITTLE POWERS...BUT THE FACT REMAINS...

DROP IN 48 star USA

Scott Snyder has written comics for both DC and Marvel, including the best-selling series BATMAN, SWAMP THING and AMERICAN VAMPIRE, and is the author of the story collection *Voodoo Heart*. He teaches writing at Sarah Lawrence College and Columbia University. He lives on Long Island with his wife, Jeanie, and his sons Jack and Emmett. He is a dedicated and un-ironic fan of Elvis Presley.

Jim Lee is a renowned comic book artist and the Co-Publisher of DC Entertainment. Prior to his current position, Lee served as DC's Editorial Director, where he oversaw WildStorm Studios and provided art for many of DC Comics' best-selling comic books and graphic novels, including ALL-STAR BATMAN AND ROBIN, THE BOY WONDER, BATMAN: HUSH, and SUPER-MAN: FOR TOMORROW. Lee also serves as the Executive Creative Director for the massively multiplayer action game *DC Universe Online* from Sony Online Entertainment. He has drawn JUSTICE LEAGUE and SUPERMAN UNCHAINED as part of DC Comics– The New 52.

Scott Williams is a veteran inker whose 30-year career has featured collaborations with many of the top pencillers of the modern comics era. Best known for his long association with superstar art-ist Jim Lee, Williams has built an award-winning and diverse body of work in the course of their 25-year partnership, ranging from *X-Men* and WILDC.A.T.S in the early days to the more current BATMAN: HUSH, ALL-STAR BATMAN AND ROBIN, THE BOY WONDER and The New 52 flagship titles JUSTICE LEAGUE and SUPERMAN UNCHAINED.

Dustin Nguyen is one of the most exciting stylists in comics today, a breath of fresh air in the gritty world of super-hero comics. After long and popular runs on DETECTIVE COMICS and STREETS OF GOTHAM, Dustin went on to write and illustrate LI'L GOTHAM, which immediately became a fan favorite. Taking its cue from TV cartoons, classic comics, and children's book illustrations, Nguyen's art synthesizes the sheer joy of comic books and the extraordinary.

Alex Sinclair grew up reading comics with his older brother, Dante. The two have many fond memories of terrorizing their sister while wearing their Batman and Robin costumes, and after 15 years as a profes-sional colorist he still considers the Dynamic Duo to be two of his favorite characters. His other work includes BATMAN: HUSH, SUPERMAN, WONDER WOMAN and JLA. He lives in San Diego with his wife, Rebecca, and four sidekicks Grace, Blythe, Meredith and Harley.